2000

REGULATION OF THE ELECTRONIC MASS MEDIA

LAW AND POLICY FOR RADIO, TELEVISION, CABLE AND THE NEW VIDEO TECHNOLOGIES

Third Edition

By

Michael Botein

Professor of Law,
New York Law School

AMERICAN CASEBOOK SERIES®

WEST GROUP

ST. PAUL, MINN., 1998

COPYRIGHT © 1979, 1991 WEST PUBLISHING CO.
COPYRIGHT © 1998 By WEST GROUP
     610 Opperman Drive
     P.O. Box 64526
     St. Paul, MN 55164–0526
     1–800–328–9352

Library of Congress Cataloging-in-Publication Data

Botein, Michael.
 Regulation of the electronic mass media : law and policy for radio, television, cable, and the new video technologies / by Michael H. Botein. — 3rd ed.
  p. cm. — (American casebook series)
 Rev. ed. of: Regulation of the electronic mass media / by Douglas H. Ginsburg, Michael Botein, and Mark D. Director. 2nd ed. c1991.
 Includes index.
 ISBN 0–314–21122–5
 1. Broadcasting—Law and legislation—United States—Cases. 2. Radio—Law and legislation—United States—Cases. 3. Television—Law and legislation—United States—Cases. 4. Cable television—Law and legislation—United States—Cases. 5. Mass media—Law and legislation—United States—Cases. I. Ginsburg, Douglas H., 1946–Regulation of the electronic mass media. II. Title. III. Series.
 KF2804.G56 1998
 343.7309'94—dc21   97–47668
                  CIP

ISBN 0–314–21122–5

TO
KRIS, LIZ, MATT and *DAISY*

*

Preface to the Third Edition

The most visible—and perhaps most important—difference between this book and the 1991 Second Edition is the absence of two well-known names on the cover: Douglas H. Ginsburg and Mark D. Director. Both have been swept up in a variety of professional and civic obligations, making it necessary for them to take what hopefully is only a temporary leave of absence. Nevertheless, much of their work from prior editions and supplements still lives in this edition. Thus only I am left to tell the tale.

And there is much to tell since the Second Edition. Indeed, developments in media law moved at a faster pace during the seven years between the Second and Third Editions than the almost fifteen between the First and Second.

Although the basics discussed in Chapters I–III remain much the same, some underlying concepts have begun to change. For example, the development of "convergence" and the passage of the 1996 Telecommunications Act have confused traditional distinctions between broadcasting, common carriage, and private radio.

Other portions of the book have changed more dramatically. Much of former Chapter IV's discussion of broadcast licensing is now obsolete, through either judicial invalidation (e.g., the old comparative hearing factors) or statutory repeal (such as radio common ownership and, to a lesser extent, cross ownership under the 1996 Telecoms Act). Similarly, although some of the attempts at structural regulation discussed in Chapter V are still at least technically on the books, control of network practices has disappeared totally.

On the other hand, the First Amendment materials in Chapters V and VI have bulked up tremendously, because of the increasing number of Supreme Court decisions. Particularly in the area of cable television and other new multichannel video media, the Court has provided an often bewildering array of doctrines or applications. Although this material is less than clear at times, it makes for good classroom discussions.

In short, welcome to a fascinating and dynamic new legal order. From a selfish point of view, however, one only can hope that the pace of change slows down somewhat between this book and the Fourth Edition—and also that my friends and colleagues will be able to rejoin us then.

Many people contributed to this book in many ways—often into the wee hours of the night. To describe each one's role even briefly would be impossible. In strictly alphabetic order, the following thus deserve special mention. Carl W. Billek, Camille Broussard, Dawn M. Fasano, Seymour I. Feig, Lesa M. Lawrence, Abraham J. Mund, Jorge A. Salinas, Roberta R. Tasley, and Michael J. Wilhelm.

MB

New York, N.Y.
January, 1998

Preface to the Second Edition

It is a dozen years since the first edition of this book was published, under the title Regulation of Broadcasting. Much has changed during that time, both in the technologies of mass communication and in the regulatory structures governing them. The Federal Communications Commission has substantially deregulated radio and television, particularly with respect to their "public trustee" functions. In 1984, Congress significantly deregulated cable systems. More recently, Congress has considered legislation that would reregulate all of these media to some extent, and has enacted a relatively large number of narrowly focused amendments to the Communications Act.

As a result of all these changes, most of the materials in the first edition have become outdated. Some have been superseded by new cases, rulemakings and secondary sources; others have no current analogue and have disappeared all together. Only materials raising the most fundamental questions, such as whether to regulate at all, and landmark court decisions bearing on the First Amendment status of the electronic media have survived intact into this edition.

The newer materials are not untested, however. Some of them appeared in the 1983–84 supplement to the first edition, which Mark Director and I edited. Much of the rest has been added incrementally over the several years for which the three current editors have collaborated, and used in multilith form both by Professor Botein and by as many as a dozen other law professors. Their experience and feedback have been very important in honing these materials to suit the law school classroom.

We begin this edition again with a Prelude that is meant to anticipate many of the principal issues in the course, but to present them in a form accessible to the beginning student. We have found it efficient to assign the Prelude and Chapter 1 as reading for the first class, and then to devote the class hour primarily to discussion of the issues raised in the Prelude. This gets students started thinking about the many preconceptions that they inevitably bring to this subject. They are all sufficiently familiar with the electronic mass media to have opinions, even if not well-informed opinions. Eliciting those views at the outset is intellectually therapeutic: it enables each student to proceed more self-consciously through the materials, and to question his or her own views and values in a constructive way.

While much of the fun of teaching, and of taking, this course derives from its relevance to the popular culture familiar to us all, it is at bottom a course in agency regulation, both economic and social, of a particular industry. As such, it involves the student deeply enough in the affairs of a single industry to appreciate the systemic nature of regulation, and the ongoing relationship between the regulator and the regulated. (In that regard, the students would be well-served by reading the trade press on a regular basis while taking the course. We recommend Broadcasting magazine for this purpose.)

Time and again, these materials take one back, in a nontechnical way, to the underlying economic issues and the forces whose clash gives rise to them. Just as frequently, one comes back to problems that do not yield nicely to an economic analysis, from the rules for political broadcasting to the regulation of television in the interests of children. We hope that you and your students find it as rewarding to grapple with these issues as have we and our students.

D.H.G.

Washington, D.C.
November, 1990

Mentors come first—in this case, Bernard Botein and Walter Gellhorn. Many colleagues also gave sage advice; but chief among them David M. Rice, who helped beat this book's outline into shape. Finally, thanks are due to several generations of law students for suffering through previous drafts of this book.

M.H.B.

New York, N.Y.

There are many who deserve gratitude and appreciation for their diverse contributions. Jim Goodale, Bob Bruce, and Jeff Cunard are enormously talented communications lawyers who have been mentors and advisors, as well as colleagues and friends. The support and forbearance of my former colleagues at Debevoise & Plimpton, my family, and my partner Annette Fields have been essential and unceasing. I want to add a special thanks to Douglas Ginsburg, who first involved me in this project more than eight years ago, when we collaborated to update the first edition of this book, and who had sufficient faith in a then-young law student to ask me—and urge me—to be involved in the ambitious and rewarding task of creating a new edition. Finally, in law and in life Gerald Director remains an inspiration.

M.D.D.

Washington, D.C.

We all wish to thank the secretaries, research assistants, paralegals, and others that assisted us in the complex and laborious task of producing this text: Steve Bazil, Sylvia Beeson, Brian Berk, John Brewer, Carol Ann Burke, Donald Falk, Bob Gillespie, Charlotte Goo, Cleveland Grant, Jessica Herman, Karen Hinson, Mary Long, Linda McGreal, Angie Mills, Deborah Ashby Moss, Abraham Mund, Paul Norris, Janel Radtke, Edury Sell, Deborah Schull, Jane Shepard, Barbara Tucker, Mary Rose Udstuen, Leonard Walczyk, Kimberly Walker, Rosemarie Wallace, and Kim Young.

*

Preface to the First Edition

This is a book about the laws governing the electronic mass media—radio, television, and cable—and the policy-making process by which those laws are formed, informed, and administered. It is intended for use in law, public policy, and communications curricula.

There could be no more auspicious moment for the publication of this book and its use in the classroom. The technologies of the electronic mass media are in a state of virtual revolution: cable television is growing apace, bringing satellite-to-cable distribution systems and two-way cable channels in its wake; over-the-air subscription television service is being licensed for the first time in 1978; home videotape recorders are now reaching the mass market; and various other developments, such as fiber optics and a new television tuning device, may soon bring about an unprecedented proliferation of new communications channels. At the same time there is increasingly wide recognition that the Communications Act of 1934 may not be an adequate regime for the regulation of present technologies and the emergence of new ones. The House Subcommittee on Communications' proposed Communications Act of 1978, H.R. 13015, has assured this issue a prominent place on the agenda of national policy debate for the next several years.

At this moment, too, the Supreme Court has shown an increased willingness to decide issues of communications law; a new majority has emerged at the Federal Communications Commission under the chairmanship of Charles Ferris; and the public interest lawyers concerned with communications issues have achieved a new sophistication in putting matters of public concern before the FCC and the reviewing courts. Not surprisingly, public awareness of and involvement in communications issues is on the ascendant, as reflected in the growing concern with the contents of mass media programs: concern with sex and violence on television, political interference with public affairs programs on public television and radio, the preservation of special formats, such as classical music, on radio, and so on.

These issues will not go away unresolved. And in their resolution there will be great consequences for the public, the affected industries, and the first amendment to the Constitution. It is my hope for this book that, through our students, it will contribute somewhat to the quality of public debate over these matters.

The materials in this book, and the questions posed, have emerged from three years of teaching the course in Regulation of Broadcasting at the Harvard Law School—to first, second, and third year law students, and to graduate students in the Harvard School of Education and in the Kennedy School of Government. Since I have found that the non-law students have very little difficulty with the legal materials involved, and often add a valuable perspective to the classroom discussion of the issues, particularly those involving content controls and economic regulation, I have no hesitancy in offering the book for use in inter-disciplinary and non-law classes.

———————

Research support for this book was provided by the Walter E. Meyer Research Professorship at the Harvard Law School, and the Harvard Faculty Project on Regulation at the Kennedy School of Government. Invaluable research assistance was provided by Neil K. Alexander, Jr., '78, and Howard Jacobson, '79, of the Harvard Law School. I am particularly grateful to Arlene Bernstein, Sheila Davidson, and Kay Smith, secretaries, who put it all together.

D.H.G.

Cambridge, Mass.
October, 1978

Summary of Contents

Table of Contents

Table of Cases

The principal cases are in bold type. Cases cited or discussed in the text are roman type. References are to pages. Cases cited in principal cases and within other quoted materials are not included.

*

REGULATION OF THE ELECTRONIC MASS MEDIA

LAW AND POLICY FOR RADIO, TELEVISION, CABLE AND THE NEW VIDEO TECHNOLOGIES

Third Edition

*

Chapter I

THE TECHNOLOGY AND ECONOMICS OF THE ELECTRONIC MEDIA

In order to deal with the electronic media, a lawyer must understand their technology and economics. This is neither surprising nor unusual. Without a general grasp of any industry's dynamics, a lawyer cannot argue policy to a tribunal, review a document, or counsel a client.

We therefore begin with an overview of technological and economic infrastructure. We also begin with the knowledge that many law students think technology and economics are irrelevant—something to be left to the technologists and economists. But the world simply does not work that way. In order to represent a cable operator, a lawyer need not know how to fix a line amplifier; but he or she must understand how many line amplifiers may be strung along a cable run.

A. TECHNOLOGY

1. MASS MEDIA

Radio and television are forms of electromagnetic energy; by comparison, fiber optic systems transmit light waves. Radio waves are not essentially different from the electrical currents that pulse through any home, except that they oscillate much more quickly and therefore have much shorter wavelengths (or, put another way, much higher frequencies).* Indeed, the initial uses of electromagnetic transmissions—the telegraph and the telephone—operated at comparatively low frequencies, not much different from those of ordinary house current.

Early experimenters discovered fairly quickly how to transmit electromagnetic signals without wires—hence radio's early moniker, "the

---

* Frequencies are measured in cycles per second—or, under modern terminology, "hertz." A kilohertz (KHz) thus is 1,000 cycles, a megahertz (MHz) 1,000 KHz, and a gigahertz (GHz) 1,000 MHz.

wireless." In 1888, Heinrich Hertz sent electromagnetic energy between two points without the use of connecting wires (and also earned the posthumous honor of having frequencies measured in terms of "hertz"). About a decade later, Guglielmo Marconi completed the basic design for point-to-point radio transmission. He envisioned radio as an alternative to telegraph service wherever cables could not be laid. In 1899, Marconi began business in the United States through the Marconi Wireless Company of America.

Marconi's system was limited to telegraphy, however, because it transmitted individual bursts of energy—dots or dashes—rather than a continuous wave. The latter, which was necessary to transmit voice or music, was developed in 1901. (Telephone companies had developed the ability to transmit audio over copper wires several decades before.) Thus, by the turn of the century, the basic technology for both broadcasting and the telephone was in place.

Radio technology has since blossomed, of course, into a variety of different voice, video, and data services—AM and FM; television; cable television; and such over-the-air subscription services as Subscription Television ("STV"), Multichannel Multipoint Distribution Service ("MMDS"), Direct Broadcast Satellite ("DBS"), and Low Power Television ("LPTV"). A brief overview of each medium may be helpful.

A simple but often misunderstood distinction is between analog and digital forms of information storage and transmission. Although the term "digital" has a certain mystique to it, it basically is just another way of transmitting intelligence—video, voice, or data. The difference is that analog technology uses changes in amplitude (AM) or frequency (FM) to carry information. By comparison, digital technology is a binary system: it breaks up intelligence–video, voice, or data–into a series of "0"s and "1"s. This has numerous advantages. First, a digital transmission is not subject to interference; if the requisite numbers of "0"s and "1"s are not received by a terminal device—including a radio or television set—it will request or wait for the proper number of digits. Second, as discussed below (p. 7), it is possible to fit 8 or more times as much digital as analog information onto a frequency, by "compressing" the digital data. Finally, because digital transmission operates in a binary world, it can transmit with considerably less power than an equivalent analog system. Until the end of the 1990s, "digital" was more a marketing than technological concept. Virtually no digital devices were available on the consumer market; the only thing digital about a digital clock radio was that it used numbers to display the time.

Until the last decade, virtually all forms of electronic information were analog—radio, television, and telephony. The advantage of analog transmission is that it requires relatively simple and inexpensive equipment. In the early days of broadcast radio, the signal was generated by passing a sound over electrically charged carbon particles in what became known as a microphone; as the particles moved, they generated different voltage levels and thus a continuously varying electrical wave.

By comparison, digital signals are binary in nature; that is, information is conveyed as a series of "0"s or "1"s, represented by the presence or absence of electrical power. A digital signal is equivalent to turning a light on and off—several billion times per second. Different combinations of "on-off" positions within a given number of digits make it possible for a binary "0–1" scheme to express numbers higher than 0 or 1. For example, in a four-digit system, 0001 might be 1, 0010 2, 0100 4, etc. A digital transmission might include a string of "on" and "off" electrical power positions.

Digital transmission has several advantages over analog. First, because the range of potential electrical values is only two—on or off—the possibility of electrical interference is relatively small; distortion from a strong electromagnetic force may knock out one or two bits, but not an entire wave—as is the case with analog signals. Second, the chance of inaccuracies is much less, because an error in storage or transmission is likely to affect only a few bits at a time. Third, it is relatively easy to build in automatic error-checking capability for digital signals, because they are transmitted in uniform clumps of four or more digits; if a receiver gets less than 4 digits at any time—or less than a certain number of four-digit clumps in a given packet—it knows that something is wrong in the transmission and requests another transmission of the information in question.

The relatively slow deployment of digital systems has been primarily a result of digital equipment's high price. Until the end of the 1990s, there was virtually no digital equipment available on the consumer electronics market.

Two trends may have begun to change this situation. First, development of increasingly sophisticated chips has required decreasing amounts of hardware to handle digital signals. Second, the increasing number of digital applications has resulted in mass manufacturing, which as always in electronics has reduced dramatically the cost of new equipment.* As discussed below, digital technology has begun to move quite successfully into the marketplace for broadcasting, cable and DBS systems.

The initial development—indeed the first century—of broadcasting thus was purely analog. Traditional analog AM and FM radio work in essentially the same way. Sound waves strike a microphone through which a steady electrical current is passing. The vibrations from the sound waves alter the electric current, which in turn modulates a "carrier wave" emitted by a transmitter. A receiver reverses the process; the modulated carrier wave changes the electric current in a receiver, which causes a speaker to reproduce the original sound waves.

AM radio is so called because it uses "amplitude modulation." The message or information is in a signal imposed upon a carrier wave, which

* For further discussion of analog and digital systems, see Graham Langley, *Telecommunications Primer* 93 *et. seq.* (1984); Peter Zorkoczy, *Information Technology* 51 *et. seq.* (1982).

has a constant frequency. In effect, the message travels along with the carrier wave, in the form of variations in its power; a radio receiver disregards the carrier wave, isolates the message, and converts it into audible form. AM radio is sometimes referred to as "standard broadcast," because it was the only form of broadcasting for many years.

Because early electromagnetic transmissions were limited to very low frequencies, AM radio received only a small portion of the spectrum—put another way, narrow frequencies or limited bandwidth. AM channels are 10 kHz wide in the United States, 9 kHz in other developed countries—thus allowing an increase in the number of stations. By comparison, FM channels are 200 KHz. Because it cannot carry the full audible range of sound, AM has relatively low fidelity compared to virtually all later transmission or recording technologies.

On the other hand, AM's status as the first over-the-air transmission technology also resulted in the allocation of low frequencies to it. A transmission's frequency is highly significant in determining its "propagation characteristics," that is, the way in which its signal travels. Low frequency transmissions travel quite far for two reasons: they hug the ground, and they reflect off the ionosphere and back down to the ground at night. (In order to avoid interference, some AM stations are authorized to operate only during the day—hence their common designation as "daytimers.") Depending upon atmospheric conditions, an AM radio transmission can travel for thousands of miles. By contrast, the higher-frequency signals used by virtually all other electronic media are "line-of-sight" in nature; with minor exceptions, they do not reach beyond the horizon.

The lower the frequency, the more favorable the propagation characteristics and the greater the range. An AM station will always carry farther than an FM or TV station with equal power and antenna height; a very high frequency ("VHF") television station (channels 2–13) will always have a better signal than an ultra high frequency ("UHF") station (channel 14 and above). By dint of an historical accident, AM radio trades off lower fidelity for greater range.

FM radio was developed in the 1930s, and was authorized to begin operation in 1941. FM's relatively wide bandwidth gives it much higher fidelity than AM. In fact, FM can carry sounds beyond the range of human hearing. By adding a second sound track and then transposing it back into the audible range, an FM receiver can offer a second or stereo channel.* FM also is much more resistant to static than is AM. FM reverses AM's trade-off by providing higher fidelity to a smaller area.

---

* An FM radio channel actually is wide enough to allow a station to carry two other "subcarriers," each one 10 Khz wide—that is, as wide as an AM channel. These subcarriers can carry audio, data, paging or other signals. A special receiver is necessary in order to receive a subcarrier, however. As of the late 1990s, FM stations leased them for $1,000 to $15,000 per month, depending upon the size of the market. Subcarriers thus offer an inexpensive (and unregulated) means of offering specialized services, ranging from stock market quotations to foreign language programming.

Broadcast television developed at about the same time as FM radio. The earliest commercial television sets created silhouettes by varying the intensity of a light shining through a rapidly spinning disk with pinholes in it. The first truly electronic television camera was developed in 1929, and experimental broadcasts began in 1941. Because of World War II, however, commercial television broadcasting did not get off the ground in the United States until the late 1940s.

As might be expected, analog television works somewhat like radio. Light enters a television camera, striking thousands of light-sensitive elements in a tube or chip. The camera scans each element and registers different amounts of reflected electrons according to the amount of light. Under the U.S. system, the camera scans each row of elements from left to right, covering all 525 rows 30 times each second; virtually all other countries use 600 or more lines, which yields a substantially higher quality picture. The reflected electrons affect the electrical energy flowing through the camera, modulating the signal, which is then either broadcast immediately or recorded for later use. In color television, each element has three cells, one for each primary color—red, blue, and green—and three separate electron sources to scan the separate color cells. At the receiver, the modulated wave alters the electrical flow in an electron gun, which projects energy onto a cathode ray tube—the set's screen. The modulated energy reproduces the light waves from the transmitter or other source.

Broadcast television requires an immensely larger piece of the electromagnetic spectrum than either AM or FM radio. A television station requires a 6 MHz channel—six times the size of the total AM radio band. In the United States, VHF television stations operate in the 54 to 216 MHz range, UHF stations in the 470 to 890 MHz range. Since UHF stations' frequencies are so much higher than VHF stations', UHF operations need greater power in order to reach the horizon, and usually do so with a lower quality signal. Moreover, most television receivers are designed for far better VHF than UHF reception. Indeed, until passage of the All Channel Receiver Act of 1962, 47 U.S.C.A. § 303(s), most U.S. television receivers did not include even a basic UHF tuner. By comparison, most other developed countries use solely UHF channels for television, in order to reserve the lower channels for governmental and private communications. They overcome the "UHF handicap" by deploying multiple directional antennas to cover relatively small areas. For example, most major European cities need fifty or more transmitters—on different frequencies—to provide half a dozen signals.

Cable television uses essentially the same NTSC transmission technology as broadcast television, except that it distributes signals through a coaxial cable rather than over the air. The main limitation on a cable system's bandwidth is not so much the cable as the associated electronics—amplifiers and the like. As of the late 1990s, a realistic limit was about one hundred channels. In the very long term, a system of fiber optic broadband networks may be able to carry thousands of channels.

A cable system receives signals from a variety of sources—local television stations, satellites, microwave relays, videocassettes—at a central processing unit called a "headend." Equipment at the headend descrambles, amplifies, and changes the frequencies of signals in preparation for their distribution. Identical technology is used in a system known as Satellite Master Antenna Television ("SMATV"), that services individual apartment houses or developments. Since SMATV operates on private property, it is not generally subject to government regulation.

A cable distribution system uses "tree and branch architecture," in which signals move "downstream" from the headend to subscribers through a series of cables, known in descending order of magnitude as "trunk," "feeder," and "drop" cables. A cable system thus resembles other traditional distribution plants, such as water, electricity, and natural gas. It is *not* a "switched" system, like a telephone local exchange carrier ("LEC"). A cable system cannot connect one subscriber with another.

A few cable systems have "two-way" or "interactive" capability, which allows subscribers to send signals back "upstream" to the headend. Although this technology has existed for a decade, at the end of the 1990s it generally remained expensive and unreliable. As a result, "pay-per-view" ordering of individual movies and sports events generally depends upon the telephone as the viewer's return link to the headend. Again, the introduction of fiber optics into the home may make truly interactive video possible in the long term. As discussed below, current "hybrid fiber-coax" ("HFC") may begin to change this during the next decade.

The cable industry originally was very much a "mom and pop" affair with local entrepreneurs setting up "community antenna television" ("CATV") systems. In more recent years, however, there has been a trend towards concentration in the industry. By the 1990s, the top four multiple systems operators ("MSOs") served half of all U.S. subscribers. In addition, a number of MSOs were vertically integrated, in that they produced their own programs and distributed them via satellite to their own and other cable systems.

The introduction of digital video technology may make greater numbers of broadcast channels available and improve picture and sound quality. Because of digital transmission's inherent nature, signals lend themselves easily to the "compression" process; the signal is squeezed in a relatively narrow bandwidth at the broadcast station, transmitted, and then "unsqueezed" at the viewer's receiver, using either a receiver designed for digital reception or a set-top adapter connected to a conventional receiver. The reason that video can be compressed into narrow channels is that in a given sequence, the information in successive frames does not normally change all that much; the signal is said to have "temporal redundancy." In an uncompressed video system, redundant picture elements are transmitted for several frames until the scene changes. In a compressed signal, one frame is compared with the frame before it, and only the differences between successive frames are transmitted. At the receiver, the entire picture, redundant elements and all, is reconstituted from the digital bit stream that has been transmitted.

Digital radio and television broadcasting is just beginning to emerge in the United States. A major problem was that the broadcasting and computer industries could not agree on a common set of standards—an important factor, since many observers believe that the same hardware ultimately will be used for video, voice, and data. The FCC began to issue licenses in 1997, in an attempt to achieve national "high definition television" ("HDTV") within a decade. *

The Commission's basic plan is that each existing television station will be allotted a new channel for digital transmission and will be allowed to retain its existing analog station. The program content on both the analog and the digital stations will be identical. Eventually, however, when digital receivers are sufficiently common, the analog transmissions will be discontinued, and the analog channels used for other services.

Video compression will be an important component of this channel swap. Each of the digital channels will be 6 MHz wide—the same bandwidth allotted for analog signals. Because of compression's great efficiency, however, approximately six digital channels can be operated in the same space as one analog channel. Hence, broadcasters will have additional bandwidth available to them, which may be employed for additional video signals or a myriad of other uses. Although lagging somewhat in development, radio also eventually may shift to digital service, capable of delivering compact disc quality sound.

Another major component of future electronic media will be "direct broadcast satellites" ("DBS"). This service essentially uses a "geostationary" space satellite which stays in a fixed position over the Earth as a 22,300 mile high antenna; because of its height, a satellite can cover up to 42 percent of the planet.

DBS became an important part of the mix of video services available in Europe by the mid–1990s. Cable was relatively undeveloped in Europe, aside from in a few countries with few broadcast television stations; as a result, even half a dozen high-quality satellite signals—some pay, some advertiser-supported—were enough to attract a substantial audience.

In the United States, DBS was just beginning to emerge as a meaningful competitor to conventional broadcasting and cable systems by the end of the 1990s. The emergence of DBS in the U.S. has been due to several factors: (a) major technological improvements; (b) development of set-top converters connected to small (i.e., 12–24 inch) home dish receiving antennae; and (c) video compression techniques. This combination of technologies has made it possible for DBS subscribers to

* For an excellent history of HDTV's political and economic evolution, see Joel Brinkley, *Defining Vision: The Battle for the Future of Television* (1997).

receive up to 500 digital television channels—by subscribing to several different DBS services. By the end of 1997, the several competing U.S. DBS systems had about 5,000,000 subscribers—as opposed to more than 65,000,000 cable subscribers. DBS suffers from the inability to deliver local television stations; if a DBS subscriber wants local news, weathers, sports, etc., he or she must rely either on local stations (usually requiring an external antenna) or subscribe to cable in addition to DBS.

There may be technological relief from this dilemma in the future. High-powered satellites can use concentrated "spot" beams to deliver one or more local station to all metropolitan areas. Also on the technological horizon is DBS radio broadcasting. For example, by having specialized receivers and antennas the size of quarter in the roofs of their cars, drivers may be able to subscribe to services with hundreds of channels.

2. TELECOMMUNICATIONS

Although this book focuses on mass media, a basic knowledge of the telecommunications is also important for two reasons. First, mass media use telecommunications for a variety of purposes, such as satellite distribution of programming to a broadcast or cable network. Second, a convergence of mass media and telecommunications is increasingly likely, as the various industries continue to overlap in their functions. If telephone companies enter the cable television market, the line between mass media and telecommunications will become increasingly hazy.

Telecommunications carriers carry not only traditional telephonic voice messages, but also data and video. Unlike the electronic mass media, telecommunications carriers offer only point-to-point communications. They do not control or create the content of the messages that they carry, and generally they are prohibited from exercising any censorship over them. Telecommunications carriers are subject to the limitations of common carriage, a rather murky notion discussed later, (p. 14)

The two most significant types of telecommunications carriers are LECs and interexchange carriers ("IXC"). LECs connect local telephone subscribers to each other, and carry interexchange calls from the exchange to the subscriber.* IXCs are also known as long distance, long-haul, or inter-LATA carriers. (A "LATA" is a local access and transport area.)

LECs are *switched* systems. Since, unlike cable television, it is not tied to tree-and-branch architecture with downstream-only capability, a switched system can connect any subscriber to any other. An LEC provides switching through a "central office," at which all subscriber lines terminate and thus can be connected with each other. (Since even a large central office normally cannot handle more than about 100,000

---

* Most LECs are Bell Operating Companies ("BOCs"), formerly owned by the American Telephone & Telegraph Company ("AT & T"). The BOCs account for more than 80 percent of U.S. local telephone service. S. Simon, After Divestiture (1985).

lines, a large LEC uses a number of central offices, which are tied together into one central processing unit for call routing within the LECs service area.)

Central offices first used human operators and then mechanical switches to connect subscribers. Modern central office switches, however, use solid state electronics to route calls, and have few moving parts; they resemble, and technologically are derived from, mainframe computers. As LECs have moved from mechanical to electronic switching, they have also incorporated into their switches the ability to handle digital signals. This is essential for handling high-speed data transmissions, as well as the digitized audio and video services that are likely in the future. The almost simultaneous break-up of AT & T and development of digital transmission have brought sweeping changes to the telecommunications industry.

IXCs are the second major component of the telecommunications system. For decades, AT & T provided virtually all long-distance service in the United States. Although AT & T is still the dominant provider, a number of other common carriers ("OCCs") such as MCI and Sprint have entered the market, with varying degrees of success. Both AT & T and the OCCs use a mixture of coaxial cable, microwave, domestic satellites, and fiber optics to carry long-haul messages. All IXCs terminate their lines at or near the central office of an LEC, which then carries the signal to the subscriber.

For the last hundred years, LECs have relied primarily upon "twisted pairs" of copper wire as a transmission technology. Copper wire has a bandwidth of about 3 to 4 KHz, making it acceptable for voice, inadequate for music, and impractical for high-speed data transmission.

The last two decades have seen significant changes in transmission technology. The single most important development has been the refinement and commercial feasibility of optical fiber. This is a very pure, flexible form of glass, capable of carrying extremely high-bandwidth, laser-generated lightwave transmissions. As of the late 1990s, commercially available fiber had a capacity of between 1.5 and 750 MHz. Some near-term uses of fiber (often with a mixture of coaxial cable) sell under the rubric of "integrated systems digital network" ("ISDN"). This is not so much an engineering term as a description of the amount and type of capacity delivered—whether analog or digital. A conventional ISDN's frequency range may be from between 128 KHz to 1.44 MHz.

This type of capacity is well within the capabilities of coaxial cable. But fiber optics in the near term may be able to offer a bandwidth of 20 to 30 gigahertz, the equivalent of 2,000 to 3,000 full video channels. Large commercial users, banks, insurance companies, and mail order houses need bandwidth of this magnitude for data transmission. Whether and when this capacity will reach the residential or small business subscriber is not clear, however, given the enormous cost of replacing existing LEC copper networks with fiber. If high-capacity fiber ever does reach the mass of the population, however, the implications for existing mass media would be significant.

For both economic and technological reasons, there has been a trend towards "convergence" of the electronic media during the last generation. Broadcasters wanted to own cable systems; LECs wanted to enter the cable and mass media industries; and cable operators wanted to provide telephone as well as data service. All of these industries felt that they could use their existing plant to provide economies of scale in entering new businesses. This provoked major litigation to test the existing limitations.

The Telecommunications Act of 1996 changed this dramatically. As discussed later (p. 213) the Act basically allowed LECs to build–but not buy–cable systems within their service areas, and to operate "open video services" (OVS) within their telephone territories

OVS basically was an image of what Congressional staff members thought would be an attractive business to the LECs and others. (There is no restriction on what firms can apply.) For the first time in U.S. media regulatory history, it creates a Griffin-like entity which is partially a common carrier and partially a programmer. (p. 78) It basically allows a multichannel operator to program at least one-third of its channels, while leasing the rest to third parties on a quasi-carrier basis.

As of the late 1990s, however, there were two major problems with OVS. First, building it turned out to be more expensive than most observers had imagined. Second, few LECs–particularly the RBOCs–were inclined to invest in it.

The drafters of the OVS provisions apparently had in mind a very definite technology–namely "hybrid fiber coax." This digital technology uses a combination of fiber optics, coaxial cable, and neighborhood switches to provide subscribers up to 500 video channels–as well as return node capability to order programs and the like. By the middle of the 1990s, no LEC or cable operator had produced a system which functioned in a consistently reliable fashion. Also, the cost of wiring up a home turned out to be much higher than many observers had expected–i.e., about $1, 600, as compared to about $600 for traditional one-way cable.

Moreover, many LECs–and particularly RBOCs–apparently found that their new-found ability to offer long-distance service might be much more profitable than OVS. Most of the RBOCs already had fiber optic connections between their major service areas, and had plant in other companies' territories through reciprocal regional calling area plans. For an RBOC to implement long-distance service within a few hundred miles of its home territory thus was relatively inexpensive–particularly with the mergers between some of the RBOCs.

Whatever the reason, by the late 1990s no RBOC had implemented OVS on a widespread basis. Their end of the convergence scenario thus appeared to be speculative at best.

At the same time, the cable industry began to retreat from the telephone business. As noted above, cable basically is a one-way medium; implementation of telephony thus would require the industry to build the equivalent of HFC plants. Because of various economic problems, the industry apparently found this to be an unattractive option.

B. ECONOMIC ORGANIZATION

1. MASS MEDIA

Types of revenue flows vary from one mass medium to another. Commercial broadcasters have depended almost exclusively upon advertising. Conversely, cable television derives its revenues almost exclusively from subscriber fees. As might be expected, however, there is always some overlap. Broadcasters get incremental revenues from a wide range of activities, such as sub-carriers, studio leasing, and the production of advertisements. Cable operators carry an increasing amount of advertising, which usually accounts for between ten and fifteen percent of a system's revenues. The cable industry's share of advertising revenues has increased steady, although it still is small in comparison to broadcasters'; in recent years, it has gone from about 10 percent to 20 percent of the industry's gross revenues–that is, several billion dollars per year out of total industry revenues of more than 20 billion dollars. Put another way, any one of the three traditional networks has more advertising revenues in a given year than the entire cable industry.

Although the cable industry still is sorting out a mix of revenue flows, advertising remains the engine that drives the broadcasting industry. Advertisers compensate broadcasters for the number of viewers in the audience. Whether on a national, regional, or local basis, advertisers pay on a "cost per thousand" ("CPM") basis, with variations for the demographic make-up of the audience. Although television CPMs are generally in the $5–$7 range, they may be significantly higher for an upscale audience. For example, women aged 25–49 are a highly valuable audience, because as a group they have the greatest purchasing power.

Broadcast advertising is a highly effective means of disseminating information about consumer products, whether one likes the message or not. But by no stretch of the imagination does it create "free" radio or television broadcasting. Sellers of goods have to factor the cost of advertising into their total cost of doing business, and recover that cost in the price of their goods. Regardless of whether cereal consumers watch the programs with the cereal advertisements, they pay for the advertisements when they buy the cereal.

The distribution of advertising revenues within the broadcasting industry is fairly complex, because of the number of different players with different economic interests.

The ultimate source of most broadcasting revenues is large vendors of consumer products. (This naturally does not include "institutional advertisers," which may intend to influence public sector decisionmakers rather than consumers.) Advertisers usually use independent advertising agencies to create commercial messages, develop a marketing plan, and buy air time for them. Advertising agencies generally receive about 15 percent of the total advertising cost in compensation.

Advertisers buy time in a variety of ways. For national television advertising, the most common method is to buy a specific number of 30–second or 1–minute periods on a network. The network generally specifies the programs in which the ads will run, and guarantees a minimum audience, with any shortfalls usually compensated for by additional "make good" ads. Network programming is no longer the dominant force in radio. Advertisers instead usually coordinate regional or national campaigns by buying air time station-by-station or through time brokers, which offer packages of advertising spot buys on groups of stations.

Until the 1960s, many advertisers bought blocks of air time from the television networks and supplied their own programming as well as advertising. The networks eventually discontinued this practice, ostensibly because it deprived them of the content control for which their affiliates were responsible to the Federal Communications Commission ("FCC"). Instead, they either produce their own programming (to the extent allowed by law), or contract for first-run rights with independent producers. Some observers believe that the networks' real motivation for taking control of programming was their perception that they could increase their total revenues per program by selling spots and avoiding controversial programming. A debate about whether direct advertiser control over programming led to higher-quality, more artistic fare has raged for the last three decades.

Networks in turn supply programming and advertisements to affiliated stations. This part of the distribution chain creates two additional and often complicated relationships. First, networks must contract with producers for the right to exhibit their programs, including royalties from reruns and resale brokerage fees. Second, the networks must attempt to have as many affiliates as possible "clear" their programs, since ad revenues depend upon the size of the audience.

Affiliation is attractive to stations for two reasons. First, they receive compensation from the network for carrying its programming. These payments are relatively small–from a few thousand dollars per hour in large markets, down to a few hundred in small ones. More important, however, the bulk of a network affiliate's revenues comes from selling the approximately two minutes of advertising time that the networks leave open for this purpose in each half hour of prime time programming. In a very large market, a one-minute spot on a network affiliate sells for up to $10,000.

Particularly with the development of inexpensive satellite transmission, both advertisers and affiliates have become less dependent upon the networks. The last decade has seen the emergence of "syndicators" that sell programs to both affiliated and independent stations. Although many syndicated programs are network re-runs, an increasingly large number are original productions made for syndication. The traditional market for syndicated programming was independent stations. Many network affiliates, however, use syndicated material either in non-prime time or instead of weak network shows.*

Public television does not air overt commercial advertisements. Nevertheless, it too is heavily dependent upon viewers, since it raises a substantial amount of its revenues by appealing to them for donations. Federal funding of public stations is provided through two institutions: the Corporation for Public Broadcasting ("CPB") and the Public Broadcasting Service ("PBS"). See 47 U.S.C. § 390 et seq. In theory, CPB's role is to define overall goals and allocate federal funds, while PBS's is to implement the production of particular programs. In practice, however, CPB at times has controlled program procurement. Moreover, in the last decade the federal government's contribution consistently has declined. By the end of the 1990s, it was down to about $300 million per year— about twenty percent of public broadcasting's total annual budget. By comparison, the Australian Broadcasting Corporation receives more than a billion dollars per year—in addition to other contributions—to serve a population of 17,000,000.

The actual amount of federal funding has remained well below the full operating costs of public television. Public stations thus raise most of their operating budgets from individual viewers and corporate donors. Because of their perennial need for funds, public stations have also developed a number of entrepreneurial activities, such as leasing their studios to commercial producers and publishing local program guides.

Subscription fees are at the opposite end of the spectrum from advertising. They have become the norm for the new video media, such as cable, MMDS, STV, and DBS. In cable, the most common practice is to offer a "tier" of "basic service" at a fixed monthly price. For example, a tier might contain about 35 to 50 channels, including local broadcast signals, "superstations" (such as WTBS or WWOR), satellite networks (such as MTV), and local access channels. (Some networks derive revenue from both subscriber fees and advertising, e.g., CNN, ESPN.) In addition, subscribers can order "pay" or "premium" services, such as Home Box Office or the Disney Channel, for an additional monthly fee. And an increasing number of systems are offering "pay-per-view" services, by which a subscriber can be billed for an individual program that he or she chooses to watch. Once again, however, these systems are not switched, and thus cannot offer true "video on demand."

Subscription fees have the natural advantage over advertising of creating a direct relationship between the viewer and the programmer. In an advertiser-supported system, a viewer gets what the advertiser, advertising agency, and programmer think he or she wants or is at least

---

* A subset of syndicated programming is "barter" material. As its name implies, in a barter transaction, the syndicator supplies a program free of charge–but with roughly two minutes of advertising per half hour already inserted. The result is that the station acquires programming without any substantial upfront capital cost, thus enabling the syndicator to sell programming that stations would not buy on a cash basis.

willing to watch. In a fee-supported system, the viewer gets what the programmer finds will generate the greatest revenues, often at high prices for viewers with intensive and specialized interests. Although a subscription system does not create a perfect match between program supply and viewer demand, it does cater more particularly to viewers' interests. Moreover, fiber optics may make it possible in the next century for consumers to view on demand any material they want.

Despite these advantages, fee-supported systems have run into political opposition. The most common concern is that subscription systems will outbid "free" television for significant events–with the most oft-cited example being the World Series. There may be some validity to this concern. By the late 1990s, cable networks already were able to buy the broadcast rights for a limited number of professional football and baseball games. Whether such "siphoning" of programs is desirable in the long run, of course, is open to debate.

2. TELECOMMUNICATIONS

Most telecommunications carriers are regulated as "common carriers." Their rates are restricted to a level necessary to cover operating expenses and to pay a sufficient dividend to attract new capital for investment. Both the FCC and state public utility commissions recently have experimented with a variety of ratesetting approaches.

The U.S. telecommunications system became substantially more complicated after AT & T's 1984 divestiture of the BOCs. Before then, AT & T had controlled more than 80 percent of all local exchange traffic and more than 90 percent of interstate traffic. In the *Modification of Final Judgment* ("*MFJ*"),* the federal District Court for the District of Columbia required AT & T to divest its local exchange carriers—the BOCs. Regional Bell Operating Companies ("RBOCs"). AT & T retained its long-distance, manufacturing, and research ("Bell Labs") units.

A common carrier's revenues derive from a rather complicated system of user fees and charges. First, telephone subscribers pay their local exchange carriers ("LECs") a monthly charge for local service. In some states, this is a flat fee, regardless of the number of calls made. Other states use a "local measured service" system, under which subscribers pay separately for each call; this avoids light users subsidizing heavy users. Many offer consumers a choice between these types of service. Regardless of the pricing mechanism, business rates traditionally are much higher than and subsidize residential rates, reflecting regulators' conscious attempt to promote universal telephone service among households.

---

* Although the *MFJ* initially was worked out by AT & T and the Department of Justice, Judge Harold H. Greene–before whom the case was pending–played a major role in fine-tuning the agreement. Judge Greene continued to play a major role in the U.S. telecommunications industry by passing upon requests for waivers of the *MFJ* as well as presiding over a general review of its terms every three years.

See, e.g., United States v. Western Electric Co., Inc., 714 F.Supp. 1 (D.D.C.1988), reversed in part 900 F.2d 283 (D.C.Cir. 1990).

Second, LECs receive substantial payments for giving the IXCs–AT & T and the OCCs–access to local subscribers through the LECs' central offices. Both long-distance carriers and subscribers pay for this connection. The long-haul carriers pay a "carrier line charge" ("CLC"), based upon the number of calls originating from or terminating at a local exchange; the local subscribers pay a flat monthly "subscriber line charge" ("SLC"), also known as an "access fee." Together, these two charges may amount to a substantial amount of an LEC's gross revenues. The FCC tried to shift the access costs from the CLC to the SLC in the 1980s in an effort to increase competition among long-distance companies. The Commission's goal was to separate local from interstate costs, in order to allow subscribers to make direct comparisons between competing long-haul carriers' rates.

Third, LECs derive revenue from other businesses, including the sale of advertising in the so-called Yellow Pages classified directories. The RBOCs' Yellow Pages gross more than $10 billion per year, or close to 10 percent of all revenues for the telecommunications industry. It is not surprising, therefore, that some RBOCs have attempted to market Yellow Pages outside of their own service areas, while some non-telephone companies have also entered the directory market.

In addition, LECs have tried to develop a variety of new revenue sources, some of which involve programming on their own telecommunications networks. These include transmission for independent "enhanced service providers," ranging from stock ticker services to "976" numbers with pre-recorded, often pornographic messages provided by third parties. The LECs also have become involved in a variety of other ventures from international communications to real estate.

As with technological changes, economic developments continue to blur the once bright line between the mass media and telecommunications services. Under the *MFJ,* both the LECs and the IXCs were straining at the bit to offer content-related services such as videotext, data bases, and the like. As noted above, the Telecommunications Act of 1996 for the first time allows RBOCs and other LECs to enter content-based businesses–either through cable or OVS. Whether these companies ultimately will choose to do so, however, is yet to be seen.

3. THE PRIVATE VALUE OF PUBLIC AUTHORIZATIONS

The Communications Act clearly states that a licensee has no property interest in its license, and that the spectrum belongs to the public. 47 U.S.C. § 309(h). This never has prevented a licensee from charging a substantial amount for agreeing to transfer its license to a third party, subject to FCC approval. In theory, the buyer of a broadcast station or mobile telephone operation receives nothing more than the right to hold (and later attempt to renew) a license. Since the Commission approves virtually all license transfers and renewals, however, licensees treat their authorizations as property rights for all practical purposes. Rupert Murdoch presumably would not have paid $500 million for a Los Angeles television station had he thought that there was any realistic possibility of its license not being renewed.

Because they are relatively scarce resources, profitable broadcast stations and cable systems sell at what appear to be high prices. As of the late 1990s, broadcast stations and cable systems usually sold at a "multiple" of their annual cash flow–4–10:1 for AM stations, 10–14:1 for FM or TV stations, and 10–20:1 for cable systems. These figures are not arbitrary, but are based upon general industry assumptions as to the future performance of the various media. For example, AM's multiple is lower than FM's because investors expect AM's audience ratings to slump relative to those of FM. These assumptions will continue to change as both mass media and telecommunications develop over the next few decades. If the country moves in the direction of a broadband fiber optic network, for example, the value of both broadcast stations and cable systems will decrease.

The economic future of the media is far from clear, but is almost certain to change in response to new technological opportunities. In all of these considerations, economics drives technology. The flashiest technology will not take hold unless it has a sound economic rationale to attract investment and provides a service that consumers are willing to pay for–as the backers of many new technologies have found to their chagrin.

C. POTENTIAL MARKET DEVELOPMENTS AND THEIR IMPLICATIONS

As noted before, towards the end of the 1990s DBS began to attract substantial numbers of subscribers in rural and some urban areas.

To be sure, before the current development of high-capacity digital satellites–such as DirecTV, Primestar, etc–a small satellite programming industry had grown up in the United States, serving roughly two million homes with "C-band" satellite receivers ten to fifteen feet in diameter. Most of these "dish" owners originally bought their equipment in order to receive pay satellite . channels without paying for them. Until the Cable Communications Policy Act of 1984, it was unclear whether "piracy" of satellite signals was illegal under the Copyright Act or otherwise. See Comment, *Private Reception of Satellite Transmission by Earth Stations*, 48 Alb.L.Rev. 426 (1984); Comment, *The Copyright Act of 1976 Served on a Satellite Dish,* 21 Willamette L.Rev. 79 (1985).

The Cable Act changed this situation significantly, by specifically allowing satellite programmers to encrypt their material and making unauthorized reception illegal. 47 U.S.C. § 605. Because paying for satellite programming generally costs more than a cable television subscription, the number of C-band receivers is unlikely to grow rapidly, except in rural areas that lack broadcast as well as cable television.

As of the mid–1990s, the more modern "Ku–Band" digital satellites gave strong indications of developing their own audiences—particularly in low-density areas which cable cannot or will not serve. Several companies entered the field, using compressed video signals in order to provide a large number of signals, i.e., 100 or more. Marketing and other problems existed, because of the relatively high cost of a Ku-band receiver: about $500 to $1,000. But some operators dealt with this by leasing or selling equipment at discounted prices. Indeed, some parts of the cable industry welcomed the advent of DBS for two reasons. First, it relieved them of their obligations to provide "universal service" to unprofitable rural and other areas. Second, many cable MSOs joined or created DBS ventures, with an eye to being the local sales representatives—thus tapping both cable and DBS revenues.

MMDS uses high-frequency microwave signals to provide up to about two dozen channels of programming–hence its nickname of "wireless cable." Its capital costs are low. MMDS thus has the economic potential to compete with cable in unwired areas, and perhaps even in cities with cable television. As of the late 1990s, however, only a few dozen low-capacity MMDS systems had begun operation.

There appear to be several reasons for this slow start. First, the FCC was slow in granting MMDS licenses, allegedly because of cable industry pressure. Second, MMDS operators had difficulty in acquiring attractive programming from the satellite networks that service the cable industry. Some observers believe that program suppliers deliberately boycotted the MMDS industry, because many of them are vertically integrated with cable systems with which MMDS would be competing. As with DBS, however, this situation seems to have changed, because of both economic and legislative pressures. Finally, potential MMDS operators feared that they could not compete head-to-head with existing cable systems, and thus were loath to enter already wired markets. In fact, a number of MMDS operations were acquired during the mid–1990s by local telephone exchange companies, as an inexpensive way of entering the video market. The experience was mixed, since a number of LECs quickly decided that the market would not yield enough profit, and just as quickly sold off their MMDS operations.

Another service along the lines of MMDS is Local Media Distribution Service (LMDS). The potential advantage of this medium is that because it operates at extremely high frequencies–e.g., 25–35 GHz–it can use enormous amounts of bandwidth without creating interference with existing RF services. Like fiber, it thus has the potential ability of providing video, voice, and data—including multiple HDTV channels–simultaneously. Although several trials during the mid–1990s indicated that LMDS was technologically feasible, there was little immediate financial interest in implementing it.

In addition to new technologies, the FCC also has expanded the number of existing radio and television services by allocating new frequencies to those services. First, the FCC created a new class of "low power television" ("LPTV") stations. These operations generally transmit with a maximum of 100 watts on the VHF band and 1,000 watts on the UHF band. These power levels are only a small fraction of those used by full-power stations, and they give LPTV a coverage radius of between two and ten miles, depending upon location, power, and antenna height.

Few LPTVs are licensed to operate in major markets, because they would interfere with existing full-power stations. Most LPTV stations operate either in rural areas or on the fringe of urban areas. This, combined with their limited power, naturally prevents them from attracting substantial audiences or advertising revenues, and few LPTV stations offer full-service broadcasting. Some LPTVs operate as local public television stations with small audiences, serving much the same function as access channels on cable television systems. Others carry satellite signals, such as music television channels. See *Comment, Low Power Television and the Doctrine of Localism: The Need to Reconcile a Medium With its Message*, 18 U.S.F. L.Rev. 505, 518 et seq. (1984).

An initially more promising development in broadcast television has been the growth in independent UHF stations. Almost 250 new "UHFs" went on the air in the early 1980s. Unlike LPTV or the new media, these stations used existing UHF allocations that previously had been considered economically unfeasible.

The new independent stations ran into several problems. First, they suffered from the usual "UHF handicap" of poor reception. Second, after cable was substantially deregulated, many were not carried by their local cable systems. Third, they could not afford to bid for attractive syndicated programming, because their audience shares and advertising revenues were too small. (Some benefited from the emergence of a fourth network, Fox, in the late 1980s, by becoming affiliates.) Not surprisingly, a number of UHF independents had failed by the end of the 1980s.

The Commission also attempted to create a variety of new frequencies for FM stations through its "Docket 80–90" proceeding (i.e., the 90th rulemaking in 1980). The FCC reevaluated its mileage separation requirements for FM stations, and found that the rules were more restrictive than necessary to avoid interference between stations. The Commission thus was able to fit in almost 700 more stations. Because of the inherent delays in the license hearing process, however, granting all the new licenses has gone slowly.

Even ten years ago, it was relatively easy to make generalizations about future directions of the electronic media. Radio had a small but secure part of the market—particularly for "drive-time" applications. Television was the major home video medium, although cable and VCRs were beginning to erode the three traditional commercial networks' prime time market shares. In terms of long-term developments, most observers predicted that major growth areas would be among independent stations in broadcasting and with cable television in multichannel media. Largely because of the *MFJ*, there seemed little prospect of major multichannel development by the most likely players, the RBOCs.

The combination of legal changes—first, the *MFJ's* gradual repeal and ultimately its nullification by the 1996 Telecommunications Act—

and the development of relatively low-cost and reliable digital transmission systems has opened up a rash of possibilities. The 1996 Act basically knocked down traditional barriers between industries.

As a result, RBOCs can enter cable, OVS, print, or other content-oriented operations. Conversely, cable operators are free to enter the local exchange and long-distance markets. As of the end of the 1990s, however, neither industry had made any definitive move towards entering the other's market.

By the late 1990s in the U.S., DBS began to pose serious competition to cable and other media. Again, however, the nature of the competition was somewhat unclear, since cable operators had ownership interests in some of the DBS systems and sold programming to all of them.

After years of keeping it in limbo, the FCC finally authorized high definition television. This in turn forced the broadcasters-both television and radio-to begin planning on new types of programming and other services to offer.

Moreover, this does not take account of new telecommunications media, such as the "personal communications services" ("PCS") frequencies which the Commission auctioned off for more than $10 billion during the late 1990s. Although these initially were viewed as a high-quality replacement for analog cellular radio, they have a variety of other uses, e.g., low-quality "picturephone" service, computer networking, and the like. Some of these applications obviously begin to look like mass media.

Finally, this analysis does not consider a whole variety of strategic alliances in the marketplace. For example, how does a regulator deal with a deal between a U.S. and U.K. international carrier, when the U.S. carrier also contracts with an international newspaper company and it in turn buys part of a U.S. DBS service? Is the entire arrangement a common carrier? A broadcaster? Or should each part be regulated separately under different legal principles? But is this possible, given the differences in domestic law, policies on cross-subsidy, and the like?

For academics, these are fascinating intellectual problems. For regulators and lawyers, they are a massive headache-particularly when clients demand predictions as to future developments. The current scenario has so many players from so many media industries that it is impossible to make any realistic predictions for the future. In most cases, the only intellectually honest answer is: who knows?

D. GLOSSARY OF ABBREVIATIONS

The following abbreviations will appear regularly in this book.

AT & T   American Telephone & Telegraph Co.
          Dominant IXC carrier, and until 1984 also the parent of
          the Bell Operating Companies
BOCs   Bell Operating Companies

	Twenty-two LECs previously owned by AT & T, before *MFJ*
CAP	Competitive access providers Companies providing local service in competition with LECs
CATV	Community antenna television, i.e. cable TV
CP	Construction permit. Initial permission to build an RF facility
CPB	Corporation for Public Broadcasting Federal agency overviewing public broadcasting
CPM	Cost per thousand Amount advertisers pay per thousand viewers
DBS	Direct broadcast satellite Satellite broadcasting to home subscribers
EIRP	Effective Isotropic Radiated Power Actual power output of station as measured at transmitter
FCC **FCC 2d**	Federal Communications Commission Reports FCC first and second series; the official reports of FCC decisions until late 1986
FCC Rcd	FCC Record Official publicaton of FCC, 1986—present
Fin-Syn	Financial interest and syndication rules Share of revenues from reruns; commission for brokering program in syndication
HAAT	Height Above Average Terrain
IXCs	Interexchange (long-distance) telecommunications carriers
KHz	Kilohertz Frequency measurement—1000 hertz (cycles) per second
LECs	Local exchange carriers Generally telephone companies; mainly BOCs
LPTV	Low power television Television stations with 5–10 mile radius of coverage
MHz	Megahertz (1 million cycles per second)
MDS	Single-channel microwave multipoint distribution service
MMDS	Multichannel multipoint distribution service "Wireless cable," with 30 analog microwave video signals
MFJ	Modification of Final Judgment: Governed divestiture of A T & T
NAB	National Association of Broadcasters Broadcast trade association
NCTA	National Cable TV Association Cable trade association
OCCs	Other common carriers IXCs other than AT & T, e.g., MCI, Sprint

PBS	Public Broadcasting System
PCS	Personal communications services Advanced RF uses, usually digital, e.g., cellular radio, computer communications
PTAR	Prime Time Access Rule Former restriction on affiliates' use of network resource
RBOCs	Regional Bell Operating Companies (also termed "Regional Holding Companies") LECs previously owned by AT & T
R.R., R.R.2d	Radio Regulation (2d) (Pike & Fischer) Looseleaf electronic communications law reporting service
SCA	Subcarrier Authorization FM or TV frequencies not used for main service, but for other data or voice transmission
SMATV	Satellite Master Antenna Television "Private cable" operations within one commonly owned facility
STV	Subscription television Single-channel pay-TV service. Now largely defunct, other than LPTV stations
UHF ("Us")	Television stations on channels 14 and above

Chapter II

THE DECISION TO REGULATE: BASIC POLICY ISSUES

The materials in this Chapter raise basic questions of broadcast regulation: Why do we have any public law in this area? Why the particular regime now embodied in the Communications Act and not some other? What others have been suggested or been tried elsewhere? What are the costs of maintaining the present system?

The historical background of the present regime in the United States is recounted in Section A. Note each different plan that was suggested for the early organization and financing of the broadcasting industry. Although all of the plans naturally reflected the peculiarities of broadcast technology, when evaluated against the course of later events they may enable you to formulate some hypotheses about the variety of possible legal responses to the emergence of a new technology. You should also note the alternatives set forth in Section B. You can test the actual and alternative approaches either in the discussion of "new communications technologies" later in this course, or elsewhere in the law school curriculum with issues such as construction blasting, electronic funds transfer, or deep seabed mining.

A. ORIGINS OF THE DECISION

As indicated below and in Chapter I, neither broadcasting nor broadcast regulation in the United States evolved from an orderly planning process. Indeed, no governmental scheme for parceling out frequencies even existed until the Radio Act of 1927. When radio began, there were no clear ideas as to either its economic base or its societal role. For example, early broadcasters differed as to whether their mission should be to sell radio receivers or commercial minutes. Indeed, the first broadcast trade association, the National Association of Broadcasters ("NAB"), initially vowed never to sell commercial advertising. But this approach, soon changed. The continuing evolution of broadcasting policy in the United States has also been driven largely by the market rather than by technological or industrial policy considerations; at least until the 1990s, new media—such as DBS—did not emerge solely because they could provide new services. One trend running through all of the discussion in this book is the interaction between "marketplace pull" and "technology push." The former usually is more significant, simply because it does not come into existence until entrepreneurs or others believe that a particular medium is capable of making a substantial profit.

The market approach naturally has both advantages and disadvantages. On the one hand, the United States' laissez faire attitude resulted in earlier development and broader use of radio broadcasting than the policy of government ownership adopted by most other countries. On the other hand, the early deployment of broadcasting locked the United States into technologies inferior to those later developed and adopted by other countries. It was no accident that the United States developed nationwide television broadcasting first, while continuing to this day to use lower-quality broadcast technology than any other Western nation. (Standards for U.S. television developed voluntarily by the National Television Standards Committee ("NTSC") are known to engineers as "Never The Same Color twice.")

At the same time, some other countries went to the other end of the spectrum. For example, the French Government originally developed television with almost twice as many lines as the U.S. system. Based upon French bistro culture, the Government reasoned that most people would watch television not at home, but rather at public places. This approach turned out to be as short-sighted as the NTSC assumptions; but since France had not moved as quickly as the U.S. in adopting standards, the Government was able to adopt new standards.

Some observers would argue that the United States still is hampered by a lack of comprehensive telecommunications policy planning, as reflected in several areas of technological development. For example, most developed nations today have AM stereo. The United States does not, arguably because the FCC consistently has refused to endorse any one technical system. Consequently, both broadcasters and manufacturers are unwilling to commit to a particular technology. Similarly, high definition television ("HDTV") has developed in both Europe and Japan, but U.S. companies did not even begin to research this technology until the late 1980s.

On the other hand, many U.S. firms seem to have been slow to take up the opportunities which new legislation and court decisions have given them. For example, the former AT & T LECs (Regional Bell Operating Companies ("RBOCs")) have shown no particular interest in offering video programming—despite their previously intense interest in entering this market. (For an excellent overview of the 1996 Telecommunications Act see Thomas G. Krattenmaker, *The Telecommunications Act of 1996,* 49 Fed. Comm. L.J. (1996).)

This recent history suggests that perceived market forces may not be enough to create an industry. A quick review of the U.S. radio industry's development may confirm this.

* * *

J. UDELSON, THE GREAT TELEVISION RACE
5–9 (1982).*

[B]y 1917 the components of a practical radio system had been fully developed. But further progress was blocked because these components could not be legally manufactured together, since their patent rights were assigned to rival corporations. These rivals included American Telephone and Telegraph, * * * General Electric, * * * American Marconi, * * * and Edwin H. Armstrong. * * *

* * *

RCA and GE arrived at cross-licensing agreements in 1919. Over the next two years cross-licensing agreements were also arranged between RCA and Westinghouse, AT & T, United Fruit, and the Wireless Specialty Company. * * * As a result of these agreements, RCA was to operate point-to-point radio communications, though not exclusively, and to market receivers, while GE and Westinghouse had exclusive rights to manufacture these receivers, 60 percent for GE and 40 percent for Westinghouse; AT & T retained exclusive rights to manufacture, lease, and sell transmitters. The result of these cross-licensing agreements was to break the patent impasse and to facilitate the development of the broadcast industry.

Westinghouse soon realized that the availability of continuous radio service would serve greatly to stimulate receiver sales, and so in October 1920 the company began operating radio station KDKA from the roof of its manufacturing plant in East Pittsburgh, Pennsylvania; soon it opened several more stations throughout the country. * * * And besides the big manufacturers, smaller operations, often run for fun or publicity, appeared all over the country; in 1922 more than six hundred stations went on the air. Sales of transmitting and receiving equipment were booming.

Yet this very success brought further patent conflicts, this time between the "radio group" headed by RCA and the "telephone group" headed by AT & T. The original cross-licensing agreements had not envisioned radio as a public broadcast medium but had only taken account of its previous point-to-point operation. * * *

* * *

But RCA was already under antitrust investigation, and AT & T was fearful of similar action against itself. Both sides therefore agreed to invoke the arbitration clause of the 1920 cross-licensing agreements. In early 1926 a three-part agreement was signed providing for a redefinition of the patent arrangements in the light of the development of widespread radio broadcasting; for AT & T to receive a monopoly for providing interconnections among stations; and for AT & T to sell its New York City station, WEAF, and its network to RCA and withdraw from broadcasting.

* * *

This brief survey of major corporate alignments in the formative years of the radio industry suggests that by 1930 the concept of the broadcast industry as a concentric set of engineering and manufacturing, programming, and networking, and promotional systems was well understood and already available as a model for the development of a similar design for television.

* * *

E. KRASNOW, L. LONGLEY & H. TERRY, THE POLITICS OF BROADCAST REGULATION
10–16 (3d ed. 1982).*

The growth of broadcasting in the early 1920s found Congress and the executive branch almost totally unprepared to meet new obligations in this field. Until 1927, Congress had passed only two laws dealing with radio: the Wireless Ship Act of 1910 and the Radio Act of 1912. Both regulated primarily ship-to-shore and ship-to-ship maritime communications. Although these acts were not designed to deal with broadcasting, then Secretary of Commerce Herbert Hoover, faced with the reality of an emerging broadcast service, attempted to use the 1912 act as a statutory basis for regulation of broadcasters' use of frequencies, hours of operation, power, and similar matters. In 1921 Hoover designated 833 kilohertz (KHz) as the frequency for broadcasting, allowing only one station in a reception area or, if more than one station desired to operate, forcing a time-sharing arrangement. In the summer of 1922 he added 750 KHz as a second broadcast frequency. Sensing the real limits of the early radio laws, however, Hoover convened the first of four broadcaster conferences in 1922 to discuss ways of controlling the use of these radio frequencies. The conferences demonstrate that, even early in its evolution, the industry played an important role in the regulatory process. After two months of study the First Radio Conference unanimously decided that regulation by private enterprise alone—self-regulation— would be inadequate and recommended legislation authorizing govern-

* © 1982 by St. Martin's Press, Inc. From *The Politics of Broadcast Regulation,* 3rd Edition, by Erwin G. Krasnow, Lawrence D. Longley and Herbert A. Terry. Reprinted with permission of St. Martin's Press, Inc.

ment control over the allocation, assignment, and use of broadcast frequencies.

* * *

While Congress continued to study the problem by holding periodic hearings, Hoover convened more industry conferences. At the Third National Radio Conference in 1924, Hoover commented: "I think this is probably the only industry of the United States that is unanimously in favor of having itself regulated." The industry had come to demand such controls as the increase in stations continued unchecked. By November 1925 more than 578 stations were on the air, and applications had been filed for 175 more. With every channel filled in urban areas, most stations were experiencing considerable interference from other stations and had been forced to work out complex time-sharing schemes.

Despite the evident need, Secretary Hoover's regulatory initiatives were repeatedly thwarted. The final blow came in 1926 when a decisive court ruling deprived him of any authority to regulate radio frequencies, power, or hours of operation. Hoover then limited the Department of Commerce to the role of a registration bureau and intensified his pleas for self-regulation.

* * *

As finally enacted, * * * the Radio Act of 1927, reflected an accommodation of interests between the House and Senate by setting up a curious division of responsibilities between the Secretary of Commerce and the new Federal Radio Commission.

* * *

The act created a Radio Commission of five members appointed by the president with the advice and consent of the Senate. The president was required to nominate one Commissioner from each of five geographical zones. * * * Having structured the FRC so carefully, Congress then launched the infant Commission with one serious handicap: it failed to give it any money! The Commission was nevertheless able to function due to a clause in the Radio Act allowing it to spend the unexpended balance in the appropriation made to the Department of Commerce under the item "wireless communications laws." The original members of the Commission were forced to do their own clerical work, and for the first four years engineers had to be borrowed from other agencies.

* * *

Throughout its short history the Radio Commission was subjected to great congressional pressure. Not really accepting the independent status of this "independent regulatory commission," Congress continually tinkered with the 1927 act. Since the Radio Commission was originally established for a period of only one year, Congress had to renew the legislation annually (or let the FRC's activities be absorbed by the Department of Commerce). This annual review gave Congress a convenient opportunity to conduct hearings and add further legislative restrictions.

* * *

Spurred by general dissatisfaction with the existing structure of governmental regulation, Congress enacted the Communications Act of 1934, which established a new, less tentative Federal Communications Commission (FCC). The Communications Act made various organizational changes from the model of the Radio Commission * * * and gave the new agency broader authority over all communications, including interstate telephone and telegraph. Title III of the 1934 act, which dealt with radio, was, however, almost identical to the Radio Act of 1927. Most important, the "public interest" criterion in the 1927 legislation was retained.

* * *

A final distinctive feature of the federal government's early regulation of broadcast stations was the focus on licensing as a primary regulatory tool. Although regulatory agencies such as the Federal Power Commission and the Interstate Commerce Commission exert control over entry by requiring proof of usefulness, the certificates of authority they issue are for indefinite terms and the certification process is secondary to the agencies' other functions of regulating profits and prices. The strong emphasis on the FCC's licensing role results in part from the fact that Congress did not expressly give the Commission the power to regulate the rates or profits of broadcast stations. It predetermined that there would be strongly fought battles over several aspects of licensing in the future: Should the "traffic cop" review such things as choices of content in making licensing decisions? What, in general, would be both the process and standards for getting licenses renewed?

Notes and Questions

1.   During the administration of the Radio Act, the Federal Radio Commission reduced the number of broadcasters from 732 to 593. The interference problem which underlay the Act was thereby solved, but it was obviously impossible to do so without benefitting some interests and harming others—at the very least those broadcasters who were eliminated from the industry.

Should the losers have been compensated for their loss? Precisely how would one value the "property" lost? Cf. 47 U.S.C. §§ 304, 307(d), 309(h)(1).

Aside from the pre–1927 broadcasters, some of whom came up winners and some losers under the licensing scheme of the Radio Act, who were the other players in the process leading to the decision to regulate? How does each interest you can identify fare under the outcome?

2.   If AT&T had successfully asserted its patents over the equipment needed by broadcasters to transmit their signals, wouldn't that have obviated the need for a governmental licensing scheme (at least for the duration of the patents)? Would there be reason to fear AT&T having such a monopoly?

Doesn't every patent intentionally bestow a monopoly on its owner? Insofar as free speech values are concerned, would you rather have the government or the telephone company controlling access to the airwaves? Isn't there a middle ground? Who controls the terms of access to the telephonic communication system: the government, the telephone company, or both? Does the effort by local telephone companies to enter cable television raise the same concerns that were raised by AT&T's early involvement in broadcasting?

3. To what extent was radio regulation based upon the notion that "government knows better"—at least in a technologically evolving and complex field? Note Professor Daniel Gifford's observations about New Deal agencies in general:

> Information scarcity provided a major justification for conferring broad discretionary powers on regulatory agencies and for judicial deference to agency judgments. Under the conventional wisdom, administrators were said to possess expertise developed from their experience in regulating as well as from their ability to draw on their staff of technicians. Because the public, the legislature, and the courts did not possess this expertise, agency judgments were said to command significant deference. * * * Because nonspecialists lacked significant information about industrial conditions, it was believed they were unqualified to interfere with the decisions of specialist administrators.

> Economic regulation of particular industries * * * was perceived at the time as casting government into the role of planner and promoter. Landis described the progression of government involvement as moving from an initial stage in which problematic behavior within a particular industrial field is brought under governmental supervision to a second stage in which "the economic well-being of an industry" becomes the chief goal of regulation. As the second stage is reached in various industries, the government assumes "supervision over the economic integrity of [these] industries and their formal development." * * *

> * * *

> Thus, by 1960, the theoretical underpinnings of administrative expertise had been largely undermined, creating a corresponding erosion in public confidence. Although critics conceded that administrators knew more about their tasks than nonspecialists, there was no longer a sound theoretical basis for believing that administrators in general knew more about the industries under their supervision than industry executives.

> * * *

> In the mid–1980s, fifty years after the arrival of the New Deal, an array of problems apparently inherent in government regulation are widely recognized. Agencies regulating single industries are susceptible to capture by the interest groups they supposedly regulate, wide grants of administrative discretion create abuses and dysfunctions whereas specific delegations create rigidities, and the institutional structures of the regulatory mechanisms tend to produce a myriad of distortions. The myth of administrative expertise has eroded and has produced a wide consensus about the beneficial effects of strengthening judicial review.
> * * *

Gifford, *The New Deal Regulatory Model: A History of Criticisms and Refinements*, 68 Minn.L.Rev. 299, 307, 316, 331 (1983).

How expert are agency officials, such as FCC commissioners? When they join the agency? When they leave it? Note that the average tenure in office of FCC commissioners is about three years, that most do not have backgrounds in communications policy, and that they generally end up in corporate jobs or private law practice after leaving the agency.

What would Professor Coase, (p. 31) think about the notion of having government officials, however well-qualified, do long-range planning for major industries? Are agency administrators better at policing or at planning?

On the other hand, how well have the FCC's license "auctions" of microwave frequencies worked out? Has the marketplace necessarily created a desireable result?

4. For another point of view on the NAB's role as a voluntary standard entity, see Mark M. MacCarthy, *Broadcasting Self–Regulation: The NAB Codes, Family Viewing Hour, and Television Violence*, 13 Cardozo Arts & Entertainment, L.J. 667 (1995).

> The NAB, founded in 1923, first attempted to regulate the industry in 1926 during the wavelength wars. The failure of this initial attempt at self-regulation is instructive in revealing the dependence of self-regulation upon an underlying scheme of government regulation.

> The NAB actively attempted to control this chaos through a voluntary standstill program. It sent to all 536 radio stations a "certificate of promise." By signing and returning this certificate to the NAB, a station agreed to operate only on wavelength and during the hours that had been assigned by the Commerce Department prior to the Attorney General's opinion. However, only 150 stations responded. In September 1926, the NAB helped to organize the National Radio Coordinating Committee, an all-industry self-regulatory body consisting of every major group involved in broadcasting. While the committee attempted to control the airwave chaos through self-regulation, it quickly realized that the real solution lay in new federal legislation.

> Despite the industry's attempt at self-regulation, this wavelength chaos endured until Congress came to the rescue. In February 1927, the President signed the Radio Act of 1927, which clearly established government authority to regulate the airwaves and assigned this responsibility to a new independent regulatory commission, the Federal Radio Commission ("FRC").

5. Consider this assessment of the Commission's track record by Henry Geller, a former FCC General Counsel, writing on the fiftieth anniversary of the Communications Act.

> An old-timer would instantly recognize Title III of the act, even though the broadcast scene has changed so drastically. * * * As to the efficacy

of the FCC's public interest regulation, the old-timer would find the following:

(i) The FCC botched its most important function—allocation of spectrum for broadcasting. It prevented superior FM service for years, and in the case of TV, unwisely mixed UHF and VHF frequencies. When this resulted in killing off UHF, the Commission did not move all TV to UHF, as it knew it should in 1953. Instead, it diddled for years, then in 1962 chose an all-channel TV law, and even today is still playing with "drop-ins" and other ways to fix an allocation plan with an obvious and fatal flaw. And it still frustrates the possible resurgence of AM by continuing to fumble with the issue of AM stereo.

H. Geller, *Communications Law—A Half Century Later*, 37 Fed.Comm.L.J. 73, 73–74 (1984).

6. As noted, some of the earliest sponsors of radio stations were manufacturers interested in spurring sales of their radio receivers. Could this have remained a viable means of supporting broadcast stations? Or wouldn't consumers rapidly have bought as many radio sets as they needed, thus leaving few future potential purchases—and thus little financial support for stations? Although there currently are more than 500 million radio receivers in the United States, consumers continue to buy about 50 million new sets per year—as "walkmen," "boom boxes," and replacement car radios proliferate.

Some other countries—most notably the United Kingdom—indirectly use the sale of radio sets as a means of financing public broadcasting, through an annual license fee on receivers. The British Broadcasting Corporation ("BBC") receives most of its funds this way, although it may need to raise money through limited advertising sales and other commercial activities in the future. Is there any economic or administrative advantage as between the private sector marking up the price of receivers and the public sector taxing the use of receivers in order to finance the broadcasting system?

Not surprisingly, many of the initial cable television entrepreneurs were retail outlets for television sets in areas of poor reception. By building cable systems, these businesspeople created a demand for sets in places where they could not previously have received a signal. In some cases, it may have been irrelevant whether their "community antenna television" (CATV) systems were profitable by themselves; cross-subsidies from sales of television sets may have more than offset CATV losses, at least in the early years. Is this economically any different from the way in which Westinghouse or the BBC financed their broadcasting activities?

7. On the early history of broadcasting generally, see E. Barnouw, *A History of Broadcasting in the United States, Vol. I: A Tower in Babel* (1966).

8. As to the process and standards for getting licenses renewed, see Chapter V.

B.   THE ONGOING POLICY DEBATE

1.   ALTERNATIVE MARKET STRUCTURES

R. COASE, THE FEDERAL COMMUNICATIONS COMMISSION

2 J.L. & Econ. 1, 14–40 (1959).*

* * *

III.   THE RATIONALE OF THE PRESENT SYSTEM

* * *

[I]t is a commonplace of economics that almost all resources used in the economic system (and not simply radio and television frequencies) are limited in amount and scarce, in that people would like to use more than exists. Land, labor, and capital are all scarce, but this, of itself, does not call for government regulation. It is true that some mechanism has to be employed to decide who, out of the many claimants, should be allowed to use the scarce resource. But the way this is usually done in the American economic system is to employ the price mechanism, and this allocates resources to users without the need for government regulation.

* * * [T]he real cause of the trouble [with frequency allocation] was that no property rights were created in these scarce frequencies. We know from our ordinary experience that land can be allocated to land users without the need for government regulation by using the price mechanism. But if no property rights were created in land, so that everyone could use a tract of land, it is clear that there would be considerable confusion and that the price mechanism could not work because there would not be any property rights that could be acquired. If one person could use a piece of land for growing a crop, and then another person could come along and build a house on the land used for the crop, and then another could come along, tear down the house, and use the space as a parking lot, it would no doubt be accurate to describe the resulting situation as chaos. But it would be wrong to blame this on private enterprise and the competitive system. A private-enterprise system cannot function properly unless property rights are created in resources, and, when this is done, someone wishing to use a resource has to pay the owner to obtain it. Chaos disappears; and so does the government except that a legal system to define property rights and to arbitrate disputes is, of course, necessary. But there is certainly no need for the kind of regulation which we now find in the American radio and television industry.

* * *

* Reprinted with permission of the Journal of Law & Economics, The University of Chicago Law School.

IV.   THE PRICING SYSTEM AND THE ALLOCATION OF FREQUENCIES

There can be little doubt that the idea of using private property and the pricing system in the allocation of frequencies is one which is completely unfamiliar to most of those concerned with broadcasting policy. * * *

This "novel theory" (novel with Adam Smith) is, of course, that the allocation of resources should be determined by the forces of the market rather than as a result of government decisions. Quite apart from the malallocations which are the result of political pressures, an administrative agency which attempts to perform the function normally carried out by the pricing mechanism operates under two handicaps. First of all, it lacks the precise monetary measure of benefit and cost provided by the market. Second, it cannot, by the nature of things, be in possession of all the relevant information possessed by the managers of every business which uses or might use radio frequencies, to say nothing of the preferences of consumers for the various goods and services in the production of which radio frequencies could be used. In fact, lengthy investigations are required to uncover part of this information, and decisions of the Federal Communications Commission emerge only after long delays, often extending to years. To simplify the task, the Federal Communications Commission adopts arbitrary rules. * * *

This discussion should not be taken to imply that an administrative allocation of resources is inevitably worse than an allocation by means of the price mechanism. The operation of a market is not itself costless, and, if the costs of operating the market exceeded the costs of running the agency by a sufficiently large amount, we might be willing to acquiesce in the malallocation of resources resulting from the agency's lack of knowledge, inflexibility, and exposure to political pressure. But in the United States few people think that this would be so in most industries, and there is nothing about the broadcasting industry which would lead us to believe that the allocation of frequencies constitutes an exceptional case.

An example of how the nature of the pricing system is misunderstood in current discussions of broadcasting policy in the United States is furnished by a recent comment which appeared in the trade journal Broadcasting:

> In the TV field, lip service is given to a proposal that television "franchises" be awarded to the highest bidder among those who may be qualified. This is ridiculous on its face, since it would mean that choice outlets in prime markets would go to those with the most money.[40]

First of all, it must be observed that resources do not go, in the American economic system, to those with the most money but to those who are willing to pay the most for them. The result is that, in the struggle for particular resources, men who earn $5,000 per annum are

40. Broadcasting, February 24, 1958, p. 200.

every day outbidding those who earn $50,000 per annum. To be convinced that this is so, we need only imagine a situation occurring in which all those who earned $50,000 or more per annum arrived at the stores one morning and, at the prices quoted, were able to buy everything in stock, with nothing left over for those with lower incomes. Next day we may be sure that the prices quoted would be higher and that those with higher incomes would be forced to reduce their purchases—a process which would continue as long as those with lower incomes were unable to spend all they wanted. The same system which enables a man with $1 million to obtain $1 million's worth of resources enables a man with $1,000 to obtain a $1,000's worth of resources. Of course, the existence of a pricing system does not insure that the distribution of money between persons (or families) is satisfactory. But this is not a question we need to consider in dealing with broadcasting policy. Insofar as the ability to pay for frequencies or channels depends on the distribution of funds, it is the distribution not between persons but between firms which is relevant. And here the ethical problem does not arise. All that matters is whether the distribution of funds contributes to efficiency, and there is every reason to suppose that, broadly speaking, it does. Those firms which used funds profitably find it easy to get more; those which do not, find it difficult. The capital market does not work perfectly, but the general tendency is clear. * * *

* * * Despite all the efforts of art dealers, the number of Rembrandts existing at a given time is limited; yet such paintings are commonly disposed of by auction. But the works of dead painters are not unique in being in fixed supply. If we take a broad enough view, the supply of all factors of production is seen to be fixed (the amount of land, the size of the population, etc.). Of course, this is not the way we think of the supply of land or labor. Since we are usually concerned with a particular problem, we think not in terms of the total supply but rather of the supply available for a particular use. Such a procedure is not only practically more useful; it also tells us more about the processes of adjustment at work in the market. Although the quantity of a resource may be limited in total, the quantity that can be made available to a particular use is variable. Producers in a particular industry can obtain more of any resource they require by buying it on the market, although they are unlikely to be able to obtain considerable additional quantities unless they bid up the price, thereby inducing firms in other industries to curtail their use of the resource. This is the mechanism which governs the allocation of factors of production in almost all industries. Notwithstanding the almost unanimous contrary view, there is nothing in the technology of the broadcasting industry which prevents the use of the same mechanism. Indeed, use of the pricing system is made particularly easy by [the fact that] the broadcasting industry uses but a small proportion of "spectrum space." A broadcasting industry, forced to bid for frequencies, could draw them away from other industries by raising the price it was willing to pay. It is impossible to say whether the result of introducing the pricing system would be that the broadcasting indus-

try would obtain more frequencies than are allocated to it by the Federal Communications Commission. Not having had, in the past, a market for frequencies, we do not know what these various industries would pay for them. Similarly, we do not know for what frequencies the broadcasting industry would be willing to outbid these other industries. All we can say is that the broadcasting industry would be able to obtain all the existing frequencies it now uses (and more) if it were willing to pay a price equal to the contribution which they could make to production elsewhere. This is saying nothing more than that the broadcasting industry would be able to obtain frequencies on the same basis as it now obtains its labor, buildings, land, and equipment.

A thoroughgoing employment of the pricing mechanism for the allocation of radio frequencies would, of course, mean that the various governmental authorities, which are at present such heavy users of these frequencies, would also be required to pay for them. This may appear to be unnecessary, since payment would have to be made to some other government agency appointed to act as custodian of frequencies. What was paid out of one government pocket would simply go into another. It may also seem inappropriate that the allocation of resources for such purposes as national defense or the preservation of human life should be subjected to a monetary test. While it would be entirely possible to exclude from the pricing process all frequencies which government departments consider they need and to confine pricing to frequencies available for the private sector, there would seem to be compelling reasons for not doing so. A government department, in making up its mind whether or not to undertake a particular activity, should weigh against the benefits this would confer, the costs which are also involved: that is, the value of the production elsewhere which would otherwise be enjoyed. In the case of a government activity which is regarded as so essential as to justify any sacrifice, it is still desirable to minimize the cost of any particular project. If the use of a frequency which if used industrially would contribute goods worth $1 million could be avoided by the construction of a wire system or the purchase of reserve vehicles costing $100,000, it is better that the frequency should not be used, however essential the project. It is the merit of the pricing system that, in these circumstances, a government department (unless very badly managed) would not use the frequency if made to pay for it. * * *

The desire to preserve government ownership of radio frequencies coupled with an unwillingness to require any payment for the use of these frequencies has had one consequence which has caused some uneasiness. A station operator who is granted a license to use a particular frequency in a particular place may, in fact, be granted a very valuable right, one for which he would be willing to pay a large sum of money and which he would be forced to pay if others could bid for the frequency. This provision of a valuable resource without charge naturally raises the income of station operators above what it would have been in competitive conditions. It would require a very detailed investigation to determine the extent to which private operators of radio and television stations have been enriched as a result of this policy. But part of the extremely high return on the capital invested in certain radio and television stations has undoubtedly been due to this failure to charge for the use of the frequency. * * *

The extraordinary gain accruing to radio and television station operators as a result of the present system of allocating frequencies becomes apparent when stations are sold. Even before the 1927 Act was passed, it was recognized that stations were transferred from one owner to another at prices which implied that the right to a license was being sold. Occasionally, references to this problem are found in the literature, but the subject has not been discussed extensively. In part, I think this derives from the fact that the only solution to the problem of excessive profits was thought to be rate regulation or profit control. * * * In any case, the determination of the rates to be charged or the level of profits to be allowed would not seem an easy matter. * * * Furthermore, rate or profit regulation with the concomitant need for control of the quality of the programs is hardly an attractive prospect.

* * *

V.   Private Property and the Allocation of Frequencies

If the right to use a frequency is to be sold, the nature of that right would have to be precisely defined. A simple answer would be to leave the situation essentially as it is now: the broadcaster would buy the right to use, for a certain period, an assigned frequency to transmit signals at a given power for certain hours from a transmitter located in a particular place. This would simply superimpose a payment on to the present system. It would certainly make it possible for the person or firm who is to use a frequency to be determined in the market. But the enforcement of such detailed regulations for the operation of stations as are now imposed by the Federal Communications Commission would severely limit the extent to which the way the frequency was used could be determined by the forces of the market.

It might be argued that this is by no means an unusual situation, since the rights acquired when one buys, say, a piece of land, are determined not by the forces of supply and demand but by the law of property in land. But this is by no means the whole truth. Whether a newly discovered cave belongs to the man who discovered it, the man on whose land the entrance to the cave is located, or the man who owns the surface under which the cave is situated is no doubt dependent on the law of property. But the law merely determines the person with whom it is necessary to make a contract to obtain the use of the cave. Whether the cave is used for storing bank records, as a natural gas reservoir, or for growing mushrooms depends, not on the laws of property, but on whether the bank, the natural gas corporation, or the mushroom concern will pay the most in order to be able to use the cave. One of the purposes of the legal system is to establish that clear delimitation of rights on the basis of which the transfer and recombination of rights can take place through the market. In the case of radio, it should be possible for someone who is granted the use of a frequency to arrange to share it with someone else, with whatever adjustments to hours of operation, power, location and kind of transmitter, etc., as may be mutually agreed upon; or when the right initially acquired is the shared use of a frequency (and in certain cases the FCC has permitted only shared usage), it should not be made impossible for one user to buy out the rights of the other users so as to obtain an exclusive usage.

The main reason for government regulation of the radio industry was to prevent interference. It is clear that, if signals are transmitted simultaneously on a given frequency by several people, the signals would interfere with each other and would make reception of the messages transmitted by any one person difficult, if not impossible. The use of a piece of land simultaneously for growing wheat and as a parking lot would produce similar results. * * * [T]he way this situation is avoided is to create property rights (rights, that is, to exclusive use) in land. The creation of similar rights in the use of frequencies would enable the problem to be solved in the same way in the radio industry.

* * *

* * * It is sometimes implied that the aim of regulation in the radio industry should be to minimize interference. But this would be wrong. The aim should be to maximize output. All property rights interfere with the ability of people to use resources. What has to be insured is that the gain from interference more than offsets the harm it produces. There is no reason to suppose that the optimum situation is one in which there is no interference. In general, as the distance from a radio station increases, it becomes more and more difficult to receive its signals. At some point, people will decide that it is not worthwhile to incur costs involved in receiving the station's signals. A local station operating on the same frequency might be easily received by these same people. But if this station operated simultaneously with the first one, people living in some region intermediate between the stations may be unable to receive signals from either station. These people would be better off if either station stopped operating and there was no interference; but then those living in the neighborhood of one of these other stations would suffer. It is not clear that the solution in which there is no interference is necessarily preferable.

* * * The reduction of interference on adjacent frequencies may require costly improvements in equipment, and operators on one frequency could hardly be expected to incur such costs for the benefit of others if the rights of those operating on adjacent frequencies have not been determined. The institution of private property plus the pricing system would resolve these conflicts. The operator whose signals were interfered with, if he had the right to stop such interference, would be willing to forego this right if he were paid more than the amount by which the value of his service was decreased by this interference or the costs which he would have to incur to offset it. The other operator would be willing to pay, in order to be allowed to interfere, an amount up to the

costs of suppressing the interference or the decrease in the value of the service he could provide if unable to use his transmitter in a way which resulted in interference. Or, alternatively, if this operator had the right to cause interference, he would be willing to desist if he were paid more than the costs of suppressing the interference or the decrease in the value of the service he could provide if interference were barred. And the operator whose signals were interfered with would be willing to pay to stop this interference an amount up to the decrease in the value of his service which it causes or the costs he has to incur to offset the interference. Either way, the result would be the same. * * *

If the problems faced in the broadcasting industry are not out of the ordinary, it may be asked why was not the usual solution (a mixture of transferable rights plus regulation) adopted for this industry? There can be little doubt that, left to themselves, the courts would have solved the problems of the radio industry in much the same way as they had solved similar problems in other industries. In the early discussions of radio law an attempt was made to bring the problems within the main corpus of existing law. The problem of radio interference was examined by analogy with electric-wire interference, water rights, trade marks, noise nuisances, the problem of acquiring title to ice from public ponds, and so on. * * * But this line of development was stopped by the passage of the 1927 Act, which established a complete regulatory system.

* * *

VI. THE PRESENT POSITION

* * *

If the aim of government regulation of broadcasting is to influence programming, it is irrelevant to discuss whether regulation is necessitated by the technology of the industry. The question does, of course, arise as to whether such regulation is compatible with the doctrine of freedom of speech and of the press. In general, this is not a question which has disturbed those who wished to see the Federal Communications Commission control programming, largely because they thought a clear distinction could be drawn between broadcasting and the publication of newspapers, periodicals, and books (for which few would advocate similar regulation). * * * The Supreme Court made the distinction between broadcasting and the publication of newspapers rest on the fact that a resource used in broadcasting is limited in amount and scarce. But, as we have seen, this argument is invalid. * * *

* * *

Mr. William Howard Taft, who was Chief Justice of the Supreme Court during the critical formative period of the broadcasting industry, is reported to have said: "I have always dodged this radio question. I have refused to grant writs and have told the other justices that I hope to avoid passing on this subject as long as possible." Pressed to explain why, he answered:

... interpreting the law on this subject is something like trying to interpret the law of the occult. It seems like dealing with something supernatural. I want to put it off as long as possible in the hope that it becomes more understandable before the court passes on the questions involved.[81]

It was indeed in the shadows cast by a mysterious technology that our views on broadcasting policy were formed. It has been the burden of this article to show that the problems posed by the broadcasting industry do not call for any fundamental changes in the legal and economic arrangements which serve other industries. But the belief that the broadcasting industry is unique and requires regulation of a kind which would be unthinkable in the other media of communication is now so firmly held as perhaps to be beyond the reach of critical examination. The history of regulation in the broadcasting industry demonstrates the crucial importance of events in the early days of a new development in determining long-run governmental policy. It also suggests that lawyers and economists should not be so overwhelmed by the emergence of new technologies as to change the existing legal and economic system without first making quite certain that this is required.

Notes and Questions

1. Be certain that you are not still subject to the "most money" illusion addressed by Professor Coase in the text following the footnote. Here is a simple illustration of the point from another, perhaps more familiar perspective:

The A Company sells razor blades. The B Company sells perfume. Each is deciding whether to buy a one-minute commercial spot on Monday Night Football for $300,000. Which is the more likely to buy this advertising resource, i.e., to be willing to pay more for it? Is that decision in any way related to how much money either firm has?

Suppose that A believes it can sell $3 million of inexpensive razor blades if it buys the time and runs its ad. Of this amount, $2,400,000 will cover the cost of producing the blades, and $300,000 will go to pay for the ad. That leaves A with a profit of $300,000.

On the other hand, B thinks that it could sell $3 million worth of expensive perfume and make perhaps $150,000 in profit after the costs of production and advertising. Clearly, A thinks that it can make more money than B if it buys the spot. Indeed, B may think the risk of loss not worth the chance to make a mere $150,000. But suppose that A doesn't have $300,000 to purchase the time? If you agreed with A's projections of sales and profits, you (or anyone else with $300,000, or 300 people with $1,000 each and so forth) would be willing to finance A's purchase of the time for $300,000, in return for taking perhaps $360,000 of the revenues which it produced—still leaving A with a profit of $240,000.

81. C.C. Dill, Radio Law 1–2 (1938). Mr. Taft was Chief Justice of the Supreme Court from 1921 to 1930. So far as I can discover, the Supreme Court did not consider any radio case while Mr. Taft was Chief Justice.

Capital markets operate along these lines to allocate the spot to the party or parties that can use it most profitably, that is, those most willing to risk that their use will be profitable. If the capital markets are open, is it possible to ascertain how much money any particular firm has, or who has the "most money"?

2.   Professor Coase suggests an open marketplace for frequencies, as a means of encouraging spectrum owners to make the highest and best use of their frequencies. What might the actual results of spectrum sales be? Professor Matthew Spitzer gives one view of this future. He begins by assuming that most advertiser-supported television would migrate to direct broadcast satellites, since they could generate larger audiences than traditional terrestrial broadcasters.

* * * Perhaps each large metropolitan area could support one or two regional stations. These stations would operate on frequencies, such as VHF, which are ill-suited to satellite broadcast and would operate at a somewhat higher power output than those broadcasting today. They would supply local news, weather, sports, and advertisements and might operate only during the morning and early evening hours when demand for local news and other information is greatest. These local broadcasters would most likely share frequencies with industrial or business users, whose demand would be greatest during weekday working hours. * * *

What would happen to "free" (i.e., advertiser-supported) television if spectrum were bought and sold in an unregulated market? Some free television would almost certainly survive, although probably not as much as exists today in major metropolitan areas. A simple example demonstrates this. Assume that there are thirty million television homes in a satellite transmitter's footprint; that a viewer must pay $.25 per half hour for a typical pay-television show; that there is a two-way mechanism capable of charging for shows; and that there are twenty television signals, competing with one another on a pay-per-view basis. Assume further that all sets are turned on and that the television homes distribute themselves equally among the signals. Further, assume that advertisers are willing to pay $.04 per home per half hour of viewing and that the pay signals have no commercials. If by switching to a free status for at least one show, one of the pay-television signals could thereby attract one-fourth of the viewers from each of the other nineteen signals, the free channel would have a viewership of 8.625 million homes and would realize revenues of $345,000 per half hour while each pay channel would realize $281,250 per half hour. Clearly, at least one channel would switch to a free signal with commercials.

* * *

In short, there probably would be a substantial mixture of financing devices, similar to those in the print medium today. Some newspapers, primarily weeklies, depend entirely upon advertiser support. Some periodicals * * * are financed almost exclusively by reader payments since they contain little or no advertising. But the vast majority of printed publications depends on a combination of advertiser and reader payments. * * *

This short excursion into the economics of newspapers, periodicals and commercial television has revealed nothing that justifies regulation of broadcast alone. Both print and broadcast experience economies of scale in the transmission phase. Each poses the difficult question of how best to deal with a naturally monopolistic bottleneck in the marketplace of ideas and requires that we choose between private ownership and some sort of public utility status. Thus, it is likely that the market structures for print and broadcast would, absent regulatory shaping, resemble one another, with firms monopolistically competing.

Matthew Spitzer, *Controlling the Content of Print and Broadcast,* 58 So.Cal. L.Rev. 1349, 1382–1384 (1985).

3.   One highly informal type of private spectrum right has arisen in the form of "pirate radio." As the jargon implies, these are usually unlicensed stations operating on ships outside of any nation's territorial waters. The FCC has had little cause to exercise jurisdiction over pirate radio, since it has authority only over offshore stations only on U.S.-registered vessels. 47 U.S.C. § 301(e). By contrast, the United Kingdom has been aggressive not only in enacting domestic legislation, but also in securing treaties against piracy. Note, *The Case of the Sarah, A Testing Ground for the Regulation of Radio Piracy in the United States,* 12 Fordham Int'l L.J. 67 (1988). One reason for the United States' apparent lack of concern in this field may be its relatively large geographic area. A comparatively low-power and directionalized offshore transmitter can fit into existing frequency allocations with little or no interference. In most proceedings against unlicensed U.S. broadcast operations, all of which have apparently been settled, FCC officials have admitted informally that the operations caused no interference to existing stations.

4.   Does the government's demand for spectrum present a special challenge to Coase's claim of efficiency for the marketplace? If the government buys spectrum from itself—e.g., a "payment" from the Defense Department to the Treasury for a "purchase" from the FCC—wouldn't it be indifferent to the price? If you think so, ask what the Defense Department must give up in order to get its frequency, in terms of an "opportunity cost." If a government agency is not likely to ask that question of itself, and would therefore be inclined to over-consume spectrum, what institutional arrangement might be used to minimize this type of misallocation? See Coase, *The Interdepartment Radio Advisory Committee,* 5 J.L. & Econ. 17 (1962); Rosenblum, *Low Visibility Decision–Making by Administrative Agencies: The Problem of Radio Spectrum Allocation,* 18 Ad.L.Rev. 19 (1965).

5.   One major question raised by Coase's thesis is why the government uses different systems to allocate different resources. For example, the government uses an auction price system to dispose of timber rights or oil leases. But the courts are available to litigants for only minimal filing fees that do not nearly cover the cost of their operation. Instead of deciding which litigation should be heard first in the "public interest," courts hear most cases approximately in the order in which they were filed. High governmental offices are allocated on a competitive—but clearly non-price—basis, known as an election. And excuse from the military draft changed from a price model during the Civil War to a public interest type of decisionmaking process, and briefly to a lottery, before its abolition in favor

of a market system in which the military competes with the private sector to attract labor.

Each type of system may make sense according to its place in history and the type of goods allocated. This still leaves the question as to how one can rationally distinguish between allocating broadcasting and mineral rights.

6. Coase observes that the present system confers vast profits upon a few chosen (lucky?) beneficiaries. Since those who purchase from an initial licensee presumably pay fair market value for their licenses, and since most initial licensees have sold their stations over the last decades, the broadcasting industry today may contain few of the original recipients of governmental largesse. In view of this fact, should the government exercise the rights reserved in Sections 304 and 309(h) of the Communications Act and auction off the right to broadcast? Even though licenses are not, at least in theory, property rights, could the government—legally or politically—justify selling licenses for which incumbent broadcasters have paid millions of dollars? Would an auction only for new frequencies be fairer? A lottery? Note the FCC's rather unhappy experience with PCS auctions.

7. Coase argues that a property rights system would have the advantage of allowing a "spectrum developer" to use frequencies in the most efficient way. This might take the form of "sub-dividing" the "spectrum property" into a variety of smaller pieces—such as a text channel on a television station's vertical blanking interval or a foreign language station on an FM station's subcarrier.

This is not terribly different from a real estate developer finding a property's "best and highest" use. In some cases, this use will be a luxury apartment building, in others, an office tower, and in still others a mixed-use building with residential, commercial and retail space. To what extent should the government second-guess the developer's decision? For example, if the "owner" of a VHF television channel decides to "subdivide" it by using digital compression to offer two or more video programs over the same bandwidth, isn't this clearly in the public interest? If the broadcaster's decision requires viewers to buy new television receivers? If the channel is offered on a "pay" basis?

2. BEYOND MARKET STRUCTURES: THE CONSTITUTIONALITY OF LICENSING

Licensing is a common means of controlling private sector conduct— from ships to saloons. In most cases, however, administrative licensing focuses on traditional public welfare concerns, usually physical health and safety, but sometimes efficient resource management. Building permits, airline routes, and fishing and hunting permits are typical applications of administrative licensing powers.

Virtually *sui generis,* however, broadcast licensing involves the government in speech, either directly or indirectly. The drafters of the 1927 Radio Act appeared to contemplate some administrative intervention in broadcasters' programming, particularly aimed at the wide variety of scams then on the air. Whether it was necessary or intended that the

FRC or the FCC use licensing as a means of content control, however, is not clear.

At least in theory, the government retains ownership of a frequency when it licenses it to a private entity. How then could the FCC adopt its policy of auctioning off licenses in the mid–1990s—especially when the Communications Act itself limited the duration of license grants? The answer lies not in the basic Act itself, but rather in the special rider which authorized the auctions in the first place.

Licensing of broadcast stations need not result in intrusive content control. For more than half a century, however, it has, and that may be unavoidable in light of the Commission's licensing power and its status as an inherently political body, whose commissioners are political appointees. If a group feels aggrieved at a station's programming—or lack thereof—it naturally seeks redress from the government agency with jurisdiction over that station. In short, it demands that the Commission "do something," on issues ranging from suppressing indecent programming to requiring children's television. In reply, it is difficult for the Commission merely to invoke free speech concerns as a reason for declining to act.

Whether the FCC should have been forced into this role is debatable. Its involvement with programming raises a number of traditional First Amendment concerns. As indicated below, however, the courts seem to play by different rules for the electronic and print media.

NEAR v. MINNESOTA
Supreme Court of the United States, 1931.
283 U.S. 697, 51 S.Ct. 625, 75 L.Ed. 1357.

MR. CHIEF JUSTICE HUGHES delivered the opinion of the Court.

Chapter 285 of the Session Laws of Minnesota for the year 1925 provides * * *:

"Section 1. Any person who * * * shall be engaged in the business of regularly or customarily producing, publishing or circulating, having in possession, selling or giving away * * *

"(b) a malicious, scandalous, and defamatory newspaper, magazine or other periodical,

—is guilty of a nuisance, and all persons guilty of such nuisance may be enjoined [in an action by the County Attorney].

"In actions brought under (b) above, there shall be available the defense that the truth was published with good motives and for justifiable ends * * *."

* * *

Under this statute, clause (b), the County Attorney of Hennepin County brought this action to enjoin the publication of what was described as a "malicious, scandalous and defamatory newspaper, magazine or other periodical," known as "The Saturday Press," published by the defendants in the city of Minneapolis. * * * [T]he articles charged in substance that a Jewish gangster was in control of gambling, bootlegging and racketeering in Minneapolis, and that law enforcing officers and agencies were not energetically performing their duties. * * * There is no question but that the articles made serious accusations. [The State district court issued a permanent injunction and the Supreme Court of Minnesota affirmed.]

This statute, for the suppression as a public nuisance of a newspaper or periodical, is unusual, if not unique, and raises questions of grave importance transcending the local interests involved in the particular action. It is no longer open to doubt that the liberty of the press, and of speech, is within the liberty safeguarded by the due process clause of the Fourteenth Amendment from invasion by state action. * * *

First. The statute is not aimed at the redress of individual or private wrongs. Remedies for libel remain available and unaffected. * * * It is aimed at the distribution of scandalous matter as "detrimental to public morals and to the general welfare," tending "to disturb the peace of the community" and "to provoke assaults and the commission of crime." In order to obtain an injunction to suppress the future publication of the newspaper or periodical, it is not necessary to prove the falsity of the charges that have been made in the publication condemned. In the present action there was no allegation that the matter published was not true. It is alleged, and the statute requires the allegation, that the publication was "malicious." But, as in prosecutions for libel, there is no requirement of proof by the State of malice in fact as distinguished from malice inferred from the mere publication of the defamatory matter. The judgment in this case proceeded upon the mere proof of publication. The statute permits the defense, not of the truth alone, but only that the truth was published with good motives and for justifiable ends. * * *

Second. The statute is directed not simply at the circulation of scandalous and defamatory statements with regard to private citizens, but at the continued publication by newspapers and periodicals of charges against public officers of corruption, malfeasance in office, or serious neglect of duty. * * *

Third. The object of the statute is not punishment, in the ordinary sense, but suppression of the offending newspaper or periodical. The reason for the enactment, as the state court has said, is that prosecutions to enforce penal statutes for libel do not result in "efficient repression or suppression of the evils of scandal." * * *

Fourth. The statute not only operates to suppress the offending newspaper or periodical but to put the publisher under an effective censorship. * * * Thus, where a newspaper or periodical has been suppressed because of the circulation of charges against public officers of official misconduct, it would seem to be clear that the renewal of the publication of such charges would constitute a contempt and that the judgment would lay a permanent restraint upon the publisher, to escape

which he must satisfy the court as to the character of a new publication. Whether he would be permitted again to publish matter deemed to be derogatory to the same or other public officers would depend upon the court's ruling. In the present instance the judgment restrained the defendants from "publishing, circulating, having in their possession, selling or giving away any publication whatsoever which is a malicious, scandalous or defamatory newspaper, as defined by law." The law gives no definition except that covered by the words "scandalous and defamatory," and publications charging official misconduct are of that class.
* * *

The question is whether a statute authorizing such proceedings in restraint of publication is consistent with the conception of the liberty of the press as historically conceived and guaranteed. In determining the extent of the constitutional protection, it has been generally, if not universally, considered that it is the chief purpose of the guaranty to prevent previous restraints upon publication. The struggle in England, directed against the legislative power of the licenser, resulted in renunciation of the censorship of the press. The liberty deemed to be established was thus described by Blackstone: "The liberty of the press is indeed essential to the nature of a free state; but this consists in laying no *previous* restraints upon publications, and not in freedom from censure for criminal matter when published. * * * "

The fact that for approximately one hundred and fifty years there has been almost an entire absence of attempts to impose previous restraints upon publications relating to the malfeasance of public officers is significant of the deep-seated conviction that such restraints would violate constitutional right. Public officers, whose character and conduct remain open to debate and free discussion in the press, find their remedies for false accusations in actions under libel laws providing for redress and punishment, and not in proceedings to restrain the publication of newspapers and periodicals. * * *

* * *

The statute in question cannot be justified by reason of the fact that the publisher is permitted to show, before injunction issues, that the matter published is true and is published with good motives and for justifiable ends. If such a statute, authorizing suppression and injunction on such a basis, is constitutionally valid, it would be equally permissible for the legislature to provide that at any time the publisher of any newspaper could be brought before a court, or even an administrative officer (as the constitutional protection may not be regarded as resting on mere procedural details), and required to produce proof of the truth of his publication, or of what he intended to publish and of his motives, or stand enjoined. If this can be done, the legislature may provide machinery for determining in the complete exercise of its discretion what are justifiable ends and restrain publication accordingly. And it would be but a step to a complete system of censorship. * * *

Equally unavailing is the insistence that the statute is designed to prevent the circulation of scandal which tends to disturb the public peace and to provoke assaults and the commission of crime. Charges of reprehensible conduct, and in particular of official malfeasance, unquestionably create a public scandal, but the theory of the constitutional guaranty is that even a more serious public evil would be caused by authority to prevent publication. * * *

For these reasons we hold the statute * * * to be an infringement of the liberty of the press guaranteed by the Fourteenth Amendment. * * *

Judgment reversed.

Mr. Justice Butler, dissenting. * * *

The Minnesota statute does not operate as a *previous* restraint on publication within the proper meaning of that phrase. It does not authorize administrative control in advance such as was formerly exercised by the licensers and censors but prescribes a remedy to be enforced by a suit in equity. In this case there was previous publication made in the course of the business of regularly producing malicious, scandalous and defamatory periodicals. The business and publications unquestionably constitute an abuse of the right of free press. The statute denounces the things done as a nuisance on the ground, as stated by the state supreme court, that they threaten morals, peace and good order. There is no question of the power of the State to denounce such transgressions. The restraint authorized is only in respect of continuing to do what has been duly adjudged to constitute a nuisance. * * * There is nothing in the statute purporting to prohibit publications that have not been adjudged to constitute a nuisance. It is fanciful to suggest similarity between the granting or enforcement of the decree authorized by this statute to prevent *further* publication of malicious, scandalous and defamatory articles and the *previous restraint* upon the press by licensers as referred to by Blackstone and described in the history of the times to which he alludes. * * *

Mr. Justice Van Devanter, Mr. Justice McReynolds, and Mr. Justice Sutherland concur in this opinion.

Notes and Questions

1. By what reasoning did the Court find a "prior restraint" in a statutory scheme that required the State to show that an offending publication already had occurred in order to obtain any relief? Would this argument be more compelling if the statute were to require the publishers to secure court approval before publishing another edition? Before beginning a new newspaper? Before buying a radio station?

2. Is it clear what the injunction here prevented the publisher from doing in the future? How would a court determine in the future whether the defendants were "publishing, circulating, having in their possession, selling or giving away any publication whatsoever which is a malicious, scandalous or defamatory newspaper, *as defined by law*" [emphasis added]. Doesn't this assume that the defendants would have at least one more day in court, to

show that a new publication was not "malicious, scandalous, or defamatory"?

3.   If the defendants could have started another publication, subject to a challenge for contempt of the injunction, would a prior restraint or a subsequent punishment have guaranteed them a more effective second day in court? As Professor Freund points out, in all cases the law "takes its bite" after publication. If the "bite" is a prison sentence, however, it is not likely that the journalist will resume publication.

4.   Would the situation be materially different if the statutory remedy were a fine? Would that depend upon the amount of the fine? On its effect on the particular publisher's ability to continue operating? By the Court's reasoning in *Near,* would imprisonment in that case also have been a "prior restraint"? If so, what does it mean to insist that "[s]ubsequent punishment for such abuses as may exist is the appropriate remedy"?

5.   Consider the following observations by Paul Freund in *The Supreme Court and Civil Liberties,* 4 Vand.L.Rev. 533, 537–39 (1951) [footnotes omitted].

> Certain distinctions commonly drawn between prior restraint and subsequent punishment will not bear analysis. It is sometimes said that prior restraint is the greater deterrent. This generality depends on the psychological aspects of the case. An injunction running against a particular individual may, to be sure, deter him more sharply than the broad command of a criminal statute; but just as possibly the underlying statutory prohibition, whether enforceable by injunction or by criminal sanctions, may have a deterrent effect not varying with the particular sanction employed. It is said, moreover, that there is a difference in the time at which the offense is passed upon, that in the case of prior restraint the offense is judged prospectively while in the case of criminal sanctions it is judged after it has been committed. But the judicial sanction takes its bite after the fact in either case, whether the sanction be fine or imprisonment for criminal violation or fine or imprisonment for violation of an injunctive or administrative order. In either case the facts of the violation are spread before a judicial tribunal after the event.

> Is there then no validity in the conventional contrast between prior restraint and subsequent penalty? Several possible differences do exist. In the first place, the identity of the trier of fact is important. There are two sets of facts to be judged: what may be called facts of coverage (including interpretation and application of the governing standards) and facts of violation. Under an outright criminal law the two coalesce into one stage, determined ordinarily by a jury and at all events according to criminal procedure. Under a licensing or injunctive scheme the one determination is made by an administrative official or by a judge, with review normally by a judge, and the other determination is made by a judge in contempt proceedings or by the processes of criminal law. To the extent that an advisory jury is used by a court at the injunctive stage, the difference between this procedure and the outright criminal sanction on the score of the trier of fact is minimized.

> Second, there may be a difference in the clarity and definiteness of the prohibition. On this point, however, no generalization is possible.

The injunctive order may in fact be just as clear and definite as a penal statute, particularly if the order is issued with respect to a designated publication. Indeed, an injunctive order in some circumstances may afford greater guidance than a penal statute. * * *

A third difference between prior restraint and subsequent punishment is suggested by this problem of interim violations. Suppose that the individual offender, rather than ultimately losing, eventually prevails on a full hearing of the constitutional issues. In a criminal trial he would of course suffer no punishment. In an injunctive or administrative proceeding, where a restraining order or temporary injunction has been issued against him or a permit withheld, but where a final injunction is ultimately denied or a permit granted, there is the serious problem of penalties for interim violations. If disobedience of the interim order is *ipso facto* contempt, with no opportunity to escape by showing the invalidity of the order on the merits, the restraint does indeed have a chilling effect beyond that of a criminal statute. To the extent, however, that local procedure allows such a defense to be raised in a contempt proceeding, the special objection to prior restraint growing out of the problem of interim activity is obviated.

In sum, it will hardly do to place "prior restraint" in a special category for condemnation. What is needed is a pragmatic assessment of its operation in the particular circumstances. The generalization that prior restraint is particularly obnoxious in civil liberties cases must yield to more particularistic analysis.

Assuming (i) that an advisory jury was required under the scheme challenged in *Near;* (ii) that the injunction prohibited "further publication of The Saturday Press"; and (iii) that no problem of "interim violations" could arise because no preliminary injunction was authorized or issued, what would a "pragmatic assessment" of the Minnesota statute's operation indicate about its constitutionality?

6. The government's interest in suppressing speech is, of course, the easiest to protect if it has a monopoly upon the media of communication, as it typically has in a totalitarian regime. Short of that, its difficulty would be minimized by requiring, under heavy penalty for failure, that the private owners of the media clear all material with government censors prior to publication. Control is still more imperfect if prior restraints are unavailable since, as may be illustrated by *New York Times Co. v. United States*, 403 U.S. 713, 91 S.Ct. 2140, 29 L.Ed.2d 822 (1971) (the "Pentagon Papers" case), some revelations, if they can only be made, are so powerful that they disable the government from taking reprisals. Once "the cat is out of the bag," not only can it not be gotten back in, but there may arise a constituency against efforts to punish its liberator.

7. After *Near,* is it fair to assume that the government may not require media to secure prior official approval before commencing or continuing operations?

8. Under this analysis, how does the FCC's licensing process fare?

TRINITY METHODIST CHURCH, SOUTH
v. FEDERAL RADIO COMMISSION

Court of Appeals of the District of Columbia, 1932.
62 F.2d 850, certiorari denied 288 U.S. 599, 53 S.Ct. 317, 77 L.Ed. 975 (1933).

GRONER, ASSOCIATE JUSTICE.

Appellant, Trinity Methodist Church, South, was the * * * operator of a radio-broadcasting station at Los Angeles. * * * The station had been in operation for several years. The Commission, in its findings, shows that, though in the name of the church, the station was in fact owned by the Reverend Doctor Shuler and its operation dominated by him. Dr. Shuler is the minister in charge of Trinity Church. * * *

In September, 1930, appellant filed an application for renewal of station license. Numerous citizens of Los Angeles protested, and the Commission * * * set the application down for hearing before an examiner. * * * [T]he Commission denied the application for renewal upon the ground that the public interest, convenience, and/or necessity would not be served by the granting of the application. Some of the things urging it to this conclusion were that the station had been used to attack a religious organization, meaning the Roman Catholic Church; that the broadcasts by Dr. Shuler were sensational rather than instructive; and that in two instances Shuler had been convicted of attempting in his radio talks to obstruct the orderly administration of public justice.

* * *

We need not stop to review the cases construing the depth and breadth of the First Amendment. * * * It is enough now to say that the universal trend of decisions has recognized the guaranty of the amendment to prevent previous restraints upon publications, as well as immunity from censorship, leaving to correction by subsequent punishment those utterances or publications contrary to the public welfare. * * * It may therefore be set down as a fundamental principle that under these constitutional guaranties the citizen has in the first instance the right to utter or publish his sentiments, though, of course, upon condition that he is responsible for any abuse of that right. *Near v. Minnesota.* * * * But this does not mean that the government, through agencies established by Congress, may not refuse a renewal of license to one who has abused it to broadcast defamatory and untrue matter. In that case there is not a denial of the freedom of speech, but merely the application of the regulatory power of Congress in a field within the scope of its legislative authority.

* * * It is too late now to contend that Congress may not regulate, and, in some instances, deny, the facilities of interstate commerce to a business or occupation which it deems inimical to the public welfare or contrary to the public interest. Everyone interested in radio legislation approved the principle of limiting the number of broadcasting stations, or, perhaps, it would be more nearly correct to say, recognized the

inevitable necessity. In these circumstances Congress intervened and asserted its paramount authority, and, if it be admitted, as we think it must be, that, in the present condition of the science with its limited facilities, the regulatory provisions of the Radio Act are a reasonable exercise by Congress of its powers, the exercise of these powers is no more restricted by the First Amendment than are the police powers of the States under the Fourteenth Amendment. * * * In either case the answer depends upon whether the statute is a reasonable exercise of governmental control for the public good.

In the case under consideration, the evidence abundantly sustains the conclusion of the Commission that the continuance of the broadcasting programs of appellant is not in the public interest. In a proceeding for contempt against Dr. Shuler, on appeal to the Supreme Court of California, that court said that the broadcast utterances of Dr. Shuler disclosed throughout the determination on his part to impose on the trial courts his own will and views with respect to certain causes then pending or on trial, and amounted to contempt of court. Appellant, not satisfied with attacking the judges of the courts in cases then pending before them, attacked the bar association for its activities in recommending judges, charging it with ulterior and sinister purposes. With no more justification, he charged particular judges with sundry immoral acts. He made defamatory statements against the board of health. He charged that the labor temple in Los Angeles was a bootlegging and gambling joint. In none of these matters, when called on to explain or justify his statements, was he able to do more than declare that the statements expressed his own sentiments. On one occasion he announced over the radio that he had certain damaging information against a prominent unnamed man which, unless a contribution (presumably to the church) of a hundred dollars was forthcoming, he would disclose. As a result, he received contributions from several persons. He freely spoke of "pimps" and prostitutes. He alluded slightingly to the Jews as a race, and made frequent and bitter attacks on the Roman Catholic religion and its relations to government. However inspired Dr. Shuler may have been by what he regarded as patriotic zeal, however sincere in denouncing conditions he did not approve, it is manifest, we think, that it is not narrowing the ordinary conception of "public interest" in declaring his broadcasts—without facts to sustain or to justify them—not within that term, and, since that is the test the Commission is required to apply, we think it was its duty in considering the application for renewal to take notice of appellant's conduct in his previous use of the permit, and, in the circumstances, the refusal, we think, was neither arbitrary nor capricious.

* * * This is neither censorship nor previous restraint, nor is it a whittling away of the rights guaranteed by the First Amendment, or an impairment of their free exercise. Appellant may continue to indulge his strictures upon the characters of men in public office. He may just as freely as ever criticize religious practices of which he does not approve. He may even indulge private malice or personal slander—subject, of

course, to be required to answer for the abuse thereof—but he may not, as we think, demand, of right, the continued use of an instrumentality of commerce for such purposes, or any other, except in subordination to all reasonable rules and regulations Congress, acting through the Commission, may prescribe.

Nor are we any more impressed with the argument that the refusal to renew a license is a taking of property within the Fifth Amendment. There is a marked difference between the destruction of physical property and the denial of a permit to use the limited channels of the air.

* * *

Affirmed.

Questions

1. Did the content of Dr. Shuler's statements over the radio differ in kind from that of "The Saturday Press" in *Near?* How? Do the differences, if any, explain or justify the different outcome in *Trinity Church?*

2. Were you persuaded by the *Trinity Church* court's distinction of *Near* and the prior restraint doctrine? On the court's reasoning, could Congress have banned the New York Times from interstate commerce or use of the mails—surely subjects within its authority—for publishing the Pentagon Papers? For publishing "defamatory and untrue matter"? See Loevinger, *Free Speech, Fairness, and Fiduciary Duty in Broadcasting*, 34 Law & Contemp. Probs. 278, 281 (1969).

3. New York Times Co. v. Sullivan, 376 U.S. 254, 84 S.Ct. 710, 11 L.Ed.2d 686 (1964), holds that the "profound national commitment to the principle that debate on public issues should be uninhibited, robust, and wide-open" requires "a federal rule that prohibits a public official from recovering damages for a defamatory falsehood relating to this official conduct unless he proves that the statement was made with 'actual malice'— that is, with knowledge that it was false or with reckless disregard of whether it was false or not * * *." This constitutional limitation on libel actions has been extended to "public figures," i.e., non-officials involved in matters "in which the public has a justified and important interest." *Curtis Pub. Co. v. Butts*, 388 U.S. 130, 87 S.Ct. 1975, 18 L.Ed.2d 1094 (1967).

(a) Is the reasoning in *Near* affected by the doctrine of *Times v. Sullivan?* Which way does it cut?

(b) Should the *Times v. Sullivan* standard for libel actions apply with equal force in broadcast license renewal proceedings? If so, would it protect the licensee in *Trinity Church?*

4. KFKB Broadcasting Ass'n v. FRC, 47 F.2d 670 (D.C.Cir.1931), upheld the denial of a renewal license to one Dr. Brinkley, who answered letters over the air by prescribing certain medicines designated only by a number. Listener-correspondents would then purchase the remedies from druggists, who had bought them from Dr. Brinkley. Is the holding in *KFKB* good law in light of Virginia State Board of Pharmacy v. Virginia Citizens Consumer Council, Inc., 425 U.S. 748, 96 S.Ct. 1817, 48 L.Ed.2d 346 (1976), under which commercial speech that is neither fraudulent nor deceptive is

protected by the First Amendment? Are there other public interest grounds on which to deny renewal of a license used in this manner?

5. Is the Church or The Saturday Press free to commence a new operation in the future? If Dr. Shuler had applied for a new license in the future, what was the likelihood of his receiving it? See the discussion as to "character qualifications." (p. 129)

6. The FCC sometimes regulates by "lifted eyebrow"—that is, through policy pronouncements that it will frown upon certain types of programming. In such a situation, the FCC's potential threat is fairly clear: (1) designation of a license renewal for hearing (with all its attendant legal fees and other costs); and (2) potentially even the "death penalty" of license non-renewal. (p. 51)

Broadcasters are also susceptible to pressure from congressional committees, which may be exercised through informal communications or more publicly through oversight hearings. Although a House or Senate committee has no direct control over a broadcaster, it can apply substantial pressure to the Commission—which may pass that pressure on to the broadcasters that initially attracted the committee's concern. Over the years, congressional committees have complained about a wide range of programming.

> * * * For example, congressional committees have often investigated individual programs with the apparent purpose of publicly castigating broadcasters rather than of enacting legislation. Programs that have been the subject of such congressional inquiry include a 1966 project that was never broadcast, entitled "Project Nassau," about gun-running by Haitian and Cuban exiles interested in the overthrow of the government of Haiti; the coverage by the three major networks of the 1968 Democratic National Convention; a 1968 documentary entitled "Hunger in America;" a 1969 two-part news report, entitled "Pot Party," about a pot party attended by university students; several allegedly staged news reports in the late '60s and early '70s; and the 1971 documentaries "The Selling of the Pentagon" and "Say Goodbye." * * * Congress also has held more general hearings into network election projections, and violent and sexual content in entertainment programming * * *.

Dyk & Goldberg, *The First Amendment and Congressional Investigations of Broadcast Programming*, 3 J.L. & Pol. 625, 630–631 (1987). Is there anything objectionable about such congressional oversight? Is Congress constitutionally obliged to delegate to an administrative agency all of its authority to regulate broadcasting as an aspect of interstate commerce? If not, would it be irresponsible to do so?

7. Finally, it is interesting to think briefly about how other countries have chosen to handle the licensing process or its equivalent. This is particularly relevant to the FCC's approach, since most of these countries had solely government-controlled broadcasting until a decade or so ago, and thus had at least the opportunity from some of the fiascos with the U.S. licensing process that will be seen.

Most regulatory agencies follow fairly similar procedures in assigning and renewing licenses. The major differences concern whether or not lengthy hearings are necessary. In most countries other than the U.S., regulatory agencies do not hold administrative "trials" to decide whether a license should be assigned or renewed.

Also because cable systems generally do not transmit over-the-air, they often are regulated in different ways from broadcasting. In France, this largely takes the form of initial approval of the creation of a "SLEC"; in the U.K., approval from OfTel and the Department of Trade and Industry ("DTI") is necessary, as well as compliance with a comprehensive set of rules. In the U.S., a cable operator first must receive a "franchise" from a state or municipal government; but it also is subject to FCC rules. Under Section 6 of the Israeli Telecommunications Law, the Minister of Communications issues concessions to potential cable operators, following an apparently conventional tender process. The Minister may include conditions in concessions as to broadcast signals to be carried, technical requirements, service areas, customer rates, and fees payable to the government. Although political infighting may delay the tender process, it can move quite quickly because of the limited procedural requirements.

Where broadcast stations are involved, of course, it is necessary to assign frequencies to particular operators in order to insure that electrical interference does not occur, as discussed in Chapter IV. Frequency assignment may be either *ad hoc* or planned. The French Conseil Superieur Audiovisuel ("CSA") follows a relatively typical approach by deciding in advance what frequencies should be available to what types of services, and then assigning particular frequencies to different companies. The first process is known generally as "allocation of frequencies," the second as "assignment of frequencies." Because its enabling statute does not require it to hold hearings, it can process competing license applications in a matter of months—rather than the years usually required in the United States.

At the same time, this naturally comes at the expense of a certain amount of procedural fairness. Under the French licensing or Israeli tender procedure, a party has only a limited opportunity to make a positive case in its favor, and usually has no chance to rebut its opponent's claims.

Given the potential abuses of the licensing process, the FCC's extensive and lengthy procedures thus may be necessary. But this creates a bit of a catch–22 situation: if a legislature gives a communications regulatory agency substantial powers, must it then create equally substantial procedural protections? If so, have the British and the Israelis done so? If not, because of what implicit assumptions?

Chapter III

THE BASES OF FCC
JURISDICTION

THE FCC IN BRIEF

Federal Communications Commission, Unpublished, 1995.

The Federal Communications Commission (FCC) is an independent United States government agency, directly responsible to Congress. The FCC was established by the Communications Act of 1934 and is charged with regulating interstate and international communications by radio, television, wire, satellite and cable. The FCC's jurisdiction covers the fifty states, the District of Columbia, and U.S. possessions.

The FCC is directed by five Commissioners appointed by the President and confirmed by the Senate for 5–year terms, except when filling an unexpired term. The President designates one of the Commissioners to serve as Chairperson. Only three Commissioners may be members of the same political party. None of them can have a financial interest in any Commission-related business.

FCC STAFF

As the chief executive officer of the Commission, the Chairman delegates management and administrative responsibility to the Managing Director. The Commissioners supervise all FCC activities, delegating responsibilities to staff units and Bureaus.

The Commission staff is organized by function. There are six operating Bureaus. The Bureaus are: Mass Media, Cable Services, Common Carrier, Compliance and Information (formerly Field Operations), Wireless Telecommunications (formerly Private Radio) and International. These Bureaus are responsible for developing and implementing regulatory programs, processing applications for licenses or other filings, analyzing complaints, conducting investigations, and taking part in FCC hearings. The staff offices are: Public Affairs, Managing Director, General Counsel, Engineering and Technology, Workplace Diversity, Legislative and Intergovernmental Affairs, Plans and Policy, Inspector General,

Communications Business Opportunities, Administrative Law Judges and the Review Board.

CABLE SERVICES

The Cable Services Bureau was established in 1993 to administer the "Cable Television Consumer Protection and Competition Act of 1992." The Bureau enforces regulations designed to ensure that cable rates are reasonable under the law. It is also responsible for regulations concerning "must carry," retransmission consent, customer services, technical standards, home wiring, consumer electronics, equipment compatibility, indecency, leased access and program access provisions. The Bureau also analyzes trends and developments in the industry to assess the effectiveness of the cable regulations.

COMMON CARRIER

The Common Carrier Bureau regulates wire and radio communications, common carriers, such as telephone, and telegraph. In addition to licensing radiotelephone circuits and assigning frequencies for their operation, the Bureau supervises charges, practices, classifications and regulations in interstate and foreign communication by radio, wire and cable; considers applications for construction of new facilities and discontinuance or reduction of service; acts on applications for mergers, and prescribes the accounting practices of communication carriers.

The Bureau also regulates rates, terms and conditions for cable television pole attachments, where such attachments are not regulated by a state and not provided by railroads or governmental or cooperatively-owned utilities.

COMPLIANCE AND INFORMATION

The Compliance and Information Bureau assures compliance with communications law, supports safety applications of radio spectrum and provides information to the Commission for affecting telecommunications policies. The Bureau operates strategically placed regional offices and field offices located across the nation, including Alaska, Hawaii and Puerto Rico. It interacts daily with military, state and local authorities in policing the airwaves to ensure free and open access by industry and the public.

The Bureau is the Commission's central source for resolving communication interference problems. It enforces rules through radio signal analysis, inspections and investigations: it supplies information to the public and provides a direct contact for both technical and non-technical inquiries.

These field offices monitor the radio spectrum to see that stations meet technical requirements, inspect stations, locate and close unauthorized transmitters, furnish direction-finding aid for aircraft or ships in distress, locate sources of interference and suggest remedial measures, do special engineering work for other government agencies, and obtain and analyze technical data for Commission use. They also perform public service activities such as participating in nationwide educational campaigns and handle general inquiries from the public.

The International Bureau was established in October 1994 to handle all FCC international telecommunications and satellite programs and policies. The Bureau represents the Commission in international conferences involving telecommunications matters such as rates, standards and development issues.

Its other primary functions include international safety and distress, space and earth stations, cable landing licenses, bilateral discussions and interaction with other international organizations. It assumes the principal representational role for Commission activities in international affairs, serves as the focal point for international activities, and advises the Commission on international matters.

The Bureau is charged with domestic administration of telecommunication provisions of treaties and international agreements to which the United States is a party. Under the Department of State's auspices, it participates in related international conferences.

MASS MEDIA

The Mass Media Bureau regulates AM, FM and television broadcast stations and related facilities. It assigns frequencies and call letters to stations, and designates operating power and sign-on times. It also assigns stations in each service within the allocated frequency bands, with specific locations, frequencies, and powers. It regulates existing stations, inspecting to see that stations are operating in accordance with rules and technical provisions of their authorizations. At renewal time, the station's records are reviewed.

Television stations are licensed for five [now eight] years and radio stations for seven [now eight] years. Licensees are obligated to comply with statutes, rules and policies relating to program content such as identifying sponsors and broadcasting information only on state-operated lotteries in their own or adjacent states. The Bureau assures that licensees make available equal opportunities for use of broadcast facilities by political candidates of opposing political candidates, station identification, and identification of recorded programs or program segments. Licensees who have violated FCC statutes, rules or policies are subject to sanctions, including loss of license and fines.

WIRELESS TELECOMMUNICATIONS (FORMERLY PRIVATE RADIO SERVICES)

The Wireless Telecommunications Bureau regulates stations serving the communications needs of business, individuals, nonprofit organizations, and state and local governments, including the following uses: private land mobile, private operational fixed microwave, aviation, marine, personal, amateur, and disaster. This Bureau is responsible for all domestic wireless telecommunications programs, except those involving satellite communications. These include Cellular Services, Personal Communications Services (PCS), Paging, and Specialized Mobile Radio, Air-to-Ground and Basic Exchange Telecommunications Radio Services.

Its Enforcement Division ensures that wireless telecommunications service providers comply with the Communications Act, statutes and Commission rules, orders and policies. Its Auction Division is responsible for conducting PCS auctions.

The Bureau also is responsible for rule making and regulatory matters concerning Public Safety, Industrial, Land Transportation and other private mobile services, Aviation, Marine, Amateur, Interactive Video Data Service (IVDS), Broadcast Auxiliary Service, Personal Radio Services, point-to-point microwave, antenna tower clearance, and the radio operator examination program.

OFFICE OF PLANS AND POLICY

The Office of Plans and Policy (OPP), is the major economic/technical policy adviser to the Commission, analyzing issues and developing long-term policy planning. OPP's Chief coordinates all policy research and development activities, both within the FCC and with other agencies; recommends budget levels and priorities for policy research programs; serves as account manager for all contract research studies funded by the Commission.

OFFICE OF THE GENERAL COUNSEL

The General Counsel advises the Commission on legal issues involved in establishing and implementing policy, handles legal questions affecting the agency's internal operations, coordinates the preparation of its legislative program and represents it in court. The OGC also assists the Commission in reviewing Review Board Decisions and, in specific cases, Initial Decisions of the Administrative Law Judges, as well as in drafting FCC decisions in adjudicatory cases.

Note: FCC Jurisdiction

Most observers tend to equate FCC regulation with licensing of over-the-air radio and television stations, probably because those are the most visible (or audible) forms of electronic communication. In fact, however, the Communications Act gives the FCC several different types of jurisdiction, some of which may not have been very clear in the minds of the Act's drafters.

First, the Commission has jurisdiction under Title III of the Act over use of "any apparatus for the transmission of energy or communications or signals by radio" in interstate or foreign commerce. 47 U.S.C. § 301. This allows the FCC to regulate any over-the-air transmitter, from television stations to CB radios. This jurisdiction may be subdivided into three distinct categories. Most visible is jurisdiction over broadcast stations, for which Title III contains special provisions. In addition, a license is necessary for any Title II common carrier—such as a domestic satellite—that uses over-the-air transmissions. As a result, the Commission regulates many common carriers under both Title II and Title III. Title III also gives the FCC jurisdiction over spectrum users that are neither Title III broadcasters nor Title II common carriers—all under the rubric of "private radio." These operations range from taxicab radios to intracorporate microwave links. The Commission has increasingly classified media as "private radio" in order to avoid the statutory requirements of broadcasting or common carrier regulation, and thus to further its deregulatory goals.

Second, under Title II the FCC has jurisdiction over common carriers. The most common examples are LECs, IXCs, and domestic satellite carriers.

Finally, the Commission has a vague type of implied jurisdiction over activities that fall within neither Title II nor Title III, but are "reasonably ancillary to the effective performance of the Commission's various responsibilities for the regulation of television." The most striking example of this is the FCC's jurisdiction over cable television.

A.   BROADCASTING

Until recently, broadcasting consisted solely of terrestrial radio and television. As the following case shows, however, the increasingly dynamic changes in the electronic media have begun to strain old definitions.

NATIONAL ASSOCIATION OF BROADCASTERS v. FCC

United States Court of Appeals, District of Columbia Circuit, 1984.
740 F.2d 1190, 239 U.S.App.D.C. 87.

[This case involved a challenge not only to the FCC's adoption of temporary rules for DBS operations, but also its grant of the first DBS license to the Satellite Television Corporation ("STC"), a subsidiary of COMSAT.]

MIKVA, CIRCUIT JUDGE:

Of the technological innovations currently revolutionizing the communications field, the most recent, and potentially the most significant, is direct broadcast satellite service. DBS involves the transmission of signals from the earth to highpowered, geostationary satellites which then beam television signals directly to individual homes equipped to receive them. Use of satellites massively extends the range of a broadcaster's voice by freeing it from the atmospheric limitations that traditionally limit terrestrial broadcasters to narrow broadcast areas; a single DBS signal will eventually be capable of reaching the entire continental United States. For this reason and others, DBS promises several significant advantages over existing television technology: high-quality service to individuals in rural or remote areas where conventional broadcasting is inefficient; the addition of many more channels even in urban areas already receiving several television signals; "narrowcasting" of programs to specialized tastes through the ability to aggregate small, widely dispersed audiences; the development of higher quality visual and audio signals through use of high-definition television signals; and television transmission of non-entertainment programming, such as medical data and educational information.

The regulatory approach to DBS taken by the [FCC], which we review today, is as novel as the technology with which it is concerned. In essence, the Commission has chosen to deregulate DBS even before the service is born. * * * We find that, on the whole, the FCC has done a commendable job in assuring that regulation in the communications field not impede new technologies that offer substantial public benefits * * * We also find, however, that in its zeal to promote this new technology, the FCC gave short shrift to certain of its statutory obligations, and we therefore vacate part of the Interim DBS regulations * * *.

BACKGROUND

In the early 1960s, the development of satellites that could transmit signals over great distances offered new promise of expanding the availability of communications services throughout the United States. To develop this satellite technology, Congress created the Communications Satellite Corporation (COMSAT), a privately run, government-subsidized company which was to provide international communications links via satellite. * * * In August 1979 * * * COMSAT announced its belief that satellite and receiver technology had advanced to the point that a commercial DBS system was feasible.

* * * On October 29, 1980, the FCC initiated a domestic proceeding to consider the prospects for United States DBS service. 45 Fed.Reg. 72719 (1980) (*1980 Notice*). The *1980 Notice* noted the rapid advances being made in DBS technology and * * * specifically sought comments on whether it [the FCC] should adopt interim DBS regulations that would permit * * * the construction of experimental DBS systems * * *. * * *

During the course of proceedings under the *1980 Notice,* [STC], a subsidiary of COMSAT and an intervenor in the present action, filed an application to construct this country's first multi-channel DBS system. * * * The Commission * * * placed the application in the DBS docket so that the question of authorizing DBS prior to [international approval] could be considered in the context of a specific DBS application. The FCC then provided additional time for interested parties to comment on DBS and on the STC application.

In June 1981, * * * the Commission released a *Notice of Proposed Policy Statement and Rulemaking.* In the *DBS Notice,* the Commission formally proposed to establish interim DBS regulations prior to [international approval] * * *. Nonetheless, according to the Commission, interim DBS rules were warranted to avoid "unnecessary delays" and to gain information that would aid in setting permanent regulatory policies. * * *

On July 14, 1982, the Commission in fact adopted interim DBS regulations (*DBS Order*). * * * Subsequently, the Commission, on October 13, 1982, granted STC's application to construct an experimental

DBS system that would provide subscription television service to the general public. *STC Decision,* 91 F.C.C.2d 953 (1982). * * *

* * *

ANALYSIS

* * *

II. *Applicability to DBS of Broadcast Restrictions*

The most innovative of the steps taken by the FCC with respect to DBS was the Commission's decision, in the service of a "flexible regulatory approach" designed to stimulate DBS technology, not to apply to DBS the major regulatory restrictions traditionally imposed on broadcasters. Central to this approach was the Commission's refusal to extend the broadcast restrictions of Title III of the Communications Act of 1934, as amended, to all DBS systems.

These statutory restrictions imposed upon broadcasters are among the most important elements of the compromise underlying passage of the 1927 Radio Act, the model for the Communications Act of 1934. As the Supreme Court has noted, when Congress decided that government regulation of the airways was needed to bring order to the chaotic and burgeoning broadcast industry, the crucial question was how to balance public and private control. Some congressmen argued that broadcasters should be treated as public utilities and thus have the obligation to act as common carriers by accepting all applicants for service on a nondiscriminatory basis. Such a pervasive access right was ultimately rejected, however, in favor of a more narrowly tailored approach in which broadcasters were required to fulfill certain well-defined public obligations. The essence of this compromise was the view that broadcasting should remain under private control in general but that certain uses of the airways, particularly political ones, were too central to democratic values to be left to the whim of the private broadcaster. Accordingly, the Radio Act imposed a specific set of restraints upon broadcasters that common carriers do not face and then, to cement the compromise, explicitly provided that a broadcaster should not be regulated as a common carrier. 47 U.S.C. § 153(h).

Among the statutory restraints that broadcasters currently face are section 312(a)(7), which requires that qualified candidates for federal office be provided reasonable access to broadcast facilities, and section 315, which provides that, if one political candidate is allowed to use a station, other qualified candidates must be given an equal opportunity to respond. Because DBS is likely to be a particularly attractive medium at least for presidential candidates, the question of how these broadcast restraints apply to DBS is of great moment.

The *DBS Order* established the following classificatory scheme for purposes of applying the Act's broadcasting rules. Those DBS applicants which propose to provide service (whether in the form of free or pay-TV) direct to homes and to "retain control over the content of the transmissions" will be treated as broadcasters. A DBS satellite owner can choose instead to operate as a common carrier, in which case satellite transmission services would have to be offered indiscriminately to the public pursuant to tariff under the provisions of Title II of the Act; a satellite owner who chooses the common carrier option will not be treated as a broadcaster. Also not treated as a broadcaster under the *DBS Order* are those who lease satellite space from a DBS common carrier and who use the leased channels to distribute programming via satellite to individual homes. These lessees, who neither own nor operate a DBS satellite, are referred to as "customer-programmers" of DBS common carriers, and it is they who control the content of the programming transmitted by a DBS common carrier.

The FCC offered three rationales for the exemption of customer-programmers from Title III. First, at the time the Communications Act was passed, Congress, according to the FCC, envisioned a system that clearly distinguished broadcasters from common carriers. * * * Because Congress did not expressly consider what type of regulation would be appropriate for a system in which an entity that wished to send signals using facilities and frequencies licensed to a common carrier would provide service directly to the public, the FCC concluded that the Communications Act did not require one who leased satellite space from a common carrier to be licensed and regulated as a broadcaster. Second, imposition on a common carrier's programmer-customers of the limited access requirements now imposed on broadcasters was said to be duplicative of the more pervasive access obligations already imposed on the carrier itself. Third, in its regulation of the common carrier MDS, * * * the Commission similarly had not required a carrier's programmer-customers, many of whom provide subscription programming services to individual residences, to be licensed or regulated as broadcasters. On the basis of these rationales, the Commission decided that it was free to determine where the public interest lay with regard to the regulatory regime imposed on DBS, and to conclude that "a flexible regulatory approach," in which customer-programmers would be unregulated for the present, would provide the Commission with experimental information that would better inform its eventual public interest judgments.

We recognize the Commission's authority to approve services on an experimental basis in an effort to gather important market data to be used in the completion of a regulatory framework. * * * But that discretion is not boundless: the Commission has no authority to experiment with its statutory obligations. We conclude that the Commission has engaged in precisely such forbidden statutory experimentation in exempting from Title III the customer-programmers of DBS common carriers.

We reach this conclusion by beginning not, as the Commission did, with the question whether Congress contemplated DBS in 1934, but rather with the language of the statute itself * * *.

Section 3(*o*) of the Communications Act defines "broadcasting" as "the dissemination of radio communications intended to be received by the public, directly or by the intermediary of relay stations." 47 U.S.C. § 153(*o*). We have previously held that the test for whether a particular activity constitutes broadcasting is whether there is "an intent for *public* distribution" and whether the programming is "of interest to the *general . . .* audience." Remarkably, the Commission did not even attempt to reconcile its approach with the statutory language or with our interpretation of that language. Nor do we believe the Commission could have done so successfully.

When DBS systems transmit signals directly to homes with the intent that those signals be received by the public, such transmissions rather clearly fit the definition of broadcasting; radio communications are being disseminated with the intent that they be received by the public. That remains true even if a common carrier satellite leases its channels to a customer-programmer who does not own any transmission facilities; in such an arrangement, someone—either the lessee or the satellite owner—is broadcasting. * * * [I]t also remains true regardless of whether a DBS system is advertiser or subscriber funded. The FCC at the time of the DBS decision was bound not to depart without reasoned explanation from its conclusion in the subscription television proceedings several years ago that

> [t]he primary touchstone of a broadcast service is the intent of the broadcaster to provide radio or television program service without discrimination to as many members of the general public as can be interested in the particular program as distinguished from a point-to-point message service to specified individuals. * * * [B]roadcasting remains broadcasting even though a segment of the public is unable to view programs without special equipment * * *.

While the FCC may be coming increasingly to the view that subscription services are not "broadcasting," a view not yet passed upon by the courts, the *DBS Order* must rise or fall upon the FCC's articulated policies at the time of the *Order*. And as the *Order* itself recognizes, those policies did not distinguish free-TV from pay-TV for purposes of defining "broadcasting." The FCC therefore cannot justify its exemption of some DBS systems from broadcast restrictions by pointing to the fact that those systems are subscriber rather than advertiser funded. * * *

The irrationality of the Commission's view of the statute, which makes ownership the touchstone of broadcasting, is illustrated by the following example. If a DBS owner broadcasts programming directly to homes, it is subject to regulation as a broadcaster; if that owner sends its programs via leased channels on another satellite, the very same programming will be immune from broadcast regulation. Through a general system of cross-leasing, all DBS systems could therefore escape Title III. * * *

Very real practical consequences could therefore follow from the FCC's exemption of common carrier DBS lessees from broadcast restrictions—consequences at odds with the basic objectives of the Communications Act. Under the *DBS Order,* a federal candidate who wanted access to a DBS system that was operated as a common carrier could not force either the satellite owner or its channel lessees to provide that access, for both would be immune from the Act's broadcast restraints; the candidate would instead have to rely on his or her purchasing power, as well as on the whim of the channel programmer, to receive access and an opportunity to respond to opponents. * * *

We therefore reject the central rationale upon which the Commission relied to exempt customer-programmers of DBS common carriers from the statutory constraints under which broadcasters must operate: the fact that Congress did not in 1934 contemplate DBS does not give the Commission a blank check to regulate DBS in any way it deems fit. * * *

The Commission's other rationales for its treatment of customer-programmers provide even less persuasive reasons for the Commission's departure from the statute's plain language. The claim that imposition of Title III obligations on channel lessees "merely would serve to duplicate the more pervasive" common carrier obligations of Title II is clearly wrong, as Title II merely requires a carrier to accept all applicants for service on a non-discriminatory basis and thus offers no surrogate for Title III requirements such as reasonable access or equal opportunity. A common carrier *cannot* guarantee political candidates reasonable access to airtime or an equal opportunity to respond to opponents, for the sine qua non of a common carrier is the obligation to accept applicants on a non-content oriented basis. Nor does the Commission's *Multipoint Distribution Service Decision, supra,* convincingly support the treatment of DBS customer-programmers. * * * The Commission in its *DBS Order* apparently relied on the fact that MDS subscribers will not be treated as broadcasters.

[The court noted that the Commission's classification of MDS as a common carrier had no real statutory basis, and that in fact the MDS industry had developed in ways that suggested that it had the characteristics of a broadcaster—hinting broadly that the Commission had misclassified MDS. The Commission's ultimate response was to classify MDS as "private radio," thus removing it from broadcasting and carriage obligations.]

* * * We hold that DBS, at least when directed at individual homes, *is* radio communication intended to be received by the general public—despite the fact that it can be received by only those with appropriate reception equipment. * * *

[The court went on to reject the FCC's suggestion that Section 301's general prohibition on transmitting without a license exempted lessee programmers from regulation, characterizing it as "post-hoc rationalizations by counsel." While non-licensee programmers were not usually regulated, the FCC could not exempt both the common carrier and the customer-programmer from broadcast regulation.]

* * *

We also do not suggest that all uses of DBS constitute broadcasting; activity that would provide non-general interest, point-to-point service, where the format is of interest to only a narrow class of subscribers and does not implicate the broadcasting objectives of the Act, need not be regulated as broadcasting. * * *

Although we vacate one portion of the *DBS Order,* the Commission's error with respect to broadcasting is sufficiently minor in the context of the *Order* as a whole that the rest of the *Order* can stand. The *DBS Order* makes clear that a DBS applicant that proposes to produce direct-to-home service and to retain control over the content of the transmissions will be treated as a broadcaster. With respect to such applicants, who comprise the great majority of DBS applicants, the *DBS Order* is thus insulated from our criticism of the FCC's failure to regulate customer-programmers. With respect to DBS applicants who propose to provide service on a common carrier basis—the set of applicants for whom our vacation of the *DBS Order* is relevant—we leave to the Commission the decision whether a generic rulemaking is required to determine how to apply broadcast restrictions to such DBS systems or whether individual application proceedings can best deal with this question.

[The court's invalidation of the customer-programmer portion of the rules did not require it to vacate the grant of the experimental DBS license to STC, since that applicant had proposed to operate as a broadcaster.]

CONCLUSION

When technology as novel as DBS confronts a statute as broadly drafted as the Communications Act of 1934, the administering agency has substantial leeway in its efforts to harmonize the two. We conclude that, on the whole, the Commission has exercised this leeway in a reasonable manner. We therefore vacate only that portion of the *DBS Order* that makes broadcast restrictions inapplicable to some DBS systems and, with the caveats noted above, affirm the rest of that Order. We also affirm in its entirety the *STC Decision.*

It is so ordered.

Notes and Questions

1. The petition to deny STC's DBS license application was filed by the National Association of Broadcasters ("NAB"), the major trade association of the broadcasting industry. Is there a certain irony here, in light of the NAB's traditional position that petitions to deny are an unfair and abusive means for citizens' groups to gain leverage over broadcasters? (p. 57)

2. Given DBS' rather slow development in the United States, the *NAB* decision had little immediate impact. Satcom never launched its DBS busi-

ness. Indeed, DBS did not begin to develop in the United States until a decade after the *NAB* case; as discussed in Chapter I (Pp .), the relevant changes seemed to have been the development of small, inexpensive Ku-band transmission and receiving equipment, as well as the interest in multichannel media already fueled by experience with cable and VCR.

The delays in implementing a new technology such as DBS illustrate some of the hazards of regulation that depends upon "technology-push" rather than economic pull: No matter how attractive a new technology may be to its proponents, including the government, it will not be relevant unless there is sufficient demand for it in the marketplace. This is just another example of the problems with technology pull versus market push; in the most favorable situation, both should be present to open up a new industry.

The Canadian government seems to have had a similar experience in its attempts to develop DBS as a form of industrial, rather than of communications, policy.

> In effect, the [Department of Communications] research program provided a "strategy for acceptance" of new technology. * * * Satellite technology development can be seen as one of the flagships of Canada's industrial policy and as providing the means of distributing Canadian and American information products. But the research program did not even consider whether Canadian policy objectives would be better served by the *absence* of a dedicated DBS system. Instead, a "new" satellite is seen to provide a resolution for policy problems that have plagued the communication sector.

Mansell, *Is Policy Research an Irrelevant Exercise?: The Case of Canadian DBS Planning*, J. Comm., Spring 1985, at 154, 162–163.

3.   The Commission apparently would restrict the definition of broadcasting to traditional terrestrial transmissions. Although not articulated very clearly, the FCC's position seems to have been that broadcasting includes only distribution systems previously denominated as such—that is, AM, FM, and TV. Does this elevate form over function? With good reason?

4.   By contrast, the court in *NAB v. FCC* seemed to focus primarily upon the medium's impact. One part of its formulation seems to involve the extent to which the medium's message is broadly cast—that is, whether the distributor wants members of the public to have easy access to its programming, presumably in order to sell advertising. This seems consistent with the Supreme Court's holding in the *Sony* case that home videotaping of a broadcast program does not infringe the copyright to that program, on the theory that most broadcasters implicitly invite viewers to tape programs, in order to expand their audiences.

5.   Is a different result indicated where a distributor provides programming only on a "pay channel" or "pay-per-view" basis? In this case, the programmer is trying to exclude at least some viewers, those unwilling to pay its charges. Would it make sense for the Commission to adopt a bright-line rule that "pay" services do not constitute broadcasting? Along these lines, it may be worth noting that most potential DBS operators propose primarily or exclusively "pay" services.

What if an entity offers some programming on a common carrier basis and other on a general public basis? Under *NAB* can a medium exist part common carrier and part broadcaster? Note the discussion of the new "open video system" ("OVS") (p. 78) created by the Telecommunications Act of 1996—and perhaps of little interest the existing media players.

6. In addition to DBS' large audience, the *NAB* court seems to focus on DBS' potential impact on political opinion, particularly in federal elections. Is this concern akin to the "pervasiveness" rationale in *Pacifica* (p. 510)? Or is the court suggesting that with any widely available medium, someone—whether carrier or "customer-programmer"—must be responsible for providing "equal opportunities" and the like? If so, how would this apply to cable and similar media? The FCC has applied the equal opportunity rules to cable programming originated by the cable system. 47 C.F.R. § 76.205; Cable Television Report and Order, 36 FCC 2d 143, 240 (1972).

B. COMMON CARRIAGE

The concept of common carriage is elusive, for a variety of reasons. First, most common carriers are public utilities, like electrical, gas, or telephone companies. Those entities require a large initial investment, but then produce units of output at a relatively low marginal cost, which results in a constantly declining average cost curve. They are often called "natural monopolies," because the average cost of producing the same output by two or more competing firms would be higher. Therefore, unless there has been a radical decline in the cost of production through use of a new technology, there is no incentive for a second firm to enter the market. Because of changes in the number of present and potential carriers, the regulatory system has begun to change from guaranteeing companies any particular return—or, for that matter, any return whatsoever—on their investments.

One of the central debates concerning telecommunications during the last few years has been whether it has lost—or, for that matter, ever had—real natural monopoly status. With the advent of low-cost and small computing as well as telecommunications technology, a number of small firms have claimed that they can serve at least some users at or below the prices of traditional local exchange carriers ("LECs"). In return, the LECs claim that these "competitive access providers" ("CAPs") merely are cream-skimming the lucrative—generally financial sector service—areas of most markets, and ignoring higher-cost, lower-price residential neighborhoods. Whoever is right, there has been a general move away from traditional forms of common carrier rate-of-return regulation, i.e., basing profits on amount of invested capital.

This traditional type of natural monopoly regulation typically guarantees the firm a return on its invested capital, in exchange for their undertaking to provide a particular service at a particular rate. Identifying a natural monopoly is sometimes difficult, however, especially if the technology of production is dynamic. For example, long distance telephone service seemed to be a natural monopoly when it depended upon copper wire as the medium of transmission. When microwave transmission became feasible, there was no longer any reason to exclude competition or to regulate the firms' rate of return and prices.

With the entry of CAPs and other forms of competition, federal and state regulatory authorities have begun to abandon traditional rate-of-return regulation. Instead, they have adopted the originally British system of "price caps." Although these systems vary from country to country and state to state, their basic premise is that a carrier has no guaranteed return on capital.* Under a price cap regime, a carrier usually may increase its prices by a combination of a consumer price and its "productivity factor"—that is, its ability to reduce costs of service.

It thus may be fair to question whether traditional rate regulation for common carriers still even exists. The deregulatory effect of price caps and the like may have made most common carrier regulation simply obsolete.

This obviously is very much a real issue in the telecommunications industry, in both local and long-distance service. But it also may have a significant impact on the status of other electronic media—most notably, perhaps, cable television.

Whether cable television is a natural monopoly probably will be debated for the next decade. Perhaps the more meaningful question is as to *what* the cable industry has a natural monopoly on. If the product is all types of video, then cable presumably has no natural monopoly; if it is multichannel video, cable may have a monopoly, except in areas served by DBS. For example, the 1992 Cable Act and the 1996 Telecommunications Act basically took the power of cable rate regulation away from local municipalities, which traditionally had exercised it. Under the 1996 Telecommunications Act, only the FCC has the jurisdiction to deal with local complaints about cable prices.

Regardless of whether cable is a traditional natural monopoly and thus subject to rate-of-return regulation, however, questions have arisen as to the propriety of imposing common carrier-style requirements upon it, as discussed below.

FCC v. MIDWEST VIDEO CORPORATION**

Supreme Court of the United States, 1979.
440 U.S. 689, 99 S.Ct. 1435, 59 L.Ed.2d 692.

Mr. Justice White delivered the opinion of the Court.

* Compare this to the later discussion of the adoption of guaranteed license renewals for broadcasters. (pp. ___) Why should there be a distinction? Of course, the carriers have only profits to lose, while the broadcasters have multi-million dollar businesses at stake. But if a carrier consistently cannot earn enough of a profit to attract new capital, it obviously is not long for this world.

** *United States v. Midwest Video Corp.*, 406 U.S. 649, 92 S. Ct. 1860, 32 L.Ed. 2d 390 (1972), sustained the FCC's "mandatory origination" rule, which required cable operators to produce local programming. That case often is referred to as "Midwest I" and this case then is commonly known as "Midwest II."

In May 1976, the Federal Communications Commission promulgated rules requiring cable television systems that have 3,500 or more subscribers and carry broadcast signals to develop, at a minimum, a 20–channel capacity by 1986, to make available certain channels for access by third parties, and to furnish equipment and facilities for access purposes. Report and Order in Docket No. 20508, 59 F.C.C.2d 294 (*1976 Order*). The issue here is whether these rules are "reasonably ancillary to the effective performance of the Commission's various responsibilities for the regulation of television broadcasting," *United States v. Southwestern Cable Co.,* 392 U.S. 157, 178, 88 S.Ct. 1994, 2005, 20 L.Ed.2d 1001 (1968), and hence within the Commission's statutory authority.

I

The regulations now under review had their genesis in rules prescribed by the Commission in 1972 requiring all cable operators in the top 100 television markets to design their systems to include at least 20 channels and to dedicate 4 of those channels for public, governmental, educational, and leased access. The rules were reassessed in the course of further rulemaking proceedings. * * * [The Commission] extended the rules to all cable systems having 3,500 or more subscribers, *1976 Order, supra.* In its 1976 Order, the Commission reaffirmed its view that there was "a definite societal good" in preserving access channels, though it acknowledged that the "overall impact that use of these channels can have may have been exaggerated in the past."

* * * Under the rules, cable systems must possess a minimum capacity of 20 channels as well as the technical capability for accomplishing two-way, non-voice communication. Moreover, to the extent of their available activated channel capacity, cable systems must allocate four separate channels for use by public, educational, local governmental, and leased-access users, with one channel assigned to each. Absent demand for full-time use of each access channel, the combined demand can be accommodated with fewer than four channels but with at least one. When demand on a particular access channel exceeds a specified limit, the cable system must provide another access channel for the same purpose, to the extent of the system's activated capacity. The rules also require cable systems to make equipment available for those utilizing public-access channels.

Under the rules, cable operators are deprived of all discretion regarding who may exploit their access channels and what may be transmitted over such channels. System operators are specifically enjoined from exercising any control over the content of access programming except that they must adopt rules proscribing the transmission on most access channels of lottery information and commercial matter. The regulations also instruct cable operators to issue rules providing for first-come, nondiscriminatory access on public and leased channels.

Finally, the rules circumscribe what operators may charge for privileges of access and use of facilities and equipment. No charge may be assessed for the use of one public-access channel. Operators may not charge for the use of educational and governmental access for the first five years the system services such users. Leased-access-channel users must be charged an "appropriate" fee. Moreover, the rules admonish that charges for equipment, personnel, and production exacted from access users "shall be reasonable and consistent with the goal of affording users a low-cost means of television access." And "[n]o charges shall be made for live public access programs not exceeding five minutes in length." Lastly, a system may not charge access users for utilization of its playback equipment or the personnel required to operate such equipment when the cable's production equipment is not deployed and when tapes or film can be played without technical alteration to the system's equipment.

The Commission's capacity and access rules were challenged on jurisdictional grounds in the course of the rulemaking proceedings. In its *1976 Order,* the Commission rejected such comments on the ground that the regulations further objectives that it might properly pursue in its supervision over broadcasting. Specifically, the Commission maintained that its rules would promote "the achievement of long-standing communications regulatory objectives by increasing outlets for local self-expression and augmenting the public's choice of programs." The Commission did not find persuasive the contention that "the access requirements are in effect common carrier obligations which are beyond our authority to impose. [T]he rules * * * adopted are reasonably related to achieving objectives for which the Commission has been assigned jurisdiction. We do not think they can be held beyond our authority merely by denominating them as somehow 'common carrier' in nature. The proper question, we believe, is not whether they fall in one category or another of regulation—whether they are more akin to obligations imposed on common carriers or obligations imposed on broadcasters to operate in the public interest—but whether the rules adopted promote statutory objectives."

Additionally, the Commission denied that the rules violated the First Amendment, reasoning that when broadcasting or related activity by cable systems is involved First Amendment values are served by measures facilitating an exchange of ideas.

On petition for review, the Eighth Circuit set aside the Commission's access, channel capacity, and facilities rules as beyond the agency's jurisdiction. 571 F.2d 1025 (1978). The Court was of the view that the regulations were not reasonably ancillary to the Commission's jurisdiction over broadcasting, a jurisdictional condition established by past decisions of this Court. The rules amounted to an attempt to impose common-carrier obligations on cable operators, the Court said, and thus ran counter to the statutory command that broadcasters themselves may not be treated as common carriers. * * *

II

The Commission derives its regulatory authority from the Communications Act of 1934. The Act preceded the advent of cable television and understandably does not expressly provide for the regulation of that medium. But it is clear that Congress meant to confer "broad authority" on the Commission * * *.

* * *

Because its access and capacity rules promote the long-established regulatory goals of maximization of outlets for local expression and diversification of programming—the objectives promoted by the rule sustained in *Midwest Video*—the Commission maintains that it plainly had jurisdiction to promulgate them. Respondents, in opposition, view the access regulations as an intrusion on cable system operations that is qualitatively different from the impact of the rule upheld in *Midwest Video*. Specifically, it is urged that by requiring the allocation of access channels to categories of users specified by the regulations and by depriving the cable operator of the power to select individual users or to control the programming on such channels, the regulations wrest a considerable degree of editorial control from the cable operator and in effect compel the cable system to provide a kind of common-carrier service. Respondents contend, therefore, that the regulations are not only qualitatively different from those heretofore approved by the courts but also contravene statutory limitations designed to safeguard the journalistic freedom of broadcasters, particularly the command of § 3(h) of the Act that "a person engaged in ... broadcasting shall not ... be deemed a common carrier." 47 U.S.C. § 153(h).[10]

We agree with respondents that recognition of agency jurisdiction to promulgate the access rules would require an extension of this Court's prior decisions. * * *

With its access rules, however, the Commission has transferred control of the content of access cable channels from cable operators to members of the public who wish to communicate by the cable medium. Effectively, the Commission has relegated cable systems, *pro tanto,* to common-carrier status. A common-carrier service in the communications context is one that "makes a public offering to provide [communications facilities] whereby all members of the public who choose to employ such facilities may communicate or transmit intelligence of their own design and choosing...." * * *

The access rules plainly impose common-carrier obligations on cable operators. Under the rules, cable systems are required to hold out dedicated channels on a first-come, nondiscriminatory basis. 47 CFR §§ 76.254(a), 76.256(d) (1977). Operators are prohibited from determining or influencing the content of access programming. § 76.256(b). And the rules delimit what operators may charge for access and use of

---

10. Section 3(h) defines "common carrier" as "any person engaged as a common carrier for hire, in interstate or foreign communication by wire or radio or interstate or foreign radio transmission of energy...." Due to the circularity of the definition, resort must be had to court and agency pronouncements to ascertain the term's meaning. *See National Association of Regulatory Utility Comm'rs v. FCC*, 173 U.S.App.D.C. 413, 423, 525 F.2d 630, 640, *cert. denied,* 425 U.S. 992, 96 S.Ct. 2203, 48 L.Ed.2d 816 (1976) * * *. [footnote relocated.]

equipment. § 76.256(c). Indeed, in its early consideration of access obligations * * * the Commission acknowledged that the result would be the operation of cable systems "as common carriers on some channels." *First Report and Order in Docket No. 18397,* 20 F.C.C.2d, at 207; see *id.,* at 202; *Cable Television Report and Order,* 36 F.C.C.2d 143, 197 (1972). In its *1976 Order,* the Commission did not directly deny that its access requirements compelled common carriage, and it has conceded before this Court that the rules "can be viewed as a limited form of common carriage-type obligation." But the Commission continues to insist that this characterization of the obligation imposed by the rules is immaterial to the question of its power to issue them; its authority to promulgate the rules is assured, in the Commission's view, so long as the rules promote statutory objectives.

Congress, however, did not regard the character of regulatory obligations as irrelevant to the determination of whether they might permissibly be imposed in the context of broadcasting itself. The Commission is directed explicitly by § 3(h) of the Act not to treat persons engaged in broadcasting as common carriers. We considered the genealogy and the meaning of this provision in *Columbia Broadcasting System, Inc. v. Democratic National Committee* (p. 316) * * * We determined, in fact, that "Congress specifically dealt with—and firmly rejected—the argument that the broadcast facilities should be open on a nonselective basis to all persons wishing to talk about public issues." * * *

The holding of the Court in *Columbia Broadcasting* was in accord with the view of the Commission that the Act itself did not require a licensee to accept paid editorial advertisements. Accordingly, we did not decide the question whether the Act, though not mandating the claimed access, would nevertheless permit the Commission to require broadcasters to extend a range of public access by regulations similar to those at issue here. The Court speculated that the Commission might have flexibility to regulate access, and that "[c]onceivably at some future date Congress or the Commission—or the broadcasters—may devise some kind of limited right of access that is both practicable and desirable." But this is insufficient support for the Commission's position in the present case. The language of § 3(h) is unequivocal; it stipulates that broadcasters shall not be treated as common carriers. As we see it, § 3(h), consistently with the policy of the Act to preserve editorial control of programming in the licensee, forecloses any discretion in the Commission to impose access requirements amounting to common-carrier obligations on broadcast systems. The provision's background manifests a congressional belief that the intrusion worked by such regulation on the journalistic integrity of broadcasters would overshadow any benefits associated with the resulting public access.[14] It is difficult to

---

14. Whether less intrusive access regulation might fall within the Commission's jurisdiction, or survive constitutional challenge even if within the Commission's power, is not presently before this Court. Certainly, our construction of § 3(h) does not put into question the statutory authority for the fairness-doctrine obligations sustained in *Red Lion Broadcasting Co. v.*

deny, then, that forcing broadcasters to develop a "nondiscriminatory system for controlling access ... is precisely what Congress intended to avoid through § 3(h) of the Act." 412 U.S. at 140 n. 9, 93 S.Ct., at 2105 (Stewart, J., concurring) * * *.

Of course, § 3(h) does not explicitly limit the regulation of cable systems. But without reference to the provisions of the Act directly governing broadcasting, the Commission's jurisdiction under § 2(a) would be unbounded. * * * Petitioners do not deny that statutory objectives pertinent to broadcasting bear on what the Commission might require cable systems to do. Indeed, they argue that the Commission's authority to promulgate the access rules derives from the relationship of those rules to the objectives discussed in *Midwest Video*. But they overlook the fact that Congress has restricted the Commission's ability to advance objectives associated with public access at the expense of the journalistic freedom of persons engaged in broadcasting.

That limitation is not one having peculiar applicability to television broadcasting. Its force is not diminished by the variant technology involved in cable transmissions. Cable operators now share with broadcasters a significant amount of editorial discretion regarding what their programming will include. * * *[17]

In determining, then, whether the Commission's assertion of jurisdiction is "reasonably ancillary to the effective performance of [its] various responsibilities for the regulation of television broadcasting," *United States v. Southwestern Cable Co.,* we are unable to ignore Congress' stern disapproval—evidenced in § 3(h)—of negation of the editorial discretion otherwise enjoyed by broadcasters and cable operators alike. Though the lack of congressional guidance has in the past led us to defer—albeit cautiously—to the Commission's judgment regarding the scope of its authority, here there are strong indications that agency flexibility was to be sharply delimited.

The exercise of jurisdiction in *Midwest Video,* it has been said, "strain[ed] the outer limits" of Commission authority. 406 U.S. at 676, 92 S.Ct. at 1874 (Burger, C.J., concurring in result). In light of the hesitancy with which Congress approached the access issue in the broadcast area, and in view of its outright rejection of a broad right of public access on a common-carrier basis, we are constrained to hold that the Commission exceeded those limits in promulgating its access rules. The Commission may not regulate cable systems as common carriers, just as it may not impose such obligations on television broadcasters. We

FCC, 395 U.S. 367, 89 S.Ct. 1794, 23 L.Ed.2d 371 (1969). * * *

17. We do not suggest, nor do we find it necessary to conclude, that the discretion exercised by cable operators is of the same magnitude as that enjoyed by broadcasters. Moreover, we reject the contention that the Commission's access rules will not significantly compromise the editorial discretion actually exercised by cable operators. At least in certain instances the access obligations will restrict expansion of other cable services. And even when not occasioning the displacement of alternative programming, compelling cable operators indiscriminately to accept access programming will interfere with their determinations regarding the total service offering to be extended to subscribers.

think authority to compel cable operators to provide common carriage of public-originated transmissions must come specifically from Congress.[19]

Affirmed.

MR. JUSTICE STEVENS, with whom MR. JUSTICE BRENNAN and MR. JUSTICE MARSHALL join, dissenting.

* * *

In my opinion the Court's holding in *Midwest Video* that the mandatory origination rules were within the Commission's statutory authority requires a like holding with respect to the less burdensome access rules at issue here. The Court's contrary conclusion is based on its reading of § 3(h) of the Act as denying the Commission the power to impose common-carrier obligations on broadcasters. I am persuaded that the Court has misread the statute.

* * *

Section 3 is the definitional section of the Act. It does not purport to grant or deny the Commission any substantive authority. Section 3(h) makes it clear that every broadcast station is not to be *deemed* a common carrier, and therefore subject to common-carrier regulation under Title II of the Act, simply because it is engaged in radio broadcasting. But nothing in the words of the statute or its legislative history suggests that § 3(h) places limits on the Commission's exercise of powers otherwise within its statutory authority because a lawfully imposed requirement might be termed a "common carrier obligation."

* * *

In my judgment, this is the correct approach. *Columbia Broadcasting System, Inc. v. Democratic National Committee, supra,* relied upon almost exclusively by the majority, is not to the contrary. In that case, we reviewed the provisions of the Communications Act, including § 3(h), which had some bearing on the access question presented. We emphasized, as does the majority here, that "Congress has time and again rejected various legislative attempts that would have mandated a variety of forms of individual access." But we went on to conclude: "That is not to say that Congress' rejection of such proposals must be taken to mean that Congress is opposed to private rights of access under all circumstances. *Rather, the point is that Congress has chosen to leave such questions with the Commission, to which it has given the flexibility to experiment with new ideas as changing conditions require.*" 412 U.S. at 122, 93 S.Ct., at 2096 (emphasis added).

19. The court below suggested that the Commission's rules might violate the First Amendment rights of cable operators. Because our decision rests on statutory grounds, we express no view on that question, save to acknowledge that it is not frivolous and to make clear that the asserted constitutional issue did not determine or sharply influence our construction of the statute. The Court of Appeals intimated, additionally, that the rules might effect an unconstitutional "taking" of property or, by exposing a cable operator to possible criminal prosecution for offensive cablecasting by access users over which the operator has no control, might affront the Due Process Clause of the Fifth Amendment. We forgo comment on these issues as well.

The Commission here has exercised its "flexibility to experiment" in choosing to replace the mandatory origination rule upheld in *Midwest Video* with what it views as the less onerous local access rules at issue here. I have no reason to doubt its conclusion that these rules, like the mandatory origination rule they replace, do promote the statutory objectives of "increasing the number of outlets for community self-expression and augmenting the public's choice of programs and types of services." And under this Court's holding in *Midwest Video,* this is all that is required to uphold the jurisdiction of the Commission to promulgate these rules. Since Congress has not seen fit to modify the scope of the statute as construed in *Midwest Video,* I would therefore reverse the judgment of the Court of Appeals for the Eighth Circuit and remand the case with instructions to decide the constitutional issue.

Notes and Questions

1. Note that the court below had placed its holding squarely on First Amendment as well as statutory grounds. Moreover, in footnote 19, the Supreme Court stated that the cable operators' constitutional claims were "not frivolous." This created substantial ambiguity and confusion, particularly because shortly after *Midwest Video* the cable industry began a campaign to be treated for First Amendment purposes as "electronic publishing." Footnote 19 thus figured prominently in a number of challenges to access and other provisions in local franchises. This litigation raged throughout the 1980's with little or no resolution. (p. 66) Recent cases have provided a bit more guidance. (pp. 404 et seq.)

2. What was the policy behind the definition of a common carrier in Section 153(h) of the Communications Act, at issue in *Midwest Video?* To protect broadcasters' rates from being regulated along common carrier rate-of return lines? To prevent carriers from charging what the market would bear, along mass media lines? In 1927, were the distinctions very clear?

3. In *Midwest Video,* was the Court concerned with the factors involved in *NAB,* i.e., the potential existence of a large audience and the effect of access time on political campaigns? If so, why did it not only fail to take the constitutional route, but also refrain from preempting state and local governments from imposing access requirements—as they had and have done quite routinely? If there is neither a constitutional nor a federalism concern at issue, why did the Court get involved in the whole mess to begin with?

4. Are there any pragmatic problems in classifying cable as a broadcaster? To what extent do the day-to-day operations of a cable system involve the notion of "journalistic discretion," as developed by the Court in cases like *Tornillo* and *CBS v. DNC?* (pp. 299, 316) A cable system normally distributes between thirty and eighty channels of programming, most of which are delivered via satellite from outside its market. Can a cable operator be expected to oversee the content of each signal on a regular basis? Moreover, most satellite-distributed programming sources contract to prevent the cable operator from canceling service on less than one month's notice, and prohibit cancellation of individual programs. If a cable operator agrees to these terms, does it fail to exercise its "journalistic discretion"? On

the other hand, how different is it from a small-town newspaper that gets most of its news from wire services?

5. To the extent that a cable operator is likened to a broadcaster under the Communications Act, does it also take on the First Amendment status of a broadcaster? Conversely, is the First Amendment status of broadcasters likely to be affected by the analogy? If the operator of a relatively passive medium such as cable has significant First Amendment rights, should not a broadcaster—with more control over content and more journalistic discretion—have more freedom of speech than in the past? Must every expansion of cable's First Amendment rights entail an increase in those of broadcasters?

6. As to more current Supreme Court attempts to define the First Amendment status of cable television access channels, see the *Denver Area* litigation. (p. 404) Among other issues, that case raises—but does not begin to resolve-the extent to which new media's First Amendment rights should be resolved by analogy to the status of existing media.

Note: Definition of a Common Carrier

With the apparent demise of traditional common carrier regulation, classification of an entity as a carrier may have increasingly less importance; "price cap" regulation begins at some point to resemble market-driven broadcast prices—particularly as LECs and IXCs become increasingly involved in program content and advertising.

Nevertheless, some background may be useful, if only to explain how the traditional regulatory scheme evolved. The common carrier concept stems from the law of bailments—a subject either not covered in law school today or given short shrift in a property course. A bailment is a delivery of personal property by the owner to a third party, with a "relation" resulting from this delivery. Bailments are nearly as old as humanity. Elaborate provisions for bailments were made in the Babylonian Code of Hammurabi and in the earliest Mosaic Codes. See *Exodus* 22:7: "If a man shall deliver unto his neighbor money or stuff to keep * * *." Roman law divided bailments into six types, which included a subdivision for "location operis mercium vehendarum"—transportation of goods for hire, and an early 20th century treatise called the carrier "by far the most important of bailees." Dobie, Handbook of the Law of Bailments and Carriers (1914).

The English courts were relatively slow in defining common carriage. In the early eighteenth century case of Gisbourn v. Hurst, 1 Salk. (Eng.) 249, 91 Eng.Rep. 220, a common carrier of goods was said to be "any man undertaking, for hire, to carry the goods of all persons indifferently." In the United States, the most commonly cited judicial definition was long that of Chief Justice Parker in Dwight v. Brewster, 18 Mass. (1 Pick.) 50, 53, 11 Am.Dec. 133 (1822): "One who undertakes, for hire or reward, to transport the goods of such as choose to employ him, from place to place." Another English case, Ingate v. Christie, 3 Car. & K. 61, 175 Eng.Rep. 463 (1850), held that: "The criterion is whether he carries for particular persons only, or whether he carries for every one. If a man hold himself out to do it for every one who asks him, he is a common carrier; but if he does not do it for every one, but carries for you or me only, that is a matter of special contract."

Under these common law principles, the courts held a variety of carriers to be common carriers: ferries, barges, canal boats, steamboats, stagecoaches, hacks, omnibuses, and carts.

In the latter half of the 19th century, railroads became the most important common carriers. Parliament passed the Railways Clauses Consolidation Act of 1845 (8 Vict. c. 20, s. 90), which provided for standardized rates and charges, and the Railway and Canal Traffic Acts of 1854 (17 & 18 Vict. c. 31) and 1888 (51 & 52 Vict. c. 25, s. 27), which outlawed preferential and discriminatory treatment. The U.S. Congress also responded, by enacting the Interstate Commerce Act of 1887, 24 Stat. 379 (1887).

Initially, telephone and telegraph companies were not treated as common carriers, because they were not deemed to carry goods in the traditional fashion. As telegraphs and telephones developed more fully towards the end of the nineteenth century, however, they were perceived as natural monopolies—thus requiring some type of regulation. More or less by default, the Interstate Commerce Commission was given jurisdiction over telecommunications, as it was the only federal regulatory authority with arguable expertise as to any type of common carrier—namely, railroads. This somewhat anomalous combination of jurisdiction over surface transportation and electronic communication ultimately ended with the transfer of common carrier jurisdiction to the newly created FCC under Title II of the Communications Act of 1934. 48 Stat. 1064 (1934). Perhaps one legacy of this earlier regulatory association lingers on: railroads were not held to be common carriers insofar as they chartered trains to people who then controlled those trains, and the same principle was later applied to dedicated telephone lines. It also may have created analogies—often ill-conceived—between transportation and telecommunications policy, e.g., the current fervor over "electronic superhighways."

Like the common law courts before them, the FCC and the courts have been unable to define common carriage very precisely. The Communications Act adds little to the common law, providing only this circular definition of a common carrier: "any person engaged as a common carrier for hire in interstate or foreign radio transmission of energy." 47 U.S.C. § 153(h). And the FCC did not break out of the circle by defining a "communications common carrier" as "any person engaged in rendering communication service for hire to the public." 47 C.F.R. § 21.2.

National Association of Regulatory Utility Commissioners v. FCC, 525 F.2d 630 (D.C.Cir.1976), cert. denied 425 U.S. 992, 96 S.Ct. 2203, 48 L.Ed.2d 816, illustrates the difficulties in applying the common carriage concept. The court there reviewed an FCC decision to allocate 30 megahertz of spectrum to "land-mobile" use, which involved two-way communication among stationary and moving operators, such as in taxi or ambulance dispatching. The Commission had made the spectrum available not only to common carriers, but also to the Specialized Mobile Radio Systems ("SMRS").

> * * * Private operations involve primarily dispatch services which the operator provides to himself, such as those provided by police departments and taxicab companies. * * * The significant action taken

under the present Order is the assimilation, with the above operations, of profit-motivated systems by an entrepreneur solely for the use of third party clients.

In authorizing the creation of * * * SMRS, the Commission seeks to deal with them precisely as it deals with the more traditional private mobile operators. Applications of all private operators including SMRS, are to be processed, up to spectrum capability, on a first-come, first-served basis. Believing that competition between many operators is the best way to hasten the development of improved technologies, the Commission seeks to treat SMRS, like all other private operators, as non-common carriers * * *. 525 F.2d at 639–640.

The court went on to review the definitions of common carriage in both the Communications Act and the Commission's Rules, concluding that they supplied little help and that "a good deal of confusion results from the long and complicated history of that concept." After reviewing the common law's treatment of common carriage, the court concluded that "the critical point is the quasi-public character of the activity involved," since the mere offering of services would include "private contract carriers," such as carriers offering dedicated lines for a single corporate entity to use in connecting its offices.

* * * What appears to be essential to the quasi-public character implicit in the common carrier concept is that the carrier "undertakes to carry for all people indifferently . . . ."

This does not mean that a given carrier's services must practically be available to the entire public. One may be a common carrier though the nature of the service rendered is sufficiently specialized as to be of possible use to only a fraction of the total population. And business may be turned away either because it is not of the type normally accepted or because the carrier's capacity has been exhausted. But a carrier will not be a common carrier where its practice is to make individualized decisions, in particular cases, whether and on what terms to deal. * * * Id. at 641.

The court ultimately concluded that SMRS were not common carriers.

In order to overturn the Commission's classification of SMRS as non-common carriers, the Court must find a substantial likelihood that SMRS will hold themselves out to serve indifferently those who seek to avail themselves of their particular services. * * * In making this determination, we must inquire, first, whether there will be any legal compulsion thus to serve indifferently, and if not, second, whether there are reasons implicit in the nature of SMRS operations to expect an indifferent holding out to the eligible user public.

As to possible regulatory compulsion, there is no indication in the proposed regulations that SMRS are to be in any way compelled to serve any particular applicant, or that their discretion in determining whom, and on what terms, to serve is to be in any way limited. The application provisions * * * say nothing about any obligation to provide services to eligible who seek them. * * *

Nor is there evidence in the administrative scheme of an implicit intent so to require. * * *

* * *

[As to whether SMRS would hold themselves out voluntarily] it appears that this inquiry must be highly speculative, both because no operating SMRS are now in existence, and because the parties have not addressed in any detail the issue of the prospective SMRS business operations.

The nature of the dispatch services which SMRS will primarily offer appear necessarily to involve the establishment of medium-to-long-term contractual relations, whereby the SMRS supply the needs of users for dispatch facilities for a period of time. In such a situation, it is not unreasonable to expect that the clientele might remain relatively stable, with terminations and new clients the exception rather than the rule. * * *

If the SMRS business is as hypothesized * * * there would appear to be little reason to expect any sort of holding out to the public at all. Moreover, even as openings arise, there may be many reasons that the operator would desire and expect to negotiate with and select future clients on a highly individualized basis. * * *

We therefore conclude that nothing in the record indicates any significant likelihood that SMRS will hold themselves out indifferently to serve the user public. * * * In so holding, we do not foreclose the possibility of future challenge to the Commission's classification, should the actual operations of SMRS appear to bring them within the common carrier definition.

Because the court held that SMRS were not common carriers, it concluded that they did not fall within the exception to federal jurisdiction for intrastate carriers, 47 U.S.C. § 152(b)(1); the Commission thus was left free to preempt state and local SMRS regulation. (For an equally diffuse discussion of common carriage by the same court in an identically captioned case, see National Association of Regulatory Utility Commissioners v. FCC, 533 F.2d 601, 174 U.S.App.D.C. 374 (D.C.Cir.1976)) ("*NARUC II*"). The court there held that data transmission services offered by cable television operators might be classified as common carriage. Since these services were offered in interstate commerce, they thus were exempt from state regulation and subject solely to the FCC's jurisdiction. This status not only prevented them from being subject to different regulatory and rate regimes from state to state, but also allowed them to concentrate their policy-making efforts on one agency—the Commission.

Common carriage is an even slipprier concept when radical changes are taking place in the industry in question. The rapidly changing nature of the telephone industry makes it particularly difficult to draw meaningful lines.

For example, as LECs begin to offer content-based services such as data bases, they look less and less like traditional common carriers. Conversely, when broadcast stations provide paging and data transmission, they start to look more like common carriers.

This makes the treatment of "hybrid" regulatory vehicles such as "open video systems" ("OVS") particularly difficult in both regulatory and First Amendment terms. As discussed later, an OVS entity may program a third of its channels, but must lease out the other one third to third parties. (pp. ___) Although both the Congress and the Commission claim that this is not a combination of mass communications and common carriage, it is somewhat difficult to see the difference.

This may be a very sensible way of enticing LECs and IXCs to build the infrastructure for broadband communications. But it raises some difficult legal issues. For example, since *Midwest Video II* seems to say that the Communications Act—and possibly the Constitution—prohibit treatment of a broadcaster as a common carrier, it is difficult to see how OVS would survive a literal reading of the case.

Questions

1. Is the policy underlying the definition of a common carrier in Section 152(b) of the Communications Act, which was involved in *National Association of Regulatory Utility Commissioners,* the same as the policy behind Section 153(h) of the Communications Act, which was involved in *Midwest Video* (p. 66)? Is it coincidental that both cases limited the Commission's power over cable systems? Were the reasons for limiting the FCC's jurisdiction the same in both cases? To what extent as the Commission simply looking for a way to impose closer scrutiny and the then new cable industry?

2. Conversely, to what extent were the Commission and the Court trying to advance the generally deregulatory goals of the 1970s and 1980s? On the one hand, *Midwest Video II* took the federal government out of the business of regulating access channels. On the other hand, *NARUC II* prevented state or local governments from regulating cable data transmission. If Julius Caesar's motto was to "divide and conquer," might the last generation's policymaker's slogan have been to "deregulate and preempt?"

C. ANCILLARY AND HYBRID JURISDICTION

The FCC's first problem with cable television was finding a jurisdictional basis upon which it could rest its regulation. As we have seen, the FCC had no explicit authority under the Communications Act of 1934. This did not deter the agency, however, and it began developing a regulatory program well before the extent of its power was clear.

C. FERRIS, F. LLOYD, & T. CASEY, CABLE TELEVISION LAW: VIDEO COMMUNICATIONS PRACTICE GUIDE

Sec. 5.03–5.05 (1983).*

Cable television developed in the late 1940s and early 1950s to fill a void in television service in rural and mid-sized communities caused by the "freeze" in television allocations and the lack of expansion in these areas following the 1952 [FCC channel allocation] decision. The early systems brought enhanced television signals into those areas where signal reception was difficult or non-existent due to topographical conditions or distance from television stations, and the population was too scarce to support its own local station.

By 1952, seventy community antenna television (CATV) systems served 14,000 subscribers. By the end of the 1950s, cable television had spread dramatically, with approximately 550 systems providing improved television reception to over 550,000 subscribing households. Throughout this period, cable acted solely as a retransmitter of broadcast television signals from local or nearby markets, and was unrestricted in its growth by federal or state regulation.

EARLY FCC REGULATORY EFFORTS

By the late 1950s and early 1960s, cable technology had vastly improved it technology. Basic channel capacity had increased from three channels in 1959 to twelve channels in 1966. In addition, more signals from distant television stations could be imported through the use of microwave relay stations. At first, when the cable systems merely enhanced the clarity of local signals or brought outlying signals to new markets where no local television service existed, cable had been seen as a benefit to broadcasting. When cable operators were no longer limited to retransmission of signals from local markets and began to bring in distant signals that competed with local signals for viewer attention, however, broadcasters in both rural and metropolitan areas began to view cable's development as a threat to their television monopolies. Thus, the short period of cooperation between cable operators and broadcasters ended abruptly at this time, and the FCC and the courts began to play an increasing role in resolving disputes between them.

Cable television does not directly use the radio spectrum to reach the viewer's home, as does broadcast television, nor did it, in its original incarnation as a retransmitter of broadcast signals, act in a manner similar to a common carrier such as the telephone or telegraph. The FCC was initially hesitant, therefore, to regulate this new industry at all. In 1959, in *Frontier Broadcasting Co.* [24 FCC 251 (1959)], the Commission refused the request of thirteen television broadcast station licensees to regulate cable as a common carrier under the Communications Act. The Commission found that cable did not fall under Title II of the Act, the title giving the FCC the power to regulate common carriers, since the "carrier" (the cable operator), rather than the individual subscriber, chose the particular message to be received. Since CATV uses wires to deliver its signal to the home instead of radio waves, the commission also held title III of the Act inapplicable.

Also in 1959, the FCC in its *Auxiliary Services Inquiry*[3] first examined the question of cable television's relationship to local broadcasting. * * * [It] decided that limiting the growth of cable was unwarranted, and imposed a "heavy burden" of proof on those broadcasters seeking to show economic injury due to the operation of cable in a local market.

* * *

The FCC never obtained a specific Congressional grant of authority to regulate cable. By 1962, however, it had changed its policy about its inherent power to do so without Congressional mandate, and it indirectly asserted its jurisdiction over cable systems by regulating microwave relay systems used to transmit distant signals to them. In *Carter Mountain Transmission Corp.*,[5] the Commission reversed its earlier position in the 1959 *Auxiliary Services Inquiry* and asserted that authorization for the use of microwave common carrier facilities would be granted only if it could be shown that there would be no direct or indirect effect from a cable system on the continued existence of a local television station operation. * * *

In 1965, the Commission issued its *First Report and Order* adopting general rules affecting the authorization of microwave-fed cable systems.[8] These rules: (1) required that such systems carry all signals of local broadcast television stations (the "must carry" rule) and (2) prohibited cable systems from carrying distant station programs that duplicated local programming during the fifteen day period before or after the local broadcast. The rules were enacted to rectify the perceived problem of "unfair or unequal competition" between cable systems and local broadcasters, and to preserve cable in its "appropriate" role as a supplement to broadcasting. * * *

By this time, the Commission was concerned not only with cable's possible effects on local rural service, but also with its potential competition with stations in larger markets. Three years earlier, Congress had passed the All–Channel Receiver Act, and the FCC promulgated rules under that Act designed to ensure the growth of UHF television stations. In adopting the 1965 *First Report and Order,* the FCC, therefore,

---

3. Inquiry into the Impact of Community Antenna Systems, TV Translators, TV "Satellite" Stations, and TV "Repeaters" on the Orderly Development of Television Broadcasting, 26 F.C.C.2d 403 (1959).

5. Carter Mountain Transmission Corp., 32 FCC 2d 459 (1962), *aff'd* 321 F.2d 359 (D.C.Cir.1963), *cert. denied* 375 U.S. 951 (1963).

8. First Report and Order in Docket Nos. 14,895 and 15,233, 38 FCC 683 (1965).

protected the UHF stations at the expense of cable television's growth in the major markets.

* * *

The FCC formally asserted its jurisdiction over all cable systems, whether microwave-fed or not, one year later in its *Second Report and Order*[14] and imposed wide-ranging and restrictive regulations on cable television. Jurisdiction was predicated on sections 2(a) and 3(a) of the Communications Act, which granted the Commission authority to regulate systems engaged in "interstate communications by wire," and the Commission's inherent authority "to prevent frustration of the regulatory scheme by CATV operations."[16]

The "must carry" local broadcast signal rules and the distant signal non-duplication requirements applied in 1965 to microwave-fed systems were extended to all cable systems. * * * In addition, a new requirement was imposed applicable to all cable systems in the top 100 markets. Prior to importing distant signals into one of these markets the cable operator had to show in an evidentiary hearing that it "would be consistent with the public interest, and particularly the establishment and health and maintenance of UHF television broadcast service."[18] The top 100 markets were selected for special attention to protect the fledgling UHF stations with the best potential for viability. In smaller markets the Commission recognized the supplementary role that cable played in enhancing broadcast service, and allowed carriage of local and distant signals thirty days after notice was given, so long as no objection was filed with the FCC.

* * * In 1968, the Supreme Court, in *United States v. Southwestern Cable Co.,* upheld the Commission's authority to promulgate the rules enacted in the *Second Report and Order.*

UNITED STATES v. SOUTHWESTERN CABLE CO.

Supreme Court of the United States, 1968.
392 U.S. 157, 88 S.Ct. 1994, 20 L.Ed.2d 1001.

Mr. Justice Harlan delivered the opinion of the Court.

These cases stem from proceedings conducted by the Federal Communications Commission after requests by Midwest Television for relief under §§ 74.1107 and 74.1109[3] of the rules promulgated by the Commission for the regulation of community antenna television (CATV) systems. Midwest averred that respondents' CATV systems transmitted the signals of Los Angeles broadcasting stations into the San Diego area, and

---

14. Second Report and Order in Docket Nos. 14,895, 15233, and 15,971, 2 FCC 2d 725 (1966), aff'd Black Hills Video Corp. v. FCC, 399 F.2d 65 (8th Cir.1968).

16. 2 FCC 2d at 734.

18. 2 FCC2d at 782.

3. 47 CFR § 74.1109 * * * provides that petitions for special relief "may be submitted informally, by letter, but shall be accompanied by an affidavit of service on any CATV system, station licensee, permittee, applicant, or other interested person * * *" * * *.

thereby had, inconsistently with the public interest, adversely affected Midwest's San Diego station.[4] Midwest sought an appropriate order limiting the carriage of such signals by respondents' systems. After consideration of the petition and of various responsive pleadings, the Commission restricted the expansion of respondents' service in areas in which they had not operated on February 15, 1966, pending hearings to be conducted on the merits of Midwest's complaints. 4 F.C.C.2d 612. On petitions for review, the Court of Appeals for the Ninth Circuit held that the Commission lacks authority under the Communications Act of 1934 to issue such an order.[6] 378 F.2d 118. We granted certiorari to consider this important question of regulatory authority. For reasons that follow, we reverse.

I.

CATV systems receive the signals of television broadcasting stations, amplify them, transmit them by cable or microwave, and ultimately distribute them by wire to the receivers of their subscribers. CATV systems characteristically do not produce their own programming, and do not recompense producers or broadcasters for use of the programming which they receive and redistribute.[10] * * *

The CATV industry has grown rapidly since the establishment of the first commercial system in 1950. * * * The statistical evidence is incomplete, but, as the Commission has observed, "whatever the estimate, CATV growth is clearly explosive in nature." Second Report and Order, 2 F.C.C.2d 725, 738, n. 15.

* * * As the number and size of CATV systems have increased, their principal function has more frequently become the importation of distant signals.[16] * * * CATV systems, formerly no more than local auxiliaries to broadcasting, promise for the future to provide a national

---

4. Midwest asserted that respondents' importation of Los Angeles signals had fragmented the San Diego audience, that this would reduce the advertising revenues of local stations, and that the ultimate consequence would be to terminate or to curtail the services provided in the San Diego area by local broadcasting stations. Respondents' CATV systems now carry the signals of San Diego stations, but Midwest alleged that the quality of the signals, as they are carried by respondents, is materially degraded, and that this serves only to accentuate the fragmentation of the local audience.

6. The opinion of the Court of Appeals could be understood to hold either that the Commission may not, under the Communications Act, regulate CATV, or, more narrowly, that it may not issue the prohibitory order involved here. We take the court's opinion, in fact, to have encompassed both positions.

10. The question whether a CATV system infringes the copyright of a broadcasting station by its reception and retransmission of the station's signals is presented in *Fortnightly Corp. v. United Artists Television, Inc.,* No. 618, now pending before the Court. [In this companion case to Southwestern, the Court held that cable systems were not subject to copyright liability for use of broadcast signals. 392 U.S. 390, 88 S.Ct. 2084, 20 L.Ed.2d 1176 (1968). As discussed later, however, the Copyright Revision Act of 1976 imposed a "compulsory copyright" scheme upon the cable industry. (p. 401)—Ed.]

16. The term "distant signal" has been given a specialized definition by the Commission, as a signal "which is extended or received beyond the Grade B contour of that station." 47 CFR § 74.1101(i). The Grade B contour is a line along which good reception may be expected 90% of the time at 50% of the locations. See 47 CFR § 73.683(a).

communications system, in which signals from selected broadcasting centers would be transmitted to metropolitan areas throughout the country.

* * *

II.

We must first emphasize that questions as to the validity of the specific rules promulgated by the Commission for the regulation of CATV are not now before the Court. The issues in these cases are only two: whether the Commission has authority under the Communications Act to regulate CATV systems, and, if it has, whether it has, in addition, authority to issue the prohibitory order here in question.

The Commission's authority to regulate broadcasting and other communications is derived from the Communications Act of 1934, as amended. The Act's provisions are explicitly applicable to "all interstate and foreign communication by wire or radio...." 47 U.S.C. § 152(a). The Commission's responsibilities are no more narrow: it is required to endeavor to "make available . . . to all the people of the United States a rapid, efficient, Nation–wide, and world-wide wire and radio communication service...." 47 U.S.C. § 151. * * * As this Court emphasized in an earlier case, the Act's terms, purposes, and history all indicate that Congress "formulated a unified and comprehensive regulatory system for the [broadcasting] industry." FCC v. Pottsville Broadcasting Co., 309 U.S. 134, 137, 60 S.Ct. 437, 439, 84 L.Ed. 656.

Respondents do not suggest that CATV systems are not within the term "communication by wire or radio." Indeed, such communications are defined by the Act so as to encompass "the transmission of . . . signals, pictures, and sounds of all kinds," whether by radio or cable, "including all instrumentalities, facilities, apparatus, and services (among other things, the receipt, forwarding, and delivery of communications) incidental to such transmission." 47 U.S.C. §§ 153(a), (b). These very general terms amply suffice to reach respondents' activities.

Nor can we doubt that CATV systems are engaged in interstate communication, even where, as here, the intercepted signals emanate from stations located within the same State in which the CATV system operates. We may take notice that television broadcasting consists in very large part of programming devised for, and distributed to, national audiences; respondents thus are ordinarily employed in the simultaneous retransmission of communications that have very often originated in other States. The stream of communication is essentially uninterrupted and properly indivisible. * * *

* * *

[The Court rejected Southwestern's argument that the FCC's attempts to secure legislation showed its lack of jurisdiction.] The Commission's requests for legislation evidently reflected in each instance both its uncertainty as to the proper width of its authority and its understandable preference for more detailed policy guidance than the Communications Act now provides. We have recognized that administrative agencies should, in such situations, be encouraged to seek from Congress clarification of the pertinent statutory provisions.

* * *

Second, respondents urge that § 152(a)[34] does not independently confer regulatory authority upon the Commission, but instead merely prescribes the forms of communication to which the Act's other provisions may separately be made applicable. Respondents emphasize that the Commission does not contend either that CATV systems are common carriers, and thus within Title II of the Act, or that they are broadcasters, and thus within Title III. They conclude that CATV, with certain of the characteristics both of broadcasting and of common carriers, but with all of the characteristics of neither, eludes altogether the Act's grasp.

We cannot construe the Act so restrictively. Nothing in the language of § 152(a), in the surrounding language, or in the Act's history or purposes limits the Commission's authority to those activities and forms of communication that are specifically described by the Act's other provisions. * * * Similarly, the legislative history indicates that the Commission was given "regulatory power over all forms of electrical communication...." Certainly Congress could not in 1934 have foreseen the development of community antenna television systems, but it seems to us that it was precisely because Congress wished "to maintain, through appropriate administrative control, a grip on the dynamic aspects of radio transmission," that it conferred upon the Commission a "unified jurisdiction" and "broad authority." * * * Congress in 1934 acted in a field that was demonstrably "both new and dynamic," and it therefore gave the Commission "a comprehensive mandate," with "not niggardly but expansive powers." We have found no reason to believe that § 152 does not, as its terms suggest, confer regulatory authority over "all interstate ... communication by wire or radio."

* * *

The Commission has reasonably found that the achievement of each of these purposes is "placed in jeopardy by the unregulated explosive growth of CATV." H.R.Rep. No. 1635, 89th Cong., 2d Sess., 7. Although CATV may in some circumstances make possible "the realization of some of the (Commission's) most important goals," First Report and Order, *supra,* at 699, its importation of distant signals into the service areas of local stations may also "destroy or seriously degrade the service offered by a television broadcaster," and thus ultimately deprive the

---

34. 47 U.S.C. § 152(a) provides that "[t]he provisions of this chapter shall apply to all interstate and foreign communication by wire or radio and all interstate and foreign transmission of energy by radio, which originates and/or is received within the United States, and to all persons engaged within the United States in such communication or such transmission of energy by radio, and to the licensing and regulating of all radio stations as hereinafter provided * * *."

public of the various benefits of a system of local broadcasting stations. In particular, the Commission feared that CATV might, by dividing the available audiences and revenues, significantly magnify the characteristically serious financial difficulties of UHF and educational television broadcasters. The Commission acknowledged that it could not predict with certainty the consequences of unregulated CATV, but reasoned that its statutory responsibilities demand that it "plan in advance of foreseeable events, instead of waiting to react to them." We are aware that these consequences have been variously estimated, but must conclude that there is substantial evidence that the Commission cannot "discharge its overall responsibilities without authority over this important aspect of television service."

* * * The Commission has reasonably found that the successful performance of these duties demands prompt and efficacious regulation of community antenna television systems. * * * [W]e therefore hold that the Commission's authority over "all interstate . . . communication by wire or radio" permits the regulation of CATV systems.

There is no need here to determine in detail the limits of the Commission's authority to regulate CATV. It is enough to emphasize that the authority which we recognize today under § 152(a) is restricted to that reasonably ancillary to the effective performance of the Commission's various responsibilities for the regulation of television broadcasting. The Commission may, for these purposes, issue "such rules and regulations and prescribe such restrictions and conditions, not inconsistent with law," as "public convenience, interest, or necessity requires." 47 U.S.C. § 303(r). We express no views as to the Commission's authority, if any, to regulate CATV under any other circumstances or for any other purposes.

III.

[The Court went on to hold that the Communications Act authorized the Commission to issue the order in question without first holding a hearing. The Court acknowledged that the provision for cease and desist orders in Section 312(b) requires a hearing, but it held that the FCC has general authority under the Act to issue such orders without invoking Section 312, particularly where necessary in order to deal with a dynamic situation.]

MR. JUSTICE WHITE, concurring in the result.

My route to reversal of the Court of Appeals is somewhat different from the Court's. Section 2(a) of the Communications Act, says that "*(t)he provisions of this chapter* shall apply to all interstate and foreign communication by wire or radio. . . ." (Emphasis added.) I am inclined to believe that this section means that the Commission must generally base jurisdiction on other provisions of the Act. This position would not, however, require invalidation of the assertion of jurisdiction before us today. Section 301, gives the Commission broad authority over broadcasting, and § 303, confers authority to "[m]ake such regulations not inconsistent with law as it may deem necessary to prevent interference between stations and to carry out the provisions of this chapter" and also the authority to establish areas or zones to be served by any station. * * *

Even if §§ 301 and 303 in themselves furnish insufficient basis for the Commission to enjoin extraneous interference with the San Diego broadcasting scheme it has authorized, § 2(a), *supra,* makes the provisions of the Act, including §§ 301 and 303, applicable to all wire and radio communication. Hence the Commission is authorized to regulate wire communications to implement the ends of §§ 301 and 303, and authorized as well to use its express authority over broadcasting to enforce its specific powers over common carriers by wire.

Notes and Questions

1.   To a certain extent, the Commission may have been boxed in by its own prior positions. As noted, in 1959 the FCC had rejected the broadcasting industry's request for regulation of cable, in part on the ground that cable was neither a carrier under Title II of the Act nor a broadcaster under Title III. Having eschewed reliance on either of the traditional bases of jurisdiction, in order to be consistent the Commission had to fall back on the "reasonably ancillary" rationale—sometimes also known as "hybrid" regulation. As will be seen later, hybrid regulation may have disappeared as an implied FCC power, but reemerged as the "open video system" requirement under the Telecommunications Act of 1996. (pp. 430–431)

2.   Note the interplay between copyright and cable. The companion case to *Southwestern* was Fortnightly Corp. v. United Artists Television, Inc., 392 U.S. 390, 88 S.Ct. 2084, 20 L.Ed.2d 1176 (1968). The Court there rejected the argument that a cable system infringes the copyright on the programs it retransmits with permission. The Court reasoned that cable transmission did not constitute a "performance" under the Copyright Act of 1909, because a cable system does not determine or change the content of the broadcast signal. Congress eventually dealt with the accommodation of copyright and cable interests in Section 111 of the 1976 Copyright Revision Act. (p. 401)

3.   The major problem with "reasonably ancillary" jurisdiction is in defining what a regulatory policy is reasonably ancillary to. The Court defines the FCC's authority only as "that reasonably ancillary to the effective performance of the Commission's various responsibilities for the regulation of television broadcasting." This seems to suggest that the test of whether a rule is "reasonably ancillary" is its utility in the Commission's regulation of the broadcast industry. If so, is it any more than a grant of authority to stifle competition for broadcasters, as the prohibition on the importation of distant signals did in *Southwestern Cable?* Ironically, in the 1980s the Commission may have been in the business of protecting cable against a whole range of new video technologies.

Southwestern represented the culmination of efforts by the Commission and the lower federal courts to confer jurisdiction over cable upon the agency. For a thorough discussion of the development of the Commission's jurisdiction over cable, see J. Fogarty & M. Spielholz, *FCC Cable Jurisdic-*

tion: From Zero to Plenary in Twenty–Five Years, 37 Fed.Comm.L.J. 113 (1984).

4. The fate of hybrid jurisdiction has been unclear for a number of years, because it seems to have been totally or partially supplanted over the years by a variety of statutes—the Cable Act of 1984, the Cable Act of 1992, and the Telecommunications Act of 1996. The Commission and the courts have had no real opportunity to pass on the question, since the statutes now cover virtually everything previously subject to hybrid jurisdiction.

For example, the "must-carry" rules upheld after much debate in *Southwestern* now are imposed by the 1992 Cable Act. Although the FCC naturally has filled in many of the holes through rulemaking proceedings, the basic policies emanate from the statute. Questions of Commission jurisdiction thus have not arisen to any substantial extent.

Similarly, the status of access channels also is now governed by the 1992 and 1996 Acts. As discussed later, the Acts impose specific access channel requirements on cable operators, subject to limited participation by state and local governments. (p. 213) And the 1996 Act went so far as to create open video systems, as a form of bureaucratic prescription for how broadband systems should allocate their channels. Whether bureaucrats' prescriptions as to how media should work is less than clear, since neither cable operators nor telephone companies initially showed any interest in building OVS.

Finally, it should be noted that the rules at issue in *Southwestern* went the way of all flesh many years ago. After the Court upheld them, the Commission made numerous changes in them. Moreover, as part of the trend towards statutory codification, the 1992 Cable Act imposed fairly specific must carry requirements—subject, of course, to the FCC's interpretation and amplification. The following excerpt describes the history before the 1992 Cable Act.

C. FERRIS, F. LLOYD & T. CASEY CABLE TELEVISION LAW: A VIDEO COMMUNICATIONS PRACTICE GUIDE
Sec. 5.04–5.05 (1983).*

REGULATION AND DEREGULATION OF CABLE IN THE 1970s

In combination, the FCC regulatory policies in the late 1960s effectively halted the growth of cable television in major markets. Although there were almost 2500 cable systems, with 4.5 million subscribers, by the end of the decade, cable television was still principally limited to rural areas and small communities on the fringe of major markets. The regulatory climate in both the Congress and the FCC was so uncertain, and the limitations on distant signal importation so severe, that investors were hesitant to enter the cable industry to provide it with the capital to enter the urban markets.

* * *

* ©1990 by Matthew Bender & Co., Inc.; reprinted with permission from *Cable Television Law*.

A significant step in resolving the cable controversy occurred in August, 1971. A second compromise measure [the "Letter of Intent"] was sent from the FCC to the Chairmen of the Senate and House Communications Subcommittees setting forth a blueprint for regulatory action.[10] The Commission reiterated its belief that the proper forum for resolution of the copyright issue was Congress or the courts, and proposed to separate the copyright issue from cable regulation so that cable could develop in the major markets without being held hostage to the competing industry pressures on Congress over copyright.

The proposals covered four main areas:

(1) television broadcasting signal carriage;

(2) access channels and minimum channel capacity;

(3) technical standards; and

(4) jurisdiction of federal and state-local governments over cable television.

* * *

THE 1971 CONSENSUS AGREEMENT AND 1972 FCC REPORT AND ORDER

The FCC's August, 1971 proposal did not initially break the deadlock between copyright holders, broadcasters and cable operators over the copyright issue. A settlement was finally achieved when the White House Office of Telecommunications Policy intervened in the fall. Representatives of all three groups were called to the White House and the so-called "Consensus Agreement" of November, 1971 resulted.[15]

The Consensus Agreement forged a compromise whereby all parties agreed to actively support cable copyright legislation in exchange for reduction of restrictions on cable television's growth in major markets. * * * This Agreement and the prior FCC Letter of Intent were incorporated into the fundamental FCC blueprint for the cable area, the 1972 *Cable Television Report and Order*.[19] In this Report, the FCC promulgated rules covering broadcast signal carriage, non-broadcast access channels, technical standards, and federal-state/local jurisdiction. The rules adopted followed in most respects the Letter of Intent.

* * *

Under the 1972 FCC regime, cable systems outside all television markets had to carry all television signals assigned to the cable community, all educational television stations within 35 miles, all translator stations in the cable community with 100 watts or more power, and all television stations "significantly viewed" in the cable community. Any other distant educational signals could be carried.

---

10. Cable Television Proposal, 31 FCC 2d 115 (1971).

15. 36 FCC 2d 284 (1972).

19. 36 FCC 2d 143, recon. 36 FCC 2d 326 (1972), *aff'd sub nom.* American Civil Liberties Union v. FCC, 523 F.2d 1344 (9th Cir.1975).

In "smaller television markets" (i.e., markets not among the top 100), mandatory carriage encompassed, in addition, all Grade B signals from stations in other smaller markets. A total of three full network stations and one independent station could be provided with a combination of local and distant signals.

The same "must carry" requirements applied to the top 100 markets (except for the requirement that cable carry Grade B signals from stations in other smaller markets). Additional independent distant signal stations (three in the top 50, two in the second 50 markets) were included in the basic service complement. Two "wild card" independent stations could also be carried in the top 50 markets above the "minimum service" standard.

* * *

Although the 1972 rules were initially heralded as the lifting of the cable "freeze," the severe restrictions they imposed on cable's ability to offer varied programming continued to protect the broadcasters' and program suppliers' interests in the major urban markets. In 1972, there were approximately 2800 cable systems serving approximately six million subscribers. Few of these subscribers were in the top television markets, and the 1972 rules so restricted cable's offerings that it remained an unattractive option for many viewers.

The cable operators' position greatly improved, however, in the ensuing years, as the FCC spent the next decade dismantling many of these complex rules, which in practice proved to be unenforceable and unnecessary.

* * *

Finally, the Commission in 1975 decided not to adopt local cable television-newspaper cross-ownership barriers, since it found that no record of abuse or trend toward monopolization of viewpoints in communities where cable systems were owned by newspapers had yet been demonstrated. It retained jurisdiction, however, in case future developments suggested that newspaper ownership restrictions would be necessary to preserve media diversity.

* * *

The FCC, meanwhile, lost a court battle which forced it to abandon entirely its pay cable restrictions. In *Home Box Office v. FCC*,[22] the Court of Appeals vacated all of the FCC's complicated pay-cable anti-siphoning rules. Most importantly, the court adopted a strict standard by which the FCC had to justify continuation of any of its regulatory restrictions on cable.

As a result of the *HBO* decision, cable systems dramatically increased their pay movie and sports offerings and subscribership increased. At this point, growth in large cities finally occurred as cable

22. 567 F.2d 9 (D.C.Cir.) (per curiam),
cert. denied, 434 U.S. 829 (1977).

systems became more attractive investments. In addition, in light of the new judicial standard announced in *HBO,* the Commission also had to justify its other regulations applying to cable television by showing actual harm to local broadcasting warranting federal protection. The eventual findings of the *Economic Inquiry,* in 1979, indicating that cable did not pose such a threat, therefore foreshadowed the further deregulation of the industry.

* * *

By the time its decision in the *Economic Inquiry* was adopted by the FCC in 1979, two important restrictions on cable remained: the distant signal carriage restrictions and the syndicated exclusivity rules. Several conclusions of the *Inquiry Report* led to the deletion of the distant signal carriage rules.

* * *

In other forums, cable in 1979 was being freed from additional FCC restrictions. The Supreme Court, in *FCC v. Midwest Video Corp.,*[75] overturned all access requirements implemented in 1976 as beyond the FCC's jurisdiction. * * *

In light of the *Midwest Video II* decision, the Commission questioned whether it had jurisdiction to continue to impose franchise fee limitations on local franchising authorities. As part of its comprehensive 1972 cable rules, the FCC had restricted municipalities to charging three percent maximum franchise fees (or five percent with Commission permission). The purpose of this limit initially was to ensure that cable operators had funds to meet the "substantial obligations" imposed by the access requirements. Since the Commission could not impose these access requirements on cable operators after *Midwest Video II,* the rationale for continuing this franchise fee limit was questioned. * * *

CABLE'S EXPANSION IN THE 1980S

* * *

By 1980, cable television's deregulation at the federal level was substantial. As a result of the findings of the 1979 *Economic Inquiry Report* and *Inquiry into Syndicated Exclusivity Rules,* the Commission concluded that "elimination of the distant signal carriage and syndicated exclusivity rules will enhance consumer welfare by promoting competition of ideas."[2] Cable systems were permitted to carry as many distant signals as their viewers demanded, and syndicated exclusivity rules were eliminated in their entirety.

Note: Whither Ancillary Jurisdiction

As the *Southwestern* Court is relatively frank in admitting, ancillary jurisdiction basically stems from somewhat protectionist needs to prevent

---

75. 440 U.S. 689 (1979).

2. Report and Order in Docket Nos. 20,-988 and 21,284, 79 FCC2d 663 (1980).

one industry from causing harm to another. (Indeed, the Commission in the 1980s arguably may have been in the business of protecting cable against a whole range of new video technologies.) But *Southwestern* represented only the culmination of efforts by the Commission and the lower federal courts to confer jurisdiction over cable upon the agency. For a thorough discussion of the development of the Commission's jurisdiction over cable, see J. Fogarty & M. Spielholz, *FCC Cable Jurisdiction: From Zero to Plenary in Twenty-Five Years*, 37 Fed. Comm. L. J. 113 (1984).

Given this paucity of cases, the boundaries of the reasonably ancillary test are less than clear. Since the doctrine has lain dormant for so long, it may have lost all or most of its vitality. And the effect upon the FCC's jurisdiction of the Cable Communications Policy Act of 1984 is less than clear. The Cable Act explicitly gives the FCC jurisdiction over a small number of matters; but it is silent as to its effect on "reasonably ancillary" jurisdiction. The Commission generally has taken the position that it retains some of its traditional jurisdiction over cable in conjunction with implied jurisdiction under the Cable Act. In American Civil Liberties Union v. FCC, 823 F.2d 1554 (D.C.Cir.1987), the court upheld the Commission's somewhat murky position.

    * * * In its *latest* formulation, [the FCC's] policy can be summarized as follows: the Commission *does* have jurisdiction to adjudicate disputes under the Cable Act's franchise fee provision, although its jurisdiction is concurrent with that of the courts. The Commission will exercise its jurisdiction only where the dispute impinges on a national policy concerning cable communications and implicates the agency's expertise. Where the dispute concerns a matter of local taxation, the FCC generally will *not* assert its jurisdiction, because the dispute's relevance to a national communications policy will tend to be "slight" and the Commission's expertise will tend not to be implicated. In these cases, the Commission will refer the dispute to "local courts," which are, in the Commission's judgment, better situated to take evidence and delve into matters of local taxation.

    Reviewing its latest formulation, we are unable to conclude that the FCC's policy of forbearance is "arbitrary, capricious, an abuse of discretion, or otherwise not in accordance with law." In contrast with several other provisions of the Cable Act, the franchise fee does not contain an explicit delegation of regulatory authority. Because the provision establishes a *uniform federal standard* for franchise fees, and because the provision has been incorporated into the Communications Act, it is clear * * * that the *ultimate* responsibility for ensuring a "national policy with respect to franchise fees lies with the federal agency responsible for administering the Communications Act. At the same time, however, the statute also appears to contemplate judicial enforcement of the franchise fee provision * * * In the absence of more explicit guidance from Congress, the FCC necessarily enjoys discretion in setting its enforcement priorities and identifying those franchise fee disputes that require Commission action. * * *"

    Our affirmance of the Commission's policy, however, is based on our assessment that the Commission has *not totally abdicated its ultimate* responsibility for enforcing the franchise fee provision. * * * [T]he

Commission has made clear that it stands ready to enforce the franchise fee provision where circumstances require Commission intervention. We thus are able to affirm the Commission's policy without fear that the Congress' efforts to establish a federal standard for franchise fees will be thwarted.

823 F.2d at 1573–1574. [emphasis in original]

The *ACLU* opinion sheds little if no light on the survival of the Commission's "reasonably ancillary" powers.

D.   RECAP: TYPES OF FCC JURISDICTION

With the enactment of the Communications Act of 1934, most observers would have assumed that media regulation consisted solely of broadcasting and common carriage—with a few grey areas for short-wave, mobile services, amateur radio and the like. Indeed, this was an extraordinarily stable analytical structure until well past the middle of the century—with the development of "new media" such as cable and then other distribution mechanisms.

Despite all of the interest in new electronic media policy, it is not clear that all that much has changed. Broadcasting still operates upon the basic licensing policies that were originally imposed by the 1927 Radio Act; like most other media—or, for that matter, most other industries—deregulation has made it subject to fewer substantive requirements. Common carriers have departed from traditional rate regulation, but still are subject to the general requirement of serving all qualified users; carriers have fewer formal requirements and may enter into content for the first time. Other media have generally operate under traditional broadcasting, carrier, or hybrid principles, e.g., cable, DBS, and OVS.

The sponsor of the 1927 Communications Act, Senator Dill, thus might find some aspects of current media regulation a bit new and anomalous; but his learning curve as to them probably would be comparatively short.

E.   FEDERAL PREEMPTION OF STATE AND LOCAL REGULATION

In addition to limitations under the Communications Act and other federal statutes, the Commission—like any other federal agencies—is subject to limitations on its preemption powers and the Tenth Amendment. At the beginning, this was not much of an issue, since broadcasting clearly was a purely interstate activity and thus not subject to any local regulations of its core activities. As an increasing number of local, intrastate media have developed—particularly cable, MMDS, and DBS—the line has not been so clear.

In a federal system of government, national policies generally take precedence over state or local laws. The Supremacy Clause of the Constitution provides that "This Constitution, and the Laws of the

United States which shall be made in pursuance thereof * * * shall be the supreme Law of the Land." U.S. Const. Art. VI, cl. 2. And since federal administrative agencies are creatures of, and creators of "the Laws of the United States," Congress may give them the power to preempt state laws, consistent with general limitations on agency powers.

The FCC's preemptive power varies with the statutory basis for its policies, and thus with the type of medium being regulated. As noted above, Title III regulation of broadcasting and other spectrum uses is exclusively federal; Section 301 states that "It is the purpose of this Act * * * to maintain the control of the United States over all the channels of radio transmission." There never has been any real doubt as to the FCC's exclusive power over licensing of over-the-air transmissions. Thus, a state law making a broadcaster liable for an act required by the Commission is preempted. For example, a licensee required to broadcast a reply message under the equal opportunities doctrine is immune from state tort liability for defamation. Farmers Educational and Cooperative Union v. WDAY, Inc., 360 U.S. 525, 79 S.Ct. 1302, 3 L.Ed.2d 1407 (1959).

The situation is not quite so clear as to common carriage. While broadcast regulation had no historical antecedents, regulation of common carriage has many, as noted before. State agencies actively regulated telephone companies well before Congress gave the FCC jurisdiction over interstate telephone service. In passing the Communications Act of 1934, Congress preserved the states' role with respect to intrastate service. Section 152(b) thus provides that:

> [N]othing in this [Act] shall be construed to apply or to give the Commission jurisdiction with respect to * * * charges, classifications, practices, services, facilities, or regulations for or in connection with intrastate communication service by wire or radio of any carrier * * *. 47 U.S.C. § 152(b).

The Act further recognizes the dual nature of telecommunications regulation by providing for "joint boards" to decide matters involving both intrastate and interstate communications. 47 U.S.C. § 410.

Despite the Act's limitations, the Commission generally has been able to expand its jurisdiction, and hence its preemptive authority, on the theory that intrastate activities affect the interstate telecommunications system. From time to time, however, the FCC has suffered setbacks in attempting to preempt state commissions. Perhaps the most severe came in Louisiana Public Service Commission v. FCC, 476 U.S. 355, 106 S.Ct. 1890, 90 L.Ed.2d 369 (1986). There the Commission required LECs to treat the cost of installing inside wiring as an expense item—and thus to recover it currently rather than over time through a charge for depreciation. The FCC was concerned that recovering this cost over time would prevent the LECs from building up the capital reserves they would need in order to expand their plants sufficiently to implement advanced telecommunications services. The Supreme Court held that Section 152(b) governed, despite any impact on the interstate telecommunications system. The Court noted:

> [W]e cannot accept [the FCC's] argument that § 152(b) does not control because the plant involved in this case is used interchangeably to provide both interstate and intrastate service, and that even if § 152(b) does reserve to the state commissions some authority over "certain aspects" of intrastate communication, it should be "confined to intrastate matters which are 'separable from and do not substantially affect' interstate communications." * * *

> * * * While it is certainly true, and a basic underpinning of our federal system, that state regulation will be displaced to the extent that it stands as an obstacle to the accomplishment and execution of the full purposes and objectives of Congress, it is also true that a federal agency may pre-empt state law only when and if it is acting within the scope of its congressionally delegated authority. * * * Section 152(b) constitutes * * * a congressional denial of power to the FCC to require state commissions to follow FCC depreciation practices for intrastate ratemaking purposes. Thus, we simply cannot accept an argument that the FCC may nevertheless take action which it thinks will best effectuate a federal policy. * * *

> Moreover, we reject the intimation—the position is not strongly pressed—that the FCC cannot help but pre-empt state depreciation regulation of joint plant if it is to fulfill its statutory obligation and determine depreciation for plant used to provide interstate service, i.e., that it makes no sense within the context of the Act to depreciate one piece of property two ways. * * * [The Act] recognizes that jurisdictional tensions may arise as a result of the fact that interstate and intrastate service are provided by a single integrated system. * * * What is really troubling respondents, of course, is their sense that state regulators will not allow them sufficient revenues. While we do not deprecate this concern, § 152(b) precludes both the FCC and this Court from providing the relief sought. * * *

> Like many statutes, the Act contains some internal inconsistencies, vague language, and areas of uncertainty. It is not a perfect puzzle into which all the pieces fit. Thus, it is with the recognition that there are not crisp answers to all of the contentions of either party that we conclude that § 152(b) represents a bar to federal pre-emption of state regulation over depreciation of dual jurisdiction property for intrastate ratemaking purposes. 476 U.S. at 373–375, 379, 106 S.Ct. at 1901–1902, 1904.

Louisiana Public Service seems to be a significant set-back to the FCC's ability to preempt state regulation solely upon the ground that intrastate activities affect the interstate network. Nevertheless, the case may be closely tied to its facts—namely, that depreciation practices have an immediate effect on intrastate rates, which are central to the regulatory responsibility of state public utilities commissions (PUCs). The FCC might have more substantial preemptive power over matters less integral to state rate setting. E.g., Public Service Com'n of Maryland v. FCC, 909 F.2d 1510 (D.C.Cir.1990) (FCC can preempt state regulation of fee LEC assesses IXC to disconnect customer's telephone for non-payment of long distance charges).

For example, the Commission may authorize an LEC to interconnect a customer in order to give it access to an IXC carrier. In Public Utility Commission of Texas v. FCC, 886 F.2d 1325 (D.C.Cir.1989), the court upheld a Commission order preempting a state PUC order that prohibited Southwestern Bell from providing local telephone lines linking the Dallas office of the Atlantic Richfield Company (ARCO), which was in Southwestern's service area, with the suburban Plano office, which was in General Telephone's area. The FCC order allowed ARCO to receive long-distance telephone calls through its microwave facility in Dallas, and then switch them through Southwestern's lines to its facility in GTE territory without using GTE lines. The Commission reasoned that:

> * * * [T]he federal interest in affirming the customer's right to interconnect in this case is substantial. If General's view were applied on a nationwide basis this could be disruptive of, and impose unacceptable burdens on, the existing communications practices and plans of many business enterprises. * * *

> * * *

> The Commission is similarly unpersuaded by [General's] assertion that this decision 'deals a severe blow' to the states' authority to determine local exchange areas. * * * [T]he customers can use the facilities at issue for both interstate and intrastate traffic, and * * * there is no way to practically separate the two for interconnection purposes. * * * 3 FCC Rcd 3089, 3091 (1988).

In affirming the Commission, the Court of Appeals circumscribed the reach of its own decision as follows:

> [I]t seems to us that, in effect, the Texas PUC threw out the interstate baby with the intrastate bath water.

> We therefore find it unnecessary in this case to accept the broad proposition that a private microwave operator has an absolute federal right of access to the public switched network at locations of its choice * * *. It is enough that the FCC established * * * the impossibility of ensuring ARCO's freedom of access to the interstate network, without pre-empting the extraordinarily broad Texas PUC's order * * *. 886 F.2d at 1334–1335.

More recently, the Eighth Circuit invalidated the FCC's rules governing contracts between local exchange carriers and other users of local switches, e.g., interexchange operators, internet service providers, online services, and the like. The court reasoned that since the 1996 Telecommunications Act provided for state-level arbitration of these disputes, the FCC had no role in setting standards for interconnection to LECs. The court did not bar the FCC, however, from suggesting procedures and criteria. Iowa Utilities Board v. FCC, 120 F.3d 753 (8th Cir.1997).

The FCC's preemptive powers thus are fairly well established as to traditional media—radio, television, and common carriers. The troublesome areas lie with the new video media—such as cable television—simply because the Commission's jurisdiction over them is less clear. As noted before, (p. 90), the FCC's "reasonably ancillary" jurisdiction over cable is tenuous if not non-existent. Whether it has significant jurisdiction under the 1992 Cable Act is also doubtful. And the less jurisdiction an agency has, the less clear is its preemptive power.

Moreover, as to the new video media, the issue of preemption has often arisen in the context of the Commission's controversial policy of deregulation. Cable is subject not only to limited federal regulation, but also to state and local authority through the franchising process. Therefore, the Commission cannot by itself free a cable system from all regulatory obligations imposed by a state or local authority.

Several types of regulation also have proven to be particularly troublesome for both the Commission and the courts—particularly in the context of cable television,

First, the Commission has changed its approach towards state/local cable regulation a number of times. The FCC initially required that a cable system secure the franchising authority's approval before raising its rate for basic service. The Commission repealed this rule within a few years of adopting it, but local governments continued setting rates. The agency ultimately resolved the issue by holding that its general regulatory framework preempted local rate regulation in the *Community Cable* case discussed below, a position that the Cable Act ultimately confirmed.

From almost the very beginning of its cable regulatory regime, the Commission preempted state or local regulation of rates for "premium"—that is, pay-per-channel or pay-per-view—services. The FCC reasoned that these services were experimental in nature, and that rate regulation might deter investment in them. Clarification of the Cable Television Rules, 46 FCC 2d 175 (1974). The FCC noted that:

> Such regulation might destroy any chance for this emerging communications service by stifling competition, setting incorrect rates, and establishing an atmosphere that deters experimentation, innovation, or speculation. We have pre-empted this area to avoid these pitfalls.

Shortly thereafter, the Commission preempted rate-setting for service tiers consisting solely of distant signals, in order to encourage the potential development of what later came to be called "superstations." Report and Order, 57 FCC 2d 625 (1975). (defined to include only signals not required to be carried under the Commission's rules).

The cable industry, having found that it could not increase charges for pay channels very rapidly without losing large numbers of subscribers, strongly supported deregulation of basic services. The Commission went to the limit of its statutory authority in an effort to preempt basic rate regulation. In Community Cable TV, Inc., 95 FCC 2d 1204 (1983), the FCC invalidated a proposed Nevada Public Service Commission order that would have set rates for all channels other than pay services; the FCC extended its preemption of rate regulation to any service tier including satellite-delivered or other non-broadcast signals. The Commission reiterated its belief that rate regulation would hinder the development of new services. It also reasoned that cable systems should not be subject to rate setting, because competitive media, such as MDS, SMATV, and DBS, were not. The FCC argued that:

> These vigorous and growing competitors in the video services market pose a new challenge to nonbroadcast programming entrepreneurs and cable system operators. This challenge is * * * to package or combine services to maximize attractiveness to consumers in different markets and in anticipation of the penetration of those local markets by other, new services. * * * The current situation requires that system operators and nonbroadcast entrepreneurs retain maximum flexibility in the marketplace to experiment with types of programming, program offerings, and methods to pay for such programs, i.e., advertisers, subscriber fees, network compensation, or a combination. Continued federal preemption is needed to preclude artificial and unnecessary skewing of the market that nonfederal regulation of entry and price could produce.

* * *

> * * * Absent a specific showing of a need for regulatory intervention * * * it is in the public interest for entrepreneurs and firms engaged in dynamic industries, such as video programming for cable television, to enjoy maximum flexibility in their responses to innovations and developments within the industry. 95 FCC 2d at 1216–1217.

The Commission's decision in *Community Cable* worked a significant change in the balance of power between cities and cable operators. For the first time, local government officials began to worry seriously about losing their regulatory power over cable.

Their concerns were increased substantially by the Supreme Court's decision in Capital Cities Cable, Inc. v. Crisp, 467 U.S. 691, 104 S.Ct. 2694, 81 L.Ed.2d 580 (1984). Capital Cities challenged an Oklahoma constitutional and statutory ban on television advertising of alcoholic beverages—including commercials on out-of-state signals carried by cable systems. Although the parties had not raised the preemption issue in the lower courts, the Supreme Court ordered it briefed and argued. The Court then invalidated the Oklahoma ban, stating that:

> The power delegated to the FCC plainly comprises authority to regulate the signals carried by cable television systems. * * * Therefore, if the FCC has resolved to pre-empt an area of cable television regulation and if this determination "represents a reasonable accommodation of conflicting policies" that are within the agency's

domain, we must conclude that all conflicting state regulations have been precluded. * * *

Accordingly, to the extent that it has been invoked to control the distant broadcast and nonbroadcast signals imported by cable operators, the Oklahoma advertising ban plainly reaches beyond the regulatory authority reserved to local authorities by the Commission's rules, and trespasses into the exclusive domain of the FCC. To be sure, Oklahoma may, under current Commission rules, regulate such local aspects of cable systems as franchisee selection and construction oversight, but, by requiring cable television operators to delete commercial advertising contained in signals carried pursuant to federal authority, the State has clearly exceeded that limited jurisdiction and interfered with a regulatory area that the Commission has explicitly pre-empted.

Quite apart from this generalized federal pre-emption of state regulation of cable signal carriage, the Oklahoma advertising ban plainly conflicts with specific federal regulations. These conflicts arise in three principal ways. First, the FCC's so-called "must-carry" rules require certain cable television operators to transmit the broadcast signals of any local television broadcasting station. * * * These "must-carry" rules require many Oklahoma cable operators * * * to carry signals from broadcast stations located in nearby States such as Missouri and Kansas. In addition, under Commission regulations, the local broadcast signals that cable operators are required to carry must be carried "in full, without deletion or alteration of any portion." * * * Consequently, those Oklahoma cable operators required by federal law to carry out-of-state broadcast signals in full, including any wine commercials, are subject to criminal prosecution under Oklahoma law as a result of their compliance with federal regulations.

Second, current FCC rulings permit, and indeed encourage, cable television operators to import out-of-state television broadcast signals and retransmit those signals to their subscribers. * * * Under Oklahoma's advertising ban, however, these cable operators must either delete the wine commercials or face criminal prosecution. Since the Oklahoma law * * * compels conduct that federal law forbids, the state can clearly "stand as an obstacle to the accomplishment and execution of the full purposes and objectives" of the federal regulatory scheme.

Finally, enforcement of the state advertising ban against Oklahoma cable operators will affect a third source of cable programming over which the Commission has asserted exclusive jurisdiction * * * often referred to as "pay cable" * * *. Although the Commission's "must-carry" and non-deletion rules do not apply to such nonbroadcast cable services, the FCC, * * * has explicitly stated that state regulation of these services is completely prohibited by federal law. * * *

Although the FCC has taken the lead in formulating communications policy with respect to cable television, Congress has considered the impact of this new technology, and has * * * acted to facilitate the cable industry's ability to distribute broadcast programming on a national basis [through creation of the compulsory copyright license].

* * * Compulsory licensing not only protects the commercial value of copyrighted works but also enhances the ability of cable systems to retransmit such programs carried on distant broadcast signals, thereby allowing the public to benefit by the wider dissemination of works carried on television broadcast signals. By requiring cable operators to delete commercial advertisements for wine, however, the Oklahoma ban forces these operators to lose the protections of compulsory licensing.

[The Court went on to reject a claim that Oklahoma's ban was justified under the Twenty–First Amendment—which had implemented Prohibition by allowing states to regulate importation and sale of alcoholic beverages. The Court held that advertising was too indirectly related to these goals to justify overriding important federal communications policies.]

The result in *Crisp* is open to question for a variety of reasons. First, the court of appeals invalidated the must-carry rules one year after the Crisp decision. See Quincy Cable TV v. FCC, (p. 352); the Supreme Court later upheld the rules in *Turner Broadcasting II*. (p. 393) Second, the Court glosses over the fact that the FCC's distant signal policy was a non-policy—namely, that the Commission had decided merely that its prior limitations were no longer necessary. Moreover, most pay channels carry little or no advertising, let alone commercials for alcoholic beverages.

Nevertheless, the decision had a dramatic effect on cable regulation, as cities came to fear that the FCC could preempt virtually any form of local regulation. The National Cable Television Association and the National League of Cities quickly reached a compromise on deregulatory legislation, and five months after *Crisp* was decided, the Congress passed the 1984 Cable Act.

Section 623 of the 1984 Cable Act specifically provided that "[a]ny Federal agency or State may not regulate the rates for the provision of cable service except to the extent provided under this section." 47 U.S.C. § 543(a). Section 623(b)(1) allowed rate regulation of basic services "in circumstances in which a cable system is not subject to effective competition," and required the Commission to define "effective competition" by rulemaking within 180 days of enactment.

This was not to last for long. The 1992 Cable Act divested local governments of all rate regulation power, and transferred it to the Commission. In turn, the FCC could delegate it back to municipalities, upon application by a local government! But since most cities are not known for proactive stances in regulatory matters, very few local governments even bothered to apply for rate regulation authority. Moreover, the Commission adopted—and then rejected—several highly complex regression analysis formulae to be used in setting rates; very few cities had either the expertise or the software to implement these

Finally, the 1996 Telecommunications Act vested cable rate regulation exclusively in the FCC; local governments' only recourse was to complain to the Commission, which then was required to decide upon the validity of the rate. 47 U.S.C. § 543(c). Since the Commission was neither equipped nor inclined to begin adjudicating potentially thousands of rate cases, it generally combined all complaints concerning one system or one MSO, and worked with the operator and the municipalities in creating a "social contract"—which sometimes involved more than just rate levels.

The whole rate regulation system was slated to become moot, in any event. The 1996 Act provided that all rate regulation—other than for the lowest "tier" of only only broadcast signals—would sunset on March 31, 1999. Local governments thus went from plenary power over cable rates in the 1980s to total disempowerment in the 1990s.

Another difficult area of cable regulation was setting the amounts which local telephone and utility companies could charge cable operators for using their poles. In the case of subscriber rate regulation, the Commission actively reached for preemptive power, as part of its deregulatory program. With pole attachment fees, however, it has explicit statutory authorization, or even encouragement, to preempt state regulation. A prime example of the latter situation involves the ability of cable operators to attach their wires to utility poles.

The continuing tension between the telephone and cable industries dates back to the 1960s. The FCC was relatively quick to discourage LECs from owning cable systems. Common Carrier Tariffs for CATV Systems, 4 FCC 2d (1966). Early on, however, LECs envisioned two quite distinct ways of profiting from cable.

First, a few LEC officials—perhaps visionary—viewed broadband communications as a logical extension of the existing telephone business. Some LECs apparently felt that inhibiting cable's growth would in the long run help telephone companies to enter the broadband business. Telephone companies thus refused to provide pole attachments for cable operators. Some refused access outright; others delayed making attachments available or performing preliminary "make ready" work; and some demanded that cable operators lease back facilities built by telephone companies, rather than constructing their own systems.

Another area of concern was pole attachment fees. Since cable systems were heavily dependent upon utility poles, particularly in the predominantly suburban and rural areas that the industry first served, they were largely captive buyers of pole attachment rights. Some LECs charged allegedly exorbitant rates. Although state public utilities commissions had jurisdiction over pole attachments, most declined to enter this already somewhat bitter confrontation.

The Commission eventually prohibited telephone companies from owning or leasing cable facilities, see General Telephone Company of the Southwest v. United States, 449 F.2d 846 (5th Cir.1971), a position it would reconsider almost two decades later. *Further Notice of Inquiry and Notice of Proposed Rulemaking*, 3 FCC Rcd 5849 (1988). The agency also encouraged the telephone companies and cable operators to negotiate a uniform pole attachment agreement. When these efforts came to naught, however, the FCC held that it lacked jurisdiction to set pole attachment rates and conditions. Memorandum Opinion and Order, 37 R.R.2d 1166 (1976).

The Congress responded by passing the Communications Act Amendments of 1978 authorizing the FCC to set rates. 47 U.S.C. § 224 gives the FCC plenary authority to regulate pole attachments, except where a state agency already has asserted jurisdiction. Section 224 provides in pertinent part that:

(b)(1) [T]he Commission shall regulate the rates, terms, and conditions for pole attachments to provide that such rates, terms, and conditions are just and reasonable * * *.

(c)(1) Nothing in this section shall be construed * * * to give the Commission jurisdiction * * * where such matters are regulated by a State.

(d)(1) [A] rate is just and reasonable if it assures a utility the recovery of not less than the additional costs of providing pole attachments, nor more than an amount determined by multiplying the percentage of the total usable space, or the percentage of the total duct or conduit capacity, which is occupied by the pole attachment by the sum of the operating expenses and actual capital costs of the utility attributable to the entire pole, duct, conduit or right-of-way.

The 1978 amendments did not by themselves resolve the pole attachment issue, as most states did not bother to take jurisdiction, and there were substantial disputes before the FCC as to the proper method of calculating pole attachment fees. In Alabama Power Company v. FCC, 773 F.2d 362 (D.C.Cir.1985), the court invalidated the Commission's rate-setting formula. Aside from the fact that the FCC had made an admitted mathematical error in that particular case, the court noted that the Commission had excluded a number of relevant items in calculating the utility's costs. The Commission quickly amended its rules to reflect the court's analysis. Attachment of Cable Television Hardware to Utility Poles, 52 Fed.Reg. 31769 (1987).

As discussed before, many leaders of the cable and telephone industries believe that eventually there will be a "convergence" of the two. If that comes to pass, presumably much of the historic friction between the two businesses will disappear, since their interests will be aligned. But the future of convergence is somewhat difficult to predict at this point.

A final area of friction between municipalities and cable operators, DBS systems, as well as MMDS facilities has been placement of antennas—particularly old-fashioned 3.5—5.0 meter C-band units. (p. 8) Quite typically, many local governments have tried to zone away aesthetically unpopular structures—only to run up against federal preemption.

Some local zoning decisions carry overtones of the ongoing warfare among competing media. To a cable operator, every home satellite receiver within its service area is a lost subscriber (unless the cable operator is also the only authorized sales agent for satellite programming in its area). The local government may face pressure on more than just aesthetic grounds.

Perhaps because local regulation of ham radio operations seems to have little economic motivation or impact, the Commission traditionally took a hands-off attitude towards local zoning activities. Guschke v. City of Oklahoma City, 763 F.2d 379 (10th Cir.1985). In its Report and Order, 50 Fed.Reg. 38,813 (1985), however, the Commission imposed a loosely-defined system of accommodation:

Few matters coming before us present such a clear dichotomy of viewpoint as does the instant issue. * * * In this situation, we believe it is appropriate to strike a balance between the federal interest in promoting amateur operations and the legitimate interests of local governments in regulating local zoning matters. The cornerstone on which we will predicate our decision is that a reasonable accommodation may be made between the two sides. * * *

Because amateur station communications are only as effective as the antennas employed, antenna height restrictions directly affect the effectiveness of amateur communications. * * * We will not, however, specify any particular height limitation below which a local government may not regulate, nor will we suggest the precise language that must be contained in local ordinances, such as mechanisms for special exceptions, variances, or conditional use permits. Nevertheless, local regulations which involve placement, screening, or height of antennas based on health, safety, or aesthetic considerations must be crafted to accommodate reasonable amateur communications, and to represent the minimum practicable regulation to accomplish the local authority's legitimate purpose.

Most courts seem to have been more than happy to leave ham operators and local governments to work out their "accommodations," and thus have been quick to remand disputes for local administrative proceedings. Thernes v. City of Lakeside Park, 779 F.2d 1187 (6th Cir.1986); Bulchis v. City of Edmonds, 671 F.Supp. 1270 (W.D.Wash. 1987).

The Commission has been somewhat more active in preempting local regulation of satellite dishes. In 1985, the FCC began a rulemaking proceeding in this area, Report and Order, 2 FCC Rcd 202 (1986), and in 1986 adopted a rule providing that:

State and local zoning and other regulations that differentiate between satellite receive-only antennas and other types of antenna facilities are preempted unless such regulations:

(a) Have a reasonable and clearly defined health, safety or aesthetic objective; and

(b) Do not operate to impose unreasonable limitations on, or prevent, reception of satellite delivered signals by receive-only antennas or to impose costs on the users of such antennas that are excessive in light of the purchase and installation costs of the equipment.

Regulation of satellite transmitting antennas is preempted in the same manner except that state and local health and safety regulation is not preempted. 47 C.F.R. § 25.104.

One commentator has suggested that the Commission lacks sufficient authority under the "theft of services" provisions of the Cable Act to preempt the field of satellite dish control. Sorrell, *Federal Preemption of State and Local Zoning Regulation of Satellite Earth Stations,* Communications and the Law, August 1987, at 40–41.

Chapter IV

REGULATION OF ENTRY: SELECTING THE LICENSEE

A. BROADCASTING: THE FCC's LICENSING PROCEDURE

As the preceding materials make clear, licensing is the FCC's primary means of controlling broadcasters. Although the Commission has other means of enforcement powers, e.g., fines, forfeitures, injunctive-style relief, none of them has the ultimate threat of refusing to grant a license for a new station (an "initial license") or denying the renewal of an existing station (a "renewal license").

Part of the difficulty in understanding the licensing process lies in the difference between initial and renewal licenses. Although in both cases the FCC exercises its power to grant or deny a particular authorization, the two types of licenses have distinctly different economic and political underpinnings. In reviewing the Commission's licensing procedures, it thus is important to understand these distinctions.

In an initial licensing proceeding, one or more firms are attempting to secure a previously unused frequency. Since a license would not affect any existing station, there is comparatively little immediate economic impact on any of the applicants—other than the legal and other fees associated with the application process. (These naturally can be quite substantial, running from several hundred thousand to several million dollars for a television station.) Initial licensing might seem to be obsolete, since virtually all attractive broadcast licenses were granted many years ago. But the Commission periodically opens up new frequencies, for broadcast and other uses; for example, in 1980, the FCC authorized almost a thousand new, albeit relatively low-powered FM frequencies. Litigation from applications for these stations still is pending.

An application for a license renewal involves an existing station, however, which may have a fair market value of hundreds of millions of dollars. Although an incumbent licensee technically does not "own" its license, it thus stands to lose huge amounts of money if the Commission fails to renew its license—hence a license renewal denial's informal moniker of "the death sentence." Moreover, since most major licensees today have acquired their stations through purchase rather than through initial licensing, major capital investments are at stake. Because the government usually does not impose forfeitures of this magnitude on private firms without severe provocation, license renewal applications are treated quite differently than requests for initial licenses.

Although the Commission and the bar long have understood and internalized this difference between initial and renewal licenses, the legal theory behind the two has tended to overlap—thus creating severe confusion, for newcomers to the field.

As will be seen, the procedures for both initial and renewal licenses have changed dramatically in the past few years, through the institution of lotteries or auctions for initial licenses, and "expectancies" for renewal licenses. Traditional application procedures still tend to govern initial licenses for broadcast stations; the Commission increasingly has used lotteries and auctions for initial licenses for non-broadcast facilities— e.g., mobile radio, cellular systems and the like. Political considerations so far seem to have precluded using these procedures for broadcast mass media purposes—apparently because of an unarticulated fear that a lottery of auction might result in license grants not in the "public interest."

At the same time, in the Telecommunications Act of 1996 the Congress finally settled the status of renewal applications. After a generation of litigation and legislation over "renewal expectancies" for incumbent licensees, in the 1996 Telecommunications Act the Congress adopted virtually automatic renewal procedures. (p. 213)

The substantive law of license applications thus has changed as to both initial and renewal applications for certain types of services. The result is that some procedures have changed little in the first 50 years, while others are new and still being fleshed out. In order to make sense of the current licensing process, it thus is necessary to understand the role of both old and new licensing procedures.

Before the advent of lotteries and auctions, the application procedures for all licenses were relatively similar. It thus may be useful to give a "nuts and bolts" overview of how one goes about applying for an initial or renewal license—one not governed by new legislation—in order to demystify somewhat the process discussed throughout this Chapter.

The first step in applying for a new license is to determine that a frequency is available. In AM this takes the form of an engineering study to show that a new station would not create undue interference. In FM and TV, the applicant must show that a frequency is authorized by a Table of Allotments. An application for a new station thus must set forth a substantial amount of information about the proposed operation's technical characteristics, including tower height, signal strength in each direction, and maps of the proposed coverage area. By contrast, the filing contains relatively little data about the station's principals—beyond their names, addresses, corporate titles, sources of financing. An application also has a substantial amount of boilerplate on points such as equal employment opportunity plans, environmental impact, and the like.

After the filing of either an initial or a renewal application, the Commission's first step is for the staff to determine whether it is "complete or substantially complete." E.g., 47 C.F.R. § 73.3564(a) (FM applications). (Because of the large number of filings, LPTV applications are held to a "letter perfect" standard—that is, they are rejected out of hand for even minor defects, with no opportunity to amend. If an application passes this preliminary review, the FCC gives public notice of "acceptance of [the] application for filing" by listing the application in the "public notices" that it releases every day).

The Commission public notices are *not* published; they are available only by picking them up at the FCC's offices at the close of each business day or through the Internet, on a somewhat hit-or-miss basis. Private services collect and mail them to interested parties at relatively hefty fees. Law firms routinely subscribe to such services or collect FCC releases themselves, in order to keep abreast of the status of their clients—and of their clients' competitors—at the FCC.

Within 30 days after an applicant files with the Commission, it must give "local public notice" of its application in order to inform potential opponents of the application's pendency. 47 C.F.R. § 73.3580. Rule 73.3580 requires that notice be given in "a newspaper of general circulation published in the community ... at least twice a week for two consecutive weeks [in a three-week period] ..." or, if such a publication is not available, in the best alternative. Within thirty days after an application has been accepted for filing, it may be amended in "minor" respects. Such amendments are "as of right," since they do not require the Commission's approval; they usually include changes in engineering specifications and the like.

In order to make an amendment after the initial thirty-day period has run, the applicant must secure permission from the FCC on a showing of "good cause." Although such later amendments may cure defects, only the application as originally filed will be considered in the event of a comparative hearing.

Acceptance of an application also starts a 30–day clock running for potential protests, known as "petitions to deny." Petitions to deny usually involve claims by competitors or citizens groups that an applicant is unqualified to hold a license.

Traditionally in the normal course of events, some initial and most renewal applications are subject to little inquiry from the Commission and encounter neither petitions to deny nor competing applications. And once again, the 1996 Telecommunications Act makes license broadcast renewals virtually automatic. Applications that do run into difficulties, however, provoke the most legal interest—and hence most of the discussion in this Chapter. Because of the recent changes in the law, most of the discussion below of renewal applications is now history; existing broadcasters effectively are not subject to competing applications at renewal time. Nevertheless, it is very important history, since it explains how the law developed into its present state. In order to understand the present—and still largely undefined regime—it thus is necessary to know how the law got there in the first place.

The traditional procedure still governs initial applications for radio and television broadcast stations. With Congressional authorization of lotteries and auctions for some services, however, the ground rules for initial applications has changed.

On a more general level, the Commission faces the task of securing maximum benefits for the public in a legal context that does not allow use of normal pricing mechanisms. To allocate broadcasting licenses "in the public interest," the allocating authority must both define "the public interest" and determine whether a particular applicant for a license will in fact serve that interest. With licenses priced near zero*— except for potential auctions of broadcast licenses—the FCC often finds itself with multiple mutually exclusive applications. In this happy circumstance, the public might still capture the benefits of competition for the license. Although it could not be paid in coin, it could be paid in kind as the would-be entrants compete to promise qualitatively superior service.

In order to capture that benefit for the public, the allocating authority must accomplish two tasks. First, it must develop a procedure by which to identify the competitor of superior promise, and inform that procedure with substantive criteria relevant to its chosen concept of the public interest. Second, it must devise a means for assuring that superior promise indeed becomes superior, or at least acceptable, performance. In the remaining portion of this Chapter you will have an opportunity to evaluate the FCC's performance in these areas and to develop your own prescriptions for meeting the particular problems encountered by the agency.

While doing that, consider the value of a lottery or auction instead of using traditional hearing procedures to choose the "best" applicant. As noted, the Commission has refrained from using either approach to mass media—particularly radio and television. For reasons that are less than clear, most politicians are concerned at using a system that does not provide reasons for its results. Part of the concern may be that mass appeal media should be held to defined standards of accountability, in order to avoid the problems of ideological bias. Another concern may be simply that politicians want to retain their ability to create obligations to broadcasters—particularly with the escalating value of broadcast time in elections.

---

* The Commission charges each applicant a filing fee and each successful applicant a grant fee as part of the government's policy of charging regulatees for the cost of regulation. These fees—at most, a few thousand dollars—are modest in relation to a station's value.

As you will see, creation of a rational decision-making process for these decisions is difficult, and none of the Commission's approaches—as discussed below—seems to have satisfied it or its clientele. Problems as to lack of standards, objectivity, and analysis have plagued the agency and its clientele for generations. Recent legislative initiatives in terms of lotteries, auctions, and renewal expectancies have mooted many of these problems. But the Commission still is the ultimate decision-maker in many licensing decisions.

1. COMPARATIVE PROCEEDINGS

a. *Initial Licensing*

Perhaps unfortunately, the Supreme Court had its first chance to define the nature of competing applications in the context of a what at least appeared to be a fairly simple contest for an initial application. (Query: did the *Ashbacker* decision below really involve an initial license application or a comparative renewal proceeding, since it involved a new entrant's attempt to dislodge an existing broadcaster?)

ASHBACKER RADIO CORP. v. FCC

Supreme Court of the United States, 1945.
326 U.S. 327, 66 S.Ct. 148, 90 L.Ed. 108.

Mr. Justice Douglas delivered the opinion of the Court.

The primary question in this case is whether an applicant for a construction permit under the Federal Communications Act is granted the hearing to which he is entitled by § 309(a) of the Act, where the Commission, having before it two applications which are mutually exclusive, grants one without a hearing and sets the other for hearing.

In March 1944 the Fetzer Broadcasting Company filed with the Commission an application for authority to construct a new broadcasting station at Grand Rapids, Michigan, to operate on 1230 kc [now Khz] with 250 watts power, unlimited time. In May 1944, before the Fetzer application had been acted upon, petitioner filed an application for authority to change the operating frequency of its station WKBZ of Muskegon, Michigan, from 1490 kc with 250 watts power, unlimited time, to 1230 kc. The Commission, after stating that the simultaneous operation on 1230 kc at Grand Rapids and Muskegon "would result in intolerable interference to both applicants," declared that the two applications were "actually exclusive." The Commission, upon an examination of the Fetzer application and supporting data, granted it in June 1944 without a hearing. On the same day the Commission designated petitioner's application for hearing. Petitioner thereupon filed a petition for hearing, rehearing and other relief directed against the grant of the Fetzer application. The Commission denied this petition, stating,

> The Commission has not denied petitioner's application. It has designated the application for hearing as required by Section 309(a) of the Act. At this hearing, petitioner will have ample opportunity to

show that its operation as proposed will better serve the public interest than will the grant of the Fetzer application as authorized June 27, 1944. Such grant does not preclude the Commission, at a later date from taking any action which it may find will serve the public interest. In re: *Berks Broadcasting Company* (WEEU), Reading, Pennsylvania, 8 FCC 427 (1941); In re: *The Evening News Association* (WWJ), Detroit, Michigan, 8 FCC 552 (1941); In re: *Merced Broadcasting Company* (KYOS), Merced, California, 9 FCC 118, 120 (1942).

Our chief problem is to reconcile two provisions of § 309(a) where the Commission has before it mutually exclusive applications. The first authorizes the Commission "upon examination" of an application for a station license to grant it if the Commission determines that "public interest, convenience, or necessity would be served" by the grant. The second provision of § 309(a) says that if, upon examination of such an application, the Commission does not reach such a decision, "it shall notify the applicant thereof, shall fix and give notice of a time and place for hearing thereon, and shall afford such applicant an opportunity to be heard under such roles and regulations as it may prescribe." It is thus plain that § 309(a) not only gives the Commission authority to grant licenses without a hearing, but also gives applicants a right to a hearing before their applications are denied. We do not think it is enough to say that the power of the Commission to issue a license on a finding of public interest, convenience or necessity supports its grant of one of two mutually exclusive applications without a hearing of the other. For if the grant of one effectively precludes the other, the statutory right to a hearing which Congress has accorded applicants before denial of their applications becomes an empty thing. We think that is the case here.
* * *

The Fetzer application was not conditionally granted pending consideration of petitioner's application. Indeed a stay of it pending the outcome of this litigation was denied. Of course the Fetzer license, like any other license granted by the Commission, was subject to certain conditions which the Act imposes as a matter of law. * * * As the Fetzer application has been granted, petitioner, therefore, is presently in the same position as a newcomer who seeks to displace an established broadcaster. By the grant of the Fetzer application petitioner has been placed under a greater burden than if its hearing had been earlier. Legal theory is one thing. But the practicalities are different. For we are told how difficult it is for a newcomer to make the comparative showing necessary to displace an established licensee. * * * Since the facility has been granted to Fetzer, the hearing accorded petitioner concerns a license facility no longer available for a grant unless the earlier grant is recalled. A hearing designed as one for an available frequency becomes by the Commission's action in substance one for the revocation or modification of an outstanding license. So it would seem that petitioner would carry as a matter of law the same burden regardless of the precise provision of the notice of hearing.

It is suggested that the Commission, by granting the Fetzer application first, concluded that the public interest would be furthered by making Fetzer's service available at the earliest possible date. If so, that conclusion is only an inference from what the Commission did. There is no suggestion, let alone a finding, by the Commission that the demands of the public interest were so urgent as to preclude the delay which would be occasioned by a hearing. * * *

* * * Whether that is wise policy or whether the procedure adopted by the Commission in this case is preferable is not for us to decide. We only hold that where two *bona fide* applications are mutually exclusive the grant of one without a hearing to both deprives the loser of the opportunity which Congress chose to give him.

In *Federal Communications Commission v. Sanders Radio Station,* 309 U.S. 470, 476, 477, 60 S.Ct. 693, 698, 84 L.Ed. 869, 875, we held that a rival station which would suffer economic injury by the grant of a license to another station had standing to appeal under § 402(b)(2) of the Act. In *Federal Communications Commission v. National Broadcasting Co.,* 319 U.S. 239, 63 S.Ct. 1035, 87 L.Ed. 1374 we reached the same conclusion where an application had been granted which would create such interference on the channel given an existing licensee as in effect to modify the earlier license. Petitioner is at least as adversely affected by the action of the Commission in this case as were the protestants in those cases. While the statutory right of petitioner to a hearing on its application has in form been preserved, it has as a practical matter been substantially nullified by the grant of the Fetzer application.

Reversed.

MR. JUSTICE BLACK and MR. JUSTICE JACKSON took no part in the consideration or decision of this case.

MR. JUSTICE FRANKFURTER, dissenting.

The extent to which administrative agencies are to be entrusted with the enforcement of federal legislation is for Congress to determine. Insofar as the actions of these agencies come under the scrutiny of judicial review, it is the business of the courts to respect the distribution of authority that Congress makes as between administrative and judicial tribunals. Of course courts must hold the administrative agencies within the confines of their Congressional authority. But in doing so they should not even unwittingly assume that the familiar is the necessary and demand of the administrative process observance of conventional judicial procedures when Congress has made no such exaction. Since these agencies deal largely with the vindication of public interest and not the enforcement of private rights, this Court ought not to imply hampering restrictions, not imposed by Congress, upon the effectiveness of the administrative process. One reason for the expansion of administrative agencies has been the recognition that procedures appropriate for the adjudication of private rights in the courts may be inappropriate for the kind of determinations which administrative agencies are called upon to make.

* * *

Questions and Problems

1. Did *Ashbacker* involve a new or renewal application? To the extent that technically two firms were competing for the same unused frequency, were initial applications at issue? But wasn't the reality of the situation that Fetzer was attempting to take away Ashbacker's monopoly on the local radio market, and was this a renewal proceeding? Put another way, if Ashbacker had not made a preemptive strike against Fetzer's application, might Fetzer have applied for Ashbacker's frequency?

2. Does this suggest that the difference between initial and renewal application procedures may not be as clear as one would like?

3. And in turn, does this suggest that the potential costs and losses involved in the case were fairly minimal, thus making a hearing not terribly onerous? After all, remember that even after its loss, Ashbacker presumably still could have filed—presumably with little opposition—for its old frequency.

4. Why do you think that Ashbacker, an existing, and presumably viable broadcaster, decided to file for the same frequency that Fetzer had applied for? The new channel did not have any better propagation characteristics, and thus was not superior from an engineering point of view. Would it make sense for Ashbacker to try to "sandbag" potential competition merely by necessitating the delay inherent in a comparative proceeding?

Assume that a client calls you with the usual tale of woe about a new station entering the market. The client tells you that her station will lose at least $100,000 per year in net revenues. She then asks you how much it would cost annually in legal fees to file and pursue a competing application against the potential entrant. Under what circumstances does it make sense for her to file a competing application, even if you advise her that the chances of winning are close to zero? Bear in mind that a comparative hearing at the FCC—and one or more trips to the court of appeals, which has become increasingly common—will often drag out a licensing proceeding for five (and sometimes more) years?

Is it ethical for a lawyer to undertake the representation in these circumstances? At what point does it cease to be ethical?

5. Suppose that the FCC in *Ashbacker* viewed the second application as a sham, and thus sought to dispose of it, and to grant Fetzer's application expeditiously? Would the Commission have fared better on appeal if it simply had labelled the Ashbacker application as "sham" from the beginning and dismissed it explicitly on that ground? By what criteria could the Commission defensibly decide that an application is made not in good faith but solely for the purpose of delay?

6. If the FCC had acted more expeditiously and granted the Fetzer application before Ashbacker had filed but after a reasonable notice period (perhaps 30 days) had run, Ashbacker would presumably have been time-

barred. But if such notice is always to be made available, then successive chain-reaction filings from contiguous areas might keep the original application open indefinitely and turn every license proceeding into a very broad-ranging inquiry indeed. The FCC has therefore established a "cut-off" policy, providing that an application will not be consolidated for hearing with previously filed applications unless it is filed before the end of the last-expiring notice period in the chain *and* before any previously filed application in the chain is designated for hearing. 47 C.F.R. § 2.337(b); see Century Broadcasting Corp. v. FCC, 310 F.2d 864, 114 U.S.App.D.C. 59 (D.C.Cir. 1962) (approving the cut-off rule in a case where 14 conflicting applications from several different communities were consolidated).

Assume that application A is received and notice of its pendency published in the Federal Register on January 10. On February 1, B files a conflicting application for a station to be located in a different town; notice appears on the same day. On February 2 the FCC designates the applications of A and B for hearing, thus barring the application of C for a station in yet another community. Is it in the public interest that the proposal to serve the third town not be considered at all? Might the operation of 47 C.F.R. § 1.227 conflict with the injunction of § 307(b) of the Act?

7. Is there ever a valid policy reason for a licensing agency to dispense with comparative proceedings altogether and grant licenses on a first-in-time basis? Assuming that minimum eligibility criteria must still be met, could such a rule be upheld as reasonably calculated to further a public interest? Consider the reason for establishing western "land rush" claims on this basis, and see United Cities Gas Co. v. Illinois Commerce Commission, 48 Ill.2d 36, 268 N.E.2d 32 (1971). Does the FCC have the authority to adopt such a rule? What is its best authority argument? See §§ 151, 303.

8. Note that the Commission has used its relatively new statutory authority to award licenses by lottery and by auction. So far, the FCC has failed to use the authority for full-power broadcast stations. What do you think the reasons for that might be? 47 U.S.C. § 309(i). Is this an improvement? Are there any policy problems in using a lottery to allocate taxicab radio licenses? Major market radio licenses?

9. It is not always obvious, by the way, whether two applications should be deemed "mutually exclusive." Consider:

> Station A, the nighttime contour of which covered only 27% of its community of license (Palm Springs, Cal.), applied for a change of frequency and transmitter site to enable it to reach 67% of the community. Meanwhile, Station B (licensed to North Las Vegas, Nev.) sought a facilities change that would require limiting Station A's potential night-time coverage, if its application were granted, to 41% of its community. Under a Commission policy favoring changes that increase coverage of the community of license, the application of A, as limited, would almost surely be granted.

Under the decision in Little Dixie Radio, Inc., 11 R.R.2d 1083 (1967) an applicant is entitled to comparative consideration per *Ashbacker* where the grant of one application would have a "substantial and material adverse effect upon the other's prospects for success." How does this standard apply to A's motion to consolidate its application proceeding with B's for comparative treatment? See KLUC Broadcasting Co., 67 FCC 2d 586 (1978).

Would it matter if A alleged that it would withdraw its application if consolidation were denied because the facilities change would not be cost-justified if it resulted in only 41% coverage? If so, how could the Commission deter opportunistic allegations of this sort?

10.   Before going on, you should stop to consider the precise question placed before the FCC by the necessity to choose between two mutually exclusive applications. Formulate that question in a manner general enough to apply to each of the following comparative contexts:

a.   A applies to establish the first radio station in a large suburb of a major city, while B would locate in the rural area beyond, which is presently able to receive the three most powerful city signals even during the day.

b.   A applies for the first license in Town, pop. 5,000; B applies for authority to service City, pop. 20,000, which is 5 miles from Town. Town has no local media, either electronic or print, but receives City's radio and television signals (one each) and its daily newspaper. All three of these media outlets are owned by City Corp.

c.   A and B have each applied for the sixty-first license to serve Chicago, Illinois. Each is a U.S. citizen with no prior broadcast experience. Because they had been partners in developing a single application before a falling-out caused them to dissolve their business partnership, they have submitted virtually identical program proposals and financial profiles.

Is there a unique answer, in each of these cases, to the generic question as you have formulated it? If not, specify any further information you would need in order to answer the question in any of the as yet unresolved hypotheticals.

11.   What happens to an existing broadcaster's frequency, when it applies for a new one? Can a third party apply for the broadcaster's present frequency, even though it is not yet vacant? This raises questions as to "contingent" applications. Assume that A files an application to move its station to a new frequency, resulting in abandonment of its old frequency if the application is granted. B then files an application for A's original frequency, contingent upon a grant of A's application for the new frequency. B can acquire no rights against A's existing frequency, and, pending satisfaction of the contingency, B's application does not receive *Ashbacker* rights as against the applications of third parties; even if the contingency is ultimately resolved, B does not acquire a preferred status against later-filed applications for A's old frequency. Jack Gross Broadcasting Co., 12 FCC 80 (1947). See Jack Mayer, *Ashbacker Rites in Administrative Practice: A Case Study of the FCC*, 24 N.Y.L.S.L.Rev. 461 (1979).

Although *Ashbacker* created the requirement of a consolidated hearing on competing applications, it did not establish any standards for deciding these cases. It thus left a substantive void, which arguably has yet to be filled—particularly, as will be seen, with regard to comparative hearings on renewal applications. As will be seen, it took Congress only fifty years to provide rules for comparative renewals in the Telecommunications Act of 1996. Although must of the FCC's and the courts' prior policies thus is moot today, it is worth a brief look, if only to understand how the Commission in particular—and regulatory agencies in general—deal with economically and politically thorny problems.

With no real policy guidance from either Congress or the courts, the Commission pretty much muddled along with a case-by-case approach to comparative hearings. By the early 1960s, however, this had become politically untenable. Several commissioners were shown to have engaged in questionable conduct, and one of them admitted receiving money from representatives of applicants in comparative proceedings. (p. 133) E.g., WKAT, Inc., 29 FCC 216, 227 (1960) (report by special master on investigation into improper conduct in comparative hearings). The FCC came under pressure on several fronts to clean up its act, and one of the products was the *1965 Policy Statement*, which follows. As noted later, the *Policy Statement* is no longer good law, but is important for historical purposes.

POLICY STATEMENT ON COMPARATIVE BROADCAST HEARINGS

Federal Communications Commission, 1965.
1 FCC 2d 393 (1965).

One of the Commission's primary responsibilities is to choose among qualified new applicants for the same broadcast facilities.[1] This commonly requires extended hearings into a number of areas of comparison. The hearing and decision process is inherently complex, and the subject does not lend itself to precise categorization or to the clear making of precedent. The various factors cannot be assigned absolute values, some factors may be present in some cases and not in others, and the differences between applicants with respect to each factor are almost infinitely variable.

Furthermore, membership on the Commission is not static and the views of individual Commissioners on the importance of particular factors may change. For these and other reasons, the Commission is not bound to deal with all cases at all times as it has dealt in the past with some that seem comparable, and changes of viewpoint, if reasonable, are recognized as both inescapable and proper.

* * *

We believe that there are two primary objectives toward which the process of comparison should be directed. They are, first, the best practicable service to the public, and, second, a maximum diffusion of control of the media of mass communications. The value of these objectives is clear. Diversification of control is a public good in a free society, and is additionally desirable where a government licensing system limits access by the public to the use of radio and television

---

1. This statement of policy does not attempt to deal with the somewhat different problems raised where an applicant is contesting with a licensee seeking renewal of license.

facilities. Equally basic is a broadcast service which meets the needs of the public in the area to be served, both in terms of those general interests which all areas have in common and those special interests which areas do not share. An important element of such a service is the flexibility to change as local needs and interests change. Since independence and individuality of approach are elements of rendering good program service, the primary goals of good service and diversification of control are also fully compatible.

Several factors are significant in the two areas of comparison mentioned above, and it is important to make clear the manner in which each will be treated.

1. *Diversification of control of the media of mass communications.*—Diversification is a factor of primary significance since, as set forth above, it constitutes a primary objective in the licensing scheme.

As in the past, we will consider both common control and less than controlling interests in other broadcast stations and other media of mass communications. The less the degree of interest in other stations or media, the less will be the significance of the factor. Other interests in the principal community proposed to be served will normally be of most significance. * * * The number of other mass communication outlets of the same type in the community proposed to be served will also affect to some extent the importance of this factor in the general comparative scale.

* * *

2. *Full-time participation in station operation by owners.*—We consider this factor to be of substantial importance. It is inherently desirable that legal responsibility and day-to-day performance be closely associated. In addition, there is a likelihood of greater sensitivity to an area's changing needs, and of programming designed to serve these needs, to the extent that the station's proprietors actively participate in the day-to-day operation of the station. This factor is thus important in securing the best practicable service. It also frequently complements the objective of diversification, since concentrations of control are necessarily achieved at the expense of integrated ownership.

We are primarily interested in full-time participation. * * *

Attributes of participating owners, such as their experience and local residence, will also be considered in weighing integration of ownership and management. [The value of] integration * * * is increased if the participating owners are local residents and if they have experience in the field. Participation in station affairs * * * by a local resident indicates a likelihood of continuing knowledge of changing local interests and needs. Previous broadcast experience, while not so significant as local residence, also has some value when put to use through integration of ownership and management.

* * *

3. *Proposed program service.*—* * * The importance of program service is obvious. The feasibility of making a comparative evaluation is not so obvious. Hearings take considerable time and precisely formulated program plans may have to be changed not only in details but in substance, to take account of new conditions obtaining at the time a successful applicant commences operation. Thus, minor differences among applicants are apt to prove to be of no significance.

The basic elements of an adequate service have been set forth in our July 27, 1960 "Report and Statement of Policy Re: Commission en banc Programming Inquiry," and need not be repeated here. * * *

* * *

4. *Past broadcast record.*—This factor includes past ownership interest and significant participation in a broadcast station by one with an ownership interest in the applicant. It is a factor of substantial importance upon the terms set forth below.

A past record within the bounds of average performance will be disregarded, since average future performance is expected. Thus, we are not interested in the fact of past ownership per se, and will not give a preference because one applicant has owned stations in the past and another has not.

We are interested in records which, because either unusually good or unusually poor, give some indication of unusual performance in the future. * * *

* * *

5. *Efficient use of frequency.*—In comparative cases where one of two or more competing applicants proposes an operation which, for one or more engineering reasons, would be more efficient, this fact can and should be considered in determining which of the applicants should be preferred. * * *

6. *Character.*—The Communications Act makes character a relevant consideration in the issuance of a license. See section 308(b), 47 U.S.C. § 308(b). Significant character deficiencies may warrant disqualification, and an issue will be designated where appropriate. * * *

7. *Other factors.*—* * * We will * * * favorably consider petitions to add issues when, but only when, they demonstrate that significant evidence will be adduced.

* * *

DISSENTING STATEMENT OF COMMISSIONER HYDE

* * *

I know of no two cases where the underlying facts are identical. I know of no two cases where differences among applicants are identical. Therefore, the significance to be given in each decision to each difference and to each criterion must of necessity vary, and must necessarily be considered in context with the other facts of the individual cases.

If the Commission has been remiss in the past in not spelling out the decisional process in each case as carefully as it should, the obvious remedy is improvement in the preparation of decisions. * * *

* * *

[The dissenting statement of Commissioner Bartley is omitted.]

CONCURRING STATEMENT OF COMMISSIONER ROBERT E. LEE

* * *

Historically, a prospective applicant hires a highly skilled communications attorney, well versed in the procedures of the Commission. This counsel has a long history of Commission decisions to guide him and he puts together an application that meets all of the so-called criteria. There then follows a tortuous and expensive hearing wherein each applicant attempts to tear down his adversaries on every conceivable front, while individually presenting that which he thinks the Commission would like to hear. The examiner then makes a reasoned decision which, at first blush, generally makes a lot of sense—but comes the oral argument and all of the losers concentrate their fire on the "potential" winner and the Commission must thereupon examine the claims and counterclaims, "weigh" the criteria and pick the winner which, if my recollection serves me correctly, is a different winner in about 50 percent of the cases.

The real blow, however, comes later when the applicant that emerged as the winner on the basis of our "decisive" criteria sells the station to a multiple owner or someone else that could not possibly have prevailed over other qualified applicants under the criteria in an adversary proceeding.* * * *

Questions

1. First, note that the *Policy Statement* is dead, for all intents and purposes. When the D.C. Circuit invalidated the use of the integration criterion (p. 122), it also held that the *Policy Statement* in general was invalid because not adopted through traditional Administrative Procedure Act rulemaking procedures. (Since the APA allows agencies to adopt policy statements without rulemaking's procedure formality, this may be a subject worth revisiting; but for now, the Commission and others treat the *Policy Statement* as void.)

2. Is the *Policy Statement* conducive to "clarity and consistency of decision"? How would you determine whether the comparative licensing process was improved by its issuance? By what criteria does it invite empirical evaluation? Cf. Anthony, *Towards Simplicity and Rationality in Comparative Broadcast Licensing Proceedings,* 24 Stan.L.Rev. 1 (1971) (proposal to award licenses and renewals on the basis of a point-scoring system).

---

* See § 310(d) (forbidding comparative proceedings in transfer situations), which was added in 1952 to disapprove a contrary Commission practice (known as the AVCO rule).—Ed.

3. Is the FCC's analysis of the integration of ownership and management sensible? If the FCC's interest in licensee performance in the public interest implies something other than simple licensee profit maximization, should it prefer the integration or separation of ownership and management? See generally A. Berle & G. Means, *The Modern Corporation and Private Property* (1932).

4. Returning to the *1965 Policy Statement,* note that Commissioner Hyde's opinion takes the majority to task for inducing applicants to fit themselves "into a mold in order to meet the Commission's preconceived standards." Is this an argument for keeping applicants in the dark about the law to which they will be subject? Or, since he advises them to consult prior FCC opinions for guidance, is it just an argument for letting the outcome of cases depend more upon the skill of counsel in divining what the FCC's opinions mean? For recognizing the futility of codification and the inevitability of incremental change, in the manner of the common law?

5. Do you think the FCC should encourage mergers among competing applicants? Is there a "public interest" reason peculiar to the context of comparative licensing to favor a mediational, merger-arranging rather than adjudicative role for the FCC? See Fuller, *Adjudication and the Rule of Law,* 54 Proceedings, Am.Soc'y.Int'l L. 1, 3–5 (1960); Botein, *Comparative Broadcast Licensing Procedures and the Rule of Law: A Fuller Investigation,* 6 Ga.L.Rev. 743 (1972).

6. Should it matter to the FCC that some or all of the applicants before it merge themselves into one of their own accord? See 47 C.F.R. § 1.525(a) (agreements between parties for amendment or dismissal of or failure to prosecute applications.). Do the "public interest" considerations vary depending upon whether the accord is reached after the comparative hearing but before the FCC administrative law judge has issued an initial decision (i.e., recommended a "winner"), or after the initial decision has been accepted for review by the Commission? Cf. the Japanese approach discussed in the *CODA.* (p. 585)

7. Assume that the facts in *Ashbacker* recurred today, and that rather than undergo an expensive comparative hearing the applicants reached an accord whereby Fetzer withdrew his application in consideration for a 33% ownership interest in and a ten-year employment contract with Ashbacker. Is the FCC powerless to prevent the parties in this way from effectively mooting the § 307(b) issue? See 47 C.F.R. § 1.525(b); cf. § 310(d) of the Act.

8. How should the FCC treat a merger agreement among applicants wherein one applicant has an option after three years to purchase the stock of the other participants? See 71 FCC 2d 295 (1979).

Note: Minority Preferences

In the *1965 Policy Statement,* the Commission placed heavy reliance upon local residence and community roots, as indicators of a licensee likely to provide diverse and relevant programming. If local residence and integration of ownership and control are indeed important, then other ties to particular parts of the community might also seem to be significant. To the extent that a large minority population exists in a market, it would thus be sensible to give a competitive advantage to an applicant which reflected the interests of that group.

The court of appeals followed precisely this reasoning in TV 9, Inc. v. FCC, 495 F.2d 929 (D.C.Cir.1973), cert. denied 419 U.S. 986, 95 S.Ct. 245, 42 L.Ed.2d 194 (1974). In that case, about 15 percent of one of the losing applicants was owned by two local Black residents. The Commission had refused to give any weight to their minority status, even though none of the other applicants included minority participation. In reversing the Commission, the court noted that:

> The minority stock ownership of an applicant serving the Orlando community is a consideration relevant to a choice among applicants of broader community representation and practicable service to the public. The credit awarded due to Mr. Perkins' participation, as a part owner, in management is not the same as credit based on broader community representation attributed to his and Dr. Smith's stock ownership and participation.

Neither the Commission nor the court seemed to be much concerned with whether this newly-created minority preference raised constitutional issues. For a history of minority preferences see Dawn McGunagle, *Metro Broadcasting, Inc. v. FCC: The Constitutionality of Minority Ownership preferences in Broadcast Licensing,* 1991 Det. C.L. Rev. (1991)

After the *TV 9* decision, the Commission, under both public and congressional pressure, created other devices to enhance minority ownership in the broadcasting and cable industries. In addition to the minority preference in comparative hearings, the Commission adopted a "distress sale" policy. This effectively allows a non-minority license holder to avoid an FCC hearing on its conduct or qualifications by selling its station to a firm controlled by minorities. (Otherwise, a licensee may not sell its facility once its license has been designated for hearing.) In order to qualify for distress sale treatment, the incumbent licensee has to sell its station before the hearing actually begins, at a price no greater than 75 percent of its fair market value. For further discussion of the *Metro* case see Antoinette Cook Bush & Marc S. Martin, *The FCC's Minority Ownership Policies from Broadcasting to PCS,* 48 Fed. Comm. L.Jj 423 (1996).

Both the minority preference and distress sale policies were challenged on constitutional grounds, and upheld by a 5–4 majority, in Metro Broadcasting, Inc. v. FCC, 497 U.S. 547, 110 S.Ct. 2997, 111 L.Ed.2d 445 (1990). Writing for the majority, Justice Brennan viewed the case as involving questions not so much of constitutionality as of congressional intent.

> * * * [W]e conclude that the interest in enhancing broadcast diversity is, at the very least, an important governmental objective and is therefore a sufficient basis for the Commission's minority ownership policies. * * * The benefits of such diversity are not limited to the members of minority groups who gain access to the broadcasting industry by virtue of the ownership policies; rather, the benefits redound to all members of the viewing and listening audience. * * *

> We also find that the minority ownership policies are substantially related to the achievement of the Government's interest. One compo-

nent of this inquiry concerns the relationship between expanded minority ownership and greater broadcast diversity; both the FCC and Congress have determined that such a relationship exists. Although we do not " 'defer' to the judgment of the Congress and the Commission on a constitutional question," * * * we must pay close attention to the expertise of the Commission and the factfinding of Congress when analyzing the nexus between minority ownership and programming diversity. * * *

Finally, we do not believe that the minority ownership policies at issue impose impermissible burdens on nonminorities. * * * [The nonminority challengers] claim that they have been handicapped in their ability to obtain [licenses] in the first instance. But * * * we find that a congressionally mandated benign race-conscious program that is substantially related to the achievement of an important government interest is consistent with equal protection principles so long as it does not impose *undue* burdens on nonminorities. * * *

In the context of broadcasting licenses, the burden on nonminorities is slight. The FCC's responsibility is to grant licenses in the "public interest," convenience, or necessity, and the limited number of frequencies on the electromagnetic spectrum means that "[n]o one has a First Amendment right to a license." *Red Lion* * * * Applicants have no settled expectation that their applications will be granted without consideration of public interest factors such as minority ownership.

Justice Stevens concurred on the ground that the policies did not "stigmatize" either minorities or nonminorities in any way. He noted that the doctrines fell "within the extremely narrow category of governmental decisions for which racial or ethnic heritage may provide a rational basis for differential treatment."

By contrast, dissenting Justice O'Connor, joined by Chief Justice Rehnquist, and Justices Scalia and Kennedy, viewed the doctrines as denying equal protection to non-minority applicants. They thought the matter was governed by Richmond v. J.A. Croson Co., 488 U.S. 469, 109 S.Ct. 706, 102 L.Ed.2d 854 (1989), which had subjected to strict scrutiny and invalidated a minority contracting set-aside provision. They expressed concern that "members of any racial or ethnic group, whether now preferred under the FCC's policies or not, may find themselves politically out of fashion and subject to disadvantageous but 'benign' discrimination."

The breadth of Metro's holding soon came under question in Adarand Constructors, Inc. v. Pena, 515 U.S. 200, 115 S.Ct. 2097, 132 L.Ed.2d 158 (1995). That case involved the constitutionality of the Small Business Administration's "8(a) program." The Small Business Act creates an indirect preference for minority and "socially and economically disadvantaged" contractors on highway construction projects; under the "8(a) program," the federal Department of Transportation (DOT) pays a general contractor up to a 10 percent override on contracts with certified minority subcontractors.

Although Adarand was the low bidder to provide guardrails for a DOT-financed highway construction project in Colorado, the general contractor nevertheless chose a minority—and more expensive—subcontractor, presumably in order to receive the override payment. Adarand sued to invalidate the subcontract as well as the general 8(a) program, arguing that it constituted invidious racial discrimination.

In a four-justice plurality opinion, Justice O'Connor cast serious doubt upon *Metro*'s continued viability. She stated that *Metro* incorrectly had used an "intermediate" rather than "strict scrutiny" standard of review, and indicated in very general terms that racial classifications would have a difficult time surviving the strict scrutiny test. She faulted *Metro*'s analysis in two major respects.

First, it turned its back on *Croson*'s explanation of why strict scrutiny of all governmental racial classifications is essential. * * *

Second, *Metro Broadcasting* squarely rejected one of the three propositions established by the Court's earlier equal protection cases, namely, congruence between the standards applicable to federal and state racial classifications, and in so doing also undermined the other two—skepticism of all racial classifications and consistency of treatment irrespective of the race of the burdened or benefitted group.* * *

* * *

In other words, such classifications are constitutional only if they are narrowly tailored measures that further compelling governmental interests. To the extent that *Metro Broadcasting* is inconsistent with that holding, it is overruled.

The plurality made clear, however, that it was not invalidating all racial classifications. It concluded by noting that:

Finally, we wish to dispel the notion that strict scrutiny is "strict in theory but fatal in fact." * * * When race-based action is necessary to further a compelling interest, such action is within constitutional constraints if it satisfies the "narrow tailoring" test this Court has set out in previous cases.

The plurality opinion offered little guidance, however, as to the type of showing necessary to establish either a "compelling interest" or "narrow tailoring." Indeed, it noted that "our decision today alters the playing field in some important respects," and remanded the case to the Court of Appeals for the Tenth Circuit to address both of these issues. At several points it suggested that the beneficiary of a racial classification must show that a racially defined benefit was necessary because of his or her past experience and present circumstances—rather than an historical "group classification."

The fifth vote for reversal came from Justice Scalia, for whom virtually no showing would be sufficient to justify a benefit based on a racial classification. In a concurring opinion, he stated:

* * * [U]nder our Constitution there can be no such thing as a creditor or a debtor race. * * * To pursue the concept of racial entitlement—even for the most admirable and benign of purposes—is to reinforce and preserve for the future mischief the way of thinking that produced race slavery, race privilege and race hatred. * * *

It is unlikely, if not impossible, that the challenged program would survive under this understanding of strict scrutiny, but I am content to leave that to be decided on remand.

The plurality opinion and Justice Scalia's concurrence provoked three dissenting statements from four justices. Several argued that the plurality had violated notions of *stare decisis* by *de facto* overruling *Metro*. Others argued for an analytical distinction between "invidious" and "benign" racial classifications. And others argued that the Constitution gave the federal government broad powers in redressing the effects of racial and other discrimination. (Interestingly enough, the plurality seemed to assume that gender preferences would continue to be subject to an "intermediate" standard of review.)

Adarand's effect as to affirmative action in general and broadcasting in particular is unclear. Although Justice Scalia presumably would be more strict in his scrutiny than the plurality, *Adarand* seems to have at least a majority in favor of "strict scrutiny"—whatever that may be in this context. Since the plurality recognized it was creating a "new playing field," further changes may be in store. Moreover, the statute in *Adarand*'s "override"— that is, bonus—provisions is quite different from the minority preferences at issue in *Metro*. First, the *Adarand* statute created a financial incentive for third parties—i.e., general contractors—to deal with minority businesses. This type of private action is somewhat different from the federal government's decision to aid minority broadcasters in *Metro*. Second, the impact of the preference was more indirect than in *Metro*. In *Adarand* the subcontractor did not receive any direct government preference, while in *Metro* the FCC granted benefits, i.e., licenses—to minority groups. At least in theory, the general contractor in *Adarand* might have decided to take a low bid instead of an override on the contract price, depending upon which yielded the greatest total profit.

Metro's scope thus may be somewhat more limited than before. But preferences presumably will continue to play a part in the FCC's licensing process for the near future. The Commission's initial reaction to *Adarand* was to delete the minority preferences from some of its auctions of personal communications services (PCS). Whether the FCC applies this on an across-the-board basis, however, remains to be seen.

Finally, while this litigation was going on, the Congress repealed one of the strongest vehicles for increasing minority ownership—namely, the "tax certificate." This basically provided that if a station owner sold to a minority enterprise, it could defer payment of capital gains taxes; in a number of cases, it effectively allowed minority companies to "outbid" non-minority competitors with lower offers, because of the tax benefits to the sellers. Congress' action appeared to be the result of claims that non-minority companies had abused the tax certificate by using companies with only token minority control to buy stations.

Note: Status of Integration Criterion

There is some real question today as to whether the integration criterion in particular or the *Policy Statement* in general still is good law. In Bechtel v. FCC, 10 F.3d 875 (D.C.Cir.1993), the court cast serious doubt upon the constitutional and statutory validity of the integration factor.

[The court first addressed three general problems underlying the Commission's integration rationale, and then went on to point up particular flaws in the agency's economic reasoning.]

1. *Lack of Permanence*

Whatever the benefits of integration, they would last only if the Commission insisted on licensees maintaining the owner-manager relation or if successful licensees tended to adopt the integrated structure of their own free will. Neither appears to be the case.

Perhaps in recognition of integration's artificiality, the Commission has done little to ensure its continuation once the promise of integration has carried an applicant to victory. On the first anniversary of the commencement of program tests, people who have won their station in a comparative hearing must report any deviations from their integration proposals. But as long as they did not misrepresent their intentions in their applications, abandonment of those proposals apparently carries no consequences. After the first anniversary, moreover, no reports are required. Similarly, while successful applicants in comparative hearings generally cannot transfer or assign their stations during the first year of operations, thereafter a licensee who had won his station through his integration proposal could "turn around and sell it ... without regard to the buyer's 'integration' or lack thereof" [albeit subject to securing the FCC's approval of the transfer of control].

* * *

2. *Lack of Evidence*

The Commission's uncertainty about the practical effects of its integration policy is not limited to the question of how long integration persists. Despite its twenty-eight years of experience with the policy, the Commission has accumulated no evidence to indicate that it achieves even one of the benefits that the Commission attributes to it. As a result, the Commission ultimately rests its defense of the integration criterion on the deference that we owe to its "predictive judgments".

* * *

Finally, it is worth noting that the "predictive judgments" at the root of the integration policy concern an area that the Commission has sometimes considered beyond its expertise. In scrutinizing integration proposals asserted by rival claimants to be illegitimate, purely formal, or otherwise inadequate, the Commission has disclaimed any "particular expertise in finance or business management" and accordingly expressed itself "reluctant to second-guess an applicant's business judgment—so long as it is, in fact, a good faith business decision." * * *

* * *

3. *Exclusion of Other Factors*

Even if integration's claimed advantages were more plausible than we find them, they would not necessarily justify the extraordinary weight that the Commission assigns to integration. The Commission has identified "two primary objectives" for its comparative process: generating "a maximum diffusion of control of the media of mass communications" and securing "the best practicable service to the public." In the typical case, the integration criterion is "the most important element of best practicable service." In other words, the Commission generally deems an applicant's integration proposal more important than his past broadcast record, his proposed program service, or the efficiency of his proposed use of frequency.

* * *

With these points in mind, we address the purported advantages of the integration criterion.

B. Incentives

1. *Financial Incentives*

The Commission asserts that stations perform better when managed by those with the "most direct financial interest" in the venture. The Commission has not defined exactly what it means by "financial interest". However the term is defined, though, the integration policy does not serve this goal.

For instance, in calculating integration credit, the Commission does not take the ownership interests of limited partners into account if all the limited partners are sufficiently insulated from influence over the partnership's affairs. * * * Accordingly, an applicant can get full integration credit even though the general partner or voting shareholder has only a small percentage of the total equity in the firm, the rest of which is held by people who will have nothing to do with the station. For example, a firm has received full integration credit where the sole general partner held only 10% of the firm's equity, for which he had paid $10. * * *

* * *

In short, whatever the benefits of ensuring that day-to-day management decisions are made by people whose money is directly on the line, the integration policy does not achieve them.

2. *Legal Accountability*

The Commission also considers it "inherently desirable" that day-to-day management decisions be made by people with "legal responsibility" for the station. * * *

It may be true, as the Commission suggests, that station owners have the most legal accountability for the station. But to a large extent they have this accountability whether or not they work at the station. Stations are not insulated from the threat of license revocation or nonrenewal, merely because they are owned by absentee investors. * * * Since absentee owners thus have strong incentives to ensure that their station complies with the relevant statutes and rules, the incremental contribution of the integration preference on this score appears trivial.

C. Interest

The Commission also asserts that integrated owners are more likely than absentee owners to have an active interest in the operation of their stations. * * *

* * * [It] is hard to see why a relatively modest differential in "interest" should overwhelm a substantial difference in experience. Although the Commission has argued that broadcast experience should be "of minor significance" because it can come with time, it is hard to imagine that anyone seriously interested in "picking winners" would so heavily downgrade the contestants' track records.

In any event, the integration criterion simply measures one form in which owners may express their interest. In general, integration credit is available only for people who hold day-to-day jobs at the station, not for those who make management decisions from afar while running other business activities too. Yet executives routinely supervise a variety of firm activities, a few hours to each, without being the least bit apathetic about the performance of any. * * *

* * *

D. Information

According to the Commission, on-site owners have better sources of information than absentee owners. * * * For example, integrated owners are more likely than absentee owners to follow station correspondence or to hear comments by station visitors.

* * * The Commission cites no evidence that station visitors are a major source of information for broadcasters, and the idea seems implausible.

* * *

Familiarity with a community seems much more likely than station visitors or correspondence to make one aware of community needs. But even long-time local residence generates at most a "qualitative" enhancement of an applicant's integration credit.

E. Objectivity

* * *

Any "objectivity" added by the integration criterion is unfortunately illusory. The Commission's scores for quantitative integration merely lend the policy a veneer of precision; every step towards the magic number is packed with subjective judgments, some generic, some ad hoc.

At a generic level, the Commission's weighting system * * * is simply a fancy way for the Commission to express its view that the values of integration fall off sharply when owner-managers work less than full-time. It has not a shred of data supporting the basic conjecture * * * .

* * *

So far as measuring ownership is concerned, the Commission's policy provides rich incentives for the adoption of firm structures that we characterized in *Bechtel I* as "strange and unnatural." After all, if a station can be acquired for legal fees and minor engineering services, and can be sold a year later for several million dollars, one would expect to see a good deal of ingenuity.

* * *

All that said, the integration preference is peculiarly without foundation. While the Commission makes it a central focus of allocation, the Commission takes no interest whatever in the matter when it comes to transfers or even in the continuing conduct of the original licensee. The Commission appears to have no evidence that the preferred structure even survives among the winners, much less that it does so among especially outstanding broadcasters. Because of applicants' incentive to create a facade of integration, and the difficulty of identifying sound business practices, even the preference's touted objectivity proves an illusion. Though we owe substantial deference to the Commission's expertise, we are forbidden to suspend our disbelief totally. We find the integration policy arbitrary and capricious.

[The court held that the pendency of a rulemaking on the status of integration did not permit the Commission to continue applying the integration policy in the interim, since it had been found to be invalid. The court remanded *Bechtel II* to the FCC, with instructions to decide upon which parties should be considered in the comparative hearing—without using the integration criterion. In the end, the Commission simply threw up its hands and abandoned the both integration policy and the *1965 Policy Statement*].

* * *

Notes and Questions

1.   Note this case's rather convoluted path in wending its way to the D.C. Circuit. A prior appeal to this court (*Bechtel I*) resulted in a remand to the Commission, with instructions for the FCC to reconsider the validity of the integration comparative criterion. The FCC responded by beginning a rulemaking proceeding, but continuing to process this case under its traditional comparative criteria—including integration. In the meantime, another D.C. Circuit panel ordered the Commission to stop applying the integration policy until it had reached a decision as to its validity. In response to the second panel's order, the FCC held that Bechtel had failed to demonstrate that continued use of the integration criterion was irrational in light of changes in the broadcast industry since the *1965 Policy Statement*. Bechtel then appealed from that order.

Remember that the *1965 Policy Statement* was not a rule, but simply a statement of precedent. A rule normally can be challenged only on a direct appeal from its adoption—within 60 days of its adoption. A policy statement has no more status, however, than any common-law-style agency case decision; it thus can be collaterally attacked by any party at any time.

This naturally raises a question as to why the agency had not adopted the *1965 Policy Statement* in the form of a rule. One answer may be that the subject matter is too intangible for codification into a rule. Another and probably more realistic explanation is that in 1965 the Commission was rushing to adopt something resembling a principled doctrine for comparative hearings because of the scandals then, and simply did not have time to comply with the Administrative Procedure Act's time and other requirements as to rulemaking.

2.   The court devotes most of its rather considerable energies to finding that particular—and sometimes rather narrow—justifications for the inte-

gration criterion do not hold water. For example: the policy does not create financial incentives for responsive programming, since absentee owners also want to maximize local audiences; an owner's presence at a station is irrelevant, since no one ever drops by to visit anyway; absentee owners may have past broadcast experience, which may be more important than integration; station owners have the same incentive to comply with the law as station managers to avoid license renewal problems.

Is any one of these potential failings by itself enough to justify holding the integration policy to be arbitrary and capricious? What ever happened to the notion of "agency expertise," as invoked successfully by the FCC in prior cases? Does the court's evaluation of how well the integration policy actually operates get it involved in second-guessing the agency?

Does the court have a more general and overarching concern with the integration policy? As noted before, the D.C. Circuit—the sole appellate forum for licensing as opposed to rulemaking decisions—has considerable expertise itself in communications law, economics, and policy. It thus may have been looking for some empirical data upon which to base the integration criterion. It obviously found very little.

3. As noted before, the FCC seems to have a recurring reluctance to producing empirical data. (To some extent, this may be a very conscious political decision, since the agency has an increasingly professional staff in its Office of Plans and Policy ("OPP")). Regardless of its motives and resources, however, the agency has done remarkably little empirical research to support its actions—from "must-carry" to SMATV economics.

To what extent did the Commission do its research job here? It acted on an intuitive conclusion that owner-operators would provide particularly good service to their communities. That type of conclusion probably sounds right to most people—particularly the New Deal types who created the FCC and instituted the notion of communications regulation. But is it accurate?

As in many other situations, the Commission apparently just didn't bother to develop an empirical basis for its conclusions. Was this the result of negligence? Or did it have a hidden agenda, as it may have had in cases like *ACT III infra*, to present as weak a case as possible to invite judicial invalidation of policies which it politically could not repeal? Once again, what are the ethical considerations in an agency's "taking a fall" on policies which it disfavors but politically cannot repeal?

Since there are no data as to the effects of integration, how would one go about finding the requisite information on some of the particular issues raised by the Commission? How would one develop data to show that viewers do not visit stations, or that owner-managers are more responsive to local needs? Is it fair to throw this burden on the agency? Is it fair to throw it upon the parties?

4. The court seems to take a dim view of the Reagan/Bush FCC's repeal of the traditional "anti-trafficking" rule, i.e., the prohibition on selling a station within three years of acquiring it. How does this relate, however, to the problem of potentially "sham" integration proposals?

In general, does the anti-trafficking policy make sense, by deterring investors from buying and selling broadcast stations as marketable goods? As the court seems to consider, however, does easy marketability of stations encourage the most economically efficient operators to take over and "turn around" marginal stations? Was this generally the experience during the "glory days" of mergers and acquisitions fueled by "junk bonds" during the late 1980s?

5.   As discussed briefly by the court, one major concern was that license applicants—particularly for the almost 800 new frequencies allocated in 1980—would use minorities as "fronts," in order to get the minority preference for entities owned by minorities. The common approach was to give a minority all of the equity in a partnership or all of the voting stock in a corporation—which in the past would have made them the owners of record for the Commission. In a typical deal, a minority might hold 51 percent of the voting stock, but be subject to buyouts through capital calls for nominal sums by non-minority owners of preferred stock. Although many licenses were granted upon such applications initially, the Commission—and particularly the administrative law judges dealing with these cases—began to invalidate or ignore these arrangements by the early 1990s.

6.   Unlike federal grant programs, the Commission's license grant procedure does not require licensees to report as to their operations or ownership. A licensee thus is free to sell its business (not its license *per se*) to the highest bidder, one year after it has established its technical qualifications—which often occurs before it even goes on the air with a full schedule of local programming.

7.   The court suggests that the Commission might impose reporting requirements—presumably on an annual basis—to determine whether station owners in fact are close to their full time to operating their stations. But this procedure seems doomed to failure. For example, how would the FCC have any accurate reading as to an owner's actual amount of management time? How would it keep records? How would it evaluate the amount of an owner's "quality time"?

8.   What is the effect of the court's decision on preferences for minority applicants, as established in *TV 9* and *Metro Broadcasting*? Since those cases reasoned to some extent that a minority owner would pay substantial attention to serving the needs of a minority audience, they and the FCC's precedents created a "qualitative" integration preference for minority applicants. In order to get this preference, however, minority applicants first had to show that they were integrated as much as their non-minority competitors.

9.   If there no longer is an integration policy, however, the status of the minority preference is less than clear. In *Metro*, the Supreme Court seemed to assume that the preference was absolute, regardless of integration and other questions. Because the Supreme Court never dealt with the details of the issue, however, it is less than clear that the minority preference would exist indepedant of a strong integration criterion.

Did the court have this problem in mind? Apparently not, even though it previously had created the minority preference in the *TV–9* case two decades ago.

Note: Character Qualifications in Broadcast Licensing

As the *Policy Statement* indicates in its rather vague way, good character is "a relevant consideration in the issuance of license." This seems like a relatively innocuous principle; presumably any regulatory regime attempts to exclude known knaves and cheats. As is altogether too typical in the broadcast licensing arena, however, defining the criterion has proved quite difficult for the FCC. The Commission has never engaged in any thorough rulemaking or other analysis of the character requirement. In fact, its first policy statement dealt only with a single aspect of the character issue. Establishment of a Uniform Policy to be Followed in Licensing of Radio Stations in Connection with Violations by an Applicant of Laws of the U.S. other than the Communications Act of 1934, as amended, 42 FCC 2d 399 (1951).

The FCC has broad authority to require information potentially relevant to the character inquiry. Section 308(b) of the Communications Act provides that "all applications for station licenses, or modifications or renewals thereof, shall set forth such facts as the Commission by regulation may prescribe as to the citizenship, *character,* and financial, technical, and other qualifications of the applicant to operate the station." 47 U.S.C. § 308(b) [Emphasis added]. Almost identical language is included in 47 U.S.C. § 319(a).

The Commission has exercised its authority to adopt a rule requiring each applicant for an AM radio license to make a "satisfactory showing" that it is of good character. 47 C.F.R. § 73.24(d). It also adopted a more general rule requiring each broadcast application to include all information required on any form, 47 C.F.R. § 73.3514, and includes "character" questions in specific broadcast application forms. E.g., Form 301, Application for Authority to Construct a New Broadcast Station or Make Changes in an Existing Station, Section II, Questions 8, 17 (June 1977); Form 303, Application for Renewal of License for Commercial TV Broadcast Station, Section II, Question 4 (June 1980).

Nothing in the legislative history of the FCC's enabling statute defines "character." In the absence of a legislative definition, the courts and the Commission have given the term a plain language interpretation. The Commission has evaluated "character" in a very general way. On one occasion, the Commission declared that the character of an applicant should be measured "by its past observance of moral, ethical, legal and professional rules of conduct." WKAT–TV Inc., 29 FCC 216, 237 (1960).

As a general proposition, there may appear to be a connection between character and future licensee performance. But good moral character is no guarantee of competent broadcast service. See e.g., Sharp and Lively, *Can the Broadcaster in the Black Hat Ride Again?: "Good Character" Requirement for Broadcast Licensees,* 32 Fed.Comm.L.J. 173, 176 (1980); and poor "character" may not necessarily result in poor broadcast service.

While the Commission has often stated that an applicant with bad character must be denied, in practice the Commission has treated character as but one factor for predicting future service. Because character inquiries have a tendency to range widely, the Commission found it necessary in 1981 to inquire whether the process had gone beyond its purpose. In the Matter of

Policy Regarding Character Qualifications in Broadcast Licensing, 87 FCC 2d 836 (1981).

In its 1986 *Policy Statement,* the Commission changed its policies—at least briefly. It concluded that it had authority to conduct "character" inquiries, but that an investigation's broad scope might not identify behavior patterns that are useful in predicting public interest performance. The Commission found that future evaluations should focus narrowly on specific traits, which would show an applicant's propensity to deal honestly with the Commission and to comply with the law. While "truthfulness" or "reliability" are desirable, the Commission said, it would be most concerned with an applicant's prior violations of the Communications Act, a Commission rule, or other laws. The basic question would be whether an applicant would deal truthfully with the Commission and comply with Commission policies. In the Matter of Policy Regarding Character Qualifications in Broadcast Licensing Amendment of Rules of Broadcast Practice and Procedure Relating to Written Responses to Commission Inquiries and the Making of Misrepresentations to the Commission by Permittees and Licensees, 102 FCC 2d 1179 (1986).

Four years later, the Commission issued a new Policy Statement, 55 Fed.Reg. 23,082 (1990), further modifying its position on character qualifications. Under the 1990 policy, the Commission will consider evidence of any felony conviction in evaluating an applicant's or licensee's character.

To implement this *Policy Statement and Order,* the Commission amended its rules by adding 47 C.F.R. § 1.17, which prohibits "any applicant, permittee or licensee" from making "any written misrepresentation or willful material omission" and 47 C.F.R. § 1.65, which requires broadcast licensees and permittees to report adverse determinations of relevant misconduct that are finally adjudicated during the term of their permit or license.

b. *License Renewal: Balancing the Interests of Incumbents and New Entrants*

One of the most difficult issues for the Commission traditionally has been comparative renewal proceedings—that is, situations in which a potential new entrant attempts to secure an existing station's license. If the agency is sympathetic to the challenger, it creates the image of being "anti-industry" or the like. On the other hand, if it is hostile to new entrants—which often are owned largely by minorities—it opens itself up to claims that it is racist, insensitive, and the like. Again, a good deal of the problem comes from the old *Ashbacker* case, which tended to confuse initial and renewal applications.

As noted at the beginning of this Chapter, there is a significant difference between applications for initial and renewal licenses. (p. 104) The competing applicants for a new license basically have little at risk other than their out-of-pocket expenses—naturally enough, comprised mainly of attorneys' fees. Although these can run into the hundreds of thousands or millions of dollars, they do not even begin to resemble the economic impact of losing an existing broadcast television license; since most major market television licensees acquired their stations through purchase rather than initial application, their investments may run into the hundreds of millions of dollars.

Once again, the Telecommunications Act of 1996 has made license challenges at renewal time virtually a non-issue. But the evolution from *Ashbacker* to the present sets out some good issues in terms of communications policy.

i. WHDH: *The Issue Framed*

We begin with a particularly difficult time in the history of the Commission. The nascent television industry was embroiled in a serious of scandals, of the visible of which was a rigged game show—later portrayed in the movie, "The Quiz Show." More substantively several FCC commissioners were involved in practices ranging from doing favors to taking money outright.

The following excerpt gives an idea of the pressures under which the FCC found itself in the late 1950s when faced with competing applications for newly authorized television frequencies. The author headed a special investigation into claims of corruption in federal administrative agencies.

BERNARD SCHWARTZ, THE PROFESSOR AND THE COMMISSIONS
198–202 (1959).*

On January 14, 1958, Baron Shacklette, our veteran chief investigator, called me from Miami and stated that Jack Anderson, Drew Pearson's principal assistant, had been telephoning people in Florida about the Channel 10 case, as well as [FCC] Commissioner Mack himself. I called Anderson, who readily told me of his phone conversation with Mack. It developed that he had got from Mack an admission that he had received money from Whiteside [a lawyer] for the winning applicant, a subsidiary of National Airlines. Anderson had secured this damaging admission by some adroit bluffing.

"I have an accountant," said Anderson, "who is prepared to testify that Whiteside has paid you money from the Grant Foster trust [a trust fund in Whiteside's custody]."

"Those were only loans," Mack blurted out. "I have borrowed money from Whiteside. This fellow I have known since he was in grammar school."

Anderson's reportorial instinct had led him to suspect that there might be money involved in the case. His telephone call to Mack obtained the key admission that money had, in fact, passed from Whiteside to Mack.

* * *

I instructed Herbert M. Wachtell and Paul S. Berger, the two young attorneys whom I had brought down to Washington, to arrange an immediate appointment with Mack. The interview was held the very next day (January 15) and secured from the commissioner the admission that he had received payments from Whiteside while the Channel 10 case was pending. Again he claimed that these were only "loans," but he conceded that he had no evidence of any repayments.

* * *

The second interview of Commissioner Mack took place in his office early in the morning of Friday, January 17, two days after the first meeting. This was the key interview, as far as the Channel 10 case was concerned, and it is the one that was wire-recorded. Drew Pearson's column about Anderson's phone conversation with Mack appeared in that morning's newspaper, but Mack was apparently the only one in Washington who had not read it.

The January 17 interview focused on the "loans" that Mack admitted receiving. The following is the crucial portion of the interview as it was described in Wachtell's and Berger's contemporaneous report to me:

> Asked how such loans had been repaid, Mr. Mack stated that, aside from the mortgage repayment previously outlined, all repayments by him to Mr. Whiteside had been in cash. Mr. Mack then advised that, in fact, he had not made full repayment to Mr. Whiteside; that the transactions could be described perhaps as "gifts, advances, or what have you"; and that while he was telling this to the writers, he would not be as frank with the committee. . . .

> Mr. Mack stated that in his opinion his account with Mr. Whiteside was at the present time about all even, in that all amounts not repaid by him to Mr. Whiteside had been "forgiven" by Mr. Whiteside. [Emphasis in original.]

In addition, Mack acknowledged that he had known that Whiteside had been brought into the case in some way by "the people from National."

In this second interview Richard Mack all but admitted himself off the FCC. He admitted that he had received substantial "loans" from an attorney whom he knew had been brought into a pending case by one of the applicants. He admitted that, if there had been any repayments by him, they had been in cash and that he had no records of such repayments. When pressed, he conceded that he had no specific recollection of ever making such cash repayments and that, in fact, all amounts not repaid had been "forgiven" by Whiteside.

The details of Mack's financial relationships with Whiteside were secured later. It developed that Mack had received directly from Whiteside checks totaling $2,650 while Mack was on the FCC. Whiteside also gave Mack a one-sixth interest in a Miami insurance firm that sold some $20,000 worth of insurance to the winning applicant in the Channel 10 case. Mack received some $10,000 from this company. In addition,

Whiteside gave to Mack all the stock interest in a loan company, from which Mack received several thousand dollars. And all this time, as Whiteside himself admitted, he was urging Mack to give National Airlines "every consideration" in its application for Channel 10.

The pressures brought by Whiteside on Commissioner Mack were only a small part of those used by the parties in the Miami Channel 10 case. In the public hearings it was brought out that a veritable galaxy of Washington luminaries were approached in an effort to influence the FCC's decision on behalf of the various parties. Colonel Katzentine had sought the help of Senators Holland, Smathers, Kefauver, Magnuson, and Wiley, as well as that of Vice President Nixon and House Minority Leader Martin. So many off-the-record contacts were made with commissioners in this case that Commissioner Mack could declare in all sincerity: "I was a little tired of talking to people about this case."

* * *

The chief representative of an apparently corrupt broadcast television system became the focus of the *WHDH* case. Although the parties' conduct on its face may have been appropriate, it raised substantial questions—at a very sensitive time—about the integrity of both the Commission and the industry.

WHDH, INC.

Federal Communications Commission, 1960.
29 FCC 205 (1960).

By the Commission:

On April 25, 1957, the Commission released a decision resolving a comparative hearing for a new television station on channel 5, Boston, Mass., in favor of WHDH, Inc., and denying the competing applications of Greater Boston Television Corp.; Massachusetts Bay Telecasters, Inc.; and Allen B. DuMont Laboratories, Inc. Appeals to the U.S. Court of Appeals for the District of Columbia Circuit were filed by Greater Boston and Massachusetts Bay, and on July 31, 1958, that court released its decision affirming the Commission on the basis of the record on which the Commission had decided the case, but remanding for inquiry into factors not in the original record.

The court noted that, subsequent to the Commission's disposition of the proceeding, testimony by a member of the Commission before the House Subcommittee on Legislative Oversight indicated that various individuals connected with some of the parties to the proceeding had conferred with him with reference to the case while the matter was still under consideration by the Commission. In light of this testimony the court remanded the case to the Commission with direction to make findings of fact [on the question of improper contacts with members of the Commission] * * *.

* * *

Originally this proceeding involved a comparison of the applications of WHDH, Inc.; Greater Boston Television Corp.; Massachusetts Bay Telecasters, Inc.; Allen B. DuMont Laboratories, Inc.; Columbia Broadcasting System; and Post Publishing Co. In the spring of 1954, shortly before the consolidation of the applications for hearing, Senator Saltonstall, at the behest of Robert B. Choate, director and vice president of the Boston Herald–Traveler Corp., publisher and editor of the Boston Herald and Traveler newspapers and president of WHDH, Inc., wrote to the Chairman of the Commission stating that the Herald–Traveler was concerned with the Commission's diversification policy as it applied to newspapers, and asked that "all applicants be given a fair and equal opportunity." In the letter no preference for any of the applicants was urged.

On October 4, 1954, George C. McConnaughey commenced his service as Chairman of the Commission. The evidence in this proceeding is concerned in large part with certain conversations held with Mr. McConnaughey by officers of two of the applicant corporations. * * *

In late 1954 or early 1955, Mr. Charles F. Mills, a friend of Choate who had previously served with McConnaughey on the Renegotiation Board, arranged a luncheon meeting for himself, Choate, and McConnaughey, who had not theretofore met. Choate told Mills that his purpose in attending the luncheon was to "size up" or form an impression of the new Chairman. At the luncheon, which took place at a Washington hotel, Choate identified himself as an applicant for a permit. Although there was no discussion of the Boston case which was then before the Commission's examiner for hearing, Choate asked how long comparative proceedings took, and what the general procedure was after an examiner made his ruling. Mr. McConnaughey did not recall having attended this luncheon.

In March or April of 1956, a second luncheon took place attended by McConnaughey, Choate, Mills, and Thomas M. Joyce, a lawyer for the Herald–Traveler Corp., who did not, however, attend the luncheon in that capacity. This meeting was some 3 months after the release of the examiner's initial decision favoring Greater Boston and some 6 months prior to the oral argument on the exceptions to that initial decision. Choate requested the luncheon for the purpose of discussing legislation with Mr. McConnaughey, although prior to the meeting he did not specify what legislation he wished to discuss. At the luncheon there was no conversation on the merits of the Channel 5 case as such, but Choate had in his possession a draft of the Dempsey amendment, which he intended to present to Mr. McConnaughey in the hope of swaying the Chairman's opposition to the then-pending Harrison–Beamer bills [seeking diversification of station ownership and limiting media concentration]. However, when Choate attempted to present the draft to McConnaughey, the latter refused to accept it or to permit discussion of the matter. Therefore, only conversation of a social nature prevailed at the luncheon.

* * *

During the years 1954–56, certain officers and stockholders of Massachusetts Bay, including Forrester A. Clark, director and vice president, communicated with prominent political figures in Washington, to advise them that there were rumors of "political activity" on the part of other applicants and to urge their neutrality. However, none of the persons contacted were asked to or did approach any Commissioner with the exception of Sherman Adams, whose only act was to call the Chairman of the Commission and advise him that there would be no interference whatever from the White House.

In February of 1956, Clark arranged a luncheon meeting with McConnaughey whereat he told the Chairman that Massachusetts Bay had no political affiliation of any kind and was only seeking fair play under the rules governing comparative hearings. In the course of this conversation, purportedly for the purpose of showing that all shades of political opinion were represented in Massachusetts Bay, Clark told McConnaughey that Arthur Fiedler, Dom DiMaggio, and John P. Marquand were stockholders. While these gentlemen all enjoy national reputations in their respective fields, Mr. Clark was not certain of the political affiliation of any of them nor did he suggest why Mr. McConnaughey might have been expected to be so aware. There was no other conversation which might be deemed as going to the merits of the case.

Subsequent to Mr. McConnaughey's appointment as Chairman of the Commission, he lunched on several occasions with Dr. Allen B. DuMont. Although Mr. McConnaughey had the impression that DuMont by his presence and demeanor sought to demonstrate that he was the sort of a responsible individual who might be expected to head a reliable organization, the conversation was confined to matters of industry wide interest on which Dr. DuMont is regarded as an authority, and did not concern the channel 5 case.

The record contains no evidence of any *ex parte* contacts of any kind on the part of Greater Boston.

* * *

We turn first to the activities of Robert Choate of WHDH.

* * * [We] conclude that Choate demonstrated an attempted pattern of influence. He indicates that his reason for the initial meeting with McConaughey was to "size up" the new Chairman but, accepting that as true as far as it goes, it does not appear to be a full disclosure of his motives. While the Herald–Traveler had a legitimate interest in the views of the new Chairman of the agency regulating its radio station and the television station it soon hoped to have, in the normal course of events, its contacts with the Commission would be conducted through its professional representatives and its appraisal of the individual Commissioners would be formulated from the opinions of these gentlemen. The record contains no persuasive explanation of why Choate felt it necessary to seek a personal relationship with McConnaughey, and we conclude that his reason was to afford the chairman an opportunity to "size him up"; that is, to demonstrate by his demeanor and presence that he was a responsible man representing responsible interests who merited favorable consideration of their application to conduct an operation in the public interest.

* * *

The very attempt to establish such a pattern of influence does violence to the integrity of the Commission's processes. Such an attack on the integrity of the processes of any adjudicatory body brings into play its inherent right to protect such processes, and one of the remedial measures available is its discretion in the voiding of any previous action that may have been tainted by such attempt. The facts revealed on this record persuade us that the Commission's processes can best be protected in this instance by exercising our discretion to void the grant to WHDH. * * * [But it was not disqualified as an applicant.]

Our conclusions as to Massachusetts Bay are not unlike those with respect to WHDH, for we deem Clark's activities to be essentially similar to Choate's. * * *

* * *

Finally, in that the previous grantee, WHDH, has not been found absolutely disqualified, we do not believe that the public interest would be served by depriving the people of Boston of the existing service during the pendency of the further proceedings ordered herein. Therefore, we shall permit WHDH to continue its operation on channel 5, but on special temporary authority.

Notes and Questions

1. The Commission appears to be concerned that Choate's actions could give at least the appearance that the comparative proceeding was tainted by *ex parte* contacts. Is it possible to tell whether the FCC had actually been compromised? If it had been, is it likely that the Commission would have volunteered the fact? Indeed, can a "fixer" ever be sure that an agency will not blow the whistle in order to avoid political embarrassment? Even if a majority of the commissioners had been contacted *ex parte* and had wanted to punish WHDH, could they have done so without harming either themselves or their colleagues, in light of their involvement? Short of intervention by an outside investigator, is it possible to test an agency's own conclusion that it did not act improperly?

Three commissioners were on the agency both in 1960 and in 1969, when the FCC ultimately took away WHDH's license, as discussed below. Two out of these three did not participate in the later decision. Does this suggest that the *ex parte* contacts may have been more extensive than the Commission acknowledged?

2.   47 C.F.R. § 1.1200 describes the Commission's *ex parte* rules as designed to deter improper communications and to maintain the utmost public confidence in Commission proceedings. To this end, these rules restrict, or require the disclosure of, any communication between persons involved in the decisionmaking process. An *ex parte* presentation is defined, at 47 C.F.R. § 1.1202(b), as:

> Any presentation [under § 1.1202(a), a communication directed to the merits or outcome of a proceeding] * * * made to decision-making personnel but, in restricted proceedings, any presentation to or from decision-making personnel * * *.

The rules divide Commission proceedings into three types: (1) those in which there are no *ex parte* restrictions (47 C.F.R. § 1.1204); (2) those proceedings classified as "non-restricted," in which *ex parte* communications may occur, but certain disclosure requirements must be met (47 C.F.R. § 1.1206); and (3) certain proceedings classified as "restricted", wherein all communications with commission staff are generally prohibited (47 C.F.R. § 1.1208).

3.   Bans on *ex parte* contacts are concerned primarily with protecting the integrity of adjudicatory proceedings—ranging from license hearings to civil litigation. *Ex parte* communications are generally accepted as part of a legislative-style process, on the theory that elected representatives have a right, or even a duty, to communicate with constituents and others. The same principles have generally been applied to administrative rulemaking, a legislative-style process, in order to allow a free flow of information.

During the last few decades, however, some lower federal courts have extended *ex parte* prohibitions to at least some rulemaking proceedings. Some cases involved proceedings that were legislative in name but adjudicatory in effect. For example, in Sangamon Valley Television Corp. v. United States, 269 F.2d 221 (D.C.Cir.1959), the court invalidated an FCC rulemaking, which would have reallocated VHF and UHF television channels, because one party had contacted Commission personnel outside of the official comment process. The Commission's decision would have had the practical effect of giving a new VHF frequency to a UHF licensee. The court of appeals held that under these circumstances *ex parte* contacts were improper even in a rulemaking, since it involved "competing private claims to a valuable privilege . . ." 269 F.2d at 223–224. In effect, the court treated the disposition of the frequency as tantamount to an adjudication. (Some of the parties' approaches to commissioners were rather crude—such as sending each one holiday turkeys.) Investigation of Regulatory Comm'ns and Agencies: Hearings Before the Special Subcomm. on Legislative Oversight of the House Comm. on Interstate and Foreign Commerce, 85th Cong., 2d Sess. 3528–29 (pt. 9) (1958) (testimony of Harry Tenenbaum); see 269 F.2d at 224.

The court of appeals seemed to expand the *Sangamon* rationale significantly in Home Box Office, Inc. v. FCC, 567 F.2d 9 (D.C.Cir.1977), cert. denied 434 U.S. 829, 98 S.Ct. 111, 54 L.Ed.2d 89, which involved a challenge to a variety of restrictions on cable systems' use of motion pictures and sporting events. The cable rules were industry-wide and—unlike the channel reallocation in *Sangamon*—did not potentially benefit any identifiable person or entity. The court nevertheless condemned the extensive *ex parte* contacts that occurred during the rulemaking, because they made it impossible for either the public or the reviewing court to evaluate the agency's rationale; the court remanded the record to the FCC to document all *ex parte* approaches so that any impropriety in the decisionmaking process would be exposed. This line of reasoning obviously had implications well beyond *Sangamon's* more limited assimilation of only some kinds of rulemaking to adjudication.

Only months after the *Home Box Office* decision, the court of appeals rejected a challenge, based upon the alleged taint of *ex parte* contacts, to the FCC's decision not to adopt proposed rules for children's television. Action for Children's Television v. FCC, 564 F.2d 458 (D.C.Cir.1977). The court noted that the case did not involve "competing private claims to a valuable privilege," and emphasized the need for input in rulemaking proceedings. See, e.g., M. Ornoff, *Ex parte Communication in Informal Rulemaking: Judicial Intervention in Administrative Procedures*, 15 U.Rich.L.Rev. 73 (1980); G. Robinson, *The Federal Communications Commission: An Essay on Regulatory Watchdogs*, 64 Va.L.Rev. 169, 227–30 (1978).

ii. Invalidation of WHDH's License.

WHDH did not acquire any long-term rights in its license. In 1969, a bare majority of the Commission voted to deny WHDH's application for a full-term license. The denial led to an immediate appeal, as well as to further legislative, administrative, and judicial actions. In Greater Boston Television Corp. v. FCC, 444 F.2d 841, 143 U.S. App. D.C. 383, certiorari denied 403 U.S. 923, 91 S. Ct. 2229, 29 L. Ed.2d 701 (1971), the court attempted to make it clear that *WHDH* was a unique case because of the past questionable practices; that message may not have gotten through to the broadcasting establishment.

1. Hearing Examiner's Decision

On August 10, 1966, Hearing Examiner Herbert Sharfman issued an exhaustive Initial Decision, in favor of granting the renewal by WHDH. He concluded that the taint of Mr. Choate's activities had passed with his death * * *.

* * *

The Examiner conceded that the position of WHDH was weak in regard to the integration criterion (participation in station management by owners), and that both BBI and Charles River were proposed by a distinguished and indeed "star-studded" group of civically active residents, offering strong claims on the score of area familiarity. The Examiner acknowledged that both BBI and Charles River proposed a diversity of excellent programs, though he offset this by noting that in the case of program proposals a new applicant enjoys a "literary advantage" over an existing operator. He further noted that the abbreviated nature of the WHDH tenure conferred by the Commission made it clear that WHDH was not entitled to a competitive advantage merely because it is a renewing station. Yet the Examiner concluded that it would be a sterile exercise to decide this case on the basis of the traditional methods of comparison of new applicants. In his view the dominant factor on balance was that the proven past record of good performance is a more reliable index of future operations in the public interest than mere promises of new applicants, which have no means of validation except as the criteria may be helpful in predicting ability to comply with proposals. The WHDH operating record was considered favorable on the whole, notwithstanding its unwillingness to grasp the nettle of some local problems. As to diversification, the Examiner concluded that while the concentration of ownership of a Boston newspaper and other broadcast facilities would probably have ruled out the WHDH application if this were an all-initial license case, in this case the preference for WHDH on past record was not materially affected.* * * *

On January 22, 1969, the Commissioner reversed the Hearing Examiner's decision, and entered an order denying the application of WHDH and granting that of BBI. 16 F.C.C.2d 1. Its Decision reviewed the comparative merits of the applications.

* * *

3.   The Commission's Action on Reconsideration

* * *

Reaction to the Commission's decision was swift. One distinguished commentator characterized it as a "spasmodic lurch toward 'the left'."[4] The television industry began organizing its forces to seek legislative reversal of what seemed to be a Commission policy * * * that placed all license holders on equal footing with new applicants every time their three-year [now five year] licenses came up for renewal. On May 19, 1969, the Commission adopted a separate Memorandum Opinion and Order on the petitions of all parties for a rehearing. 17 F.C.C.2d 856.

* * *

The Commission added a closing paragraph to clarify that this was not an ordinary renewal case since "unique events and procedures * * * place WHDH in a substantially different posture from the conventional applicant for renewal of broadcast license." The FCC noted that WHDH's operation, although conducted some 12 years, has been for the most part under temporary authorizations. It did not receive a license to operate a TV station until September 1962, and then for only 4 months, because of the Commission's concern with the "inroads made by WHDH upon the rules governing fair and orderly adjudication." And in the renewal proceeding the FCC expressly ordered that new applications

---

* The fourth applicant, Greater Boston Television Corp. (II), was disqualified for failing to surmount two preliminary (non-comparative) questions: it had not made an independent evaluation of the community's program needs, nor had it been able to secure its proposed antenna site. [Ed.]

4. Jaffe, *WHDH: The FCC and Broadcasting License Renewals*, 82 Harv.L.Rev. 1693, 1700 (1969).

could be filed for a specified 2–month period, which was done and a proceeding held thereon.

* * *

If the case were before us solely on the Decision adopted by the Commission on January 22, 1969—susceptible of the construction that the 1965 Policy Statement was applicable to all renewal proceedings—we would be presented with a different question. While the "forfeiture" terminology invoked by WHDH may be more of a conclusion than a reason, and while this statute does not reflect the same concern for "security of certificate" that appears in other laws, there would be a question whether the Commission had unlawfully interfered with legitimate renewal expectancies implicit in the structure of the Act. In addition, a question would arise whether administrative discretion to deny renewal expectancies, which must exist under any standard, must not be reasonably confined by ground rules and standards—a contention that may have increased significance if First Amendment problems are presented on renewal application by a newspaper affiliate, including the possibility that TV proceedings may come to involve overview of newspaper operations. * * *

* * *

The Commission's 1970 Policy Statement carries a proviso, * * * indicating that it is inapplicable to "those unusual cases, generally involving court remands, in which the renewal applicant, for sui generis reasons, is to be treated as a new applicant." (p. 144) In such cases the applicant's record will be examined, but subject to the comparative analysis called for by the 1965 Policy Statement.

We think the distinction drawn by the Commission, in both this case and the 1970 statement, providing for special consideration of certain renewal applicants, as in remand cases, as if they were new applicants, to be reasonable both generally and in its application to the case before us.

* * * The Commission stayed within the range of sound discretion when it adopted, as successive remedial measures, voiding the original grant to WHDH (though not void ab initio); remanding for a comparative reevaluation of the original applicants; confining the grant given to WHDH as the better of the original applicants to a mere 4—month operating license; providing for a reopening period of two months, in order to permit a comparative evaluation with new applicants proposing to serve the public interest.

While the precise nature of the forthcoming comparative evaluation was not spelled out in detail, WHDH certainly has no basis for suggesting it had an assurance of being treated by the same criteria as those generally accorded to renewal applicants.

* * *

There being no impediment in the content or shape of the record due to lack of fair notice, certainly we cannot say the Commission was unreasonable when in the last analysis it used the tainted overtures of WHDH as a reason for fresh consideration of all applicants, without any special advantage to WHDH by virtue of its operation under lawful but temporary authority. This is what the law seeks to ensure whenever selection of a contender must be made after a hearing, although one of the applicants has been given temporary authority, either without a hearing at all because of emergency, or after a proceeding subject to a defect. * * *

In between these extremes are possibilities like a comparative hearing with a demerit assigned to WHDH; that was done by the Commission in its Decision of September 25, 1962, which, however, left the Commission with the conviction that while it would still make a grant to WHDH, a customary 3–year grant was not in the public interest.

The Commission's action in exposing WHDH to another public hearing with new applicants, a hearing scheduled soon after the date of its order, is a disadvantage from the viewpoint of WHDH, but we cannot say it was contrary to the public interest. After this court's remand, to take account of Choate's death, the Commission set a course that retained its order for a hearing with new applicants, but avoided a specific demerit for WHDH in that comparative consideration. This was preferable to an approach wherein a demerit would be inserted into the comparison with new applicants, preferable both for WHDH and, it would seem, for the public interest.[38] WHDH insists, however, on an approach which would give it all the rights and expectancies of an ordinary renewal applicant. In the ordinary case such expectancies are provided in order to promote security of tenure and to induce efforts and investments, furthering the public interest, that may not be devoted by a licensee without reasonable security. This position does not fairly characterize the situation of a licensee which, by virtue of its officer's impropriety, has been given only temporary operating authority of one kind or another (including the 4–month license). This was the conclusion of both the Hearing Examiner and the Commission * * * and we think it within the range of reasonable discretion.

The determination that in certain cases a renewal application must be conducted on the basis of a new comparative consideration is not necessarily a "punishment" for wrongdoing. The same result may follow even where the ineptitude and errors of the Commission may be more to blame than the licensee for the state of affairs precipitating that result. The central consideration is that there is a special class of cases where this method of reaching the optimum decision in the public interest may

---

38. When an applicant is required to bear a demerit assigned for non-comparative reasons, the public may wind up being denied the services of a superior broadcaster. Where that demerit is not necessary for deterrent reasons, it would seem counter-productive. As to the final comparative hearing the blend of deterrence and public interest in selecting the broadcaster was accomplished by requiring WHDH to face a de novo comparative hearing, but without a continuing demerit.

be fairly invoked without undercutting whatever expectancies may attach in general to licensees seeking renewal.

The Commission's action in pitting WHDH against its rivals for fresh comparative consideration is not negatived by its * * * 1962 issuance, * * * of a 4–month license rather than some other kind of temporary operating authority * * *. The 4–month license did not operate to make WHDH a conventional applicant for renewal, and that is the core of its position in this court.

The Commission did not try, as WHDH suggests, to erase the operating record and experience of WHDH and its principals. In effect what it did was to hold WHDH to a higher comparative standard than that required of renewal applicants generally in order to be able to invoke a past record as a reason for rejecting the promise of better public service by new applicants. The Hearing Examiner considered that a good record of past performance was a more reliable indicator of public service than glowing promise. The Examiner was not as impressed as the Commission by the reliability of criteria as indicators validating the likelihood of performance. Also, he does not seem to have taken into account the problem that his approach provided in effect a "built-in-lead" from actual operation, although he disclaimed any right of WHDH to a privileged position as an applicant for renewal. The Commission, on the other hand, was more concerned with keeping the parties as close as possible to a new application situation, without undue advantage acquired from the physical fact of operation under a temporary authorization.

We think the course adopted by the Commission cannot be considered as arbitrary or unreasonable, or as in violation of legislative mandate. * * * On the unique facts presented, WHDH was neither a new applicant nor a renewal applicant as those terms are generally construed. Since these orthodox classifications, and the rules generally pertaining to each, were not meaningfully available to the Commission on these facts, that body soundly formulated an intermediate position for the instant case. There was no error.

* * *

Affirmed.

Notes and Questions

1. To say that *WHDH* shocked the broadcast industry would be an understatement. Broadcasters read the court decision as putting any incumbent's license in jeopardy, if an applicant could make a credible claim to offer better service. Was this a realistic appraisal of the court's opinion? If it was not, might there be any political benefit in exaggerating the effect of the decision? Note the court's own description of the reaction to the Commission's decision:

While the Commission's decision was on appeal to this court, the legislative pressure continued to build. A bill, introduced by Senator Pastore, Chairman of the Communications Subcommittee of the Senate

Commerce Committee, proposed to require a two hearing procedure, wherein the issue of renewal would be determined prior to and to the exclusion of the evaluation of new applications. On January 15, 1970, the Commission issued a new Policy Statement, which, while retaining the single hearing approach, provided that the renewal issue would be determined first, in a proceeding in which new applicants would be able to appear to the extent of calling attention to the license holder's failings. Only upon a refusal to renew would full comparative hearings be held.

The Policy Statement set forth that a licensee with a record of "solid substantial service" to the community, without serious deficiencies, would be entitled to renewal notwithstanding promise of superior performance by a new applicant. This was said to provide predictability and stability of broadcast operations, yet to retain the competitive spur since broadcasters will wish to ensure that their service is so "substantial" as to avoid the need for comparative proceedings.

The Commission expressly stated that its policy statement "is inapplicable, however, to those unusual cases, generally involving court remands, in which the renewal applicant, for sui generis reasons, is to be treated as a new applicant." In such case the license holder cannot obviate the comparative analysis called for by the established Policy Statement (1965). 444 F.2d at 849–50.

Note that the 1970 Policy Statement was adopted almost intact by Section 204 of the Telecommunications Act of 1996 (pp. ___).

2.   On what basis did the Commission and the court distinguish *WHDH* from cases subject to the *1970 Policy Statement?* Does the distinction remove from the case the "question whether the Commission had unlawfully interfered with legitimate renewal expectancies implicit in the structure of the Act?" (p. 213) Is it clear that such expectancies are implicit in the structure of an Act that is explicitly (e.g., § 309(h)) to the contrary?

3.   Did the court of appeals in fact recognize the existence of some type of "renewal expectancy" for broadcasters? See also *Central Florida Enterprises v. FCC*, (p. 152). Did it seem to contemplate some type of presumption in favor of the incumbent? What is the relevance here of its emphasis on the fact that WHDH's only license was the four-month short-term grant?

4.   Are you persuaded that the 1962 grant of a 4–month license was "not necessarily a punishment for wrongdoing" by WHDH? What does the court view it as? Why does it discuss the policy and possibility of deterrence? Cf. B. Cole & M. Oettinger, Reluctant Regulators 213 (1978): "Designating a license renewal for hearing is considered by both key [FCC] staff people and most commissioners almost as drastic as taking a license away." Presumably, then, setting a license down for a second *comparative* hearing, which is inherently more expensive and more threatening, is a still more "drastic" measure.

Excursus

Innocente brings an action for libel in which his prior reputation is a major determinant of the damage award. Reasonably fearing a nominal award of six cents, he attempts to bribe the judge. After conviction for the attempted subornation, Innocente is sentenced as follows: he is to spend four months on probation, after which there will be a probation revocation proceeding to determine whether he should remain at large or be executed. The issue in that proceeding will be whether "the public interest" is better served by his demise.

Is the analogy to *WHDH* sound? Are the (present) values of one's life, of one's liberty, and of one's property equally a function of the security of tenure one enjoys from the state?

iii.   *Congressional Reaction and Judicial Intervention.*

The *1970 Policy Statement* seemed to serve as a sop to most broadcasters, but it met with a rather negative reaction from the Circuit Court of Appeals for the D.C. Circuit, which invalidated it on statutory grounds. Citizens Communications Center v. FCC, 447 F.2d 1201, 145 U.S.App.D.C. 32 (D.C.Cir.1971).

J.   SKELLY WRIGHT, CIRCUIT JUDGE:

* * * [P]etitioners in these consolidated cases challenge the legality of the "Policy Statement on Comparative Hearings Involving Regular Renewal Applicants," * * * and by its terms made applicable to pending proceedings. Briefly stated, the disputed Commission policy is that in a hearing between an incumbent applying for renewal of his radio or television license and a mutually exclusive applicant, the incumbent shall obtain a controlling preference by demonstrating substantial past performance without serious deficiencies. Thus if the incumbent prevails on the threshold issue of the substantiality of his past record, all other applications are to be dismissed without a hearing on their own merits.

* * * Without reaching petitioners' other grounds for complaint, we hold that the 1970 Policy Statement violates the Federal Communications Act of 1934, as interpreted by both the Supreme Court and this court.

* * *

III

Superimposed full length over the preceding historical analysis of the "full hearing" requirement of Section 309(e) of the Communications Act is the towering shadow of *Ashbacker, supra,* and its progeny, perhaps the most important series of cases in American administrative law. * * * Although *Ashbacker* involved two original applications, no one has seriously suggested that its principle does not apply to renewal proceedings as well. This court's opinions have uniformly so held, as have decisions of the Commission itself.

It is not surprising, therefore, that the Commission's 1970 Policy Statement implicitly accepts *Ashbacker* as applicable to renewal proceedings. To circumvent the *Ashbacker* strictures, however, it adds a twist: the Policy Statement would limit the "comparative" hearing to a single issue—whether the incumbent licensee had rendered "substantial" past performance without serious deficiencies.[32] * * * Challenging applicants would thus receive no hearing at all on their own applications, contrary to the express provision of Section 309(e) which requires a "full hearing."

* * *

The Policy Statement purports to strike a balance between the need for "predictability and stability" and the need for a competitive spur. It does so by providing that the qualifications of challengers, no matter how superior they may be, may not be considered unless the incumbent's past performance is found not to have been "substantially attuned" to the needs and interests of the community. Unfortunately, instead of stability the Policy Statement has produced *rigor mortis*. For over a year now, since the Policy Statement substantially limited a challenger's right to a full comparative hearing on the merits of his own application, not a single renewal challenge has been filed.

Petitioners have come to this court to protest a Commission policy which violates the clear intent of the Communications Act that the award of a broadcasting license should be a "public trust." * * * Our decision today restores healthy competition by repudiating a Commission policy which is unreasonably weighted in favor of the licensees it is meant to regulate, to the great detriment of the listening and viewing public.

Wherefore it is ORDERED: that the Policy Statement, being contrary to law, shall not be applied by the Commission in any pending or future comparative renewal hearings * * *.

[The concurring opinion of Judge MacKinnon is omitted.]

Questions and a Note on Legislation

1. Has the court devised an approach truly consistent with *Ashbacker?* Would it be sensible to do so?

2. What must and what can the FCC do in comparative renewal hearings after the *Citizens* case? Must it apply the *1965 Policy Statement* even if its validity still was clear? Can even the superior performance of an incumbent be considered in the analytic framework of that policy? If so, could the FCC solve its problem by making prior broadcast experience a minimum qualification for applicants? If it cannot do that, can it give it a preference, or even "merit" toward a preference, without betraying *Ashbacker?*

3. The court referred to but did not need to reach the petitioners' first amendment argument(s) against the *1970 Policy Statement*. What would the argument(s) be? Whose free speech interests could be invoked: the petitioners'? the incumbent broadcasters'? the public's?

---

32. "such as rigged quizzes, violations of the Fairness Doctrine, overcommercialization, broadcast of lotteries, violation of racial discrimination rules or fraudulent practices as to advertising." [Footnote relocated but unchanged.]

Congress: The Other Player

The Pastore bill, S. 2004, 91st Cong., 1st Sess. (1969), was co-sponsored by 22 Senators; the House version had 118 sponsors. But, according to the court in *Citizens:*

> [T]he bill was bitterly attacked in the Senate hearings by a number of citizens groups testifying, *inter alia,* that the bill was racist, that it would exclude minorities from access to media ownership in most large communities, and that it was inimical to community efforts at improving television programming.
>
> The impact of such citizen opposition measurably slowed the progress of S. 2004. Then, without any formal rule making proceedings, the Commission suddenly issued its own January 15, 1970 Policy Statement and the Senate bill was thereafter deferred in favor of the Commission's "compromise."
>
> Indeed, Senator Pastore, then Chairman of the Subcommittee on Communications, in announcing that the subcommittee would take no further action until the Policy Statement had a fair test, said, "It's a step in the right direction. All I ever wanted to do right along was to make sure that a good licensee had a reasonable chance to stay in business, without harassment. The FCC policy * * * will have a salutary effect. It will discourage those engaged in piracy."

From this sequence of events, isn't it fairly clear that the Congress had acted, without legislating but through an exercise of its oversight power, to approve—indeed to induce—the *1970 Policy Statement?* Wasn't the 1970 policy—that is, a congressional policy incorporated informally into the Act— therefore incapable of being set aside by a court on the ground of repugnance to the statute itself? The courts acknowledge the congressional approval implicit in long administrative practice known to but left undisturbed by Congress; even greater weight may be accorded if the statute was amended in other respects but the disputed practice allowed to continue. Why not acknowledge the obvious congressional, or at least committee, imprimatur here? Doesn't failure to do so deprive the broadcasting industry of the benefit of its bargain, as described rather explicitly by Commissioner Johnson?

In any event, it only took the Congress 25 years to overrule *Citizens* and adopt the *Policy Statement* almost word for word in the 1996 Telecommunications Act (p. 213)

c.   *The Search for Manageable Standards*

In the wake of the unsuccessful *1970 Policy Statement* and *Citizens,* the Commission and the court of appeals continued their ping-pong diplomacy approach towards quantifying the renewal expectancy. One of the primary vehicles for this process was the *Central Florida* litigation, which involved a competing application for the license of WESH–TV, owned by Cowles Broadcasting, Inc.

In 1969, Cowles filed for renewal of WESH–TV's license. Central Florida Enterprises, Inc. filed a competing application, alleging various improprieties on Cowles' part. On review, the court of appeals described the allegations as follows.

a.   The Main Studio Move

Commission rules require that "[t]he main studio of a television broadcast station shall be located in the principal community to be served." WESH–TV's city of assignment is Daytona Beach, and the station had always had a studio just outside the city * * *. In addition, WESH–TV maintained "auxiliary" studios in Winter Park, just outside Orlando. Since 1960, the station had been authorized to identify as a Daytona Beach–Orlando station, although the Commission stressed that Daytona remained the city of assignment and "principal city." * * *

* * *

b.   Mail Fraud

Cowles is a wholly owned subsidiary of Cowles Communications, Inc. (CCI). During the license period, CCI also published Look Magazine and owned five other subsidiaries, each in the business of obtaining magazine subscriptions. The five subsidiaries conducted so-called "paid during service" (PDS) operations in which subscribers paid installments of the purchase price over the life of the subscription.

After a few years, complaints arose of improper sales and collection practices by the PDS companies. * * * In 1970, after being informed that the Justice Department intended to investigate the entire PDS industry, CCI initiated negotiations which resulted in *nolo contendere* pleas by the five PDS subsidiaries to fifty counts of mail fraud, and a consent decree against the five companies, guaranteed by CCI, enjoining specific sales and collection practices.

Central Florida Enterprises, Inc. v. FCC, 598 F.2d 37, 45 (D.C.Cir. 1978).

In addition, Central Florida claimed that it should receive credit on two criteria under the *1965 Policy Statement*. It claimed superiority on diversification, since it had no other media outlets, while CCI had several other radio and television stations as well as stock interests in The New York Times Company and other newspapers. Central Florida also claimed a preference for integration of ownership and management.

The Commission adopted the Administrative Law Judge's findings that the studio move had been innocent and that little wrongdoing should be attributed from CCI's other subsidiaries to Cowles Broadcasting. On the diversification issue, the Commission found that Central Florida was clearly superior, but concluded that Cowles was entitled to a renewal expectancy because its service was "superior." The court of appeals reversed and remanded, on the ground that the Commission had failed to give a reasoned basis for its finding of the renewal expectancy. The court noted that:

In a comparative inquiry evidence of past performance is ordinarily relevant only insofar as it predicts whether future performance will be better or worse than that of competing applicants. The Commission nowhere articulated how Cowles' unexceptional, if solid, past performance supported a finding that its future service would be better than Central's. In fact, as we have noted, *Central prevailed on each of the questions supposedly predicting which applicant would better perform*—the same criteria the Commission uses for this purpose in nonrenewal comparative hearings. * * * [Emphasis in original.]

In light of this we leave to conjecture what leap of faith would be required to find that Cowles prevailed in the overall inquiry. On remand, the Commission will have to reconsider its manner of deriving a preference under the best practicable service criterion, and if appropriate, how such a preference should be balanced against other factors in the more general public interest inquiry. * * * 598 F.2d at 55.

On remand, the Commission once again found for Cowles, and Central Florida again appealed. Central Florida Enterprises, Inc. v. FCC, 683 F.2d 503, 221 U.S.App.D.C. 162 (D.C.Cir.1982).

WILKEY, CIRCUIT JUDGE:

* * * On remand, while the FCC has again concluded that the license should be renewed, it has also assuaged our concerns that its analysis was too cursory and has adopted a new policy for comparative renewal proceedings which meets the criteria we set out in *Central Florida I*. Accordingly, and with certain caveats, we affirm the Commission's decision.

* * *

On remand the Commission has followed our directives and corrected, point by point, the inadequate investigation and analysis of the four factors cutting against Cowles' requested renewal. The Commission concluded that, indeed, three of the four merited an advantage for Central Florida, and on only one (the mail fraud issue) did it conclude that nothing needed to be added on the scale to Central's plan or removed from Cowles'. We cannot fault the Commission's actions here.

We are left, then, with evaluating the way in which the FCC weighed Cowles' main studio move violation and Central's superior diversification and integration, on the one hand, against Cowles' substantial record of performance on the other. This is the most difficult and important issue in this case, for the new weighing process which the FCC has adopted will presumably be employed in its renewal proceedings elsewhere. * * *

* * *

We believe that the formulation by the FCC in its latest decision, however, is a permissible way to incorporate some renewal expectancy while still undertaking the required comparative hearing. The new policy, as we understand it, is simply this: renewal expectancy is to be a factor weighed with all the other factors, and the better the past record, the greater the renewal expectancy "weight." [Emphasis deleted.]

In our view [states the FCC], the strength of the expectancy depends on the merit of the past record. Where, as in this case, the incumbent rendered substantial but not superior service, the "expectancy" takes the form of a comparative preference weighed against [the] other factors. . . . An incumbent performing in a superior manner would receive an even stronger preference. An incumbent rendering minimal service would receive no preference.

* * *

If a stricter standard is desired by Congress, it must enact it. We cannot: the new standard is within the statute.

The reasons given by the Commission for factoring in some degree of renewal expectancy are rooted in a concern that failure to do so would hurt broadcast *consumers*.

* * *

We are relying, then, on the FCC's commitment that renewal expectancy will be factored in for the benefit of the public, not for incumbent broadcasters. In subsequent cases we must judge the faithfulness of the FCC to that commitment, for, as the Supreme Court has said, "It is the right of the viewers and listeners, not the right of the broadcasters, which is paramount." * * *

There is a danger, of course, that the FCC's new approach could still degenerate into precisely the sort of irrebuttable presumption in favor of renewal that we have warned against. But this did not happen in the case before us today, and our reading of the Commission's decision gives us hope that if the FCC applies the standard in the same way in future cases, it will not happen in them either. The standard is new, however, and much will depend on how the Commission applies it and fleshes it out. Of particular importance will be the definition and level of service it assigns to "substantial"—and whether that definition is ever found to be "opaque to judicial review," "wholly unintelligible," or based purely on "administrative 'feel.'"

In this case, however, the Commission was painstaking and explicit in its balancing. The Commission discussed in quite specific terms, for instance, the items it found impressive in Cowles' past record. It stressed and listed numerous programs demonstrating Cowles' "local community orientation" and "responsive[ness] to community needs," discussed the percentage of Cowles' programming devoted to news, public affairs, and local topics, and said it was "impressed by [Cowles'] reputation in the community. * * * Moreover, the record shows no complaints. . . ." The Commission concluded that "Cowles' record [was] more than minimal," was in fact " 'substantial,' *i.e.,* 'sound, favorable and substantially above a level of mediocre service which might just minimally warrant renewal.' "

The Commission's inquiry in this case did not end with Cowles' record, but continued with a particularized analysis of what factors weighed against Cowles' record, and how much. The FCC investigated fully the mail fraud issue.[29] It discussed the integration and diversification disadvantages of Cowles and conceded that Central had an edge on these issues—"slight" for integration, "clear" for diversification. But it reasoned that "structural factors such as [these]—of primary importance in a new license proceeding—should have lesser weight compared with the preference arising from substantial past service."

Finally, with respect to the illegal main studio move, the FCC found that "licensee misconduct" in general "may provide a more meaningful basis for preferring an untested challenger over a proven incumbent." The Commission found, however, that here the "comparative significance of the violation" was diminished by the underlying facts * * *.

* * *

Having listed the relevant factors and assigned them weights, the Commission concluded that Cowles' license should be renewed. * * *

We are somewhat reassured by a recent FCC decision granting, for the first time since at least 1961, on comparative grounds the application of the challenger for a radio station license and denying the renewal application of the incumbent licensee.[38] In that decision the Commission found that the incumbent deserved no renewal expectancy for his past program record and that his application was inferior to the challenger's on comparative grounds. Indeed, it was the incumbent's preferences on the diversification and integration

---

29. The Commission concluded on the mail fraud issue that the subsidiaries involved in the mail fraud and Cowles "are linked only by their . . . relationship with" their common parent.

The broadcast facilities were not used to promote mail fraud and there was no integration of operating personnel between the [subsidiaries involved in mail fraud] and broadcast subsidiaries. Consequently, we adhere to our conclusion that the activities of the [former] *do not portend Cowles' likely future performance* as a broadcast licensee. Therefore, neither disqualification nor a comparative demerit is warranted.

The Commission also found that there was no basis to conclude that the principal common officers of Cowles and the implicated subsidiaries participated in or encouraged any misconduct, and that the mail fraud inquiry had not been curtailed in any significant way—two other reservations we had in *Central Florida I.* We think the Commission's findings here are adequately supported.

38. *In re Applications of Simon Geller and Grandbanke Corp.,* FCC Docket Nos. 21104–05 (Released 15 June 1982). We intimate no view at this time, of course, on the soundness of the Commission's decision there; we cite it only as demonstrating that the Commission's new approach may prove to be more than a paper tiger.

factors which were overcome (there, by the challenger's superior programming proposals and longer broadcast week). The Commission found that the incumbent's "inadequate [past performance] reflects poorly on the likelihood of future service in the public interest." Further, it found that the incumbent had no "legitimate renewal expectancy" because his past performance was neither "meritorious" nor "substantial."

We have, however, an important caveat. In the Commission's weighing of factors the scale mid-mark must be neither the factors themselves, nor the interests of the broadcasting industry, nor some other secondary and artificial construct, but rather the intent of Congress, which is to say the interests of the listening public. All other doctrine is merely a means to this end, and it should not become more. * * *

* * *

We hope that the standard now embraced by the FCC will result in the protection of the public, not just incumbent licensees. And in today's case we believe the FCC's application of the new standard was not inconsistent with the Commission's mandate. Accordingly the Commission's decision is

Affirmed.

Notes and Questions.

1. What was the Commission's second and new opinion based upon? Were there any new facts? Did the FCC reopen the record and hold any new hearings? If not, what is the basis for the Commission's "particularized analysis"?

2. If one were a betting person, presumably one might add up the odds—in terms of the respective merits and demerits—as follows:

Issue	Cowles	Central
studio move	minor demerit	—
mail fraud	minor demerit	—
diversification	clear demerit	clear advantage
integration	slight demerit	slight advantage

Although it is impossible to assign any type of even quasi-mathematical weight to each of these characterizations, it seems fair to conclude that Cowles has at least two arguable law violations against it, and is subject to a "clear" demerit on diversification and a "slight" demerit on integration— the two areas assigned primary importance by the *Policy Statement*. Even forgetting about the impact of the violations, therefore, Cowles would seem to be less favored than Central. Moreover, Cowles has no claim to a "renewal expectancy" based upon superior prior performance. Nevertheless, the Commission holds—and the court affirms—that incumbency is enough to offset a clear and a slight demerit.

What does the result suggest about the significance of even a weak renewal expectancy? Could even an incumbent's mediocre past performance defeat a challenger's identifiable advantages on the two most significant comparative factors? If this is the case, would Cowles's renewal expectancy have overridden even "clear" advantages for Central on both diversification and integration? And if this is the case, would "superior" past performance defeat virtually any showing by a challenger?

3. Is it surprising that competing applications on renewal have become an endangered species in the last decade? And now are virtually prohibited by the 1996 Telecommunications Act? (p. 213)

4. Although only indirectly at issue in *Central Florida,* one of the few sure ways to lose a license is to misrepresent facts to the Commission. Not surprisingly, the agency takes an exceedingly dim view of licensees who lie to it. (One may question, of course, whether a licensee's misrepresentation is more important than its service to the public.) As with the somewhat related issue of character, the FCC's standards lack a certain amount of precision. As one commentator has noted:

> The "harder" cases involve some—although not always a great deal of—ambiguity. It is here that the FCC would be expected to develop a thoughtful approach to intent—to work out factors to be considered in each case, or to suggest inferences to be drawn in situations lacking conclusive documentary evidence. But the FCC's decisions drift on a sea of subjectivity; ambiguity becomes exculpatory. In many of these "harder cases," the Commission adopts one of at least four modes of analysis. Useful labels for these modes are: (a) psychoanalytic; (b) literalist; (c) "administrative feel"; and (d) "human frailty." Each enables the decision-maker to avoid the imposition of the ultimate sanction.

Murchison, *Misrepresentation and the FCC,* 37 Fed.Comm.L.J. 403, 419–420 (1985).

Note: Of Time and the Comparative Renewal The RKO Litigation

As is probably already evident from the *WHDH* and *Cowles* cases, comparative hearings do not lend themselves to speedy resolutions. *WHDH* lasted almost two decades from beginning to end, *Cowles* more than one decade. One reason is that comparative hearings involve complex and often intangible issues, which are subject to litigation at three administrative and two judicial levels.

Another and perhaps more cynical explanation may lie in the economics of administrative litigation. If an incumbent receives supracompetitive profits, it has both the incentive and the ability to fight to preserve them. To the extent that the incumbent's profits minus attorneys' fees exceed the return that the incumbent would otherwise receive from an alternative investment of the proceeds it would get from selling the station, it makes economic sense to continue to litigate. Whether a lawyer has a duty to caution against, or even to abandon what he or she views as dilatory litigation is not commonly addressed.

The *RKO* litigation—also more than two decades in length—is a prime example of the problem of delay. In 1965, RKO, a subsidiary of General Tire and Rubber, applied for renewal of its license for KHJ–TV, Channel 9, Los Angeles. Fidelity Television, Inc. filed a timely competing application. The

Commission designated a comparative hearing. In 1969, the Hearing Examiner (now known as an administrative law judge) granted Fidelity's application and denied RKO's. RKO General, Inc. (KHJ–TV), 44 FCC 2d 149 (Init.Dec.1969).

While RKO was appealing this decision to the full Commission, competing applicants challenged RKO's license renewal for WNAC–TV, Channel 7, Boston. RKO General, Inc. (WNAC–TV), 20 FCC 2d 846 (1969). In the Boston proceeding, the Commission designated for hearing issues as to anticompetitive practices by RKO and its parent company, General Tire. General Tire allegedly had conditioned its purchases of products upon a seller's agreement to purchase advertising time on RKO stations. RKO General, Inc. (WNAC–TV), 78 FCC 2d 1, 38–47 (1980). The Los Angeles hearing had touched on those reciprocal trade dealings, but not as broadly as the subsequent Boston proceeding. The Broadcast Bureau therefore asked the Commission to reopen the Los Angeles hearing for consideration of new evidence being developed in Boston, and of an additional issue as to some RKO witnesses' candor in the Los Angeles hearing on the alleged reciprocity.

Instead of reopening the Los Angeles proceeding, the Commission made Fidelity a party to the Boston case. RKO General, Inc. (KHJ–TV), 31 FCC 2d 70, 74 (1971). The Commission reasoned that this procedure would protect Fidelity's right to adduce new evidence as to RKO's fitness, if the Commission reversed the Hearing Examiner's decision in favor of Fidelity. If the Commission affirmed the Hearing Examiner's decision, however, any evidence against RKO in Boston would be immaterial to the Los Angeles proceeding.

After some prodding by the court of appeals, see Fidelity Television, Inc. v. FCC, 502 F.2d 443, 446–447 (D.C.Cir.1974), in late 1973 the FCC finally decided RKO's Los Angeles appeal. RKO General, Inc. (KHJ–TV), 44 FCC 2d 123 (1973). Reversing the Hearing Examiner's conclusion in favor of Fidelity, the Commission held that RKO's license should have been renewed on the basis of the hearing record. Relying heavily once again on the renewal expectancy, the Commission held 3–2 that RKO and Fidelity were equal, noting that "credit must be given in a comparative renewal proceeding, when the applicants are otherwise equal, for the value to the public in the continuation of the existing service." Id. at 137. Recognizing that further character evidence against RKO might arise in the Boston proceeding, however, the Commission left open the possibility that Fidelity ultimately might be entitled to the Los Angeles license. The Commission ordered that "the application of Fidelity ... is deemed to be denied, subject to whatever action may be deemed appropriate following resolution of the matters in the Boston proceeding." Id. at 138.

The Commission moved to dismiss Fidelity's appeal from this order on the ground that the order was merely preliminary, since it had not denied Fidelity's application within the meaning of 47 U.S.C. § 402(b)(1). In Fidelity Television, Inc. v. FCC, 502 F.2d 443 (D.C.Cir.1974), the court of appeals disagreed, holding that the challenged order was immediately reviewable. The court reasoned that the FCC had approved RKO's renewal application subject to possible change only upon termination of the Boston proceeding. Id. at 448–53. When the court later reviewed the order on the merits, it held that the FCC "did not commit reversible error" in renewing RKO's license and denying Fidelity's application for a construction permit. Fidelity Television, Inc. v. FCC, 515 F.2d 684, 702 (D.C.Cir.1975), cert. denied 423 U.S. 926, 96 S.Ct. 271, 46 L.Ed.2d 253. The court noted, however, that its affirmance was "conditional (as was the Commission's decision) on the ultimate outcome of the Boston proceedings." Id. at 703 n. 45.

At this point in the *RKO* saga, a full decade had passed since Fidelity had first filed its competing application. In this time, only the Los Angeles case had proceeded to a final determination on the merits. Yet the litigation was just beginning in earnest.

Shortly after the court's decision in the Los Angeles case, new questions as to RKO's fitness arose in the Boston proceeding. The Securities and Exchange Commission alleged that a variety of undisclosed domestic and overseas actions by RKO's parent, General Tire, violated the securities laws. The SEC proceeding resulted in a consent decree on May 10, 1976, requiring General Tire to undergo an operational review by five non-management directors, culminating in a special report. This July 1, 1977 report documented wide-ranging corporate misconduct. The report concluded that deficient recordkeeping and accounting practices had caused inaccuracies in RKO's financial disclosures to the Commission. In 1978, before the FCC could act upon the report, RKO and the two competing Boston applicants proposed a settlement, whereby RKO would assign its license to a new entity composed of the two other applicants.

This proposed settlement was contingent upon the FCC's finding that RKO qualified to be a broadcast licensee. This development made participation in the Boston proceeding crucial for Fidelity and for Multi–State Communications, Inc., an applicant competing for RKO's New York City license, and thus unattractive to RKO and the two Boston applicants. The FCC ultimately allowed Fidelity and Multi–State to participate on all issues as to RKO's fitness as a broadcast licensee. RKO General, Inc. (WNAC–TV), 78 FCC 2d 1, 24 (1980).

On the merits, the Commission found RKO unfit to be a licensee of the Boston television station. 78 FCC 2d 1 (1980). The Commission based its finding on three independent grounds: (1) reciprocal trade practices; (2) inaccurate financial reports; and (3) lack of candor in the Boston proceeding. In a companion decision, the FCC held that these three factors also disqualified RKO as a licensee of Channel 9 in Los Angeles. The Commission thereupon ordered further pleadings on whether to grant Fidelity's application, since it was the only other applicant. RKO General, Inc. (KHJ–TV), 78 FCC 2d 355 (1980). See also RKO General Inc., (WOR–TV), 78 FCC 2d 357 (1980) (disqualifying RKO, on basis of the above three factors, as licensee of the New York television station).

On review the court of appeals rejected two of the three disqualifying factors. RKO General, Inc. v. FCC, 670 F.2d 215 (D.C.Cir.1981), cert. denied 456 U.S. 927, 102 S.Ct. 1974, 72 L.Ed.2d 442 (1982). The court held that the record did not support the findings as to the reciprocal conduct or the financial misrepresentations. The court upheld the Commission's reliance upon RKO's lack of candor during the Boston proceeding as a basis for disqualifying RKO, but stressed that RKO's lack of candor in the Boston proceeding could not automatically justify denial of its Los Angeles or New

York City licenses. Instead, the court directed further proceedings with respect to those two licenses, in order to give RKO an opportunity to demonstrate that its performance in Los Angeles and New York City merited different treatment. RKO was ultimately able to keep its New York City license, through special legislation granting an automatic five-year license to any New York station relocating to New Jersey. Multi–State Communications, Inc. v. FCC, 728 F.2d 1519 (D.C.Cir.1984).

Meanwhile, in 1980 two companies had petitioned to intervene in the Los Angeles proceeding, after the Commission attempted to disqualify RKO as a Los Angeles licensee. The Commission denied these requests. RKO General, Inc. (KHJ–TV), 94 FCC 2d 879, 54 R.R.2d 53 (1983), affirmed Multi–State Communications, Inc. v. FCC, 728 F.2d 1519, 234 U.S.App.D.C. 285 (D.C.Cir.1984).

A few months after the court of appeals had affirmed the Commission's Boston decision, the FCC awarded WNAC–TV's license to NETV Inc., a company formed by the two groups that had challenged RKO's license. NETV began operating the station as WNEV–TV in May, 1982.

In response to another court decision, the FCC lifted its moratorium on competing applications for RKO's remaining stations. The licenses attracted scores of competing applicants, spawning nine comparative hearings.

With the *WNAC–TV* and *WOR–TV* cases resolved, Administrative Law Judge Edward J. Kuhlmann took up the case of KHJ–TV in June of 1983, and conducted a comprehensive hearing into RKO's basic qualifications to be a licensee. This proceeding was separate from the multiple comparative hearings before other administrative law judges. Judge Kuhlman was first to decide RKO's basic qualifications, after which the comparative cases would proceed.

The parties to the *KHJ–TV* case tried to preempt the FCC proceeding with a settlement agreement in November 1985. Group W Broadcasting, not a party to the case, agreed to pay RKO $212 million and Fidelity $98 million to acquire the station. This deal eventually fell through, however, because of delay. In 1987, Disney agreed to pay $217 million to RKO and $103 million to Fidelity, which the Commission approved. RKO General, Inc. (KHJ–TV), 3 FCC Rcd 5057 (1988).

In 1986, the FCC proposed that RKO work out a comprehensive settlement with the 69 remaining applicants for its 13 other stations. It also put a temporary freeze on the comparative hearings.

In order to help move things along, the Commission took the novel step of appointing the Chief of the Mass Media Bureau [formerly Broadcast Bureau] as a mediator. RKO was unable to reach a comprehensive settlement, however, by the FCC's deadline of January 31, 1987. Only one station sale actually resulted from the mediation—WHBQ(AM), Memphis, a perennial money loser. Broadcasting, February 9, 1987, at 22. Nonetheless, the FCC continued to encourage settlements. After the attempt at a comprehensive settlement failed, the FCC reactivated the comparative renewal proceedings.

In the meantime, RKO's corporate parent, Gencorp (formerly General Tire), decided to get out of the broadcasting business, and began to sell its fourteen television and radio stations. By the summer of 1987, in addition to the Disney purchase of KHJ–TV Los Angeles for $320 million, WOR–TV New York–Secaucus and WHBQ–TV Memphis had been sold to MCA for $387 million and $50 million respectively. Eleven additional AM and FM radio stations with an estimated total worth of over $225 million were yet to be sold, and were the subject of the Bureau Chief's further unsuccessful attempt at mediation of these settlement agreements. *Broadcasting*, August 17, 1989, at 35.

In an August 1987 decision, Judge Kuhlmann found RKO unfit to hold broadcast licenses and denied the renewal applications for all of its 14 stations. Judge Kuhlmann found that RKO had filed false and misleading financial reports and that its radio networks had billed advertisers fraudulently. After all this sound and fury, the Commission ultimately turned to an *ad hoc* position, approving sales of RKO stations on an individual basis. Indeed, it employed precisely this approach in allowing the sale of KHJ–TV to Disney. RKO General, Inc. (KHJ–TV), 3 FCC Rcd 5057 (1988). Despite years of litigation and mediation, the FCC allowed RKO to make individual sales at "distress" but still profitable prices. In the end, RKO was able to sell all of its properties except the Boston television station.

The remarkable two-decade *RKO* saga raises fundamental questions about the procedural as well as the substantive aspects of comparative hearings. Is the delay inherent? Is it deliberately manufactured by an incumbent? And what is the proper role of counsel for the incumbent, other parties, and the Commission?

One unique sidelight to the *RKO* imbroglio was the almost successful intervention of the Commission on an informal level as a mediator. Is this role preferable to the traditional, formal adjudicatory approach? Can the same agency deal effectively with both mediation and litigation? Even in the same case? Does an unsuccessful attempt at mediation—regardless of any effort to prevent communication between the mediators and the litigators on the staff—compromise the Commission in a later adjudication?

Note: Congress Steps in on Renewal Expectancies

As noted at the beginning, most of the foregoing discussion as to renewal—rather than initial—applications now is history. Nevertheless, it is significant in terms of explaining how the FCC deals with complex licensing issues.

In the end, the Congress stepped in and took the whole renewal license issue out of both the Commission's and the courts' hands. Although only a relatively small part of the Telecommunications Act of 1996—which dealt broadly with entry of cable into telephone and the reverse—Section 204 of the Act provided that:

SEC. 204. BROADCAST LICENSE RENEWAL PROCEDURES.

(a) Renewal Procedures.—

(1) Amendment.—Section 309 (47 U.S.C. 309) is amended by adding at the end thereof the following new subsection:

"(k) Broadcast Station Renewal Procedures.—

"(1) Standards for renewal.—If the licensee of a broadcast station submits an application to the Commission for renewal of such license, the Commission shall grant the application if it finds, with respect to that station, during the preceding term of its license—

"(A) the station has served the public interest, convenience, and necessity;

"(B) there have been no serious violations by the licensee of this Act or the rules and regulations of the Commission; and

"(C) there have been no other violations by the licensee of this Act or the rules and regulations of the Commission which, taken together, would constitute a pattern of abuse.

"(2) Consequence of failure to meet standard.—If any licensee of a broadcast station fails to meet the requirements of this subsection, the Commission may deny the application for renewal in accordance with paragraph (3), or grant such application on terms and conditions as are appropriate, including renewal for a term less than the maximum otherwise permitted.

"(3) Standards for denial.—If the Commission determines, after notice and opportunity for a hearing as provided in subsection (e), that a licensee has failed to meet the requirements specified in paragraph (1) and that no mitigating factors justify the imposition of lesser sanctions, the Commission shall—

"(A) issue an order denying the renewal application filed by such licensee under section 308; and

"(B) only thereafter accept and consider such applications for a construction permit as may be filed under section 308 specifying the channel or broadcasting facilities of the former licensee.

"(4) Competitor consideration prohibited .-In making the determinations specified in paragraph (1) or (2), the Commission shall not consider whether the public interest, convenience, and necessity might be served by the grant of a license to a person other than the renewal applicant.".

* * *

More than fifty years after the initial *Ashbacker* decision, the Congress thus imposed a renewal expectancy. The irony of the situation may be that no one ever really doubted the existence of the expectancy—but rather that nobody felt it had sufficient competence to adopt it as a matter of law.

To what extent is Section 204 similar to the 1970 Policy Statement which was invalidated in *Citizens Communications Center*? Aside from the fact that Section 204 has a statutory basis, is there really any distinction in terms of policy? Under the statute is there still such a thing as a comparative renewal proceeding? If a challenger must knock out the incumbent first, isn't any later procedure an *initial* comparative hearing? Also, does a challenger get any credit for deposing the incumbent? If not, why would it do so?

Given the requirement for petitioners to deny to win an "inverse summary judgment" (p. 172), does the new statutory language really make that much of a difference? Would you expect to see substantially fewer competing applications in the future? Or does Section 204 pretty much express the reality of competing applications today?

And how does this apply to petitions to deny?

2. THE PETITION TO DENY

a. *Economic Competition*

Although a competing application and a petition to deny may be functionally the same today, they reflect different histories and ideologies. Unlike a competing application, a petition to deny claims not that the moving party is better qualified than the incumbent licensee, but rather than the incumbent does not deserve the grant or renewal of a license. As will be seen, the grounds for petitions to deny vary dramatically, from economic injury to employment discrimination to inadequate programming.

Since most broadcasting and other over-the-air licenses were initially granted many years ago, the petition to deny is usually directed at an existing licensee's renewal application. (This is not always the case, of course, since the Commission periodically authorizes new services, such as direct broadcast satellites, or expands the number of frequencies within an existing band. For example, in 1983 the FCC created almost a thousand new relatively low-powered FM radio stations in a proceeding known as "Docket 80–90." *Report and Order*, 94 FCC 2d 152 (1983)).

As usual, the Communications Act is vague as to the requirements for a petition to deny. Section 309(d)(1), states merely that:

> Any party in interest may file with the Commission a petition to deny any application * * *. * * * The petition shall contain specific allegations of fact sufficient to show that the petitioner is a party in interest and that a grant of the application would be prima facie inconsistent with [the public interest]. Such allegations of fact shall, except for those of which official notice may be taken, be supported by affidavit of a person or persons with personal knowledge thereof.
> * * *

Although the Communications Act apparently contemplated petitions to deny from the very beginning, very few were actually filed. Failure to use this procedure may have stemmed largely from an initial uncertainty regarding the definition of a "party in interest."*

In broader terms, the concept of standing to sue was particularly unclear in the administrative context. Indeed, the development of doctrines relating to standing before the FCC was instrumental in developing general notions of standing in administrative law.

---

* The requirements for standing before the Commission are less clear than those for standing in court. In the *United Church of Christ* case, (p. 166), the court of appeals seems to indicate that the tests are identical. But this does not necessarily follow, since the Commission is an Article I entity and the court an Article III tribunal.

Until the 1960's, audience-based organizations simply did not exist. If listeners and viewers could not or did not assert their objections to licensees' activities, who else would? Perhaps because of the lack of any other "audience participation," in FCC v. Sanders Brothers Radio Station, 309 U.S. 470, 60 S.Ct. 693, 84 L.Ed. 869 (1940), the Supreme Court held that competitors of a new station had standing to file a petition to deny.

January 20, 1936, the Telegraph Herald, a newspaper published in Dubuque, Iowa, filed with the petitioner [FCC] an application for a construction permit to erect a broadcasting station in that city. May 14, 1936, the respondent, who had for some years held a broadcasting license for, and had operated, Station WKBB at East Dubuque, Illinois, directly across the Mississippi River from Dubuque, Iowa, applied for a permit to move its transmitter and studios to the last named city and to install its station there. August 18, 1936, respondent asked leave to intervene in the Telegraph Herald proceeding, alleging in its petition, inter alia, that there was an insufficiency of advertising revenue to support an additional station in Dubuque and insufficient talent to furnish programs for an additional station; that adequate service was being rendered to the community by Station WKBB and there was no need for any additional radio outlet in Dubuque and that the granting of the Telegraph Herald application would not serve the public interest, convenience, and necessity. Intervention was permitted and both applications were set for consolidated hearing.

The respondent and the Telegraph Herald offered evidence in support of their respective applications. The respondent's proof showed that its station had operated at a loss; that the area proposed to be served by the Telegraph Herald was substantially the same as that served by the respondent and that, of the advertisers relied on to support the Telegraph Herald station, more than half had used the respondent's station for advertising. * * *

[The Commission held that since no electrical interference would necessarily result from the two stations' operations, and since both stations were financially and technically capable of operating, both applications should be granted.]

First. We hold that resulting economic injury to a rival station is not in and of itself, and apart from considerations of public convenience, interest, or necessity, an element the petitioner must weigh and as to which it must make findings in passing on an application for a broadcasting license. * * *

Plainly it is not the purpose of the Act to protect a licensee against competition but to protect the public. * * *

This is not to say that the question of competition between a proposed station and one operating under an existing license is to be entirely disregarded by the Commission, and, indeed, the Commission's practice shows that it does not disregard that question. It may have a vital and important bearing upon the ability of the applicant adequately to serve his public; it may indicate that both stations— the existing and the proposed—will go under, with the result that a portion of the listening public will be left without adequate service; it may indicate that, by a division of the field, both stations will be compelled to render inadequate service. These matters, however, are distinct from the consideration that, if a license be granted, competition between the licensee and any other existing station may cause economic loss to the latter. * * *

We conclude that economic injury to an existing station is not a separate and independent element to be taken into consideration by the Commission in determining whether it shall grant or withhold a license.

Second. It does not follow that, because the licensee of a station cannot resist the grant of a license to another, on the ground that the resulting competition may work economic injury to him, he has no standing to appeal from an order of the Commission granting the application. * * *

The petitioner insists that as economic injury to the respondent was not a proper issue before the Commission it is impossible that [the statute] was intended to give the respondent standing to appeal, since absence of right implies absence of remedy. This view would deprive subsection (2) of any substantial effect.

Congress had some purpose in enacting section 402(b)(2). It may have been of opinion that one likely to be financially injured by the issue of a license would be the only person having a sufficient interest to bring to the attention of the appellate court errors of law in the action of the Commission in granting the license. It is within the power of Congress to confer such standing to prosecute an appeal.

We hold, therefore, that the respondent had the requisite standing to appeal and to raise, in the court below, any relevant question of law in respect of the order of the Commission. * * *

[The Court also rejected arguments that the evidence before the Commission was improper and that the FCC had erred in not disclosing some filings by KFBB speedily enough.] 309 U.S. at 471–77, 60 S.Ct. at 695–98.

At first blush, *Sanders Brothers* seems to create an internal inconsistency: it holds that economic harm from a new station is not a ground for denying a license, but then allows the very same competitive injury as the basis for the injured competitor's standing. The resolution of the apparent conflict, of course, is that the incumbent licensee may challenge the potential competitor only upon non-economic, public interest grounds. For example, it is not at all uncommon for an incumbent licensee to petition to deny a new entrant on the ground that the latter's programming or employment practices are inadequate.

Why did the Court allow a licensee to challenge a new station on grounds having nothing to do with the licensee? As the Court hints, the answer is simply that in 1940 there were no other parties with enough of an "interest" to go through a long and complex litigation. Public interest groups did not exist, and the whole notion of the "private attorney general" was unheard of. Schneyer, *An Overview of Public Interest Law Activity in the Communications Field*, 1977 Wis.L.Rev. 619. Although the Court obviously knew that an incumbent licensee's motives would be selfish, the need for some representation of the public interest apparently outweighed the need that it be selfless.

It is important to understand the potential for delay created by the petition to deny. Incumbent broadcasters have an incentive to delay—even if they cannot prevent—competitive new entry. As brought out in our discussion of competing applications, if the value of delayed competition is greater than the legal fees involved, filing a petition to deny makes eminently sound economic sense.

The Court in *Sanders Brothers* acknowledges that the FCC would be properly concerned if competitive entry would cause both stations to fail or to operate at substandard levels. Why the concern? Is this result any more or less likely to occur in broadcasting than in other industries, such as retailing? Should entry into that field be similarly restricted then? Compare Meeks, *Economic Entry Controls in FCC Licensing: the Carroll Case Reappraised,* 52 Iowa L.Rev. 236 (1966) with Note, Economic Injury in FCC Licensing: The Public Interest Ignored, 67 Yale L.J. 135, 141–145 (1957).

Moreover, shouldn't competition lead to better, rather than to worse service? Monopoly, not competition, is usually thought to harm consumers. Are broadcasters just perverse in this respect? Along these lines, consider this comment from Comanor & Mitchell, *The Costs of Planning: The FCC and Cable Television*, 15 J.L. & Econ. 177, 178–179 (1972) (emphasis in original):

> A dominant feature of *planning by regulation* is that the regulatory authorities have only limited power for their task. While they can require that certain actions be taken, they generally have no funds at their command to subsidize or pay for desired results. What they can do is to protect the monopoly position of the firm in certain markets, precisely so that these funds can be used to subsidize projects—desired by the regulators—which are not self-sustaining. What they can provide is the protection required for internal subsidization. [emphasis on original.]

The *Sanders Brothers* Court's casual dictum about the relationship between economic impact and the public interest was largely ignored, until Carroll Broadcasting Co. v. FCC, 258 F.2d 440 (D.C.Cir.1958). In that case, Carroll filed a petition to deny West Georgia Broadcasting Company's application for an AM station in Bremen, Georgia—twelve miles away from Carroll's station in Carrollton, Georgia. The towns had populations of 2,300 and 8,600 respectively, in an area with an almost exclusively agrarian economy. The Commission refused to designate an economic impact issue under *Sanders Brothers,* and Carroll appealed. The court gave *Sanders Brothers* its first—and perhaps only—expansive reading.

On this issue the Commission held that "Congress had determined that free competition shall prevail in the broadcast industry" and that "The Communications Act does not confer upon the Commission the power to consider the effect of legal competition except perhaps" in Section 307(b) cases. Hence, said the Commission, "it is unnecessary for us to make findings or reach conclusions on this issue." Moreover, the Commission said, pursuant to other decisions by it, as a matter of policy "the possible effects of competition will be disregarded in passing upon applications for new broadcast stations."

* * *

Thus, it seems to us, the question whether a station makes $5,000, or $10,000, or $50,000 is a matter in which the public has no interest so long as service is not adversely affected; service may well be improved by competition. But, if the situation in a given area is such that available revenue will not support good service in more than one station, the public interest may well be in the licensing of one rather than two stations. To license two stations where there is revenue for only one may result in no good service at all. So economic injury to an existing station, while not in and of itself a matter of moment, becomes important when on the facts it spells diminution or destruction of service. At that point the element of injury ceases to be a matter of purely private concern.

* * *

So in the present case the Commission had the power to determine whether the economic effect of a second license in this area would be to damage or destroy service to an extent inconsistent with the public interest. Whether the problem actually exists depends upon the facts, and we have no findings upon the point.

This opinion is not to be construed or applied as a mandate to the Commission to hear and decide the economic effects of every new license grant. It has no such meaning. We hold that, when an existing licensee offers to prove that the economic effect of another station would be detrimental to the public interest, the Commission should afford an opportunity for presentation of such proof and, if the evidence is substantial, i.e., if the protestant does not fail entirely to meet his burden, should make a finding or findings.

* * *

The Commission says it lacks the "tools"—meaning specifications of authority from the Congress—with which to make the computations, valuations, schedules, etc., required in public utility regulation. We think no such elaborate equipment is necessary for the task here. As we have just said, we think it is not incumbent upon the Commission to evaluate the probable economic results of every license grant. * * *

The Commission clearly was not enthusiastic about having to undertake the type of economic analysis contemplated by the court—even on the relatively unsophisticated level suggested. The FCC's concerns are easy to understand. For example, assume that an incumbent makes the following presentation to the agency:

a) Present Annual Advertising Income		$1,000,000
b) Present Expenses		$ 900,000
Debt service	$200,000	
Salaries	$300,000	
Heat, light, rent	$100,000	
Program rights	$100,000	
General & Administrative	$200,000	

The incumbent would appear to have made a prima facie showing the market will support only one station at even a moderate profit level. (Well-run radio stations in major markets commonly return net revenues of 20 to 30 percent of gross.) But other considerations may be relevant. What if the debt service reflects a loan from the owner's minor children, at ten points above the prime rate? Or if salaries consist of $75,000 apiece for the General Manager and her husband, with the remaining $50,000 constituting payments to local students at the minimum wage? And what exactly *is* "general and administrative?"

Moreover, there is the problem of estimating the *potential* advertising market in the area. It is obviously difficult to predict how many additional advertising dollars may lurk in a market—let alone how many advertisers would be attracted to a new station's format. It is not surprising, therefore, that the Commission resisted making the *Carroll* type of inquiry—or that the parties in *Carroll* quickly settled after the remand.

Despite these conceptual and practical problems, litigants continued to raise *Carroll* or related issues on a regular basis. For example, in WLVA, Inc. (WLVA–TV), Lynchburg, Va. v. FCC, 459 F.2d 1286 (D.C.Cir.1972), the court upheld the FCC's refusal to consider WLVA's opposition to an application to increase power by an affiliate of the same network in a nearby community. The court upheld the Commission's finding that WLVA's projections of lost network compensation and national advertising sales revenues were too speculative to support a *Carroll* hearing, and that it had failed to make any showing of diminished public service programming.

Although *Carroll's* practical impact has been relatively minor,* it has the conceptual breadth to affect a wide variety of situations. Perhaps

---

* Interestingly enough, some other federal regulatory agencies applied *Carroll*-like principles with gusto to regulated industries. See, e.g., Delta Air Lines v. CAB, 228

most intriguing is whether *Carroll* could apply to *intermedia* as well as *intramedia* competition. For example, could a cable operator petition to deny grant of a license to an MMDS ("wireless cable") operator, on the ground that it would provide direct competition to the cable operator for both basic and pay services? Could a terrestrial broadcaster oppose authorization of a DBS facility?

In National Association of Broadcasters v. FCC, 740 F.2d 1190 (D.C.Cir.1984), (p. 57), the NAB challenged the Commission's promulgation of DBS rules and grant of a DBS license to STC, a subsidiary of COMSAT. The court rejected the application of *Carroll* to intermedia competition.

> * * * The *Carroll* doctrine and its subsequent codification at 47 U.S.C. § 309 were never intended for a situation such as the one presented here. * * * The purpose of a *Carroll* hearing is to allow the FCC to make a focused inquiry into the validity in a particular case of the general presumption that competition furthers the public interest.
>
> That very purpose, however, has already been satisfied in this case. Before granting STC's license application, the FCC in the DBS proceedings engaged in extended rulemaking in which a central issue was whether DBS service, in light of its potential impact on local broadcasting, was in the public's net interest. The *DBS Order* concluded that, for the country as a whole, DBS competition was in the public interest * * *. * * * Thus, a *Carroll* hearing under these circumstances would force the agency to redecide in an evidentiary hearing the very question it has already resolved through informal rulemaking. It was never the aim of *Carroll* to force such duplicative hearings. * * *

Only if there were convincing reasons to expect that the conclusions of the *DBS Order* were inapplicable to the particular region of the country for which a DBS license was sought would there be any basis for considering whether a *Carroll* hearing was needed; we are hard pressed to imagine how such a situation could arise * * *. * * *

Although the *NAB* decision rested upon the particular circumstance that the FCC had determined generically that DBS would not have an impact on local broadcasting contrary to the public interest, economic impact seems to be increasingly irrelevant in licensing decisions—as only makes sense in a pro-competitive, deregulatory era. It may remain highly important as a means of creating standing, however, particularly if, as seems to be the case, public interest groups are decreasingly taking advantage of the standing discussed in the next subsection.

F.2d 17 (D.C.Cir.1955). And while the FCC was edging away from *Carroll,* the Australian Broadcasting Tribunal was adopting it!

b. *Standing of Listeners and Viewers*

Because standing was initially based upon economic injury, individual viewers and citizens groups had little or no hand in the renewal process—no "audience participation," as then-Judge Burger later would term it. The point was not so much that masses of aggrieved citizens wanted to strip local stations of their licenses. Although a petition to deny a license renewal ultimately can lead to that result, its more significant use is to give local citizens groups some leverage in dealing with their local broadcast stations. If nothing else, defending a petition to deny can be extremely costly and time-consuming for a licensee; the filing or threat of a petition is thus an effective means of getting a station owner's attention. Whether this is a desirable process is open to debate, of course, as suggested by the following exchange from the *Proceedings of the Mass Communications Law Section*, Association of American Law Schools (1977).

Charles Firestone, Director, Communications Law Program, UCLA Law School:

> Of course, the movement started out as a civil rights movement and groups were generally started by people who wanted more programming for blacks—which evolved into more for women or for a particular ethnic group. In this area usually the groups want three things: (1) access to more programming that is relevant to them, seeing themselves on the screen so they and others can relate to it more; (2) more employment for their ethnic group or sex; and (3) more and more commonly they want ownership of the media. * * *

> * * * There are two different situations in which to use the petition to deny. In one, you really are trying to get a station's license taken away; this is really the only way you are going to get it. In the other, you want to make your point and the broadcaster refused to listen unless you go for the jugular—which is the license, the pocketbook. Sometimes just by bringing a case and putting pressure on a station, the group's goals are achieved.

> This was the reason that the petition to deny was used in the very beginning. It then became a little bit counterproductive; the petition to deny was often very hard for a group to use, since they had to get the substantiation; and for various other reasons it was just too much.

Erwin G. Krasnow, General Counsel, National Association of Broadcasters:

> Broadcasters are, of course, very concerned about the tactics of citizens groups. Some observers look at the statistics—the relatively low number of stations that are designated for hearing—and claim that broadcasters are over-reacting. Licensees of broadcast stations don't look at it in such a related way. * * * They worry that a valuable investment may be dissipated away in legal fees and protracted hearings or—God forbid—by losing their license (broad-

casters call it the "death penalty". * * * Virtually all broadcasters will associate the phrase "petition to deny" with the word "aggravation." * * *

Then there are these phony citizen groups. * * * They frequently call themselves a coalition, and they say that x number of organizations belong to the coalition. * * * What really upsets broadcasters and their counsel is a group that claims to be a coalition and names the groups—and the groups don't even know that a petition has been filed. * * *

It is especially difficult to deal with attempts at extortion. And it happens. I was involved in a case where we reported the incident to the FCC. A Chicano group met with the General Manager of KWGN–TV, Denver, and after a few margaritas the head of the Chicano group said, "We'll withdraw the petition to deny and all of our charges about programming and unemployment if you give us $15,000," to which my client initially responded, "Do you want that in a check or in cash?" * * * I have had experience with other instances of attempted extortion. One woman, who filed a petition to deny, said to the general manager: "If you'll make me program manager of your station, God will bless station XYZ." .

A 1966 case opened this Pandora's box by articulating the position, probably implicit in *Sanders Brothers,* that listeners have standing.

OFFICE OF COMMUNICATION OF UNITED CHURCH OF CHRIST v. FCC

United States Court of Appeals, District of Columbia Circuit, 1966.
359 F.2d 994, 123 U.S.App.D.C. 328.

BURGER, CIRCUIT JUDGE:

This is an appeal from a decision of the Federal Communications Commission granting to the Intervenor a one-year renewal of its license to operate television station WLBT in Jackson, Mississippi. Appellants filed with the Commission a timely petition to intervene to present evidence and arguments opposing the renewal application. The Commission dismissed Appellants' petition and, without a hearing, took the unusual step of granting a restricted and conditional renewal of the license. Instead of granting the usual three-year renewal, it limited the license to one year from June 1, 1965, and imposed what it characterizes here as "strict conditions" on WLBT's operations in that one-year probationary period.

The questions presented are (a) whether Appellants, or any of them, have standing before the Federal Communications Commission as parties in interest under Section 309(d) of the Federal Communications Act to contest the renewal of a broadcast license; and (b) whether the Commission was required by Section 309(e) to conduct an evidentiary hearing on the claims of the Appellants prior to acting on renewal of the license.

Because the question whether representatives of the listening public have standing to intervene in a license renewal proceeding is one of first impression, we have given particularly close attention to the background of these issues and to the Commission's reasons for denying standing to Appellants.

BACKGROUND

The complaints against Intervenor embrace charges of discrimination on racial and religious grounds and of excessive commercials. As the Commission's order indicates, the first complaints go back to 1955 when it was claimed that WLBT had deliberately cut off a network program about race relations problems on which the General Counsel of the NAACP was appearing and had flashed on the viewers' screens a "Sorry, Cable Trouble" sign. In 1957 another complaint was made to the Commission that WLBT had presented a program urging the maintenance of racial segregation and had refused requests for time to present the opposing viewpoint. Since then numerous other complaints have been made. * * *

To block license renewal, Appellants filed a petition in the Commission urging denial of WLBT's application and asking to intervene in their own behalf and as representatives of all other television viewers in the State of Mississippi. The petition stated that the Office of Communication of the United Church of Christ is an instrumentality of the United Church of Christ, a national denomination with substantial membership within WLBT's prime service area. It listed Appellants Henry and Smith as individual residents of Mississippi, and asserted that both owned television sets and that one lived within the prime service area of WLBT; both are described as leaders in Mississippi civic and civil rights groups. Dr. Henry is president of the Mississippi NAACP; both have been politically active. Each has had a number of controversies with WLBT over allotment of time to present views in opposition to those expressed by WLBT editorials and programs. Appellant United Church of Christ at Tougaloo is a congregation of the United Church of Christ within WLBT's area.

The petition claimed that WLBT failed to serve the general public because it provided a disproportionate amount of commercials and entertainment and did not give a fair and balanced presentation of controversial issues, especially those concerning Negroes, who comprise almost forty-five per cent of the total population within its prime service area; it also claimed discrimination against local activities of the Catholic Church. * * *

The Commission denied the petition to intervene on the ground that standing is predicated upon the invasion of a legally protected interest or an injury which is direct and substantial and that "petitioners * * * can assert no greater interest or claim of injury than members of the general public." * * * The one-year renewal was on conditions which plainly put WLBT on notice that the renewal was in the nature of a probationary grant * * *

STANDING OF APPELLANTS[8]

The Commission's denial of standing to Appellants was based on the theory that, absent a potential direct, substantial injury or adverse effect from the administrative action under consideration, a petitioner has no standing before the Commission and that the only types of effects sufficient to support standing are economic injury and electrical interference. It asserted its traditional position that members of the listening public do not suffer any injury peculiar to them and that allowing them standing would pose great administrative burdens. * * *

What the Commission apparently fails to see in the present case is that the courts have resolved questions of standing as they arose and have at no time manifested an intent to make economic interest and electrical interference the exclusive grounds for standing. *Sanders,* for instance, granted standing to those economically injured on the theory that such persons might well be the only ones sufficiently interested to contest a Commission action. * * *

The Commission's rigid adherence to a requirement of direct economic injury in the commercial sense operates to give standing to an electronics manufacturer who competes with the owner of a radio-television station only in the sale of appliances, while it denies standing to spokesmen for the listeners, who are most directly concerned with and intimately affected by the performance of a licensee. Since the concept of standing is a practical and functional one designed to insure that only those with a genuine and legitimate interest can participate in a proceeding, we can see no reason to exclude those with such an obvious and acute concern as the listening audience. This much seems essential to insure that the holders of broadcasting licenses be responsive to the needs of the audience, without which the broadcaster could not exist.

There is nothing unusual or novel in granting the consuming public standing to challenge administrative actions [citing cases granting standing to consumers of coal, electricity, and margarine, and to railroad passengers]. * * *

These "consumer" cases were not decided under the Federal Communications Act, but all of them have in common with the case under review the interpretation of language granting standing to persons "affected" or "aggrieved." The Commission fails to suggest how we are to distinguish these cases from those involving standing of broadcast "consumers" to oppose license renewals in the Federal Communications Commission. The total number of potential individual suitors who are consumers of oleomargarine or public transit passengers would seem to be greater than the number of responsible representatives of the listening public who are potential intervenors in a proceeding affecting a

---

8. All parties seem to consider that the same standards are applicable to determining standing before the Commission and standing to appeal a Commission order to this court. See Philco Corp. v. FCC, 103 U.S.App.D.C. 278, 257 F.2d 656 (1958), cert. denied, 358 U.S. 946, 79 S.Ct. 350, 3 L.Ed.2d 352 (1959); Metropolitan Television Co. v. U.S., 95 U.S.App.D.C. 326, 221 F.2d 879 (1955). We have, therefore, used the cases dealing with standing in the two tribunals interchangeably.

single broadcast reception area. Furthermore, assuming we look only to the commercial economic aspects and ignore vital public interest, we cannot believe that the economic stake of the consumers of electricity of public transit riders is more significant than that of listeners who collectively have a huge aggregate investment in receiving equipment.[17]
* * *

Nor does the fact that the Commission itself is directed by Congress to protect the public interest constitute adequate reason to preclude the listening public from assisting in that task. The Commission of course represents and indeed is the prime arbiter of the public interest, but its duties and jurisdiction are vast, and it acknowledges that it cannot begin to monitor or oversee the performance of every one of thousands of licensees. Moreover, the Commission has always viewed its regulatory duties as guided if not limited by our national tradition that public response is the most reliable test of ideas and performance in broadcasting as in most areas of life. * * *

The theory that the Commission can always effectively represent the listener interests in a renewal proceeding without the aid and participation of legitimate listener representatives fulfilling the role of private attorneys general is one of those assumptions we collectively try to work with so long as they are reasonably adequate. When it becomes clear, as it does to us now, that it is no longer a valid assumption which stands up under the realities of actual experience, neither we nor the Commission can continue to rely on it. * * *

The Commission's attitude in this case is ambivalent in the precise sense of that term. While attracted by the potential contribution of widespread public interest and participation in improving the quality of broadcasting, the Commission rejects effective public participation by invoking the oft-expressed fear that a "host of parties" will descend upon it and render its dockets "clogged" and "unworkable." The Commission resolves this ambivalence for itself by contending that in this renewal proceeding the viewpoint of the public was adequately represented since it fully considered the claims presented by Appellants even though denying them standing. It also points to the general procedures for public participation that are already available, such as the filing of complaints with the Commission, the practice of having local hearings, and the ability of people who are not parties in interest to appear at hearings as witnesses. In light of the Commission's procedure in this case and its stated willingness to hear witnesses having complaints, it is difficult to see how a grant of formal standing would pose undue or insoluble problems for the Commission.

We cannot believe that the Congressional mandate of public participation which the Commission says it seeks to fulfill was meant to be

---

17. According to Robert Sarnoff of NBC the total investment in television by American viewers is 40 billion dollars, a figure perhaps twenty times as large as the total investment of broadcasters. FCC, Television Network Program Procurement, H.R.Rep. No. 281, 88th Cong., 1st Sess. 57 (1963). Forty billion dollars would seem to afford at least one substantial brick in a foundation for standing.

limited to writing letters to the Commission, to inspection of records, to the Commission's grace in considering listener claims, or to mere non-participating appearance at hearings. We cannot fail to note that the long history of complaints against WLBT beginning in 1955 had left the Commission virtually unmoved in the subsequent renewal proceedings, and it seems not unlikely that the 1964 renewal application might well have been routinely granted except for the determined and sustained efforts of Appellants at no small expense to themselves. * * *

We recognize the risks * * * [that] regulatory agencies, the Federal Communications Commission in particular, would ill serve the public interest if the courts imposed such heavy burdens on them as to overtax their capacities. * * * In order to safeguard the public interest in broadcasting, therefore, we hold that some "audience participation" must be allowed in license renewal proceedings. We recognize this will create problems for the Commission but it does not necessarily follow that "hosts" of protestors must be granted standing to challenge a renewal application or that the Commission need allow the administrative processes to be obstructed or overwhelmed by captious or purely obstructive protests. The Commission can avoid such results by developing appropriate regulations by statutory rulemaking. * * *

The responsible and representative groups eligible to intervene cannot here be enumerated or categorized specifically; such community organizations as civic associations, professional societies, unions, churches, and educational institutions or associations might well be helpful to the Commission. These groups are found in every community; they usually concern themselves with a wide range of community problems and tend to be representatives of broad as distinguished from narrow interests, public as distinguished from private or commercial interests.

* * *

We are aware that there may be efforts to exploit the enlargement of intervention, including spurious petitions from private interests not concerned with the quality of broadcast programming, since such private interests may sometimes cloak themselves with a semblance of public interest advocates. But this problem, as we have noted, can be dealt with by the Commission under its inherent powers and by rulemaking.

[The court went on to hold that the petitioners had made a sufficient showing to warrant an evidentiary hearing, and remanded the case to the Commission for further proceedings.]

Notes and Questions

1. Following a hearing on remand, the Commission granted WLBT a full three-year renewal, finding that the petitioners had failed to prove their charges against the licensee. Petitioners again appealed, and the court again reversed. Office of Communication of United Church of Christ v. FCC, 425 F.2d 543 (D.C.Cir.1969). The court held that the Commission had improperly

placed the burden of proof on the petitioners and had treated them with "pervasive impatience—if not hostility—which made fair and impartial consideration impossible." Finding that "The administrative conduct reflected in this record is beyond repair," the court declined to remand the case again. Instead, it vacated the grant of the license and directed the Commission to invite applications for the license. The ensuing licensing process lasted for more than a decade.

2.   How could the FCC go about granting standing only to "responsible and representative" groups in a community? Require a bond? Set minimum membership limits, in absolute or per capita terms? In fact, the National Association of Broadcasters petitioned the FCC to require petitioners to deny to disclose the names of all of their members. Any problems with this?

3.   *UCC* gives petitioners the right to file a petition to deny, but not the right to a hearing. As indicated, in order to have a hearing designated, a petitioner must demonstrate that there is a "substantial and material question of fact" as to the licensee's performance. Moreover, a petitioner must do so without the aid of any compulsory process; the normal tools of discovery are available only after a hearing has been designated. This puts a rather severe burden upon a typical petitioner. Indeed, the procedure is almost the opposite of that in a conventional civil lawsuit, in which the complainant has access to compulsory process from the beginning of the proceeding and can use it in an attempt to defeat a motion for summary judgment. In a sense, the Commission has imposed a form of "inverse summary judgment"—that is, the petitioner must prove its case in order to get discovery. The court of appeals has rejected several attempts to force the Commission to provide pre-hearing discovery. E.g., National Black Media Coalition v. FCC, 589 F.2d 578 (D.C.Cir.1978). Does this help explain the relatively small number of hearings designated by the Commission on petitions to deny? For a discussion of the notion of standing as a new media see Frank P. Darr, *Converging Media Technologies and Standing At The Federal Communications Commission*, 7 Harv.J.L. & Tech.I (1993).

4.   *United Church of Christ* may not be quite as broad a grant of standing as it seemed a decade ago. In general, the federal courts have attempted to cut back the scope of standing by requiring a petitioner to show that it suffers direct harm from a governmental action, e.g., an environment group which is unable to use a particular piece of parkland. E.g., Lujan v. Defenders of Wildlife, 504 U.S. 555, 112 S.Ct. 2130, 119 L.Ed.2d 351 (1992).

This in turn has lead courts to narrow somewhat the scope of standing in petitions to deny cases. In many situations, the more modern approach makes little or no difference with broadcasting cases, since the petitioners are local viewers with a tangible and obvious interest—such as the those in *United Church of Christ*. But in some cases, petitioners may not be able to show the requisite harm and causation, as indicated in the *Branton* case below.

BRANTON v. FCC

United States Court of Appeals, District of Columbia, 1993.
993 F.2d 906, cert. denied 511 U.S. 1052, 114 S.Ct. 1610, 128 L.Ed.2d 338 (1994).

Before BUCKLEY, WILLIAMS, and D. H. GINSBURG, CIRCUIT JUDGES.

D.H. GINSBURG, CIRCUIT JUDGE

This is a petition for review of a letter ruling of the Federal Communications Commission refusing to take action against National Public Radio for allegedly broadcasting "obscene, indecent, or profane" language in violation of 18 U.S.C. S 1464. We hold that the petitioner lacks standing under Article III of the Constitution to challenge the FCC's decision.

I. BACKGROUND

In the early evening of February 28, 1989, NPR's news show "All Things Considered" ran a report on the trial of John Gotti, the alleged leader of an organized crime syndicate in New York. The report featured a tape recording of a wiretapped phone conversation between Gotti and an associate. In the 110–word passage that NPR excerpted from the tape recording for broadcast, Gotti used variations of "the f___ word" ten times. He used it to modify virtually every noun and in one instance even a verb ("I'll f___ing kill you"). NPR made no effort, such as substituting bleeps for any or all of these references, to render the passage less offensive to persons of ordinary sensibility.

Peter Branton, who heard the broadcast and was offended, filed a complaint with the Mass Media Bureau of the FCC. The Bureau concluded that the broadcast material in question was "not actionably indecent" and did not provide "the necessary legal basis for further Commission action" pursuant to 18 U.S.C. S 1464. Mr. Branton then wrote to the Commission asking how he could appeal the Bureau's decision. The Commission treated his letter as an Application for Review and, in a brief letter ruling (over one dissent), affirmed the Bureau's decision. The Commission explained that the Gotti tape was part of a "bona fide" news story; indeed, it had been introduced as evidence in the criminal trial that was the subject of that story. The Commission also noted its long-standing reluctance "to intervene in the editorial judgments of broadcast licensees on how best to present serious public affairs programming to their listeners." Letter Ruling, 6 FCC Rcd. 610 (1991).

Mr. Branton now petitions for judicial review of the agency's decision not to proceed against NPR.

* * *

II. ANALYSIS

In order to establish standing under Article III, a complainant must allege (1) a personal injury-in-fact that is (2) "fairly traceable" to the defendant's conduct and (3) redressable by the relief requested. The alleged injury must be "distinct and palpable," not "conjectural" or "hypothetical." Application of these familiar principles leads us to conclude that the petitioner lacks standing to seek review of the FCC no-action letter at issue here.

A.   *Injury-in-fact*

In order to challenge official conduct one must show that one "has sustained or is immediately in danger of sustaining some direct injury" in fact as a result of that conduct. This component of the standing doctrine serves both "to assure that concrete adversariness which sharpens the presentation of issues," and to prevent the federal courts from becoming "continuing monitors of the wisdom and soundness of Executive action...."

The petitioner in this case alleges that he was injured because he was subjected to indecent language over the airwaves. While an offense to one's sensibilities may indeed constitute an injury, see FCC v. Pacifica, a discrete, past injury cannot establish the standing of a complainant, such as Branton, who seeks neither damages nor other relief for that harm, but instead requests the imposition of a sanction in the hope of influencing another's future behavior. * * *

If the petitioner suffers any continuing injury, we suppose it is in the nature of the increased probability that, should the NPR broadcast go unsanctioned, he will be exposed in the future to similar indecencies over the airwaves. Under established Supreme Court precedent, however, this marginal increase in the possibility of a future harm does not meet the "immediacy" requirement for Article III standing.

* * *

[I]n Lujan v. Defenders of Wildlife, 119 L.Ed.2d 351, 112 S.Ct. 2130 (1992), the Court held that an environmental group lacks standing to challenge policies that will allegedly result in the extinction of endangered species if the group can not establish that its members will visit the habitat of those species in the near future. * * *

In the present case, the possibility that the petitioner will again "some day" be exposed to a broadcast indecency lacks the imminence required under * * * Defenders of Wildlife. It is mere conjecture that a radio station will again broadcast, at a time when the petitioner is listening, indecencies that would be proscribed under 18 U.S.C. S 1464 (as he would have us interpret that statute). While there is, of course, some chance that somewhere, at some time, the petitioner may again be exposed to a broadcast indecency as a result of the Commission's decision, that possibility seems to us far too remote and attenuated to establish a case or controversy under Article III.

* * *

UCC is not controlling in the present case for two reasons. First, the appellants in UCC alleged that the licensee in question was engaged in a continuing pattern of inappropriate and discriminatory broadcasting, which the FCC by renewing its license had in effect extended. In contrast, the appellant in the present case challenges an FCC determination regarding an isolated indecency broadcast at a single moment in the past. He does not allege a continuing course of misconduct, and there is simply too little reason to believe that the harm to him will ever recur. A listener who alleges that a broadcaster has repeatedly violated the indecency standard might be in a better position to argue that he is subject to a continuing harm or at least an increased likelihood of the harm recurring.

Second, in the years since UCC, the Supreme Court has repeatedly emphasized the "immediacy" element of the injury-in-fact requirement. See Defenders of Wildlife. Accordingly, UCC must be understood as a creature of the context from which it arose, *viz.* a license renewal proceeding, which is inherently future oriented.

In sum, the petitioner fails to demonstrate that the FCC's decision not to take action against NPR causes him an injury that is sufficiently "immediate" to establish his standing to challenge that decision. The marginal increase in the probability that he will be exposed to indecent language in the future if NPR is not sanctioned is simply too slight to generate a case or controversy proper for resolution by an Article III court.

B.   Causation/Redressability

Even if the harm to the petitioner here were sufficiently immediate to make out an Article III "injury," he would not be able to show that his injury "fairly can be traced to the challenged action" and would be "redressed by a favorable decision." Causation and redressability are separate requirements, as is apparent in a case * * * where the relief requested goes beyond mere cessation of the official conduct being challenged to include additional relief. The two requirements tend to merge, however, in a case such as this where the requested relief consists solely of the reversal or discontinuation of the challenged action.

* * *

In the present case, it is at least equally conjectural whether the FCC's proceeding against the alleged broadcast indecency of February 28, 1989 would cause any radio station(s) in the petitioner's area to broadcast any fewer indecent programs in the future. As in the cases discussed above, any favorable impact of the official action that the complainant seeks to compel depends utterly upon the actions of "third parties not before the court," whose behavior is difficult to predict.

* * *

Without some reason to believe that the level of broadcast indecency is significantly affected by the possibility of incurring an FCC sanction, we lack a sufficient basis for the exercise of the federal judicial power. A court is rightly reluctant to enter a judgment which may have no real consequence, depending upon the putative cost-benefit analyses of third parties over whom it has no jurisdiction and about whom it has almost no information.

III. CONCLUSION

This dispute between the petitioner and the FCC falls outside the constitutional domain of the federal courts. The petitioner fails to establish a justiciable case or controversy because his asserted injury is too attenuated and improbable and because this injury neither resulted from the challenged Government decision nor would be remedied by a reversal of that decision. Accordingly, the petition for review is

Dismissed.

Notes and Questions.

1. The court clearly is attempting to bring the standards for intervention before the Commission more in line with the current administrative law of standing. But has it ever been clear that intervention and standing are the same concept? Indeed, didn't the court in *United Church of Christ* brush over the question of standing for judicial review in a short footnote? Is there a difference between a citizen's independant judicial challenge to an administrative policy—particularly one of taxing or spending, as noted below—and a complaint to an agency about a regulated firm's conduct? Does a petitioner need to show more or less permanent effect to complain to the FCC about the behavior of an entity subject to ongoing licensing and periodic license renewals? Also, the court refers several times to action by the "Executive Branch." Are standing principles of challenge Executive action necessarily relevant to independant regulatory agencies?

2. Even under general administrative law principles, why isn't there "injury in fact" here? Are Mr. Branton's concerns as "speculative" as those in *Defenders of Wildlife*? As the court notes, there the petitioners alleged only that they might visit areas with endangered species in the future. Is it as unlikely as the court suggests that Mr. Branton may be subjected to another offensive National Public Radio broadcast in the future? Is there any showing that Mr. Branton is moving away from the objectionable station's service area? In any event, NPR is a national service; unless Mr. Branton were to leave the country, he thus might run into its obnoxious broadcasts at any point in the future. Indeed, is it more likely than not that NPR will air similar programs in the future? Its past run-ins with Congress on questions of programming judgment indicate that it has a taste for controversial material.

3. If Mr. Branton did not suffer injury in fact from the offensive broadcast, why was there standing in *Pacifica* and similar cases? After all, the complainant in Pacifica was just passing through New York City when he tuned in the George Carlin monologue; unlike NPR, Pacifica is not a national satellite-fed network, but just a small group of commonly owned stations. (p. 510) Under this court's reasoning, shouldn't the Commission have heaved out Pacifica from the start (a result which might have had much to commend itself in terms of the Commission's doctrinal development)?

4. Is it clear that there could be no "damages or other relief" here? Obviously the FCC would not have denied a license renewal based solely on Mr. Branton's complaint. But could it not have taken other action? For example, in *Pacifica*, the Commission merely "associated" a copy of its decision with the licensee's renewal file—a seemingly minor step, but one which the parties thought significant enough to litigate up to the Supreme Court.

5. Or, does the court focus more upon notions of "zone of interests" and "immediacy"? As to the "zone" issue, doesn't petitioner have a fairly straightforward position, since he has a right to expect at least "channeling" of indecent material? As to immediacy, remember *Pacifica*'s emphasis on the "intrusive" nature of broadcasting.

6. Is the court's reliance on taxing and spending cases as to the causation issue appropriate? After all, hasn't the Supreme Court made clear that these are unique situations, because of the discretionary legislative-style nature of taxation, and thus that only a very narrow class of challenges is appropriate? E.g., Flast v. Cohen, 392 U.S. 83, 88 S.Ct. 1942, 20 L.Ed.2d 947 (1968).

7. The court maintains that its standard does not represent a departure from *United Church of Christ*. But is it clear that the Jackson, Mississippi television viewers would have sufficient "injury in fact" under the Branton standard? Would they be able to show that they would be subject to a "continuous pattern" of discriminatory and inadequate service in the future? To be sure, they had monitored WLBT for several years, and had records as to a number of fairness doctrine violations and racist programs. Would Mr. Branton have had a stronger position if he had bided his time and kept a log of NPR programming which he deemed offensive? How many offensive programs would he have had to identified in order to have standing?

Or is the court simply loath to tamper with *UCC*, because of its emotionally charged connection with the civil rights movement? Even if *UCC* no longer is sound law, is there any compelling reason for doing away with it, especially since the anticipated flood of petitions to deny has turned into a trickle? Is this a form of jurisprudential tokenism?

B. ALTERNATIVE SELECTION PROCEDURES

As the foregoing materials indicate, the Commission has had notably little success in rationally conducting the licensing process in general and the comparative hearing in particular. Observers have proposed a variety of means for improving the comparative process. Some focus primarily upon changes in existing procedural or substantive law. For example, Professor Anthony argues strongly in favor of reducing the number of comparative criteria, in order to make them more understandable and workable. (p. 117)

Others favor total abandonment of the comparative process, on the ground that no amount of tinkering will improve it very much. As seen before, Professor Coase's theory of property rights in frequencies contemplates transfer of spectrum by a bidding or auction approach; aside from doing away with a problematic procedure, this approach has the advantage of returning some of the license's value to the government—at least when it is sold the first time. The auction has never had much political appeal, however, at least as to radio and television licenses.

One highly attractive approach has been the lottery, which makes no pretense to reasoned decisionmaking. Unless an applicant is given a preference (as discussed below), its fate is totally random.

Until recently, the lottery was largely a matter of academic discussion. In 1991, however, Congress passed the first in a series of Communications Act amendments, allowing the Commission to use lotteries. Section 309(i) provided:

> If there is more than one application for any initial license or construction permit which will involve any use of the electromagnetic spectrum, then the Commission, after determining that each such application is acceptable for filing, shall have authority to grant such license or permit to a qualified applicant through the use of a system of random selection.

The original statute also required the Commission to give "significant preferences" to people or groups "which are underrepresented in the ownership of telecommunications facilities or properties." Pub.L. No. 97–35, 95 Stat. 357, 736–737 (1981).

The Commission, however, had difficulty in interpreting this language. The establishment of the scheme, the identity of groups eligible for lottery preferences, and the meaning of the term "significant preferences," raised serious obstacles to the Commission's implementation of the lottery procedure authorized in the statute. See Report and Order, 89 F.C.C.2d 257, 279–82 (1982). The Commission thus asked Congress for more specific guidance in order to effectuate the preferences. In 1982, Congress responded with a revised lottery statute; it deleted the scheme for preferences to "underrepresented" groups or individuals. In the amended statute Congress provided for preferences in awarding authorizations for "any media of mass communication" for "applicants, the grant to which . . . would increase the diversification of ownership of the media of mass communications. . . ." Congress also created an additional significant preference for "any applicant controlled by a member or members of a minority group." 47 U.S.C. § 309(i)(3)(A). It defined minority group to include "Blacks, Hispanics, American Indians, Alaskan natives, Asians, and Pacific Islanders." 47 U.S.C. § 309(i)(3)(C)(ii).

In interpreting the new law, the Commission observed that Congress had directed "a narrowly drawn preference scheme" that contained only two kinds of preferences. Considering Congress' language, and its legislative history, the Commission concluded that women were not entitled to preferences under either the media ownership provision or the minority group provision.

Since "includes" is a term of enlargement and not of limitation, the Commission determined that in the context of Section 309, the term referred to people belonging either to "out" groups, or to racial and ethnic minorities. The Commission concluded that women as a class were not enough like any of the enumerated groups to constitute a "minority group," and thus that the statute excluded them from preferences. See Pappas v. FCC, 807 F.2d 1019 (D.C.Cir.1986) (affirming).

The Commission initially used the lottery solely to award non-broadcast licenses (such as MMDS). Because of the high visibility of broadcast licenses, the FCC seemed somewhat reluctant to hand them out by chance. Nevertheless, Congress clearly had authorized the agency to use lotteries for broadcast licenses. Indeed, noting the overwhelming backlog of LPTV license applications, Congress expressly stated its desire that LPTV licensees be chosen by lottery. H.R.Rep No. 765, 97th Cong., 2d Sess. 38–39 (1982), reprinted in 1982 U.S.Code Cong. & Admin. News at 2282–83. The LPTV lottery scheme was implemented in Random Selection Lotteries, Second Report and Order, 93 FCC 2d 952 (1983).

Later on, the Commission took steps toward choosing broadcast licenses by lottery. In a Notice of Proposed Rule Making, 4 FCC Rcd 2256 (1989), the Commission reasoned that lotteries would be superior to the current system for several reasons. First, they would simplify the broadcast licensing process by obviating the need to apply numerous criteria and by sidestepping adjudicatory and hearing procedures. The criteria for consideration of applications would be reduced to the Section 309(i) preferences. And for much the same reasons, decisions would be more objective.

Second, the FCC's experience in using lotteries in licensing for LPTV, cellular radio, MMDS, and the like seemed to show that a lottery speeds the processing of license applications. For example, the lottery had allowed the Commission to process over 23,000 LPTV applications and to grant over 2500 permits since September, 1983. By speeding up the licensing process, service could begin sooner, thus benefiting the public. And at the same time, a lottery would reduce administrative costs for both the Commission and the applicants.

Third, the FCC found no reason to believe that a lottery system would reduce the quality of licensees, based on its experience with other non-comparative license grants—such as assignments, settlements, and LPTV lotteries. The Commission also believed that a lottery system would further the public interest goals of Section 309(i)—minority ownership and diversification of media ownership.

Although LPTV is the only mass medium subject to a lottery, a general mass media lottery procedure exists in 47 C.F.R. §§ 1.1601–1.1604, 1.1621–3. Under that procedure, a lottery determines the "tentative selectee" among mutually exclusive applications prescreened for acceptability. Preferences are given to applicants for minority ownership and diversification of ownership; an applicant with a preference has additional chances to be selected on the basis of its preference.

In LPTV, each applicant receives a set of consecutive numbers (a number block) from a series of numbers. To the extent a preference exists, it is reflected by an adjustment in the size of the number block assigned. A number from the numerical series is then randomly produced and the applicant with the number block containing the winning number becomes the tentative selectee. After the tentative selectee has been chosen, petitions to deny may be filed against it. This procedure has apparently been effective in the LPTV lottery.

One drawback to the lottery procedure is that by stimulating the amount of interest and number of applications, it also increases the number of sham filings. As in other areas of licensing, the value of the authorization encourages entrepreneurs to engage in what might be termed "spectrum speculation." To encourage only legitimate applicants to file, LPTV applications were subject to a "complete and sufficient" standard. The FCC also imposed hefty filing and hearing designation fees.

In order to inhibit speculative applications, the Commission also requires LPTV applicants to provide detailed ownership information designed to identify the real party in interest. Applicants must disclose corporate officers and directors, as well as their ownership interests in the applicant. LPTV applicants must also certify that "no agreement, either explicit or implicit, has been entered into for the purposes of transferring or assigning to another party, any station construction permit or license or interest therein that is awarded as a result of random selection or lottery." 47 C.F.R. § 2133.

Of the variety of alternatives to the comparative proceeding, only the lottery seems to have any appeal to decisionmakers. Although a lottery makes no attempt at reaching a traditionally reasoned decision, it dispenses mass justice in a relatively quick and inexpensive way. And its provisions for minority groups insure that it does more than just perpetuate existing patterns of media ownership. Whether it is superior to other alternatives—such as an auction—is hard to assess, at least until those procedures receive realistic field trials.

Perhaps because the FCC's experience with the lottery-particularly with LPTV—was relatively favorable, the Congress also authorized the agency to allocate frequencies by means of auctions. Although the legislation would have authorized the Commission to put radio and television frequencies up for auction, as with lotteries the Commission declined to do so. Again, political and economic reasons may have made this unattractive.

At the same time, the agency undertook an aggressive campaign to sell licenses for various types of non-media licenses—primarily licenses for personal communications services (PCS), paging, and wireless computer as well as other links. The Commission held a number for auctions for different types of applications, and as of 1996 had received more than $10 billion dollars. (From the FCC's point of view, this had little or no immediate effect, since the revenues went directly to the Treasury.)

At first, this seemed like a "win-win" situation. Politicians were enamoured of the auctions' ability to help reduce the deficit and plug budgetaay holdes—particularly in what seemed to be a relatively painless way, at least for the federal government. Coasian advocates saw auctions as an ultimate vindication of Chicago School economics.

By the late 1990's, however, the auctions had begun to show only mixed success, for several reasons—most of the attributable to the FCC's structure of the sales.

First, the Commission required a rather hefty down payment—usually ten percent of the total purchase price—from winning bidders. In sales of large frequency blocks—e.g., 20–30 Mhz—in major urban areas, this often amounted to more than a hundred million dollars. Moreover, additional payments for the rest of the purchase price were due over a ten-year period.

At the same time, the agency required the new licensees to "build out" fairly large portions of their systems within the first few years of operation. Many buyers saw this as virtually doubling the cost of entering PCS or other businesses, by imposing first the auction fee and then the normal cost of starting up a new and untried business. Their complaints naturally were a bit self-serving, since they naturally had been aware of both the payment and build-out requirements before they entered the auction.

Minority groups also did not fare well with the auction. They lacked the billion-dollar warchests to buy and then build major market PCS operations. Although the Commission had planned for this to some extent by setting aside frequencies in most major markets for minority entrepreneurs, it eventually retreated from this after the *Adarand* decision. (p. 120) Moreover, minority groups generally were unable to raise sufficient capital for even relatively limited services. For example, the Commission auctioned off one-half Mhz frequencies in the Interactive Video Distribution Service ("IVDS")—a band suitable for limited PCS operations and paging. More than two-thirds of the licenses were sold to minority enterprises. But virtually all of them ultimately defaulted or sold their licenses to non-minority companies, because they lacked the working capital to launch their systems.

As the above suggests, the core of the problem with the auction may have been that the bidders' expectations as to potential profits simply were too high. Much of the responsibility for this naturally falls on the bidders. At the same time, however, the Commission may have encouraged a land rush, without taking into account the real costs for the bidders—and particularly the minority bidders.

Although the FCC was stung by the results of this first round of auctions, it shows no intent to abandon the process. In the future, it thus may work out a more feasible—or at least acceptable—of using the system which Coase proposed almost 40 years ago.

C. CABLE TELEVISION: FRANCHISEE SELECTION

Cable television franchising is analogous in several respects to both initial and renewal broadcast licensing. Perhaps most significant, cable renewal franchising started out without any notion of a "renewal expectancy," like that just seen in the broadcast context. In the 1984 Cable Act, however, the cable industry was given an explicit statutory renewal expectancy, while the broadcasting industry was still fighting the issue through the courts.

Since the economics underlying cable and broadcasting are different, one might expect their basic authorization procedures to differ. A substantial investment in physical plant—and periodic total rebuilding every ten to fifteen years—characterizes the cable but not the broadcast industry. And perhaps as a result of this phenomenon, cable franchises generally run fifteen or more years, while broadcast television licenses are only eight (or, until recently, five) years in duration. Cable's greater investment in plant might militate in favor of some utility-type of permanence, in order to encourage continued maintenance and upgrading. Cable's already-lengthy franchises, however, by guaranteeing an operator's ability to operate its plant for its full useful life, arguably constitute enough protection.

Local Regulation to 1984. A more important fact of life for cable is that it is subject to regulation by local city councils, rather than by a federal administrative agency. Since local legislators are elected officials, politics naturally must—and should—play a major role in their decision-making. This is not to suggest that they engage in improper or corrupt activities; only a handful of such scandals has emerged in the history of cable franchising. It does indicate, however, that their agendas may be somewhat different than those of Washington-based appointed officials. And for better or worse, they lack the staff or the "expertise" of traditional regulatory agencies.

In cable's early days, during the 1950s and 1960s, neither cable operators nor cities gave much thought to the content or legal status of franchising. Cable was new enough that long-term franchises had not yet begun to come up for renewal. Moreover, initial franchise proceedings generally were not competitive in nature; only rarely did more than one firm apply for a community's franchise. As a result, the whole notion of a comparative proceeding was foreign to the process.

This began to change as cable became a financially attractive industry in the 1970s. With the advent of satellite-delivered pay channels, cable operators started to have cash flows of forty to sixty percent of revenue. The value of franchises escalated. (As a rough indication of the change over the years, in 1970 most well-run cable systems sold for the equivalent of about $500 per subscriber; by 1990, prices were between

$2,000 and $2,500 per subscriber. This price seemed to decline, however, during the late 1990s.)

Just as with television broadcast licenses during the *WHDH* days, a successful applicant ended up with an authorization saleable for many times the cost of the application procedure. This naturally encouraged firms to apply for cable franchises in any potentially lucrative market. And at this time, most large cities were still without cable, because of the difficulties of underground cabling and the lack of unique programming to sell. This situation did not last for long. Many local governments moved quickly to franchise cable systems in the mid–1970s, partly because their citizens demanded service, and partly because they were anxious for revenues from franchise fees.

By the mid–1970s, any cable franchising process in a substantial community was sure to attract a number of applicants, generally large multiple systems operators ("MSOs"). For the first time, competition entered into the cable franchising process—bringing with it what the industry quaintly dubbed "franchise wars."

Most cities responded to MSOs' overtures by initiating some form of comparative bidding process. Fears of legal and political reprisals usually dissuaded city governments from simply making an outright award. Because the relevant regulatory authority was a local legislative body rather than a regulatory agency, however, these procedures generally tended to be rather open-ended in nature; they lacked the formality or dignity of an FCC hearing procedure, with review by the full Commission and potentially by the court of appeals.

Since most cities had neither experience nor expertise with cable, their first step generally was to hire an outside consulting firm. Regardless of whether a local government actually followed its consultant's advice, merely seeking it added a degree of legitimacy to the whole franchising process. In fact, cable consulting became a small growth industry in the late 1970s. A number of firms with a mixture of economic, technological, and legal expertise grew up almost overnight— fueled by the fact that most MSOs were willing to reimburse a city for consulting expenses, as a condition of moving the franchising process along.

Most initial franchising procedures began with the issuance of a "request for proposals" ("RFP"), usually prepared by the city's consultant. Although RFPs naturally differed from one community to another, they basically amounted to a wish list of services from, and a demand for background information on, the applicants. As time went on, both RFPs and responses became increasingly sophisticated. For example, the bids in New York City's initial franchising process for the outer four boroughs were several volumes apiece.

If the written information was as lengthy as in comparative broadcast proceedings, the hearings certainly were not. As legislators, city council members generally had no taste for drawn-out trial-type proceedings. Most franchise hearings thus gave each applicant an hour or so to state its case, and an opportunity for limited questioning by local legislators, staff, and consultants. The process thus resembled a zoning board meeting more than an FCC hearing. Many observers have compared it to a beauty contest.

For a brief time, the Commission attempted to impose some procedural limitations upon local governments. In the initial version of its comprehensive 1972 cable television rules, the FCC had included a short laundry list of items for local governments to consider. Rule 76.31 required each franchise agreement to: (1) state that a "full public proceeding affording due process" had taken place; (2) require "significant construction within one year"; (3) have a "reasonable duration" (no more than fifteen years); (4) make rates subject to approval; and (5) "specify procedures" for resolving subscriber complaints. Cable Television Report and Order, 36 FCC 2d 143, 222 (1972). The Commission quickly encountered difficulty in administering these provisions for thousands of communities, and repealed them.

Particularly in the absence of any procedural or substantive guidelines, the final city council decisions were virtually always "political." Local legislators were generally concerned not so much with finding the most efficient operator in order to maximize benefits to citizens, but rather with making the most politically advantageous decision in order to further their careers. In some cases, this meant choosing the applicant with the most high-tech "bells and whistles" on its system. This resulted in systems' having studio facilities, two-way data transmission, and security systems that often went virtually unused—but that subscribers ended up paying for. (Indeed, later studies indicated that local governments almost consistently chose high-tech options over low-priced service.) Other forms of political input were more direct; campaign contributions and the like did not go unnoticed. And some MSOs were highly innovative in making themselves attractive to city councils, agreeing to supply services ranging from busing for the elderly to drug rehabilitation programs.

The initial franchising process thus became comparative at least for a time. But local officials seemed to have used far different criteria than the FCC, with its statutory fact finding requirements and its insulation from direct electoral politics.

By the early 1980s, most major cities had granted franchises, and thus the wave of initial franchising came to an end. About this time, the MSOs began to confront a hard but uncomfortable fact: many of their new franchise areas were unprofitable. Demand for pay services had not grown nearly as much as expected. Rates for "basic" services had risen very little, because of difficulties in securing increases from local governments. And the "franchise wars" had left a legacy of expensive and onerous obligations. Even though the MSOs had not only bid these terms, but had fallen all over each other in offering the lushest packages, at least publicly they now identified franchise obligations as the source of their financial woes.

Some MSOs decided to get rid of onerous franchise terms immediately, through a process glibly dubbed "renegotiation"—a threat to turn off a system unless a local government amended the franchise to delete expensive obligations. Others relied on increasing FCC pre-emption to loosen up local control of rates. But virtually the entire industry tried to use the renewal process—which began for most MSOs in the late 1980s—as a time for retrenchment.

There was virtually no statutory or common law governing cable franchise renewals. Since a franchise is essentially just a glorified easement agreement, cities generally were under few limitations as to renewal; presumably they could decide not to renew for any reason or for no reason at all. In some of the relatively rare non-renewal situations, MSOs brought antitrust actions based on arguments that cities were monopolists which had refused to deal. None of these ever went to a full decision, so the effectiveness of the argument is difficult to gauge. At the same time, local citizens and groups appeared to have none of the standing rights in franchise renewals that they had acquired in broadcast license renewals. Most cities excluded them from the renewal process, except for occasional service on some type of non-binding citizens advisory panel. Although some observers suggested that citizens should have rights as third party beneficiaries of the underlying franchise contract, only one court ever seems to have given this approach any credence. New York Citizens Committee on Cable TV v. Manhattan Cable TV, Inc., 651 F.Supp. 802 (S.D.N.Y.1986).

The Cable Act of 1984. Because of its concerns about the potential dangers of the renewal process, in the early 1980s the cable industry began a multi-pronged attack on local governmental powers. First, it convinced the Commission to begin preempting many aspects of local cable regulation, including all rate regulation for non-broadcast signals. Since the Commission had already embarked upon an extensive program of cable deregulation, preemption of local powers—the only remaining regulation—amounted to deregulation. (p. 96)

Second, the industry began extensive lobbying efforts for federal statutory limitations on a variety of local government powers—particularly focusing on franchise renewals. Initially, the industry's proposal was largely deregulatory, and did little more than preempt state and local regulation. See S. 66, 98th Cong., 1st Sess. (1983). The National Cable Television Association ("NCTA") apparently realized however, that it could not move legislation through Congress unilaterally, and in 1983 initiated negotiations with the National League of Cities ("NLC").

At first, the NLC was not interested; the NCTA seemed to have little bargaining power. In the summer of 1984, the cities' position changed dramatically in the wake of Capital Cities Cable, Inc. v. Crisp, 467 U.S. 691, 104 S.Ct. 2694, 81 L.Ed.2d 580 (1984). In a much misunderstood opinion, the Court invalidated, on preemption grounds, an Oklahoma statute that prohibited cable systems from carrying liquor advertisements. The Court based its holding on the effect of federal copyright legislation as well as FCC rules concerning signal carriage; but many observers—particularly local governmental interests—interpreted the decision as giving the FCC *carte blanche* to continue preempting municipal jurisdiction over cable. The NLC therefore found new reason to negotiate over federal cable legislation. The NLC, the NCTA, then-Congressman Timothy Wirth, and his House Telecommunications Subcommittee staff launched a series of negotiations that culminated in House passage of H.R. 4103, 98th Cong., 2d Sess. (1984), the Cable Communications Policy Act of 1984. (The Act is codified in various parts of Titles 5, 6, and 7 of the Communications Act.)

One of the most hotly contested provisions of the Act was the renewal provision, which imposed both substantive and procedural limitations upon a local government's ability to deny renewal of a franchise. A city must renew if a franchisee can show that:

(A) the cable operator has substantially complied with the material terms of the existing franchise and with applicable law;

(B) the quality of the operator's service including signal quality, response to consumer complaints, and billing practices, but without regard to the mix, quality, or level of cable services or other services provided over the system, has been reasonable in light of community needs;

(C) the operator has the financial, legal, and technical ability to provide the services, facilities, and equipment as set forth in the operator's proposal; and

(D) the operator's proposal is reasonable to meet the future cable-related community needs and interests, taking into account the cost of meeting such needs and interests. 47 U.S.C. § 546(c)(1).

The meaning of this provision is unclear, since there have been only a few lower court decisions to date. Nevertheless, the plain language and legislative history of the provision indicate that its purpose was substantially to foreclose local governments' discretion in denying franchise renewals. Unless the four criteria above are interpreted very expansively, any vaguely competent cable operator should be entitled to renewal.

Moreover, the procedure mandated by the statute makes it less likely that a city will throw a franchise into jeopardy. Under 47 U.S.C. §§ 546(a), (b), in order to conduct franchise denial proceedings, a city must take the following steps: (1) begin reviewing a franchisee's performance during a "window" 30 to 36 months before franchise termination; (2) receive a renewal proposal from the incumbent cable operator; and then (3) "commence an administrative proceeding after providing prompt public notice." This type of endeavor requires a city to do a considerable amount of planning and exercise a foresight that is not routine for municipal officials. (By way of contrast, a competing applicant or petitioner to deny in the broadcast context need file only thirty days before a license expires.) In addition, the formalities of a renewal proceeding may be enough to deter any but the most serious city officials. And finally, the Act provides for judicial review of a city's action in federal district court, with apparently *de novo* consideration of the city's "compliance with the procedural requirements of this section." 47 U.S.C. § 546(e).

The renewal provisions of the Cable Act seem to offer a strong renewal expectancy to cable operators. And interestingly enough, the cable industry seems to have secured it a decade before the 1996 Act's relief for broadcasters.

Chapter V

REGULATING MARKET STRUCTURE

In regulating the structure of the mass media market, the FCC has attempted to promote diverse ownership of media outlets on the premise that diverse ownership will result in diverse content. Structural regulation thus represents an indirect attempt by the government to influence the content of the mass media; unlike the behavioral regulations discussed in Chapter VII, it entails no direct control over the operation of a media outlet.

This is not to suggest that structural regulation has no impact on speakers or speech. A rule very well may have the impact—whether intended or incidental—of preventing a particular person or point of view from owning communications facilities. For example, consider the attempt to keep Mr. Rupert Murdoch from owning both a television station and a daily newspaper in New York City. (See p. 211)

Regardless of its effect on speech, one question raised by structural regulation is whether it is an effective means of accomplishing its stated purpose. In the 1980s, the FCC began to question whether its many structural rules had led to a diversity of views being expressed in the electronic mass media. If the rules were not producing diverse views or programs that are responsive to different constituencies, then the continued need for them was drawn into doubt. If the only remaining effect of structural regulation was to prevent concentration of ownership and thereby to encourage competition, it was not clear why the FCC should lay down special rules for the media rather than relying upon the general antitrust laws.*

A second important question is whether structural regulation is free of the constitutional concerns raised by many behavioral regulations. Is it less problematic for the government entirely to deny a would-be speaker access to media ownership than to regulate the behavior of

---

* In 1990, the Supreme Court endorsed the validity of the view that diverse—there, minority—ownership can serve as a proxy for diverse speech. See Metro Broadcasting, Inc. v. FCC, 497 U.S. 547, 110 S.Ct. 2997, 111 L.Ed.2d 445 (1990).

licensed operators? In general, there has been less constitutional criticism of structural regulation than of behavioral regulation, but you should ask yourself whether that is appropriate or correct.

This chapter examines three broad structural policies. The first is to promote a system of local broadcasting. Principally through licensing and spectrum allocation policies, the FCC has sought to encourage local ownership of stations in the hope that they would therefore be more responsive to the communities that they serve. Until recently, the Commission had a complex system of preferences in awarding new licenses for applicants "integrating" ownership and management; the courts have invalidated this in a series of decisions. (See p. 122) The FCC also chose to license a large number of less powerful, local broadcast outlets, rather than a small number of very powerful, national or regional outlets; each community, thus, would have one or more broadcast stations of its own.

The second set of policies concerns limits on common ownership or control of mass media outlets. The FCC's various restrictions on ownership concentration are intended to ensure that media ownership is widely dispersed.

Finally, the FCC has applied a number of policies to limit the influence that programming networks have on the content of broadcast outlets. While recognizing that large national networks, such as ABC, CBS, and NBC, can contribute valuable programming and expertise that might not otherwise be possible, until recently the FCC attempted to prevent these networks from controlling the majority of what is available to listeners and viewers. The Commission repealed the most significant rules in the early 1990s under judicial pressure. Moreover, the Telecommunications Act of 1996 invalidated most limitations on common ownership of broadcast stations. (See p. 203)

As you will see, these policies are compatible and frequently interconnected. An important question, however, is whether they have impeded powerful market forces, possibly to the detriment of the public. Would some greater degree of ownership concentration yield scale economies that would benefit viewers and listeners? Conversely, has the FCC admirably resisted economic pressures in seeking to carry out its statutory obligations? As you read the materials that follow, you should consider whether the recent relaxation of the structural regulations under the 1996 Telecommunications Act reflects dissatisfaction with their effectiveness or a decision that it is not productive to resist market forces.

A. LOCALISM

1. TRADITIONAL POLICY

In their study of television regulation, Roger G. Noll, Merton J. Peck, and John J. McGowan identified four general objectives underlying licensing, the FCC's most important economic decision:

(1) what has come to be known as the FCC's 'local service' objective—the establishment of stations in as many localities as possible;

(2) achievement of an acceptable level of diversity in program content;

(3) fulfillment of broadcasting's role as public servant; and

(4) the maintenance of an acceptable level of competition.

Economic Aspects of Television Regulation 99 (1973).

At the less general level at which more particularized corollary policies must be articulated and implemented, these objectives often conflict. In *Carroll Broadcasting,* (p. 161), for example, there was a potential conflict perceived between the maintenance of any competition and fulfillment of a public service role for broadcasting. In the comparative licensing criteria, where all four of the objectives are arguably represented, the conflict arises at the operational level of choosing between different applicants that are thought to represent different contributions to localism (local ownership and locally-originated programs), diversity in programming, public service (based on past broadcasting record), and competition (diversification of ownership).

One of the often unexamined issues in local programming is whether, and why viewers want it—or should want it. Some local programs probably attract viewers because they involve intensely local types of activities, e.g., membership groups (such as religious organizations) with a substantial and committed number of local members; city or county-wide sporting events; or news of events in a viewer's immediate community. If programming lacks this sort of attraction, however, does it have any necessary value in terms of localism? For example, how many viewers would prefer a telecast of a local high school orchestra to that of the Vienna Philharmonic—aside from those whose children or friends may perform in the "local" version?

Note: The FCC, the Local Service Obligation, and Frequency Allocations

With the passage of the Radio Act of 1927, Congress charged the Federal Radio Commission ("FRC") with the complex task of eliminating the chaotic interference then endemic on the AM broadcast band. The FRC had to deal with a number of conflicting congressional goals. One was to provide a local station for every community in the nation that could support one, another to serve rural portions of the nation as well. To provide local community service would require many, low-power stations. These, however, could not hope to reach the rural hinterlands with their signals. To serve the rural areas would require a spectrum allocated among a much smaller number of high-powered stations.

The Clear Channel Debate. The FRC consulted a group of engineers on the formulation of an allocation plan in light of these constraints and goals. The engineers proposed creating fifty "clear channel" frequencies, each of which would be assigned to only one station at night. These stations would guarantee nighttime service to much of the rural portion of the nation, which at that time was largely unserved. These same fifty stations would be the dominant stations during the day, but other stations would be licensed for daytime operation on the same frequencies. Other frequencies, the engineers proposed, could then be licensed at lower power to serve small communities. This scheme would still have required the FRC to eliminate many of the stations operating in 1928, or at least to force them to share the broadcast day on the same frequency.

The FRC adopted a compromise position between the engineers' proposal and the existing broadcasters' opposition to any reallocation. It created forty clear channels, and 34 "regional" channels to accommodate 125 full-time stations; it also left space for an additional 150 full-time "local" stations.

The clear channel stations were licensed up to 25 kilowatts, with experimental authorization up to 50 kilowatts. Some members of the industry further encouraged the FRC to license "superpower" stations that could serve vast areas of the country on a clear channel. Foremost among them was Powel Crosley, Jr., the owner of station WLW in Cincinnati; and in 1934, the FRC licensed WLW experimentally at 500 kilowatts—ten times the usual power limit for clear channel stations

For Crosley, the experiment may have been too successful. The station became immensely profitable from the sale of advertising. Moreover, Crosley also used WLW to market inexpensive radios; although the purchasers might have difficulty receiving other stations, they could count on a strong signal from "superpower" WLW. In 1936, an FCC survey revealed that WLW was the first choice of listeners in 13 states, and the second choice in another 6 states. Inevitably, other clear channel stations clamored for authorization to go "superpower" too.

Crosley's success, and his anti-labor editorial policies, eventually raised opposition in Washington. Senator Burton Wheeler of Montana, who saw "superpower" as the advent of a new monopoly (and for the same reason opposed multiple ownership, networks, and even "clear channels") sponsored a Senate resolution, passed in 1938, against licensing any station for more than 50 kw. In 1939, the FCC terminated the WLW experiment, reduced the station's authorization to 50 kw, and denied all pending applications for higher power operation.

The FCC returned to these issues in 1946, but reached no conclusion for fifteen years. Technical advances had increased greatly the number of AM stations, but as of 1958, 20 million Americans were still without primary nighttime service. Meanwhile, network dominance of radio had all but disappeared with the advent of television. In 1961, the Commission assigned one additional station (using directional antennae) on 13 of the 25 clear channels still unduplicated, in hopes of reducing the nation's nighttime "white areas"—those without primary AM service. The FCC deferred a decision on authorizing "superpower" on the unduplicated channels, at least in part because of the 1938 Wheeler Resolution and the opposition of most of the radio industry.

In 1975, the Commission reopened the matter. It conceded that the 1961 changes had brought primary nighttime service to only 300,000 additional persons, and that it simply did not know how many were newly served by FM. The issues respecting superpower thus remained much the same as they had been in the 1930s.

The Commission ultimately terminated the exclusive nighttime authorizations of 11 of the 25 Class I–A AM stations and renewed the restrictions on nighttime use of the other 14 channels, which had already been required to share their frequencies with one or two other stations. Clear Channel Broadcasting, 78 FCC 2d 1345 (1980) (Report and Order). The Commission estimated that this amendment of its rules would allow it to authorize 100 additional AM stations and to increase the number of local, minority-owned, and non-commercial outlets. The new stations' signals would cause only minimal interference to the signals of the 50 kw Class I–A stations and would do so only at the outer boundaries of their reach. The court of appeals affirmed the Commission's choice as "reasoned decisionmaking" made in accordance with its statutory obligation to balance "competing demands for a scarce radio spectrum." *Loyola University v. FCC*, 670 F.2d 1222 (D.C.Cir. 1982).

Local Service Reborn: Television. In the late 1940s and early 1950s, the FCC again had to face the policy choice between local service and national coverage, this time in the context of television. The Commission opted again for a locally-oriented approach, which it believed was required by the Act, and which surely appealed to its radio-bred image of broadcasting as a community-oriented service much like a local newspaper. The FCC again rejected the alternative of powerful regional stations, which could have provided as many as six VHF channels for most of the country, in favor of a scheme of lower-power local stations. This permitted more towns to have their own stations, but reduced the number of channels the average viewer could receive. The Commission created a "Table of Assignments," allocating at least one channel to 1,274 different communities in a manner designed to avoid interference among the stations using the same channels in different towns. The Table reflected the following priorities:

(1) to provide at least one television service to all parts of the United States;

(2) to provide each community with at least one television broadcast station;

(3) to provide a choice of at least two television services to all parts of the United States;

(4) to provide each community with at least two television broadcast stations; and

(5) to assign any channels remaining under the foregoing priorities to the various communities depending upon their size, geographical location, and the number of television services available to such community from television stations located in other communities.

Sixth Report and Order, Television Allocations, 41 FCC 148, 167 (1952).

The Commission rejected the proposal to reserve some of the higher UHF frequencies for "stratovision," a method of telecasting from an airborne transmitter, which could "supply about 81 percent of the area of the United States with one signal," 41 FCC at 216, bringing substantial additional service to rural areas at the cost of local ground-based stations. Once again, some concern was expressed by both the Senate Interstate Commerce Committee and the Commission as to the possibly "monopolistic" effects of stratovision.**

The DuMont Television Network opposed the Commission's heavy emphasis on providing local service in constructing the Table of Allocations. DuMont had suggested that the FCC assign four VHF stations to as many major markets as possible, at the sacrifice of some local stations in smaller communities, which would still be able to receive service through these more powerful metropolitan stations; this pattern arguably would have made a fourth national network immediately feasible—instead of waiting fifty years for Fox and other entrants—thereby fostering greater competition. The Commission, however, was "of the view that healthy economic competition" would exist under its *Table of Allocations*, which allowed for three stations in a large number of markets. 41 FCC at 171–72.

As noted in Chapter I, (p. 2), the FCC eventually did move in the direction of creating separate local and regional television service by authorizing LPTV. Although LPTV may be too little and too late, its basic concept is to allow stations with limited range to fill in local service gaps left by the authorization of higher-power regional stations. As discussed below, cable television systems also have begun to provide a measure of local coverage.

Notes and Questions

1. The Commission has calculated that if twelve unduplicated clear channel stations were authorized to operate at 750 kw, they would provide a minimum of four skywave (nighttime) services to virtually the entire nation, eliminating most white areas, and extend daytime primary service into areas lacking it. Clear Channel Broadcasting, 24 FCC 303, 315 (1958). How would you argue that the FCC has the authority, and perhaps even the obligation, to authorize some stations to increase their operating power substantially?

On what criterion or criteria should competing applicants for superpower authority be chosen? Should broadcasters whose nighttime service would have to compete with the newly strengthened signals be heard to object? Cf. *Carroll Broadcasting v. FCC*, (p. 161) If such authority is granted to broadcasters, could a system for the voluntary (paid) exchange of present broadcasting "rights" or authorizations be devised? See Note, *Power to Some People: The FCC's Clear Channel Allocation Policy*, 44 So.Cal.L.Rev. 811, 844–46 (1971).

2. Did the FCC, in rejecting the regionally oriented proposal of DuMont, with its potential to support four television networks, and in favoring local service instead, reasonably balance the conflicts among its various objectives?

3. As a technical matter, the national television policy could have been to have six or seven national channels. Each could originate programming from a different part of the country, if that was desired, for distribution—by cable, microwave, or satellite—to local or regional transmitters that would

---

** Query: are the issues raised by strato-
vision the same as or analogous to those
now raised by DBS?

broadcast the signal to receivers just as they do at present. See Noll, Peck & McGowan, *supra*, at 116. (This would create over-the-air "superstations," not unlike those currently distributed by cable systems.) Indeed, it may have been possible to combine a nationwide six-channel system with a local or regional origination capacity to be used, during certain designated hours, to bring the benefits of localism to at least a substantial part of the population. In fact, the French television networks that were privatized in the late 1980s have adopted this type of approach.

The British Broadcasting Corporation operates a two-channel national network, along with local production centers that not only feed the network but also provide specialized programming to such diverse regions of the United Kingdom as Northern Ireland, Wales, and Scotland. The eight regional stations also produce daily news and weekly regional affairs and sports programs. BBC Handbook 198, 205 (1977). At the other end of the spectrum is Israel, which has one private and one public national channel—mainly running foreign programming. To what extent does this explain the 95 percent take-up rate of Israeli homes passed by cable?

4. Think about how allocation of more high-powered television stations to regional markets—along the lines of the DuMont proposal perhaps—might have increased television service, admittedly at the cost of local stations. Remember that "co-channel" (that is, same-channel) VHF television stations cannot be located closer than approximately 200 air miles apart, while "adjacent channel" (that is, next-channel) stations must be separated by about 150 air miles. Allocation of channels along the lines of the *Sixth Report and Order* thus makes it impossible to locate more than about three or four stations in a regional center—other than major urban areas such as New York or Los Angeles.

But try playing media policymaker and look at some other alternatives. What would happen if you clustered seven stations at the center, and distributed the other five to the outlying areas? What might your configuration look like? Would this be better or worse in terms of service than the *Sixth Report and Order?* Note that in most developed countries the average number of channels available to almost all citizens is about six. Note also that most of these signals are delivered by a variety of low-power UHF stations, each of which has relatively geographic coverage. It is not uncommon for cities of 100,000 in other countries to have even two or three sets of transmitters located on different sides in order to provide almost complete coverage while avoiding interference.

5. Local Service in Comparative Hearings. Section 307(b) of the Communications Act states that the Commission should seek a "fair, efficient, and equitable distribution of radio service" among the various "States and communities" when allocating broadcast licenses for use of the radio spectrum. The Section 307(b) issue has not been confined to the problem of clear channels and the television (and FM) *Tables of Assignment*; it appears also in the context of comparative hearings for new station licenses.

In FCC v. Allentown Broadcasting Corp., 349 U.S. 358, 75 S.Ct. 855, 99 L.Ed. 1147 (1955), the Commission had granted a construction permit for an AM station in Easton, Pa., to Easton Publishing Co., and denied the mutually exclusive application of Allentown Broadcasting Co., which proposed to operate in Allentown, Pa. Neither of the proposed stations would be able to serve the other community. "Allentown had three local stations; Easton only one. The Commission recognized that Allentown was a city almost triple the size of Easton and growing at a greater pace, but held that Easton's need for a choice between locally originated programs was decisive." 349 U.S. at 360, 75 S.Ct. at 857. The Court ruled that the FCC, in awarding AM licenses between mutually exclusive applicants for different communities, could select one community over another on the basis of the former's need under Section 307(b), without first determining the relative ability of each applicant to serve its own community.

Under the authority established in the *Allentown* case, the Commission adopted a policy for determining when a comparative applicant for an AM license in a suburb of a larger community could obtain a preference on the ground that it would provide the first local service to the suburb. Policy Statement on Section 307(b) Considerations for Standard Facilities Involving Suburban Communities, 2 FCC2d 190 (1965). The Commission emphasized its policy of preferring first local service—that is, the first station actually located in and licensed to a given community regardless of the number of other signals received in the community—over multiple local service to any other community. All too frequently, in its view, suburban stations that place a strong signal over the metropolitan area "tend to seek out national and regional advertisers and to identify themselves with the entire metropolitan area rather than with the particular needs of their specified communities." This defeats the local service objective that dictated placing stations in the suburbs to serve peculiarly local needs. To resolve the dilemma, the FCC erected a rebuttable presumption that a suburban applicant in a metropolitan area with multiple local service intending to place a strong signal over the larger community should be treated as an applicant for the larger community for Section 307(b) purposes. Therefore, it would not be entitled to a preference for providing "first local service." It follows from this policy that, in a comparative hearing between applicants from the same or multiple suburban communities lacking a first local service, one proposing to transmit a weak signal that would not encompass the larger community would be preferred on the Section 307(b) ground to others proposing a strong signal. Does this make sense?

The rules were adopted in order to identify and reject applicants who listed a small community while intending to use the license to compete in a nearby major market. The Commission subsequently determined that its procedures were unduly harsh on applicants, that they tended to deter suburban applications, and that they were used by established urban stations to block competition. In 1983, the rules were repealed. Suburban Community Policy and Berwick Doctrine, 53 R.R.2d 681 (1983).

6. Since cable now passes about 90 percent of U.S. homes and has more than 65 percent of households as subscribers, and DBS is beginning to accumulate at least several million subscribers, is the whole service issue now moot, since most viewers can have 50–150 channels? To what extent, though, does either cable or DBS have the capacity to deliver local programming—either produced by it or by existing terrestrial television stations? Are any potential limitations significant by comparison to the existing allocation scheme?

7. Taking this one step further, what is the impact of the "National Information Infrastructure" (a/k/a) ("electronic superhighway") on concerns about both number of available signals and localism? If "fiber-to-the home" eventually puts several hundred or thousand channels into all or most households, would the marketplace necessarily provide large numbers of both national and local programs? If this ultimately turns out to be the case, what would be the impact on regulation of existing terrestrial broadcasting?

8. Consider the objections to the FCC's localism policies raised by the excerpt that follows. (Although the facts are dated, the points that they support remain valid.)

R. NOLL, M. PECK & J. MCGOWAN, ECONOMIC ASPECTS OF TELEVISION REGULATION

98–120 (1973).*

This provision [local station allocation] underlies what has come to be known as the FCC's "local service" objective—achievement of an acceptable level of diversity in program content and fulfillment of broadcasting's role as public servant. As noted above, the FCC's fourth major objective is the maintenance of an acceptable level of competition. The problem is that these four objectives are conflicting. Recognition of this conflict is crucial to comprehension of the dilemmas the FCC has faced. * * * An idealized view of FCC policy making would put all four objectives on a par, with the FCC making difficult tradeoffs between them in each of its decisions. But the record shows little willingness to subordinate the local service objective to any of the other goals. In dogged pursuit of localism the FCC has paid a high price in terms of its other objectives. * * *

The benefits of localism have proved to be relatively small. * * * The fact remains that almost all of the programming broadcast over the local station has a national focus. The network affiliates, which constitute the vast majority of VHF stations, rely on the networks for 82 percent of their prime time programming. Of the remaining 18 percent, a high proportion is devoted to non-network films and other national programming. Outside of prime time the reliance is less * * * but the pattern is much the same. Few local programs other than local news and weather and sports are offered. Independent stations are not much different. Most of their programming is new or rerun syndications and movies * * *.

* * *

One other rationale for local stations is that they serve as an advertising medium for local merchants. Here the localism role is somewhat more important, but the broadcasters still earn 80 percent of their revenue from either network or spot messages of national advertisers. Paradoxically, independent stations earn more of their revenue from national advertising than do network affiliates. * * *

* 1973 by The Brookings Institution. Reprinted by permission.

The reasons for the failure of the original FCC vision are not hard to find. Local programming is not as profitable for station owners as national programming. The difference in profitability simply reflects the fact that a program of the same quality shown nationally is obviously much cheaper per viewer. A typical half-hour evening network show costs at least $90,000 to produce, but, with an average share of the nationwide audience, the individual station in a market with a million homes can afford only $1,500 for program costs—an amount sufficient to produce only a low-quality talk show with minimum salaries for production and performing talent and with guests who are generally volunteers. For the most part the viewing audience prefers highly professional talent—professional football rather than local high school games, for example. Locally produced programs, therefore, have low audience ratings, and their advertising revenues are correspondingly low. Consequently, they must operate on very small budgets—which act further to reduce their audiences—even though they are often much more expensive per viewer than national programming.

This combination of significantly higher costs and lower revenues means that station owners are attracted to the more profitable national programs. The exception is local news and weather, which often draws good audiences, is cheap to produce, and hence, is reasonably profitable.
* * *

* * *

The preceding analysis is quite critical of the FCC's emphasis on localism and the costs it imposes on society in limitations on viewer choice and the lack of competition for networks and affiliates. Yet the policy itself is understandable in terms of the legislative origins of broadcast regulation. What is less obvious is the rationale behind the FCC's continued adherence to localism in the face of the heavy cost it exacts in diversity and the paucity of local programming undertaken by the stations themselves.

* * *

Note: Cable Television as a Local Outlet

The FCC derived its localism policies primarily from the mandate of Section 307(b) of the Communications Act, which does not apply to cable television systems because they do not need radio broadcast licenses to operate. Prior to the Cable Act of 1984, therefore, the Commission lacked any obvious statutory basis for authority to impose "local service" requirements on cable television systems. As early as 1960, however, the growth of cable television as a video distribution medium made the Commission concerned about the continued viability of the "localism" objectives that it had pursued through the licensing of local broadcast outlets. Viewers that subscribed to cable service would often connect their televisions to the cable and disconnect the rooftop antennas that enabled them to receive off-air broadcast stations. As a result, if the cable system did not carry the signals of the local broadcast stations, increased subscription to cable television service would result in reduced viewership of local broadcast services. In the "worst-case" scenario, local broadcasters, suffering from reduced viewership, would be unable to sell sufficient advertising to meet their costs of operation; with them would fail the Commission's localism policies.

For many years, the Congress, courts, and Commission have struggled with a difficult policy decision about how to accommodate (or even encourage) the growth of cable television without setting the stage for the demise of the local broadcasting industry.

Cable television systems increasingly have implemented public, educational, and governmental "access" ("PEG") channels, which carry both local and other public interest programming. Although these channels have survived both legal and funding threats, it still is not clear whether they will develop a substantial enough presence to become the primary providers of local programming. This is true to any even greater extent with newer media, such as DBS and "open video systems." (p. 78)

One might argue that the government simply should not choose among competing technologies; it should let viewers in the marketplace decide what video services they want and how they want to receive those services. Otherwise, in effect it imposes the failures of broadcast regulation upon cable and other new media. Would such an approach be consistent with the requirements of Section 307(b) of the Communications Act? Must the Commission ensure that a system of local broadcast outlets survives?

B. OWNERSHIP

1. TRADITIONAL CONCERNS

The Commission historically has attempted to prevent undue "concentration of control"—that is, ownership of too many print and broadcast media. Obviously enough, the immediate problem here is defining "too much"—something which the FCC never has been able to do very effectively.

Before dealing with these materials, note that they are largely historical and theoretical in nature. As discussed later (p. 213), provisions in the Telecommunications Act of 1996 repealed major aspects of the concentration rules—as well as many other aspects of traditional communications regulation.

Part of both the past and present dilemma in applying concentration rules comes from the fact that concerns about ownership have at least two separate ideological underpinnings. First, concentration may result in anti-competitive effects. For example, if a firm owns the only newspaper and the leading television station in a market, it may be able to force programmers to sell for less than the market price, and advertisers to pay more. A firm with market power thus may be able to operate simultaneously in different product markets as a monopsonist (buying at less than competitive prices) and as a monopolist (selling at supra-competitive prices.)

The second ideological concern is somewhat akin that behind localism: namely a quasi-constitutional policy in favor of maximizing diverse speech. This proceeds from the general structural regulation policy that a large number of speakers will result in increase the number of viewpoints. As noted at the beginning of this Chapter, however, there is no hard evidence that diverse structure creates diverse content.

The existence of these two parallel but sometimes inconsistent policies often has led to confusion in formulating and applying rules as to concentration of control. This has been particularly true over the last decade, with the introduction of new—particularly multichannel—media. To a very real extent, the Commission's contemporary reasoning is based not just on changes in the existing broadcast industry, but also on the development of new media. In its Report and Order, Multiple Ownership of AM, FM and Television Broadcast Stations, 100 FCC 2d 17 (1984), the agency defined the relevant media as follows.

25.   The record in this proceeding supports the conclusion that the information market relevant to diversity concerns includes not only TV and radio outlets, but cable, other video media, and numerous print media as well. * * *

30.   We conclude that, in terms of viewpoint diversity, the market includes a wide variety of active, energetic organs engaged in the dissemination of ideas, and that these instruments include not simply television and radio, but also cable, videocassette recorders, newspapers, magazines, books, and, when they are in operation, MDS, STV, LPTV and DBS, all of which should be considered when evaluating diversity concerns.

For analytical purposes, concentration of control breaks down into two major sub-issues: common ownership and cross ownership. As its label suggests, common ownership refers to an essentially horizontal situation, in which one firm owns a variety of the same media in different geographic markets, e.g., group ownership of newspaper, television stations, or radio broadcasters. By contrast, cross ownership involves vertical ownership of different media in the same location—classically, newspapers, radio, and television stations in the same market.

Sometimes, of course, the lines blur a bit. The same firm may be involved in both common and cross ownership, by owning a number of local media combinations around the country. This was particularly common in the past. Newspapers often were the first—and thus most successful—radio licensees in the their markets. And as with old wine in new bottles, they naturally moved into television when it matured. It thus was less than surprising that the leading national newspaper chains acquired AM, FM, and television in their local markets. As discussed later, many of these situations broke up under the pressure of FCC "anti-duopoly" rules and competitive market pressure during the 1970s and 1980s, thus leaving substantially less newspaper/television cross ownership than before. Moreover, the 1996 Telecommunications Act does not appear to immunize print/electronic cross-ownership, as it does radio/television cross-interests (p. 202)

Interestingly enough, comparatively few cross-owners made major, long-term entry into cable television; although a number of them acquired their local franchises during the 1950s and 1960s, virtually all had sold out to cable MSOs by the 1980s. The reason for this phenomenon are less than clear; very simplistically, after fifty years of single-channel experience, operation of a multi-channel medium may have been foreign to newspaper-based firms.

a. Common Ownership

The Commission had a long and complex history of attempting to deal with common ownership. As indicated by the material below, it made relatively radical changes to its rules every decade or so, and really never established firm reasoning or policies. The Commission's own description of its regulatory history in this area highlights this, in the following discussion from its Notice of Proposed Rulemaking, Multiple Ownership of AM, FM, and Television Broadcast Stations, 95 FCC 2d 360 (1983).

2.   Although multiple ownership of stations had been a feature of the broadcast industry since its earliest days, it was not until the late 1930's that the Commission began to focus its attention on this aspect of industry organization. The Commission's considerations came at a time when there was a significant expansion of Federal governmental activity and a corresponding lack of belief in the efficacy of the competitive marketplace. * * *

3.   When the Commission adopted rules governing the new commercial FM service in June, 1940, * * * for the first time the Commission established a limit on the number of licenses which could be held under common control. The limit was six stations. The Commission subsequently stated that the purpose of the new rules was "[t]o obviate possible monopoly, and encourage local initiative." In 1940 the Commission also promulgated similar rules for television, which was still being treated as an experimental service, but set the maximum number of stations which could be owned at three. When rules authorizing television broadcasting as a regular commercial service were adopted in April, 1941, these restrictions were retained. In May, 1944, the maximum number of television stations which could be controlled by one owner was increased to five in response to a National Broadcasting Co. ("NBC") petition.

4.   Two years later, the Commission established a de facto seven station limit for AM when it denied CBS' application to purchase an eighth such station, KQW in San Jose. The Commission asserted that concentration of control, "particularly in AM," was "not a factor of the absolute number of stations alone," but also depended on "the powers and frequencies of the stations." CBS already owned six 50,000–watt clear channel stations, as well as a

5,000–watt regional station. While the decision indicated that the Commission would in AM matters consider all the factors involved in a given case, it in fact set a numerical line by which future Commission actions were measured.

5. The decision in the KQW case also reflected the ambivalence about network ownership of broadcast stations which has colored many subsequent Commission ownership deliberations. * * *

6. Thus, by the mid–1940s, the Commission had established the broad outline of what were to be the basic elements of its ownership regulations for several decades. There were to be local and national ownership limitations—regional regulations would come later—with special attention sometimes given to the role of networks. The Commission had also established use of a pattern of analysis in which it generally merged its consideration of action necessary to prevent economic concentration, essentially an antitrust matter, with concerns regarding diversity of information sources, a First Amendment issue, and frequently utilized a relatively unsophisticated approach to these merged issues. * * *

* * *

B. The "Seven Station" Rule Making

8. * * * [I]n August, 1948, the Commission initiated a proceeding which for the first time proposed formal restrictions on the number of AM stations under common control. The number suggested for AM was seven, the KQW figure. No changes were proposed in the existing ceilings of six FM and five TV stations * * *. * * *

9. * * * The Commission's Order adopted the limits of seven AM and five TV stations as proposed. The AM limit was kept at seven, the Commission said, so that the existing holdings of such stations would not be "unduly disrupted." The Commission found that a seven station limit was "consistent with the historical development of AM broadcasting and the tremendous expansion that has been achieved almost entirely within the framework of that limitation." The six station FM rule was stated to have been raised to AM's level of seven "because of their interrelationship and the present status of FM's growth." The TV limit was maintained at five because in the Commission's "judgment based on extensive experience with the problems of multiple ownership," it had "proven practicable and desirable."

10. In adopting the "seven station rule," the Commission acknowledged the arguments by some parties that the proposed rules were arbitrary because they did not take into account "class and size of stations, geographical locations, populations served, and similar factors." Because of these adverse comments, it had "considered alternatives to the outstanding proposal." However, it had determined as a result of a study of existing multiple ownership that

"any proposal to limit multiple ownership on the basis of such factors as class of station or geographic location" was "either unsatisfactory or unworkable." * * *

* * *

15. On September 17, 1954, * * * the television rule [was modified] to allow for ownership of seven stations, a maximum of five being VHF, [the remainder being UHF]. * * *

———

Note on the Reconsideration

On reconsideration, the Commission added an audience reach limitation to the twelve-station rule. Thus, an individual or group may not have an attributable interest in more than 12 television stations or in any lesser number of stations that reaches an aggregate of 25% of the national audience calculated on the basis of Arbitron ADI television households. 100 FCC 2d 74, 57 R.R.2d 966 (Gen Dkt. No. 83–1009, *Memorandum Opinion and Order*) (1984). The Commission also adopted a "UHF discount" policy, concluding that "while there has been demonstrable progress in the viability of UHF television, the inherent physical limitations of this medium should be reflected in our national multiple ownership rules." (The 1996 Telecommunications Act seems to contemplate an expanded version of this doctrine in terms of both common and cross ownership). (p. 213) Consequently, the FCC decided that an individual or entity would be charged with only 50% of the television households in any market in which it had an attributable interest in a UHF station.

Finally, the FCC adopted a provision to encourage minority ownership of broadcast stations. Despite its continuing belief that the multiple ownership rules should not "serve as the primary mechanisms to promote minority ownership in television and radio broadcasting," the FCC decided that an individual or group may have an attributable interest in up to 14 stations in each broadcast service, provided that two stations are controlled by members of a minority group. With respect to television stations, the audience-reach cap would be 30%, provided that at least 5% of that audience reach was attributable to minority-controlled stations.

In separate statements, both Commissioner Dawson and Commissioner (later Chairman) Patrick questioned the adoption of the separate cap for minority-controlled stations. As phrased by Patrick, "[i]f the public interest is threatened by concentrating the ownership of 14 stations in a single owner, how is that threat obviated by the race of the owner?" Patrick went on to suggest that the Commission might waive its twelve-station/25% cap in specific instances where a party could show "that the acquisition would contribute to diversity. * * * Such a process would allow the Commission to focus on whether our compelling interest in promoting diversity of viewpoints is furthered. And it would avoid the Commission's granting of preferences based solely on race without regard to whether diversity will be furthered."

All of these provisions changed quite dramatically in 1996.

In addition to its sweeping changes in regulation of common carriers and cable systems, the Telecommunications Act of 1996 also radically deregulated several aspects of broadcasting—particularly ownership limitations. In terms of common ownership, it virtually eliminated prior restrictions in several respects.

Section 202(a) of the Act completely did away with caps on radio station ownership, by "eliminating any provisions limiting the number of AM or FM broadcast stations which may be owned or controlled by one entity nationally." Although it remains to be seen how the industry ultimately will react to this, within a year of the Act's passage a number of radio groups already had accumulated more than 400 stations apiece and were planning yet further acquisitions.

The conventional wisdom seemed to be that operation of a large number of stations, combined with the Act's relaxation of local cross-ownership (p. 205) would create substantial economies of scale in areas such as program acquisition, advertising sales, and accounting. Several large new groups in effect were planning to become wholly owned national radio networks somewhat along the European model—something which never had existed in the United States. To a certain extent, their approach thus was based on "cutting out the middleman" in terms of local affiliates.

The Act also largely eliminated cross-ownership restrictions on television. Section 202(c) provided that firms could own an unlimited *number* of stations. Unlike the Act's radio provisions, however, it continued to impose a cap on the percentage of the country's *population* which one firm could cover.

(c) Television Ownership Limitations.—

(1) National ownership limitations.—The Commission shall modify its rules for multiple ownership set forth in section 73.3555 of its regulations (47 C.F.R. 73.3555)—

(A) by eliminating the restrictions on the number of television stations that a person or entity may directly or indirectly own, operate, or control, or have a cognizable interest in, nationwide; and

(B) by increasing the national audience reach limitation for television stations to 35 percent.

The population cap was probably the most hotly contested part of the Act's broadcast provisions. Some groups wanted to retain the existing 25 percent limitation, in order to protect small and minority businesses. Others wanted to remove it totally, in order to encourage more firms to enter the industry through group and/or network ownership. The debate centered on cap of between a 25 percent and 50 percent, with 35 percent ultimately adopted as a compromise.

The result is that firms can own an unlimited number of television stations, subject to the 35 percent audience cap. To a lesser extent than with radio, firms began to acquire large numbers of television stations—albeit often UHF operations, with relatively small audiences, in order to stay within the 35 percent limitation. Within a year of the Act's passage, some group owners had two or three dozen stations. Again, the industry's reasoning relied largely upon economies of scale and networking opportunities; the latter was bolstered by the entry of yet two more new networks, Warner and Paramount. Moreover, legislators had made it clear that the 35 percent limitation would be subject to reevaluation at some unspecified point in the future.

These radical changes in common ownership policy raise a number of questions.

Once again, how much is too much? A group owner with 400 radio stations or 50 television stations seems quite large by traditional standards. But is it, given the fact that it would have only 4 percent of all U.S. radio and 5 percent of all U.S. television stations? Are there really economies of scale? See Harvey Levin, *infra*. And as to television, is the sheer number of stations relevant, as long as there is an audience cap? Would there be a difference it if group owner acquired all of its 50 stations in markets with particular ethnic groups, thus covering perhaps 90 percent of the nation's Hispanic or Asian population? And is there a countervailing consideration in the possible development of yet more new networks, to provide competition to the existing "big three" (or four?)

What is the effect of both radio and television consolidation on existing independent and network stations? By eliminating the "middleman," will group owners eliminate both localism and diversity? Will they create "networks" or other organizations along the lines of those in Europe? Is group ownership necessarily inconsistent with either localism or diversity? Even if it is, given the doubts voiced above as to these values, is the trade-off worthwhile?

And as a continuing theme, what is the effect on these considerations of the multichannel media? If cable provides effective access opportunities, is localism as relevant as it once might have been? If the combination of cable, DBS, and MMDS delivers large numbers of channels, are fears as to diversity still important? But should cable have to pay for broadcasting's sins?

Although the Congress did not give many reasons—other than political ones—for the 1996 Telecommunications Act's new policies as to common ownership, is it possible yet to evaluate them very effectively?

Notes and Questions

1. (a) Do you agree or disagree with the premise that diversification of ownership will promote diverse programming and viewpoints? If so, what considerations support the decision to raise the seven-station limit to twelve stations? In fact, if the premise is valid, shouldn't the FCC adopt a one-station rule? Alternatively, should the FCC limit ownership only within a particular market and leave concerns about national concentration to the antitrust laws? Are the antitrust laws adequate to guard against concentration at all levels—national, regional, and local?

(b) Do you accept the contention that there are benefits from group ownership that must be balanced against the benefits from diversification? Should the realization of scale economies be permitted to impede or dilute the First Amendment-related objective of promoting a diversity of views in the media? If the issue is one of balancing benefits and detriments, why would the FCC initially have proposed allowing the rules to sunset after six years?

(c) How might the FCC address the needs of children, or the elderly, or the homeless—who, for practical reasons, might be unable to acquire or operate a broadcast station?

(d) Absent the premise that diverse ownership contributes to the diversity of speech, what justification is there for having any ownership rules? In its decision to adopt the twelve-station limit, the FCC concluded that "if the rule were repealed immediately and in its entirety, a significant restructuring of the broadcast industry might occur before all ramifications of such a change became apparent." Thus, the twelve-station rule was adopted "out of an abundance of caution." Is this a proper basis for agency action that restricts competition? Does such agency action serve the "public interest?"

2.   Is it relevant that there are more broadcast outlets today than there were when the seven-station rule was adopted? Does it matter if a substantial portion of these stations are group-owned or are affiliated with one of the national networks? Do other media, such as STV, DBS, and SMATV, contribute to diversity of programming and viewpoints? Does it matter that many of these new distribution outlets supply relatively little original programming? Should the FCC consider trends in the growth or decline of other information outlets, such as magazines, newspapers, books, and newsletters?

3.   The Commission suggested that higher ratings for the local news programs of group-owned stations means that such stations "do a superior job of responding to viewer demands for news." Do you agree? Suppose an independent station that runs a game show opposite these news programs has the highest rating in the market for the time period. Is that independent station doing a better job of meeting viewer demands for television programming? If no stations provide programming that is of interest to small groups of viewers in a market, such as minorities or children, should the FCC attempt to ensure that these viewers' interests are served? Are the multiple ownership rules an effective way of addressing this type of concern?

4.   Enforcement of the FCC's ownership limits can occur in a number of ways. First, an ownership issue might arise in the context of an initial licensing or a renewal proceeding. An interested party might file a petition to deny, alleging that an applicant's ownership of the station at issue would violate one of the ownership rules. Second, the issue might be raised as a challenge to an application to transfer control or to assign a license, either of which requires prior FCC approval. Finally, a complaint might be lodged with the FCC alleging that a licensee is operating in violation of the FCC's ownership rules.

Assuming that the Commission finds a violation, it can take any of several actions. The Commission can deny any application that, if granted, would put the licensee in violation of the ownership rules. The FCC can also order a licensee to divest one or more properties in order to come into compliance with the ownership rules. Under appropriate circumstances, the FCC may grant a waiver of the applicable rule, on either a temporary or permanent basis, if it concludes that the public interest would be served thereby. Finally, the FCC may permit a party to use a voting trust to cure an ownership violation.

5. In addition to concerns about diversity, the FCC has devoted some attention to antitrust analysis—the possibility that a large group owner could cause economic harm to smaller owners, advertisers, and the viewing public. Antitrust analysis typically requires a definition of the relevant product and geographic markets. What do you think the relevant product and geographic markets should be? Which media should be included? Should the analysis be conducted on a market-by-market or on a national basis? And what economic harm should be considered? Inasmuch as viewers receive television programming free of charge, how might the public be harmed? Are the antitrust laws sufficient to redress instances of price fixing, predatory pricing, or other anticompetitive behavior that might affect advertisers or smaller station owners?

b. *Cross Ownership*

If possible, cross ownership generally has been more of a political hot potato for the Commission than common ownership. First, it often allowed one old, long-dominant firm to dominate the political and ideological life of a community. Second, it confirmed A.J. Liebling's axiom that "freedom of the press belongs to those who have one," and thus almost by definition excluded racial and ethnic minorities. The FCC's most stringent attack on cross-ownership came in its "one-to-a-customer" rule in 1970, which (prospectively only) prevented one firm from having more than one print or electronic medium in a market.

In adopting the one-to-a-market rule in 1970, 47 C.F.R. § 73.3555(b), the FCC said:

> 16. Basic to our form of government is the belief that "the widest possible dissemination of information from diverse and antagonistic sources is essential to the welfare of the public." (Associated Press v. United States, 326 U.S. 1, 20 (1945)). * * *

> 17. * * * [C]entralization of control over the media of mass communications is, like the monopolization of economic power, per se undesirable. * * *

> 18. It is accordingly firmly established that in licensing the use of the radio spectrum for broadcasting, we are to be guided by the sound public policy of placing into many, rather than few hands, the control of this powerful medium of public communication. * * * 22 FCC 2d 306, 310.

Does the Commission's 1984 decision reject this "sound public policy"? Does the decision provide a rationale for rejecting it? What is that rationale? Could the FCC better achieve the identified policy objectives by awarding licenses for short terms on the basis of a random selection process (such as a lottery)? Might the policy goals be better achieved by requiring that station licensees provide others in society with access to the airwaves? What other mechanisms might be used to promote the better operation of the "marketplace of ideas"? Should the FCC or any governmental authority try to "engineer" such a marketplace by awarding rights to enter the market?

7. In the document, the Commission stated that "the more correct focus for addressing viewpoint diversity and economic competition concerns is the number and diversity of information and advertising outlets in local markets * * *." The 1996 Telecommunications Act effectively has done away with restrictions on common and cross ownership among radio stations. If the marketplace functions in a way that best serves the public interest, what is left for the FCC to do? Even before the new Act, the Commission took an increasingly relaxed approach to cross ownership—largely through waivers.

(a) In 1988, the Commission relaxed its radio duopoly rule to permit slight signal overlaps. It permitted common ownership of more than one commercial AM or FM station serving that same market, provided that the "principal city" signal contours of the stations do not overlap. Amendment of Section 73.3555 of the Commission's Rules, the Broadcast Multiple Ownership Rules, 4 FCC Rcd 1723 (1988) (*First Report and Order*).

(b) Also in 1988, the FCC relaxed its one-to-a-market rule, stating that it would "look favorably" upon requests to waive the one-to-a-market rule in the 25 largest media markets, if the particular market at issue has at least 30 different broadcast "voices" (i.e., 30 different owners of radio and television stations). Where this "Top 25 Markets/30 Voices" standard is not met, the FCC said it would consider waiver requests on a case-by-case basis "in light of our diversity and competition concerns." Amendment of Section 73.3555 of the Commission's Rules, the Broadcast Multiple Ownership Rules, 4 FCC Rcd. 1741 (1988) (Second Report and Order). In dissent, Commissioner Dennis argued for a more stringent standard for granting a waiver. She would have limited waivers solely to markets where there are at least 10 television stations, 45 voices, and 65 total stations, e.g., Los Angeles, New York, Chicago. Do you favor Commissioner Dennis' waiver standard? How much diversity is enough?

(c) In the past, the FCC has waived the ownership rules where the overlap is *de minimis*, such as where an applicant seeks to acquire stations in Ohio and Michigan with signals that overlap largely in sparsely populated areas and over Lake Erie. Applications of the Shareholders of Storer Communications, Incorporated, (Transferor) and Subsidiaries of SCIPSCO, Inc. (Transferee), 59 R.R.2d 611 (1985). What about an applicant proposing to acquire television stations serving New York City and Philadelphia, both of which can be received in parts of New Jersey? Does it matter that residents in the parts of New Jersey served by these stations do not have any local New Jersey television stations to serve them? Silver King Broadcasting of Vineland, Inc., 2 FCC Rcd 324, 61 R.R.2d 1117 (1986); Applications of Capital Cities Communications, Inc., 59 R.R.2d 451 (1985) (acquisition of ABC).

8. (a) Concern with the viability of independent UHF television stations has been a theme running throughout the multiple ownership proceedings and, indeed, throughout the Commission's policy structure

for almost three decades. See, e.g., V. Mosco, The Regulation of Broadcasting in the United States: A Comparative Analysis (1975). The discount for the audience reached by a UHF station is just the latest example of this policy. The FCC long had a similar policy for FM stations. Consequently, the FCC exempted AM–FM combinations from its duopoly rules. The exemption remains in place today, although the continued viability of independent AM stations has now become the focus of concern. First Report and Order, 4 FCC Rcd 1723 (1989).

(b) In 1975, the FCC adopted rules prohibiting broadcast-"daily" newspaper combinations in the same market. 50 FCC 2d 1046 (1975), codified at 47 C.F.R. § 73.3555(c). A significant point of contention was whether to require that all existing newspaper-broadcast combinations be broken up. Over a strong dissent from Commissioner Glen Robinson, the FCC decided to require that only the most "egregious" combinations be ended by 1980 through divestiture of either the newspaper or the broadcast station. Divestiture was confined to markets where the only daily newspaper and the only commercial broadcast station—radio or television—were co-owned. The Commission accepted the proposition that common ownership provided economies of scope that, if lost, might cause some local news outlets to fail; it appeared to be particularly concerned about the possibility that divestiture might cause some newspapers to fail. The Commission stated generally:

> Requiring divestiture could reduce local ownership as well as the involvement of owners in management as many sales would have to be [to] outside interests. The continuity of operation would be broken as the new owner would lack the long knowledge of the community and would have to begin raw. Local economic dislocations are also possible as a result of the vast demand for equity capital and wide-scale divestiture could increase interest rates and affect selling price too.

Did these considerations require that divestiture be limited to the "most egregious" cases? Are these factors relevant only to ownership arrangements that were in existence at the time the Commission adopted the rules? Would any of these factors support the grant of a waiver to permit a new broadcast-newspaper combination to be formed?

Commissioner Robinson objected that "whatever the general public interest merits of subsidization of newspapers I do not think that this is, in itself, a proper concern of the FCC." Do you agree or disagree? What is the basis for the Commission's concern about newspapers? Does it have statutory authority to regulate newspaper ownership? For a comparative view see Townsend, *Regulation of Newspaper Broadcasting, Media Cross–Ownership in Canada*, 33 U.N.B.L.J. 261 (1984).

(c) Consider the relevance to the FCC's broadcast-newspaper policies of congressional policy as expressed in the Newspaper Preservation Act of 1970, 15 U.S.C. § 1801 *et seq.* The scale economies to be had from a joint newspaper operating arrangement, especially as between a morning and an afternoon newspaper, are more obviously substantial than are those available from newspaper-broadcast station common ownership. The latter still may be significant, however. But cf. Harvey Levin, *Broadcast Regulation and Joint Ownership of Media* 91–100 (1960) (1940–52 data show economies not significant).

In markets where a newspaper's entry into broadcasting would not create a monopoly of the local advertising media, and therefore no monopoly profit potential, there would seem to be no incentive other than the expectation of scale economies for a newspaper to enter into this field as opposed to any other. See Caldwell, *Principles Governing the Licensing of Broadcasting Stations*, 79 U.Pa.L.Rev. 113, 153 (1930) (similarities, scale economies); compare Lago, *The Price Effects of Joint Mass Communication Media Ownership*, 16 Antitrust Bull. 789 (1971) (joint media ownership without effect on prices for national advertising in either newspapers or television), with Owen, *Newspaper and Television Station Joint Ownership*, 18 Antitrust Bull. 787 (1973) (newspaper-owned TV stations charge 15% more than otherwise for national advertising). On the other hand, newspapers (like networks) with experience in radio broadcasting may have perceived a special opportunity to realize the rents accruing from experience by entering the television field, as well as the scale economies of joint radio-television operations. See generally Sterling, *Newspaper Ownership of Broadcast Stations*, 1920–68, 46 Journalism Q. 227 (1969).

In any event, newspaper companies and radio stations were strongly motivated to enter television. Newspapers obtained 50 of the first 142 television station construction permits issued through 1952, and radio stations got many of the rest; interestingly, only eight stations went to licensees with no other communications interests (including motion pictures, networks, and national magazines). These early licenses tended to be for the largest markets, where there were multiple stations and the least reason to expect that an advertising monopoly could be established.

Note that the Newspaper Preservation Act contemplates the elimination of competition in the advertising market, where the realization of scale economies (from joint solicitation, for example) is not likely to be significant. Can this tolerance of non-competitive pricing be adequately explained by observing that if all but one of the contracting newspapers were to fail, see § 4(b), pricing would not be competitive anyway?

(d) The Commission has authorized temporary waivers and, in one case, a permanent waiver, of the broadcast-newspaper rule. The permanent waiver involved the owner of a grandfathered newspaper-television station combination in Chicago, which sold the station but retained a right to repurchase it and kept a significant role in the station's operation. When the buyer of the station was later liquidated, the FCC permitted the original owner to reacquire and keep the station. Field Communications, 65 FCC 2d 959 (1977).

(e) The Cowles Family owns the two daily newspapers and an AM, an FM, and a TV station in Spokane, Wash.

(i) From 1974–1977 one of the Cowles' papers listed the daily programming of local radio stations in order of channel sequence. It listed the programming on television stations in the order in which the stations had entered the market. In each case, programs on its stations appeared first as a result. Is this an abuse of cross-ownership? Does it warrant divestiture or some lesser sanction?

(ii) Suppose the paper now begins to print a captioned picture highlighting one television show each day. More than half of these pictures are from the owned station's programs. Is this an abuse warranting divestiture? Some lesser sanction? None of the FCC's business? See KHQ, Inc., 87 FCC 2d 705, 50 R.R.2d 21 (1981).

(f) See also the *News America* decision (p. 212)

9. The relationship between the antitrust laws and FCC regulatory policy is rather complex. Although the Commission may incorporate antitrust considerations into its articulation of the "public interest," it does not have exclusive or primary jurisdiction of antitrust issues involving broadcasters; the government or a private plaintiff may bring suit under the antitrust laws without, or indeed in spite of, any prior resort to the FCC. See United States v. Radio Corp. of America, 358 U.S. 334, 79 S.Ct. 457, 3 L.Ed.2d 354 (1959); Sangster, *A Tale of Two Standards: Antitrust, the Public Interest, and the Television Industry*, 6 Hastings Comm/Ent L.J. 887 (1984).

Since the 1970s it has not been uncommon for the Department of Justice to appear before the FCC, perhaps because it perceives the courts as somewhat deferential to the FCC's public interest determination notwithstanding the agency's lack of authority to preclude the antitrust issue. Alternatively, the administrative may be more convenient than the judicial forum, with its more informal evidentiary rulings, and especially its ability to address issues categorically in rulemaking; this obviates the need both for multiple adjudications and for proof of specific violations of the law. See Lee, *The FCC and Regulatory Duplication: A Case of Overkill?*, 51 Notre Dame Law. 235, 245 (1975) (DOJ not an appropriate party in adjudications); cf. Barrow, *Antitrust and the Regulated Industry: Promoting Competition in Broadcasting*, 1964 Duke L.J. 282 (proposal to obligate DOJ to intervene before FCC, estoppel of separate antitrust action); compare McClatchy Newspapers, Inc., 61 FCC 2d 279, 38 R.R.2d 980 (1976) (DOJ petition to deny, on grounds of monopolization, denied), with *Westinghouse Broadcasting Co.* (Petition for Rulemaking filed Nov. 23, 1976) (DOJ memorandum in support of a broad inquiry into network program origination practices). Other limitations on the ownership of media outlets include the following. First, an individual or entity may not own or control a cable television system and have an attributable interest in a local broadcast station with a signal that overlaps all or part of the community served by the cable system. 47 U.S.C. § 533(b); 47 C.F.R. § 76.501(a)(2). Second, an individual or entity may not own or control a cable television system and have an attributable interest in a national television network. 47 C.F.R. § 76.501(a)(1). The FCC proposed to eliminate this rule, 47 Fed.Reg. 39,212 (1982), but has taken no final action.

Finally, the 1996 Telecommunications Act broke down barriers betweeen LECs and home entertainment industries, such as cable and DBS. As noted later, (pp. 430–431), the Act's chosen instrument was "open video systems" ("OVS")—a hybrid multichannel medium which has attracted little interest.

Broadcasting and common carriage have historically been distinct businesses, providing different types of information. The former has carried audio and video programming, the latter voice (traditional telephone) and data services (including telex, teletext, and facsimile). During the 1980s, the distinctions eroded notably. Broadcasting increasingly was used to transmit data through subcarrier or vertical blanking interval services; common carriers offered videoconferencing and, but for the cable-telco rules, would have offered multi-channel video programming. Cable television arguably stood in the middle of the confusion. Cable's product seemed like the familiar television service offered by broadcasters; but cable's high-capacity, wire-delivered service that consisted primarily of video programs from unaffiliated sources, had many similarities to common carriage.

10. Can the Commission, consistent with the First Amendment, prohibit a broadcaster from "speaking" in a thirteenth market because it is licensed to speak in twelve other markets? Would a similar rule limiting the number of newspapers owned by a single publisher be constitutional? Is it a proper (or desirable?) role for the government to protect the public from excessively powerful speakers? Were the Commission's rules defensible on the ground that they create opportunities for a larger number of speakers to contribute their voices to the mass media? Does that rationale extend to the Commission's prohibiting a telephone company from adding its own voice (by selecting video programs that it will deliver to customers) to the voices of others transmitted over the telephone network?

The Supreme Court examined the constitutionality of the Commission's ownership rules for the first and only time in FCC v. National Citizens Committee for Broadcasting, 436 U.S. 775, 98 S.Ct. 2096, 56 L.Ed.2d 697 (1978) (*NCCB*). The case involved a challenge to the rule prohibiting broadcast-local newspaper combinations. Only a small portion of Justice Marshall's lengthy opinion squarely addressed the constitutional question. In response to the argument that the rules "violate the First Amendment rights of newspaper owners," Justice Marshall wrote:

> * * * We cannot agree, for this argument ignores the fundamental proposition that there is no "unbridgeable First Amendment right to broadcast comparable to the right of every individual to speak, write, or publish." Red Lion Broadcasting Co. v. FCC, [p. 316] * * *.

The physical limitations of the broadcast spectrum are well known. Because of problems of interference between broadcast signals, a finite number of frequencies can be used productively; this number is far exceeded by the number of persons wishing to broadcast to the public. In light of this physical scarcity, Government allocation and regulation of broadcast frequencies are essential, as we have often recognized. * * * No one here questions the need for such allocation and regulation, and, given that need, we see nothing in the First Amendment to prevent the Commission from allocating licenses so as to promote the "public interest" in diversification of the mass communications media.

* * *

As we wrote in National Broadcasting, [319 U.S. 190, 63 S.Ct. 997, 87 L.Ed. 1344 (1943)], "the issue before us would be wholly different" if "the Commission [were] to choose among applicants upon the basis of their political, economic or social views." 319 U.S., at 226, 63 S.Ct., at 1014. Here the regulations are not content related; moreover, their purpose and effect is to promote free speech, not to restrict it.

* * *

In the instant case, far from seeking to limit the flow of information, the Commission has acted, in the Court of Appeals' words, "to enhance the diversity of information heard by the public without on-going government surveillance of the content of speech." * * * 555 F.2d, at 954. The regulations are a reasonable means of promoting the public interest in diversified mass communications; thus they do not violate the First Amendment rights of those who will be denied broadcast licenses pursuant to them. * * *

(a) You should reconsider this rather conclusory constitutional analysis after reading the materials in Chapter VI.

(b) For a different analysis of the rules upheld in *NCCB*, see Mills, et al., *The Constitutional Consideration of Multiple Media Ownership Regulation by the FCC*, 24 Am.U.L.Rev. 1217 (1975); Lee, *Antitrust Enforcement, Freedom of the Press and the "Open Market": The Supreme Court on the Structure and Conduct of Mass Media*, 32 Vand.L.Rev. 1251 (1979); Emord, *The First Amendment Invalidity of FCC Ownership Regulations*, 38 Cath.U.L.Rev. 401 (1989).

12. After becoming an American citizen, Rupert Murdoch, whose companies had broadcast and publishing operations throughout Australia, Europe, and North America (but no U.S. broadcast stations) formed the Fox Television Network. As part of the development of the Fox Network, Murdoch's News America Corp. acquired television stations in New York City and Boston; News America owned daily newspapers in those cities and, therefore, requested and received temporary waivers of the newspaper-broadcast cross-ownership rule. In such situations, the FCC customarily granted a temporary waiver of its ownership rules so that the owner of the co-located properties would not be required to make an immediate sale at a deeply discounted price. See Report and

Order, 50 FCC 2d 1046, 1076 n. 25 (1975); Metromedia Radio & Television, Inc., 102 FCC 2d 1334, 1353 (1985), affirmed Health & Medicine Policy Research Group v. FCC, 807 F.2d 1038 (D.C.Cir.1986) (discussing the FCC's waiver policies.) News America was unable to sell either of the Boston properties before the expiration of its waiver, however, and required an extension of the waiver to avoid violating the FCC's rules.

Before News America applied to the FCC for an extension of the waiver, Congress adopted appropriations legislation that included the following provision:

> [N]one of the funds appropriated [for the federal government for fiscal year 1988] * * * may be used to repeal, to retroactively apply changes in, or to begin or continue a reexamination of [its newspaper-television cross-ownership rule] * * *, or to extend the time period of current grants of temporary waivers to achieve compliance with such rule * * *.

When News America subsequently requested a waiver extension, the FCC denied the request, citing the limitation in the appropriations legislation. News America brought suit in federal court to strike down the legislation.

One focus of congressional attention when Congress acted had been Rupert Murdoch, who, according to some congressmen, was building a U.S. media empire because the FCC had little interest in enforcing its ownership rules. Senator Hollings, the author of the waiver provision in the legislation, originally stated that the action was directed specifically against Mr. Murdoch. 134 Cong.Rec. S63 (daily ed. Jan. 26, 1988). He later contended that the provision was meant to be general in its application. 134 Cong.Rec. S139 (daily ed. Jan. 27, 1988). When Congress acted, the News America waivers were the only ones outstanding.

(a) The court of appeals held that the legislation was unconstitutional, noting that "Congress has denied a single publisher/broadcaster the opportunity to ask the FCC to exercise its discretion to extend its waivers." News America Pub. v. FCC, 844 F.2d 800, 815 (D.C.Cir.1988). What is the relevance of the legislation's affecting only a single publisher/broadcaster? Consider these questions again after you have read the materials in Chapter VI.

(b) In a dissent, Judge Spottswood Robinson argued that the legislation properly served a legitimate congressional purpose and was therefore constitutional:

> If the aim is to preserve the cross-ownership rule, and the waiver extensions endanger the rule, then a prohibition on extensions of waivers—albeit only current ones—does serve the [asserted] purpose * * *.

* * *

To be sure, Congress could have brought future waivers within the purview of the [legislation], but that is not to say that its failure to do so renders this enactment unconstitutional. Rather, Congress may deal with immediate threats as they arise.

844 F.2d at 820, 821. Judge Robinson went on to suggest that broader congressional action, which had the effect of banning all waivers, could be constitutionally more problematic. Do you agree with his views?

As with common ownership, the Telecommunications Act of 1996 changed the ground rules for cross-ownership significantly. It basically repealed the "one-to-a-market" restriction, except perhaps as to print/broadcast combinations.

While the FCC's prior rules had restricted local radio and television cross-ownership to one extent or another, the Act allowed not unlimited, but higher degrees of cross-interests than before. As to radio, Section 202(b) provided a sliding scale of local cross-ownership, based upon the number of radio stations in the market.

Note: 1996 Act's New Ownership Restrictions

(b) Local Radio Diversity.—

(1) Applicable caps.—The Commission shall revise section 73.3555(a) of its regulations (47 C.F.R. 73.3555) to provide that—

(A) in a radio market with 45 or more commercial radio stations, a party may own, operate, or control up to 8 commercial radio stations, not more than 5 of which are in the same service (AM or FM);

(B) in a radio market with between 30 and 44 (inclusive) commercial radio stations, a party may own, operate, or control up to 7 commercial radio stations, not more than 4 of which are in the same service (AM or FM);

(C) in a radio market with between 15 and 29 (inclusive) commercial radio stations, a party may own, operate, or control up to 6 commercial radio stations, not more than 4 of which are in the same service (AM or FM); and

(D) in a radio market with 14 or fewer commercial radio stations, a party may own, operate, or control up to 5 commercial radio stations, not more than 3 of which are in the same service (AM or FM), except that a party may not own, operate, or control more than 50 percent of the stations in such market.

(2) Exception.—Notwithstanding any limitation authorized by this subsection, the Commission may permit a person or entity to own, operate, or control, or have a cognizable interest in, radio broadcast stations if the Commission determines that such ownership, operation, control, or interest will result in an increase in the number of radio broadcast stations in operation.

As discussed above in relation to common ownership, much of the rationale for local cross-ownership may involve apparent reductions in transactions costs. Indeed, these may be more realistic in cross-ownership than in common ownership situations. For example, six stations presumably can process their scheduling and billing less expensively together than separately.

Moreover, and not surprisingly, shortly after passage of the Act many group owners not only increased their national ownership but also bought a number of stations in the same market. There thus may be—or perceived to be—economies by combining both national and local functions. Indeed, a number of firms moved quickly to acquire multiple stations in large and medium-sized markets, along with their previously—noted expansion in terms of national station ownership.

It is less than clear, however, how easing of radio cross-ownership restrictions will impact on concerns as to localism and diversity. In very large markets like New York or Los Angeles, there might be little impact because even ownership of eight stations—roughly 20 percent to total radio licensees—would have little impact. Moreover, increased cross-ownership arguably might be the price of keeping marginal—particularly AM—stations on the air, resulting in a net long-term increase in voices—and hence localism and diversity. This may be tempered by the fact that many new local cross-owners also have bought enough stations for national coverage, as noted above. And a high degree of common and cross ownership may result in problems of monopsony and monopoly as to producers and advertisers.

The effect of easing the cross-ownership rules also may vary with the size of a market. For example, in the very largest markets, an entity cannot acquire more than 20 percent (8 of 45) radio stations. In smaller markets, however, a firm may own more than one-third (5 of 14) stations. As usual, the reasoning behind particular numbers is less than clear. But it seems strange to allow one firm to control more of a limited than a large number of voices. Indeed, the Act presumably would allow one company to own 3 out of seven radio stations in an area-not an unusual situation in smaller markets.

Finally, the Act also opened the way for the Commission to allow cross-ownership of broadcast television stations. As noted above, the FCC already had begun to move in this direction as to ownership of VHF and UHF stations. Section 202(C)(2) of the Act directed the Commission to engage in rulemaking to determine across-the-board rules for local television cross-ownership, by providing that:

(c) Television Ownership Limitations.

* * *

(2) Local ownership limitations.—The Commission shall conduct a rule-making proceeding to determine whether to retain, modify, or eliminate its limitations on the number of television stations that a person or entity may own, operate, or control, or have a cognizable interest in, within the same television market.

Again, it is not clear how the Commission will deal with this in even the near-term future. It seems reasonable to assume, however, that its tradition-ally limited policy in favor of allowing cross-ownership between major VHF and "failing" UHF stations will expand in the future.

The FCC's traditional common and cross ownership policies always have been less than precise. Ironically, the agency just had begun to clarify them when the 1996 Telecommunications Act became law. Although the Act's ownership provisions seem relatively clear on their face, they will require years of FCC interpretation to become reliable legal principles.

2. LIMITATIONS ON ALIEN OWNERSHIP

Section 310(b) of the Act explicitly prohibits more than 25 percent foreign ownership of a common carrier or broadcast station—but not a cable operator, apparently just an historical oversight. Very often these determinations turn on complex factual decisions as to personal and financial relationships between individuals. For example, in *Spanish International Communications Corporation,* (1986), the Administrative Law Judge went through dozens of pages describing the relations among the U.S. and alien parties. In fact, that decision relies heavily, if not exclusively, on the financial and personal relationships between the foreign investors and the U.S. licensees. This is not a terribly precise method of attributing "representation"—let alone actual ownership. It relies heavily upon a decisionmaker's potentially subjective views of his personal and professional relationships. A short taste follows.

27. *Background.* SIN, Inc., a Delaware corporation, is a Spanish-language television network which is also engaged in the business of national spot advertising sales representation * * *. It was formed in 1962, essentially to act as sales representative for KWEX–TV, KMEX and several Mexican border stations, and to distribute Spanish language programs to other stations in the U.S.

* * *

29. In 1971, 25% of the stock of Spanish International Network, Inc. was issued to Reynold Anselmo pursuant to an earlier understanding between him and the senior Azcarraga * * *; 75% remained in the name of Emilio Azcarraga Milmo * * *. At present, the company is 75% owned by Televisa, a Mexican corporation, and 25% by Mr. Anselmo * * *. SIN's three directors are Mr. Azcarraga * * *, Mr. Anselmo, and Alejandro Sada * * *. Like Azcarraga, Mr. Sada is a citizen of Mexico.

* * *

32. Televisa, which owns 75% of SIN, is a Mexican corporation with its principal place of business in Mexico * * *. It is a television network [that owns stations in Mexico and produces programming.] * * * Televisa is owned 58.25% by the Azcarraga[s] * * *.

* * *

34. SIN is Televisa's United States program distributor, accounting for one percent of Televisa's gross sales * * *, with four percent covering from all exports to foreign countries. * * *

40. *SIN as Program Source.* In 1972 SIN became the chief source of programming for the SICC stations (and later for Bahia and Seven Hills), obtaining most of it from Protele, an exporting subsidiary of Televisa. Prior to that time programming had been acquired from Teleprogramas (Anselmo's employer from 1954 until 1963) and later (1967) from V.T. Latin. Both companies were controlled by Azcarraga, Sr.

41. SIN provides basically all of the programming aired by the Licensees;[11] the percentage ranging from about 75% to 90% * * *. Although the general managers of the Licensee stations were involved in the selection of programs, both Mexican and non-Mexican, it was Anselmo who purchased them for the stations and negotiated the rates * * *. Daniel Villanueva, general manager then, as now, of KMEX in Los Angeles (as well as a shareholder, director and officer of SICC, Bahia and Seven Hills) indicated that he thought of SIN as being Anselmo and assumed a connection between them and Televisa * * *. Anselmo stated that in programming negotiation he did not think about which entity he represents, but attempted to do the best thing for all of them * * *. On SIN's behalf, he also decided what markup to charge the Licensee stations and informed the Licensee Boards * * *. [The opinion goes on to describe the contractual agreements between SIN and the Licensees, which, as discussed below, treat the Licensees less favorably than other outlets for SIN's programming.]

* * *

Business and Financial Relationships Between Licensee Principals and Mexican Nationals

80. *The Azcarragas and Anselmo.* [The Azcarragas gave Anselmo substantial loans to permit him to acquire ownership interests in the SICC stations.] * * *

81. In some cases, Azcarraga V. or a company in which he held an ownership interest, would also advance monies directly to the stations. In those instances, an amount representing Anselmo's and the other shareholders' shares of the payment, in accordance with each one's percentage ownership of the station, would be charged as a loan to the shareholder. Anselmo's share of such loans amounted to approximately $208,440 * * *.

85. Except for * * * [a small] initial * * * [investment], every investment in the stations made by Anselmo in the early days was financed by Azcarraga V. * * *. This was not the case with respect to Anselmo's investment in the Miami station, SICC's final acquisition. Anselmo's interest was not depended [sic] on loans * * *. Thereafter, Anselmo received no financial assistance from Azcarraga or other Mexican interests. He did, however, borrow $127,000 from

---

11. The term "Licensees" is used herein to include SICC, Bahia and Seven Hills.

SIN in 1976 to invest in the San Francisco station license to Bahia two years earlier * * *.

87.   In addition to the foregoing, in 1967 Azcarraga V. guaranteed the $92,000 mortgage on Anselmo's home. * * * The Azcarraga family, or companies in which they held an ownership interest, also bore many of Anselmo's living expenses after he moved to New York in 1963. * * *

90.   *Azcarraga Vidaurreta and SICC.* * * * [It] was the understanding, which Azcarraga V. always adhered to, that he would provide the rogramming to the stations and defer any payment therefor. * * *

91.   * * * [I]n the early 1960's an account was established at Frost National Bank in San Antonio, Texas, for the San Antonio and Los Angeles stations to draw upon * * *. As a requirement for the bank's financing the stations in this manner, funds equal to 50% of the amount to be loaned to the individual stations were to be placed in a joint time deposit account as a collateral deposit. * * * Each stockholder [of the station] was charged with his share of the collateral deposit account in accordance with his stock ownership in the respective stations. At such time as the loans made by the Frost Bank were repaid by the stations, the collateral representing Anselmo's * * * shares would be released and returned to Azcarraga V. * * *.

92.   *Azcarraga Vidaurreta and Other SICC Principals.* Azcarraga V. also financed early investors in the SICC stations other than Anselmo * * *.

[The opinion goes on at length to catalogue various financial, business, and other relationships between the Azcarraga family and the principals and employees of SICC, Bahia, and Seven Hills.]

The ALJ eventually held that the overall pattern of relationships constituted alien ownership, and thus violated Section 310. The existing owners were forced into a distress sale.

In a slightly more concrete contest, the significance of non-equity financial relationships arose in a somewhat more concrete context in the litigation below. Unlike the *Spanish International* analysis, however, the Commission's decision is based almost exclusively upon the significance of capital contributions.

FOX TELEVISION STATIONS, INC.

Federal Communications Commission, 1995.
77 Rad. Reg. 2d (P & F) 1043.

MEMORANDUM OPINION AND ORDER

By the Commission: Commissioner Quello concurring and issuing a statement.

1. Fox Television Stations, Inc. ("FTS") seeks renewal of its license for station WNYW–TV (Channel 5) in New York City.[6] The Metropolitan Council of NAACP Branches ("Metro NAACP") has petitioned to deny the renewal. * * *

I. Introduction

2. On May 23, 1994, FTS informed the Mass Media Bureau that The News Corporation Ltd. ("News Corp."), an Australian company, owns more than 99 percent of the corporate equity capital of FTS's parent company, Twentieth Holdings Corporation ("THC"), even though News Corp. owns only 24 percent of THC's voting stock. To determine whether the renewal application may be granted, we must therefore assess that ownership structure in light of Section 310(b)(4) of the Communications Act * * * We must also decide whether the application should be designated for hearing based on other issues raised by Metro NAACP.

[The Commission explained the license application's representations as to THC's' stock structure as follows:

> THC will issue two classes of stock, one common and one preferred. The preferred stock will exercise 76% of the vote on all matters; and the remaining 24% of the vote will be exercised by the common stock.

Murdoch held the preferred stock, and News Corp. the common stock. The effect of the arrangement was to give voting control to Murdoch— independent of his arguable *de facto* control of News Corp. Murdoch had become a U.S. citizen at the time of the application; News Corp. was and remained an Australian corporation.]

3. More specifically, this case presents the following issues: (1) whether News Corp.'s ownership of 99 percent of the capital contributed to THC exceeds Section 310(b)(4)'s benchmark of 25 percent of the "capital stock" of the company; (2) whether, if News Corp.'s interest is deemed to exceed the benchmark, FTS has intentionally concealed that fact or misrepresented its compliance with the statute in applications and other filings submitted to the Commission beginning in 1985; (3) whether News Corp. exercises de facto control over FTS or whether Rupert Murdoch, the Chairman of News Corp., controls FTS as the representative of News Corp.; and (4) if we find that FTS's alien ownership exceeds the benchmark, that FTS is under alien control, or that FTS has lacked candor, what remedial action, if any, is appropriate.

* * *

6. The six [FTS] stations were WNYW–TV (formerly WNEW–TV) in New York City, New York; KTTV–TV in Los Angeles, California; WFLD–TV in Chicago, Illinois; WTTG–TV in Washington, D.C.; KDAF–TV (formerly KRLD–TV) in Dallas, Texas; and KRIV–TV in Houston, Texas.

II. SUMMARY

5. * * * For the reasons set forth below, we deny Metro NAACP's Petition to Deny, and grant FTS's renewal application conditioned upon FTS's election either (1) to submit information demonstrating that the level of FTS's foreign ownership is consistent with the public interest; or (2) to come into compliance with the foreign ownership benchmark of Section 310(b)(4).

6. We find that News Corp.'s ownership of THC's "capital stock" exceeds the 25 percent foreign ownership benchmark established in Section 310(b)(4). THC wholly owns the licensee, FTS. Although News Corp. owns only 24 percent of the total number of outstanding shares of THC stock, News Corp. contributed over 99 percent of the capital invested in THC and is entitled to virtually all of the economic incidents of THC's operation. In these circumstances, we conclude that the statute requires us to evaluate not only the number of shares of stock held by alien owners, but also the amount of equity capital contributed by such owners. Such an approach effectuates the statutory objective, and will enable the Commission to perform a bona fide analysis of alien ownership. This decision is also consistent with the Commission's prior decisions * * *

7. Even though FTS exceeds the ownership benchmark, we do not conclude that FTS intentionally misrepresented or concealed that fact. Although there are some disputed issues as to subsidiary or "proximate" facts, the totality of the evidence before us does not present a substantial and material question of fact on the ultimate issue of whether FTS misrepresented the facts or lacked candor in its 1985 transfer application or any of its subsequent filings with this Commission. We reach this decision after careful review of the voluminous documentary and testimonial evidence and the parties' lengthy submissions.

8. We recognize that our reported interpretations of Section 310(b)(4) at the time FTS filed its original application in 1985 did not clearly indicate that a foreign corporation's equity capital contributions were of decisional significance to the Commission in determining a corporate parent's compliance with the statutory benchmark. Thus, although the Commission had held that capital contributions were relevant in the limited partnership context, the totality of the circumstances leads us to conclude that FTS did not believe that it had a duty to disclose the amount of equity capital contributed to THC by foreign interests, and thus FTS did not intentionally conceal this information in an effort to deceive the Commission.

9. We further find that Murdoch, by virtue of his controlling voting interest in THC, exercises *de jure* control over that company and its wholly-owned subsidiary, FTS. Moreover, the record shows that Murdoch was in charge of THC's day-to-day operations and dominated its corporate affairs. While FTS and THC are subsidiaries of News Corp. for financial reporting purposes, the totality of the evidence demonstrates that Murdoch, a United States citizen, nonetheless exercises *de facto*

control over THC. We reject the contention that as a consequence of his position with News Corp., Murdoch is acting as a representative of alien interests.

10.   The Commission holds that News Corp.'s 99 percent capital contribution to THC exceeds the 25 percent benchmark. A licensee is permitted to exceed the benchmark, however, where the Commission expressly finds that the "public interest" would be served. Absent such a public interest finding, FTS must comply with the benchmark.

* * *

III.   ALIEN OWNERSHIP OF FTS EXCEEDS THE BENCHMARK ESTABLISHED IN SECTION 310(B)(4)

* * *

32.   We conclude that THC's foreign ownership exceeds the statutory ownership benchmark because approximately 99 percent of the company's equity capitalization was provided by a foreign corporation. In so concluding, we recognize that the Commission's prior decisions have directly addressed the relevance of capital contributions in determining compliance with the ownership limitations in the context of limited partnerships, and although the rationale of those decisions may also apply in the corporate context, no Commission decision has clearly explained how the ownership benchmark should be computed for corporations or the extent to which capital contributions may be material to that computation. Accordingly, in this decision, we set forth the legal basis for our conclusion that the amount of alien capital contributed to a corporation is a relevant consideration in deciding whether the ownership benchmark is exceeded and, in particular, why it is relevant to THC's corporate structure.

A.   The Ownership Benchmark Applies to Beneficial Ownership Interests

33.   The statutory benchmark at issue in this case applies to a "corporation . . . of which more than one-fourth of the capital stock is owned of record or voted by . . . a corporation organized under the laws of a foreign country." 47 U.S.C. § 310(b)(4). The issue here is whether News Corp., an Australian corporation, has an interest in THC's "capital stock owned of record or voted" that exceeds the benchmark.

* * *

35.   In some contexts, counting the number of shares of outstanding stock owned of record by aliens yields an accurate assessment of the extent of alien ownership interests in a corporation. Thus, in some circumstances, it is an appropriate method for determining compliance with the Section 310(b)(4) ownership benchmark. We do not agree, however, that in all circumstances the method FTS advocates for determining ownership interests comports with common sense or congressional intent.

36. In enacting the statutory language in question, Congress clearly indicated its concern with the extent to which aliens possess substantial ownership interests in corporations, in addition to and independent of alien voting interests. Using a simple "count the shares" approach may not accurately reflect the actual extent of alien ownership interests in a corporation, particularly when the corporation issues more than one class of stock, and those classes have widely divergent characteristics. Accordingly, to carry out Congress's intention that the extent of alien ownership interests be fairly evaluated, the Commission must construe the benchmark in a manner that considers factors in addition to the number of alien-owned shares of stock where the distribution of shares of stock is not proportionate to equity interests. Thus, the Commission should consider the amount of foreign capital contributions to a corporation in determining compliance with the statutory ownership benchmark.

* * *

42. FTS's insistence that we calculate the ownership benchmark only by counting the number of shares of stock issued to aliens, regardless of the class or nature of such stock, could, in some instances, yield results that bear no relationship to an alien's actual ownership interest in a corporate holding company or licensee. For example, a corporate applicant's parent company could issue four shares of stock, all of which vote, but three of which are purchased by United States citizens for $1 each, while an alien pays $1 billion for the remaining share. Under FTS's interpretation, this arrangement would comply with both the voting and ownership benchmarks of Section 310(b)(4). Presumably, FTS's approach would also find compliant an arrangement where the parent company issues two classes of stock with disparate voting attributes. For example, if United States citizens held three shares of Class A stock entitled to one vote per share, and an alien held one share of Class B stock entitled to three votes per share, the benchmarks would be satisfied under FTS's theory, since the alien's single share constitutes only 25 percent of the number of outstanding shares of "capital stock", notwithstanding its right to cast 50 percent of the votes.

43. Indeed, THC's own corporate structure provides a vivid example of the potential pitfalls of FTS's methodology. It would allow nominal compliance with the 25 percent statutory ownership benchmark, even though News Corp. has virtually all of the beneficial ownership interest in THC. * * * We cannot construe the statutory language in a manner that effectively eviscerates the statutory restrictions. Congress could not have envisioned every circumstance that might arise, and where a simple "count the shares" methodology leads to patently absurd results that defeat the congressional intent, we intend to fill any such voids in the law consistent with the underlying congressional purpose.

B. *Capital Contributions as "Capital Stock"*

45. Because News Corp.'s true ownership interest in THC is not revealed by simple reference to the total number of shares of stock it

holds, we must determine an alternative method for quantifying News Corp.'s ownership of THC's "capital stock." We believe that evaluating News Corp.'s equity capital contributions to the corporation * * * is the best way to quantify the extent of News Corp.'s ownership interest consistent with the congressional intent and the statutory language.

46. Using equity capital contributions to measure ownership interests in corporations is consistent with and reflects the customary method by which corporate ownership interests were measured at the time of Section 310(b)'s enactment. Traditionally, shareholders' ownership interests in corporations correspond to the amounts of their capital contributions. These contributions are acknowledged through the issuance of stock certificates or "shares" that represent those interests. * * *

* * *

48. In summary, it is evident from the legislative history of Section 310(b) that Congress intended the Commission to undertake a bona fide assessment of the extent of foreign ownership interests in corporations. Therefore, consistent with congressional intent, we shall construe the statutory benchmark language relating to capital stock in a manner that permits a bona fide analysis. Where, as here, the ownership of corporate shares does not correspond to the beneficial ownership of the corporation, we will not be bound by a formalistic and formulaic "count the shares" approach that understates the true extent of alien ownership.

49. We recognize that in certain situations, equity capital contributions may not fairly measure the true extent of an ownership interest. For example, such a methodology might not reflect "sweat equity" invested by shareholders, or could present other problems when applied to widely-held corporations. Should such issues arise, we will evaluate them on a case-by-case basis.

[The Commission went on at considerable length to consider indications as to News Corp.'s alleged misrepresentations, and ultimately dismissed the claims.]

* * *

VIII. BENCHMARK COMPLIANCE FOR PUBLIC INTEREST WAIVER

* * *

177. FTS has argued in the course of this proceeding that, in the event the Commission determines that its ownership structure exceeds the benchmark, the Commission should nevertheless approve its renewal application under the public interest standard of Section 310(b)(4). Among other public interest considerations, FTS maintains the following: it has established a fourth broadcast network; reduced the dominance of the three existing networks, thereby improving the position of local stations relative to the networks and providing competitive choices for advertisers, program suppliers and viewers; promoted the viability of UHF television stations; facilitated local news programming; and made available increased children's programming. FTS also suggests that the

public interest implications of its ownership structure should be analyzed in light of Murdoch's *de jure* and *de facto* control of THC and by FTS's assertion that Murdoch has *de facto* control of News Corp. Metro NAACP, on the other hand, has disputed certain of these statements and whether they justify a public interest finding.

178. These factors, including the arguments concerning them raised by FTS and Metro NAACP, will be considered as part of our public interest determination. * * * We therefore decline to make a public interest determination at this time and shall allow further submissions on this issue.

[In a concurring statement, Commissioner Quello stated that he found FTS to be 76 percent owned by Rupert Murdoch, a U.S. citizen, and thus that there was no alien ownership issue. He also rejected arguments as to possible misrepresentations, and indicated that he would favor grant of a public interest waiver on the record before the Commission.]

Notes and Questions

1. Shouldn't this be an easy case, since News Corp.'s CEO, Rupert Murdoch, was a U.S. citizen? Is the citizenship of the corporation or of its chief executive—and arguably controlling shareholder—at issue? Although Murdoch's change from Australian to U.S. citizenship presumably was a convenient way to allow him to form FTS, is there any question about the validity of his change? After all, the Court of Appeals for the District of Columbia Circuit previously had accepted it. On the other hand, does the ease of Murdoch's change in citizenship raise some questions about the rationality of Section 310's requirements in the first place? Would he have been any less likely to engage in propaganda after his transmogrification?

2. What is the relationship between News Corp., THC, and FTS? Who owns how much of each corporation?

3. Why is News Corp.'s "equity capital contribution" of decisional significance? *Per se*, does the investment give News Corp. any more power than a simple loan? Is it important to know what, if any conditions were attached to the "contribution?" For example, it is not uncommon for debt instruments to give lenders the right to take control of a company if it does not produce specified financial results. Was there such a provision here? Would it have made any difference?

4. To what extent does a "contribution" create the same type of relationship as in Spanish International? Even if it does not create direct legal control—which the FCC finds it to in *Fox*—does it create some form of personal relationship? Some type of moral obligation? Is it possible to measure this type of interest very accurately?

5. Despite the adoption of recent changes to both the General Agreement on Trade and Tariffs ("GATT") and the World Trade Organization's ("WTO's") telecommunications provisions, Section 310(b) remains largely intact. Although the WTO agreement prohibits signatory nations—including the U.S.—from imposing alien ownership limitations, the Congress refused to amend the statute. The Commission has found administrative means,

however, of reaching the WTO's goals. Most important, it has construed the 24 percent limitation on alien holding companies to create a rebuttable presumption that any WTO signatory is entitled to a waiver. (But note that the FCC may not waive the 20 percent limitation on direct alien ownership, thus requiring the use of an intermediary holding company.) In addition, the Commission imposed an "equal communications opportunity" ("ECO") requirement of showing that a company's home country allowed entry by U.S. firms; but the burden of proof is on a objector.

6. What type of "public interest" showing must FTS make? Is it enough for it to show that it created new competition in both network and independent television? That it encouraged the development of a potential fifth and sixth national network? How, if at all, does that take away from the alleged evils of alien ownership?

3.   CHANGES IN OWNERSHIP: PRIOR APPROVALS AND THE MEDIA MARKETPLACE

Acquisitions and dispositions of radio and television stations can create regulatory nightmares. Section 310(d) of the Communications Act bars any changes in ownership without prior FCC approval. This limitation is a complement to the scheme for initial licensing; it is intended to ensure that scarce licenses are not transferred into the hands of unfit parties. Typically, the prior approval requirement simply imposes some delay on the transaction—the approval process can take months. For the lawyer, this means planning ahead; deals can fall apart in the latter stages if the FCC approval process has not been moved along deliberately while other details are being wrapped up.

In some situations, the prior approval requirement is not simply a matter of timing. Because the statute requires approval of a "transfer of control," one must know what constitutes control and when such control has changed. The Commission, unfortunately, has said repeatedly that the concept of control cannot be defined and must be decided on a case-by-case basis in light of the relevant facts. In short, the Commission knows a change of control when it sees it—at which point it may be too late for the licensee (and its unfortunate lawyer) to request a prior approval. Under the circumstances, communications lawyers have to develop their own sense of when a change of control might be occurring.

Another problem created by the prior approval requirement is that some transactions simply will not work if they must be held up while everyone waits for the FCC to give its consent. In such circumstances, the Communications Act becomes an almost impenetrable—even if unintended—obstacle to a transaction. Indeed, when hostile tender offers arose as a threat to incumbent managements of publicly traded companies in the 1980s, many potential target companies acquired FCC licensees just to shield themselves from hostile tender offers—which are made much more difficult by the risk of substantial delay.

The material that follows explores both of these problems. First, the court of appeals considers the meaning of Section 310(d) to determine whether a proxy contest causes a change of control in an FCC-regulated company. In the next selection, a Commission policy statement seeks to accommodate within the prior approval process the needs of companies that are involved in time-sensitive transactions.

As you read this material and the notes that follow, consider the degree to which the timing of a change of control can be "manipulated" to accommodate certain corporate objectives. Is either the Commission or the court straining to read the statute so that the Communications Act is not a significant obstacle to contemporary corporate dealmaking?

a. *"Control"*

Stephen F. Sewell, *Assignments and Transfers of Control of FCC Authorizations Under Section 310(d) of the Communications Act of 1934*, 43 Fed. Comm. L. J. 277, 285–293 (1991).

An assignment occurs when the license moves from one entity to another. For example, the Commission approved the assignment of the license of station WOR–TV from RKO General, Inc., to GTH–101, Inc. In a transfer of control, the licensee remains the same, but the owners of the licensee change. A transfer of control occurred, for example, when General Electric bought the stock of RCA, Inc., giving General Electric control of RCA and its subsidiary, NBC. NBC held the licenses in question before and after the purchase of RCA's stock, but NBC is now controlled by General Electric, not by RCA. Within the communications bar, an assignment may be described as an asset sale, and a transfer of control as a stock sale. As far as Commission rules and policies are concerned, there are no significant differences between assignments and transfers of control. There may be important differences for individual applicants; for example, tax consequences.

The statute also refers to the assignment or transfer of "any rights" under a license or permit. The Commission stated in Turner Broadcasting System, Inc., that "the 'rights' referred to go to the ownership and operation of licensed stations." In that case, the Board of Directors of CBS, Inc., had amended its bylaws and entered into agreements with banks in order to fend off hostile takeover attempts. Turner Broadcasting System contended that the CBS Board had transferred "rights" within the meaning of the Act without prior Commission approval. The Commission found, however, that the amendments and agreements did not change ownership of the corporation, nor did they affect the operation of CBS stations. Consequently, the Commission concluded that its prior approval was not required under section 310(d) of the Act.

A "right" under section 310(d) does not include the assignment of a contractual right to buy a station. Thus, if a licensee sold an option to buy its station, the subsequent sale of that option to a third party does not require Commission approval, although a later exercise of that option would. The Commission has also ruled that section 310(d) does not apply to the assignment of a lease of the transmitting equipment used by a broadcast station, in contrast to the license to operate that equipment. The right to vote a controlling block of stock, however, even where the buyer of that right grants voting control to the seller by a proxy, is a "right" under the license that cannot pass without the Commission's prior approval.

* * * [T]he Avco amendment, the last clause of section 310(d), barred the procedure under which "the Commission [had] subjected assignment applications to the type of comparative consideration employed in passing on initial applications for permits or licenses." Accordingly, the contention that a party would allegedly provide better service than the buyer proposed in an application cannot be considered under the Avco amendment. In some cases involving hostile takeovers of licensees, the Commission has granted its permission to two entities to acquire control, one friendly and one hostile. In such cases, the Commission found each buyer basically qualified, so that stockholders could determine which proposal was more advantageous to them. There was no Commission comparison between the two buyers, however, and the Avco amendment did not prohibit consideration of the second-filed application.

Section 310(d) makes specific reference to section 308 of the Act, which requires written applications for Commission authorizations. In turn, section 309 applies to applications filed under section 308. Section 309 specifies the procedures to be used for various kinds of authorizations. Section 309(b) provides that no application "for an instrument of authorization in the broadcasting or common carrier [and other specified] services ... shall be granted by the Commission earlier than thirty days following issuance of public notice" of acceptance of the application for filing. Within that 30–day period, interested parties may file petitions to deny the application, under section 309(d). Only the kinds of applications specified in section 309(b) are subject to the plenary 30–day wait/petition-to-deny procedures. All other applications can be acted upon as soon as they are processed.

* * *

Even in those services that generally require the use of plenary procedures, assignment and transfer applications may be processed under summary procedures in specified circumstances. * * * In the broadcast services, however, applications that fall within the 309(c)(2)(B) exemptions are filed on FCC Form 316, commonly referred to as the "short form." Broadcast applications that do not qualify under the exemptions are filed on "long-form" applications; FCC Form 314 (assignments) and FCC Form 315 (transfers of control). Consequently, cases dealing with broadcast applications may refer to "long-form" or "short-form" procedures.

STORER COMMUNICATIONS, INC. v. FCC

United States Court of Appeals, District of Columbia Circuit, 1985.
763 F.2d 436.

PER CURIAM. * * * [The FCC] determined that, in the specific circumstances presented here where a committee of minority shareholders of Storer Communications, Inc. ("Storer") mounted a proxy contest with the purpose of replacing the existing board of directors, any resulting change in control would not constitute a "substantial change" in control requiring full compliance with the pre-grant application approval procedures of 47 U.S.C. § 309. The Commission concluded that the public interest would be satisfied by Commission review of the shareholder committee's actions pursuant to a modified version of the FCC's "short form" transfer of control application procedures. We affirm the Commission's decision.

I. BACKGROUND

Section 310(d) of the Communications Act ("the Act"), 47 U.S.C. § 310(d), provides in pertinent part:

"No * * * station license, or any rights thereunder, shall be transferred, assigned, or disposed of in any manner, voluntarily or involuntarily, directly or indirectly, *or by transfer of control of any corporation holding such * * * license,* to any person except upon application to the Commission and upon finding by the Commission that the public interest, convenience, and necessity will be served thereby." (emphasis added).

Section 304(b) of the Act provides that before certain license applications can be granted, including applications for the assignment or transfer of a license, the Commission must issue a public notice followed by a 30–day waiting period in which, pursuant to Section 309(d), any "party in interest" may file a petition to deny the application. Section 309(c) of the Act, however, provides that certain types of applications, e.g., transfers not involving a "substantial change" in control, are excepted from the procedures set forth in Section 309(b). Pursuant to Commission regulations, applications for a transfer subject to the notice and 30–day waiting period of Section 309(b) are filed on FCC Form 315 ("long form") whereas applications falling within one of the exceptions listed in Section 309(c) are filed on FCC Form 315 ("short form"). See 47 C.F.R. § 73.3540 (1984). Applications filed on the short form are not subject to the 30–day waiting period, petitions to deny, or the potential of a hearing which are entailed in applications filed on the long form.

The events culminating in the present action began on March 19, 1985, when a shareholder group, known as The Committee for Full Value of Storer Communications, Inc. ("the Committee"), notified the Commission by letter that it had acquired ownership or voting rights in 5.3 percent of Storer's stock and that it intended to conduct a proxy contest to replace Storer's existing board of directors with a new slate of nominees. * * * The Committee's nominees pledged, if elected, to implement a program to maximize the value of the shareholders' investment in Storer by selling the company's assets and distributing the net proceeds to the shareholders. In its letter of notification, the Committee asserted its position that the election of a new board of directors by existing shareholders would not be a transfer of control requiring prior Commission consent under the Act. The Committee, however, further stated:

> "We are mindful that in the past, the Commission has used the 'short form' application for consent to transfer control (FCC Form 316) as a means to act on such proposals. Despite our view that the 'short form' is unnecessary, we enclose for your convenience an original and two copies of a completed form. If the Commission considers the form to be necessary, it is respectfully requested that the application be granted as expeditiously as possible."

Storer filed a petition for dismissal of the application on the grounds that control of Storer rested in the existing board of directors; consequently replacing the existing board with a new board "would constitute a voluntary de facto transfer of control" which could be accomplished only with prior Commission consent pursuant to long-form, not short-form, procedures.

On March 29, 1985, the FCC's Mass Media Bureau ("the Bureau"), finding that ultimate control of the corporation rested with the shareholders and not the board, agreed with the Committee's position that no transfer of control requiring prior Commission approval was at issue in the proposed election of a new board. The Bureau, nonetheless, granted the Committee's short-form application "to remove any uncertainty as to [the Committee's] authority to proceed." Storer filed a petition for review on April 1, 1985, seeking full Commission review of the Bureau's decision. On April 25, 1985, the Commission issued its opinion reversing the Bureau in part by finding a cognizable transfer of control but upholding the Committee's right to proceed in its proxy solicitation without the necessity of first undergoing the long-form approval process. Storer then filed this appeal pursuant to 42 U.S.C. § 402(b).

II. DISCUSSION

* * *

* * * At issue here is Section 309(c)(2)(B) excepting transfers involving Commission:

> "consent to an involuntary assignment or transfer under Section 310(d) of this title or to an assignment or transfer thereunder which does not involve *a substantial change in ownership or control*."

What constitutes a substantial change in control is not defined in the statute.

In this case, the Commission, faced with a question of first impression, considered the relevant factors and reached a reasoned conclusion with respect to the facts of this particular adjudicatory proceeding which presented a need for prompt action. The Commission noted that this decision was limited to the specific circumstances of this case and in no way prejudiced the Commission's adoption of alternate procedures in the future. * * * On the facts presented, we cannot say that the Commission acted arbitrarily, capriciously, or abused its discretion.

The Commission cited a number of considerations which, taken as a whole, led it to conclude that the change in control was not "substantial." The Commission first noted that the Committee proposed only to solicit proxies for the election of new directors. The Committee did not propose any change in stock ownership or any change in the voting rights of the shareholders. The shareholders, thus, retained their ultimate right of control. Under the applicable corporation laws of Ohio, the shareholders must elect a board of directors annually and 25% of the shareholders may at any time call a special meeting to remove the board. The Commission further noted that any subsequent decision by the newly-elected board to liquidate the assets of the company would require a two-thirds vote of the shareholders and would be subject to prior Commission approval pursuant to the long-form procedures. Thus, the Commission concluded that the shareholders retained ultimate control and that any change in the composition of the board at the annual shareholders' meeting would result from the shareholders' exercise of their substantial control, not a transfer of that control.

* * *

* * * [T]he test generally applied by the Commission in the past for determining whether a transfer constitutes a substantial change in control has linked a substantial change in control to some transfer of stock or on-going voting interests. The Commission's regulations setting forth the types of transfers or assignments which can properly be filed on a short form (FCC Form 316) further supports the finding that the Commission's established practice is to consider changes in control nonsubstantial if not accompanied by some change in ownership or voting rights. See 47 C.F.R. § 73.3540(f) (1984). The Commission specifically found 47 C.F.R. § 73.3540(f)(5) analogous to the matter at issue in this case. That section provides that an "[a]ssignment or transfer from a corporation to a wholly owned subsidiary thereof or vice versa, or where there is an assignment from a corporation to a corporation owned or controlled by the assignor shareholders without substantial change in their interests" is a nonsubstantial change in control which may be filed on a short form (FCC Form 316).

This is not to say that a substantial change in control may never occur without some change in ownership or voting rights, but only that this is a major factor in determining whether a substantial change has occurred. * * * There may be varying degrees of working control exercised at different levels of the corporation. Corporate officers or station managers may exercise substantial day-to-day working control; yet FCC approval would not be required before a corporation was allowed to replace such personnel. Directors may also change on an evolutionary basis, e.g., several directors may retire or resign over the course of a year. The Commission only requires that such evolutionary changes be reported on an annual Ownership Report.

The Commission, thus, is required to engage in making fine distinctions with respect to gradations of control in determining whether any particular transfer of control is a substantial change. We find that the Commission's reliance on whether a transfer of control is accompanied by a change of ownership or voting rights as a major factor aiding in the determination of whether a change is substantial to be entirely reasonable. In the present case, the shareholders could elect the new board members at the annual meeting and subsequently decide not to approve their liquidation plan or even to remove them and reseat the old board. On the other hand, an incumbent board or executive officer who has actual working control which is backed up by significant ownership interests or voting rights possesses a measurably greater degree of control—one which is not exercised solely by the grace of others possessing the ultimate authority or control.

* * *

Appellants also focus on the declared objective of the new board if elected: to liquidate the company. Appellants argue that breaking up Storer through a liquidation may not be in the public interest. Appellants in effect assert that the Commission must review the stated policies of the nominees versus the policies of the incumbent board. Congress, however, explicitly prohibited such comparative evaluation in the review of transfer applications. *See* 47 U.S.C. § 310(d) ("the Commission may not consider whether the public interest, convenience, and necessity might be served by the transfer, assignment, or disposal of the permit or license to a person other than the proposed transferee or assignee."). * * * The Commission's modified short-form procedure adequately assured that the proposed nominees were qualified. In fact, Storer has raised no material question as to the qualifications of the nominees.

We note that the modified short-form procedure adopted does not leave appellant and intervenors completely without a forum for comment or recourse in the case of a Commission mistake. The rules provide for the filing of informal objections before the application is granted. See 47 C.F.R. § 73.3587 (1984). The statute also provides a safety valve through petitions for reconsideration, see 47 U.S.C. § 405, and revocation, see 47 U.S.C. § 312.

Finally, we find that the Commission reasonably resolved a number of competing policy considerations in this case. There was a need for prompt action in the face of a pending proxy contest. * * *

Whereas the long-form review only required a 30–day waiting period, if petitions to deny are filed, it may take the Commission a significant additional period of time to consider the filings and determine whether a hearing is necessary. For tactical reasons, proxy contests are often not begun until within weeks prior to a shareholder meeting. Requiring long-form review could very well result in unduly insulating incumbent directors from challenge.[5] Such a result would not only be inconsistent with federal securities law protecting corporate democracy but also with the purposes of Section 309. Section 309 pre-grant procedures were drafted in order to prevent parties from using the Commission's procedures for purposes of delay and to minimize the burden on Commission resources. * * * The Commission did not act unreasonably or improperly by taking these factors into consideration in reaching its final determination.

Note: Time Brokerage Agreements Compared

Under a "time brokerage" contract, a licensee allows a third party— usually another local broadcaster—to program its station. While no stock or assets change hands, control of the lessor's station arguably may change, as discussed in Michael E. Lewyn, *Whan is Time Brokerage a Transfer of Control? The FEE'c Regulation of Local Marketing Agreements and the Need for Rulemaking*, 6 Fordham Intell. Prop. Media & Ent. L.J. 1. (1995).

In order to save their stations, many licensees entered into time brokerage agreements which dramatically differed from the time brokerage agreements of the 1950s and 1960s. Instead of giving a broker a few hours a week, many 1990s agreements allowed the broker to "purchase 100% of the available broadcast time from the other station for a flat monthly fee, and act as the programmer and sales representative for that station." While 1960s time brokers were often small ethnic broadcasters, 1990s time brokers often have been prospective purchasers, and many 1990s agreements have given the broker an option to purchase the brokered station. Time brokerage arguably has saved weak television and radio stations by allowing them to jointly operate facilities with other stations and thereby reduce expenses.

Before 1989, "it was widely assumed that the type of agreement which provided for the brokering of a substantial portion of a station's time, would violate section 310(d) of the Communications Act and attendant FCC policies." In 1989, however, the FCC repealed its prohibition against "one station brokering time on another station in the same market." Shortly thereafter, the FCC staff began to approve "modern" LMAs. For example, in Russo, the Bureau upheld a time brokerage agreement involving competing stations even though the agreement provided that the broker would program 20 hours per day of programming and have an option to purchase the brokered station. The Bureau found that the licensee had retained control of its station because, among other factors, it had "(1) 'retained its manage-

---

5. The Commission, of course, acknowledges that it would be obliged to require long-form review despite this result if it were necessary to satisfy the terms of Section 309. * * * Having determined that Section 309 did not require long-form review under the circumstances of this case, however, the Commission properly took into account various considerations in determining the appropriate procedure to require.

ment personnel, including its General Manager, Business Manager, Traffic Director, Executive Secretary, and Chief Engineer' ... (2) retained, by written contract, full authority over programming and personnel ... and (3) retained control over station financing, leaving the broker merely the ordinary 'profit of advertising revenues over brokerage fee.' " The FCC also noted that the LMA provided that the brokered licensee would have full authority over the station, including the right to reject or preempt programming and advertisements and the right to supervise all personnel through its General Manager and Chief Engineer.

After Russo, brokered licensees have been able to obtain nearly all of their programming from time brokers. Not surprisingly, over the past five years, the FCC has approved more time brokerage agreements than it has rejected.

The FCC, however, has declined to adopt any broad rules governing time brokerage on the ground that the question of whether a licensee has "lost control" over a station is one that is most appropriately addressed on a case-by-case basis. Under this "case-by-case" inquiry, the FCC will typically address the extent of the broker's control over the brokered station's finances, personnel, and programming. If the broker rather than the brokered licensee controls station finances, personnel or programming, the licensee has violated § 310(d) by transferring control of its station without FCC permission.

———

In order to comply with § 310(d) of the Communications Act, a licensee must retain ultimate control over station personnel, programming and finances. However, a licensee may delegate day-to-day control over all three areas, as long as the licensee continues to set policies guiding station operations. Although contract terms may be relevant, provisions that "purport to retain control in the licensee, if not actually exercised, will not ensure protection where the FCC believes that the totality of the circumstances indicate that there has been an unauthorized transfer of control."

b. Tender Offers

Tender offers—and particularly hostile ones—raise particular problems, because of tension between the communications and securities laws. As discussed by Sewell, this has resulted in the Commission's adopting the complex set of rules set forth below.

The Commission has also adopted special procedures for parties seeking to acquire control of corporate licensees by tender offer. Unlike a proxy contest where a party seeks control by persuading shareholders to vote for a new slate of directors, the offeror seeks control by asking shareholders to sell, or "tender," their shares to the offeror at a specified price. Federal securities laws recognize that tender offers perform a useful function by keeping existing management alert or by weeding out inefficient management. Delays in the tender-offer process aid existing management by affording it time to erect defensive barriers. It is federal policy, therefore, to avoid delay caused by government review of tender offers. Federal statutes provide, for example, that the Securities and Exchange Commission must make its review promptly and that the Antitrust Division of the Justice Department or the Federal Trade Commission must make a review within a short time for compliance with antitrust laws.

Ordinarily, if a person sought to acquire a majority of a licensee's stock, plenary procedures would be required, including the required 30–day statutory waiting period and potential petitions to deny. The Commission established a mechanism for quick review in recognition of the stated need for expedition in tender offer cases involving communications licensees. These procedures were first set out in One Two Corporation, and later refined in subsequent rulings and in Tender Offers. Under those procedures, the offeror requests a special temporary authorization pursuant to section 309(f) of the Act to permit an independent trustee to collect the stock and to run the licensee temporarily, subject to several limitations. The information on which to base a judgment as to the trustee's qualifications and the conformance of the trust with Commission requirements are filed on a short-form application. The application is, however, only a convenient information-gathering device: the Commission grants or denies the temporary authorization, not the short-form application. Because there is no statutory 30–day waiting period, temporary authorizations can be acted on promptly. If less than a half of the shares are tendered, the tendered shares will be returned to the stockholders and the offer ends. If the tender offer is successful, the shares will be purchased and the Commission will move on to the next step, which is consideration of a long-form application transferring control of the licensee from the trustee to the offeror. If the offeror is found qualified, the application will be granted. If not, the trustee is obligated to find another buyer for the shares that can pass Commission muster.

The pace of hostile takeover attempts of communications companies has slowed recently. The last case in which the Commission issued a temporary authorization to a trustee for a hostile tender offeror was in 1988.

––––––––

Following the decision in the *Storer* case, the Commission initiated a proceeding to devise policies applicable to transfer requests filed in connection with proxy contests and tender offers that involved companies holding FCC licenses.

In the resulting *Policy Statement*, an excerpt from which follows, the Commission stated that it sought to further four broad objectives. First, of course, it had to remain consistent with the requirement of the

Communications Act that it pre-approve transfers of control over a licensee. Second, approval procedures should avoid unnecessary delay. Third, any approval procedures should promote "government neutrality" in corporate control contests. Finally, the FCC sought to accommodate, to the extent possible, other federal and state laws and policies concerning corporations. In particular, the Commission referred to the Williams Act, 15 U.S.C. §§ 78m(d)–(e) & 78n(d)–(f), and other state and federal statutes that seek to protect the rights of shareholders and promote government neutrality in takeover contests.

In Section II of the Policy Statement, the Commission adopted procedures for proxy contests involving transfers of control. The Commission noted that whether a particular proxy contest involves a transfer of control is, of course, a fact-specific issue and has to be decided on a case-by-case basis. It noted the Storer proxy contest, which involved an effort to replace the entire board of a publicly-held company, as an example of a proxy contest that would involve a transfer of control. In such situations, the short-form application procedure approved of and described in *Storer* could be used. For proxy contests not involving a change of control, the Commission would simply continue to require that any resulting changes in the composition of the board of directors be reported to the FCC as part of the licensee's annual ownership report.

TENDER OFFERS AND PROXY CONTESTS

Federal Communications Commission, 1986.
59 R.R.2d 1536.

Petition for rev. dismissed sub nom. Office of Communication of the United Church of Christ v. FCC 826 F.2d 101 (D.C.Cir.1987).

* * *

III. TENDER OFFERS

A. Introduction

19. * * * [T]he prior approval requirements contained in Section 310(d) of the Communications Act are fully applicable to tender offers conveying control to the offeror.[76] The procedures set forth in this Policy Statement have been designed to conform both to the letter and to the spirit of Section 310(b). In this regard, we believe that Congress intended to afford interested parties the opportunity to challenge the qualifications of the purchaser of controlling stock in a corporate licensee. We also believe that Congress intended for this Commission to carefully evaluate the qualifications of these purchasers. We emphasize, therefore, that we shall require strict adherence to the long-form procedures, including the opportunity for public comment, before we will permit the ultimate purchaser to assume control of the licensee.

---

76. This proceeding is limited to tender offers which convey control to the purchaser; the appropriate procedures governing the use of tender offers which do not result in a change of control are beyond the scope of this proceeding. * * *

20. Contrary to the position of certain parties, however, we reject the notion that adherence to the dictates of the Communications Act precludes administrative flexibility or mandates that we ignore other important policy considerations, including those that are embodied in the statutes of the United States. As described in greater detail below, tender offers involving publicly held licensees are subject to the requirements of the Williams Act in addition to those of the Communications Act. In formulating the appropriate procedures for Commission review of license transfers which arise in connection with tender offers, we reject the contention that adherence to the requirements of the Communications Act forecloses accommodation of the securities laws or that the formulation of communications policies—with myopic disregard of other important national policy objectives—furthers the public interest.[77] Indeed, in order to fully comply with the requirements of the Communications Act, we have an obligation to consider all relevant factors in determining the public interest, including the national policy underlying the Williams Act.

B. *The Williams Act*

[The Commission summarized the requirements of the Williams Act. Among the most pertinent requirements are that (1) stockholders who tender their shares may withdraw them after 60 days from the start of the tender offer if the offeror has not consummated the tender offer by that time and (2) under SEC rules, a tender offer generally must remain open for at least 20 days. Accordingly, the FCC stated, its prior approval procedures should permit a tender offeror to close its tender after 20 days and, in any event, should not impose a delay of more than 60 days. The FCC also stated that the Williams Act was designed to promote government neutrality and reflected a congressional decision that the government should not impede tender offers; and the Commission's own policies should be consistent with these congressional policies.]

C. *Infirmities in the Long–Form Procedures*

27. We believe that the use of the long-form procedures, standing alone, would effectively frustrate the goal of governmental neutrality embodied in the securities laws and our policies. While a person seeking control of a communications entity can initiate a tender offer for a licensee without our prior consent, he or she cannot acquire *de jure* or *de facto* control through the purchase of tendered stock until after the Commission grants approval of a license transfer application. The use of the long-form procedures, however, necessarily entails significant delay. The Commission is prohibited from granting the long-form application prior to the expiration of a 30–day period in which persons opposing the transfer have an opportunity to voice their objections. If petitions to deny are filed, and if the parties submit responsive pleadings, the

---

77. [Although the Williams Act applies only to companies with publicly held securities, we] * * * expect that the procedures set forth in this Policy Statement will be applied to situations involving licensees which are not publicly held.

pleading period alone would extend for almost 60 days. Furthermore, as a contested transfer application may involve a myriad of complex issues, additional time would be necessary for the Commission to evaluate the merits of the pleadings. Finally, the Commission must institute a hearing in order to resolve any substantial questions of fact.

28.   The delays inherent in the long-form process impede the objective of governmental neutrality embodied in the Williams Act and our policies. In fact, the use of this procedure would unduly favor the incumbent management of a licensee at the expense of a challenger in several respects. First, use of the long-form procedures would make acceptance of tender offers extremely unattractive to shareholders. The regulatory delays inherent in the long-form process would require stockholders who elect to accept the offer to tie up their assets for an indeterminate but prolonged period of time. Further, since the offer would of necessity be conditioned upon Commission approval of the transfer of control, those shareholders would have no guarantee that the tender offeror would be able to purchase their stock even at the expiration of the protracted long-form process.

29.   Second, even if the offeror was able to persuade shareholders to tender their stock, the use of the protracted long-form procedure would impede the efforts of the offeror by precluding him or her from consummating the transaction prior to the time in which tendering shareholders are free to withdraw their shares. For purposes of securities regulation, the filing of a transfer application with this Commission triggers the commencement of the tender offer. As a result, the stockholders who have tendered their stock have a statutory right to withdraw their shares after the expiration of the 60–day period. The Williams Act, therefore, provides the offeror with a positive incentive to purchase the tendered shares prior to the expiration of the 60–day period in order to prevent shareholders from being able to exercise their statutory right of withdrawal. If the tender offer involves a communications company, however, the offeror would be barred from purchasing the tendered stock until after the Commission affirmatively grants approval of the transfer application if long-form procedures were required. Since it is extremely unlikely, particularly in contested cases, for the Commission to render a decision on the transfer within the 60–day–time period, the tender offeror would be prevented, solely by the delay inherent in our regulatory procedures, from completing the transaction before shareholders choosing to tender their stock possessed the statutory right to withdraw their acceptance. As a consequence, the regulatory process would thwart the efforts of tender offerors.

32.   Several parties suggest that we can ameliorate the deleterious effects of regulatory delay by expediting the long-form process. We question both the propriety and the efficacy of this proposal. We are precluded by statute from shortening the thirty-day period for the filing of petitions to deny and, consequently, our ability to prescribe an abbreviated pleading cycle is sharply constrained. While we have the authority to reduce the deadlines for the submission of responsive

pleadings, we believe that it would be unwise for us to contract these periods. As noted above, the deadlines for the submission of oppositions and replies are ten days and five days, respectively. In determining whether or not to shorten the pleading cycle, we must balance the benefits derived from expedition against the danger that a contracted pleading cycle would impede the ability of interested parties to make their views known. In this regard, we believe that any meaningful reduction of these already abbreviated deadlines would only minimally affect regulatory delay but would likely hinder the ability of interested parties to effectively participate in a transfer proceeding. Further, we reject the proposal of several commenters that we impose upon ourselves the stringent five-day deadline in which to consider the pleadings and render a decision. It is critically important for the Commission to evaluate the potentially complex issues in a transfer application careful-ly. We are concerned that the artificial constraints of a mandatory, abbreviated deadline would impede our ability to perform this task with the deliberation necessary to effectively discharge our regulatory respon-sibilities. * * *

* * *

D. Trust Mechanism

34. In light of the difficulties concerning the use of the long-form procedure in the context of a tender offer, we believe that it is appropri-ate for us to formulate an alternative procedural approach. In this regard, we find that a bifurcated procedure, which utilizes an interim voting trust as a supplement to the long-form process, is the appropriate procedural mechanism to govern our consideration of applications for transfers of control arising in the context of a tender offer.

35. Under this procedure we shall require the simultaneous sub-mission of a long-form and a short form application. We shall expect that a copy of the completed and executed trust agreement will accompany the short form application. Our expedited review of the information contained in the short form application will permit the consummation of the tender offer in a timely manner and minimize the danger that our regulatory process will be used to aid either side in the battle for corporate control. This additional, accelerated procedure will be limited in scope to a determination as to whether we should permit the offeror to purchase the tendered stock subject to the limitations of a voting trust. After review of the information submitted in short form applica-tion,[123] under our authority under Section 309(f) of the Communications Act, we will consider whether to grant a special temporary authority

---

123. We shall require this informational short form application to be submitted on behalf of both the tender offeror and the trustee. We will require this application to contain sufficient information on the quali-fications of the trustee to permit us to make a determination that the grant of tempo-rary authorization is in the public interest. Moreover, while we shall consider the infor-mation contained in the short form applica-tion prior to the 30–day period in which petitions to deny can be filed on the long form application, we intend to permit the submission of informal objections to the short form application and we will consider any oppositions that are filed.

("STA") to an independent trustee. Under the STA, the trustee will be empowered to collect the tendered stock and, subject to certain prescribed limitations described below, to vote this stock pending Commission consideration of the qualifications of the tender offeror. We note that we have the authority to take corrective action in the event that the trustee acts in a manner which is either inconsistent with the principles enunciated in this Policy Statement or is contrary to the authorization granted by this Commission. In this regard, for example, we could impose sanctions upon the trustee directly or take action in the context of the pending long-form application.

36.   During the pendency of the long-form proceeding, we shall not permit the offeror to exercise any control of the tendered stock nor shall we permit him or her to attempt to influence, either directly or indirectly, the actions of the independent trustee. Moreover, during this interim period, interested parties will be given the full panoply of procedural rights attendant to the long-form process, including the opportunity to petition the Commission to deny the transfer application and to participate in any evidentiary hearings which may be necessary to resolve disputed questions of fact. It is only after the approval of the long-form application[128] that the tender offeror will be authorized to exercise control over the licensee.

37.   A number of parties contend that the utilization of a voting trust would inherently prejudge the outcome of the long-form application, thereby making Commission approval of the long-form application virtually inevitable. In this regard, certain parties argue that the consummation of the offer would render impossible a return to the status quo ante; other commenters contend that the uncertainties arising as to control in the target company between the time in which the Commission disapproves the transaction and the ultimate disposition of the stock to alternative purchasers would inexorably place pressure upon the Commission to approve the transfer of control to the offeror. In addition, certain parties assert that the Commission would feel pressure to approve the final transfer in order to avoid the possible financial injury to the offeror or to other shareholders resulting, *inter alia,* from the "distress sale" character of the sale of stock to alternative parties.

38.   We are very cognizant of the fact that the strict impartiality of our processes is a matter of paramount importance and we fully intend to preserve such impartiality. For several reasons, however, we take issue with the assertion that the grant of a temporary authorization to an independent trustee would adversely affect our neutrality in evaluating the merits of the offeror.

39.   First, we disagree that a condition precedent to the use of a voting trust mechanism is, or should be, the ability of the Commission to

---

128. If we determine, at the expiration of the long form process, that it is not in the public interest to grant the long form application, the tendered stock will remain subject to the voting trust until the trustee has the opportunity to arrange for the disposition of the stock and the Commission has approved, if necessary, the qualifications of the purchaser or purchasers selected by the trustee. * * *

return to the status quo ante in the event that the long-form application of the tender offeror is disapproved. By accepting the tender offer, existing stockholders have made the decision that it is in their best interest to sell their stock holdings. In our view, it is neither necessary nor appropriate for the Commission to return control over the corporation to persons who have affirmatively taken action to relinquish their ownership interests in the company.

40.   Second, contrary to the assertions of certain parties, we do not believe that a decision by the Commission to disapprove the long-form application of the offeror would create a vacuum of control. During the pendency of the long-form review of the offeror, we have granted authority to the trustee—not to the tender offeror—to exercise control over the tendered stock but within carefully crafted limits so as to preserve the status quo to the fullest extent possible. In the event that we disapprove the application of the offeror, we expect that the trustee will simply continue to exercise control until the stock is ultimately transferred. Because the procedures adopted in this proceeding have been specifically designed to assure continuity if the offeror is disqualified, we do not believe that our ability to render an unbiased decision will be affected by the alleged uncertainty resulting from a denial of the long-form application.

41.   Third, we also find unpersuasive the contention that we lack the ability to render an impartial decision because the trustee will be forced to sell the tendered stock at a low price, thereby adversely affecting both the offeror and other stockholders. In the event that the offeror is disqualified, we will provide the trustee with the authority to dispose of the stock in an orderly manner, thereby minimizing the possibility of "distress sale" pricing; as a consequence, we believe that the allegations of financial harm are speculative. Further, to the extent that there is a risk of financial loss to the offeror potentially resulting from the disapproval of the long-form application, we believe that this risk is one which the offeror must be prepared to assume.

42.   Fourth, the procedures adopted in this proceeding have been carefully crafted to attenuate the danger of possible prejudice in the long-form proceeding. The grant of an STA is given to a trustee who does not have an interest in receiving long-form authorization and who is expected to relinquish control whether the Commission decides to grant or to deny the long-form application of the offeror. * * *

* * *

E.   Special Temporary Authority

45.   We believe that we have the requisite statutory authority to grant an STA to the trustee. Notwithstanding the general procedures prescribed by Section 309(b), Section 309(f) of the Communications Act authorizes us to grant a temporary authorization in exceptional circumstances. Specifically, where a long-form application is on file with the Commission, we are empowered under Section 309(f) to grant an STA if

we determine that "extraordinary circumstances existing requiring temporary operations in public interest," and we further determine that "delay in the institution * * * of temporary operations would seriously prejudice the public interest."

46.   We find that these criteria are met in the exceptional situation in which a tender offer is used as a means to obtain control of a communications corporation. * * * Without the use of an expedited procedure which provides temporary authorization to the trustee, our regulatory processes would effectively result in precluding the use of tender offers as a means by which to obtain control over communications companies. This, in turn, would deprive shareholders of these companies of the ability to consider tender offers.

59.   * * * [W]e believe that Section 309(f) provides a sufficient legal basis to support the grant of an STA to a trustee pending our consideration of the long-form application of a tender offeror. While this authorization will permit the trustee to vote the tendered stock and take other actions consistent with the voting trust agreement, the STA which we grant to the trustee will not empower him or her to exercise plenary power over the tendered stock. To the contrary, the public interest requires us to impose certain limitations upon the powers of the trustee over matters relating to the licensee. We believe further that the trustee, in exercising the powers conferred upon him or her by the STA over the affairs of the licensee, should act independently; as a consequence, we shall impose certain restrictions governing the relationship between the trustee and the offeror. In addition, we shall place restrictions on the offeror designed to limit his or her ability to exercise control over the licensee prior to completion of the long-form procedures. * * *

F.   Limitations Arising From the Use of the Trust Mechanism

60.   *Limitations Placed Upon the Offeror*—Section 310(d) requires the Commission to approve the qualifications of the offeror under the long-form process before the offeror can assume control over the licensee. The procedures adopted in this proceeding permit the offeror to purchase, through a trust mechanism, an amount of stock which would be sufficient to convey control over the licensee; consequently, we believe that Section 310(d) mandates that restrictions be placed upon the offeror to prevent him or her from exercising control, directly or indirectly, before the requisite regulatory approvals are obtained. Accordingly, from the time that the tender offer is consummated—that is, from the time shares are purchased which would be sufficient to pass either *de jure* or *de facto* control of a licensee to the tender offeror[187]—the offeror will be strictly prohibited from either becoming involved in, or seeking to influence, directly or indirectly, the operation or management of the

187. The restrictions noted would extend until the expiration of the authority granted to the trustee pursuant to the STA. We find that restrictions imposed upon the offeror prior to the consummation of the tender offer could operate to favor incumbent management at the expense of the offeror, thereby frustrating our goal of assuring strict regulatory neutrality in takeover contests.

corporation. In this regard, the offeror may not nominate a director as his or her representative or attempt to influence the trustee's selection of Board members. In addition, the offeror shall be required to place all his or her existing stock holdings in trust at or before the consummation of the tender offer.

61. We believe that only those regulatory restraints which are necessary to promote the objectives underlying Section 310(d) of the Communications Act should be placed upon the offeror. In this regard, the imposition of regulatory restrictions which do not further statutory objectives, in our view, would both unnecessarily burden the offeror and would constitute unwarranted governmental interference in the marketplace. For example, before consummation of the tender offer, the offeror will not be restricted from exercising voting rights in existing stock interests or from taking any other actions he or she deems appropriate to promote a successful takeover bid, providing such actions do not amount to an exercise of *de facto* control of the licensee. Additionally, the offeror will not be obligated to place his or her existing stock holdings in trust prior to the time the tender offer is consummated.

62. *Insulation Between the Trustee and the Tender Offeror*—In addition to direct limitations on the offeror, we believe that additional prescriptions concerning the relationship between the offeror and the trustee are essential to ensure that the trustee will be able to act independently in exercising the powers granted pursuant to the STA. It is particularly important that there be limitations precluding the tender offeror from indirectly exercising control over a licensee, by means of his or her influence over the trustee, during the pendency of the long-form process. The best method of safeguarding the independence of the trustee is to require strict separation between the trustee and the offeror.

63. * * * [W]e believe it would be inappropriate for us to grant an STA to a trustee if that trustee either has any direct or indirect familial ties or business relationships, apart from the trust agreement, with the offeror, related entities or its principals, officers, or directors. In addition, the same type of insulation criteria would apply to any director who may be elected by the trustee.

64. * * * [We will] prohibit the offeror from communicating with the trustee on matters relating either to the management or operations of the corporation. Because an offeror could influence the licensee by communicating with the trustee on matters relating to the management and operations of the company, we deem it appropriate to impose an absolute ban on such communications.

65. We do not believe, however, that it furthers the public interest to completely prohibit all communications between the offeror and the trustee. The offeror, with his or her significant financial investment, has a legitimate interest in matters involving the corporation and certain types of communications would not adversely affect our regulatory objectives. In McCarthy, we specifically permitted the trustee to send

written information to the offeror regarding the management or operations of the company. Because the mere receipt of written reports from the trustee would not provide the offeror with the means by which to influence corporate affairs, we do not find it is necessary to prohibit the trustee from sending such reports to the offeror informing him or her about matters relating to the company. We also do not believe that there is any reason to prohibit communications between the trustee and the offeror relating to the purchase of tendered stock, as the exchange of information on the mechanics of implementing the tender offer would not convey the ability to influence the licensee. We note, however, that * * * during the time in which the STA is in effect, we will proscribe all oral communications between the offeror and the trustee.

66. *Limitations Placed Upon the Powers of the Trustee*—* * * [T]he trustee should recognize that he or she receives a special temporary authorization for a limited purpose—that of a temporary conservator or caretaker charged with preserving the nature and character of the corporation in order to facilitate our consideration of the long-form license transfer to the ultimate purchaser. Moreover, to the extent that a trustee concludes that his or her responsibilities to this agency might conflict with contractual or other private fiduciary obligations to the offeror, the trustee should recognize that the former obligations are paramount.

67. * * * Because the policies adopted in this proceeding must accommodate situations in which the offeror is hostile to current management as well those in which no such hostility exists, we believe that the trustee requires a certain degree of flexibility in the manner in which he or she exercises control over the corporation. Accordingly, * * * [t]he trustee will be permitted, for example, to participate in the election of the Board of Directors. The trustee may elect to serve as a director personally and may fully vote the tendered stock in corporate elections of the Board.

68. The need for flexibility, however, must be balanced against the limited purpose and temporary duration of the trust. The trustee is a temporary steward with a limited mission who has not been subject to long-form review. As a consequence, it is essential that we provide specific guidance as to the trustee's proper role. In this regard, we expect the trustee to act, whenever possible, and except where necessary to promote the three objectives set forth below, in a manner which preserves the status quo and maintains the general character of the corporation. The trustee is, therefore, presumptively disallowed from undertaking, initiating or supporting any significant departures from existing corporate operations or practices. In addition, unless it is necessary to further one of the three principles herein addressed, the trustee should not discharge key employees, such as news anchors, where such action may effectuate a significant change in the nature of the business.

69. As noted above, we believe that three broad principles must guide the trustee's participation in the management and operations of

the company as well as the manner in which he or she exercises the power granted by the STA. First, the trustee has a general obligation to safeguard the assets of the corporation.[207] As a fiduciary of the offeror, the trustee has the responsibility to assure that the assets remain available for transfer to the offeror if the long-form application is approved. In addition, as we stated in the Notice, "the trustee should also be able to protect the buyer from unwarranted or imprudent actions by the existing Board or management, such as voting themselves overly generous benefits or wasting corporate assets."

70. Second, the trustee should exercise his or her power in a manner which assures the continuity of broadcast operations. In this regard, we believe that the trustee should be able to replace officers, directors or employees who have either resigned or whose actions or proposed actions are inconsistent with the proper discharge of the trustee's obligations. Actions of the trustee which are incompatible with this objective would be inconsistent with the nature and purpose of the interim authority granted to the trustee and would be prohibited. For example, while persons who control communications companies generally possess the power to surrender a broadcast license, an STA would not empower the trustee to take that action.

71. Third, we believe that the trustee must act in a manner which facilitates the underlying long-form transaction. From the offeror's perspective, the purpose of the trust is to provide a mechanism which enables an offeror to use a tender offer as a means by which to obtain a controlling ownership interest in a communications company. The trustee is obliged to act in a manner which furthers that purpose. For example, we expect that the trustee would take all actions that are necessary to consummate the tender offer, to hold the stock pending Commission review of the qualifications of the tender offeror and to transfer that stock after the completion of the long-form procedure if the Commission approves the qualifications of the offeror. If the long-form application of the offeror is denied, we expect the trustee to act promptly to obtain alternative buyers for the tendered stock.[211]

* * *

IV. CONCLUSION

77. * * * [T]his Policy Statement is intended to provide a framework for the regulatory treatment of tender offers and proxy contests involving Commission licensees or companies with controlling interests in Commission licensees. The adoption of this Policy Statement, however, is not intended to foreclose the Commission, in a particular proceed-

---

207. The primary obligation of the trustee is to conserve, rather than to enhance, corporate assets and, in this regard, we anticipate that the trustee will act cautiously.

211. In the event that the Commission denies the long-form application of the offeror, it is the responsibility of the trustee promptly to find an alternative purchaser or purchasers for the tendered stock either by means of private placement or public offering of the shares. We believe that the trustee should not be required to obtain the approval of the offeror prior to the sale of the stock.

ing, from adopting a different approach if warranted in specific circumstances.

* * *

Notes and Questions

1. What does it mean to have an "insubstantial" transfer of control? What makes a transfer "substantial"? Do you agree with the distinction drawn by the FCC in the *Storer* case between transfers that involve a change of ownership and those that do not?

2. In the *Storer* case, the stockholders could have replaced the board of directors, thereby expressing their preference for a change in the company's future direction. Suppose that a company has a staggered board, so that it would take several years for the stockholders to replace a majority of the board. Suppose, also, that the company's charter and by-laws require an 80% vote to remove a director or to call a special stockholder meeting to remove or elect directors. Under these circumstances, might a proxy contest intended to replace the current board represent a "substantial" transfer of control? Is a proxy contest to replace the board a less "substantial" transfer where a small number of very powerful stockholders control a majority of the voting power of the company's stock?

3. For many years, the FCC has often been called upon to decide whether an unauthorized transfer or assignment has taken place. These cases provide a helpful, but by no means comprehensive backdrop for today's much more complex and sophisticated media marketplace. The FCC practitioner is frequently called upon to advise whether a proposed transaction will require prior FCC approval and, if so, whether approval can be obtained without being subjected to the formal notice-and-comment procedure. Consider the following situations in which the FCC has been required to decide whether an unauthorized transfer or assignment took place:

(a) An individual who held a broadcast station construction permit received FCC permission to transfer the permit to a newly formed corporation. The individual held 55% of the corporation's outstanding common stock. The Lorain Journal Co., a newspaper publisher, held the remaining common stock and all of the preferred stock (which carried no voting rights). After the transfer, the Journal provided 100% of the financing for construction and initial operation of the station. The loan documents prohibited the licensee corporation from spending more than $1000 without approval of the directors, two of whom were representatives of the Journal. A Journal representative was also required to co-sign all checks of the corporation. Has the Journal assumed control of the broadcast station without FCC permission? WWIZ, Inc., 36 FCC 2d 561 (1964), aff'd sub nom. Lorain Journal Co. v. FCC, 351 F.2d 824 (D.C.Cir.1965), cert. denied 383 U.S. 967, 86 S.Ct. 1272, 16 L.Ed.2d 308 (1966).

(b) A company interested in buying a radio station, before getting FCC permission to acquire the station, pays off all of the station's indebtedness, arranges for the station to hire a new general manager, causes the station to change its program format, and supervises all station spending. Has a transfer of control occurred? Voice of Reason, Inc., 37 FCC 2d 686 (Rev.Bd. 1972).

(c) John Kluge, president, chairman of the board, and chief executive officer of Metromedia, Inc., was deemed to have *de facto* control of Metromedia, even though it was a publicly-owned company and Mr. Kluge held less than a majority of the outstanding voting shares. By virtue of his stock ownership, Mr. Kluge long had the power to nominate a majority of the board of directors. He also served as the proxy for management, voting all of the shares for which proxies are given. Mr. Kluge was consistently identified in documents filed with the Securities and Exchange Commission as the person in control of Metromedia. Mr. Kluge sought to acquire the company in a leveraged buy-out. As a result of the buy-out, Mr. Kluge would own more than 92% of Metromedia's outstanding voting shares. Metromedia filed a short-form application (Form 316) with the FCC requesting approval of the transfer from John Kluge (*de facto*) to John Kluge (*de jure*). What result? Is the transfer substantial or insubstantial? Does it matter that more than 50% of Metromedia shares will be changing hands? Metromedia, Inc., 98 FCC 2d 300 (1984), recon. denied 56 R.R.2d 1198 (1984), affirmed sub nom. California Ass'n of the Physically Handicapped, Inc. v. FCC, 778 F.2d 823 (D.C.Cir. 1985). See also Barnes Enterprises, Inc., 55 FCC 2d 721 (1975); Clay Broadcasters, Inc., 21 R.R.2d 442 (1971).

(d) Loews Corp. acquired 24.91% of the common stock of CBS, Inc. The acquisition made Loews the largest single holder of CBS stock, which is publicly traded. As a result, Loews could have a significant impact on the outcome of any stockholder vote, including the election of directors. Lawrence Tisch, chairman of Loews, allegedly expressed his interest in controlling CBS. As part of an agreement between CBS and Loews, under which Loews agreed not to acquire a larger equity interest in CBS, Mr. Tisch was named to the CBS board, which consisted primarily of outside directors. At a highly contentious meeting, the CBS board decided to replace the President and CEO of the company and named Mr. Tisch as interim President and CEO. William S. Paley, the founder of CBS and its second largest stockholder (with approximately 8% of the stock), was named acting Chairman. Mr. Tisch was also appointed head of a "management committee," consisting primarily of outside directors.

Fairness in Media ("FIM"), a group that had criticized CBS programming as politically too liberal, filed a petition with the FCC contending that Loews and Mr. Tisch had taken control of CBS in violation of Section 310(d) of the Communications Act. What result? Is CBS controlled by its stockholders or by its board of directors? Letter to William S. Paley, 1 FCC Rcd 1095, 61 R.R.2d 413 (1986). Tisch subsequently was named President and CEO on a full-time basis and also took over as Chairman. FIM again alleged an unauthorized transfer of control. What result? Direction Letter Regarding Control of CBS, Inc., 2 FCC Rcd 2274, 62 R.R.2d 852 (1987).

(e) McCaw Cellular Communications, Inc., a U.S. corporation, had various wholly-owned subsidiaries that held FCC licenses to provide cellular telephone service. It entered into an agreement with British Telecom USA ("BTA"), a U.S. corporation that is a wholly-owned subsidiary of British Telecom, a company then controlled by the government of the United Kingdom and one of two providers of telephone service in the U.K. Under the agreement, BTA would acquire voting and non-voting stock of McCaw with approximately 22% of the outstanding voting power. BTA would also be entitled to designate four of McCaw's 19 directors. The McCaw family, which includes the members of McCaw's senior management, would own 68% of the outstanding voting power. Through various shareholder agreements, Craig McCaw would control the majority of the votes on any matter submitted to a vote of shareholders and would be entitled to designate 10 members of the McCaw board. Craig McCaw would also continue to control McCaw's management and could buy out BTA's interest in McCaw, or require BTA to sell that interest, if significant board disputes occurred four times in a year.

Under the agreement, BTA must give its prior consent before the McCaw board can take any of the following actions:

- amend McCaw's charter or by-laws in any way that would impair BTA's rights under the agreement;

- issue a large number of new shares of McCaw stock;

- enter into non-telecommunications related businesses in the United Kingdom; or

- sell, transfer, or otherwise dispose of substantial cellular telephone assets.

Did BTA assume control of McCaw? McCaw Cellular Communications, Inc.,4 FCC Rcd. 3784 (1989). See also News International, plc, 97 FCC 2d 349, 357–58 (1984) (minority stockholder's right to approve changes to charter and by-laws); Intercontinental Radio Inc., 56 R.R.2d 1565, 1567 (1985) (covenants not to compete).

4. Because Section 309 applies to certain non-broadcast FCC licenses (common carrier and aeronautical radio licenses), acquisitions of companies other than broadcast companies are subject to the FCC's prior approval requirements. For example, cellular telephone companies with substantial investments in common carrier radio licenses may not be acquired without prior FCC approval. See, e.g., CNCA Acquisition Corp., 64 R.R.2d 947 (1988).

5. Does the *Policy Statement* achieve a reasonable accommodation between the Communication Act and the federal securities laws? Alternatively, has the Commission distorted the Communications Act in order to encourage the development of a vigorous market for media acquisitions? For example, does a tender offer create an "extraordinary circumstance" warranting special Commission action? In his dissent, Commissioner Quello argues that Congress should amend the Communications Act to resolve the conflicts among various federal policies. Is this not an appropriate role for the Commission? Would it be appropriate for the Commission to take the position that the special "public trustee" obligations imposed upon FCC licensees prohibit the Commission from acting to facilitate rapid hostile acquisitions of media companies?

6. A central point of controversy raised by the Policy Statement is whether Section 309(f) authorizes the Commission to grant an STA to the trustee for a tender offeror. After reading Section 309(f), consider the following arguments:

(a) A number of parties suggested that Section 309(f) was intended to be used only when an extraordinary technical or financial situation required special Commission action in order to permit a broadcast station to continue operating and thereby serving the public. A tender offer, it was argued, is not the kind of dire situation that threatens a loss of service.

(b) In 1982, Congress amended Section 309(f) to substitute the word "temporary" for the word "emergency." A number of parties argued that the change was not intended to affect the applicability of Section 309(f), and that a tender offer simply did not involve a situation requiring the grant of "emergency" operating authority.

(c) When the *Policy Statement* was appealed, the court of appeals dismissed the challenge as unripe, suggesting that the FCC's authority to grant an STA should be tested, if at all, in the context of a specific transaction. The court stated, "Were we to decide the issue of authority now, * * * we would have to decide whether no tender offer or every tender offer would fit under section 309(f). But the correct answer to this question * * * could also be 'some.'" Office of Communication of the United Church of Christ v. FCC, 826 F.2d 101, 106 (D.C.Cir.1987). In dissent, Chief Judge Wald argued that the tender offer policy exceeds the Commission's statutory authority.

> * * * Based on my reading of the language and the legislative history of his section, I believe Congress intended § 309(f) to be used only when the FCC needed to put or keep broadcast stations in operation temporarily so that they might inform citizens of impending disasters or "extraordinary" political events. I cannot conclude that Congress intended to allow the FCC to invoke its "safety-value" authority of § 309(f) merely because it found the regular statutory "long-form" procedures were too cumbersome for broadcast license transfers resulting from a tender offer. Even if the FCC's new tender offer procedures might be extremely wise as a matter of policy, this court is bound by the plain language and clear intent of Congress. * * *

7. The *Policy Statement* has become the basis for numerous so-called "two-step" transfer applications. The Step 1 application (a short-form application) involves a request for an STA in order to permit a trustee to assume control of the target company upon completion of a successful tender offer. The Step 2 application (a long-form application) requests FCC consent to the transfer of the tendered stock from the trustee to the offeror so that the offeror can take control of the target company.

(a) Shortly after the FCC issued its *Policy Statement*, Macfadden Acquisition Corp. launched a hostile tender offer for John Blair & Co., a diversified company that owned a number of television stations. Macfadden submitted applications to the FCC for a "two-step" transfer. Upon completion of the successful tender for control of Blair, an independent trustee would acquire the Blair stock, remove the entire Blair board of directors, and appoint a new board of three directors. Two of the new directors would be Macfadden principals, and the third would be the trustee. All responsibility to oversee the broadcast operations of Blair would be vested solely in the trustee, who would act as a "committee of one." The other two directors would oversee the sale of Blair's non-broadcast assets to help reduce the debt that would be incurred by Macfadden in order to pay for the Blair stock. Is the proposal consistent with the *Policy Statement*? See Macfadden Acquisition Corp., 60 R.R.2d 339 (1986). If the trustee is obligated to restructure the target company or sell off non-broadcast assets in order to raise the money with which the offeror will take down the shares tendered, does the trust arrangement preserve the "status quo" as required by the Policy Statement?

(b) Is a trustee independent if the law firm in which the trustee is a partner represents companies that have a financial interest in the bidder or the target? Suppose the trustee is prohibited from having any dealings with such clients and from gaining access to any files concerning the clients? Does it matter if a portion of the trustee's compensation from the law firm might be attributable to the fees paid by such clients? Macfadden Acquisition Corp., 60 R.R.2d 873 (1986).

(c) The battle for control of Blair proved to be a bitter struggle in which the Commission's two-step transfer procedures played a central role. Reliance Capital Group, L.P., through a wholly-owned subsidiary, J.B. Acquisition Corp., entered the takeover battle as a "white knight" and launched a tender offer for Blair with the support of the Blair management. Originally, Reliance proposed to name four of the seven members of Blair's board as trustees for the Step 1 transfer. In this situation, where the bidder and the target are cooperating to effect the transfer, can the target's directors be considered "independent" trustees? J.B. Acquisition Corp., 60 R.R.2d 1095 (1986).

A majority of the outstanding Blair stock was tendered to Reliance. As Reliance's tender offer was about to expire, however, the FCC had not yet approved Reliance's Step 1 transfer arrangement. The FCC was bombarded with bitter pleadings from Macfadden challenging every aspect of Reliance's Step 1 proposals. Rather than extend its tender offer and raise the possibility that tendering stockholders would withdraw their tendered shares and tender them to Macfadden, Reliance "accepted" the tendered shares but did not pay for them before receiving FCC approval of the trust arrangement. (Under the federal securities laws, acceptance of tendered shares extinguishes a tendering shareholder's right to withdraw its shares.) After its Step 1 application was approved, Reliance paid for the accepted shares. Macfadden charged that acceptance of the tendered shares, which constituted a controlling interest in Blair, constituted an unauthorized transfer of control. Does it matter that before accepting the shares, Reliance renounced any right to vote the shares prior to the time it paid for them? J.B. Acquisition Corp., 60 R.R.2d 1288 (1986).

(d) In considering a Step 1 application, the FCC has said that it will not examine the qualifications of the offeror to become a licensee. In an effort to minimize objections to the trust arrangement, offerors have tended to select as trustees former politicians, public servants, and corporate executives with unimpeachable backgrounds. Among the trustees that have been approved by the FCC are former New York Governor Hugh Carey, former U.S. Senator Eugene McCarthy, former FCC Commissioner Anne Jones, and former Secretary of the Treasury, G. William Miller. Should such an ad hoc trustee be as acceptable to the FCC as an institutional trustee, such as a bank trust department or a trust company?

(e) Despite the FCC's stated intent not to consider the offeror's qualifications as a licensee, a Step 1 application is typically met with numerous allegations about the "evils" of the offeror and its proposed acquisition. Should the Commission grant a Step 1 application if there are allegations that, if proved true, would lead the FCC to deny the Step 2 application? In such a circumstance, does the trust serve the "public interest"? How much evidence regarding the FCC's qualifications would be sufficient to justify a denial of the Step 1 application?

(f) Raider X launches a hostile tender offer to acquire a media conglomerate, Huge Media Co., which owns both broadcast stations and cable television systems. Cable systems are subject to state and local franchising procedures, many of which include requirements for prior approval of a transfer of control. Raider X files a two-step transfer application with the FCC and receives an STA permitting the use of a trust to hold tendered shares of Huge Media Co. Can Raider X complete the tender offer and deposit the tendered shares with the trustee if state and local approvals for the cable franchises have not also been obtained? Can—or should—the FCC grant an STA in a situation where state and local approvals are also necessary and have not yet been obtained? If Raider X must wait for the state and local approvals—some of which could take months—wouldn't the FCC's two-step procedure be effectively useless in situations involving cable television companies? Is this a problem, given the FCC's new statutory powers over other aspects of cable regulation, e.g., rates?

This question became a central point of contention in the Time–Warner–Paramount battle in 1989. Paramount launched a hostile tender offer for Time, Inc. (which would have frustrated the proposed Time Warner merger sought by their respective managements). A large number of state and local franchising authorities filed pleadings with the Commission arguing that the Commission could not—or, at least, should not—grant Paramount an STA and implicitly endorse the transaction before all necessary state and local approvals had been obtained. Do you agree? Paramount ended its bid for Time before the Commission had a chance to resolve the issue finally. See CNCA Acquisition Corp., 64 R.R.2d 947 (1988) (stating that the Commission need not await state approval before issuing an STA to permit the hostile acquisition of a cellular telephone licensee).

Professor McGinty has offered as an alternative to takeovers the notion of using bankruptcy as an effective means of protecting shareholders. Park McGinty, *The Twilight of Fiduciary Duties on the Need for Shareholder Self-help in an Age of Formalistic Proceduralism*, 46 Emory L.J. 168 (1997).

C. LIMITING NETWORK INFLUENCE

1. NETWORK–AFFILIATE RELATIONS

Networking in a rudimentary form involving as few as two stations was the subject of experimentation as early as 1923. By 1927, the year of the original Radio Act, the National Broadcasting Co. (NBC) had been formed as a subsidiary of RCA and was operating two network systems (the "Red" and "Blue" networks), and the Columbia Broadcasting

System (CBS) was operating a third. The Mutual Broadcasting System was formed in 1934 as a cooperative venture among its affiliates.

In the years before television, radio networks offered a full schedule of programs to their affiliates. As television developed after World War II, however, advertising revenues, and hence programing resources, were drawn away from radio and into the new medium. As a result, radio broadcasting now depends upon inexpensive recorded music and live talk formats, with networking limited primarily to news and feature services, and regional or national sports distribution.

In contrast, television stations affiliated with one of the national networks take a very substantial portion of their programming from the network, and network affiliation is the largest single determinant of a station's financial well-being. The so-called "independent" or unaffiliated stations as a group have been financially precarious and, outside of the few largest markets, remain so. (Many independent stations labor under the additional obstacle of being on the UHF band, although the growth of the Fox Television Network has helped put some struggling independents on a sound economic footing.)

The FCC's concern with the consequences of the economic relationship between networks and affiliates first surfaced in 1938, when the Commission authorized an investigation to determine whether special regulations applicable to radio stations engaged in "chain broadcasting" were advisable.* As a result of that inquiry, the Commission issued the Report on Chain Broadcasting, Commission Order No. 37, Dkt. 5060 (May 1941) and the regulations described in the following case. The current regulations governing network affiliation appear at 47 C.F.R. § 73.132 (AM); 47 C.F.R. § 73.232 (FM); and 47 C.F.R. § 73.658 (a)–(i) (TV).

As you read the Supreme Court opinion in *National Broadcasting Co. v. United States,* consider the relationship between the various regulations and the competition, localism, and diversity objectives discussed in the previous sections of this chapter. Which goals are being pursued? Which ones are being sacrificed?

a.   History

NATIONAL BROADCASTING
CO. v. UNITED STATES

Supreme Court of the United States, 1943.
319 U.S. 190, 63 S.Ct. 997, 87 L.Ed. 1344.

Mr. Justice Frankfurter delivered the opinion of the Court.

* * *

---

* The Mutual Broadcasting System had requested the investigation, complaining that it had difficulty in obtaining affiliates for its planned national network due to NBC and CBS dominance of local stations. See Howard, *Multiple Broadcast Ownership: Regulatory History*, 27 Fed.Comm. B.J. 1, 5 (1974).

These suits were brought on October 30, 1941, to enjoin the enforcement of the Chain Broadcasting Regulations promulgated by the Federal Communications Commission. * * *

* * * The Regulations, which the Commission characterized in its Report as "the expression of the general policy we will follow in exercising our licensing power," are addressed in terms to station licensees, and applicants for station licenses. They provide, in general, that no licenses shall be granted to stations or applicants having specified relationships with networks. Each Regulation is directed at a particular practice found by the Commission to be detrimental to the "public interest," and we shall consider them *seriatim*. * * *

The Commission found that at the end of 1938 there were 660 commercial stations in the United States, and that 341 of these were affiliated with national networks. 135 stations were affiliated exclusively with the National Broadcasting Company, Inc., known in the industry as NBC, which operated two national networks, the "Red" and the "Blue." NBC was also the licensee of 10 stations. * * * 102 stations were affiliated exclusively with the Columbia Broadcasting System, Inc., which was also the licensee of 8 stations. * * * [Seventy-four] stations were under exclusive affiliation with the Mutual Broadcasting System, Inc. In addition, 25 stations were affiliated with both NBC and Mutual and 5 with both CBS and Mutual. These figures, the Commission noted, did not accurately reflect the relative prominence of the three companies, since the stations affiliated with Mutual were, generally speaking, less desirable in frequency, power, and coverage. It pointed out that the stations affiliated with the national networks utilized more than 97% of the total night-time broadcasting power of all the stations in the country. NBC and CBS together controlled more than 85% of the total night-time wattage, and the broadcast business of the three national network companies amounted to almost half of the total business of all stations in the United States.

The Commission recognized that network broadcasting had played and was continuing to play an important part in the development of radio. "The growth and development of chain broadcasting," it stated, "found its impetus in the desire to give widespread coverage to programs which otherwise would not be heard beyond the reception area of a single station. Chain broadcasting makes possible a wider reception for expensive entertainment and cultural programs and also for programs of national or regional significance which would otherwise have coverage only in the locality of origin. Furthermore, the access to greatly enlarged audiences made possible by chain broadcasting has been a strong incentive to advertisers to finance the production of expensive programs. * * * But the fact that the chain broadcasting method brings benefits and advantages to both the listening public and to broadcast station licensees does not mean that the prevailing practices and policies of the networks and their outlets are sound in all respects, or that they should not be altered. * * * "

The Commission found that eight network abuses were amenable to correction within the powers granted it by Congress:

Exclusive affiliation of station. The Commission found that the network affiliation agreements of NBC and CBS customarily contained a provision which prevented the station from broadcasting the programs of any other network. The effect of this provision was to hinder the growth of new networks, to deprive the listening public in many areas of service to which they were entitled, and to prevent station licensees from exercising their statutory duty of determining which programs would best serve the needs of their community. * * *

[The only current Commission regulation addressing this situation applies to television service. See 47 C.F.R. § 73.658(a). The Commission repealed the radio networking rules (other than those limiting territorial exclusivity) in 1977.]

Territorial exclusivity. The Commission found another type of "exclusivity" provision in network affiliation agreements whereby the network bound itself not to sell programs to any other station in the same area. The effect of this provision, designed to protect the affiliate from the competition of other stations serving the same territory, was to deprive the listening public of many programs that might otherwise be available. If an affiliated station rejected a network program, the "territorial exclusivity" clause of its affiliation agreement prevented the network from offering the program to other stations in the area. * * * [See 47 C.F.R. §§ 73.132 (AM) and 73.232 (FM). See also 47 C.F.R. § 73.658(b) (TV).]

Term of affiliation. The standard NBC and CBS affiliation contracts bound the station for a period of five years, with the network having the exclusive right to terminate the contracts upon one year's notice. The Commission, relying upon § 307(d) of the Communications Act of 1934, under which no license to operate a broadcast station can be granted for a longer term than three years, found the five-year affiliation term to be contrary to the policy of the Act * * *. * * *

Option time. The Commission found that network affiliation contracts usually contained so-called network optional time clauses. Under these provisions the network could upon 28 days' notice call upon its affiliates to carry a commercial program during any of the hours specified in the agreement as "network optional time". For CBS affiliates "network optional time" meant the entire broadcast day. * * *

In the Commission's judgment these optional time provisions in addition to imposing serious obstacles in the path of new networks, hindered stations in developing a local program service. The exercise by the networks of their options over the station's time tended to prevent regular scheduling of local programs at desirable hours. * * *

The Commission undertook to preserve the advantages of option time, as a device for "stabilizing" the industry, without unduly impairing the ability of local stations to develop local program service. [It] called for the modification of the option-time provision in three respects: the minimum notice period for exercise of the option could not be less than 56 days; the number of hours which could be optioned was limited; and specific restrictions were placed upon exercise of the option to the disadvantage of other networks. * * * [See 47 C.F.R. § 73.658(d).]

Right to reject programs. The Commission found that most network affiliation contracts contained a clause defining the right of the station to reject network commercial programs. The NBC contracts provided simply that the station "may reject a network program the broadcasting of which would not be in the public interest, convenience, and necessity." NBC required a licensee who rejected a program to "be able to support his contention that what he has done has been more in the public interest than had he carried on the network program." * * *

While seeming in the abstract to be fair, these provisions, according to the Commission's finding, did not sufficiently protect the "public interest." As a practical matter, the licensee could not determine in advance whether the broadcasting of any particular network program would or would not be in the public interest. * * *

* * *

The Commission undertook * * * to formulate the obligations of licensees with respect to supervision over programs * * *.

Network ownership of stations. The Commission found that NBC, in addition to its network operations, was the licensee of 10 stations, 2 each in New York, Chicago, Washington, and San Francisco, 1 in Denver, and 1 in Cleveland. CBS was the licensee of 8 stations, 1 in each of these cities: New York, Chicago, Washington, Boston, Minneapolis, St. Louis, Charlotte, and Los Angeles. These 18 stations owned by NBC and CBS, the Commission observed, were among the most powerful and desirable in the country, and were permanently inaccessible to competing networks. * * *

The Commission stated that if the question had arisen as an original matter, it might well have concluded that the public interest required severance of the business of station ownership from that of network operation. But since substantial business interests have been formed on the basis of the Commission's continued tolerance of the situation, it was found inadvisable to take such a drastic step. The Commission concluded, however, that "the licensing of two stations in the same area to a single network organization is basically unsound and contrary to the public interest," and that it was also against the "public interest" for network organizations to own stations in areas where the available facilities were so few or of such unequal coverage that competition would thereby be substantially restricted. [See 47 C.F.R. § 73.658(f).]

* * *

Control by networks of station rates. The Commission found that NBC's affiliation contracts contained a provision empowering the network to reduce the station's network rate, and thereby to reduce the compensation received by the station, if the station set a lower rate for non-network national advertising than the rate established by the contract for the network programs. Under this provision the station could not sell time to a national advertiser for less than it would cost the advertiser if he bought the time from NBC. * * *

The Commission concluded that "it is against the public interest for a station licensee to enter into a contract with a network which has the effect of decreasing its ability to compete for national business. We believe that the public interest will best be served and listeners supplied with the best programs if stations bargain freely with national advertisers." [See 47 C.F.R. § 73.658(h).]

[The remainder of the opinion, which focuses on the Commission's statutory and constitutional authority to regulate use of the radio frequency spectrum is omitted.]

Affirmed.

MR. JUSTICE BLACK and MR. JUSTICE RUTLEDGE took no part in the consideration or decision of these cases.

[The dissent of MR. JUSTICE MURPHY, with which MR. JUSTICE ROBERTS noted his agreement, is omitted.]

Notes and Questions

1. In 1977, the rules relating to dual networking, exclusive network affiliation, term of affiliation, time optioning, stations's right to reject programs, and network control over station rates were repealed and replaced by a more general *Statement of Policy on Network Radio*. This action was taken in recognition of the "increase * * * in aural broadcast stations," the "lessened economic importance of networks in radio," and the "change in the nature" of the network service, from one of half-hour or longer entertainment programs to one of short periodic segments of news and information. Network Broadcasting by Standard (AM) and FM Broadcast Stations, 40 R.R.2d 80, 84 (1977).

2. The prohibition on network ownership of multiple stations in the same service and market was supplemented by the more general prohibition of duopoly ownership by any licensee, which in turn was repealed by the 1996 Telecommunications Act. (p. 213)

The dual radio network operations of NBC were severed in 1943, in response to the FCC's threat of action, thus causing the FCC to suspend the prohibition on dual radio network operations. The Blue Network was spun off and, in 1945, became the ABC radio network. As reflected in 47 C.F.R. § 73.658(g), the prohibition of dual network operation applies to television.

3. How significant an impact were the Chain Broadcasting Regulations likely to have on the continuing network-affiliate relationship? Wouldn't the likely answer be a function of the particular licensee's market characteristics—particularly the number of local stations and thus potential affiliates? (According to the brief of the Mutual Broadcasting System, which supported the regulations, only twenty-one cities were fully served by four or more

commercial stations, i.e., fully encompassed by the signals of four such stations with unrestricted hours of operation.) What is their likely significance, then, as adapted for television? See B. Owen, J. Beebe, and W. Manning, Jr., *Television Economics* 97–98 (1974).

Should the Commission limit network ownership of, or involvement in media other than broadcast radio or television? Why or why not? Consider the FCC's proposal to eliminate the network-cable television cross-ownership ban, and the 1996 Telecommunications Act's implementation of the policy. Is it significant that when Congress adopted the 1984 Cable Act and the 1996 Telecommunications Act, it included prohibitions on cable-telephone company and cable-broadcast television cross-ownership, but did not include a cable-network cross-ownership limitation? See 47 U.S.C. § 533. For an excellent discussion of the cable/telco problem, see Allen S. Hammond, IV, *Regulating Broadband Communications Networks*, 9 Yale J. Reg. 181 (1992).

4. The Chain Broadcasting Regulations initially were applied to television in their original form, which was devised for radio. As a result of the Commission's *Report on Network Broadcasting* (1957) (the "Barrow Report"), however, the FCC completely banned option time in television and prohibited television networks from representing their affiliates in the sale of non-network time, i.e., spot advertising sales. See 47 C.F.R. §§ 73.658(d) & (i).

(a) What was the economic function of option time? The significance of its prohibition? See Besen & Soligo, *The Economics of the Network–Affiliate Relationship in the Television Broadcasting Industry,* 63 Am. Econ.Rev. 259 (1973); cf. Salant, Fisher, and Brooks, *The Functions and Practices of a Television Network*, 22 Law & Contemp. Probs. 584, 603 (1957).

(b) Why do you suppose the Commission prevents television networks from representing their non-owned affiliates in the national spot market? What are the advantages and disadvantages of such representation?

2. NETWORK SUPPLY

a. *Syndication and Financial Participation*

In 1970, the Commission adopted the financial interest and syndication ("fin-syn") rules. Report and Order in Docket No. 12782, 23 FCC 2d 382, on recon. 25 FCC 2d 318 (1970), affirmed sub nom. Mount Mansfield Television, Inc. v. FCC, 442 F.2d 470 (2d Cir.1971). The rules, which are set forth at 47 C.F.R. § 73.658(j), prohibited broadcast television networks from (1) acquiring financial interests in programming produced by others, except the right to air the program on the network and (2) syndicating a program (or having an interest in any syndication arrangement) for off-network carriage. Networks were permitted, however, to syndicate, or participate in the syndication of, network-produced programs for transmission outside of the United States.

The Commission adopted the rules because of concerns about network dominance of the television program production business. From 1957 to 1968, the percentage of prime-time network programming provided by independent producers declined to approximately 4% from 33%. The networks were controlling program production both through their own production activities and through co-production arrangements, in which independent companies produced the programs and then licensed to the networks first-run rights as well as various syndication rights. According to the Commission's 1970 decision, "network judgment in choosing new programs is substantially influenced by their acquisition of subsidiary interests in the programs chosen." In other words, the public was receiving those programs that the networks judged would have the greatest profit potential—taking account of both their appeal to the network audience and the syndication rights, domestic and foreign, that the network could obtain from licensing off-network exhibition. According to the Commission, this created a conflict of interest for the networks; "good" programming might not make the network schedule unless the program producer was willing to give the network a substantial interest in the program's overall revenue potential.

As a political matter, fin-syn represented a battle between two powerful factions—the television networks and Hollywood (or, more generally, the creative film/video community). The fin-syn rules determined how the revenues from television programming would be apportioned among these groups. For the Commission, the decision to adopt the fin-syn rules required it to make a difficult judgment about how best to stimulate the development and production of a large number of diverse programs (the "public interest" objective it said it was pursuing). You can imagine that the decision had to be made amid relentless lobbying, as well as political "power-brokering," given the enormous amounts of money at stake.

After more than a decade under the fin-syn rules, the Commission proposed that they be repealed, or at least substantially relaxed. The result, and the reasons for the change in the Commission's decision, are set forth in the decision that follows.

AMENDMENT OF THE SYNDICATION AND FINANCIAL INTEREST RULES

Federal Communications Commission, 1983.
94 FCC 2d 1019, 54 R.R.2d 457.

* * *

2.   A brief description of the process of network program development will help place these rules and this proceeding in perspective. The prime time entertainment series that are aired on the networks are generally produced by the major film studios, major independent producers of a small number of their own programs, but their production activity is limited by the respective consent decrees that each has entered into with the Department of Justice. [pp. 288–289]

3.   The process of developing an entertainment series varies among the networks, although there are some common elements. In general, program ideas come from network development departments or producers. A producer can either present an idea directly to a network or to the

network through an agent or major studio. A program passes through four stages of development: 1) the treatment; 2) a pilot script; 3) a pilot; and 4) series production. The network development departments finance the first three stages and may terminate the process at any point. The financial terms negotiated between networks and producers at the developmental stages vary greatly, but may include fees, delivery dates, options and possibly the license fee if the program should become a series. Since pilots are expensive, relatively few are made in proportion to the number of treatments and scripts ordered by the networks, and only a fraction of the pilots that are made become series. * * *

4. The producer of a TV series is paid a license fee by the network for each episode produced. The license fee entitles the network to exclusive rights to air the program for a period of time. * * * License fees can be renegotiated during the run of a series.

5. Successful network programs have value beyond their network run. They can be sold to individual stations through the syndication market. Syndicators may be studios, multiple station groups, advertisers or companies set up specifically to act as syndicators. Under individual contract terms, off-network syndication may begin following the expiration of the licensing network's exclusivity protection for each episode. The most important characteristic common to all off-network syndicated programs is that they have achieved successful network runs in prime time. For a program to be syndicatable, it must have run long enough on the network to have approximately 80–100 episodes. The large number of episodes is required because the off-network syndicated series is usually broadcast daily, in the same time period, a practice known as stripping.

6. The rights to syndicate a program are often negotiated early in the production process. An established producer may even be able to obtain a cash advance from a syndicator based on prospective syndication of a series. The negotiations between producers and syndicators focus on the basic arrangements for dividing syndication revenues, the duration of the syndication rights, the territory where the program may be sold, and any cash advances. A syndicator operates by contacting stations individually and, if enough stations are willing to buy a particular program, then the off-network show feasibly can go into syndication. The price a station pays for a syndicated show is largely dependent on the station's market size. * * *

[The Commission's summary of the fin-syn rules is omitted.]

SUMMARY OF TENTATIVE DECISION AND REQUEST FOR FURTHER COMMENTS

10. Our own review of the rules and the responses to the *Notice* in this proceeding have persuaded us that the rules are in need of very substantial revision. While the continuation of some measure of regulatory control relating to the licensing and use of off-network program-

ming does appear to be appropriate, it does not appear that the financial interest rule is either necessary or desirable. * * *

* * *

125. After considering all the available evidence, we have concluded that the extent to which the conditions hypothesized above accurately characterize today's media marketplace is very much in doubt. First, there is evidence that the three networks do in fact compete with each other. * * * Second, there has been an expansion in the number of television outlets and network services that has caused an increase in the number of program purchasers and an increased demand for new programming. As a result, the network share in total program expenditures has declined over the years * * * To say that networks control the programs they buy is clearly true, but alternative program purchasers are developing to which program suppliers can turn should the networks try to lower the price they offer to program suppliers.

127. The available evidence also leads us to the conclusion that collusion among the networks would be difficult to achieve and maintain. * * *

131. **Effectiveness of the Rules.** * * * [W]e must conclude that the rules are unnecessary if the networks have no demonstrable monopsony power. * * * Of additional concern, however, is whether, even if the networks did have a significant degree of market power, the rules effectively would preclude the networks from exercising it. Our analysis leads us to believe that the financial interest and syndication rules are unlikely to curb any network market power that could exist. The fundamental reason leading us to this conclusion is that the rules do not modify the source of any such market power, viz., the structure of the market. The market structure is defined by the fact that there are only three broadcast networks. * * * The rules do not change the networks' control over the nature of the programs they choose to purchase for broadcast. Even with the rules in place, each network selects which program it will air and which it will not and thus holds veto power over any content it does not wish to air. Accordingly, producers' fear of losing creative control of their programs if the networks regain a financial interest appears unfounded.

———

In the end, it took judicial intervention to put the fin-syn rules to a quiet death. In the following case, Judge Posner took a rather dim view of the Commission's old "network dominance" theories, and essentially made it impossible for the FCC to create a new set of rules which would pass at least his muster.

SCHURZ COMMUNICATIONS, INC. v. FCC

United States Court of Appeals, Seventh Circuit, 1992.
982 F.2d 1043.

POSNER, CIRCUIT JUDGE.

In 1970 the Federal Communications Commission adopted "financial interest and syndication" [commonly known as "fin-syn"] rules designed to limit the power of the then three television networks—CBS, NBC, and ABC—over television programming. *Network Television Broadcasting*, 23 F.C.C.2d 382, 387 (1970), aff'd under the name of *Mt. Mansfield Television, Inc. v. FCC*, 442 F.2d 470 (2d Cir.1971). Each of the three networks consisted (as they still do) of several television stations, in key markets, owned and operated by the network itself, plus about two hundred independently owned stations electronically connected to the network by cable or satellite. In exchange for a fee paid them by the network, these affiliated stations broadcast programs that the network transmits to them, as well as to its owned and operated stations, over the interconnect system. The networking of programs intended for the early evening hours that are the "prime time" for adult television viewing gives advertisers access to a huge number of American households simultaneously, which in turn enables the networks to charge the high prices for advertising time that are necessary to defray the cost of obtaining the programming most desired by television viewers.

The financial interest and syndication rules adopted in 1970 forbade a network to syndicate (license) programs produced by the network for rebroadcast by independent television stations—that is, stations that were not owned by or affiliated with the network—or to purchase syndication rights to programs that it obtained from outside producers, or otherwise to obtain a financial stake in such programs. If the network itself had produced the program it could sell syndication rights to an independent syndicator but it could not retain an interest in the syndicator's revenues or profits.

Many syndicated programs are reruns, broadcast by independent stations, of successful comedy or dramatic series first shown on network television. Very few series are sufficiently successful in their initial run to be candidates for syndication. Independent stations like to air five episodes each week of a rerun series that originally had aired only once a week or less, so unless a series has a first run of several years—which few series do—it will not generate enough episodes to sustain a rerun of reasonable length. The financial interest and syndication rules thus severely limited the networks' involvement in supplying television programs other than for their own or their affiliated stations.

The concern behind the rules was that the networks, controlling as they did through their owned and operated stations and their affiliates a large part of the system for distributing television programs to American households, would unless restrained use this control to seize a dominating position in the production of television programs. That is, they would lever their distribution "monopoly" into a production "monopoly." They would, for example, refuse to buy programs for network distribution unless the producers agreed to surrender their syndication rights to the network. For once the networks controlled those rights, the access of independent television stations, that is, stations not owned by or affiliated with one of the networks, to reruns would be at the sufferance of the networks, owners of a competing system of distribution. * * *

The Commission hoped the rules would strengthen an alternative source of supply (to the networks) for independent stations—the alternative consisting of television producers not owned by networks. The rules would do this by curtailing the ability of the networks to supply the program market represented by the independent stations, and by protecting the producers for that market against being pressured into giving up potentially valuable syndication rights. And the rules would strengthen the independent stations (and so derivatively the outside producers, for whom the independent stations were an important market along with the networks themselves) by securing them against having to purchase reruns from their competitors the networks.

The basis for this concern that the networks, octopus-like, would use their position in distribution to take over programming, and would use the resulting control of programming to eliminate their remaining competition in distribution, was never very clear. If the networks insisted on buying syndication rights along with the right to exhibit a program on the network itself, they would be paying more for their programming. (So one is not surprised that in the decade before the rules were adopted, the networks had acquired syndication rights to no more than 35 percent of their prime-time series, although they had acquired a stake in the syndicator's profits in a considerably higher percentage of cases.) If the networks then turned around and refused to syndicate independent stations, they would be getting nothing in return for the money they had laid out for syndication rights except a long-shot chance—incidentally, illegal under the antitrust laws—to weaken the already weak competitors of network stations. Nor was it clear just how the financial interest and syndication rules would scotch the networks' nefarious schemes. If forbidden to buy syndication rights, networks would pay less for programs, so the outside producers would not come out clear winners— indeed many would be losers. Production for television is a highly risky undertaking, like wildcat drilling for gas and oil. Most television entertainment programs are money losers. The losses are offset by the occasional hit that makes it into syndication after completing a long first run. The sale of syndication rights to a network would enable a producer to shift risk to a larger, more diversified entity presumptively better able to bear it. The resulting reduction in the risks of production would encourage new entry into production and thus give the independent stations a more competitive supply of programs. Evidence introduced in this proceeding showed that, consistent with this speculation, networks in the pre–1970 era were more likely to purchase syndication rights from small producers than from large ones.

Whatever the pros and cons of the original financial interest and syndication rules, in the years since they were promulgated the structure of the television industry has changed profoundly. The three networks have lost ground, primarily as a result of the expansion of cable television, which now reaches 60 percent of American homes, and videocassette recorders, now found in 70 percent of American homes. Today each of the three networks buys only 7 percent of the total video and film programming sold each year, which is roughly a third of the percentage in 1970. (The inclusion of films in the relevant market is appropriate because videocassettes enable home viewers to substitute a film for a television program.) And each commands only about 12 percent of total television advertising revenues. Where in 1970 the networks had 90 percent of the prime-time audience, today they have 62 percent, and competition among as well as with the three networks is fierce. They are, moreover, challenged today by a fourth network, the Fox Broadcasting Corporation, which emerged in the late 1980s.

Notwithstanding the fourth network, which might have been expected to reduce the number of independent stations by converting many of them to network—Fox network—stations, the number of independent stations has increased fivefold since 1970. At the same time, contrary to the intention behind the rules yet an expectable result of them because they made television production a riskier business, the production of prime-time programming has become more concentrated. There are 40 percent fewer producers of prime-time programming today than there were two decades ago. And the share of that programming accounted for directly or indirectly by the eight largest producers, primarily Hollywood studios—companies large enough to bear the increased risk resulting from the Commission's prohibition against the sale of syndication rights to networks—has risen from 50 percent to 70 percent.

* * *

In 1983 the Commission issued a tentative decision agreeing with the staff, proposing radical revisions in the rules leading to their eventual repeal, but inviting further public comments on the details of its proposals. Tentative Decision and Request for Further Comments in Docket 82–345, 94 F.C.C.2d 1019 (1983). The networks, the Commission found in the tentative decision, had lost any significant monopoly or market power that they may once have had. The financial interest and syndication rules were hampering the entry of new firms into production by blocking an important mechanism (the sale of syndication rights) by which new firms might have shifted the extraordinary risks of their undertaking to the networks.

Mainly as a result of congressional pressure*, there was no follow-up to the tentative decision. The question what to do about the rules

---

* As well as, perhaps an undocumented 20–minute meeting between the then-

remained in limbo until 1990, when the Commission at the request of the Fox network initiated a fresh notice-and-comment rulemaking proceeding. After receiving voluminous submissions from the various segments of the television industry, the Commission held a one-day hearing, after which it issued an opinion, over dissents by two of the five commissioners, including the chairman, promulgating a revised set of financial interest and syndication rules. In re Evaluation of the Syndication and Financial Interest Rules, 56 Fed. Reg. 26242 (May 29, 1991), on reconsideration, 56 Fed. Reg. 64207 (Nov. 22, 1991).

The new rules are different from the old and also more complicated. They define "network" as an entity that supplies at least 15 hours of prime-time programming to interconnected affiliates. They take off all restrictions on nonentertainment programming (that is, news and sports), and most restrictions on nonprime-time programming and on syndication for the foreign as distinct from the domestic market. But in a provision that has no counterpart in the old rules, the new ones provide that no more than 40 percent of a network's own prime-time entertainment schedule may consist of programs produced by the network itself. The new rules unlike the old permit a network to buy domestic syndication rights from outside producers of prime-time entertainment programming—provided, however, that the network does so pursuant to separate negotiations begun at least 30 days after the network and the producer have agreed on the fee for licensing the network to exhibit the program on the network itself. Even then the network may not do the actual syndication; that is, it may not arrange for the distribution of the programming to the independent stations; it must hire an independent syndicator for that. And it may acquire syndication rights only in reruns, not in first-run programs, and thus it may not distribute first-run programming other than to its network stations. This restriction applies to foreign as well as to domestic syndication unless the program is not intended for exhibition in the U.S. at all. * * *

* * * Although the Commission conceded that the networks may already have lost so much of their market power as no longer to pose a threat to competition as it is understood in antitrust law, it concluded that some restrictions remain necessary to assure adequate diversity of television programming. The Commission's chairman, understandably irate because the majority had ignored most of the points in his long and detailed dissent, predicted that the majority's decision would "produce a milestone case on what constitutes arbitrary and capricious decisionmaking." The new rules were not stayed, and became effective in May of last year. * * *

* * *

Chairman of the FCC and the then-President, Ronald Reagan, who had some ties to Hollywood.—Ed.

Although the television industry is less complex than some and its product is well known even to federal judges, there are more than enough technical aspects to the industry, involving such things as the modes of financing and contracting and the effects of market structure and practices on television fare, to enforce judicial diffidence. Moreover, economists do not agree on the relation between monopoly or competition, on the one hand, and the quality or variety of an industry's output, on the other, so that it is difficult to obtain a theoretical perspective from which to evaluate the Commission's claims about that relation.

* * *

From what we have said so far, it should be apparent that the networks have no hope of proving to our satisfaction that the Commission is without any power to restrict the networks' participation in television programming. Even if we were persuaded that it would be irrational to impute to the networks even a smidgen of market power, the Commission could always take the position that it should carve out a portion of the production and distribution markets and protect them against the competition of the networks in order to foster, albeit at a higher cost to advertisers and ultimately to consumers, a diversity of programming sources and outlets that might result in a greater variety of perspectives and imagined forms of life than the free market would provide. That would be a judgment within the Commission's power to make.

The difficult question presented by the petitions to review is not whether the Commission is authorized to restrict the networks' participation in program production and distribution. It is whether the Commission has said enough to justify, in the face of the objections lodged with it, the particular restrictions that it imposed in the order here challenged. One might be tempted as an original matter to treat an administrative rule as courts treat legislation claimed to deny substantive due process, and thus ask whether on any set of hypothesized facts, whether or not mentioned in the statement accompanying the rule, the rule was rational. And then the new financial interest and syndication rules would have to be upheld. But that is not the standard for judicial review of administrative action. It is not enough that a rule might be rational; the statement accompanying its promulgation must show that it is rational—must demonstrate that a reasonable person upon consideration of all the points urged pro and con the rule would conclude that it was a reasonable response to a problem that the agency was charged with solving.

The new rules flunk this test. The Commission's articulation of its grounds is not adequately reasoned. Key concepts are left unexplained, key evidence is overlooked, arguments that formerly persuaded the Commission and that time has only strengthened are ignored, contradictions within and among Commission decisions are passed over in silence. The impression created is of unprincipled compromises of Rube Goldberg complexity among contending interest groups viewed merely as clamoring suppliants who have somehow to be conciliated. * * * The possibility of resolving a conflict in favor of the party with the stronger case, as distinct from throwing up one's hands and splitting the difference, was overlooked. The opinion contains much talk but no demonstration of expertise, and a good deal of hand-wringing over the need for prudence and the desirability of avoiding "convulsive" regulatory reform, yet these unquestioned goods are never related to the particulars of the rules—rules that could have a substantial impact on an industry that permeates the daily life of this nation and helps shape, for good or ill, our culture and our politics. The Commission must do better in articulating their justification. Perhaps the attempt to do so will result in significant modifications in the rules. Not all remands result in the reinstatement of the original decision with merely a more polished rationalization.

* * * Stripped of verbiage, the opinion, like a Persian cat with its fur shaved, is alarmingly pale and thin. It can be paraphrased as follows. The television industry has changed since 1970. There is more competition—cable television, the new network, etc. No longer is it clear that the networks have market power in an antitrust sense, which they could use to whipsaw the independent producers and strangle the independent stations. So there should be some "deregulation" of programming—some movement away from the 1970 rules. But not too much, because even in their decline the networks may retain some power to extort programs or program rights from producers. The networks offer advertisers access to 98 percent of American households; no competing system for the distribution of television programming can offer as much. Anyway the Commission's concern, acknowledged to be legitimate, is not just with market power in an antitrust sense but with diversity, and diversity is promoted by measures to assure a critical mass of outside producers and independent stations. So the networks must continue to be restricted—but less so than by the 1970 rules. The new rules will give the networks a greater opportunity to participate in programming than the old ones did, while protecting outside producers and independent stations from too much network competition.

* * *

The new rules, like their predecessors, appear to harm rather than to help outside producers as a whole (a vital qualification) by reducing their bargaining options. It is difficult to see how taking away a part of a seller's market could help the seller. One of the rights in the bundle of rights that constitutes the ownership of a television program is the right to syndicate the program to nonnetwork stations. The new rules restrict—perhaps, as a practical matter, prevent—the sale of that right to networks. How could it help a producer to be forbidden to sell his wares to a class of buyers that may be the high bidders for them? It is not as if anyone supposed that syndication rights, like babies or human freedom or the vital organs of a living person, should not be salable at all. They are freely salable—except to networks. Since syndication is the riskiest component of a producer's property right—for its value depends on the distinctly low-probability event that the program will be a smash hit on network television—restricting its sale bears most heavily on the smallest, the weakest, the newest, the most experimental producers, for they are likely to be the ones least able to bear risk. It becomes understandable why the existing producers support the financial interest and syndication rules: the rules protect these producers against new competition both from the networks (because of the 40 percent cap) and from new producers. * * *

This analysis of risk and its bearing on competition in the program industry is speculative, theoretical, and may for all we know be all wet—though it is corroborated by the increasing concentration of the production industry since the rules restricting the sale of syndication rights were first imposed in 1970. The Commission was not required to buy the analysis. But as the analysis was more than plausible and had been pressed upon it by a number of participants in the rulemaking proceeding—including a putatively disinterested Justice Department that in the past had frequently seen the bogeyman of monopoly lurking everywhere, as well as the Commission's own chairman—the Commission majority was not entitled to ignore it. Not even to consider the possibility that the unrestricted sale of syndication rights to networks would strengthen the production industry (the industry—not necessarily its present occupants) and thereby increase programming diversity by enabling a sharing between fledgling producers and the networks of the risks of new production was irresponsible. For if the argument about risk sharing is correct, the rules are perverse; by discouraging the entry of new producers into the high-risk prime-time entertainment market, they are likely to reduce the supply of programs to the independent stations and so reduce diversity both of program sources and of program outlets. The Commission's stated desiderata are competition and diversity. The rules adopted by the Commission in order to achieve these desiderata have the remarkable property—if the risk-sharing argument that the Commission did not deign to address is correct—of disserving them both.

[The court went on to debunk the Commission's notion that the networks still had the power to force producers to deal with them, even if the networks had lost market power.]

The difficulty is that if the networks do have market power, the new rules (in this respect like the old) do not seem rationally designed to prevent its exercise. A rule telling a person he may not do business with some firm believed to have market power is unlikely to make the person better off. * * * If he could do better by selling syndication rights to someone else he would not accede to such unfavorable terms as the network offered.

If this is right, the new rules, at least insofar as they restrict network syndication, cannot increase the prices that producers receive. All they can do is increase the costs of production by denying producers the right to share risks with networks.

* * *

Everything that we have said about the effect of forbidding producers to sell syndication rights to networks may be wrong. That we freely grant. But the argument we have sketched—an argument vigorously pressed upon the Commission by the networks——is sufficiently persuasive to have placed a burden of explanation on the Commission. It did not carry the burden. It did not mention the objection.

* * *

[The court then went on to discuss the Fox Network's argument that it not be subject to the same rules as the "big three," in order to give it more incentive and room to grow. The court suggested that the Commission treat Fox separately, at least in terms of the financial interest and syndication rules.]

The Commission's treatment of precedent was also cavalier. An administrative agency is no more straitjacketed by precedent than a court is. It can reject its previous decisions. But it must explain why it is doing so. This is an aspect of the duty mentioned earlier of rational explanation; a rational person acts consistently, and therefore changes course only if something has changed. [The court chastised the FCC for not explaining why its 1983 conclusion that the networks lacked market power was not at least as valid in 1991.]

* * *

Finally, while the word diversity appears with incantatory frequency in the Commission's opinion, it is never defined. At argument one of the counsel helpfully distinguished between source diversity and outlet diversity (as had the Commission itself in previous decisions).

* * *

Almost everyone in this country either now has or soon will have cable television with 50 or 100 or even 200 different channels to choose among. With that many channels, programming for small audiences with specialized tastes becomes entirely feasible. It would not have been surprising, therefore, if the Commission had taken the position that diversity in prime-time television programming, or indeed in over-the-air broadcasting generally, was no longer a value worth promoting. It did not take that position. Instead it defended its restrictions on network participation in programming on the ground that they promote diversity. But it made no attempt to explain how they do this. It could have said, but did not, that independent television stations depend on reruns, which they would prefer to get from sources other than the networks with which they compete, and—since reruns are the antithesis of diversity—they use their revenue from reruns to support programming that enhances programming diversity. It could have said that programs produced by networks' in-house facilities are somehow more uniform than programs produced by Hollywood studios. It didn't say that either. It never drew the link between the rules, which on their face impede the production of television programs—not only by constraining negotiations between networks and outside producers but also by reducing the networks' incentive to produce by limiting the extent to which a network can exhibit its own programs in prime time—and the interest in diverse programming. The Commission may have thought the link obvious, but it is not. The rules appear to handicap the networks and by handicapping them to retard new entry into production; how all this promotes programming diversity is mysterious, and was left unexplained in the Commission's opinion.

That opinion, despite its length, is unreasoned and unreasonable, and therefore, in the jargon of judicial review of administrative action, arbitrary and capricious. The Commission's order is therefore vacated and the matter is returned to the Commission for further proceedings. The Commission may of course reopen the record of the rulemaking proceeding to receive additional comments if that will help it reach an articulate reasoned decision.

Questions

1. Why didn't the FCC just repeal what it viewed as an outdated rule in 1983? Who was President at that time? Although Judge Posner refers to "congressional pressures," were there perhaps other and more powerful ones?

2. What is the role of "diversity" in network regulation? As seen before, isn't diversity generally almost akin to "localism?" Given their nationwide audiences, are networks likely candidates to provide much in the way of diversity—or, under present jargon "narrowcasting?" Do their economic constraints allow this? Is it an accident that few programs such as "All in the Family" ever made it to network television? E.g., Geoffrey Cowan, See *No Evil* (1978) (explaining the rather strange politics which allowed Norman Lear to sell "All in the Family" and similar programs to CBS.)

3. Note that the on remand the Commission did not attempt to develop a more complete "administrative record." Instead, on April 1, 1993, it abandoned the "new" fin-syn rules and adopted a phased repeal of the "old" ones.

4. One of Judge Posner's basic problems with the FCC is that it did not consider the pro-competitive aspects of allowing networks to put money "up front" for new programs, as a means of enabling small producers to secure sufficient capital to create new programs. If a potential program is sufficiently attractive, however, a producer should have no difficulty in finding potential investors. At least in theory, the only difference between dealing with the networks and with individual investors would be the ease of raising capital and the transactions costs involved. Indeed, Professor Ron Coase— one of the gurus of the "Chicago School" law and economics jurisprudence which Judge Posner helped bring to fruition—observed as much in his seminal article on marketplace allocation of broadcast licenses. As seen before, "[I]n the struggle for particular resources, men who earn $5,000 per annum are every day outbidding those who earn $50,000 per annum." Does Judge Posner suggest a reason why this phenomenon has not occurred with

program production? If not, what might it be, other than excessive transaction costs?

5. Judge Posner notes that the number of major program producers has declined since adoption of the original fin-syn rules in 1970. Has this necessarily resulted from the dearth of network up front money? To what extent has there been a change in the production community from major studios to smaller, "start-up" operations? Is it relevant that many producers have entered the production market by catering to low-cost, low-end cable satellite networks? (As noted below, these operations have at best minuscule market shares as compared to the traditional networks.) Might this migration thus have taken place regardless of whether the fin-syn rules had been in place?

Indeed, the last few years have seen a reverse movement of programs from cable to broadcasting—at least in the syndication marketplace. Less than memorable examples include "The Morton Downey Show." Regardless of one's view about the merits of programs like this, does this indicate a viable syndicated marketplace for syndicated programming?

6. Despite the Commission's noise about the networks' declining market shares and lack of market power, is it clear that at least the "big three" have lost significant market position as to all types of programming? Judge Posner notes that the networks buy only about 7 percent of all independently produced programming, and generally have about 20 percent of the U.S. prime time audience. By comparison, however, the most successful cable networks (e.g., ESPN, CNN) do well to get more than 4 percent of the audience, even during major events such as the "Gulf War," during which CNN provided coverage substantially before the major networks.

In terms of defining the relevant product (i.e., advertising) market, are single-digit market shares on cable networks very attractive to mass marketers, such as manufacturers of automobiles, home products, and cosmetics? With the advent of cable and other "narrowcast" media, are there thus two different advertising markets—one for traditional mass appeal programming, and another for "niche" products? Do the major networks still have a hold on nationwide mass advertising? Should they thus be subject to any restraints? If so, what? Did the Commission punt by simply getting out of the fin-syn regulatory business?

7. Does Judge Posner hold that the FCC was just wrong, or merely that it did not adequately document its decision? Although he suggests that the agency might be able to find a "rational basis" on remand, was that a realistic expectation? (As indicated above, on remand the Commission made no attempt to find an empirical basis for its decision.) As discussed in relation to the "indecency" and cable "must-carry" cases, would a deregulatory FCC have a real incentive to create a record for upholding rather than repealing distasteful regulations?

Along these lines, during the last decade the Commission has had a reversal rate of more than 50 percent on appeal. What does this say about the FCC's view of judicial review? What does this say about courts' views of the FCC?

8. In his previous career as a professor at the University of Chicago Law School, Judge Posner was a founder of what commonly is known as the "Chicago School" or the "Law and Economics" jurisprudence. This school of thought relies heavily upon the writings of Professor Ronald Coase, as discussed above. (p. 31) Regardless of one's views as to the validity of this approach, it has had a major impact upon U.S. legal—and particularly regulatory—thinking.

In evaluating the FCC's fin-syn rulemaking actions, Judge Posner clearly is less than a fan of the agency's decisionmaking process. But there could be two-and perhaps coterminous—reasons for his discomfort. First, he might have believed that the agency had failed to articulate a rational basis for its action. Second, he might have believed that the FCC basically was incompetent in this area, because of various political pressures, and thus could not have made a rational decision.

From Judge Posner's opinion, is it possible to tell which—or both—alternatives governed? In the long run, does it make any difference?

Is this another situation in which there is a strained "partnership" between the FCC and the reviewing courts? Compare the tension between the Commission and the D.C. Circuit as to comparative license proceedings.

9. On appeal from the Commission's adoption of the new 1993 fin-syn rules, the Seventh Circuit resoundingly upheld the FCC's action against a variety of complaints about allowing the networks to produce and syndicate any amount of programming. National Broadcasting Company v. Capital Cities/ABC, Inc., 29 F.3d 309 (7th Cir.1994). The court basically reasoned that the Commission had acted reasonably in rejecting its own prior rationale and in adopting the court's analysis. Judge Posner noted:

> On remand the Commission did not attempt to offer a more convincing rationalization for the 1991 rules, or tinker with them around the edges, though either would have been a predictable response. Instead it threw out the rules, convinced that the objections to them were unanswerable. Except for reporting requirements which concern no one, the Commission decided that as of (as it has turned out) November 1995 there will be no fin-syn rules. The networks will be free to compete in the television program market on terms of complete equality with the independent producers and syndicators.

> It is a remarkable about-face for an agency that for half a century has treated the independent television stations as sensitive plants requiring high fences to keep out network predators. * * * [The independent producers and stations] are wrong to argue that the Commission had to explain why it agreed with the criticisms of the 1991 rules made in our previous opinion. If it believed that the reasoning underlying the rules had been erroneous, it had to say why; that is true; but rather than set forth its reasons at length it could say, as in effect it did, "for the reasons set forth in the Seventh Circuit's opinion." It did not have to add, "because those reasons are sound." Administrative agencies, like courts, are generally in the position of choosing between competing positions rather than creating new positions ex nihilo. * * * If as happened here * * * an agency is persuaded by a court's reasoning to alter its course, it can adopt that reasoning, and then the adequacy of

the agency's new position will depend on the adequacy of the adopted reasoning.

The quarrel of the independent producers and stations, therefore, is not with the Commission, but with our previous opinion, which furnished a rationale for deregulation that the Commission has adopted. Yet they have not taken direct issue with any of the central points in that opinion. Their argument is not that the opinion was wrong, but that the Commission could not adopt the reasoning of the opinion without explaining why it was adopting that reasoning. The only answer the Commission could have given, however, was the one it did give—that it agreed with the opinion. Whether this was a rational response depends only on whether the reasoning in our previous opinion was rational. We are given no reason to suppose that it was not.

Is the court here engaged in a bit of micro-management? Did it effectively rewrite the Commission's policy for it? If so, would there be anything wrong with that?

b. *Competition in Program Production*

The final major component of the Commission's network regulations was the Prime Time Access Rule ("PTAR"). As discussed below, this basically was intended to create an incentive for network-affiliated stations to buy independently produced programs to fill at least part of prime time; the corollary was that it would give independent stations a an opportunity to compete with *network* reruns against the affiliates, thus turning the tables somewhat. As described by the Commission in Prime Time Access Rule, 50 FCC 2d 829 (1975), PTAR applied as follows:

2.   In substance, the provisions of the new rule, effective September 8, 1975, are as follows:

(a) Network-owned or affiliated stations in the 50 largest markets (in terms of prime time audience for all stations in the market) may present no more than three hours of network or off-network programs (including movies previously shown on a network) during the hours of prime time 7:00–11:00 p.m. E.T. and P.T., 6:00–10:00 p.m. C.T. and M.T.

(b) Certain categories of network and off-network programming are not to be counted toward the three-hour limitation; these are generally:

— Network or off-network programs designed for children, public affairs programs or documentary programs.

— Special news programs dealing with fast-breaking news events, on-the-spot coverage of news events or other material related to this coverage, and political broadcasts by or on behalf of legally qualified candidates for public office.

— Regular half-hour network news programs when immediately adjacent to a full hour of locally produced news or public affairs programming.

— Runovers of live network coverage of sports events, where the event has been reasonably scheduled to conclude before prime time.

— For stations in the Mountain and Pacific time zones, when network prime time programming consists of a sports or other live program broadcast simultaneously throughout the United States, these stations may schedule programming as though the live network broadcast occupies no more of their prime time than that of stations in the other time zones.

— Broadcasts of international sports events (such as the Olympics), New Year's Day college football games, or other network programming of a special nature (except other sports or motion pictures) when the network devotes all of its evening programming time, except for brief "fill" material, to the same programming.

(c) Another provision includes definitions of the terms "programs designed for children" and "documentary programs".

* * *

15. As to the matter of network dominance, it is readily apparent that, as far as network control over station time is concerned, it is reduced by the requirement of cleared or access time, and that certain public advantages have resulted. These include the local programming activities which have been stimulated. * * * It may be that these programs in some cases would have been presented anyhow, and possibly at a reasonably desirable hour in prime or fringe time; but their presentation in high-audience hours is certainly facilitated by the rule * * *. These showings afford tangible evidence of the benefits flowing from the rule. * * * Also of significance in this connection is the fact that affiliated stations are able to retain all of the revenues from access program time (less the amount they spend for programming, typically no more than 33% according to earlier material herein) compared to about 30% which they typically get from the networks for network time. Thus, they have more money from which to support local programming efforts. We find it an important and valid consideration.

16. Also of considerable importance is the encouragement of a body of new syndicated programming, which independent stations may use as well as affiliated stations, by making prime time available for its presentation. Such a body of programming has developed. While [various opponents] * * * urge that this is not of significance (being game shows, foreign imports or other network "retreads"), it is premature to make any final judgment at this time as to the character of this programming (assuming that such a judgment is ever appropriate). * * *

17. On balance, we conclude that the rule also has other benefits. These include the increased opportunity for non-national

advertisers as well as an optional outlet for national advertisers who may choose to use spot rather than network messages. There is increased programming of a public service character presented by ABC as a result of its greater profitability under the rule. Finally, there is the emergence of successful distributors who are able to finance their own and others' production of network and non-network programs * * *. As a result there is now an increased number of producers active in prime time. * * *

* * *

A substantial amount of such programming is produced locally and presented in access time, one of the important benefits of the rule as already mentioned. As to the networks, there is a substantial amount of public affairs programming (and similar news documentary material) in prime time on all three networks, but no regularly scheduled material, whereas before the rule both CBS and NBC had regular prime-time programs of this nature, and it is also noted that some such network programming occurs outside of prime time. We conclude, therefore, that the rule constitutes an inhibition on the networks' exercise of this highly important part of their activities, fulfillment of part of their journalistic function to advise and inform the public concerning matters of public importance, and that this added benefit outweighs the impingement on access time. This exemption is a codification and extension of the existing waiver for one-time network news and public affairs programs which has been in effect throughout the rule's history. That exemption has not been used to an inordinate extent by the networks. * * *

33. Documentaries as defined herein also, of course, include other programs, such as National Geographic and Jacques Cousteau specials and the America series, both network and off-network programs. * * * In sum, in view of the obvious informational value of documentary programs, the benefit to the public from facilitating the presentation thereof outweighs in importance what might be termed an increase in network dominance (to the extent these are network programs) and an incursion into the full availability of 3 hours a night of cleared time for other new material. * * *

34. We expect the networks, and licensees in their acceptance of network programs and use of off-network material, to keep such programming to the minimum consistent with their programming judgments as to what will best serve the interests of the public generally. * * * We attach particular importance to the programming opportunities available on Saturday in the access time period. We do so because of the significance of existing local programming efforts in this time period, and the fact that this time offers the most significant opportunity for hour-long access programs [since there is no network news broadcast at 7:00 E.T.]. We caution networks to avoid any incursion into this period unless there are compelling

public interest reasons for so doing. If there are extensive deviations from these precepts, the exemption may have to be revisited.

35.   In acting herein to permit an increase of network programming of certain types, we are only opening up an option for licensees to use such additional network material if, in light of their programming judgments as licensee-trustees meeting the needs, tastes, interests and problems of their coverage areas, they deem it appropriate to do so. Our purpose is to make available to licensees programming which, to some extent, was removed from prime time or caused to be run at a much later hour. There is intended no requirement, or even a suggestion, that such additional network programming should be carried in order for a licensee to carry out properly his programming obligations.

* * *

D.   Off–Network and Feature Film Restrictions

49.   As to the off-network restriction, we find that repeal or relaxation is not warranted, except to the limited extent adopted herein and discussed above. It is readily apparent that elimination of this restriction would lead to a large-scale incursion into cleared time by use of off-network material, sharply reducing the availability of time to sources of new non-network material. While the off-network aspects of the rule do constitute a restraint which is not directly related to present network dominance, the drastic impact on our objective of encouraging the development of new material would obviously be completely disserved.

50.   We have decided to modify prior provisions regarding the use of feature films in access time. Under the changes made here, we eliminate the restriction on movies which have been shown by a station in the same market within a two-year period. At the same time, however, the new rule bars any feature film which has ever appeared on a network from the access period. If a movie has never appeared on a network, it may now be presented during the access hour, regardless of when or whether it has ever appeared on a station in the same market. If it appeared on a network—whether or not made for television—it is barred. We believe that this will ease the administration of this portion of the rule for licensees, motion picture distributors, and the Commission. * * *

53.   Network news following a full hour of local news. The new rule (§ 73.658(k)(3)) codifies the existing waiver for a half-hour of regular network news if it is preceded by a full hour of local news or local public affairs programming. * * *

[Discussion of the exemptions for sports runovers, special network programming, and special network news coverage, and of time zone problems with live coverage of special events, is omitted. These regulations appear at 47 C.F.R. § 73.658(k)(2)–(6).]

* * *

[The concurring statements of Chairman Wiley and Commissioners Reid and Robert E. Lee are omitted.]

DISSENTING STATEMENT OF COMMISSIONER GLEN O. ROBINSON

I. INTRODUCTION

* * *

The revised rule plainly reflected the Commission's ambivalence between curbing network dominance over programming on the one hand and retaining network programs (the kind for which waivers had been granted) on the other. * * * There appears to be no recognition that each part of the modified rule undercuts the other. Access is good, but it does not produce the kind of programming which we like so we have to provide the opportunity for such programming; we like such programming but if we see too much of it we see it as evidence of "network dominance" since it can only be supplied by network brokers.

* * *

II. THE CONCEPT OF NETWORK DOMINANCE

* * *

Presumably, network dominance refers to the power which three national brokers of local station time and national programming have in selecting the nation's television program menu. In general, program suppliers must deal with one of these three network companies or forego national distribution of their product. This limited number of potential buyers, it is asserted, presents the real threat of arbitrariness in program selection and the denial of access to program suppliers with new ideas. A second form of "network dominance" which emerges in the discussion of the rule is the ability of networks to persuade local affiliates to clear time for network programming. As networks expand their activities to new day parts, they progressively preempt the local station's ability to make its own program choices. The rule would return this choice to the stations, if for only one hour per day.

Unfortunately, there appears to be only a limited understanding that the chief cause of "network dominance," making inevitable some form of network power, derives from the Commission's own television frequency allocations. * * * It is a basic economic fact that, with a few exceptions, programs receiving less than national exposure cannot hope to compete for audiences with those achieving network distribution. If network distribution were not national, program budgets would have to be much lower per dollar of advertising generated. Network distribution allows the most efficient use of television advertising revenues in the stimulation of program production.

A network is more than a mere broker of station time. It is also an investor in programming. By agreeing in advance to commit its local affiliates to a given program series, and by guaranteeing program suppliers a sum certain (in the form of a license fee) for a number of programs well in advance of exhibition, the network makes possible the investment of $250,000 or more per hour of entertainment fare. Without this "preselling," producers would not commit themselves to such program budgets.

To the extent that the Commission laments the decline in station program selection and the growth of "network dominance" in this process, it laments the development of efficient program brokerage. In this sense, what has been obtained from the prime time access rule is just what should have been expected: a fragmented array of low-cost, low-quality programs offered to local stations directly by producers without the intervention of a broker. Enormous energies and expenses are required in this distribution process—expenses which are diverted directly from program budgets.

As time passes, it may be possible for program brokers to develop for just the access period. If this were to happen, however, we would be no closer to the goals which the majority hopes to attain than we were with PTAR I or II. Since market forces would distill no more than three such brokers from the set of current program distributors, the *best* that can be realistically hoped for is the development of a new triopoly, which would "dominate" the access period. Unfortunately, this optimum is likely to be difficult to accomplish if there are any scale economies in performing network brokerage. A mere seven hours per week may not be sufficient to make efficient use of the personnel required to establish and enforce affiliate contracts, negotiate for program rights, select and schedule new program series and perform various research functions. The result may well be that a much greater share of the revenues for this period will be diverted to these brokerage functions than is true for the three existing networks.

At some point it is necessary to submit to the limitations of the real world. * * *

III. PROGRAM ACCESS, QUALITY, AND DIVERSITY

Searching through the current access period programming in pursuit of the gems which the three networks are supposed, in their capriciousness, to avoid, is a frustrating business. No definition of program quality seems to me congruent with the current run of access programs, an opinion which appears to be widely shared—by Commissioners, television critics and quite a few viewers. Of course measures of quality are elusive at best, and one's interpretation of the prudence of continuing the rule cannot depend solely upon comparisons between network and access programs. In particular I am mindful of the First Amendment restrictions that preclude us from judging the merits of the access rule by engaging in critical review of, say, "Bowling for Dollars" or "Let's Make a Deal."* However, a major premise of the rule was, and is, that it would promote diversity—by promoting new sources of programming, reflecting different ideas and creative energies. I assume we can, without affronting the First Amendment, ask whether this goal has been or can be achieved under the rule.

* * *

The market for access programs has already begun to distinguish the programs with audience appeal from those with little value to viewers. A few series * * * dominate the access market while myriad other programming ventures realize very limited sales and are dropped by syndicators. This trend will continue * * *. Only those programs achieving full national distribution, obtaining clearance in a large proportion of markets, will be able to cover the costs of production, which syndicators will soon find beginning to escalate. Thus, one of the purported benefits of the rule—the large number of programs available for the period (in contrast to the twenty-one hours available from networks if they programmed the full access period) will soon evaporate as the rule assumes a more permanent appearance.

The Commission should not lament this decline in the number of access programs as it develops. It is only through the process of funneling the total national advertising revenues available for the period into program budgets of a smaller set of programs exhibited in every market that suppliers of access programs will be able to compete for resources with those supplying network fare and to offer quality programs. In short, quantity and quality are inversely related in this market through their interaction in the program budgets of suppliers. * * *

* * *

VI. THE CHOICES FACED BY THE COMMISSION

* * *

If we wish to commit ourselves seriously to reducing "network dominance," I believe we have to focus our attention on the basic source of the problem: the limited number of economically competitive television stations in each market. What is wanted is a means to increase the number of stations. * * *

* * *

Unless the Commission confronts the issue of network *economic power* head-on, it will simply sit as a constant arbitrator among groups competing for the scarcity rents which it has created by its allocations

---

* In 1974–75 over 65 percent of the programs in the access period were game shows—a five-fold increase over the last pre-PTAR period, 1970–71, when the figure was 11 percent. In the 1974–75 season, 17 of the top 22 access shows (accounting for 87 percent of all *syndicated* access programming) had been broadcast before the access rule, [and] 16 had been broadcast (as network programs) before the access rule. Many of these shows, in fact, continue to be produced with network facilities (and some are still broadcast as network shows). [Footnote relocated]

plan and the current access rule. The Commission should not be forced to determine how these rents should be divided between large Hollywood motion picture companies and smaller purveyors of game shows. Rather, it should carry out its authority to increase competitive outlets in a manner which prevents the development of monopoly power. If it is unwilling to do this, it should simply return to the status quo ante, allowing the three national network companies to program as much or as little of the prime time period as they wish. This last is obviously the most realistic option at this point; and in light of the past few years' experience, together with what I believe are the demonstrable facts of economic life, I think the Commission should embrace it.

Notes and Questions

1. The three television networks, whose market dominance is the primary target of the PTAR, took widely disparate positions in the PTAR II proceeding: CBS sought repeal of the rule, NBC "supported the PTAR II compromise" that was adopted, and ABC was a "strong supporter" of the original (PTAR I) rule. What might explain this array of views?

2. (a) Among the benefits claimed for PTAR, the FCC found that affiliated stations fared better financially, thus giving them "more money from which to support local programming efforts." ¶ 15. Is the FCC's premise plausible? Assuming it is, does the Commission's conclusion follow?

(b) The Commission also found that "network dominance is obviously reduced by the reduction in network prime time programming." Yet the Commission had before it a staff report stating:

> Overall network power has been strengthened, not weakened, by the [PTAR]. Network originated programming has become scarce, resulting in greater advertiser demand for commercial minutes within prime-time programming. It has, in addition, strengthened the networks' bargaining position with program producers, who are now required to compete for fewer prime-time network hours.

A. Pearce, The Economic Consequences of the FCC's Prime–Time Access Rule on the Broadcasting and Program Production Industries 1 (1973). Which statement employs the more meaningful criterion of network power?

3. On review, the court of appeals did not reach the merits of the Commission's 1974 action; it decided only that the changes were implemented too precipitously, and enjoined the Commission from making any changes to the PTAR before September 1975. National Ass'n of Independent Television Producers and Distributors v. FCC, 502 F.2d 249 (2d Cir.1974) (*NAITPD I*). The decision was remanded to the Commission to determine an appropriate effective date. The court also suggested that the Commission develop a clearer position on three matters: (1) the argument that the rule works to increase, rather than decrease, network dominance; (2) the effect of the rule on competition; and (3) the potential for the rule to have a serious adverse impact on Hollywood as a result of the reduced time made available

for network programming. The Commission's abbreviated responses to the first two issues are clearly stated in the preceding Report and Order; with respect to the third issue, the Commission decided that the available evidence was inconclusive.

PTAR II was reviewed in National Association of Independent Television Producers and Distributors v. FCC, 516 F.2d 526 (2d Cir.1975) (NAITPD II). First the court (1) upheld the basic PTAR concept against the argument that it had failed to achieve its purposes; (2) rejected the First Amendment attack on PTAR II's scheme of exceptions based on program type; but (3) directed the agency (a) to formulate a broad definition of "public affairs programs," and (b) not to entertain waiver or other petitions requesting it to determine whether particular programs fall within the exempted categories, but instead to allow licensees to determine for themselves whether programming fit those categories.

The court also (4) held that "so long as the FCC permits movies never seen on a television network to be played in cleared access time, it must also permit movies which have been shown on network to be played in that time," id. at 543; and (5) read paragraph 34 as an unlawful delegation to licensees of the Commission's "policing duty" under the public interest standard of § 307(d), and required that the Commission "either withdraw its admonition concerning Saturday programs or make the exempted categories wholly unavailable to licensees in access time on Saturdays." Finally, the court (6) directed the FCC to consider in conjunction with the effective date for PTAR II, "a ceiling on total hours allowed for the exempted network programs in the light of the number of independent programs for first-run syndication then available for early production."

On remand the Commission declined to impose an overall ceiling on the use of network or off-network material qualifying for exemption as children's documentary, or public affairs programming, and responded to the court's mandate concerning the Saturday access hour, the use of feature films, and the definition of "public affairs programs." As thus amended, the PTAR rules appear at 47 C.F.R. § 73.658(k).

5.   Does Commissioner Robinson's dissenting statement suggest that no fin-syn rule or PTAR is likely to achieve the objective of limiting network dominance? Do you agree with his thesis? If so, should the Commission repeal these rules and pursue some other type of regulation? What alternative policies might be pursued? Should the Commission simply abandon these rules and permit the growth of alternative media to contain network dominance? What can the Commission do to confront network power "head on," as urged by Commissioner Robinson?

In the end, the Commission found PTAR to have little if any positive effect, largely because of the reasons noted in Commissioner Robinson's dissent. After various attempts to redesign the rule, it just scrapped it.

IN RE REVIEW OF THE PRIME
TIME ACCESS RULE

Federal Communications Commission, 1995.
11 FCC Rcd. 546, 1995 WL 449873.
July 31, 1995 Released; Adopted July 28, 1995.

By the Commission: Commissioner Barrett concurring and issuing a statement; Commissioner Chong issuing a statement.

I. INTRODUCTION

1. The Commission's Prime Time Access Rule ("PTAR") generally prohibits network-affiliated television stations in the top 50 television markets ("Top 50 Market Affiliates") from broadcasting more than three hours of network programs (the "network restriction") or former network programs (the "off-network restriction") during the four prime time viewing hours (i.e., 7 to 11 p.m. Eastern and Pacific times; 6 to 10 p.m. Central and Mountain times). The rule exempts certain types of programming (e.g., runovers of live sporting events, special news, documentary and children's programming, and certain sports and network programming of a special nature) which are not counted toward the three hours of network programming. PTAR was promulgated in 1970 in response to a concern that the three major television networks—ABC, CBS and NBC—dominated the program production market, controlled much of the video fare presented to the public, and inhibited the development of competing program sources. The Commission believed that PTAR would increase the level of competition in program production, reduce the networks' control over their affiliates' programming decisions, and thereby increase the diversity of programs available to the public. PTAR also came to be viewed as a means of promoting the growth of independent stations in that they did not have to compete with Top 50 Market Affiliates in acquiring off-network programs to air during the access period.

2. On October 20, 1994, the Commission adopted a Notice of Proposed Rule Making ("Notice") in this docket to conduct an overall review of the continuing need for PTAR given the profound changes that have occurred in the television industry since 1970. As we stated in the Notice, inherent in our regulatory mandate is the continuing responsibility to review our rules and policies to determine whether, in light of prevailing market conditions, such rules and policies continue to serve the public interest. * * *

3. Based on this record, we conclude that PTAR should be extinguished. The three major networks do not dominate the markets relevant to PTAR. There are large numbers of sellers and buyers of video programming. Entry, even by small businesses, is relatively easy. There are a substantially greater number of broadcast programming outlets today than when PTAR was adopted in 1970 due to the growth in numbers of independent stations. In addition, nonbroadcast media have proliferated. Viewers can choose from program offerings on cable, so-

called "wireless" cable, satellite television systems, and VCRs. Under these market conditions, PTAR is no longer needed to promote the development of non-network sources of television programming. We also find, given these market conditions, and the record before us, that the role is not warranted as a means of promoting the growth of independent stations and new networks, or of safeguarding affiliate autonomy. Indeed, the rule generates costs and inefficiencies that are not now offset by substantial, if any, benefits.

4. We thus find that the public interest warrants the repeal of PTAR. In scheduling repeal of the rule, we believe a one-year transition period is appropriate to provide parties time to adjust their programming strategies and business arrangements prior to the elimination of a regulatory regime that has been in place for 25 years. We consequently will make repeal of PTAR effective August 30, 1996.

II. BACKGROUND

A. The Structure of the Industry

5. We begin by summarizing briefly how the market for the purchase and sale of television programs operates. Television stations obtain programming for delivery to their viewers in a variety of ways. First, stations that affiliate with a television network obtain an entire package or schedule of programming directly from their network. This network "feed" is delivered to affiliated stations via satellite. Affiliated stations then broadcast the network programming to their local audiences. Some of the network feed is comprised of programs produced in-house by the network, such as the nightly national news and some entertainment programming. Much of the network feed, however, consists of programs produced by independent program production companies, with the network acting as a broker between these suppliers and its affiliated stations.

6. Affiliated television stations also program portions of the broadcast day independently of their network. They air locally originated programming, primarily local news, public affairs, and sports programming. They also obtain programming from suppliers called "syndicators," entities that sell programming to television stations, primarily on an individual basis. In contrast to a network feed which supplies a schedule of network programming pursuant to an agreement between the network and a station, a syndicator licenses programs for exhibition on a station-by-station, program-by-program basis.

* * *

8. Recently, two new networks have been launched. The United Paramount Network ("UPN"), owned by subsidiaries of Chris–Craft Industries, Inc., began service on January 16, 1995, with 96 affiliates. UPN had 67 percent coverage through primary affiliates and an additional 16 percent coverage through secondary affiliations for a total coverage of 83 percent. * * * WB, affiliated with Warner Brothers (which, in turn, is owned by Time Warner), began broadcasting on

January 11, 1995, with 47 affiliates and superstation WGN. WB has a national reach of 78 percent, with 18 percent of this reach achieved through cable delivery on WGN. Neither Fox, UPN, nor WB, however, falls within the definition of "network" for purposes of PTAR. None offers more than fifteen hours of prime time programming per week, a prerequisite for a "network" as defined for purposes of the PTAR rules.

9.   There are now over 450 local commercial broadcast stations that are not affiliated with the ABC, CBS, or NBC networks. While these stations have traditionally been called "independent" stations, approximately 300 of these commercial stations are now affiliated with and obtain several hours of prime-time programming from the Fox, UPN, or WB networks. Approximately 150 of these stations are affiliated with Fox. Some of these stations have dual affiliations. In addition to airing this network programming, independent stations air some locally originated programming. Much of their programming, however, is obtained from program producers or syndicators. These programs include movies previously shown in theaters, television series previously aired on network affiliates (i.e., off-network programs such as reruns of The Cosby Show), and series produced for first-run viewing on the independent stations (e.g., Star Trek: The Next Generation).

B.   The History of PTAR

* * *

12.   PTAR was adopted as a structural mechanism to promote the Commission's diversity goals. * * * PTAR is an indirect effort to promote program diversity by seeking to increase the variety of program sources (i.e., source diversity), and, as some parties argue, program distributors, i.e., outlet diversity. The rule as originally conceived was not designed to promote a certain kind of speech, but to increase the variety of non-network speakers. The Commission subsequently carved out exceptions to the rule so that the rule would not prevent the broadcast during the access period of certain types of programming that served the public interest, e.g., children's programming and news and public affairs programming.

13.   PTAR has been subject to criticism over the years. Several observers have faulted the rule for not achieving its goal of improving the television industry's economic structure and performance.[23] In fact, they maintain that it has had the unintended effect of lowering the quality and diversity of access-period programming. The Commission itself was prompted to reexamine the need for the rule shortly after it was initially adopted. It ultimately retained the rule in a 1975 decision, rejecting a number of arguments for repeal by stating that it was "persuaded that the rule has not yet been fully tested."[26] A number of

---

23.   23 See Thomas G. Krattenmaker & Lucas A. Powe, Jr., Regulating Broadcast Programming 72–74 (1994); Krattenmaker, "The Prime Time Access Rule: Six Commandments for Inept Regulation," 7 Comm/Ent L.J. 19 (1984).

26.   PTAR III, 50 FCC 2d at 837.

Commissioners nonetheless expressed reservations about continuing the rule. In 1980, the Commission's Network Inquiry Special Staff concluded that PTAR should be repealed because, among other things, it did not appear to further any Commission policy to regulate in the public interest.[28]

* * *

III.   THE FRAMEWORK FOR ASSESSING THE CONTINUING NEED FOR PTAR

* * *

19.   Specifically, we assess the continuing need for PTAR as follows: First, we will evaluate whether the networks dominate the markets relevant to the rule, or would be likely to dominate them in the absence of PTAR. Second, we assess the costs imposed by the rule. Third, taking into account our findings regarding whether the networks dominate and the costs of the rule, we analyze whether the rule is necessary as a means of pursuing the benefits of fostering independent programming, promoting the growth of independent stations and new networks, and safeguarding affiliate autonomy. In particular, we assess whether PTAR provides public interest benefits by altering competitive opportunities in the following three ways:

* First, by carving out a portion of prime time to be used for non-network use, the rule made it easier for independent producers to sell their programming to Top 50 Market Affiliates.

* Second, the rule provided independent stations with more programming choices than affiliates in an effort to foster their growth and that of new networks.

* Third, the rule reduced the networks' role in dictating their affiliates' prime-time programming choices by forbidding Top 50 Market Affiliates from broadcasting more than three hours of network or off-network programming during prime time.

20.   Examining the evidence taken from the record before us, we conclude that repeal of PTAR will not jeopardize the competition and diversity goals that prompted the Commission to adopt the rule in 1970. The networks and their affiliates do not dominate video programming distribution or the video programming production market and are unlikely to do so without PTAR. The record also indicates that PTAR is no longer warranted as a means of providing independent stations a competitive advantage. Moreover, repeal of the rule will not threaten the station base or jeopardize the further development of the new networks, WB and UPN. Finally, the record does not support the argument that affiliates need the rule to reduce the networks' asserted ability to control affiliate programming choices.

---

28. Network Inquiry Special Staff, New Television Networks: Entry, Jurisdiction, Ownership and Regulation Vol. I at 510–13 (1980) ("Network Inquiry Study"). See Notice, 9 FCC Rcd at 6336 (describing study).

21.   This conclusion is consistent with our 1993 decision to repeal the fin/syn rules, which was upheld on appeal by the U.S. Court of Appeals for the Seventh Circuit.[38] We determined that repeal of the fin/syn rules was warranted given the increased competition facing the networks and the conditions in the television programming marketplace. These conditions included the decline in network audience share since the fin/syn rules were adopted, the increasing demand for television programming created by the emergence of the Fox network and cable networks and the growth of independent television stations, the intense competition among the three established networks for programming, and the increasing ability of first-run distribution to be a fully comparable alternative to network distribution for program producers. Based upon these findings we eliminated a number of the fin/syn rules immediately and set a timetable for repeal of the remainder.

* * *

IV.   THE NETWORKS AND THEIR AFFILIATES DO NOT DOMINATE MARKETS RELEVANT TO PTAR

23.   The Commission's adoption of PTAR in 1970 was premised on a view that the three networks dominated television programming. The parties debate whether this remains true today. Proponents of the rule argue that the networks still dominate. Advocates of repeal argue that the networks do not dominate programming. Our analysis of the record leads us to conclude that neither the networks nor their affiliates dominate video programming distribution or the video programming production market.

A.   Video Programming Distribution

* * *

27.   Even with this narrow description of video programming distribution that is limited to the video programming offered by local broadcast stations, there are substantially more distribution outlets today than in 1970. The total number of commercial and non-commercial television stations has increased 78 percent, from 862 stations in 1970 to 1,532 stations as of January 1, 1995. The number of commercial independent stations (which rely mostly on syndicated programming, including for their prime-time schedules) has grown by almost 450 percent, from 82 in 1970, to over 450 in February 1994. Moreover, in 1970, the Top 50 PTAR Markets had 70 independent stations, or, on average, 1.4 per market. In 1994, the Top 50 PTAR Markets had 278 independent stations, or, on average, 5.6 per market. In short, in 1970, television viewers in the Top 50 PTAR Markets had access, on average to 4.4 commercial VHF and UHF stations. By 1994, that number had more than doubled to 8.9. (Including noncommercial stations, the per market average again more than doubled from 5.7 to 11.6.) Hence, even without considering other potentially competitive media outlets, the number of

38. Capital Cities/ABC, Inc. v. FCC, 29 F.3d 309 (7th Cir.1994).

competing stations in the markets subject to PTAR has increased very substantially.

* * *

31. We thus conclude that, even focussing narrowly on local broadcast video programming distribution, the three networks and their affiliates cannot singly or jointly dominate video program distribution in the Top 50 PTAR Markets. This is a strong conclusion because the inclusion of additional television alternatives such as cable, satellite systems, video dialtone, etc. would serve to make domination by the networks and their affiliates even less likely.

* * *

V. THE COSTS OF PTAR

* * *

40. PTAR harms not only networks and affiliates, but the producers of network programming. The off-network restriction has had the unintended effect of discouraging investment in prime-time programming. Producers rely to a great extent on their ability to sell reruns of their programs, i.e., off-network programs, to recoup their costs and to earn a profit. The license fee the networks pay for the right to air prime-time entertainment programs often does not cover the costs of producing these programs. The network license fee usually covers only 70 percent of the producer's costs, resulting in production deficits for network programming. The off-network restriction, however, diminishes producers' ability to recoup costs by artificially restraining the prices of off-network programming. It does so by eliminating the Top 50 Market Affiliates from the range of potential purchasers of this programming. By reducing demand, the prices for off-network shows are reduced. PTAR provides a corresponding subsidy to producers of first-run syndicated programs in the form of higher prices and to certain independent stations in the form of higher ratings. The Commission believes that PTAR produces costs and inefficiencies to viewers that are larger than the benefits, if any, of PTAR to viewers.

41. Reduced prices for off-network shows will naturally have the effect of lowering the return on network programming, thus reducing the quantity and quality of such programming that a non-PTAR market would otherwise produce. In this respect, television programs can be likened to durable goods. Like any durable good, restrictions on future availability and uses will reduce the value of the good. Program producers will be induced to reduce the quantity of programming they sell because PTAR reduces the size of the secondary market for those programs. This may result in fewer episodes of each series. In some cases, there may be sufficiently few episodes that the series does not qualify for syndication. We are persuaded that by reducing the prices of

off-network programming, PTAR's off-network restriction also tends to reduce the quality of prime-time series.

* * *

45. We are persuaded that there are efficiency costs to retaining PTAR. PTAR does deprive the networks and their affiliates of the opportunity to take advantage of the efficiencies networks provide. The record does not provide reliable estimates of the size of the welfare loss to consumers due to PTAR. But it is safe to say that, by altering the normal functioning of the market, PTAR generally produces inefficiencies that impose significant costs on the consumer. This is particularly the case with respect to the off-network restriction. The logical connection between restricting the size of the market for network television programs as PTAR does and reduced investment (both quantitatively and qualitatively) in that programming is too clear to be ignored.

VI.   Analyzing the Public Interest Need for Ptar

A.   *Increasing Opportunities for Independent Programmers*

* * *

49. Without judging the quality of particular programs, we agree that PTAR, by eliminating network programming, may have resulted in the loss of efficiencies that the networks and their affiliates may have enjoyed in the absence of the rule. We note, however, that there are many variables that affect the number of program producers and program types in the market, with or without PTAR. It is also possible that the competitive advantage first-run producers gain in the access period from PTAR may help them finance first-run shows that air in other dayparts and thus leads to greater diversity in this respect. In fact, the syndication market as a whole has produced an increasing number of new first-run programs, growing from 45 first-run syndicated programs sold in 1970 to 250 in 1990. Nevertheless, we recognize the limits of regulatory efforts to promote program diversity, and realize that PTAR prevents the use of network efficiencies during the access hour.

* * *

51. We no longer believe PTAR is necessary to provide this opportunity under today's market conditions. We reached a similar conclusion in eliminating the fin/syn rules' restriction on network acquisition of financial interest and syndication rights in network prime time entertainment programming. In reaching this conclusion, we dealt with the same source diversity concerns * * *

* * *

53. Repeal of PTAR will subject suppliers of first-run syndicated programming to greater competition during the access period. A Top 50 Market Affiliate may, for example, decide to acquire the rights to broadcast an off-network program during this period, or demand that the first-run syndicator lower its price to induce the station to carry its

programming rather than off-network fare. This competition in today's marketplace can provide incentives to provide more innovative, higher quality programming, all of which benefits the consumer.

* * *

59. To the extent off-network or network programming would displace first-run syndicated programs from the Top 50 Market Affiliates, first-run programs should be able to find a place on independent stations, not to mention other outlets such as cable. In such an event, independent stations will have an incentive to air first-run programming to counter-program the affiliate's programming; an independent station will be motivated to air, for example, such programs as Hard Copy in response to the affiliate who shows reruns of Cheers. Indeed, many independents already broadcast first-run programs in prime time opposite network broadcasts; among non-Fox independent stations in the top–50 markets, 39 percent of prime time hours were first-run syndication.

* * *

B. Fostering the Growth of Independent Stations and New Networks

64. The Commission's central purpose in adopting PTAR in 1970 was to promote the growth of independent program producers. * * * We conclude that today PTAR is no longer necessary to promote independent program sources. The record before us, as well as the decision in our fin/syn proceeding, shows that there is a healthy supply of independently produced programs available to the television industry.

* * *

[The Commission went on to reject claims that stations needed PTAR in order to help offset the "UHF handicap", that is, relatively inferior reception for UHF as opposed to VHF stations. The FCC noted that: (1) improved tuner technology had increased the quality of UHF signals; (2) cable carriage gave UHF stations the same quality as VHF; and (3) PTAR was not an appropriate regulatory vehicle for resolving UHF's problems. The agency also noted that independent stations in general would not necessarily suffer from the repeal of PTAR; although repeal might result in higher prices for off-network programming, the Commission stated that this was a normal consequence of changing to a competitive marketplace.]

* * *

107. We note that we are not concerned with the relative bargaining position of networks and their affiliates to the extent it merely affects the distribution of profits between the parties. Rather, the public interest is implicated where network leverage prevents an affiliate from fulfilling its public interest obligations, such as broadcasting programming responsive to local interests, or distorts the normal market incentive to air programming according to viewer preferences.

108. We think these issues are best addressed in the context of our rules governing a station's right to reject network programming, the filing of affiliation agreements, and our other rules regarding the network-affiliate relationship. The Commission has initiated a comprehensive review of these rules. * * *

VII. SUMMARY OF FINDINGS AND TRANSITION

* * *

116. Transition. * * * As noted above, the record before us provides strong support for repeal of the rule. A transition consequently is not necessary to take a "wait and see" approach in order to test, and possibly revisit, the conclusion we reach today. We do, however, believe a short transition period is appropriate to allow "industry participants to adjust to the changing economic conditions that might result" from repeal of PTAR. The PTAR regulatory scheme has been in place for over two decades, during which time members of the industry have come to rely on the structure imposed by that scheme. Eliminating that structure precipitously may have disruptive effects as the marketplace adjusts to the deregulated environment. A one-year transition will give parties time to adjust their business plans and contractual arrangements prior to repeal of the rule and moderate an unnecessarily abrupt impact on affected stations.

* * *

124. We will thus schedule repeal of the rule in its entirety for August 30, 1996. This will provide ample time for publication of this Report and Order in the Federal Register before the one-year transition period commences. It also allows this period to end prior to the start of the 1996–97 television season.

Commissioner Barrett concurred, stating that a longer transition period might be appropriate in light of the many contracts already in place for syndicated programming.

Commissioner Chong filed a separate statement, arguing that a shorter transition period would be appropriate, since PTAR served no purpose in the current market.

Notes and Questions

1. Why and how does PTAR help independent stations in general? UHF stations in particular? Producers?

2. Does the Commission suggest that this type of assistance is not a valid goal for a regulatory policy? Or does the FCC indicate that PTAR is not an appropriate or efficient means of achieving this goal? Is the difference between these two positions necessarily very clear?

3. Although the networks have lost massive amounts of audience share during the last two decades, is it clear that they have no significant market power? After all, on a combined basis the three major networks still have a larger prime time audience than cable television and independent stations

put together. Indeed, more cable subscribers watch the three major networks than any other type of programming; the weakest of the three major networks generally has an audience share three to four times that of the strongest cable network.

4.   Is there still a certain cachet to first-run network exhibition? After all, it brings with it exposure to the largest possible audience, as well as perhaps a certain imprimatur—albeit a declining one—left over from the three major networks' glory days? Even the Commission seems to indicate that consumers perceive network programming as high-quality.

5.   Along these lines, is it significant that off-network shows often end up on independent stations or cable networks, but that programs produced by the independents or cable hardly ever migrate to broadcasting—and virtually never to network television?

6.   What is the potential harm for the independent stations in PTAR's repeal? That they will have to pay more for off-network programs, because of increased bidding? If so, presumably their new competitors are network affiliates, which now are free to carry off-network programming during the "access" period. Is there anything unfair about more intense bidding? Do affiliates have any unfair advantage in buying programming? If so, why? Because they tend to be VHF stations, and thus to have large prime-time audiences? Because they are network affiliates, and thus can cross-subsidize the purchase of access programming from advertising profits on other network programs? But if the networks have lost their dominance, are the affiliates still able to extract supra-competitive profits for commercials on network programming?

7.   Does it make sense for the FCC to take a "conservative" position in not considering various multichannel media as competition for the networks? After all, many observers believe that cable television has been at least as responsible as independent stations in decreasing the three major networks' audiences.

8.   The amount of economic literature on this topic is vast, even though it is not referred to in the edited version above of the FCC's decision. Every interest group basically hired the best economists that money could buy to produce voluminous studies to support their positions. Although the documents naturally conflict with each other, they provide a wealth of economic data and analysis.

Note: Antitrust Aspects

In 1972, the United States filed antitrust actions against ABC, CBS, and NBC. The complaints, which were dismissed without prejudice, and then refiled in 1974, alleged that the networks violated Section 1 (contracts in unreasonable restraint or trade) and Section 2 (monopolization, or attempt to monopolize) of the Sherman Act. The relevant market was alleged to be that for "television entertainment programs exhibited on [each respective network] during prime evening hours."

The specification in United States v. CBS, Inc., Civ. Action No. 74–3599 (C.D.Cal., filed December 10, 1974), is found in the following paragraphs:

18.   Pursuant to said offenses, defendant CBS:

(a) has used its control over access to the broadcasting time of the CBS Television Network during prime evening hours;

(i) To exclude television entertainment programs in which CBS had no ownership interest from broadcast on the CBS Television Network during prime evening time;

(ii) To compel outside program suppliers to grant to it financial interests in television entertainment programs produced by them;

(iii) To refuse to offer program time alone to advertisers and other outside program suppliers;

(iv) To control the prices paid by CBS for television exhibition rights to motion picture feature films distributed by non-network motion picture distributors;

(v) To obtain a competitive advantage over other producers and distributors of television entertainment programs and of motion picture feature films; and

(b) has entered into a contract with National General, then owner and operator of the second largest chain of theaters in the United States, for exclusive distribution in the United States of all theatrical motion picture films produced by CBS.

20. The effects of the aforesaid offenses, among others, have been and are as follows:

(a) Ownership and control of television entertainment programs broadcast during prime evening hours on the CBS Television Network has been concentrated in defendant CBS;

(b) Competition in the production, distribution and sale of television entertainment programs, including feature films, has been unreasonably restrained;

(c) Competition in the sale of television entertainment programs to the CBS Television Network by outside program suppliers of said programs has been unreasonably restrained;

(d) The viewing public has been deprived of the benefits of free and open competition in the broadcasting of television entertainment programs.

———

The government initially sought an order prohibiting each network from (1) obtaining any interest (other than for the first-run right of exhibition) in any television entertainment programs, including feature films, produced by others; (2) engaging in syndication of any such programs; (3) offering over the network any such programs produced by the network itself or any other commercial television network; and (4) offering any other commercial network programs produced by it.

The government then, however, entered into a somewhat more modest proposed consent decree with NBC (1) embodying the FCC's financial interest and syndication rules; (2) limiting certain terms that may be bargained for in purchasing programs from independent producers, e.g., terms requiring the use of NBC's production facilities; (3) prohibiting reciprocal dealings in the purchase and sale of programs from or to other networks; (4) limiting the option rights and exclusive exhibition rights NBC can negotiate with independent producers; and (5) limiting, for ten years, the amount of NBC-produced programming that NBC may exhibit in the various dayparts, as follows:

> Max. hours/week Daypart
> 2½ Prime time (6–11 p.m.)
>   Day time (9 a.m.–6 p.m.)
> 11 Fringe Time (11 p.m.–6 a.m.)

The last provision, like certain others, was to be effective only if ABC and CBS were subjected to the same terms, either by consent or after litigation.

The NBC consent decree was approved. United States v. National Broadcasting Co., Inc., 449 F.Supp. 1127 (C.D.Cal.1978), affirmed 603 F.2d 227 (9th Cir.), cert. denied sub nom. CBS, Inc. v. United States, 444 U.S. 991, 100 S.Ct. 521, 62 L.Ed.2d 419 (1979).

CBS and ABC subsequently entered into consent decrees that for periods of 10 to 15 years (1) limit them to producing for themselves no more than 21½ hours of programming per week and no more than 2½ hours of prime time programming (other than certain specials); (2) prohibit them from acquiring an interest other than network exhibition rights in a program produced by an independent supplier; and (3) prohibit them from engaging in foreign or domestic syndication. United States v. CBS, Inc., 1980–81 Trade Cas. (CCH) ¶ 63,594 (1980); United States v. ABC, Inc., 1981–1 Trade Cas. (CCH) ¶ 64,160 (1980).

Questions

1.   What effect would FCC repeal of the financial interest and syndication rules have in light of these consent decrees? What continuing significance does the PTAR have? Certain provisions in the decrees, most notably the ones limiting the networks' in-house program production, expired in November 1990. How, if at all, should this change affect the FCC's evaluation of the fin-syn rules. (p. 256)

2.   As counsel to the Government, how would you have responded to the networks' various arguments against the consent decree? What position should the FCC have taken on the proposed decree, assuming that it was to be consistent with its own prior decisions?

3.   Notice that the NBC consent decree separately limits the amount of daytime, prime time, and nighttime (11:00 p.m.—9:00 a.m.) network-produced programming per week. Does this make any sense when one considers

that entertainment programs can be distributed over the network at any time for delayed broadcast by the affiliates?

4. Should the government seek to prohibit a network-owned and operated station ("O & O") from producing programs for sale to other affiliates or to one of the other networks? A group of O & Os producing a program for sale to the network? Would such a provision give non-network owned groups, including affiliates, an unfair advantage?

Chapter VI

BEHAVIORAL REGULATION: THE CONSTITUTIONAL FRAMEWORK

The late Ithiel de Sola Pool set forth a rather ominous view of contemporary communications policy, suggesting that courts and regulators coping with technological change lack a broad perspective. In Professor Pool's view, the era of robust debate, in which the mass media served as an open and free vehicle for individuals to communicate with the masses, was drawing to a close as more and more communication depends on electronic impulses, rather than ink impressions. Pool mourned the "decline" of the First Amendment, particularly at a time when society viewed itself as being increasingly dependent on access to, and the movement of, information.

A. INTRODUCTION

In Chapters VI and VII we examine whether regulation of the electronic media has come at the expense of traditional First Amendment values or has reflected an effort to adapt these values to a new technological setting. As you read these materials, consider whether you agree with Professor Pool's assertion, in the first selection below, that because of regulation, "an unabridged right of citizens to speak without controls may be endangered." One might argue, to the contrary, that many of the policies examined in earlier chapters are intended to preserve, rather than to impede, the "marketplace of ideas" and the ability of individuals to speak freely. Certainly the FCC believed that its efforts to promote diversity and localism were based upon notions of a pluralistic and free society. Professor Pool suggests, however, that it may be impossible to have a truly free society once the government has become involved in making decisions about access to and use of the mass media—even if the government takes great pains to act in a neutral and fair manner.

What, then, are we to conclude about laws that require licenses for parades or for street corner speeches, or that punish littering (including the careless disposal of pamphlets), or that restrict the use of sound trucks in residential neighborhoods, or that prevent X-rated movie theaters from being operated in certain parts of a town? Where is the line between the abridgement of speech and the avoidance of anarchy? Is the line increasingly more difficult to draw when speech is broadcast into the air and sent through wire or fiber networks into millions of homes, rather than shouted on the street corner or left at the local newsstand?

ITHIEL DE S. POOL
TECHNOLOGIES OF FREEDOM

1–10 (1983)*.

* * * [N]ew technologies of electronic communication may now relegate old and freed media such as pamphlets, platforms, and periodicals to a corner of the public forum. Electronic modes of communication that enjoy lesser rights are moving to center stage. The new communication technologies have not inherited all the legal immunities that were won for the old. When wires, radio waves, satellites, and computers became major vehicles of discourse, regulation seemed to be a technical necessity. And so, as speech increasingly flows over those electronic media, the five-century growth of an unabridged right of citizens to speak without controls may be endangered. * * *

* * *

Both civil libertarians and free marketers are perturbed at the expanding scope of communications regulations. After computers became linked by communications networks, for example, the FCC spent several years figuring out how to avoid regulating the computer industry. The line of reasoning behind this laudable self-restraint, known as deregulation, has nothing to do, however, with freedom of speech. Deregulation, whatever its economic merits, is something much less than the First Amendment. The Constitution, in Article 1, Section 8, gives the federal government the right to regulate interstate commerce, but in the First Amendment, equally explicitly, it excludes one kind of commerce, namely communication, from government authority. Yet here is the FCC trying to figure out how it can avoid regulating the commerce of the computer industry (an authority Congress could have given, but never did) while continuing to regulate communications whenever it considers this necessary. The Constitution has been turned on its head.

The mystery is how the clear intent of the Constitution, so well and strictly enforced in the domain of print, has been so neglected in the electronic revolution. The answer lies partly in changes in the prevailing concerns and historical circumstances from the time of the founding fathers to the world of today; but it lies at least as much in the failure of Congress and the courts to understand the character of the new technologies. Judges and legislators have tried to fit technological innovations under conventional legal concepts. The errors of understanding by these scientific laymen, though honest, have been mammoth. They have sought to guide toward good purposes technologies they did not comprehend.

* * *

The erosion of traditional freedoms that has occurred as government has striven to cope with problems of new communications media * * * is a story of how, in pursuit of the public good, a growing structure of controls has been imposed. * * *

A hundred and fifty years from now, today's fears about the future of free expression may prove * * * alarmist * * *. But there is reason to suspect that our situation is * * * ominous. * * * [N]ew and mostly electronic media have proliferated in the form of great oligopolistic networks of common carriers and broadcasters. Regulation was a natural response. Fortunately and strangely, as electronics advances further, another reversal is now taking place, toward growing decentralization and toward fragmentation of the audience of the newest media. The transitional era of giant media may nonetheless leave a permanent set of regulatory practices implanted on a system that is coming to have technical characteristics that would otherwise be conducive to freedom.

* * *

The interaction over the past two centuries between the changing technologies of communication and the practice of free speech, I would argue, fits a pattern that is sometimes described as "soft technological determinism." Freedom is fostered when the means of communication are dispersed, decentralized, and easily available, as are printing presses or microcomputers. Central control is more likely when the means of communication are concentrated, monopolized, and scarce, as are great networks. But the relationship between technology and institutions is not simple or unidirectional, nor are the effects immediate. Institutions that evolve in response to one technological environment persist and to some degree are later imposed on what may be a changed technology. The First Amendment came out of a pluralistic world of small communicators, but it shaped the present treatment of great national networks. Later on, systems of regulation that emerged for national common carriers and for the use of "scarce" spectrum for broadcasting tended to be imposed on more recent generations of electronic technologies that no longer require them.

Simple versions of technological determinism fail to take account of the differences in the way things happen at different stages in the life cycle of a technology. When a new invention is made, such as the telephone or radio, its fundamental laws are usually not well understood. It is designed to suit institutions that already exist, but in its early stages if it is to be used at all, it must be used in whatever form it proved experimentally to work. Institutions for its use are thus designed around

a technologically determined model. Later, when scientists have comprehended the fundamental theory, the early technological embodiment
becomes simply a special case. Alternative devices can then be designed
to meet human needs. Technology no longer need control. A 1920s
motion picture had to be black and white, silent, pantomimic, and shown
in a place of public assembly; there was no practical choice. A 1980s
video can have whatever colors, sounds, and three-dimensional or syn-
thetic effects are wanted, and can be seen in whatever location is desired.
In the meantime, however, an industry has established studios, theaters,
career lines, unions, funding, and advertising practices, all designed to
use the technology that is in place. Change occurs, but the established
institutions are a constraint on its direction and pace.

* * *

The key technological change, at the root of the social changes, is
that communication, other than conversation face to face, is becoming
overwhelmingly electronic. Not only is electronic communication growing faster than traditional media of publishing, but also the convergence
of modes of delivery is bringing the press, journals, and books into the
electronic world. One question raised by these changes is whether some
social features are inherent in the electronic character of the emerging
media. Is television the model of the future? Are electromagnetic pulses
simply an alternative conduit to deliver whatever is wanted, or are there
aspects of electronic technology that make it different from print—more
centralized or more decentralized, more banal or more profound, more
private or more government dependent?

The electronic transformation of the media occurs not in a vacuum
but in a specific historical and legal context. Freedom for publishing has
been one of America's proudest traditions. But just what is it that the
courts have protected, and how does this differ from how the courts
acted later when the media through which ideas flowed came to be the
telegraph, telephone, television, or computers? What images did policy
makers have of how each of these media works; how far were their
images valid; and what happened to their images when the facts
changed?

In each of the three parts of the American communications system—
print, common carriers, and broadcasting—the law has rested on a
perception of technology that is sometimes accurate, often inaccurate,
and which changes slowly as technology changes fast. Each new advance
in the technology of communications disturbs a status quo. It meets
resistance from those whose dominance it threatens, but if useful, it
begins to be adopted. Initially, because it is new and a full scientific
mastery of the options is not yet at hand, the invention comes into use in
a rather clumsy form. Technical laymen, such as judges, perceive the
new technology in that early, clumsy form, which then becomes their
image of its nature, possibilities, and use. This perception is an incubus
on later understanding.

The courts and regulatory agencies in the American system (or other authorities elsewhere) enter as arbiters of the conflicts among entrepreneurs, interest groups, and political organizations battling for control of the new technology. The arbiters, applying familiar analogies from the past to their lay image of the new technology, create a partly old, partly new structure of rights and obligations. The telegraph was analogized to railroads, the telephone to the telegraph, and cable television to broadcasting. The legal system thus invented for each new technology may in some instances, like the First Amendment, be a *tour de force* of political creativity, but in other instances it may be less worthy. The system created can turn out to be inappropriate to more habile forms of the technology which gradually emerge as the technology progresses. This is when problems arise, as they are arising so acutely today.

Historically, the various media that are now converging have been differently organized and differently treated under the law. The outcome to be feared is that communications in the future may be unnecessarily regulated under the unfree tradition of law that has been applied so far to the electronic media. The clash between the print, common carrier, and broadcast models is likely to be a vehement communications policy issue in the next decades. Convergence of modes is upsetting the trifurcated system developed over the past two hundred years, and questions that had seemed to be settled centuries ago are being reopened, unfortunately sometimes not in a libertarian way.

* * *

* * * The specific question to be answered is whether the electronic resources for communication can be as free of public regulation in the future as the platform and printing press have been in the past. * * *

* * *

* * * It would be dire if the laws we make today governing the dominant mode of information handling in such an information society were subversive of its freedom. The onus is on us to determine whether free societies in the twenty-first century will conduct electronic communication under the conditions of freedom established for the domain of print through centuries of struggle, or whether that great achievement will become lost in a confusion about new technologies.

Chapters IV and V focused on regulatory policies aimed at fostering a diversity of voices by affecting the structure and composition of the electronic media marketplace. In adopting and applying these "structural" regulations, the government avoided becoming directly involved in deciding what would be said in the media; nonetheless, the government has had a significant impact on who is able to "speak." Because structural regulations do not directly involve the government in making decisions about the transmission of a specific program, viewpoint, statement, or idea, they are often characterized as "content neutral." Yet, it would seem that a regulation that affects the identity of the speaker has at least an indirect impact on the content of the speech.

Perhaps the distinction between the structural regulations examined earlier and the "behavioral" regulations discussed in this and the next chapter is one of degree—the degree to which regulation involves the government in making decisions about content. Structural regulation arguably involves less direct government incursion into matters of content than does behavioral regulation. Is regulation of content less objectionable when it is accomplished by indirection? Or might less direct regulation be *more* objectionable because it is more amenable to use in a deceitful or clandestine manner? Why accept either approach to government regulation of content?

The First Amendment states that "Congress shall make no law * * * abridging the freedom of speech, or of the press."* What does this seemingly flat prohibition mean as a practical matter? If it really means that Congress shall make "no law," then almost the entire Communications Act, and all the structural and behavioral regulations adopted to implement it, might be unconstitutional. The First Amendment protection of speech has not been applied in a broad or literal way, of course, although some scholars and jurists (most notably Justice Black) have maintained that it is an absolute bar to the regulation of speech—which places great pressure upon the definition of "speech." (Do you see why?)

In interpreting the First Amendment's command and applying it to a changing society, the courts have faced the difficult task of trying to fashion a jurisprudence that permits society to "abridge" speech to the degree necessary to advance other compelling interests. For example, the courts have upheld laws that restrain speech that causes personal injury, or threatens national security, or is considered "obscene" by community standards.

The courts have had a particularly difficult time deciding how to apply the First Amendment's command to the electronic media. Initially, as we saw in Chapter II, the courts faced the question of whether the government could license the use of the electromagnetic spectrum at all. More recently, with the development of cable television, the courts have confronted the similar issue of whether state and local authorities can limit the number of franchises to use public rights-of-way for cable installation. In addition, the courts have had to address, in a myriad of contexts, the constitutional limits on regulation of "electronic speech."

We begin our examination of regulations concerned directly with the content of "programming" by exploring the courts' changing—and often confusing—rationales for permitting or prohibiting varying degrees of

* The First Amendment applies by its terms to the federal government. It has been held applicable to the states (and their respective subdivisions, such as city and town governments) through incorporation into the due process clause of the Fourteenth Amendment.

behavioral regulation. An initial question is why the electronic media should be treated differently from, for example, print media. To the extent that the courts permit greater regulation of electronic speech, than in the analogous print context, what competing interests are being advanced and how does regulation advance them? (If broadcasting is different from print for purposes of the First Amendment—and cable television or MMDS is seemingly different from broadcasting—then the constitutional spectrum becomes almost confounding.)

The materials in Chapters VI and VII raise three broad issues. First, what justifications, if any, exist for applying "special" or "peculiar" First Amendment standards to the electronic media? Second, as a result, what are the constitutional limits to behavioral regulation? Finally, within those constitutional limits, what types of behavioral regulation make sense or are effective? In thinking about these questions, keep in mind Professor Pool's skepticism about the benefits of having the government involved at all in "managing" the development of communications technology. Are we really following a path toward a less free and open society, or are we merely searching for ways to preserve freedom in the face of technological change?

B. A FIRST AMENDMENT STANDARD FOR BROADCASTING

As will become quite evident from the cases below, the courts use a number of different constitutional tests in dealing with the First Amendment status of electronic media regulatory policies. The principal tension is between a "strict scrutiny" and "intermediate level of scrutiny" test. The former revolves primarily upon whether a rule is "content specific" in its application; if it is—that is, if it singles out a particular type of speech for regulation—only an overwhelmingly powerful government interest will save it. On the other hand, if a rule is "content neutral"— namely, if it does not impact upon a particular type of speech—it is subject to the more relaxed intermediate level, which at least nominally developed in the *O'Brien* case in 1968. (p. 333)

Moreover, these broad distinctions are complicated still further in the context of the electronic media, because of a largely unarticulated sense that they somehow are different from traditional print media. Chief Justice Taft's reluctance to become involved in broadcasting cases still may have some vitality; indeed, it may have been extended to increasingly complex "new" media such as cable and DBS.

This is particularly evident in content or behavioral regulation. One normally would assume that imposition of a right of reply would be subject to strict scrutiny, and would come crashing down given the less than overwhelming government interest in insuring that the public hears both sides of local political disputes. The result in *Tornillo* below thus is hardly surprising. On the other hand, at roughly the same time the same Court held that the FCC could require broadcasters to give reply time, because of the "scarcity doctrine" articulated in *Red Lion*—which seems to be a slightly different version of what became known as intermediate scrutiny. And as the later cable cases show, the *O'Brien* case seems to have created numerous variations as its progeny.

This is not too surprising. By its very nature, public law in general and the First Amendment in particular deal with such broad concepts and differing policies that consistency is devoutly to be hoped for but rarely achieved. It may be useful to keep this general proposition in mind while perusing the materials below.

MIAMI HERALD PUBLISHING CO. v. TORNILLO

Supreme Court of the United States, 1974.
418 U.S. 241, 94 S.Ct. 2831, 41 L.Ed.2d 730.

Mr. Chief Justice Burger delivered the opinion of the Court.

The issue in this case is whether a state statute granting a political candidate a right to equal space to reply to criticism and attacks on his record by a newspaper, violates the guarantees of a free press.

I

In the fall of 1972 appellee * * * was a candidate for the Florida House of Representatives. On September 20, 1972, and again on September 29, 1972, appellant printed editorials critical of appellee's candidacy. In response to these editorials appellee demanded that appellant print verbatim his replies * * *. Appellant declined to print the appellee's replies, and appellee brought suit in Circuit Court, Dade County, seeking declaratory and injunctive relief and actual and punitive damages in excess of $5,000. The action was premised on Florida Statute § 104.38 (1973), a "right of reply" statute which provides that if a candidate for nomination or election is assailed regarding his personal character or official record by any newspaper, the candidate has the right to demand that the newspaper print, free of cost to the candidate, any reply the candidate may make to the newspaper's charges.[2]* * * Appellant sought a declaration that § 104.38 was unconstitutional. After an emergency hearing requested by appellee, the Circuit Court * * * held that § 104.38 was unconstitutional as an infringement on the freedom of the press under the First and Fourteenth Amendments to the Constitution. The Circuit Court concluded that dictating what a newspaper must print was no different from dictating what it must not print. The Circuit

---

2. "104.38 *Newspaper assailing candidate in an election; space for reply*—If any newspaper in its columns assails the personal character of any candidate for nomination or for election in any election, or charges said candidate with malfeasance or misfeasance in office, or otherwise attacks his official record, or gives to another free space for such purpose, such newspaper shall upon request of such candidate immediately publish free of cost any reply he may make thereto in as conspicuous a place and in the same kind of type as the matter that calls for such reply, provided such reply does not take up more space than the matter replied to. Any person or firm failing to comply with the provisions of this section shall be guilty of a misdemeanor of the first degree, punishable as provided in § 775.082 or § 775.083."

Judge viewed the statute's vagueness as serving "to restrict and stifle protected expression." * * *

On direct appeal, the Florida Supreme Court reversed, holding that § 104.38 did not violate constitutional guarantees. It held that free speech was enhanced and not abridged by the Florida right-of-reply statute, which in that court's view furthered the "broad societal interest in the free flow of information to the public." * * *

III

A

* * *

Appellant contends the statute is void on its face because it purports to regulate the content of a newspaper in violation of the First Amendment. Alternatively it is urged that the statute is void for vagueness since no editor could know exactly what words would call the statute into operation. It is also contended that the statute fails to distinguish between critical comment which is and which is not defamatory.

B

* * *

Access advocates submit that although newspapers of the present are superficially similar to those of 1791 the press of today is in reality very different from that now in the early years of our national existence. * * * Newspapers have become big business and there are far fewer of them to serve a larger literate population. Chains of newspapers, national newspapers, national wire and news services, and one-newspaper towns,[13] are the dominant features of a press that has become noncompetitive and enormously powerful and influential in its capacity to manipulate popular opinion and change the course of events. Major metropolitan newspapers have collaborated to establish news services national in scope. Such national news organizations provide syndicated "interpretive reporting" as well as syndicated features and commentary, all of which can serve as part of the new school of "advocacy journalism."

The elimination of competing newspapers in most of our large cities, and the concentration of control of media that results from the only newspaper's being owned by the same interests which own a television station and a radio station, are important components of this trend toward concentration of control of outlets to inform the public.

* * *

13. "Nearly half of U.S. daily newspapers, representing some three-fifths of daily and Sunday circulation, are owned by newspaper groups and chains, including diversified business conglomerates. One-newspaper towns have become the rule, with effective competition operating in only 4 percent of our large cities." Background Paper by Alfred Balk in Twentieth Century Fund Task Force Report for a National News Council, A Free and Responsive Press 18 (1973).

The obvious solution, which was available to dissidents at an earlier time when entry into publishing was relatively inexpensive, today would be to have additional newspapers. But the same economic factors which have caused the disappearance of vast numbers of metropolitan newspapers, have made entry into the marketplace of ideas served by the print media almost impossible. It is urged that the claim of newspapers to be "surrogates for the public" carries with it a concomitant fiduciary obligation to account for that stewardship. From this premise it is reasoned that the only effective way to insure fairness and accuracy and to provide for some accountability is for government to take affirmative action. The First Amendment interest of the public in being informed is said to be in peril because the "marketplace of ideas" is today a monopoly controlled by the owners of the market.

* * *

IV

However much validity may be found in these arguments, at each point the implementation of a remedy such as an enforceable right of access necessarily calls for some mechanism, either governmental or consensual. * * *

* * *

Appellee's argument that the Florida statute does not amount to a restriction of appellant's right to speak because "the statute in question here has not prevented the *Miami Herald* from saying anything it wished" begs the core question. Compelling editors or publishers to publish that which " 'reason' tells them should not be published" is what is at issue in this case. The Florida statute operates as a command in the same sense as a statute or regulation forbidding appellant to publish specified matter. Governmental restraint on publishing need not fall into familiar or traditional patterns to be subject to constitutional limitations on government powers. Grosjean v. American Press Co., 297 U.S. 233, 244–245 (1936). The Florida statute exacts a penalty on the basis of the content of a newspaper. The first phase of the penalty resulting from the compelled printing of a reply is exacted in terms of the cost in printing and composing time and materials and in taking up space that could be devoted to other material the newspaper may have preferred to print. It is correct, as appellee contends, that a newspaper is not subject to the finite technological limitations of time that confront a broadcaster but it is not correct to say that, as an economic reality, a newspaper can proceed to infinite expansion of its column space to accommodate the replies that a government agency determines or a statute commands the readers should have available.

Faced with the penalties that would accrue to any newspaper that published news or commentary arguably within the reach of the right-of-access statute, editors might well conclude that the safe course is to avoid controversy. Therefore, under the operation of the Florida statute, political and electoral coverage would be blunted or reduced. Government-enforced right of access inescapably "dampens the vigor and limits the variety of public debate," New York Times Co. v. Sullivan, 376 U.S., at 279. * * *

Even if a newspaper would face no additional costs to comply with a compulsory access law and would not be forced to forego publication of news or opinion by the inclusion of a reply, the Florida statute fails to clear the barriers of the First Amendment because of its intrusion into the function editors. A newspaper is more than a passive receptacle or conduit for news, comment, and advertising.[24] The choice of material to go into a newspaper, and the decisions made as to limitations on the size and content of the paper, and treatment of public issues and public officials—whether fair or unfair—constitute the exercise of editorial control and judgment. It has yet to be demonstrated how governmental regulation of this crucial process can be exercised consistent with First Amendment guarantees of a free press as they have evolved to this time. Accordingly, the judgment of the Supreme Court of Florida is reversed.

It is so ordered.

MR. JUSTICE BRENNAN, with whom MR. JUSTICE REHNQUIST joins, concurring.

I join the Court's opinion which, as I understand it, addresses only "right of reply" statutes and implies no view upon the constitutionality of "retraction" statutes affording plaintiffs able to prove defamatory falsehoods a statutory action to require publication of a retraction. * * *

MR. JUSTICE WHITE, concurring.

* * *

To justify this statute, Florida advances a concededly important interest of ensuring free and fair elections by means of an electorate informed about the issues. But prior compulsion by government in matters going to the very nerve center of a newspaper—the decision as to what copy will or will not be included in any given edition—collides with the First Amendment. * * *

The constitutionally obnoxious feature of § 104.38 is not that the Florida Legislature may also have placed a high premium on the protection of individual reputational interests; for government certainly has "a pervasive and strong interest in preventing and redressing attacks upon reputation." Rosenblatt v. Baer, 383 U.S. 75, 86 (1966). Quite the contrary, this law runs afoul of the elementary First Amendment propo-

---

24. "[L]iberty of the press is in peril as soon as the government tries to compel what is to go into a newspaper. A journal does not merely print observed facts the way a cow is photographed through a plate-glass window. As soon as the facts are set in their context, you have interpretation and you have selection, and editorial selection opens the way to editorial suppression. Then how can the state force abstention from discrimination in the news without dictating selection?" 2 Z. Chaffee, Government and Mass Communications 633 (1947).

sition that government may not force a newspaper to print copy which, in its journalistic discretion, it chooses to leave on the newsroom floor.

* * *

Notes and Questions

1.   Did the Court implicitly find that the Florida statute was unconstitutionally vague?

2.   Could a monopoly newspaper be compelled to carry "legal notices," publication of which in a newspaper of general circulation is arguably required by the due process standard of "best practicable notice under the circumstances," or by Fed.R.Civ.P. 71A(d)(3)(ii) (condemnation of property, owner unavailable for personal service)?

3.   (a) Prior to *Tornillo,* there was a considerable literature urging the need for a private right of access. Perhaps the leading essay was Barron, *Access to the Press—A New First Amendment Right,* 80 Harv.L.Rev. 1641 (1967). And, as the *Tornillo* Court noted in a passage omitted here, the plurality opinion in Rosenbloom v. Metromedia, Inc., 403 U.S. 29, 47 & n. 15, 91 S.Ct. 1811, 1821 & n. 15, 29 L.Ed.2d 296 (1971) (Brennan, J.), had observed that some states had adopted retraction or right-of-reply statutes, stating that "[i]f the States fear that private citizens will not be able to respond adequately to publicity involving them, the solution lies in the direction of ensuring their ability to respond, rather than in stifling public discussion of matters of public concern."

(b) What is the constitutional status of such defamation "retraction" statutes in light of the reasoning in *Tornillo?* Does a judicial order to print a retraction amount also to "[c]ompelling editors or publishers to publish that which 'reason' tells them should not be published"? Are the countervailing considerations stronger when the original publication has first been proved in court to be false? Should it matter whether the defamed plaintiff is a public figure, barred by New York Times Co. v. Sullivan, 376 U.S. at 279–83, 84 S.Ct. at 725–27, from recovering from a publisher that was neither malicious nor reckless in printing the libel.

Consider also the view of Judge Boreman, in J.P. Stevens & Co. v. NLRB, 406 F.2d 1017 (4th Cir.1968) (dissenting), where the court enforced the Board's order that the employer assemble its employees and read them a Board-dictated notice listing unfair practices that would violate the labor laws and promising not to engage in them:

> Even the convicted felon can never be made to confess that he has violated the law and he can, and often does, deny guilt; indeed, at every opportunity he may proclaim that he has been unjustly convicted.

> The forcing of such declarations, in the nature of confessions or recantations, is not a matter to be lightly regarded. The feeling and the resolution of free men against forced utterances can become extremely intense. Over many centuries they have suffered oppressions rather than admit wrongdoing which they deeply and devoutly believed they had not committed. * * *

Judge Learned Hand clearly expressed the thought in the following terms: * * *. Forcibly to compel anyone to declare that the utterances of any official, whoever he may be, are true, when he protests that he does not believe them, has implications which we should hesitate to believe Congress could ever have intended. * * * [W]e can very well understand the sense of outrage which anyone may feel at being forced publicly to declare that he has committed even a minor dereliction of which in his heart he does not believe himself guilty.

4. Are the considerations mentioned in *Tornillo* equally relevant to the constitutionality of a right to reply to a broadcast? Are there stronger reasons for recognizing such a right? The Court had considered this question five years before the *Tornillo* decision. *Tornillo* does not cite the earlier case, which follows. (Note that *Red Lion* involves solely the fairness doctrine, *not* the right to "equal opportunities" (commonly known as "equal time") under Section 315 of the Act.)

RED LION BROADCASTING CO. v. FCC

Supreme Court of the United States, 1969.
395 U.S. 367, 89 S.Ct. 1794, 23 L.Ed.2d 371.

Mr. Justice White delivered the opinion of the Court.

The Federal Communications Commission has for many years imposed on radio and television broadcasters the requirement that discussion of public issues be presented on broadcast stations, and that each side of those issues must be given fair coverage. This is known as the fairness doctrine, which originated very early in the history of broadcasting and has maintained its present outlines for some time. It is an obligation whose content has been defined in a long series of FCC rulings in particular cases, and which is distinct from the statutory requirement of § 315 of the Communications Act that equal time be allotted all qualified candidates for public office. Two aspects of the fairness doctrine, relating to personal attacks in the context of controversial public issues and to political editorializing, were codified more precisely in the form of FCC regulations in 1967. The two cases before us now, which were decided separately below, challenge the constitutional and statutory bases of the doctrine and component rules. *Red Lion* involves the application of the fairness doctrine to a particular broadcast, and *RTNDA* arises as an action to review the FCC's 1967 promulgation of the personal attack and political editorializing regulations, which were laid down after the *Red Lion* litigation had begun.

I.

A.

The Red Lion Broadcasting Company is licensed to operate a Pennsylvania radio station, WGCB. On November 27, 1964, WGCB carried a 15–minute broadcast by the Reverend Billy James Hargis as part of a "Christian Crusade" series. A book by Fred J. Cook entitled "Goldwater—Extremist on the Right" was discussed by Hargis, who said that Cook had been fired by a newspaper for making false charges against city officials; that Cook had then worked for a Communist-affiliated publication; that he had defended Alger Hiss and attacked J. Edgar Hoover and the Central Intelligence Agency; and that he had now written a "book to smear and destroy Barry Goldwater." When Cook heard of the broadcast he concluded that he had been personally attacked and demanded free reply time, which the station refused. After an exchange of letters among Cook, Red Lion and the FCC, the FCC declared that the Hargis broadcast constituted a personal attack on Cook; that Red Lion had failed to meet its obligation under the fairness doctrine as expressed in Times–Mirror Broadcasting Co., 24 P & F Radio Reg. 404 (1962), to send a tape, transcript, or summary of the broadcast to Cook and offer him reply time; and that the station must provide reply time whether or not Cook would pay for it. [The court of appeals affirmed.]

B.

Not long after the *Red Lion* litigation was begun, the FCC issued a Notice of Proposed Rule Making, 31 Fed.Reg. 5710, with an eye to making the personal attack aspect of the fairness doctrine more precise and more readily enforceable, and to specifying its rules relating to political editorials. * * * [T]he rules were held unconstitutional in the *RTNDA* litigation by the Court of Appeals for the Seventh Circuit, on review of the rule-making proceeding, as abridging the freedoms of speech and press.

As they now stand amended, the regulations read as follows:

Personal attacks; political editorials.

(a) When, during the presentation of views on a controversial issue of public importance, an attack is made upon the honesty, character, integrity or like personal qualities of an identified person or group, the licensee shall, within a reasonable time and in no event later than 1 week after the attack, transmit to the person or group attacked (1) notification of the date, time and identification of the broadcast; (2) a script or tape (or an accurate summary if a script or tape is not available) of the attack; and (3) an offer of a reasonable opportunity to respond over the licensee's facilities.

* * *

(c) Where a licensee, in an editorial, (i) endorses or (ii) opposes a legally qualified candidate or candidates, the licensee shall, within 24 hours after the editorial, transmit to respectively (i) the other qualified candidate or candidates for the same office or (ii) the candidate opposed in the editorial (1) notification of the date and the time of the editorial; (2) a script or tape of the editorial; and (3) an offer of a reasonable opportunity for a candidate or a spokesman of the candidate to respond over the licensee's facilities: *Provided, however,* that where such editorials are broadcast within 72 hours prior to the day of the election, the licensee shall comply with the provisions of this paragraph sufficiently far in advance of the broadcast to enable the candidate or candidates to have a reasonable opportunity to prepare a response and to present it in a timely fashion. 47 C.F.R. §§ 73.123, 73.300, 73.598, 73.679 (all identical).

C.

Believing that the specific application of the fairness doctrine in *Red Lion,* and the promulgation of the regulations in *RTNDA,* are both authorized by Congress and enhance rather than abridge the freedoms of speech and press protected by the First Amendment, we hold them valid and constitutional, reversing the judgment below in *RTNDA* and affirming the judgment below in *Red Lion.*

II.

The history of the emergence of the fairness doctrine and of the related legislation shows that the Commission's action in the *Red Lion* case did not exceed its authority, and that in adopting the new regulations the Commission was implementing congressional policy rather than embarking on a frolic of its own.

A.

* * *

There is a twofold duty laid down by the FCC's decisions * * *. The broadcaster must give adequate coverage to public issues * * *, and coverage must be fair in that it accurately reflects the opposing views. * * *

B.

* * *

The fairness doctrine finds specific recognition in statutory form, is in part modeled on explicit statutory provisions relating to political candidates, and is approvingly reflected in legislative history.

In 1959 the Congress amended the statutory requirement of § 315 that equal time be accorded each political candidate except for certain appearances on news programs, but added that this constituted no exception "from the obligation imposed upon them under this Act to operate in the public interest and to afford reasonable opportunity for the discussion of conflicting views on issues of public importance." This language makes it very plain that Congress, in 1959, announced that the phrase "public interest," which had been in the Act since 1927, imposed a duty on broadcasters to discuss both sides of controversial public issues. In other words, the amendment vindicated the FCC's general view that the fairness doctrine inhered in the public interest standard * * * Here, the Congress has not just kept its silence by refusing to overturn the administrative construction, but has ratified it with positive legislation. * * *

The objectives of § 315 themselves could readily be circumvented but for the complementary fairness doctrine ratified by § 315. The section applies only to campaign appearances by candidates, and not by family, friends, campaign managers, or other supporters. Without the fairness doctrine, then, a licensee could ban all campaign appearances by candidates themselves from the air and proceed to deliver over his station entirely to the supporters of one slate of candidates, to the exclusion of all others. In this way the broadcaster could have a far greater impact on the favored candidacy than he could by simply allowing a spot appearance by the candidate himself. It is the fairness doctrine as an aspect of the obligation to operate in the public interest, rather than § 315, which prohibits the broadcaster from taking such a step.

* * * [W]e cannot say that when a station publishes personal attacks or endorses political candidates, it is a misconstruction of the public interest standard to require the station to offer time for a response rather than to leave the response entirely within the control of the station which has attacked either the candidacies or the men who wish to reply in their own defense. When a broadcaster grants time to a political candidate, Congress itself requires that equal time be offered to his opponents. It would exceed our competence to hold that the Commission is unauthorized by the statute to employ a similar device where personal attacks or political editorials are broadcast by a radio or television station.

In light of the fact that the "public interest" in broadcasting clearly encompasses the presentation of vigorous debate of controversial issues of importance and concern to the public; the fact that the FCC has rested upon that language from its very inception a doctrine that these issues must be discussed, and fairly; and the fact that Congress has acknowledged that the analogous provisions of § 315 are not preclusive in this area, and knowingly preserved the FCC's complementary efforts, we think the fairness doctrine and its component personal attack and political editorializing regulations are a legitimate exercise of congressionally delegated authority. * * *

III.

A.

Although broadcasting is clearly a medium affected by a First Amendment interest, differences in the characteristics of new media justify differences in the First Amendment standards applied to them.[15] Joseph Burstyn, Inc. v. Wilson, 343 U.S. 495, 503 (1952). For example, the ability of new technology to produce sounds more raucous than those of the human voice justifies restrictions on the sound level, and on the hours and places of use, of sound trucks so long as the restrictions are reasonable and applied without discrimination.

15. The general problems raised by a technology which supplants atomized, relatively informal communication with mass media as a prime source of national cohesion and news were discussed at considerable length by Zechariah Chafee in Government and Mass Communications (1947). Debate on the particular implications of this view for the broadcasting industry has continued unabated. * * *

Just as the Government may limit the use of sound-amplifying equipment potentially so noisy that it drowns out civilized private speech, so may the Government limit the use of broadcast equipment. The right of free speech of a broadcaster, the user of a sound truck, or any other individual does not embrace a right to snuff out the free speech of others.

When two people converse face to face, both should not speak at once if either is to be clearly understood. But the range of the human voice is so limited that there could be meaningful communications if half the people in the United States were talking and the other half listening. Just as clearly, half the people might publish and the other half read. But the reach of radio signals is incomparably greater than the range of the human voice and the problem of interference is a massive reality. The lack of know-how and equipment may keep many from the air, but only a tiny fraction of those with resources and intelligence can hope to communicate by radio at the same time if intelligible communication is to be had, even if the entire radio spectrum is utilized in the present state of commercially acceptable technology.

* * *

Where there are substantially more individuals who want to broadcast than there are frequencies to allocate, it is idle to posit an unbridgeable First Amendment right to broadcast comparable to the right of every individual to speak, write, or publish. If 100 persons want broadcast licenses but there are only 10 frequencies to allocate, all of them may have the same "right" to a license; but if there is to be any effective communication by radio, only a few can be licensed and the rest must be barred from the airwaves. It would be strange if the First Amendment, aimed at protecting and furthering communications, prevented the Government from making radio communication possible by requiring licenses to broadcast and by limiting the number of licenses so as not to overcrowd the spectrum.

* * *

By the same token, as far as the First Amendment is concerned those who are licensed stand no better than those to whom licenses are refused. A license permits broadcasting, but the licensee has no constitutional right to be the one who holds the license or to monopolize a radio frequency to the exclusion of his fellow citizens. There is nothing in the First Amendment which prevents the Government from requiring a licensee to share his frequency with others and to conduct himself as a proxy or fiduciary with obligations to present those views and voices which are representative of his community and which would otherwise, by necessity, be barred from the airwaves.

This is not to say that the First Amendment is irrelevant to public broadcasting. On the contrary, it has a major role to play as the Congress itself recognized in § 326, which forbids FCC interference with "the right of free speech by means of radio communication." Because of the scarcity of radio frequencies, the Government is permitted to put restraints on licensees in favor of others whose views should be expressed on this unique medium. But the people as a whole retain their interest in free speech by radio and their collective right to have the medium function consistently with the ends and purposes of the First Amendment. It is the right of the viewers and listeners, not the right of the broadcasters, which is paramount. * * * It is the purpose of the First Amendment to preserve an uninhibited marketplace of ideas in which truth will ultimately prevail, rather than to countenance monopolization of that market, whether it be by the Government itself or a private licensee. * * * "[S]peech concerning public affairs is more than self-expression; it is the essence of self-government." It is the right of the public to receive suitable access to social, political, aesthetic, moral, and other ideas and experiences which is crucial here. That right may not constitutionally be abridged either by Congress or by the FCC.

B.

* * *

Nor can we say that it is inconsistent with the First Amendment goal of producing an informed public capable of conducting its own affairs to require a broadcaster to permit answers to personal attacks occurring in the course of discussing controversial issues, or to require that the political opponents of those endorsed by the station be given a chance to communicate with the public. Otherwise, station owners and a few networks would have unfettered power to make time available only to the highest bidders, to communicate only their own views on public issues, people and candidates, and to permit on the air only those with whom they agreed. There is no sanctuary in the First Amendment for unlimited private censorship operating in a medium not open to all. * * *

C.

It is strenuously argued, however, that if political editorials or personal attacks will trigger an obligation in broadcasters to afford the opportunity for expression to speakers who need not pay for time and whose views are unpalatable to the licensees, then broadcasters will be irresistibly forced to self-censorship and their coverage of controversial public issues will be eliminated or at least rendered wholly ineffective. Such a result would indeed be a serious matter, for should licensees actually eliminate their coverage of controversial issues, the purposes of the doctrine would be stifled.

At this point, however, as the Federal Communications Commission has indicated, that possibility is at best speculative. The communications industry, and in particular the networks, have taken pains to present controversial issues in the past, and even now they do not assert that they intend to abandon their efforts in this regard. It would be better if the FCC's encouragement were never necessary to induce the broadcasters to meet their responsibility. And if experience with the administration of these doctrines indicates that they have the net effect of reducing rather than enhancing the volume and quality of coverage, there will be time enough to reconsider the constitutional implications. The fairness doctrine in the past has had no such overall effect.

* * *

E.

* * *

The rapidity with which technological advances succeed one another to create more efficient use of spectrum space on the one hand, and to create new uses for that space by ever growing numbers of people on the other, makes it unwise to speculate on the future allocation of that space. It is enough to say that the resource is one of considerable and growing importance whose scarcity impelled its regulation by an agency authorized by Congress. Nothing in this record, or in our own researches, convinces us that the resource is no longer one for which there are more immediate and potential uses than can be accommodated, and for which wise planning is essential. * * *

Even where there are gaps in spectrum utilization, the fact remains that existing broadcasters have often attained their present position because of their initial government selection in competition with others before new technological advances opened new opportunities for further uses. Long experience in broadcasting, confirmed habits of listeners and viewers, network affiliation, and other advantages in program procurement give existing broadcasters a substantial advantage over new entrants, even where new entry is technologically possible. These advantages are the fruit of a preferred position conferred by the Government. * * *

In view of the scarcity of broadcast frequencies, the Government's role in allocating those frequencies, and the legitimate claims of those unable without governmental assistance to gain access to those frequencies for expression of their views, we hold the regulations and ruling at issue here are both authorized by statute and constitutional.[25] * * *

Not having heard oral argument in these cases, Mr. Justice Douglas took no part in the Court's decision.

Notes and Questions on Red Lion

1. The fairness doctrine and the related "political broadcasting" requirements are discussed in Chapter VII. In 1987, the FCC concluded that continued enforcement of the fairness doctrine was contrary to the First Amendment. Do you agree with the Court that Congress, in adding Section

---

25. We need not deal with the argument that even if there is no longer a technological scarcity of frequencies limiting the number of broadcasters, there nevertheless is an economic scarcity in the sense that the Commission could or does limit entry to the broadcasting market on economic grounds and license no more stations than the market will support. Hence, it is said, the fairness doctrine or its equivalent is essential to satisfy the claims of those excluded and of the public generally. * * *

315 to the Act, "ratified" the FCC's interpretation of the public interest standard to include the fairness doctrine? If it did, then does the Commission have the authority to abandon the doctrine?

2. (a) Compare the Court's reliance on the "scarcity of broadcast frequencies" to justify the regulation upheld in *Red Lion* with its decision in *Tornillo* that even if "entry into the marketplace of ideas served by the print media [is] almost impossible," the government could not impose a right of reply on newspapers. Can you reconcile the two positions? Is it relevant that there are many more broadcasters than there are daily newspapers—both nationally and in most local communities? Is it true—or constitutionally relevant—that broadcasting has a greater impact than newspapers on public affairs and the public's perception of society? If broadcasting is generally a more "powerful" medium, does this justify more or less regulation of broadcasting? Compare the reasoning behind limitations on "indecent programming."

(b) What is the relevance of the fact that the government licenses broadcasters but not newspapers? Recall that the rationale for licensing was technological—to avoid interference. If a sudden and dramatic shortage of newsprint developed, due to war or natural disaster, for example, such that the government undertook to allocate supplies at controlled prices in the interest of assuring some to each publisher, could the government also require that each newspaper cover all sides of controversial issues?

(c) Was the Court looking at the appropriate "marketplace of ideas" in evaluating whether the fairness doctrine was constitutional? Is it enough to conclude that broadcast frequencies are "scarce"? Relative to what? Does it matter whether a particular broadcaster presents unbalanced coverage of public issues so long as other broadcasters and newspapers provide more balanced coverage—or coverage that is unbalanced in another direction? Must each broadcaster be its own "marketplace of ideas"? How does the introduction of multi-channel media such as cable television or DBS affect this analysis? Are the new media relevant, for constitutional purposes?

(d) Must the Court's conclusion in *Red Lion* give way when technology overcomes—or reduces—scarcity? The impact of the FCC's 1985 evaluation of the fairness doctrine on the Court's "scarcity" rationale is discussed later. Consider also the *League of Women Voters* case. (p. 337)

(e) When the Supreme Court upheld the FCC's Chain Broadcasting Rules in 1943, see *National Broadcasting Co.*; it briefly considered First Amendment objections to the networking restrictions:

> * * * If [the Rules abridge a network's free speech rights], it would follow that every person whose application for a license to operate a station is denied by the Commission is thereby denied his constitutional right of free speech. * * * Unlike other modes of expression, radio inherently is not available to all. That is its unique characteristic, and that is why, unlike other modes of expression it is subject to government regulation. * * * But Congress did not authorize the Commission to choose among applicants upon the basis of their political, economic, or social views, or upon any other capricious basis. If it did, or if the Commission by [the Chain Broadcasting Rules] proposed a choice among applicants upon some such basis, the issue before us would be wholly

different. The question here is simply whether the Commission [may constitutionally] * * * refuse licenses to persons who engage in specified network practices (a basis for choice which we hold is comprehended within the statutory criterion of "public interest") * * *. The right of free speech does not include * * * the right to use the facilities of radio without a license. * * * Denial of a license on [the ground that it would be contrary to the Chain Broadcasting Rules] * * * is not a denial of free speech.

Does the reasoning of *National Broadcasting Co.* support the result in *Red Lion*? Is there a constitutionally significant distinction between the Chain Broadcasting Rules and the fairness doctrine? Does the fairness doctrine raise the kind of "wholly different" issue that the Court noted in affirming the Chain Broadcasting Rules?

3. Henry Geller has concluded that "there is a direct conflict between *Tornillo* and *Red Lion,*" but rather lamely defends the fairness doctrine nonetheless as a "necessary incident" to the fact of government licensing lest minority groups and interests be "denied the right to express their views over the broadcast media." Geller, Does *Red Lion* Square with *Tornillo?*, 29 U.Miami L.Rev. 477 (1975). Putting aside the apparent *non sequitur*, what empirical assumption is he making? Is it plausible?

4. (a) A more imaginative defense of the Court's decisions is offered by Professor Bollinger, who suggests that "it is the *First Amendment itself* that justifies this differential treatment of mass communications technologies" in order simultaneously to realize "the benefits of two distinct constitutional values * * *: access in a highly concentrated press and minimal governmental intervention." This could "theoretically" have been accomplished by requiring public access to the pages of newspapers and instead deregulating broadcasting, but the order of their development has brought us to the opposite resting point. Bollinger, *Freedom of the Press and Public Access: Toward a Theory of Partial Regulation of the Mass Media,* 75 Mich.L.Rev. 1, 36 (1976) (emphasis in original).

A premise of Professor Bollinger's argument is that access in fact furthers a First Amendment goal: "It seeks to neutralize the disparities that impede the proper functioning of the 'market-place of ideas,' to equalize opportunities within our society to command an audience and thereby to mobilize public opinion, and in that sense to help realize democratic ideals."

Viewed with an eye on this premise, "partial regulation of the mass media" can be roughly evaluated as a success or failure. Has the broadcast press, governed by the fairness doctrine, equalized opportunities to mobilize public opinion? Can you think of some instances when it has done so, i.e., where a minority view found expression on the electronic soap box and acquired a following? Do they involve local or national issues?

(b) We will return to Professor Bollinger's thesis, and to the question of its continuing vitality in the years since *Red Lion,* in Chapter VII, when we discuss the FCC's decision to stop enforcing the fairness doctrine.

5. Was the Court in *Red Lion* equating editorial discretion with "unlimited private censorship"? Is any privately owned mass medium truly "open to all"? Would it be preferable for the mass media to be government-

owned, rather than licensed to individuals and then subject to public use pursuant to government command?

6. Does the concern in *Red Lion* for the rights of viewers, as opposed to the rights of licensees, represent a populist view of the First Amendment, in which the Court is advocating the right of the public to self-definition through use of public resources such as the electromagnetic spectrum? That view would seem to be consistent with the policy of localism enshrined in the Communications Act. Under that view of the First Amendment, should local broadcasters be a forum for the exchange of ideas, or a reflection of accepted local attitudes, or both? Does the regulation upheld in *Red Lion* actually further the populist vision of the First Amendment? Or does the fairness doctrine "sterilize" the broadcast medium by making each broadcaster a neutral in the war of ideas? Can an advertiser-supported medium, such as over-the-air commercial television, ever be expected to be anything but neutral on controversial issues of public importance? Might the role of a combatant be better performed by low-power television stations? Cable television systems? Do newspapers play such a role, or are they expected to provide detached and objective information about public issues?

7. In evaluating the constitutional theory advanced by *Red Lion*, consider the following three hypotheses about the effects of the fairness doctrine:

A. By requiring presentation of all sides to a controversy, the doctrine deprives the broadcast press of a discrete political voice and disables it from performing in the historic role of the press—for which it received constitutional protection—that of an independent check on governmental arrogations of power. Broadcasters are deterred from taking strong positions because they then must confound themselves by giving circulation to the oppositing view. Hence, there is no William Randolph Hearst, no William Loeb or I.F. Stone, no *National Review* or *New Republic* of broadcasting. Indeed, anyone with strong views would lay better claim to his soul by staying out of the broadcasting business and assuming among the powers of the press. Whatever can be said for "access," then, it is purchased at this price: the press is half free and half slave, and it is the potentially more potent half, not surprisingly, that the government has chosen to enslave.

How does this impact on the 1996 Telecommunications Act's creation of "open video systems," which are partially carriers and partially content providers? (p. 430)

B. On the contrary, the fairness doctrine hardly affects the content of broadcasting at all, and what effect it has is salutary. First, the operative word in proposition (A) is "business." Broadcasting is a business, primarily an entertainment business since entertainment is profitable and discussion of public affairs is not (or not as much so). Thus, left to their own devices—as they largely are by the FCC—broadcasters shun political debate; even if relieved of the fairness doctrine, they surely would not adopt as their own controversial views that offend any significant number of viewers.

Second, to the extent that broadcasters do present controversy, either by choice or in response to the Commission's subtle pressure, as government licensees they should give a balanced presentation. Otherwise they give the appearance, and invite the reality, of government "censorship"; as has been pointed out, "the government could select licensees on the basis of its preferences for their demonstrated political view, and could foreclose access to the media for all those views it disapproved." Marks, *Broadcasting and Censorship: First Amendment Theory After Red Lion*, 38 Geo.Wash.L.Rev. 974, 992 (1970). Accordingly, the fairness doctrine should be seen as a governmental abjuration of power over the press.

C. Both of the prior views fail to appreciate the significance of the fact that broadcasting is licensed by the government. As Bernard Kilgore, the President of *The Wall Street Journal,* said in a speech in 1961, "no matter how loose the reins may be, * * * the argument that freedom of the press protects a licensed medium from the authority of the government that issues the license is double talk. * * * [I]f we try to argue that freedom of the press can somehow exist in a medium licensed by the government we have no argument against a licensed press." *Quoted in* Kalven, *Broadcasting and the First Amendment,* 10 J.Law & Econ. 1, 16 (1967). This accounts for broadcasting's non-participation in debates over public affairs. Indeed, in the Watergate scandal when *The Washington Post* performed the traditional role of the press as a check on government, it found its jointly-owned television station, WTOP, in a license challenge instigated in the White House. And the three networks were the objects of direct intimidation by the government (as recounted in detail by Thomas Whiteside in *Annals of Television: Shaking the Tree, The New Yorker,* Mar. 17, 1975, at 41). (Whiteside was a Nixon Administration official in charge of White House media policy.) That was possible only because the networks are licensees in their capacity as owners of some of the largest television and radio stations, according to Whiteside.

It is no explanation at all that broadcasting is a business; so is a newspaper or a magazine. Yet, among the free press some publishers find that they can make money without devoting their pages entirely to entertainment or presenting a "balanced" view of public affairs. William Randolph Hearst sold a lot of newspapers, and publications like those mentioned in proposition (A) are often run with an eye not to maximizing profits but to spreading a view, often at large personal costs to their backers. Not so with broadcasters, and the reason isn't the fairness doctrine; it's licensing. Indeed, many of the most reputable and influential newspapers in the country have followed *The New York Times*' example in opening their pages to submitted essays rebutting their editorials, and carry letters to the editor, and columnists reflecting a spectrum of political views. To some unlicensed publishers, that is, a self-imposed variant of the fairness doctrine seems to be good business and good journalism. "Fairness" is not the cause of the broadcasters' political blandness; licensing is.

8. (a) The late Professor Harry Kalven's comments speak to proposition (C):

> The speech problems posed by broadcasting are probably not unique, but belong to a category that is hard to capture. Various analogies come to mind and suggest the possibility of working toward a firmer theory of how communications problems of this type ought to be handled. * * *

> Take the town meeting which is often thought of as a model of free speech in operation. If the Chairman is keeping order he has problems

somewhat like those of broadcasting. Not everyone can talk at once nor can they talk too long since time is scarce nor can they talk far off the point. *The speakers are in effect 'licensed' by the chairman,* yet no one has ever said that this spoiled the game. What is understood by us all here is an implicit standard limiting the chairman to noncontent regulation. He may supervise the program but only in this critically limited sense. Probably the FCC can go somewhat farther, but it may prove profitable to play with the analogy of the FCC as the chairman of the meeting.

Then consider cases like Cox v. New Hampshire, 312 U.S. 569 (1941), holding that it is constitutional to require licensing of parades to avoid having two parades on the same corner at the same time. Here again is an analogy to the Roberts Rules of Order of the town meeting and another firm example of the compatibility, at times, of licensing with freedom of speech and press. The case has not yet arisen, but what would we think if the state were to choose between competing parades on the grounds that it preferred the quality or public service of the one parade over the other. 10 J.Law & Econ., at 47 (emphasis in original; footnotes omitted).

(b) But cf. Marks, supra, 38 Geo.Wash.L.Rev. at 986–87: "As between mutually exclusive applications for parade permits to use Fifth Avenue on St. Patrick's Day—one by the DAR and one by the St. Patrick's Day Committee—the latter would be preferred "on the grounds that its parade offered the better public service that day. The choice would reflect the government's estimate of the community's desire and expectation * * *." Do you agree?

Marks continues in response to Professor Kalven's analogy of the town meeting, with broadcasters as the townspeople and the FCC as the moderator:

But it is wrong to equate each speaker, rather than the meeting as a whole, to a broadcast station. Like a local station, the meeting is a forum serving community needs. The role of the chairman of the meeting is analogous to the licensee's: he himself can speak on any issue, but he cannot exclude other speakers on the basis of their viewpoints. The expectation is the same as the one implicit in the fairness doctrine, that fairness results from a multiplicity of viewpoints, none of which is prevented from being heard.

Who should prevail in this war of analogies? Is it significant that Marks says "fairness" results from a multiplicity of viewpoints, rather than "truth"?

9. (a) The Court stresses the superior right of "the public to receive suitable access to social, political, aesthetic, moral, and other ideas * * *." Who should determine the degree of access that is "suitable"—the broadcaster, the public, the FCC, or someone else? Why "suitable" rather than "reasonable," or "unfettered," or "unlimited" access? What significance, if any, do you assign to the fact that the Court chose to endorse a qualified— and necessarily subjective—access standard? Does the standard provide room for a different conclusion as the characteristics of the market change, e.g., because many new media outlets enter the market?

(b) The following two cases may shed light upon what the Court believes is "suitable" access.

COLUMBIA BROADCASTING SYSTEM, INC. v. DEMOCRATIC NATIONAL COMMITTEE

Supreme Court of the United States, 1973.
412 U.S. 94, 93 S.Ct. 2080, 36 L.Ed.2d 772.

MR. CHIEF JUSTICE BURGER delivered the opinion of the Court.

We granted the writs of certiorari in these cases to consider whether a broadcast licensee's general policy of not selling advertising time to individuals or groups wishing to speak out on issues they consider important violates the Federal Communications Act of 1934, * * * or the First Amendment.

The complainants in these actions are the Democratic National Committee (DNC) and the Business Executives' Move for Vietnam Peace (BEM), a national organization of businessmen opposed to United States involvement in the Vietnam conflict. In January 1970, BEM filed a complaint with the Commission charging that radio station WTOP in Washington, D.C., had refused to sell it time to broadcast a series of one-minute spot announcements expressing BEM views on Vietnam. WTOP, in common with many, but not all, broadcasters, followed a policy of refusing to sell time for spot announcements to individuals and groups who wished to expound their views on controversial issues. WTOP took the position that since it presented full and fair coverage of important public questions, including the Vietnam conflict, it was justified in refusing to accept editorial advertisements. WTOP also submitted evidence showing that the station had aired the views of critics of our Vietnam policy on numerous occasions. * * *

Four months later, in May 1970, DNC filed with the Commission a request for a declaratory ruling:

> That under the First Amendment to the Constitution and the Communications Act, a broadcaster may not, as a general policy, refuse to sell time to responsible entities, such as the DNC, for the solicitation of funds and for comment on public issues.

DNC claimed that it intended to purchase time from radio and television stations and from the national networks in order to present the views of the Democratic party and to solicit funds. Unlike BEM, DNC did not object to the policies of any particular broadcaster but claimed that its prior "experiences in this area make it clear that it will encounter considerable difficulty—if not total frustration of its efforts—in carrying out its plans in the event the Commission should decline to issue a ruling as requested." DNC cited Red Lion Broadcasting Co. v. FCC, 395 U.S. 367 (1969), as establishing a limited constitutional right of access to the airwaves.

In two separate opinions, the Commission rejected respondents' claims that "responsible" individuals and groups have a right to purchase advertising time to comment on public issues without regard to whether the broadcaster has complied with the Fairness Doctrine. * * *

* * * The Commission did, however, uphold DNC's position that the statute recognized a right of political parties to purchase broadcast time for the purpose of soliciting funds. The Commission noted that Congress had accorded special consideration for access by political parties, see 47 U.S.C. § 315(a), and that solicitation of funds by political parties is both feasible and appropriate in the short space of time generally allotted to spot advertisements.[1]

A majority of the Court of Appeals reversed the Commission, holding that "a flat ban on paid public issue announcements is in violation of the First Amendment, at least when other sorts of paid announcements are accepted." Recognizing that the broadcast frequencies are a scarce resource inherently unavailable to all, the court nevertheless concluded that the First Amendment mandated an "abridgeable" right to present editorial advertisements. The court reasoned that a broadcaster's policy of airing commercial advertisements but not editorial advertisements constitutes unconstitutional discrimination.* The court did not, however, order that either BEM's or DNC's proposed announcements must be accepted by the broadcasters; rather, it remanded the cases to the Commission to develop "reasonable procedures and regulations determining which and how many 'editorial advertisements' will be put on the air." * * *

I

Mr. Justice White's opinion for the Court in Red Lion Broadcasting Co. v. FCC, 395 U.S. 367 (1969), makes clear that the broadcast media pose unique and special problems not present in the traditional free speech case. * * * Congress and its chosen regulatory agency have established a delicately balanced system of regulation intended to serve the interests of all concerned. The problems of regulation are rendered more difficult because the broadcast industry is dynamic in terms of technological change * * *.

Thus, in evaluating the First Amendment claims of respondents, we must afford great weight to the decisions of Congress and the experience of the Commission. * * *

* * *

II

* * *

1. The Commission's [rulings] * * * in favor of DNC's claim that political parties should be permitted to purchase air time for solicitation of funds were not appealed to the Court of Appeals and are not before us here.

* In the court of appeals' view, broadcasters were subject to the requirements of the First Amendment because, having been granted use of part of the public domain and regulated as "fiduciaries of the people," they are instrumentalities of the government.—Ed.

The legislative history of the Radio Act of 1927, the model for our present statutory scheme, reveals that in the area of discussion of public issues Congress chose to leave broad journalistic discretion with the licensee. Congress specifically dealt with—and firmly rejected—the argument that the broadcast facilities should be open on a nonselective basis to all persons wishing to talk about public issues. Some members of Congress—those whose views were ultimately rejected—strenuously objected to the unregulated power of broadcasters to reject applications for service. * * * They regarded the exercise of such power to be "private censorship," which should be controlled by treating broadcasters as public utilities. * * *

* * * [In 1934] Congress after prolonged consideration adopted § 3(h) [Section 153(h)], which specifically provides that "a person engaged in radio broadcasting shall not, insofar as such person is so engaged, be deemed a common carrier." [The Court noted that Section 326 of the Communications Act specifically prohibits censorship by the Commission.]

From these provisions it seems clear that Congress intended to permit private broadcasting to develop with the widest journalistic freedom consistent with its public obligations. Only when the interests of the public are found to outweigh the private journalistic interests of the broadcasters will government power be asserted within the framework of the Act. License renewal proceedings, in which the listening public can be heard, are a principal means of such regulation.

Subsequent developments in broadcast regulation illustrate how this regulatory scheme has evolved. Of particular importance, in light of Congress' flat refusal to impose a "common carrier" right of access for all persons wishing to speak out on public issues, is the Commission's "Fairness Doctrine," which evolved gradually over the years spanning federal regulation of the broadcast media. * * *

* * *

III

[The Chief Justice, here joined only by Justices Stewart and Rehnquist, argued that broadcasters' editorial policies and judgments should not be considered governmental actions subject to the restraint of the First Amendment.]

IV

There remains for consideration the question whether the "public interest" standard of the Communications Act requires broadcasters to accept editorial advertisements or, whether, assuming governmental action, broadcasters are required to do so by reason of the First Amendment. * * *

The Commission was justified in concluding that the public interest in providing access to the marketplace of "ideas and experiences" would scarcely be served by a system so heavily weighted in favor of the financially affluent, or those with access to wealth. Even under a first-come-first-served system, proposed by the dissenting Commissioner in these cases, the views of the affluent could well prevail over those of others, since they would have it within their power to purchase time more frequently. Moreover, there is the substantial danger * * * that the time allotted for editorial advertising could be monopolized by those of one political persuasion.

* * *

If the Fairness Doctrine were applied to editorial advertising, there is also the substantial danger that the effective operation of that doctrine would be jeopardized. To minimize financial hardship and to comply fully with its public responsibilities a broadcaster might well be forced to make regular programming time available to those holding a view different from that expressed in an editorial advertisement; indeed, BEM has suggested as much in its brief. The result would be a further erosion of the journalistic discretion of broadcasters in the coverage of public issues, and a transfer of control over the treatment of public issues from the licensees who are accountable for broadcast performance to private individuals who are not. The public interest would no longer be "paramount" but, rather, subordinate to private whim * * *.

Nor can we accept the Court of Appeals' view that every potential speaker is "the best judge" of what the listening public ought to hear or indeed the best judge of the merits of his or her views. All journalistic tradition and experience is to the contrary. For better or worse, editing is what editors are for; and editing is selection and choice of material. That editors—newspaper or broadcast—can and do abuse this power is beyond doubt, but that is no reason to deny the discretion Congress provided. * * * [The Court went on to note that the exercise of discretion by broadcast "editors" is limited by the licensing scheme, which can result in a license revocation for failure to serve public needs and interests.] No such accountability attaches to the private individual, whose only qualifications for using the broadcast facility may be abundant funds and a point of view.

The Court of Appeals * * * suggested that broadcasters could place an "outside limit on the total amount of editorial advertising they will sell" and that the Commission and the broadcasters could develop" 'reasonable regulations' designed to prevent domination by a few groups or a few viewpoints." * * *

By minimizing the difficult problems involved in implementing such a right of access, the Court of Appeals failed to come to grips with another problem of critical importance to broadcast regulation and the First Amendment—the risk of an enlargement of Government control over the content of broadcast discussion of public issues. This risk is inherent in the Court of Appeals' remand requiring regulations and procedures to sort out requests to be heard—a process involving the very editing that licensees now perform as to regular programming.

Under a constitutionally commanded and Government supervised right-of-access system urged by respondents and mandated by the Court of Appeals, the Commission would be required to oversee far more of the day-to-day operations of broadcasters' conduct, deciding such questions as whether a particular individual or group has had sufficient opportunity to present its viewpoint and whether a particular viewpoint has already been sufficiently aired. Regimenting broadcasters is too radical a therapy for the ailment respondents complain of.

* * *

The rationale for the Court of Appeals' decision imposing a constitutional right of access on the broadcast media was that the licensee impermissibly discriminates by accepting commercial advertisements while refusing editorial advertisements. The court relied on decisions holding that state-supported school newspapers and public transit companies were prohibited by the First Amendment from excluding controversial editorial advertisements in favor of commercial advertisements. The court also attempted to analogize this case to some of our decisions holding that States may not constitutionally ban certain protected speech while at the same time permitting other speech in public areas.

* * *

Those decisions provide little guidance, however, in resolving the question whether the First Amendment requires the Commission to mandate a private right of access to the broadcast media. In none of those cases did the forum sought for expression have an affirmative and independent statutory obligation to provide full and fair coverage of public issues, such as Congress has imposed on all broadcast licensees. In short, there is no "discrimination" against controversial speech present in this case. The question here is not whether there is to be discussion of controversial issues of public importance on the broadcast media, but rather who shall determine what issues are to be discussed by whom, and when.

* * *

Conceivably at some future date Congress or the Commission—or the broadcasters—may devise some kind of limited right of access that is both practicable and desirable. Indeed, the Commission noted in these proceedings that the advent of cable television will afford increased opportunities for the discussion of public issues. * * *

* * * [T]he history of the Communications Act and the activities of the Commission over a period of 40 years reflect a continuing search for means to achieve reasonable regulation compatible with the First Amendment rights of the public and the licensees. * * * At the very least, courts should not freeze this necessarily dynamic process into a constitutional holding.

The judgment of the Court of Appeals is

Reversed.

MR. JUSTICE STEWART, concurring.

* * *

II

* * *

The First Amendment and the public interest standard of the statute are not coextensive. The two are related in the sense that the Commission could not "in the public interest" place a requirement on broadcasters that constituted a violation of their First Amendment rights. The two are also related in the sense that both foster free speech. But we have held that the Commission can under the statute require broadcasters to do certain things "in the public interest" that the First Amendment would not require if the broadcasters *were* the Government. For example, the Fairness Doctrine is an aspect of the "public interest" regulation of broadcasters that would not be compelled or even permitted by the First Amendment itself if broadcasters were the Government.

If the "public interest" language of the statute were intended to enact the substance of the First Amendment, a discussion of whether broadcaster action is governmental action would indeed be superfluous. For anything that Government could not do because of the First Amendment, the broadcasters could not do under the statute. But this theory proves far too much, since it would make the statutory scheme, with its emphasis on broadcaster discretion and its proscription on interference with "the right of free speech by means of radio communication," a nullity. Were the Government really operating the electronic press, it would, as my Brother DOUGLAS points out, be *prevented* by the First Amendment from selection of broadcast content and the exercise of editorial judgment. It would not be permitted in the name of "fairness" to deny time to any person or group on the grounds that their views had been heard "enough." Yet broadcasters perform precisely these functions and enjoy precisely these freedoms under the Act. The constitutional and statutory issues in these cases are thus quite different.

* * *

Even though it would be in the public interest for the respondents' advertisements to be heard, it does not follow that the public interest requires *every* broadcaster to broadcast them. And it certainly does not follow that the public interest would be served by *forcing* every broadcaster to accept any particular kind of advertising. In the light of these diverse broadcaster policies—and the serious First Amendment problem that a contrary ruling would have presented—there are surely no "compelling indications" that the Commission misunderstood its statutory responsibility.

III

* * *

Those who wrote our First Amendment put their faith in the proposition that a free press is indispensable to a free society. They believed that "fairness" was far too fragile to be left for a Government bureaucracy to accomplish. History has many times confirmed the wisdom of their choice.

This Court was persuaded in *Red Lion* to accept the Commission's view that a so-called Fairness Doctrine was required by the unique electronic limitations of broadcasting, at least in the then-existing state of the art. Rightly or wrongly, we there decided that broadcasters' First Amendment rights were "abridgeable." But surely this does not mean that those rights are nonexistent. And even if all else were in equipoise, and the decision of the issue before us were finally to rest upon First Amendment "values" alone, I could not agree with the Court of Appeals. For if those "values" mean anything they should mean at least this: If we must choose whether editorial decisions are to be made in the free judgment of individual broadcasters or imposed by bureaucratic fiat, the choice must be for freedom.

[The concurring opinions of Justice White and of Justice Blackmun, with whom Justice Powell joined, are omitted.]

MR. JUSTICE DOUGLAS, concurring in the judgment.

While I join the Court in reversing the judgment below, I do so for quite different reasons.

My conclusion is that TV and radio stand in the same protected position under the First Amendment as do newspapers and magazines. The philosophy of the First Amendment requires that result, for the fear that Madison and Jefferson had of government intrusion is perhaps even more relevant to TV and radio than it is to newspapers and other like publications. That fear was founded not only on the specter of a lawless government but of government under the control of a faction that desired to foist its views of the common good on the people.

* * *

II.

* * *

It is said that TV and radio have become so powerful and exert such an influence on the public mind that they must be controlled by Government. Some newspapers in our history have exerted a powerful—and some have thought—a harmful interest on the public mind. But even Thomas Jefferson, who knew how base and obnoxious the press could be, never dreamed of interfering. For he thought that government control of newspapers would be the greater of two evils. * * *

Of course there is private censorship in the newspaper field. But for one publisher who may suppress a fact, there are many who will print it.

But if the Government is the censor, administrative *fiat,* not freedom of choice, carries the day.

* * *

MR. JUSTICE BRENNAN, with whom MR. JUSTICE MARSHALL concurs, dissenting.

* * *

I

[Justice Brennan here argued that broadcasters should, like the government, be governed by the First Amendment with respect to the particular subject involved in these cases, *viz.* a broadcaster's ability to adopt a policy of "refus[ing] absolutely to sell any advertising time to those wishing to speak out on controversial issues." The factors on which he based his opinion are summarized in his conclusion:]

Thus, given the confluence of these various indicia of "governmental action"—including the public nature of the airwaves, the governmentally created preferred status of broadcasters, the extensive Government regulation of broadcast programming, and the specific governmental approval of the challenged policy—I can only conclude that the Government "has so far insinuated itself into a position" of participation in this policy that the absolute refusal of broadcast licensees to sell air time to groups or individuals wishing to speak out on controversial issues of public importance must be subjected to the restraints of the First Amendment.

II

* * * In fulfilling their obligations under the Fairness Doctrine * * * broadcast licensees have virtually complete discretion, subject only to the Commission's general requirement that licensees act "reasonably and in good faith," "to determine what issues should be covered, how much time should be allocated, which spokesmen should appear, and in what format." * * * Given this doctrinal framework, I can only conclude that the Fairness Doctrine, standing alone, is insufficient—in theory as well as in practice—to provide the kind of "uninhibited, robust, and wide-open" exchange of views to which the public is constitutionally entitled.

As a practical matter, the Court's reliance on the Fairness Doctrine as an "adequate" alternative to editorial advertising seriously overestimates the ability—or willingness—of broadcasters to expose the public to the "widest possible dissemination of information from diverse and antagonistic sources." As Professor Jaffe has noted, "there is considerable possibility the broadcaster will exercise a large amount of self-censorship and try to avoid as much controversy as he safely can." Indeed, in light of the strong interest of broadcasters in maximizing their audience, and therefore their profits, it seems almost naive to expect the majority of broadcasters to produce the variety and controversality of material necessary to reflect a full spectrum of viewpoints.

Stated simply, angry customers are not good customers and, in the commercial world of mass communications, it is simply "bad business" to espouse—or even to allow others to espouse—the heterodox or the controversial. As a result, even under the Fairness Doctrine, broadcasters generally tend to permit only established—or at least moderated—views to enter the broadcast world's "marketplace of ideas."

Moreover, the Court's reliance on the Fairness Doctrine as the *sole* means of informing the public seriously misconceives and underestimates the public's interest in receiving ideas and information directly from the advocates of those ideas without the interposition of journalistic middlemen. * * *

Our legal system reflects a belief that truth is best illuminated by a collision of genuine advocates. Under the Fairness Doctrine, however, accompanied by an absolute ban on editorial advertising, the public is compelled to rely *exclusively* on the "journalistic discretion" of broadcasters, who serve in theory as surrogate spokesmen for all sides of all issues. This separation of the advocate from the expression of his views can serve only to diminish the effectiveness of that expression. Indeed, we emphasized this fact in *Red Lion* * * *.

* * *

III

* * *

This is not to say, of course, that broadcasters have *no* First Amendment interest in exercising journalistic supervision over the use of their facilities. On the contrary, such an interest does indeed exist, and it is an interest that must be weighed heavily in any legitimate effort to balance the competing First Amendment interests involved in this case. In striking such a balance, however, it must be emphasized that these cases deal *only* with the allocation of *advertising* time—air time that broadcasters regularly relinquish to others without the retention of significant editorial control. Thus, we are concerned here, not with the speech of broadcasters themselves, but, rather, with their "right" to decide which *other* individuals will be given an opportunity to speak in a forum that has already been opened to the public.

* * *

IV

Finally, the Court raises the specter of administrative apocalypse as justification for its decision today. The Court's fears derive largely from the assumption, implicit in its analysis, that the Court of Appeals mandated an *absolute* right of access to the airwaves. In reality, however, the issue in these cases is not whether there is an *absolute* right of access but, rather, where there may be an *absolute denial* of such access. * * *

* * * I must agree with the conclusion of the Court of Appeals that although "it may unsettle some of us to see an antiwar message or a

political party message in the accustomed place of a soap or beer commercial * * * we must not equate what is habitual with what is right—or what is constitutional. A society already so saturated with commercialism can well afford another outlet for speech on public issues. All that we may lose is some of our apathy."

Notes and Questions

1.   What does the Court hold in *CBS v. DNC?* Consider the following possibilities:

A.   The First Amendment prohibits the government from interfering with the editorial judgments of broadcasters, whether those judgments broaden or constrict third-party access to the airwaves.

B.   The First Amendment is not relevant to the case because the editorial judgments of broadcasters are not "government actions" subject to the constraints of the First Amendment.

C.   A government policy requiring broadcasters to accept some or all editorial advertisements does not violate the First Amendment.

D.   Broadcasters may decide not to accept some or all editorial advertisements without violating the First Amendment.

E.   The "public interest" standard of the Communications Act does not require that broadcasters air some or any editorial advertisements.

F.   The "public interest" standard does not require the Commission to ensure that some or all editorial advertisements are aired by broadcasters.

G.   The "public interest" standard is intended to protect the editorial judgments of broadcasters from scrutiny by the Commission, except in the context of license renewal proceedings.

H.   Both the First Amendment and the "public interest" standard protect broadcasters from being compelled to carry certain advertisements.

Is there *any* majority holding on either the constitutional issue or the statutory issue? Justice Brennan suggests there is no majority holding on the constitutional question. In his view, some of the Justices have concluded that the First Amendment is not relevant to deciding whether a broadcaster can refuse to air all editorial advertisements, while other of the Justices have decided that although the First Amendment is applicable to a broadcast licensee's decision to refuse to carry editorial advertisements, such a policy does not violate the First Amendment. Do you agree with his analysis?

If there is no constitutional holding in the case, has the Court concluded anything more than the following: the Communications Act permits the Commission to respect—and to protect—the editorial decisions of individual broadcasters? If this is the Court's holding, can it be squared with the decision in *Red Lion,* where the Court upheld a policy that restricts the editorial discretion of broadcasters? Can the fairness doctrine fairly be viewed as a policy that preserves broadcasters' editorial discretion—at least as compared to a right of access to the airwaves for third parties? Read together, do *Red Lion* and *CBS v. DNC* mean that the Communications Act and the First Amendment give the Commission very broad discretion to regulate the conduct of broadcasters?

2.   Would an FCC rule prohibiting broadcasters from airing any editorial advertisements be lawful? Cf. *League of Women Voters,* (p. 337), in which the Court considers the provision of the Communications Act that prohibits public broadcasters from airing editorials.

3.   Eight years after deciding *CBS v. DNC,* the Court faced the question of whether broadcasters could be required to grant access to third parties. Is this the same question that the Court considered in deciding *CBS v. DNC* ? Or did the Court really decide whether a broadcaster could refuse access? Is there any substantive difference between the two questions? In this subsequent examination of access, the Court reached a strikingly different conclusion. Why?

CBS, INC. v. F.C.C.

Supreme Court of the United States, 1981.
453 U.S. 367, 101 S.Ct. 2813, 69 L.Ed.2d 706.

CHIEF JUSTICE BURGER delivered the opinion of the Court.

* * *

I

A

On October 11, 1979, Gerald M. Rafshoon, President of the Carter–Mondale Presidential Committee, requested each of the three major television networks to provide time for a 30–minute program between 8 p.m. and 10:30 p.m. on either the 4th, 5th, 6th, or 7th of December 1979. The Committee intended to present, in conjunction with President Carter's formal announcement of his candidacy, a documentary outlining the record of his administration.

The networks declined to make the requested time available. Petitioner CBS emphasized the large number of candidates for the Republican and Democratic Presidential nominations and the potential disruption of regular programming to accommodate requests for equal treatment, but it offered to sell two 5–minute segments to the Committee, one at 10:55 p.m. on December 8 and one in the daytime. Petitioner American Broadcasting Cos. replied that it had not yet decided when it would begin selling political time for the 1980 Presidential campaign, but subsequently indicated that it would allow such sales in January 1980. Petitioner National Broadcasting Co., noting the number of potential requests for time from Presidential candidates, stated that it was not prepared to sell time for political programs as early as December 1979.

On October 29, 1979, the Carter–Mondale Presidential Committee filed a complaint with the Federal Communications Commission, charging that the networks had violated their obligation to provide "reasonable access" under § 312(a)(7) of the Communications Act of 1934, as amended. Title 47 U.S.C. § 312(a)(7), as added to the Act, 86 Stat. 4, states:

The Commission may revoke any station license or construction permit—

* * *

(7) for willful or repeated failure to allow reasonable access to or to permit purchase of reasonable amounts of time for the use of a broadcasting station by a legally qualified candidate for Federal elective office on behalf of his candidacy.

At an open meeting on November 20, 1979, the Commission, by a 4-to-3 vote, ruled that the networks had violated § 312(a)(7). In its memorandum opinion and order, the Commission concluded that the networks' reasons for refusing to sell the time requested were "deficient" under its standards of reasonableness, and directed the networks to indicate by November 26, 1979, how they intended to fulfill their statutory obligations. 74 F.C.C.2d 631.

B

The Court of Appeals affirmed the Commission's orders, 202 U.S.App.D.C. 369, 629 F.2d 1 (1980), holding that the statute created a new, affirmative right of access to the broadcast media for individual candidates for federal elective office. As to the implementation of § 312(a)(7), the court concluded that the Commission has the authority to independently evaluate whether a campaign has begun for purposes of the statute, and approved the Commission's insistence that "broadcasters consider and address all non-frivolous matters in responding to a candidate's request for time." For example, a broadcaster must weigh such factors as: "(a) the individual needs of the candidate (as expressed by the candidate); (b) the amount of time previously provided to the candidate; (c) potential disruption of regular programming; (d) the number of other candidates likely to invoke equal opportunity rights if the broadcaster grants the request before him; and, (e) the timing of the request." And in reviewing a broadcaster's decision, the Commission will confine itself to two questions: "(1) has the broadcaster adverted to the proper standards in deciding whether to grant a request for access, and (2) is the broadcaster's explanation for his decision reasonable in terms of those standards?"

* * *

Finally, the Court of Appeals rejected petitioners' First Amendment challenge to § 312(a)(7) as applied, reasoning that the statute as construed by the Commission "is a constitutionally acceptable accommodation between, on the one hand, the public's right to be informed about elections and the right of candidates to speak and, on the other hand, the editorial rights of broadcasters." In a concurring opinion adopted by the majority, Judge Tamm expressed the view that § 312(a)(7) is saved from constitutional infirmity "as long as the [Commission] * * * maintains a very limited 'overseer' role consistent with its obligation of careful neutrality. * * * "

II

We consider first the scope of § 312(a)(7). Petitioners CBS and NBC contend that the statute did not impose any additional obligations on broadcasters, but merely codified prior policies developed by the Federal Communications Commission under the public interest standard. The Commission, however, argues that § 312(a)(7) created an affirmative, promptly enforceable right of reasonable access to the use of broadcast stations for individual candidates seeking federal elective office.

A

The Federal Election Campaign Act of 1971, which Congress enacted in 1972, included as one of its four Titles the Campaign Communications Reform Act (Title I). Title I contained the provision that was codified as 47 U.S.C. § 312(a)(7).

* * * In unambiguous language, § 312(a)(7) authorizes the Commission to revoke a broadcaster's license

> for willful or repeated failure to allow reasonable access to or to permit purchase of reasonable amounts of time for the use of a broadcasting station by a legally qualified candidate for Federal elective office on behalf of his candidacy.

It is clear on the face of the statute that Congress did not prescribe merely a general duty to afford some measure of political programming, which the public interest obligation of broadcasters already provided for. Rather, § 312(a)(7) focuses on the individual "legally qualified candidate" seeking air time to advocate "*his* candidacy," and guarantees him "reasonable access" enforceable by specific governmental sanction. Further, the sanction may be imposed for "willful or repeated" failure to afford reasonable access. This suggests that, if a legally qualified candidate for federal office is denied a reasonable amount of broadcast time, license revocation may follow even a single instance of such denial so long as it is willful; where the denial is recurring, the penalty may be imposed in the absence of a showing of willfulness.

* * *

Under the pre–1971 public interest requirement, compliance with which was necessary to assure license renewal, some time had to be given to political issues, but an individual candidate could claim no personal right of access unless his opponent used the station and no distinction was drawn between federal, state, and local elections. * * * By its terms, however, § 312(a)(7) singles out legally qualified candidates for *federal* elective office and grants them a special right of access on an individual basis, violation of which carries the serious consequence of license revocation. The conclusion is inescapable that the statute did more than simply codify the pre-existing public interest standard.

B

The legislative history confirms that § 312(a)(7) created a right of access that enlarged the political broadcasting responsibilities of licensees. * * *

* * *

C

* * *

Since the enactment of § 312(a)(7), the Commission has consistently construed the statute as extending beyond the prior public interest policy. In 1972, the Commission made clear that § 312(a)(7) "now imposes on the overall obligation to operate in the public interest *the additional specific requirement* that reasonable access and purchase of reasonable amounts of time be afforded candidates for Federal office." Use of Broadcast and Cablecast Facilities by Candidates for Public Office, 34 F.C.C.2d 510, 537–538 (1972) (1972 Policy Statement) (emphasis added). Accord, Public Notice Concerning Licensee Responsibility Under Amendments to the Communications Act Made by the Federal Election Campaign Act of 1971, 47 F.C.C.2d 516 (1974).[8]

* * *

The Commission's repeated construction of § 312(a)(7) as affording an affirmative right of reasonable access to individual candidates for federal elective office comports with the statute's language and legislative history and has received congressional review. Therefore, departure from that construction is unwarranted. * * *

D

In support of their narrow reading of § 312(a)(7) as simply a restatement of the public interest obligation, petitioners cite our decision in Columbia Broadcasting System, Inc. v. Democratic National Committee, 412 U.S. 94, 93 S.Ct. 2080, 36 L.Ed.2d 772 (1973), which held that neither the First Amendment nor the Communications Act requires broadcasters to accept paid editorial advertisements from citizens at large.

* * *

However, "the language of an opinion is not always to be parsed as though we were dealing with language of a statute." * * * The qualified observation that § 312(a)(7) "essentially codified" existing Commission practice was not a conclusion that the statute was in all respects coextensive with that practice and imposed no additional duties on broadcasters. In *Democratic National Committee,* we did not purport to rule on the precise contours of the responsibilities created by § 312(a)(7)

8. No request for access must be honored under § 312(a)(7) unless the candidate is willing to pay for the time sought.

since that issue was not before us. Like the general public interest standard and the equal opportunities provision of § 315(a), § 312(a)(7) reflects the importance attached to the use of the public airwaves by political candidates. Yet we now hold that § 312(a)(7) expanded on those predecessor requirements and granted a new right of access to persons seeking election to federal office.

[In Part III of the opinion, the Court concluded that the Commission's implementation of the access obligations of Section 312(a)(7) was not arbitrary or capricious and that its policies clearly covered the conduct of the petitioners in the case.

IV

* * * [P]etitioners assert that § 312(a)(7) as implemented by the Commission violates the First Amendment rights of broadcasters by unduly circumscribing their editorial discretion. * * * Petitioners argue that the Commission's interpretation of § 312(a)(7)'s access requirement disrupts the "delicate balanc[e]" that broadcast regulation must achieve. We disagree.

A licensed broadcaster is "granted the free and exclusive use of a limited and valuable part of the public domain; when he accepts that franchise it is burdened by enforceable public obligations." Office of Communication of the United Church of Christ v. FCC, 123 U.S.App. D.C. 328, 337, 359 F.2d 994, 1003 (1966). * * *

The First Amendment interests of candidates and voters, as well as broadcasters, are implicated by § 312(a)(7). We have recognized that "it is of particular importance that candidates have the * * * opportunity to make their views known so that the electorate may intelligently evaluate the candidates' personal qualities and their positions on vital public issues before choosing among them on election day." Indeed, "speech concerning public affairs is * * * the essence of self-government." The First Amendment "has its fullest and most urgent application precisely to the conduct of campaigns for political office." Section 312(a)(7) thus makes a significant contribution to freedom of expression by enhancing the ability of candidates to present, and the public to receive, information necessary for the effective operation of the democratic process.

Petitioners are correct that the Court has never approved a *general* right of access to the media. * * * Nor do we do so today. Section 312(a)(7) creates a *limited* right to "reasonable" access that pertains only to legally qualified federal candidates and may be invoked by them only for the purpose of advancing their candidacies once a campaign has commenced. The Commission has stated that, in enforcing the statute, it will "provide leeway to broadcasters and not merely attempt *de novo* to determine the reasonableness of their judgments * * *." * * * If broadcasters have considered the relevant factors in good faith, the Commission will uphold their decisions.* * * * Further, § 312(a)(7) does not

* Among the factors that may be considered are the candidate's stated purpose for seeking air time, the amount of time previously sold to the candidate, the disruptive

impair the discretion of broadcasters to present their views on any issue or to carry any particular type of programming.

Section 312(a)(7) represents an effort by Congress to assure that an important resource—the airwaves—will be used in the public interest. We hold that the statutory right of access, as defined by the Commission and applied in these cases, properly balances the First Amendment rights of federal candidates, the public, and broadcasters.

The judgment of the Court of Appeals, is

Affirmed.

Notes and Questions

1.   Does *CBS v. FCC* overrule the earlier *CBS v. DNC* decision? Was the same question before the Court in the two cases?

Does the Court's interpretation of Section 312(a)(7) render inoperative its earlier assertion that Congress, in the Communications Act, refused to regulate broadcasters as common carriers? Is the decision in *CBS v. FCC* consistent with the command of Section 3(h) of the Communications Act, which states that a broadcaster shall not "be deemed a common carrier"?

2.   Do you accept the proposition that the First Amendment will accommodate preferential access for a "legally qualified" *federal* candidate? Should the First Amendment be interpreted to permit favored treatment for the speech rights of the people who adopt legislation that determines the scope of broadcast regulation? Is their inherent conflict of interest of any constitutional significance? Why should access be limited to *federal* candidates, as compared to state or local candidates? Recall footnote 21 in *CBS v. DNC,* where the Court despairs of finding any principled distinction between political parties and others: Is the federal/state distinction drawn by Section 312(a)(7) a principled one?

3.   (a) Can you reconcile the Court's analysis of the "proper balance between private and public control" of broadcasting in *CBS v. DNC* with the Court's position in *Red Lion* that in striking the appropriate First Amendment balance, it is the rights of the audience, not of the broadcasters, that are paramount? Does the Court's analysis in Section IV of *CBS v. FCC* provide a basis for reconciling the reasoning in *CBS v. DNC* with that of *Red Lion?* What constitutional principle would you draw from the three cases, when read together?

(b) Professor Laurence Tribe has stated that *CBS v. DNC* "took a step away from *Red Lion* by its treatment of broadcasters as part of the 'press' with an important editorial function to perform * * *." American Constitutional Law 1005 (2d ed. 1988). What kind of a "press" does the *Red Lion* Court have in mind when it speaks, in Part IV of the opinion, about the "accountability" of the broadcast medium? Does *CBS v. FCC* represent a step back toward *Red Lion?*

impact on regular programming, and the likelihood of requests by rivals under Sec-   tion 315(a) (equal opportunities).—Ed.

(c) In *CBS v. DNC* the Court clearly was concerned about opening a Pandora's box if it read the Communications Act or the First Amendment to compel or to permit a right of access for paid editorial announcements. If the Court had upheld the access right, would it have transformed broadcasting into a soapbox for the wealthiest speakers? (Given the market for broadcast stations, isn't broadcasting an outlet for the wealthiest speakers anyway? What is, can, or should be done to counteract the economic limits to access to broadcasting? Recall the "most money" illusion.) How would a broadcaster ensure the availability of a responsive message? If no responsive message could be found, would the broadcaster be required to provide it in order to satisfy its fairness doctrine obligations? The Court in *CBS v. FCC* relied heavily on the fact that Section 312(a)(7) creates a limited access right. Should this matter? What is the constitutional principle on which to distinguish a general right of access from a right of access for legally qualified federal candidates?

(d) In *CBS v. FCC* the Court referred to *Tornillo* only in Part IV, when it noted that it has "never approved a *general* right of access to the media." Is it fair to say that the Court views *CBS v. FCC* as being entirely consistent with *Tornillo*? Alternatively, is *Tornillo* irrelevant to the question the Court faced in the case?

(e) In a dissenting opinion, in which Justices Rehnquist and Stevens joined, Justice White (the author of the Court's opinion in *Red Lion*) argued that the FCC's rules for implementing the Section 312(a)(7) right of reasonable access contravened "the longstanding statutory policy of deferring to editorial judgments that are not destructive of the goals of the Act." Justice White wrote:

> * * * [S]uch a policy would require acceptance of network or station decisions on access as long as they are within the range of reasonableness, even if the Commission would have preferred different responses * * *. * * * [T]he Commission seriously misconstrued the statute when it assumed that it had been given authority to insist on its own views as to reasonable access even though this entailed rejection of media judgments representing different but nevertheless reasonable reactions to access requests.

Is Justice White's view more consistent with *Red Lion*? (By the way, do you think the networks' responses in this case were "reasonable"? Justice White thought so.)

(f) Does Justice Brennan's dissenting opinion in *CBS v. DNC* provide any principle on which "to balance the competing First Amendment interests involved"? Does it lend support—albeit unintentionally—to Justice Douglas's concurring view in the case that the whole notion of government scrutiny of media content "puts the head of the camel inside the tent and enables administration after administration to toy with TV or radio in order to serve its sordid or benevolent ends"?

4. What do you make of the view that the decisions of broadcasters represent "governmental action" for purposes of constitutional analysis? Under this view, could a broadcaster constitutionally exercise any editorial discretion? May the government do so in publishing the newspapers of the armed forces?

5. In Chapter VII, we will return to Sections 312(a)(7) and 315 (and the FCC's related rules and policies) in order to examine how the statutory provisions have been applied in practice—and with what consequences.

6. The Court's "standard" of First Amendment protection for broadcasting is not clearly stated in any of its fairness doctrine decisions. It is clear, however, that broadcasters have some lesser degree of protection than the Court affords newspapers in *Tornillo*. In *Red Lion*, the Court stated that "differences in the characteristics of new media justify differences in the First Amendment standards applied to them." What "standard" did it adopt in *Red Lion?* Did it apply the same "standard" in *CBS v. DNC?* (Consider what the Court meant when it said "courts should not freeze this necessarily dynamic process [of searching for an appropriate, limited right of access to the broadcast medium] into a constitutional holding.") What about in *CBS v. FCC?* The *League of Women Voters* decision, (p. 337), represents the Court's most recent comprehensive consideration of the First Amendment standard applicable to broadcasting. How, if at all, does it differ from *Red Lion, CBS v. DNC,* or *CBS v. FCC?* So what is the First Amendment standard applicable to broadcasting?

7. The Court's decision in *United States v. O'Brien,* which is discussed in the following *Note*, contains a First Amendment standard that has often been used to determine the constitutionality of regulations applicable to the electronic mass media. After you have read the *Note*, consider whether *O'Brien* should be used to define the First Amendment rights of the electronic media.

Notes and Questions on the Protection of Expressive Conduct Under United States v. O'Brien

In 1968, the Court considered whether a statute that made it a crime to "knowingly destroy[ ] * * * [or] mutilate[ ]" a draft card was constitutional. United States v. O'Brien, 391 U.S. 367, 88 S.Ct. 1673, 20 L.Ed.2d 672 (1968). While participating in a demonstration against the Vietnam War, David O'Brien burned his draft card. During his criminal trial, O'Brien argued that the statute unconstitutionally abridged speech and served no legitimate legislative purpose. The Supreme Court upheld the statute.

The Court first noted that it did not consider the case to involve a facial challenge to the constitutionality of the statute:

> We note at the outset that the 1965 Amendment plainly does not abridge free speech on its face, and we do not understand O'Brien to argue otherwise. * * * [The statute] on its face deals with conduct having no connection with speech. It prohibits the knowing destruction of certificates issued by the Selective Service System, and there is nothing necessarily expressive about such conduct. The Amendment does not distinguish between public and private destruction, and it does not punish only destruction engaged in for the purpose of expressing views. * * * A law prohibiting destruction of Selective Service certificates no more abridges free speech on its face than a motor vehicle law prohibiting the destruction of drivers' licenses, or a tax law prohibiting the destruction of books and records.

The Court went on to consider whether the statute, as applied to O'Brien, abridged his speech in violation of the First Amendment. O'Brien argued that the constitution was intended to protect all modes of expression, including "communication of ideas by conduct." In response, the Court wrote:

We cannot accept the view that an apparently limitless variety of conduct can be labeled "speech" whenever the person engaging in the conduct intends thereby to express an idea. However, even on the assumption that the alleged communicative element in O'Brien's conduct is sufficient to bring into play the First Amendment, it does not necessarily follow that the destruction of a registration certificate is constitutionally protected activity. This Court has held that when "speech" and "nonspeech" elements are combined in the same course of conduct, a sufficiently important governmental interest in regulating the nonspeech element can justify incidental limitations on First Amendment freedoms. To characterize the quality of the governmental interest which must appear, the Court has employed a variety of descriptive terms: compelling; substantial; subordinating; paramount; cogent; strong. Whatever imprecision inheres in these terms, we think it clear that a government regulation is sufficiently justified [1] if it is within the constitutional power of the Government; [2] if it furthers an important or substantial government interest; [3] if the governmental interest is unrelated to the suppression of free expression; and [4] if the incidental restriction on alleged First Amendment freedoms is no greater than is essential to the furtherance of that interest. We find that the 1965 Amendment to § 12(b)(3) of the Universal Military Training and Service Act meets all of these requirements, and consequently that O'Brien can be constitutionally convicted for violating it.

In evaluating the draft card burning law against the four-part constitutional test, the Court made the following determinations:

The constitutional power of Congress to raise and support armies and to make all laws necessary and proper to that end is broad and sweeping. * * *

We think it apparent that the continuing availability to each registrant of his Selective Service certificates substantially furthers the smooth and proper functioning of the system that Congress has established to raise armies. We think it also apparent that the Nation has a vital interest in having a system for raising armies that functions with maximum efficiency and is capable of easily and quickly responding to continually changing circumstances. For these reasons, the Government has a substantial interest in assuring the continuing availability of issued Selective Service certificates.

It is equally clear that the 1965 Amendment specifically protects this substantial governmental interest. We perceive no alternative means that would more precisely and narrowly assure the continuing availability of issued Selective Service certificates than a law which prohibits their willful mutilation or destruction. * * * The 1965 Amendment prohibits such conduct and does nothing more. In other words, both the governmental interest and the operation of the 1965 Amendment are limited to the noncommunicative aspect of O'Brien's conduct. The governmental interest and the scope of the 1965 Amendment are limited to preventing harm to the smooth and efficient functioning of the Selective Service System. When O'Brien deliberately rendered unavailable his registration certificate, he willfully frustrated this governmental interest. For this noncommunicative impact of his conduct, and for nothing else, he was convicted.

The case at bar is therefore unlike one where the alleged governmental interest in regulating conduct arises in some measure because the communication allegedly integral to the conduct is itself thought to be harmful. In Stromberg v. People of State of California, 283 U.S. 359, 51 S.Ct. 532, 75 L.Ed. 1117 (1931), for example, this Court struck down a statutory phrase which punished people who expressed their "opposition to organized government" by displaying "any flag, badge, banner, or device". Since the statute there was aimed at suppressing communication it could not be sustained as a regulation of noncommunicative conduct.

In a brief concurring opinion, Justice Harlan sought to limit the applicability of the Court's decision. Referring to the Court's statement of the four-part test, he wrote:

I wish to make explicit my understanding that this passage does not foreclose consideration of First Amendment claims in those rare instances when an "incidental" restriction upon expression, imposed by a regulation which furthers an "important or substantial" governmental interest and satisfies the Court's other criteria, in practice has the effect of entirely preventing a "speaker" from reaching a significant audience with whom he could not otherwise lawfully communicate. This is not such a case, since O'Brien manifestly could have conveyed his message in many ways other than by burning his draft card.

While the Court's decision, on its own, may seem unremarkable, there is much debate over when it is appropriate to apply the four-part *O'Brien* test.

1.   (a) The four-part test of the *O'Brien* case has been applied broadly to assess the constitutionality of laws and regulations that impose an "incidental" burden on speech. When does government action burden speech only "incidentally"? Does the *O'Brien* test become inappropriate when government action burdens speech directly? Intentionally? Substantially?

(b) What do you think the Court meant by requiring that a regulation be "unrelated to the suppression of free expression" in order to pass constitutional muster? If a regulation incidentally burdens speech, is it "unrelated" to the suppression of that speech? Consider the Court's assertion that the prohibition on draft card destruction was "limited to the noncommunicative aspect of O'Brien's conduct." What does this mean? Can speech and conduct be separated? How?

(c) Is legislative intent relevant to the constitutionality of a law or regulation affecting a mass medium? What would constitute an "improper" intent if legislators and regulators are trying to balance competing—and legitimate—interests, such as those of broadcast licensees, viewers, and unlicensed persons wanting to express themselves over the medium?

(d) Perhaps the most important part of the *O'Brien* test is the require-ment that the suppression be "no greater than is essential" to further the government interest. Does this mean that if a court can dream up *any* less burdensome alternative, the regulation in question must be struck down or narrowed? What do you think the Court meant by including this part of the constitutional test? Were the regulations upheld in *Red Lion* and *CBS v. FCC* sufficiently narrow? Consider this question as you read the cases involving cable television, below at (p. 349).

2. Do you agree with Justice Harlan that the Court's opinion in *O'Brien* does not immunize a regulation that, even if it furthers an impor-tant or substantial interest, deprives a speaker of any opportunity to communicate? Consider this reading of *O'Brien* again in the next section of this chapter, in which the constitutionality of cable franchising is examined.

3. Consider Professor Tribe's critique of the constitutional analysis that distinguishes between the regulation of "speech plus" and pure speech, in light of the *O'Brien* opinion:

> The trouble with the distinction between speech and conduct is that it has less determinate content than is sometimes supposed. All commu-nication except perhaps that of the extrasensory variety involves con-duct. Moreover, if the expression involves talk, it may be noisy; if written, it may become litter. So too, much conduct is expressive, * * *. Expression and conduct, message and medium, are thus inextricably tied together in all communicative behavior * * *. It is thus not surprising that the Supreme Court has never articulated a basis for its distinction; it could not do so * * *.

> Meaning might be poured into the speech-conduct dichotomy by reference to a system of free expression that permits the identification of acts that should be protected by the First Amendment. Government would be guilty of impermissibly abridging speech or petition within the First Amendment's meaning, * * * if the regulation is properly under-stood as suppressing a disfavored viewpoint or idea. Thus, a rule forbidding "outdoor sleeping as a means of protesting homelessness," but permitting all other outdoor sleeping, would surely be an abridge-ment of speech * * *.

> The harder problem arises when a law is not directed at anything resembling speech *or* at the views expressed, but when its enforcement nonetheless serves to inhibit speech. If any such effect is merely inciden-tal, no First Amendment issue should be deemed to arise.

* * *

> * * * [A]ctivities not ordinarily thought to have any particularly expressive dimension * * * might properly *acquire* such a dimension in a specific regulatory context where the regulation is promulgated in response to what is generally understood to be expressive use of the activities in question. * * *

> When the acts that trigger a rule's enactment and that occasion its invocation in the case at hand are both intended to express, and understood by their audience to express, a particular message, it is necessary to subject the rule and its enforcement to some degree of First

Amendment scrutiny. All that follows is that the government must meet some version of the least restrictive alternative test—a relaxed version, * * * when the Court does not deem the activities in question particularly significant to the system of free expression. * * *

American Constitutional Law 827–32 (2d ed. 1988) (footnotes omitted). Under this view, do you think *O'Brien* was decided correctly or incorrectly? How would this speech/conduct analysis be applied to *Red Lion? CBS v. FCC?* On what basis should a court make the judgments suggested by Professor Tribe? Are these judgments that you think should be made by a court? See Ely, *Democracy and Distrust* 105–16 (1980); Nimmer, *The Meaning of Symbolic Speech Under the First Amendment*, 21 U.C.L.A. L.Rev. 29 (1973); Note, *Symbolic Conduct*, 68 Colum.L.Rev. 1091 (1968).

4.   (a) The State of Minnesota imposed an annual use tax on ink and newsprint. The tax exempted the first $100,000 in materials each year for each user, thereby exempting most small publishers from any tax liability. (Just 14 of almost 400 publishers in the state paid any tax.) The Minneapolis Star and Tribune had to pay more than $600,000 in a single year as a result of the use tax—almost two-thirds of the total tax proceeds collected that year. The paper challenged the constitutionality of the statute.

Should the statute be judged under the *O'Brien* test as an incidental burden on speech? Does it matter that there was no evidence of any intent by the state to censor or influence the content of newspapers? If *O'Brien* should apply, what result? See Minneapolis Star and Tribune Co. v. Minnesota Com'r of Revenue, 460 U.S. 575, 103 S.Ct. 1365, 75 L.Ed.2d 295 (1983) (the statute unconstitutionally discriminates against newspapers and larger publishers; although the State's interest in raising revenue is important, there are much less burdensome alternatives, such as a generally applicable business tax).

(b) In the *Minneapolis Star* decision, the Supreme Court wrote that "differential treatment [of the press], unless justified by some special characteristic of the press, suggests that the goal of the regulation is not unrelated to suppression of expression, and such a goal is presumptively unconstitutional." Does this sound like language appropriate for judging the constitutionality of an "incidental" burden on speech? Is broadcasting "the press"? Does broadcasting have "special characteristics" that would warrant "differential treatment", e.g., spectrum scarcity? If so, what standard of constitutional scrutiny should be used to judge broadcast regulations—the *O'Brien* test? Is the reasoning of *Red Lion* consistent with *O'Brien,* which was decided a year earlier?

FCC v. LEAGUE OF WOMEN VOTERS OF CALIFORNIA

Supreme Court of the United States, 1984.
468 U.S. 364, 104 S.Ct. 3106, 82 L.Ed.2d 278.

JUSTICE BRENNAN delivered the opinion of the Court.

Moved to action by a widely felt need to sponsor independent sources of broadcast programming as an alternative to commercial broadcasting, Congress set out in 1967 to support and promote the development of noncommercial, educational broadcasting stations. A keystone of Congress' program was the Public Broadcasting Act of 1967, 47 U.S.C. § 390 *et seq.*, which established the Corporation for Public Broadcasting, a nonprofit corporation authorized to disburse federal funds to noncommercial television and radio stations in support of station operations and educational programming. Section 399 of that Act, as amended * * * forbids any "noncommercial educational broadcasting station which receives a grant from the Corporation" to "engage in editorializing." * * * In this case, we are called upon to decide whether Congress, by imposing that restriction, has passed a "law ... abridging the freedom of speech, or of the press" in violation of the First Amendment of the Constitution.

I

A

* * * [T]he Public Broadcasting Act of 1967 * * * established the basic framework of the public broadcasting system of today. Titles I and III of the Act authorized over $38 million for continued HEW construction grants and for the study of instructional television. Title II created the Corporation for Public Broadcasting (CPB or Corporation), a nonprofit, private corporation governed by a bipartisan Board of Directors appointed by the President with the advice and consent of the Senate. The Corporation was given power to fund "the production of ... educational television or radio programs for national or regional distribution," 47 U.S.C. § 396(g)(2)(B) (1976 ed.), to make grants to local broadcasting stations that would "aid in financing local educational ... programming costs of such stations," § 396(g)(2)(C), and to assist in the establishment and development of national interconnection facilities. § 396(g)(2)(E).[4] Aside from conferring these powers on the Corporation, Congress also adopted other measures designed both to ensure the autonomy of the Corporation and to protect the local stations from governmental interference and control. For example, all federal agencies, officers, and employees were prohibited from "exercis[ing] any direction, supervision or control" over the Corporation or local stations, § 398, and the Corporation itself was forbidden to "own or operate any television or radio broadcast station," § 396(g)(3), and was further required to "carry out its purposes and functions ... in ways that will most effectively assure the maximum freedom ... from interference with or control of program content" of the local stations. § 396(g)(1)(D).

B

Appellee Pacifica Foundation is a nonprofit corporation that owns and operates several noncommercial educational broadcasting stations in five major metropolitan areas. Its licensees have received and are pres-

---

4. In accordance with the Act, an interconnection system was formally developed in 1969 when the Public Broadcasting Service (PBS) was created. Today, PBS is a private, nonprofit membership corporation governed by a Board of Directors elected by its membership, which consists of the licensees of noncommercial, educational television stations located throughout the United States. * * * National Public Radio (NPR) was established in 1970 and performs an analogous service for public radio stations.

ently receiving grants from the Corporation and are therefore prohibited from editorializing by the terms of § 399, as originally enacted and as recently amended.[7] In April 1979, appellees brought this suit in the United States District Court for the Central District of California challenging the constitutionality of former § 399. * * * While the suit was pending before the District Court, Congress, as already mentioned, *see* n. 7, *supra,* amended § 399 by confining the ban on editorializing to noncommercial stations that receive Corporation grants and by separately prohibiting all noncommercial stations from making political endorsements, irrespective of whether they receive federal funds. Subsequently, appellees amended their complaint to reflect this change, challenging only the ban on editorializing.[9]

The District Court granted summary judgment in favor of appellees, holding that § 399's ban on editorializing violated the First Amendment. * * * The FCC appealed from the District Court judgment directly to this Court pursuant to 28 U.S.C. § 1252. We * * * now affirm.

II

We begin by considering the appropriate standard of review. * * * Section 399 plainly operates to restrict the expression of editorial opinion on matters of public importance, and, as we have repeatedly explained, communication of this kind is entitled to the most exacting degree of First Amendment protection. Were a similar ban on editorializing applied to newspapers and magazines, we would not hesitate to strike it down as violative of the First Amendment. But, as the Government correctly notes, because broadcast regulation involves unique considerations, our cases have not followed precisely the same approach that we have applied to other media and have never gone so far as to demand that such regulations serve "compelling" governmental interests. At the same time, we think the Government's argument loses sight of concerns that are important in this area and thus misapprehends the essential meaning of our prior decisions concerning the reach of Congress' authority to regulate broadcast communication.

The fundamental principles that guide our evaluation of broadcast regulation are by now well established. First, we have long recognized that Congress, acting pursuant to the Commerce Clause, has power to regulate the use of this scarce and valuable national resource.[11] * * *

7. § 399 in its current form provides in full:

"No noncommercial educational broadcasting station which receives a grant from the Corporation for Public Broadcasting under subpart C of this part may engage in editorializing. No noncommercial educational broadcasting station may support or oppose any candidate for public office." 47 U.S.C. § 399.

9. In their amended complaint, appellees did not challenge the provision in § 399 prohibiting all noncommercial edu-

cational broadcasting stations from "support[ing] or oppos[ing] any candidate for public office." * * * We therefore express no view of the constitutionality of the second sentence in § 399. * * *

11. * * * The prevailing rationale for broadcast regulation based on spectrum scarcity has come under increasing criticism in recent years. * * * We are not prepared, however, to reconsider our longstanding approach without some signal from Congress or the FCC that technological developments have advanced so far that some revision of

Second, Congress may, in the exercise of this power, seek to assure that the public receives through this medium a balanced presentation of information on issues of public importance that otherwise might not be addressed if control of the medium were left entirely in the hands of those who own and operate broadcasting stations. * * *

Finally, although the Government's interest in ensuring balanced coverage of public issues is plainly both important and substantial, we have, at the same time, made clear that broadcasters are engaged in a vital and independent form of communicative activity. As a result, the First Amendment must inform and give shape to the manner in which Congress exercises its regulatory power in this area. * * * Indeed, if the public's interest in receiving a balanced presentation of views is to be fully served, we must necessarily rely in large part upon the editorial initiative and judgment of the broadcasters who bear the public trust.

Our prior cases illustrate these principles. In *Red Lion*, for example, we upheld the FCC's "fairness doctrine"—which requires broadcasters to provide adequate coverage of public issues and to ensure that this coverage fairly and accurately reflects the opposing views—because the doctrine advanced the substantial governmental interest in ensuring balanced presentations of views in this limited medium and yet posed no threat that a "broadcaster [would be denied permission] to carry a particular program or to publish his own views."[12]

* * *

Thus, although the broadcasting industry plainly operates under restraints not imposed upon other media, the thrust of these restrictions has generally been to secure the public's First Amendment interest in receiving a balanced presentation of views on diverse matters of public concern. As a result of these restrictions, of course, the absolute freedom to advocate one's own positions without also presenting opposing viewpoints—a freedom enjoyed, for example, by newspaper publishers and soapbox orators—is denied to broadcasters. But, as our cases attest, these restrictions have been upheld only when we were satisfied that the restriction is narrowly tailored to further a substantial governmental interest, such as ensuring adequate and balanced coverage of public issues. Making that judgment requires a critical examination of the interests of the public and broadcasters in light of the particular circumstances of each case.

the system of broadcast regulation may be required. [Footnote relocated.]

12. * * * Of course, the Commission may, in the exercise of its discretion, decide to modify or abandon these rules, and we express no view on the legality of either course. As we recognized in *Red Lion*, however, were it to be shown by the Commis-sion that the fairness doctrine "[has] the net effect of reducing rather than enhanc-ing" speech, we would then be forced to reconsider the constitutional basis of our decision in that case.

As discussed later, (p. 476), the Commis-sion eventually did repeal the Fairness Doc-trine, largely on First Amendment grounds.—Ed.

III

We turn now to consider whether the restraint imposed by § 399 satisfies the requirements established by our prior cases for permissible broadcast regulation. Before assessing the Government's proffered justifications for the statute, however, two central features of the ban against editorializing must be examined, since they help to illuminate the importance of the First Amendment interests at stake in this case.

A

First, the restriction imposed by § 399 is specifically directed at a form of speech—namely, the expression of editorial opinion—that lies at the heart of First Amendment protection. In construing the reach of the statute, the FCC has explained that "although the use of noncommercial educational broadcast facilities by licensees, their management or those speaking on their behalf for the propagation of the licensee's own views on public issues is therefore not to be permitted, such prohibition should not be construed to inhibit any *other* presentations on controversial issues of public importance." The Commission's interpretation of § 399 simply highlights the fact that what the statute forecloses is the expression of editorial opinion on "controversial issues of public importance." * * *

The editorial has traditionally played precisely this role by informing and arousing the public, and by criticizing and cajoling those who hold government office in order to help launch new solutions to the problems of the time. Preserving the free expression of editorial opinion, therefore, is part and parcel of "a profound national commitment . . . that debate on public issues should be uninhibited, robust, and wide-open." New York Times Co. v. Sullivan, 376 U.S. 254, 270, 84 S.Ct. 710, 721, 11 L.Ed.2d 686 (1964). As we recognized in Mills v. Alabama, 384 U.S. 214, 86 S.Ct. 1434, 16 L.Ed.2d 484 (1966), the special place of the editorial in our First Amendment jurisprudence simply reflects the fact that the press, of which the broadcasting industry is indisputably a part, carries out a historic, dual responsibility in our society of reporting information and of bringing critical judgment to bear on public affairs. Indeed, the pivotal importance of editorializing as a means of satisfying the public's interest in receiving a wide variety of ideas and views through the medium of broadcasting has long been recognized by the FCC; the Commission has for the past 35 years actively encouraged commercial broadcast licensees to include editorials on public affairs in their programming. Because § 399 appears to restrict precisely that form of speech which the Framers of the Bill of Rights were most anxious to protect—speech that is "indispensable to the discovery and spread of political truth"—we must be especially careful in weighing the interests that are asserted in support of this restriction and in assessing the precision with which the ban is crafted.

Second, the scope of § 399's ban is defined solely on the basis of the content of the suppressed speech. A wide variety of noneditorial speech "by licensees, their management or those speaking on their behalf," is plainly not prohibited by § 399. Examples of such permissible forms of speech include daily announcements of the station's program schedule or over-the-air appeals for contributions from listeners. Consequently, in order to determine whether a particular statement by station management constitutes an "editorial" proscribed by § 399, enforcement authorities must necessarily examine the content of the message that is conveyed to determine whether the views expressed concern "controversial issues of public importance." * * *

* * *

B

In seeking to defend the prohibition on editorializing imposed by § 399, the Government urges that the statute was aimed at preventing two principal threats to the overall success of the Public Broadcasting Act of 1967. According to this argument, the ban was necessary, first, to protect noncommercial educational broadcasting stations from being coerced, as a result of federal financing, into becoming vehicles for Government propagandizing or the objects of governmental influence; and, second, to keep these stations from becoming convenient target for capture by private interest groups wishing to express their own partisan viewpoints. By seeking to safeguard the public's right to a balanced presentation of public issues through the prevention of either governmental or private bias, these objectives are, of course, broadly consistent with the goals identified in our earlier broadcast regulation cases. But, in sharp contrast to the restrictions upheld in *Red Lion* or in *CBS, Inc. v. FCC,* which left room for editorial discretion and simply required broadcast editors to grant others access to the microphone, § 399 directly prohibits the broadcaster from speaking out on public issues even in a balanced and fair manner. The Government insists, however, that the hazards posed in the "special" circumstances of noncommercial educational broadcasting are so great that § 399 is an indispensable means of preserving the public's First Amendment interests. We disagree.

(1)

When Congress first decided to provide financial support for the expansion and development of noncommercial educational stations, all concerned agreed that this step posed some risk that these traditionally independent stations might be pressured into becoming forums devoted solely to programming and views that were acceptable to the Federal Government. That Congress was alert to these dangers cannot be doubted. * * *

The intended role of § 399 in achieving these purposes, however is not as clear. * * *

More importantly, an examination of both the overall legislative scheme established by the 1967 Act and the character of public broadcasting demonstrates that the interest asserted by the Government is not substantially advanced by § 399. First, to the extent that Federal financial support creates a risk that stations will lose their independence through the bewitching power of governmental largesse, the elaborate structure established by the Public Broadcasting Act already operates to insulate local stations from governmental interference. Congress not only mandated that the new Corporation for Public Broadcasting would have a private, bipartisan structure, but also imposed a variety of important limitations on its powers. The Corporation was prohibited from owning or operating any station, it was required to adhere strictly to a standard of "objectivity and balance" in disbursing federal funds to local stations, and it was prohibited from contributing to or otherwise supporting any candidate for office.

The Act also established a second layer of protections which serve to protect the stations from governmental coercion and interference. Thus, in addition to requiring the Corporation to operate so as to "assure the maximum freedom [of local stations] from interference with or control of program content or other activities," the Act expressly forbids "any department, agency, officer, or employee of the United States to exercise any direction, supervision, or control over educational television or radio broadcasting, or over the Corporation or any of its grantees or contractors...." * * *

Even if these statutory protections were thought insufficient to the task, however, suppressing the particular category of speech restricted by § 399 is simply not likely, given the character of the public broadcasting system, to reduce substantially the risk that the Federal Government will seek to influence or put pressure on local stations. An underlying supposition of the Government's argument in this regard is that individual noncommercial stations are likely to speak so forcefully on particular issues that Congress, the ultimate source of the stations' federal funding, will be tempted to retaliate against these individual stations by restricting appropriations for all of public broadcasting. But, as the District Court recognized, the character of public broadcasting suggests that such a risk is speculative at best. There are literally hundreds of public radio and television stations in communities scattered throughout the United States and its territories. Given that central fact, it seems reasonable to infer that the editorial voices of these stations will prove to be as distinctive, varied, and idiosyncratic as the various communities they represent. More importantly, the editorial focus of any particular station can fairly be expected to focus largely on issues affecting only its community. Accordingly, absent some showing by the Government to the contrary, the risk that local editorializing will place all of public broadcasting in jeopardy is not sufficiently pressing to warrant § 399's broad suppression of speech.

* * *

Furthermore, the manifest imprecision of the ban imposed by § 399 reveals that its proscription is not sufficiently tailored to the harms it seeks to prevent to justify its substantial interference with broadcasters' speech. Section 399 includes within its grip a potentially infinite variety of speech, most of which would not be related in any way to governmen-

tal affairs, political candidacies, or elections. Indeed, the breadth of editorial commentary is as wide as human imagination permits. But the Government never explains how, say, an editorial by local station management urging improvements in a town's parks or museums will so infuriate Congress or other federal officials that the future of public broadcasting will be imperiled unless such editorials are suppressed.
* * *

The Government appears to recognize these flaws in § 399, because it focuses instead on the suggestion that the source of governmental influence may well be state and local governments, many of which have established public broadcasting commissions that own and operate local noncommercial educational stations. The ban on editorializing is all the more necessary with respect to these stations, the argument runs, because the management of such stations will be especially likely to broadcast only editorials that are favorable to the state or local authorities that hold the purse strings. The Government's argument, however, proves too much. First, § 399's ban applies to the many private noncommercial community organizations that own and operate stations that are not controlled in any way by state or local government. Second, the legislative history of the Public Broadcasting Act clearly indicates that Congress was concerned with "assur[ing] complete freedom from any *Federal Government influence.*" * * *

Finally, although the Government certainly has a substantial interest in ensuring that the audiences of noncommercial stations will not be led to think that the broadcaster's editorials reflect the official view of the government, this interest can be fully satisfied by less restrictive means that are readily available. To address this important concern, Congress could simply require public broadcasting stations to broadcast a disclaimer every time they editorialize which would state that the editorial represents only the view of the station's management and does not in any way represent the views of the Federal Government or any of the station's other sources of funding. * * *

* * *

(2)

Assuming that the Government's second asserted interest in preventing noncommercial stations from becoming a "privileged outlet for the political and ideological opinions of station owners and managers" is legitimate, the substantiality of this asserted interest is dubious. The patent overinclusiveness and underinclusiveness of § 399's ban "undermines the likelihood of a genuine [governmental] interest" in preventing private groups from propagating their own views via public broadcasting. If it is true, as the Government contends, that noncommercial stations remain free, despite § 399, to broadcast a wide variety of controversial views through their power to control program selection, to select which persons will be interviewed, and to determine how news reports will be presented, then it seems doubtful that § 399 can fairly be said to advance any genuinely substantial governmental interest in keeping controversial or partisan opinions from being aired by noncommercial stations.

* * * If the vigorous expression of controversial opinions is, as the Government assures us, affirmatively encouraged by the Act, and if local licensees are permitted under the Act to exercise editorial control over the selection of programs, controversial or otherwise, that are aired on their stations, then § 399 accomplishes only one thing—the suppression of editorial speech by station management. It does virtually nothing, however, to reduce the risk that public stations will serve solely as outlets for expression of narrow partisan views. * * *

* * *

We therefore hold that even if some of the hazards at which § 399 was aimed are sufficiently substantial, the restriction is not crafted with sufficient precision to remedy those dangers that may exist to justify the significant abridgment of speech worked by the provision's broad ban on editorializing. The statute is not narrowly tailored to address any of the Government's suggested goals. Moreover, the public's "paramount right" to be fully and broadly informed on matters of public importance through the medium of noncommercial educational broadcasting is not well served by the restriction, for its effect is plainly to diminish rather than augment "the volume and quality of coverage" of controversial issues. Nor do we see any reason to deny noncommercial broadcasters the right to address matters of public concern on the basis of merely speculative fears of adverse public or governmental reactions to such speech.

[The dissenting opinions of Justices WHITE and REHNQUIST are omitted.]

JUSTICE STEVENS, dissenting.

The court jester who mocks the King must choose his words with great care. An artist is likely to paint a flattering portrait of his patron. The child who wants a new toy does not preface his request with a comment on how fat his mother is. Newspaper publishers have been known to listen to their advertising managers. Elected officials may remember how their elections were financed. By enacting the statutory provision that the Court invalidates today, a sophisticated group of legislators expressed a concern about the potential impact of Government funds on pervasive and powerful organs of mass communication. One need not have heard the raucous voice of Adolf Hitler over Radio Berlin to appreciate the importance of that concern.

As Justice White correctly notes, the statutory prohibitions against editorializing and candidate endorsements rest on the same foundation. In my opinion that foundation is far stronger than merely "a rational basis" and it is not weakened by the fact that it is buttressed by other provisions that are also designed to avoid the insidious evils of government propaganda favoring particular points of view. The quality of the interest in maintaining government neutrality in the free market of ideas—of avoiding subtle forms of censorship and propaganda—outweigh the impact on expression that results from this statute. Indeed, by simply terminating or reducing funding, Congress could curtail much more expression with no risk whatever of a constitutional transgression.

* * *

I

* * *

The Court does not tell us whether speech that endorses political candidates is more or less worthy of protection than other forms of editorializing, but it does iterate and reiterate the point that "the expression of editorial opinion" is a special kind of communication that "is entitled to the most exacting degree of First Amendment protection."

Neither the fact that the statute regulates only one kind of speech, nor the fact that editorial opinion has traditionally been an important kind of speech, is sufficient to identify the character or the significance of the statute's impact on speech. Three additional points are relevant. First, the statute does not prohibit Pacifica from expressing its opinion through any avenue except the radio stations for which it receives federal financial support. It eliminates the subsidized channel of communication as a forum for Pacifica itself, and thereby deprives Pacifica of an advantage it would otherwise have over other speakers, but it does not exclude Pacifica from the marketplace for ideas. Second, the statute does not curtail the expression of opinion by individual commentators who participate in Pacifica's programs. The only comment that is prohibited is a statement that Pacifica agrees or disagrees with the opinions that others may express on its programs. Third, and of greatest significance for me, the statutory restriction is completely neutral in its operation—it prohibits all editorials without any distinction being drawn concerning the subject matter or the point of view that might be expressed.

II

The statute does not violate the fundamental principle that the citizen's right to speak may not be conditioned upon the sovereign's agreement with what the speaker intends to say. On the contrary, the statute was enacted in order to protect that very principle—to avoid the risk that some speakers will be rewarded or penalized for saying things that appeal to—or are offensive to—the sovereign. The interests the statute is designed to protect are interests that underlie the First Amendment itself.

In my judgment the interest in keeping the Federal Government out of the propaganda arena is of overriding importance. That interest is of special importance in the field of electronic communication, not only because that medium is so powerful and persuasive, but also because it is the one form of communication that is licensed by the Federal Government. When the Government already has great potential power over the electronic media, it is surely legitimate to enact statutory safeguards to make sure that it does not cross the threshold that separates neutral regulation from the subsidy of partisan opinion.

The Court does not question the validity of the basic interests served by § 399. Instead, it suggests that the statute does not substantially serve those interests because the Public Broadcasting Act operates in many other respects to insulate local stations from governmental interference. In my view, that is an indication of nothing more than the strength of the governmental interest involved here—Congress enacted many safeguards because the evil to be avoided was so grave. * * *

* * *

III

I respectfully dissent.

Notes and Questions

1. What constitutional standard does the Court apply in *League of Women Voters?* How, if at all, does it differ from the standard applied in the *Red Lion* case? Do you agree that in *CBS v. DNC* the regulation that was overturned simply went too far in favor of the rights of listeners and viewers, as compared to those of licensees?

2. (a) Do you agree with the Court that the balance of interests weighs in favor of broadcasters in this case? Justice Brennan makes much of the fact that Section 399 of the Communications Act is "directed at a form of speech—namely, the editorial opinion—that lies at the heart of First Amendment protection." "Preserving the free expression of editorial opinion * * * is part and parcel," he adds, quoting New York Times Co. v. Sullivan, 376 U.S. 254, 270, 84 S.Ct. 710, 721, 11 L.Ed.2d 686 (1964), "of a 'profound national commitment . . . that debate on public issues should be uninhibited, robust, and wide-open.' "Is the fairness doctrine, as upheld in *Red Lion,* consistent with preserving a robust debate? If, in accordance with the fairness doctrine, each licensee is to serve as a town meeting for the debate of controversial issues, should the chairman of the meeting be permitted to editorialize?

3. The Court characterizes Section 399 as an express and intentional restraint on a particular type of speech: the restriction "is specifically directed at * * * editorial opinion * * *." Is this a fair characterization of legislative intent or motive? Could one view the fairness doctrine in similar terms—that is, the licensee's right to address the audience on the controversial issues covered by the fairness doctrine is *conditioned* on its willingness to present both sides of the issue? Is the conditional right of speech embodied in the fairness doctrine constitutionally acceptable, whereas the flat ban in Section 399 simply goes too far? Why?

4. The Court does not think very highly of the government's suggestion that Section 399 was intended to prevent noncommercial stations from becoming vehicles for government propaganda. In the Court's view, Section 399 is not particularly well-designed to achieve this goal. (Why might Congress limit only the federal government's involvement in noncommercial broadcasting?) If the statute were well-suited for this purpose, however, do

you think the Court might uphold it? Is the Court likely to be more concerned about "disguised" government control of television stations—exercised through the appropriations power—than it would be about explicit control—exercised through a law or regulation that expressly restricts certain speech?

5. What does the Court believe is an appropriate role for the federal government to play in affecting the content of a noncommercial television station? Suppose the Congress required that every noncommercial television station set aside one hour of each day for use by the government to broadcast programs selected by a special committee of the Congress. Do you think the Court would uphold or overturn the statute? On what grounds?

6. Note the Court's suggestion about the use of a disclaimer to make clear that a licensee's editorial does not necessarily represent the view of the government. Should there be equal concern about the opposite impression, i.e., that the government's views are presented as if they were merely those of the licensee? Suppose the Congress passed a law requiring noncommercial stations to run a disclaimer before any editorial, stating that the station is supported by government funds and that the opinions expressed by the station may be influenced, in whole or in part, by the government. Would the law be constitutional? What about a law requiring that if a government owns or controls a noncommercial station license, its interest must be made clear?

7. Is Justice Stevens' dissent convincing? Is Section 399 an effective way of ensuring that the government does not allocate funds only to those speakers with which it agrees? Suppose the Congress provided additional funds to noncommercial stations that carried at least ten hours of programming each week teaching basic science and math skills; and that for one year additional funds were allocated to stations that devoted more than two hours per week to coverage of events in Eastern Europe. Would either one of these decisions be permissible, in Justice Stevens' view? In your view? Does Justice Stevens want noncommercial stations to be sterile outlets for the dissemination of noncontroversial programming?

8. Do political endorsements present a greater or lesser danger for government influence over noncommercial station licensees? What do you think Justice Stevens' view of the endorsement ban is? Is that view consistent with the thrust of his dissent?

9. In its balancing of interests in the various broadcast decisions, which of the following interest groups is receiving the most and which the least weight: licensees; non-licensees wishing to speak; listeners and viewers; the federal government; state and local governments; candidates for federal office; candidates for state or local office; elected federal officials; elected state and local officials? Does the First Amendment require such a weighing of interests? If not, is there anything about broadcasting, unlike newspapers, that justifies such a weighing of competing interests? Is it "fair" to condition receipt of a broadcast license on a licensee's willingness to serve as a "fiduciary" for the public? Is it constitutional? Can a fiduciary be a "speaker," with a view of its own?

10. The struggle to define the scope of constitutional protection applicable to broadcasters is replicated—and magnified—in the courts' efforts to

decide the proper constitutional status of cable television. If broadcasters, who are licensed to use the public airwaves as public trustees, are not considered "full-fledged" speakers, then cable system operators, who at least initially appeared to be running utilities as opposed to electronic newspapers, seem destined to receive even less constitutional protection. Cable television, particularly in its earliest days, functioned primarily as a wire conduit for the retransmission of other people's programming. For constitutional purposes, cable television did not seem to be adding any new "voices." (Should the editorial function of program selection be viewed as creating a new "voice," or is the creation of original programming the only activity that gives rise to a substantial claim for First Amendment protection?) Thus, the medium's need for protection from government regulation of or affecting speech was arguably slight. The appeal of cable, in the view of many, was that its multichannel capacity could provide a video outlet for a large number of speakers who could never gain access to the public over the limited number of broadcast television stations. The next section of this Chapter traces the ongoing debate about whether the First Amendment should advance the rights of non-operators to have access to cable systems or the rights of operators to program their systems by performing the traditional—and constitutionally protected—function of editors. As you read the cases, consider whether the First Amendment will permit an accommodation of both perspectives.

C. THE UNCERTAIN CONSTITUTIONAL STATUS OF CABLE TELEVISION

1. Background

As a relatively new medium, cable television had virtually no constitutional framework during its development. On the one hand, it was not a broadcaster, since it did not use over-the-air frequencies. On the other, it was not a common carrier, since it did not make its channels available to third parties. Particularly during cable's early days, the courts thus had great difficulty in finding appropriate First Amendment doctrines to govern it.

Possibly because nothing else seemed to fit, the quasi-*O'Brien* intermediate scrutiny was pressed into service. The first significant discussion of the test came in *Home Box Office, Inc. v. FCC*, 567 F.2d 9 (D.C.Cir.1977), certiorari denied 434 U.S. 829, 98 S. Ct. 111, 54 L.Ed.2d 89.

At the heart of these cases are the Commission's "pay cable" rules. [47 CFR § 76.225 (1976).] The effect of these rules is to restrict sharply the ability of cablecasters to present feature film and sports programs if a separate program or channel charge is made for this material. In addition, the rules prohibit cablecasters from devoting more than 90 percent of their cablecast hours to movie and sports programs and further bar cablecasters from showing commercial advertising on cable channels on which programs are presented for a direct charge to the viewer. * * *

* * * The purpose of these limitations [which originally were developed to apply to subscription broadcast television, FCC Docket 18397, 20 FCC 2d 201 (1969)] was twofold. First, the Commission had agonized over both its authority to dedicate one or more channels from the electronic spectrum to subscription operations and the desirability of doing so. Such channels are scarce, and opponents of subscription television had argued that they should be used for conventional programming which would, of course, be free to all viewers. * * * A second reason for restricting the feature films, sports events, and series programs that could be shown on subscription television was the Commission's fear that the revenue derived from subscription operations would be sufficient to allow subscription operators to bid away the best programs in these categories, thus reducing the quality of conventional television. By limiting the subscription operator to material that would not otherwise be shown on television, the Commission hoped both to prevent such "siphoning" and to enhance the diversity of program offerings on broadcast television as a whole.

* * *

III.   FIRST AMENDMENT

* * *

Applying *O'Brien* here, we cannot say that the pay cable rules were intended to suppress free expression. The narrow purpose exposed by the Commission—protecting the viewing rights of those not served by cable or too poor to pay for cable—is neutral. Indeed, it is not unlike a regulation quieting hecklers or enforcing order on the radio spectrum. As in those situations, the conduct regulated would otherwise blot out transmission of a message, regardless of its content, to at least a segment of its potential audience. Also like those cases, both those whose conduct is restrained by the regulation and those who benefit by it have First Amendment rights, although here the right is one to receive, rather than transmit, information. True, unlike the heckler the person able to pay for cable television does not interrupt transmission of a message to all who might hear it; specifically, he does not affect his own First Amendment rights or those of others served by cable. That only one segment of an audience benefits from the pay cable rules does not, however, at least in this case, require a different result for, as we shall now show, execution of the Commission's purpose in favoring one group would not necessarily deny material to the other or affect the range of ideas that are presented to either group.

* * *

The speech of cablecasters, while undoubtedly inhibited, is similarly free from restrictions abridging freedom of expression. The rules clearly have no effect on traditional broadcast modes of persuasive speech such as news broadcasts or editorials. Nor do they affect films which the cablecaster has himself produced. Moreover, they do not even affect the cablecaster's ability to exhibit the work of others so long as no per-channel or per-program fee is charged. The sole effect of the rules is to prohibit the cablecaster from exhibiting for a separate fee the artistic work of others. Finally, no claim is made here that this narrow exclusion prevents the cablecaster from making an effective presentation of his views, nor for that matter is any claim made that cablecaster "endorsement" of the views of a particular film adds importantly to the message of the filmmaker.

Despite our conclusion that content regulations are not at issue here, we nonetheless hold that the rules as promulgated and as put into effect by the Commission cannot be squared with *O'Brien's* other requirements and, consequently, they violate the First Amendment. The no-advertising and 90–percent rules clearly violate *O'Brien's* first criterion. Not only do they serve no "important or substantial . . . interest," they serve no purpose which will withstand scrutiny on this record. The sports and features films rules fare no better. We have already concluded that the Commission has not put itself in a position to know whether the alleged siphoning phenomenon is a real or merely a fanciful threat to those not served by cable. Instead, the Commission has indulged in speculation and innuendo. *O'Brien* requires that "an important or substantial governmental interest" be demonstrated, however—a requirement which translates in the rulemaking context into a record that convincingly shows a problem to exist and that relates the proffered solution to the statutory mandate of the agency. The record before us fails on both scores. Moreover, we doubt that the Commission's interest in preventing delay of motion picture broadcasts could be shown to be important or substantial on any record.

Finally, we think the strategy the Commission has pursued in implementing its interest in preventing siphoning creates a restriction "greater than is essential to the furtherance of that interest." *Id.* The Commission's approach to preserving the present quantity and quality levels of broadcast television has not been to set such levels directly. Instead, the Commission has sought to divide film and sports material into that suitable for broadcasting and that which can be shown, if at all, only on cable, and has left broadcasters free to choose from among the former without any competition from cable television. Even assuming that such a scheme is reasonable, a position contested by a number of petitioners, it is nonetheless very clear that, if such a strategy is to be used, the rules must be closely tailored to the end to be achieved so that material not broadcast (because it is unsuitable or unsalable) is readily available to cablecasters. Otherwise the rules will curtail the flow of programming to those served by cable and willing to pay for it, with a consequent loss of diversity and unnecessary restriction of the First Amendment rights of producers, cablecasters, and viewers.

2. DEVELOPMENT OF DOCTRINE

As the cable industry developed and litigation increased, a few general propositions began to come clear. The two main areas of dispute were "must carry" signals and "access channels"—both of which will be revisited. To a very real extent, they are mirror images of each other.

The must carry rules require cable television operators to carry all signals deemed to be "local"—a term whose meaning has changed almost a dozen times in the history of cable regulation. The access regulations allow local franchising authorities (usually municipalities) to impose upon cable operators requirements of offering "public," "educational," and/or "governmental" ("PEG") channels for use by third parties. The must carry rules thus require carriage of broadcasters, the PEG franchise provisions other third parties. Since both requirements take away channels on which a cable operator otherwise could display attractive programming, they are quite understandably unpopular with cable operators.

To set the stage for contemporary cases, it thus may be useful to look at some excerpts from early cases involving must carry and PEG access requirements. The District of Columbia Circuit invalidated the FCC's must carry rules twice before; as will be seen (p. 370), the *Turner Broadcasting* case seemed to say that they might be constitutional. The second opinion came in Quincy Cable TV, Inc. v. FCC, 768 F.2d 1434 (D.C.Cir.), 768 F.2d 1434, certiorari denied 476 U.S. 1169, 106 S.Ct. 2889, 90 L.Ed.2d 977 (1986).

In short, here, no less than in *Home Box Office,* the FCC has failed to "put itself in a position to know" whether the problem the rule seeks to cure—the destruction of free, local television—"is a real or merely a fanciful threat." That approach, we have concluded falls far short of the burden the government must affirmatively bear to prove the substantiality of the interest served by the rules. Although in some instances "complete factual support ... for the Commission's judgment or prediction is not possible or required," FCC v. National Citizens Committee for Broadcasting, 436 U.S. 775, 813, 98 S.Ct. 2096, 2121, 56 L.Ed.2d 697 (1978), as we now explain, the particular circumstances of this constitutional challenge make continued deference to the Commission's concededly unsupported determinations plainly inappropriate.

We note first that, in sharp and unexplained contrast to its defense of the must-carry rules, the Commission itself now applies a far more rigorous standard of proof before crediting the broadcast industry's inevitable refrain that regulation is essential to protect it from the deleterious effects of new video technologies. As a matter of explicit agency policy, the Commission will consider such regulation only if presented with "hard evidence" that the new technology "will have a critically adverse effect on existing broadcast service." *DBS Inquiry,* 90 FCC 2d at 689. * * * In light of the Commission's express unwillingness to premise intrusive regulations on unsubstantiated speculation, we find it difficult to sustain the suggestion that we defer to the Commission's admittedly unproven belief that the must-carry rules in fact serve the substantial interest of protecting local broadcasting.

Moreover, this is demonstrably not an instance in which "complete factual support ... for the Commission's judgment or prediction is not possible...." *FCC v. National Citizens Committee for Broadcasting, supra,* 436 U.S. at 814, 98 S.Ct. at 2121. When the FCC first asserted jurisdiction 20 years ago, the cable industry was in its infancy and its impact on local broadcasting could not be gauged with accuracy. In that historical context, courts faced with nonconstitutional claims concerning the breadth of the FCC's jurisdiction consistently and appropriately deferred to the Commission's admittedly speculative fears that the advent of cable television would displace local broadcasting. Nearly two decades have now passed, and the Commission has shown itself capable of the most sophisticated analysis of the effects of cable in conventional television. See *Economic Inquiry Report,* 71 FCC 2d at 673. And yet, even in the context in of a serious constitutional challenge, a context in which it must affirmatively bear the burden of proof, it continues to rely on precisely the kind of "speculative allegations" it expressly refuses to credit elsewhere. At some point, especially where First Amendment rights are at stake, the Commission must do more than ask us to defer to its "more or less intuitive model" and "collective instinct" to sustain its assertion that a rule is both necessary and important. Where, as here, the Commission itself has expressly acknowledged that its regulatory premises are susceptible of empirical proof and, in fact, has demanded such proof as a prerequisite of regulation in analogous contexts, we believe that point has passed.

* * *

B. *The Congruence Between Means and Ends*

Even were we to conclude that the Commission adequately demonstrated the substantiality of the interest served by the must-carry rules, we could uphold their validity only if the restriction on activity protected by the First Amendment were "no greater than is essential to the furtherance of that interest." * * *

Fully aware of the breadth of the agency's discretion and the concomitant limits on the scope of our review, our analysis leaves us with no doubt that the must-carry rules, as currently drafted, represent a "fatally overbroad response" to the perceived fear that cable will displace free, local television. * * *

1.

In the Commission's own words, the must-carry rules are designed to "maintain the availability of local broadcast service to both those who [are] cable subscribers and those who [are] not." * * *

Thus, and the distinction is critical, the rules seek to protect local broadcasting and not local broadcasters. * * *

2.

But, if the goal is to preserve "localism" and not "local broadcasters," the must-carry rules are "grossly" overinclusive. The rules indiscriminately protect each and every broadcaster regardless of the quantity of local service available in the community and irrespective of the number of local outlets already carried by the cable operator. The 18th station is entitled to carriage no less than the first even if its programming is virtually duplicative of the viewing fare already transmitted over the cable system. Indeed, it is entitled to carriage even if it carries no local programming at all.[52]

* * *

It may well be that in some circumstances requiring carriage of the 18th broadcast station is consistent with the objective of preserving free, community-oriented television. And we certainly do not mean to imply that there is such a thing as too many communicative outlets in a given community. It is not the fact of the 18th station that is troubling, but the fact that it is guaranteed a channel even if carriage effectively bumps a cable programmer, regardless of the extent it impinges on the cable operator's editorial autonomy, and irrespective of whether it thwarts viewer preferences. Given the substantial First Amendment costs implicit in this sweeping guarantee, the Commission must make some effort to move beyond the amorphous in defining the interest served by the must-carry rules. * * *

3.

In addition to their complete indifference to the quantity of local television already available either over the air or on the cable system itself, the rules' overinclusiveness lies in their indiscriminate protection of every broadcaster regardless of whether or to what degree the affected cable system poses a threat to its economic well-being. Indeed, the Commission has expressly taken the position that the "financial health" of the broadcaster is irrelevant to its absolute right to occupy a channel on the local cable system. *First Report and Order*, 38 FCC at 713. This blanket protection, by sweeping even the most financially secure broadcaster under the rules' beneficent mantle, reaches well beyond the rules' asserted objective of assuring

---

52. This prospect is by no means entirely academic. Under the Commission's recently revised approach, broadcast licensees need no longer provide specified amounts of community-oriented programming, but instead can rely, at least in part, on the offerings of other local stations to satisfy their programming obligations. * * * Perhaps spurred by this change, several broadcasters have announced plans to provide a full day of music videos, programming that, of course, is devoid of any local orientation at all. * * *

that the advent of cable technology not undermine the financial viability of community-oriented, free television.

* * *

IV. CONCLUSION

Regulation of emerging video technologies requires a delicate balancing of competing interest[s]. On the one hand, a regulatory framework that throttles the growth of new media or otherwise limits the number and variety of outlets for expression is likely to run afoul of the First Amendment's central mission of assuring "the widest possible dissemination of information from diverse and antagonistic sources," * * *. On the other hand, unfettered growth of new video services may well threaten other deeply ingrained societal values. In particular, the complete displacement of expressive outlets attuned to the needs and concerns of the communities they serve not only would contravene a long-standing historical tradition of a locally oriented press but might itself disserve the objective of diversity.

The *Preferred* case presented the Supreme Court with an opportunity to establish a First Amendment standard for cable television. The Court chose instead to issue a somewhat cryptic opinion that merely confirmed the existence of significant First Amendment concerns in the context of cable television regulation. Los Angeles v. Preferred Communications, Inc., 476 U.S. 488, 106 S.Ct. 2034, 90 L.Ed.2d 480 (1986). Then–Justice Rehnquist, writing for the Court, concluded as follows:

We agree with the Court of Appeals that respondent's complaint should not have been dismissed, and we therefore affirm the judgment of that court; but we do so on a narrower ground than the one taken by it. The well pleaded facts in the complaint include allegations of sufficient excess physical capacity and economic demand for cable television operators in the area which respondent sought to serve. The City, while admitting the existence of excess physical capacity on the utility poles, the rights-of-way, and the like, justifies the limit on franchises in terms of minimizing the demand that cable systems make for the use of public property. * * *

We of course take the well-pleaded allegations of the complaint as true for the purpose of a motion to dismiss. * * * We are unwilling to decide the legal questions posed by the parties without a more thoroughly developed record of proceedings in which the parties have an opportunity to prove those disputed factual assertions upon which they rely.

We do think that the activities in which respondent allegedly seeks to engage plainly implicate First Amendment interests. * * * [T]hrough original programming or by exercising editorial discretion over which stations or programs to include in its repertoire, respondent seeks to communicate messages on a wide variety of topics and in a wide variety of formats. We recently noted that cable operators exercise "a significant amount of editorial discretion regarding what their programming will include." Cable television partakes of some of the aspects of speech and the communication of ideas as do the traditional enterprises of newspaper and book publishers, public speakers and pamphleteers. Respondent's proposed activities would seem to implicate First Amendment interests as do the activities of wireless broadcasters, which were found to fall within the ambit of the First Amendment in *Red Lion Broadcasting Co. v. FCC,* even though the free speech aspects of the wireless broadcasters' claim were found to be outweighed by the government interests in regulating by reason of the scarcity of available frequencies.

Of course, the conclusion that respondent's factual allegations implicate protected speech does not end the inquiry. "Even protected speech is not equally permissible in all places and at all times." * * * Moreover, where speech and conduct are joined in a single course of action, the First Amendment values must be balanced against competing societal interests. We do not think, however, that it is desirable to express any more detailed views on the proper resolution of the First Amendment question raised by the respondent's complaint and the City's responses to it without a fuller development of the disputed issues in the case. We think that we may know more than we know now about how the constitutional issues should be resolved when we know more about the present uses of the public utility poles and rights-of-way and how respondent proposes to install and maintain its facilities on them.

Justice Blackmun, joined by Justices Marshall and O'Connor, in a short concurring opinion underscored that the Court was not deciding anything beyond the relevance of the First Amendment:

I join the Court's opinion on the understanding that it leaves open the question of the proper standard for judging First Amendment challenges to a municipality's restriction of access to cable facilities. Different communications media are treated differently for First Amendment purposes. * * * In assessing First Amendment claims concerning cable access, the Court must determine whether the characteristics of cable television make it sufficiently analogous to another medium to warrant application of an already existing standard or whether those characteristics require a new analysis. As this case arises out of a motion to dismiss, we lack factual information about the nature of cable television. Recognizing these considerations, * * * the Court does not attempt to choose or justify any particular standard. It simply concludes that, in challenging Los Angeles' policy of exclusivity in cable franchising, respondent alleges a cognizable First Amendment claim.

Before *Preferred,* was there any doubt that cable television "plainly implicate[s] First Amendment interests"? Did the Supreme Court do anything more than frame the question for decision?

Contrast the *Quincy* court's reasoning with that just a few years before in a case upholding the constitutionality of state PEG access rules. Berkshire Cablevision of Rhode Island, Inc. v. Burke, 571 F.Supp. 976 (D.R.I.1983), vacated as moot 773 F. 2d 382 (1st Cir.1985).

This case involves important questions concerning the First Amendment rights of cable television operators. At issue is the constitutionality of regulations promulgated by the Rhode Island Division of Public Utilities and Carriers ("DPUC"); the contested features require:

1.   the cable television operator to provide, of the total available channels, at least one channel each for access by members of the public, educational institutions and government agencies;

2.   the cable television operator to construct an institutional/industrial network which will permit origination and transmission, for a fee, of programming at institutions and public buildings, including schools and religious institutions within the service territory.

The plaintiff, Berkshire Cablevision of Rhode Island, Inc. ("Berkshire"), is an applicant for a certificate to provide cable television service to Newport County, Rhode Island. It seeks a declaration that the regulations are unconstitutional as violative of the First and Fourteenth Amendments to the United States Constitution, and a permanent injunction prohibiting any hearings thereunder.

The defendant Edward Burke, Administrator of the DPUC, is responsible for the regulation of cable television in Rhode Island and is sued in his official capacity.

For the reasons which follow, the injunction and declaration of unconstitutionality are denied.

* * *

[The court here reviews Midwest Video Corp. v. FCC, 571 F.2d 1025 (8th Cir.1978), affirmed 440 U.S. 689, 99 S.Ct. 1435, 59 L.Ed.2d 692 (1979) and Home Box Office, Inc. v. FCC, 567 F.2d 9 (D.C.Cir.1977), cert. denied 434 U.S. 829, 98 S.Ct. 111, 54 L.Ed.2d 89, noting that in both cases the courts rejected the application of the "broadcast" standard of First Amendment jurisprudence to cable television.]

With all due deference to the Eighth and District of Columbia Circuits, I respectfully disagree with their analysis of the constitutionality of the access requirements for cable television systems. Newspapers and cable television cannot be equated. More to the point, the two media are constitutionally distinguishable. Although a cable operator's selection of its programming is similar to the editorial function of a newspaper publisher or a television broadcaster, this similarity does not mean that each medium is entitled to the same measure of First Amendment protection. * * *

CATV and newspapers first differ in that only the latter have historically operated virtually free from any form of government control over their content.[2] As Justice White noted in his concurrence in *Miami Herald Publishing Co. v. Tornillo*: "According to our accepted jurisprudence, the First Amendment erects a virtually insurmountable barrier between government and the print media so far as government tampering, in advance of publication, where news and editorial content is concerned." It was in this historical setting that the Tornillo court struck down the Florida right-of-access law.

Cable television does not have a similar history of freedom from government regulation over either its operations or the content of its programming. Indeed, government franchising of the cable television industry is virtually indispensable. For example, since constructing a cable television system requires use of the public streets or telephone poles, the government has a substantial interest in limiting the number of cable operators who build cable systems.

Of course, the flip side to government franchising is that it insulates cable operators from unnecessary competition. The award of a franchise serves as a rational way of choosing which cable operator will provide cable television service within a particular service area. Cable operators often compete for a cable franchise but very rarely develop competing cable systems for the same service area. Such a franchising system recognizes the economic realities of the cable industry, which, as a practical matter, create a "natural monopoly" for the first cable operator to construct a cable system in a given service area. Testimony in this case established that to construct the Newport County cable system would cost approximately seven million dollars. Because of these start-up costs and the nature of the cable television market, cable systems have operated largely free from competition.

* * *

* * * [O]ne basic issue in the instant case is whether or not economic "scarcity" is a constitutionally sufficient rationale for the regulation of cable television. It is the opinion of this court that the Tenth Circuit has developed the more sensible approach to the question. [See Community Communications Co. v. City of Boulder, 660 F.2d 1370 (10th Cir.1981), cert. dismissed 456 U.S. 1001, 102 S.Ct. 2287, 73 L.Ed.2d 1296 (1982) (concluding that cable's "economic monopoly" provided constitutional justification for some added degree of regulation).] While it is true that the Supreme Court has rejected economic scarcity as a basis for the regulation of newspapers, the lack of any access requirement for newspapers

---

2. Newspapers are subject, however, to antitrust laws, Associated Press v. United States, 326 U.S. 1, 65 S.Ct. 1416, 89 L.Ed. 2013 (1945), labor laws, Associated Press v. NLRB, 301 U.S. 103, 57 S.Ct. 650, 81 L.Ed. 953 (1937), and "ordinary forms of taxation." Grosjean v. American Press Co., 297 U.S. 233, 250, 56 S.Ct. 444, 449, 80 L.Ed. 660 (1936).

simply does not prevent a member of the general public from expressing his opinions *in that same medium,* which in such a case is print, of course. Any person may distribute a written message in the form of a leaflet, pamphlet, or other relatively inexpensive form of "publication." In contrast, a resident of Newport County who does not have seven million dollars to develop his own cable system is shut out of that medium with no way to express his ideas with the widely acknowledged power of the small screen. Quite frankly, I am unwilling to say that the Supreme Court would ignore this distinction were the issue to come before it.

The result is that *Red Lion,* the seminal case of contemporary communications law, retains its vitality in the high-tech world of cable television. To be sure, the scarcity rationale for governmental regulation here takes a somewhat different form, but the goal remains the same as in 1969: to *promote* the First Amendment by making a powerful communications medium available to as many of our citizens as is reasonably possible. For this court, at least, scarcity is scarcity—its particular source, whether "physical" or "economic,"[10] does not matter if its effect is to remove from all but a small group an important means of expressing ideas.

* * *

Rhode Island's mandatory access rules are content-neutral. The regulations mandate that all individuals be given the opportunity to appear on cable television on a nondiscriminatory first-come, first-served basis. While the access regulations are not intended to restrict the free speech rights of cable operators, their incidental effect is to limit cable operators' editorial control over their channels. Accordingly, the Court concludes the regulations must be examined under the test enunciated in *United States v. O'Brien.*

The mandatory access requirements serve substantial governmental interests. The regulations are intended to assure community participation in cable television production and programming. It has been noted that "[i]f cable is to become a constructive force in our national life, it must be open to all Americans. There must be relatively easy access . . . for those who wish to promote their ideas, state their views, or sell their goods and services. . . . This unfettered flow of information is central to freedom of speech and freedom of the press which have been described correctly as the freedoms upon which all of our other rights depend." Cabinet Committee on Cable Communications, [Report to the President, CABLE at 19 (1974)] * * * Furthermore, enabling all segments of society to participate in cable television programming promotes the

---

10. Still other types of medium "scarcity" are at least theoretically possible to justify content regulation. For example, a cable system guaranteed an exclusive franchise for a particular area by the appropriate government agency would establish what might be labeled "legal" scarcity. That is, other potential speakers, even those with sufficient funds to establish their own cable systems, would be shut out of the market, in this case by law.

"First Amendment goal of producing an informed public capable of conducting its own affairs...." *Red Lion,* 395 U.S. at 392, 89 S.Ct. at 1807.

The incidental restriction of mandatory access requirements on cable operators' First Amendment freedoms is not greater than is essential to the furtherance of these governmental objectives. Rhode Island requires cable operators only to set aside no more than seven of their 50 or more channels for public access. Cable operators retain complete editorial control over the remaining channels and can use any of these channels to express their own views. Mandatory access regulations thus result in only a minimal intrusion on cable operators' First Amendment activities.

Mandatory access requirements are even less intrusive on First Amendment freedoms than the fairness doctrine upheld by the Supreme Court in *Red Lion.* Because the fairness doctrine requires broadcasters to present both sides of every issue of public importance, broadcasters may choose to avoid coverage of controversial issues rather than be forced to devote considerable time to opposition spokesmen. Mandatory access requirements, by contrast, do not pose such a threat; they require only that all individuals be given an opportunity to air their views on a first-come, first-served basis. Access requirements, therefore, further, rather than inhibit, the presentation of important, controversial issues.

In sum, the mandatory access requirements are a sensible accommodation of the rights of individuals to express themselves, the editorial freedom of cable television operators and the rights of viewers to receive information. The regulations recognize "the legitimate claims of those unable to gain access ... for expression of their views." *Red Lion.* Accordingly, the Court holds that Rhode Island's mandatory access regulations do not violate the First Amendment.

* * *

Notes and Questions

1. Although the court of appeals vacated the *Berkshire* decision as moot because the plaintiff abandoned its effort to secure a cable franchise, 773 F.2d 382 (1st Cir.1985), the district court's opinion is cited often by proponents of access requirements.

2. Should the fact that a medium has not historically been free from government regulation affect the degree of constitutional protection to which it is entitled? In a footnote omitted here, the *Berkshire* court argues in essence that the special protection afforded to newspapers is an historical anomaly that developed to preserve the contributions of reporters and editors to vigorous public debate. Also, although the district court does not mention the fact, most "newspapers" at the time of the Revolution were short, weekly, newsletter type publications, owned by splinter political parties. To a very real extent, regulation of these publications thus was a direct attack on political organizations. The judge notes that the Supreme

Court has refused to extend the reasoning of *Tornillo* to privately owned shopping centers (which, the Supreme Court has held, are not protected by the First Amendment from a state law requirement that they provide access for leafletting on their premises). See PruneYard Shopping Center v. Robins, 447 U.S. 74, 100 S.Ct. 2035, 64 L.Ed.2d 741 (1980). Is a cable system more like a shopping center or a newspaper in constitutionally relevant respects?

3. The court in *Berkshire* disagrees with the Eighth and District of Columbia Circuits, both of which concluded that the "scarcity" rationale applicable to broadcasting cannot be used to justify regulation of cable television. "Economic scarcity," it says, is a constitutional justification for the access regulations challenged by the plaintiff. Note the observation that "government franchising * * * insulates cable operators from unnecessary competition." Is the government keeping out only "unnecessary" competition, or is it creating the monopoly that gives rise to the court's constitutional "scarcity" analysis? If cable is a "natural monopoly," as is accepted by the Tenth Circuit in *Community Communications* (see also Omega Satellite Products Co. v. City of Indianapolis, 694 F.2d 119 (7th Cir.1982)), does that constitutionally justify access regulation?

Is it persuasive to argue, as in *Berkshire,* that scarcity of newspapers does not justify a newspaper access requirement because anyone can distribute a leaflet, but that scarcity of cable television is different, because few people have the resources to operate a cable system? What if Newport County were served by an LPTV station that accepted third-party programming? Does it matter that almost any individual can buy or rent a home video camera to produce programming that is the equivalent of a "video leaflet" and distribute it to any viewer with access to a VCR? If, as the *Berkshire* court states, *Red Lion* is intended to "mak[e] a powerful communications medium available to as many citizens as is reasonably possible," why does it not apply to newspapers? Is it because leaflets are an adequate substitute for an article in a newspaper? Are home-produced video cassettes any more or less adequate substitutes for cable television programming? Can you think of some better justification for the access requirements upheld in *Berkshire?*

4. Should access regulations be tested under the four-part standard of *O'Brien?* Does a regulation that requires that one form of channel use (nondiscriminatory public access) be substituted for another (a service of the cable operator's choice) impose only an "incidental" burden on speech? Should access regulations be considered "time, place, and manner" rules that are properly applied to public forums? Why is cable television a public forum? If a cable operator that must set-aside one or more access channels cannot carry a particular programming service because of limited channel capacity of its system, have the access regulations "[left] open ample alternative channels of communication"?

5. When the Supreme Court had an opportunity to address the constitutionality of access requirements, it failed to reach the issue, deciding only that the Eighth Circuit Court of Appeals had correctly concluded that the FCC lacked statutory authority to impose such requirements. The Court noted, however, that the First Amendment questions were "not frivolous." FCC v. Midwest Video Corp., 440 U.S. 689, 708 n. 19, 99 S.Ct. 1435, 1446 n. 19, 59 L.Ed.2d 692 (1979).

6. As the *Berkshire* court notes, the Eighth Circuit drew a constitutional distinction between mandatory access and local origination ("LO") requirements. It concluded that the latter were less objectionable because "[t]he cable operator retained ultimate control over who used his facilities and which programs he would actually air." See *Midwest Video*, 571 F.2d at 1055. Do you agree or disagree with the distinction? Is the distinction more or less valid than the distinction between the fairness doctrine obligations upheld in *Red Lion* and the access requirements invalidated in *CBS v. DNC*? Is *CBS v. FCC* relevant?

Another court of appeals upheld the constitutionality of local access requirements in Chicago Cable Communications v. Chicago Cable Comm'n, 879 F.2d 1540 (7th Cir.1989). The case involved a challenge to the Chicago Cable Commission's decision to fine three affiliated cable television service corporations (collectively, "CCTV") $60,000 for violating the LO provisions of their identical franchise agreements with the City. Those agreements required the franchisees both to produce and to show a certain amount of LO programming per week. (During the relevant period, CCTV was to program and transmit four-and-one-half hours of LO programming each week.) CCTV, together with another Chicago franchisee, was also required to pledge up to $6,000,000 to produce this programming for 15 years and to equip and staff an LO production facility. CCTV was required to submit to the Commission monthly reports on its LO scheduling. After some controversy about whether CCTV was meeting its LO obligations, the Commission issued a notice of violation. CCTV disputed the Commission's claims, but the Commission, after a hearing, voted to fine CCTV.

(a) On appeal, CCTV argued, among other things, that the LO rules violated the First Amendment. The court rejected CCTV's First Amendment arguments:

> The court below concluded that the appropriate framework for analysis in this case was provided by *United States v. O'Brien.*

> CCTV's scheduling plainly implicates First Amendment interests, for cable operators exercise "a significant amount of editorial discretion regarding what their programming will include." * * * We adhere to our position that "there are enough differences between cable television and the non-television media to allow more government regulation of the former." *Omega Satellite Prod.* * * * As other courts have held, *O'Brien* is an appropriate standard-bearer for dealing with questions of local regulation of cable television. This is especially so here, where CCTV was only required to present four and one-half hours weekly of local origin programming.

> Our adoption of an *O'Brien* test in the cable context does not justify abandoning First Amendment scrutiny due to the fact that cable operators require use of a public right of way or that the "natural monopoly characteristics" of cable create economic constraints on competitors comparable to the physical constraints imposed by the limited size of the electromagnetic spectrum. * * *

> A proper analysis under *O'Brien* begins with an appraisal of whether the interest to be served by a governmental measure is truly substan-

tial.* If it is, the next relevant step is to determine the fact-based issue of whether the means chosen are congruent with the desired end, or whether they are too broadly tailored to pass constitutional muster. Since the municipal code and franchise requirement's LO requirements implicate the second and fourth parts of the *O'Brien* test, we now proceed to show that they have been met by defendants.

1. *Substantiality of Governmental Interest*

The Commission and City contend that these minimal LO rules serve the interest of preserving free, locally oriented television and provide an outlet for community expression and choice of programming. The four and one-half hour local programming requirement is said to improve communications between the citizens and the City as well as encouraging participation of minorities in the economic opportunities created by cable television. On the other hand, CCTV claims that there is no governmental interest furthered by regulating the content of LO programming.

Yet substantial governmental interests are at stake and fostered by LO programming requirements. In *United States v. Midwest Video Corp.*, the Court held that the Federal Communications Commission could require cable operators to have facilities available for local production. * * * This origination rule would reasonably further the goals of "increasing the number of outlets for community self-expression and augmenting the public's choice of programs * * *." Similarly, the LO requirements in this case assure community participation in the production and programming of cable television.

Promotion of community self-expression can increase direct communication between residents by featuring topics of local concern. Encouragement of "localism" certainly qualifies as an important or substantial interest. * * *

An additional interest fostered by the defendants' LO requirement is the provision of jobs for residents of Chicago. Production of programming in the City provides career opportunities as well as potential internships for students studying communications at local schools. All of the above objectives of the LO rules are important and substantial concerns of the City, thereby satisfying the relevant second prong of *O'Brien*.

2. *The Congruence Between Means and Ends*

The pertinent fourth tier of the *O'Brien* test focuses on the congruence between the means chosen by the Commission to regulate cable television and the end it seeks to achieve. While the Commission has adequately demonstrated the substantiality of the interest served by the LO rules, their validity also depends on whether these restrictions were "no greater than is essential to the furtherance of that interest." *Quincy Cable*, * * *. Because the municipal code's and franchise agreement's

---

* The court accepted the district court's conclusion that the defendants had the constitutional power to adopt the regulations in question and had acted in furtherance of an interest unrelated to the suppression of free expression—the "first" and "third" prongs of the *O'Brien* test.—Ed.

LO requirements may be characterized as content-related, they "may be sustained only if the government can show that the regulation is a precisely drawn means of serving a compelling state interest." Or, put another way, is each of the restrictions no greater than is essential to the furtherance of that interest?

* * *

Cable programming, like other forms of the electronic media, is an economically scarce medium. * * * As a result the government, which serves as the representative of cable customers, is duty-bound to recognize the effects of "medium scarcity" by ensuring that the few programmers who are granted a franchise make optimum use of it. With this in mind, it is within the City's rights, arguably its responsibilities, to proffer some requirements guaranteeing that the cable customers are, to the extent possible, accorded a range of programming from the franchisee, since the cable viewing public has no other channel to which to turn.

Finally, it is worth noting that CCTV is required to broadcast just four and a half hours of local origination programming per week. The City is not seeking a dominant interest in CCTV's cable programming, nor even a substantial interest, but simply a few hours a week. * * * CCTV is not required by the municipal code or franchise agreement to cablecast any specific program, kind of show, or editorial viewpoint. As long as the particular episode is geared to Chicago—be it sports, politics, news, weather, entertainment, etc.—CCTV has full discretion over what it may desire to transmit. This restriction on CCTV's control in meeting the minimal LO requirements does not divest it of discretion * * *. The limited restriction at issue is really no greater than essential to further substantial City interests. It cannot be gainsaid that substantial interests of the community are well served by requiring some local programming. Considering the benefits to the community, this four and one-half hour weekly obligation is sufficiently modest to avoid First Amendment prohibition. * * *

Would the court's reasoning support local access, just as much as local origination, requirements? What is the basis for the court's conclusion that a substantial governmental interest is being advanced? Would a requirement of six or ten hours of LO each week be narrowly tailored? What about LO on one of thirty-two channels, on a full-time basis? What about one of seventy-two channels?

Can a city make a governmental channel available for full-time use by a commercial entity? When New York tried to do so, the courts were quick to find violations not only of the 1992 Act, but also of the First Amendment. Time Warner Cable of New York City v. New York City, 943 F.Supp. 1357 (S.D.N.Y.1996).

(b) Consider whether the following constitutional analysis of public access applies only to channel set-aside requirements, or whether it also would apply to LO requirements such as those upheld in the *Chicago Cable* case:

* * * The [franchising] Ordinance requires all CTV operators to provide eight leased access channels to unaffiliated persons at negotiated rates. The Ordinance also requires three public and educational channels and two governmental channels ("PEG" access), which the franchisees can satisfy by collaborating to provide a single set of such channels.

Clearly, if such access requirements were applied to the traditional press, such as newspapers, they would violate the First Amendment. * * * This Court has already concluded that the justification for such governmental intrusion into the broadcast media, the physical scarcity of radiowaves, is inapplicable to the instant case. Finding that " 'the analogy [of cable television] to more traditional media is compelling,' "this Court concluded that, except for its impact on the public domain, "the defendant Cities as a matter of law have failed to persuade this Court that there are any other differences attributable to cable television that can justify a degree of First Amendment protection similar to that applied to the broadcast medium."

Accordingly, the rationale in Miami Herald v. Tornillo and Pacific Gas [& Electric Co. v. Public Utilities Com'n of California, 475 U.S. 1, 106 S.Ct. 903, 89 L.Ed.2d 1 (1986) (plurality op.)] applies to the access requirements in the instant case. The Cities attempt to distinguish *Miami Herald* and *Pacific Gas* on the ground that the access requirements in those cases were triggered by the newspapers' content, while the access channels here are imposed automatically on all CTV operators regardless of any other programming they cablecast. The Cities read these cases too narrowly.

Regardless of how the Cities attempt to characterize the access channels, their result is undeniable: a CTV operator will be forced to cablecast material by other speakers that it might otherwise choose not to present. * * * [S]uch forced access has two independent, impermissible effects on a cable operator's right to speak.

First, forcing a speaker to communicate the views of another undoubtedly impacts the content of the speech of the primary speaker. In the case of the traditional press, and in this Court's opinion CTV operators, this impact is inconsistent with the principles of the First Amendment. The Cities cannot deny that the PEG channels, which are directly or indirectly controlled by city government,[3] could very well provide a conduit for criticism of the CTV operator. Even the leased commercial access channels, over which the CTV operators have control, carry the impermissible risk of affecting the programming of the CTV operator.

Admittedly, the access channels provide other cable speakers regular and constant access that is not necessarily dependent on the content of any franchisee's speech. The content sought to be cablecast by the access users, however, will be influenced by what the franchisee cable-

---

3. The content of the government-access channel is obviously under the direct control of the city governments. The Cities do note, however, that an *"independent"* community access organization ("CAO") will regulate the public and educational access channels. A simple reading of the Ordinances' relevant provisions, however, leaves this Court with grave doubts about how "independent" the CAO will be from the City Council and City Manager.

casts (why cablecast programming that is already on another channel?), and the reverse is also certain to be true: the material on the access channels will influence what the franchisee presents on its channels. This indirect effect is no less impermissible than the direct effect of a right-to-reply statute in *Miami Herald.*

The second impermissible effect of forced access channels is an intrusion into a CTV operator's considerable editorial functions, which results regardless of whether the access would force a speaker to forego the communication of a particular opinion or material. * * *

Because the Ordinance's access requirements must be characterized as content-based, they "may be sustained only if the government can show that the regulation is a precisely drawn means of serving a compelling state interest."

The Cities have simply not met this burden. * * * The access channels forced upon plaintiff by the Cities carry the inherent risk that a franchisee's speech will be chilled and the direct, undeniable impact of intruding into the franchisee's editorial control and judgment of what to cablecast and what not to cablecast. Neither result can be tolerated under the First Amendment in the name of an "attitude that government knows best how to fine tune the flow of information to which [the people] have access."

Century Federal, Inc. v. City of Palo Alto, 710 F.Supp. 1552, 1554–55 (N.D.Cal.1987).

Do LO requirements "force" speech? They require a cable operator to carry speech about a particular topic—in general, the community being served. PEG and leased access requirements do not require a cable operator to produce or transmit any type of programming. They simply require that the cable operator refrain from programming one or more channels. Under the reasoning in *Century Federal,* which type of access is constitutionally more offensive? Should LO and public access be distinguished as a constitutional matter? Why?

7. The constitutional analysis may differ for different types of cable television regulations. Consider the following cases, which examine the constitutionality of refusing to grant a franchise to an applicant, rather than merely imposing conditions on the franchise that is to be granted.

(a) Cable television ordinances that limit to one the number of franchises per geographic area were overturned in Group W Cable, Inc. v. City of Santa Cruz, 669 F.Supp. 954 (N.D.Cal.1987), and Century Federal Inc. v. City of Palo Alto, 648 F.Supp. 1465 (N.D.Cal.1986) (*"Century Federal II "*). Are ordinances that require all cable television operators to be franchised, but do not limit the number of franchises that may be granted, equally vulnerable to constitutional attack?

(b) Where, as a result of litigation challenging an exclusive franchise arrangement, additional operators are permitted to begin serving parts of a city or county, what justification is there for continued detailed regulation of cable television? Should the "original" cable system operator, which built its system on the assumption that it would have an exclusive service right, be able to sue a franchising authority for breach of contract? Should it receive damages? Should the original operator be permitted to escape from the terms of its franchise agreement? Is there any constitutional basis for treating the original cable operator differently from subsequent market entrants?

(c) May the "original" operator's franchise contain a "most favored nation" clause, requiring the city to impose the existing franchise's burdens on a new entrant? To give the original operator the benefit of any new deregulatory provisions?

(d) The court in *Century Federal* compared a universal service requirement with a regulation requiring a newspaper or bookstore "to deliver or be located in a particular geographic area of the community." Does the First Amendment prevent a government from seeking to ensure that remote or poor sections of a community are not disadvantaged because of the economics of information delivery? Should the government pay a cable operator to make it financially attractive for the operator to wire remote or poor sections of town? Federal and state governments have developed elaborate schemes for subsidizing the cost of telephone service for low-income individuals and rural residents—so-called "universal service." The justification is that the value of access to the telephone network is increased for all as its reach is extended; in other words, those who would call the subsidized telephone users are benefitted as well by their being subsidized. Is there a related argument that cable television should not be unavailable to those who are unable to pay? Is it like the case for "free" public education?

3. Erie Telecommunications Inc. (ETI) was awarded a franchise in 1980 to provide cable television service to Erie, Pennsylvania. The franchise agreement was typical of urban system franchises awarded at the time. It included provisions requiring payment to the city of an annual franchise fee, the set-aside of certain channel capacity for public access use, the provision of television production equipment and facilities to foster access programming, and the payment of specified amounts to support the access activities. Following passage of the 1984 Cable Act, and after operating under the franchise agreement for some time, ETI sued the city, claiming that certain provisions of the franchise agreement were invalid because they violated the First Amendment. Specifically, ETI claimed that any fees in excess of the cost of regulation represented an unconstitutional tax—or license fee—on speech, and that the various access requirements were unconstitutional. The district court rejected both First Amendment challenges. Erie Telecommunications, Inc. v. City of Erie, 659 F.Supp. 580 (W.D.Pa.1987). It concluded that the franchise fees were permissible charges for the use of public rights-of-way, not taxes having the effect of a prior restraint on speech (and, therefore, not within the Supreme Court's reasoning in the *Minneapolis Star* case, and it upheld the access requirements under the *O'Brien* standard.

The court of appeals affirmed the district court on the narrow ground that ETI had knowingly waived its constitutional rights. 853 F.2d 1084 (3d Cir.1988). The court noted that in 1984, ETI and the city had been parties to litigation brought by an unsuccessful applicant for the Erie cable franchise. In settlement of that lawsuit, all parties, including Erie, executed a complete and comprehensive release of the city from all claims "in any way relating to, directly or indirectly, the franchise together with any and all litigation arising from, or in connection with, said Agreement including, but not limited to, the pending action from the beginning of the world to the date of these presents." Although certain provisions of the franchise agreement might be interpreted to be inconsistent with the 1984 Cable Act, the court said it would not limit the scope of the release to effectuate federal cable television policies.

In the *Chicago Cable* case, the court of appeals distinguished *Erie* and found no barrier to hearing the cable system operator's First Amendment challenge to the LO requirements. The court reasoned as follows:

> [I]n this case the only contract was the initial franchising agreement, a significant distinction from *Erie* [in which there was an express release], and serious reservations arise when a local government with a virtual monopoly on cable access conditions a franchise contract with a cable programmer on a stipulation that the programmer waive certain constitutional rights * * *.

Chicago Cable, 879 F.2d at 1548 n. 6.

A Note and Questions:

In Search of Constitutional Standards for Electronic Mass Media

As illustrated by the cases in this Chapter, the courts have almost unanimously rejected the application of a "broadcast" standard of constitutional protection to cable television. Although the courts—including the Supreme Court—have not provided an entirely clear statement of the standard applicable to broadcast speech, it is apparent that broadcasting receives somewhat less constitutional protection than print or non-spectrum-using speech. In deciding how much less, you might want to consider again the degree to which the *League of Women Voters* decision is more or less protective of broadcast speech than is *Red Lion*.

What additional modicum of protection could—or should—be afforded to broadcast speech? Does—or should—the standard applicable to broadcasting affect the degree of constitutional protection given to cable television? Is a standard of protection a function of deciding how to balance the competing interests in using a medium of mass communication? What about the courts' concerns about economic factors, such as the economic impact of cable television on free broadcast service, and the economics of competition in providing cable service?

Where in this unsettled area of constitutional jurisprudence do cable television and other new video media fit? As we have seen, the only principle widely accepted thus far is that the First Amendment applies differently to media having different characteristics. Do you agree with this assertion as a starting point? What is the basis for such a notion, which admittedly has much practical appeal? And what are the "characteristics" that have constitutional import? Perhaps a court should consider only a stark, distinguishing characteristic, such as the Supreme Court found in 1943 when it concluded that

> [u]nlike other modes of expression, radio inherently is not available to all. This is its unique characteristic, and that is why, unlike other modes of expression, it is subject to governmental regulation.

National Broadcasting Co. v. United States, 319 U.S. 190, 226, 63 S.Ct. 997, 1014, 87 L.Ed. 1344 (1943).

We will consider whether courts should draw First Amendment distinctions among the new media, such as teletext, videotex, MDS, DBS, and SMATV. Should teletext, which uses a portion of a broadcast signal, be treated like traditional broadcast services? Should videotex be treated like a common carrier service because it is distributed over a telephone system? What is MDS, if it looks like broadcast television but uses a non-broadcast radio frequency? Is there any basis for distinguishing between SMATV and cable television? What about distinguishing among DBS, satellite-delivered cable television services (such as Home Box Office), and network television, which is distributed to network-affiliated stations primarily via satellite?

Despite the multiplicity of options for communicating ideas, the courts have tended to apply only two readily identifiable First Amendment standards when considering the constitutionality of a government law or regulation.

The first doctrine is traditional "strict scrutiny" as applied to speakers and the press: invalidation of any content-specific regulation.

The second standard is the four-part *O'Brien* test, on which many courts have relied in order to assess the constitutionality of various cable television regulations. In some instances, the courts may have applied *O'Brien* more broadly than the Supreme Court intended. It is not entirely clear that *O'Brien* has been applied only to regulations that are aimed at the "conduct" aspect of a combined speech and conduct activity. Perhaps this is because the speech and non-speech elements of some activities cannot always be separated—at least not readily. For example, *O'Brien* might be applied more easily to regulation of the construction of a cable television system, than to regulation of channel use or franchise eligibility. Since the *O'Brien* doctrine has received so many different interpretations from the courts, however, it is somewhat difficult to predict how it may apply to a particular situation.

Should *O'Brien* be used as a constitutional standard applicable to certain media, such as cable television, that are thought to deserve somewhat less protection than is afforded by the strict scrutiny approach? Is *O'Brien* more or less protective than *Red Lion?* Than *League of Women Voters?* Recall *Quincy Cable,* in which the court of appeals questioned the propriety of applying *O'Brien* but does not resolve the issue.

The public forum doctrine, although not literally a constitutional "standard," has also been applied in some constitutional cases involving cable television or other electronic media, in an effort to define the terms of the constitutional debate. This standard has been used to judge the constitutionality of government regulations regarding the use of public property for expressive purposes. Under public forum jurisprudence, the courts have identified three classifications for public property: the "traditional public forum," which is property such as parks and street corners that has long been kept open for expressive uses; the "limited public forum," which is property that the government has made or caused to be made available for expressive uses; and the "non-public forum," which is basically all other property. If property is within either of the first two classifications, courts have permitted both content-based regulations that are narrowly tailored to advance a compelling government interest and "reasonable," content-neutral "time, place, and manner" regulations. Property within the third classification may be subjected, so far as the First Amendment is concerned, to almost any type of regulation that is not intended merely to suppress particular speech.

In the case of cable television, public forum analysis can prove useful; utility poles and rights-of-way, which are necessary conduits for cables, are almost always some type of public forum. Regulations on the use of this public property are subject to careful limits that guard against government censorship. See, e.g., Southeastern Promotions, Ltd. v. Conrad, 420 U.S. 546, 95 S.Ct. 1239, 43 L.Ed.2d 448 (1975) (concluding that the government could not refuse to permit the musical "Hair" to be presented in a municipal theater—a public forum—because of concerns that the show's nudity and "obscenity" would be inconsistent with the government's policy of using the theater for "cultural advancement [and] clean and healthful entertainment"). Ultimately, however, public forum analysis is not a dispositive constitutional standard. Once it is decided that the use of a public forum is involved, a court still must determine whether the regulation at issue represents a constitutional assertion of government power. To do this, it will typically apply either strict scrutiny or the *O'Brien* standard.

What the courts have given us is an ill-defined and shifting continuum of constitutional analyses, ranging from a highly suspect view of prior restraints on newspaper publishing to a much more flexible approach to many broadcast regulations—with cable television receiving an intermediate level of treatment. Is there some unifying principle to make sense out of decisions as seemingly disparate as *Red Lion, Tornillo,* and *League of Women Voters,* or *CBS v. DNC* and *CBS v. FCC?* Where in this continuum should the other new electronic media fit? Should we, perhaps, be rethinking the utility of developing a special First Amendment jurisprudence for each medium, and be focusing more closely on finding some clear principles by which to apply the constitutional command that "Congress shall make no law * * * abridging the freedom of speech, or of the press * * * "?

During the middle of the 1990s, for the first time the Supreme Court tried to define First Amendment doctrine for the new media. You can judge the success of its efforts from the following cases.

TURNER BROADCASTING SYSTEM, INC. v. FCC

Supreme Court of the United States, 1994.
512 U.S. 622, 114 S.Ct. 2445, 129 L.Ed.2d 497.

JUSTICE KENNEDY announced the judgment of the Court and delivered the opinion of the Court, except as to Part III–B.

Sections 4 and 5 of the Cable Television Consumer Protection and Competition Act of 1992 require cable television systems to devote a portion of their channels to the transmission of local broadcast television stations. This case presents the question whether these provisions abridge the freedom of speech or of the press, in violation of the First Amendment.

The United States District Court for the District of Columbia granted summary judgment for the United States, holding that the challenged provisions are consistent with the First Amendment. Because issues of material fact remain unresolved in the record as developed thus far, we vacate the District Court's judgment and remand the case for further proceedings.

I

A

The role of cable television in the Nation's communications system has undergone dramatic change over the past 45 years. Given the pace of technological advancement and the increasing convergence between cable and other electronic media, the cable industry today stands at the center of an ongoing telecommunications revolution with still undefined potential to affect the way we communicate and develop our intellectual resources.

[The Court's discussion of the history and characteristics of cable television is omitted.]

* * *

B

* * * At issue in this case is the constitutionality of the so-called must-carry provisions, contained in §§ 4 and 5 of the [Cable Television Competition and Consumer Protection] Act [of 1992, Pub. L. 102–385, 106 Stat. 1460 (1992 Cable Act or Act)], which require cable operators to carry the signals of a specified number of local broadcast television stations.

Section 4 requires carriage of "local commercial television stations," defined to include all full power television broadcasters, other than those qualifying as "noncommercial educational" stations under § 5, that operate within the same television market as the cable system. § 4, 47 U.S.C. §§ 534(b)(1)(B), (h)(1)(A) (1988 ed., Supp. IV). Cable systems with more than 12 active channels, and more than 300 subscribers, are required to set aside up to one-third of their channels for commercial broadcast stations that request carriage. § 534(b)(1)(B). Cable systems with more than 300 subscribers, but only 12 or fewer active channels, must carry the signals of three commercial broadcast stations. § 534(b)(1)(A).

If there are fewer broadcasters requesting carriage than slots made available under the Act, the cable operator is obligated to carry only those broadcasters who make the request. If, however, there are more requesting broadcast stations than slots available, the cable operator is permitted to choose which of these stations it will carry. § 534(b)(2). The broadcast signals carried under this provision must be transmitted on a continuous, uninterrupted basis, § 534(b)(3), and must be placed in the same numerical channel position as when broadcast over the air. § 534(b)(6). Further, subject to a few exceptions, a cable operator may not charge a fee for carrying broadcast signals in fulfillment of its must-carry obligations. § 534(b)(10).*

Section 5 of the Act imposes similar requirements regarding the carriage of local public broadcast television stations, referred to in the Act as local "noncommercial educational television stations." 47 U.S.C. § 535(a) (1988 ed., Supp. IV). A cable system with 12 or fewer channels must carry one of these stations; a system of between 13 and 36 channels must carry between one and three; and a system with more than 36 channels must carry each local public broadcast station requesting carriage. §§ 535(b)(2)(A), (b)(3)(A), (b)(3)(D). The Act requires a cable operator to import distant signals in certain circumstances but provides protection against substantial duplication of local noncommercial educational stations. See §§ 535(b)(3)(B),(e). As with commercial broadcast stations, § 5 requires cable system operators to carry the program schedule of the public broadcast station in its entirety and at its same over-the-air channel position. §§ 535(g)(1),(g)(5).

Taken together, therefore, §§ 4 and 5 subject all but the smallest cable systems nationwide to must-carry obligations, and confer must-carry privileges on all full power broadcasters operating within the same television market as a qualified cable system.

C

Congress enacted the 1992 Cable Act after conducting three years of hearings on the structure and operation of the cable television industry. * * *. The conclusions Congress drew from its factfinding process are recited in the text of the Act itself. See §§ 2(a)(1)-(21). In brief, Congress found that the physical characteristics of cable transmission, compounded by the increasing concentration of economic power in the cable industry, are endangering the ability of over-the-air broadcast television stations to compete for a viewing audience and thus for necessary operating revenues. Congress determined that regulation of the market for video programming was necessary to correct this competitive imbalance.

In particular, Congress found that over 60 percent of the households with television sets subscribe to cable, § 2(a)(3), and for these households cable has replaced over-the-air broadcast television as the primary provider of video programming. § 2(a)(17). This is so, Congress found, because "most subscribers to cable television systems do not or cannot maintain antennas to receive broadcast television services, do not have input selector switches to convert from a cable to antenna reception system, or cannot otherwise receive broadcast television services." *Ibid.* In addition, Congress concluded that due to "local franchising requirements and the extraordinary expense of constructing more than one

---

* Cable operators have an alternative to must-carry, by negotiating with broadcasters for "retransmission consent." Usually cable operators have traded channels for new satellite signals in exchange for con- sent. The statute was upheld in Time Warner v. FCC, 56 F. 3d 151 (D.C.Cir.1995), cert. denied ___ U.S. ___, 116 S. Ct. 911, 133 L.Ed.2d 842 (1996)—Ed.

cable television system to serve a particular geographic area," the overwhelming majority of cable operators exercise a monopoly over cable service. § 2(a)(2). "The result," Congress determined, "is undue market power for the cable operator as compared to that of consumers and video programmers." *Ibid.*

According to Congress, this market position gives cable operators the power and the incentive to harm broadcast competitors. The power derives from the cable operator's ability, as owner of the transmission facility, to "terminate the retransmission of the broadcast signal, refuse to carry new signals, or reposition a broadcast signal to a disadvantageous channel position." § 2(a)(15). The incentive derives from the economic reality that "cable television systems and broadcast television stations increasingly compete for television advertising revenues." § 2(a)(14). By refusing carriage of broadcasters' signals, cable operators, as a practical matter, can reduce the number of households that have access to the broadcasters' programming, and thereby capture advertising dollars that would otherwise go to broadcast stations. § 2(a)(15).

Congress found, in addition, that increased vertical integration in the cable industry is making it even harder for broadcasters to secure carriage on cable systems, because cable operators have a financial incentive to favor their affiliated programmers. § 2(a)(5). Congress also determined that the cable industry is characterized by horizontal concentration, with many cable operators sharing common ownership. This has resulted in greater "barriers to entry for new programmers and a reduction in the number of media voices available to consumers." § 2(a)(4).

In light of these technological and economic conditions, Congress concluded that unless cable operators are required to carry local broadcast stations, "there is a substantial likelihood that ... additional local broadcast signals will be deleted, repositioned, or not carried," § 2(a)(15); the "marked shift in market share" from broadcast to cable will continue to erode the advertising revenue base which sustains free local broadcast television, §§ 2(a)(13)-(14); and that, as a consequence, "the economic viability of free local broadcast television and its ability to originate quality local programming will be seriously jeopardized." § 2(a)(16).

* * *

II

There can be no disagreement on an initial premise: Cable programmers and cable operators engage in and transmit speech, and they are entitled to the protection of the speech and press provisions of the First Amendment. Through "original programming or by exercising editorial discretion over which stations or programs to include in its repertoire," cable programmers and operators "seek to communicate messages on a wide variety of topics and in a wide variety of formats." *Los Angeles v. Preferred Communications, Inc.*, 476 U.S. 488, 494, 90 L. Ed. 2d 480, 106

S. Ct. 2034 (1986). By requiring cable systems to set aside a portion of their channels for local broadcasters, the must-carry rules regulate cable speech in two respects: The rules reduce the number of channels over which cable operators exercise unfettered control, and they render it more difficult for cable programmers to compete for carriage on the limited channels remaining. Nevertheless, because not every interference with speech triggers the same degree of scrutiny under the First Amendment, we must decide at the outset the level of scrutiny applicable to the must-carry provisions.

A

We address first the Government's contention that regulation of cable television should be analyzed under the same First Amendment standard that applies to regulation of broadcast television. It is true that our cases have permitted more intrusive regulation of broadcast speakers than of speakers in other media. * * *. But the rationale for applying a less rigorous standard of First Amendment scrutiny to broadcast regulation, whatever its validity in the cases elaborating it, does not apply in the context of cable regulation.

The justification for our distinct approach to broadcast regulation rests upon the unique physical limitations of the broadcast medium. See *FCC v. League of Women Voters of Cal.*, 468 U.S. 364, 377, 82 L. Ed. 2d 278, 104 S. Ct. 3106 (1984); * * *. * * * The scarcity of broadcast frequencies * * * required the establishment of some regulatory mechanism to divide the electromagnetic spectrum and assign specific frequencies to particular broadcasters. * * *

Although courts and commentators have criticized the scarcity rationale since its inception, we have declined to question its continuing validity as support for our broadcast jurisprudence, and see no reason to do so here. The broadcast cases are inapposite in the present context because cable television does not suffer from the inherent limitations that characterize the broadcast medium. Indeed, given the rapid advances in fiber optics and digital compression technology, soon there may be no practical limitation on the number of speakers who may use the cable medium. Nor is there any danger of physical interference between two cable speakers attempting to share the same channel. In light of these fundamental technological differences between broadcast and cable transmission, application of the more relaxed standard of scrutiny adopted in *Red Lion* and the other broadcast cases is inapt when determining the First Amendment validity of cable regulation. * * *

This is not to say that the unique physical characteristics of cable transmission should be ignored when determining the constitutionality of regulations affecting cable speech. They should not. * * *. But whatever relevance these physical characteristics may have in the evaluation of particular cable regulations, they do not require the alteration of settled principles of our First Amendment jurisprudence.

Although the Government acknowledges the substantial technological differences between broadcast and cable, * * *, it advances a second argument for application of the *Red Lion* framework to cable regulation. It asserts that the foundation of our broadcast jurisprudence is not the physical limitations of the electromagnetic spectrum, but rather the "market dysfunction" that characterizes the broadcast market. Because the cable market is beset by a similar dysfunction, the Government maintains, the *Red Lion* standard of review should also apply to cable. While we agree that the cable market suffers certain structural impediments, the Government's argument is flawed in two respects. First, as discussed above, the special physical characteristics of broadcast transmission, not the economic characteristics of the broadcast market, are what underlies our broadcast jurisprudence. * * *. Second, the mere assertion of dysfunction or failure in a speech market, without more, is not sufficient to shield a speech regulation from the First Amendment standards applicable to nonbroadcast media.

* * *

B

At the heart of the First Amendment lies the principle that each person should decide for him or herself the ideas and beliefs deserving of expression, consideration, and adherence. * * * Our precedents thus apply the most exacting scrutiny to regulations that suppress, disadvantage, or impose differential burdens upon speech because of its content. * * *. Laws that compel speakers to utter or distribute speech bearing a particular message are subject to the same rigorous scrutiny. * * *. In contrast, regulations that are unrelated to the content of speech are subject to an intermediate level of scrutiny, * * *, because in most cases they pose a less substantial risk of excising certain ideas or viewpoints from the public dialogue.

Deciding whether a particular regulation is content-based or content-neutral is not always a simple task. We have said that the "principal inquiry in determining content-neutrality . . . is whether the government has adopted a regulation of speech because of [agreement or] disagreement with the message it conveys." *Ward v. Rock Against Racism*, 491 U.S. 781, 791, 105 L. Ed. 2d 661, 109 S. Ct. 2746 (1989). * * *. The purpose, or justification, of a regulation will often be evident on its face. * * *. But while a content-based purpose may be sufficient in certain circumstances to show that a regulation is content-based, it is not necessary to such a showing in all cases. * * *. Nor will the mere assertion of a content-neutral purpose be enough to save a law which, on its face, discriminates based on content. * * *.

As a general rule, laws that by their terms distinguish favored speech from disfavored speech on the basis of the ideas or views expressed are content-based. * * *. By contrast, laws that confer benefits or impose burdens on speech without reference to the ideas or views expressed are in most instances content-neutral. See, e.g. *City Council of Los Angeles v. Taxpayers for Vincent*, 466 U.S. 789, 804, 80 L. Ed. 2d 772, 104 S. Ct. 2118 (1984) (ordinance prohibiting the posting of signs on public property "is neutral—indeed it is silent—concerning any speaker's point of view").

C

Insofar as they pertain to the carriage of full power broadcasters, the must-carry rules, on their face, impose burdens and confer benefits without reference to the content of speech. Although the provisions interfere with cable operators' editorial discretion by compelling them to offer carriage to a certain minimum number of broadcast stations, the extent of the interference does not depend upon the content of the cable operators' programming. The rules impose obligations upon all operators, save those with fewer than 300 subscribers, regardless of the programs or stations they now offer or have offered in the past. Nothing in the Act imposes a restriction, penalty, or burden by reason of the views, programs, or stations the cable operator has selected or will select. The number of channels a cable operator must set aside depends only on the operator's channel capacity, * * *; hence, an operator cannot avoid or mitigate its obligations under the Act by altering the programming it offers to subscribers. Cf. *Miami Herald Publishing Co. v. Tornillo*, 418 U.S., at 256–257 (newspaper may avoid access obligations by refraining from speech critical of political candidates).

The must-carry provisions also burden cable programmers by reducing the number of channels for which they can compete. But, again, this burden is unrelated to content, for it extends to all cable programmers irrespective of the programming they choose to offer viewers. * * *. And finally, the privileges conferred by the must-carry provisions are also unrelated to content. The rules benefit all full power broadcasters who request carriage—be they commercial or noncommercial, independent or network-affiliated, English or Spanish language, religious or secular. The aggregate effect of the rules is thus to make every full power commercial and noncommercial broadcaster eligible for must-carry, provided only that the broadcaster operates within the same television market as a cable system.

* * *

That the must-carry provisions, on their face, do not burden or benefit speech of a particular content does not end the inquiry. Our cases have recognized that even a regulation neutral on its face may be content-based if its manifest purpose is to regulate speech because of the message it conveys.** *

Appellants contend, in this regard, that the must-carry regulations are content-based because Congress' purpose in enacting them was to promote speech of a favored content. We do not agree. Our review of the Act and its various findings persuades us that Congress' overriding objective in enacting must-carry was not to favor programming of a particular subject matter, viewpoint, or format, but rather to preserve access to free television programming for the 40 percent of Americans without cable.

In unusually detailed statutory findings, * * *, Congress explained [its reasons for enacting the must-carry rules]. * * * Congress concluded that absent a requirement that cable systems carry the signals of local broadcast stations, the continued availability of free local broadcast television would be threatened. * * *. Congress sought to avoid the elimination of broadcast television because, in its words, "such programming is . . . free to those who own television sets and do not require cable transmission to receive broadcast television signals," § 2(a)(12), and because "there is a substantial governmental interest in promoting the continued availability of such free television programming, especially for viewers who are unable to afford other means of receiving programming."

By preventing cable operators from refusing carriage to broadcast television stations, the must-carry rules ensure that broadcast television stations will retain a large enough potential audience to earn necessary advertising revenue—or, in the case of noncommercial broadcasters, sufficient viewer contributions, see § 2(a)(8)(B)—to maintain their continued operation. In so doing, the provisions are designed to guarantee the survival of a medium that has become a vital part of the Nation's communication system, and to ensure that every individual with a television set can obtain access to free television programming.

This overriding congressional purpose is unrelated to the content of expression disseminated by cable and broadcast speakers. Indeed, our precedents have held that "protecting noncable households from loss of regular television broadcasting service due to competition from cable systems," is not only a permissible governmental justification, but an "important and substantial federal interest." *Capital Cities Cable, Inc. v. Crisp,* 467 U.S. 691, 714, 81 L. Ed. 2d 580, 104 S. Ct. 2694 (1984); see also *United States v. Midwest Video Corp.,* 406 U.S. 649, 661–662, 664, 32 L. Ed. 2d 390, 92 S. Ct. 1860 (1972) (plurality opinion).

The design and operation of the challenged provisions confirm that the purposes underlying the enactment of the must-carry scheme are unrelated to the content of speech. The rules * * * do not penalize cable operators or programmers because of the content of their programming. They do not compel cable operators to affirm points of view with which they disagree. They do not produce any net decrease in the amount of available speech. And they leave cable operators free to carry whatever programming they wish on all channels not subject to must-carry requirements.

Appellants and the dissent make much of the fact that, in the course of describing the purposes behind the Act, Congress referred to the value of broadcast programming. In particular, Congress noted that broadcast television is "an important source of local news[,] public affairs programming and other local broadcast services critical to an informed electorate," § 2(a)(11); see also § 2(a)(10), and that noncommercial television "provides educational and informational programming to the Nation's citizens." § 2(a)(8). We do not think, however, that such references cast any material doubt on the content-neutral character of must-carry. That Congress acknowledged the local orientation of broadcast programming and the role that noncommercial stations have played in educating the public does not indicate that Congress regarded broadcast programming as more valuable than cable programming. Rather, it reflects nothing more than the recognition that the services provided by broadcast television have some intrinsic value and, thus, are worth preserving against the threats posed by cable. * * *

The operation of the Act further undermines the suggestion that Congress' purpose in enacting must-carry was to force programming of a "local" or "educational" content on cable subscribers. The provisions, as we have stated, benefit all full power broadcasters irrespective of the nature of their programming. * * *

* * *

We likewise reject the suggestion, advanced by appellants and by Judge Williams in dissent, that the must-carry rules are content-based because the preference for broadcast stations "automatically entails content requirements." * * *. It is true that broadcast programming, unlike cable programming, is subject to certain limited content restraints imposed by statute and FCC regulation. But it does not follow that Congress mandated cable carriage of broadcast television stations as a means of ensuring that particular programs will be shown, or not shown, on cable systems.

As an initial matter, the argument exaggerates the extent to which the FCC is permitted to intrude into matters affecting the content of broadcast programming. * * *

* * *

D

Appellants advance three additional arguments to support their view that the must-carry provisions warrant strict scrutiny. * * *

1

Appellants maintain that the must-carry provisions trigger strict scrutiny because they compel cable operators to transmit speech not of their choosing. Relying principally on *Miami Herald Publishing Co. v. Tornillo*, * * *, appellants say this intrusion on the editorial control of cable operators amounts to forced speech which, if not *per se* invalid, can be justified only if narrowly tailored to a compelling government interest.

Tornillo affirmed an essential proposition: The First Amendment protects the editorial independence of the press. * * * Because the right of access at issue in *Tornillo* was triggered only when a newspaper elected to print matter critical of political candidates, it "exacted a penalty on the basis of ... content." * * *. We found, and continue to recognize, that right-of-reply statutes of this sort are an impermissible intrusion on newspapers' "editorial control and judgment." * * *.

* * * Moreover, by affording mandatory access to speakers with which the newspaper disagreed, the law induced the newspaper to respond to the candidates' replies when it might have preferred to remain silent. See *Pacific Gas & Electric Co. v. Public Utilities Comm'n of Cal.*, 475 U.S. 1, 11, 89 L.Ed. 2d 1, 106 S.Ct. 903 (1986) (plurality opinion).

The same principles led us to invalidate a similar content-based access regulation in *Pacific Gas & Electric*. At issue was a rule requiring a privately-owned utility, on a quarterly basis, to include with its monthly bills an editorial newsletter published by a consumer group critical of the utility's ratemaking practices. Although the access requirement applicable to the utility, unlike the statutory mechanism in *Tornillo*, was not triggered by speech of any particular content, the plurality held that the same strict First Amendment scrutiny applied. Like the statute in *Tornillo*, the regulation conferred benefits to speakers based on viewpoint, giving access only to a consumer group opposing the utility's practices. * * *. The plurality observed that in order to avoid the appearance that it agreed with the group's views, the utility would "feel compelled to respond to arguments and allegations made by the [the group] in its messages to [the utility's] customers." * * *. This "kind of forced response," the plurality explained, "is antithetical to the free discussion the First Amendment seeks to foster." * * *.

Tornillo and *Pacific Gas & Electric* do not control this case for the following reasons. First, unlike the access rules struck down in those cases, the must-carry rules are content-neutral in application. They are not activated by any particular message spoken by cable operators and thus exact no content-based penalty. * * *. Likewise, they do not grant access to broadcasters on the ground that the content of broadcast programming will counterbalance the messages of cable operators. Instead, they confer benefits upon all full power, local broadcasters, whatever the content of their programming. * * *.

Second, appellants do not suggest, nor do we think it the case, that must-carry will force cable operators to alter their own messages to respond to the broadcast programming they are required to carry. * * *. Given cable's long history of serving as a conduit for broadcast signals, there appears little risk that cable viewers would assume that the broadcast stations carried on a cable system convey ideas or messages endorsed by the cable operator. Indeed, broadcasters are required by federal regulation to identify themselves at least once every hour, * * *, and it is a common practice for broadcasters to disclaim any identity of viewpoint between the management and the speakers who use the broadcast facility. Cf. *PruneYard Shopping Center v. Robins*, 447 U.S. 74, 87, 64 L. Ed. 2d 741, 100 S. Ct. 2035 (1980) (noting that the views expressed by speakers who are granted a right of access to a shopping center would "not likely be identified with those of the owner"). Moreover, in contrast to the statute at issue in *Tornillo*, no aspect of the must-carry provisions would cause a cable operator or cable programmer to conclude that "the safe course is to avoid controversy," * * *, and by so doing diminish the free flow of information and ideas.

Finally, the asserted analogy to *Tornillo* ignores an important technological difference between newspapers and cable television. Although a daily newspaper and a cable operator both may enjoy monopoly status in a given locale, the cable operator exercises far greater control over access to the relevant medium. A daily newspaper, no matter how secure its local monopoly, does not possess the power to obstruct readers' access to other competing publications—whether they be weekly local newspapers, or daily newspapers published in other cities. Thus, when a newspaper asserts exclusive control over its own news copy, it does not thereby prevent other newspapers from being distributed to willing recipients in the same locale.

The same is not true of cable. When an individual subscribes to cable, the physical connection between the television set and the cable network gives the cable operator bottleneck, or gatekeeper, control over most (if not all) of the television programming that is channeled into the subscriber's home. Hence, simply by virtue of its ownership of the essential pathway for cable speech, a cable operator can prevent its subscribers from obtaining access to programming it chooses to exclude. A cable operator, unlike speakers in other media, can thus silence the voice of competing speakers with a mere flick of the switch.

The potential for abuse of this private power over a central avenue of communication cannot be overlooked. * * *. The First Amendment's command that government not impede the freedom of speech does not disable the government from taking steps to ensure that private interests not restrict, through physical control of a critical pathway of communication, the free flow of information and ideas. * * *

2

Second, appellants urge us to apply strict scrutiny because the must-carry provisions favor one set of speakers (broadcast programmers) over another (cable programmers). Appellants maintain that as a consequence of this speaker preference, some cable programmers who would have secured carriage in the absence of must-carry may now be dropped. Relying on language in *Buckley v. Valeo*, 424 U.S. 1, 46 L. Ed. 2d 659, 96 S. Ct. 612 (1976), appellants contend that such a regulation is presumed invalid under the First Amendment because the government may not "restrict the speech of some elements of our society in order to enhance the relative voice of others." *Id.*, at 48–49.

* * *

Our holding in *Buckley* does not support appellants' broad assertion that all speaker-partial laws are presumed invalid. Rather, it stands for the proposition that speaker-based laws demand strict scrutiny when they reflect the Government's preference for the substance of what the favored speakers have to say (or aversion to what the disfavored speakers have to say). * * *

The question here is whether Congress preferred broadcasters over cable programmers based on the content of programming each group offers. The answer, as we explained above, * * * is no. Congress granted must-carry privileges to broadcast stations on the belief that the broadcast television industry is in economic peril due to the physical characteristics of cable transmission and the economic incentives facing the cable industry. Thus, the fact that the provisions benefit broadcasters and not cable programmers does not call for strict scrutiny under our precedents.

3

Finally, appellants maintain that strict scrutiny applies because the must-carry provisions single out certain members of the press—here, cable operators—for disfavored treatment. * * *. In support, appellants point out that Congress has required cable operators to provide carriage to broadcast stations, but has not imposed like burdens on analogous video delivery systems, such as multichannel multipoint distribution (MMDS) systems and satellite master antenna television (SMATV) systems. Relying upon our precedents invalidating discriminatory taxation of the press, * * *. appellants contend that this sort of differential treatment poses a particular danger of abuse by the government and should be presumed invalid.

Regulations that discriminate among media, or among different speakers within a single medium, often present serious First Amendment concerns. * * *

It would be error to conclude, however, that the First Amendment mandates strict scrutiny for any speech regulation that applies to one medium (or a subset thereof) but not others. * * * [H]eightened scrutiny is unwarranted when the differential treatment is "justified by some special characteristic of" the particular medium being regulated. * * *.

The must-carry provisions, as we have explained above, are justified by special characteristics of the cable medium: the bottleneck monopoly power exercised by cable operators and the dangers this power poses to the viability of broadcast television. Appellants do not argue, nor does it appear, that other media—in particular, media that transmit video programming such as MMDS and SMATV—are subject to bottleneck monopoly control, or pose a demonstrable threat to the survival of broadcast television. It should come as no surprise, then, that Congress decided to impose the must-carry obligations upon cable operators only.

* * *

III

A

In sum, the must-carry provisions do not pose such inherent dangers to free expression, or present such potential for censorship or manipulation, as to justify application of the most exacting level of First Amendment scrutiny. We agree with the District Court that the appropriate standard by which to evaluate the constitutionality of must-carry is the intermediate level of scrutiny applicable to content-neutral restrictions that impose an incidental burden on speech. See *Ward v. Rock Against Racism*, 491 U.S. 781, 105 L. Ed. 2d 661, 109 S. Ct. 2746 (1989); *United States v. O'Brien*, 391 U.S. 367, 20 L. Ed. 2d 672, 88 S. Ct. 1673 (1968).

To satisfy the *O'Brien* standard, a regulation need not be the least speech-restrictive means of advancing the Government's interests. "Rather, the requirement of narrow tailoring is satisfied 'so long as the . . . regulation promotes a substantial government interest that would be achieved less effectively absent the regulation.' " Narrow tailoring in this context requires, in other words, that the means chosen do not "burden substantially more speech than is necessary to further the government's legitimate interests."

Congress declared that the must-carry provisions serve three interrelated interests: (1) preserving the benefits of free, over-the-air local broadcast television, (2) promoting the widespread dissemination of information from a multiplicity of sources, and (3) promoting fair competition in the market for television programming. * * *. None of these interests is related to the "suppression of free expression," * * *, or to the content of any speakers' messages. And viewed in the abstract, we have no difficulty concluding that each of them is an important governmental interest. * * *.

* * *

Likewise, assuring that the public has access to a multiplicity of information sources is a governmental purpose of the highest order, for it promotes values central to the First Amendment. * * *. Finally, the Government's interest in eliminating restraints on fair competition is always substantial, even when the individuals or entities subject to particular regulations are engaged in expressive activity protected by the First Amendment. * * *

B

* * *

Thus, in applying *O'Brien* scrutiny we must ask first whether the Government has adequately shown that the economic health of local broadcasting is in genuine jeopardy and in need of the protections afforded by must-carry. Assuming an affirmative answer to the foregoing question, the Government still bears the burden of showing that the remedy it has adopted does not "burden substantially more speech than is necessary to further the government's legitimate interests." On the state of the record developed thus far, and in the absence of findings of fact from the District Court, we are unable to conclude that the Government has satisfied either inquiry.

* * *

That Congress' predictive judgments are entitled to substantial deference does not mean, however, that they are insulated from meaningful judicial review altogether. On the contrary, we have stressed in First Amendment cases that the deference afforded to legislative findings does "not foreclose our independent judgment of the facts bearing on an issue of constitutional law." * * *. This obligation to exercise independent judgment when First Amendment rights are implicated is not a license to reweigh the evidence *de novo*, or to replace Congress' factual predictions with our own. Rather, it is to assure that, in formulating its judgments, Congress has drawn reasonable inferences based on substantial evidence. * * *

The Government's assertion that the must-carry rules are necessary to protect the viability of broadcast television rests on two essential propositions: (1) that unless cable operators are compelled to carry broadcast stations, significant numbers of broadcast stations will be refused carriage on cable systems; and (2) that the broadcast stations denied carriage will either deteriorate to a substantial degree or fail altogether.

As support for the first proposition, the Government relies upon a 1988 FCC study showing, at a time when no must-carry rules were in effect, that approximately 20 percent of cable systems reported dropping or refusing carriage to one or more local broadcast stations on at least one occasion. * * *. The record does not indicate, however, the time frame within which these drops occurred, or how many of these stations were dropped for only a temporary period and then restored to carriage. The same FCC study indicates that about 23 percent of the cable operators reported shifting the channel positions of one or more local broadcast stations, and that, in most cases, the repositioning was done for "marketing" rather than "technical" reasons. * * *

* * *

Without a more substantial elaboration in the District Court of the predictive or historical evidence upon which Congress relied, or the introduction of some additional evidence to establish that the dropped or repositioned broadcasters would be at serious risk of financial difficulty, we cannot determine whether the threat to broadcast television is real enough to overcome the challenge to the provisions made by these appellants. We think it significant, for instance, that the parties have not presented any evidence that local broadcast stations have fallen into bankruptcy, turned in their broadcast licenses, curtailed their broadcast operations, or suffered a serious reduction in operating revenues as a result of their being dropped from, or otherwise disadvantaged by, cable systems.

The paucity of evidence indicating that broadcast television is in jeopardy is not the only deficiency in this record. Also lacking are any findings concerning the actual effects of must-carry on the speech of cable operators and cable programmers, i.e., the extent to which cable operators will, in fact, be forced to make changes in their current or anticipated programming selections; the degree to which cable programmers will be dropped from cable systems to make room for local broadcasters; and the extent to which cable operators can satisfy their must-carry obligations by devoting previously unused channel capacity to the carriage of local broadcasters. The answers to these and perhaps other questions are critical to the narrow tailoring step of the *O'Brien* analysis, for unless we know the extent to which the must-carry provisions in fact interfere with protected speech, we cannot say whether they suppress "substantially more speech than ... necessary" to ensure the viability of broadcast television. * * *. Finally, the record fails to provide any judicial findings concerning the availability and efficacy of "constitutionally acceptable less restrictive means" of achieving the Government's asserted interests. * * *

In sum, because there are genuine issues of material fact still to be resolved on this record, we hold that the District Court erred in granting summary judgment in favor of the Government. * * *

The judgment below is vacated, and the case is remanded for further proceedings consistent with this opinion.

It is so ordered.

[The concurring opinion of Justice Blackmun is omitted.]

Justice Stevens, concurring in part and concurring in the judgment.

* * *

While I agree with most of Justice Kennedy's reasoning, and join Parts I, II(C), II(D), and III(A) of his opinion, I part ways with him on the appropriate disposition of this case. In my view the District Court's judgment sustaining the must-carry provisions should be affirmed. The District Court majority evaluated §§ 4 and 5 as content-neutral regulations of protected speech according to the same standard that Justice Kennedy's opinion instructs it to apply on remand. In my view, the District Court reached the correct result the first time around.

As Justice Kennedy recognizes, * * *, findings by the Congress, particularly those emerging from such sustained deliberations, merit special respect from this Court. Accorded proper deference, the findings in § 2 are sufficient to sustain the must-carry provisions against facial attack. * * *

Justice Kennedy asks the three-judge panel to take additional evidence on such matters as whether the must-carry provisions really respond to threatened harms to broadcasters, whether §§ 4–5 "will in fact alleviate these harms in a direct and material way," * * *, and "the extent to which cable operators will, in fact, be forced to make changes in their current or anticipated programming selections," * * *. While additional evidence might cast further light on the efficacy and wisdom of the must-carry provisions, additional evidence is not necessary to resolve the question of their facial constitutionality.

* * *

It is thus my view that we should affirm the judgment of the District Court. Were I to vote to affirm, however, no disposition of this appeal would command the support of a majority of the Court. An accommodation is therefore necessary. * * *. Accordingly, because I am in substantial agreement with Justice Kennedy's analysis of the case, I concur in the judgment vacating and remanding for further proceedings.

JUSTICE O'CONNOR, with whom JUSTICE SCALIA and JUSTICE GINSBURG join, and with whom JUSTICE THOMAS joins as to Parts I and III, concurring in part and dissenting in part.

* * * By reserving a little over one-third of the channels on a cable system for broadcasters, [the 1992 Act] * * * ensured that in most cases it will be a cable programmer who is dropped and a broadcaster who is retained. The question presented in this case is whether this choice comports with the commands of the First Amendment.

I

A

The 1992 Cable Act implicates the First Amendment rights of two classes of speakers. First, it tells cable operators which programmers they must carry, and keeps cable operators from carrying others that they might prefer. * * *

Second, the Act deprives a certain class of video programmers—those who operate cable channels rather than broadcast stations—of access to over one-third of an entire medium. * * *. A cable programmer that might otherwise have been carried may well be denied access in favor of a broadcaster that is less appealing to the viewers but is favored by the must-carry rules. * * *

* * *

I agree with the Court that some speaker-based restrictions—those genuinely justified without reference to content—need not be subject to strict scrutiny. But looking at the statute at issue, I cannot avoid the conclusion that its preference for broadcasters over cable programmers is justified with reference to content. The findings, enacted by Congress as § 2 of the Act, and which I must assume state the justifications for the law, make this clear. * * *

* * *

Preferences for diversity of viewpoints, for localism, for educational programming, and for news and public affairs all make reference to content. They may not reflect hostility to particular points of view, or a desire to suppress certain subjects because they are controversial or offensive. They may be quite benignly motivated. But benign motivation, we have consistently held, is not enough to avoid the need for strict scrutiny of content-based justifications. * * *. The First Amendment does more than just bar government from intentionally suppressing speech of which it disapproves. It also generally prohibits the government from excepting certain kinds of speech from regulation because it thinks the speech is especially valuable. * * *

This is why the Court is mistaken in concluding that the interest in diversity—in "access to a multiplicity" of "diverse and antagonistic sources," * * *—is content neutral. Indeed, the interest is not "related to the suppression of free expression," * * *, but that is not enough for content neutrality. * * * The interest in ensuring access to a multiplicity of diverse and antagonistic sources of information, no matter how praiseworthy, is directly tied to the content of what the speakers will likely say.

B

The Court dismisses the findings quoted above by speculating that they do not reveal a preference for certain kinds of content * * *. I cannot agree. * * *

* * * [I]t does not seem likely that Congress would make extensive findings merely to show that broadcast television is valuable. The controversial judgment at the heart of the statute is not that broadcast television has some value—obviously it does—but that broadcasters should be preferred over cable programmers. The best explanation for the findings, it seems to me, is that they represent Congress' reasons for adopting this preference; and, according to the findings, these reasons rest in part on the content of broadcasters' speech. To say in the face of the findings that the must-carry rules "impose burdens and confer benefits without reference to the content of speech," * * *, cannot be correct, especially in light of the care with which we must normally approach speaker-based restrictions. * * *

It may well be that Congress also had other, content-neutral, purposes in mind when enacting the statute. But we have never held that the presence of a permissible justification lessens the impropriety of relying in part on an impermissible justification. * * *

C

* * *

The interest in localism, either in the dissemination of opinions held by the listeners' neighbors or in the reporting of events that have to do with the local community, cannot be described as "compelling" for the purposes of the compelling state interest test. It is a legitimate interest, perhaps even an important one—certainly the government can foster it by, for instance, providing subsidies from the public fisc—but it does not rise to the level necessary to justify content-based speech restrictions.

* * *

The interests in public affairs programming and educational programming seem somewhat weightier, though it is a difficult question whether they are compelling enough to justify restricting other sorts of speech. We have never held that the Government could impose educational content requirements on, say, newsstands, bookstores, or movie theaters; and it is not clear that such requirements would in any event appreciably further the goals of public education.

But even assuming arguendo that the Government could set some channels aside for educational or news programming, the Act is insufficiently tailored to this goal. To benefit the educational broadcasters, the Act burdens more than just the cable entertainment programmers. It equally burdens CNN, C–SPAN, the Discovery Channel, the New Inspirational Network, and other channels with as much claim as PBS to being educational or related to public affairs.

* * *

III

Having said all this, it is important to acknowledge one basic fact: The question is not whether there will be control over who gets to speak over cable—the question is who will have this control. Under the FCC's view, the answer is Congress, acting within relatively broad limits. Under my view, the answer is the cable operator. Most of the time, the cable operator's decision will be largely dictated by the preferences of the viewers; but because many cable operators are indeed monopolists, the viewers' preferences will not always prevail. Our recognition that cable operators are speakers is bottomed in large part on the very fact that the cable operator has editorial discretion. * * *

I have no doubt that there is danger in having a single cable operator decide what millions of subscribers can or cannot watch. And I have no doubt that Congress can act to relieve this danger. In other provisions of the Act, Congress has already taken steps to foster competition among cable systems. * * *. Congress can encourage the creation of new media, such as inexpensive satellite broadcasting, or fiber-optic networks with virtually unlimited channels, or even simple devices that would let people easily switch from cable to over-the-air broadcasting. And of course Congress can subsidize broadcasters that it thinks provide especially valuable programming.

Congress may also be able to act in more mandatory ways. If Congress finds that cable operators are leaving some channels empty— perhaps for ease of future expansion—it can compel the operators to make the free channels available to programmers who otherwise would not get carriage. * * *. Congress might also conceivably obligate cable operators to act as common carriers for some of their channels, with those channels being open to all through some sort of lottery system or timesharing arrangement. Setting aside any possible Takings Clause issues, it stands to reason that if Congress may demand that telephone companies operate as common carriers, it can ask the same of cable companies; such an approach would not suffer from the defect of preferring one speaker to another.

* * *

[The opinion of JUSTICE GINSBURG, concurring in part and dissenting in part, is omitted.]

Notes and Questions

1. What, ultimately, is the Court's holding about the constitutionality of the must-carry rules? Does Justice Stevens' "accommodation," to produce a fifth vote that created the Court's majority, weaken the validity or persuasive value of the holding?

2. (a) Does the Court define the "level" of First Amendment scrutiny applicable to cable television? What is that level? Does a single constitutional standard apply to all types of regulations of cable television, or only to certain types? If distinctions are to be drawn, what are the bases for such distinctions? For example, can educational and governmental access requirements survive the decision in *Turner Broadcasting*? What arguments would you make in support of such access obligations? In opposition?

(b) The Court expressly rejects the argument that cable television should be subjected to the relaxed level of First Amendment scrutiny applicable to broadcasters. How does the level of constitutional scrutiny applied to the must-carry rules differ from the test used in the *League of Women Voters* case? Would the result have been any different if the Court were asked to analyze the constitutionality of a must-carry type rule applicable to broadcasters?

(c) What would be the result if the Court, after the decision in *Turner Broadcasting*, were to evaluate a must-carry type regulation made applicable to a print medium, such as newspapers? Does the Court's discussion in Section II.D.1 of the majority opinion provide an answer? Do you accept the Court's analysis, in which it found that the reasoning of *Tornillo* and *Pacific Gas & Electric* should not control the disposition of this case?

(d) Was it possible to gauge the true meaning of the Court's holding until the issues on remand were finally resolved? In other words, is it more important to know whether the constitutional standard will be applied in a rigorous or loose fashion, than to know simply what the standard is?

3. How important is cable television's status as a "bottleneck" distribution medium to the analysis of its First Amendment rights? Consider the Court's statement that "[t]he First Amendment's command that government not impede the freedom of speech does not disable the government from taking steps to ensure that private interests not restrict, through physical control of a critical pathway of communication, the free flow of information and ideas." Would this provide a constitutional justification for even some content-based restrictions on the "speech" of cable television operators? Would it justify analysis of content-based cable regulations under the *O'Brien* test, rather than strict scrutiny? Does it mean that economic justifications for speech regulation, which were rejected in the case of the newspaper industry by the decision in *Tornillo*, may be permissible in the case of the cable television industry? Compare Preferred Communications, Inc. v. Los Angeles, 13 F.3d 1327, 74 Rad. Reg. 2d (P & F) 508, 511–12 (9th Cir.1994) (affirming, again, a trial court's decision to strike down the exclusivity portion of a cable franchise, but concluding that the holding in *Tornillo* does not resolve the constitutional issue: "Unlike newspapers, a

'cable company must significantly impact the public domain in order to operate.' ... The economic oddities of cable, coupled with the burden on public resources caused by the entry—and exit—of additional operators may arguably justify some limitations on the number of operators.... [However], the one operator/one area limitation is not narrowly tailored to advance [the city's] ... interest [in avoiding 'traffic disruption and visual blight'].'").

4. (a) Compare the reasoning in Sections I.C and II.D.2 of the majority opinion with the reasoning in Sections I.A and I.B of Justice O'Connor's opinion. Which analysis do you find more persuasive on the question of whether the must-carry rules should be evaluated as content-based or content-neutral restrictions on speech? Do you think the majority would have struck down the must-carry rules if it had found them to be content-based restrictions on speech? Would the Court have applied a strict scrutiny test to such a content-based law? Consider note 6 in the majority opinion, in which the Court expressly avoided confronting some of the more difficult aspects of the must-carry rules.

(b) Do you think the Court reasonably evaluated the impact of must-carry on the carriage interests of non-broadcast programmers in deciding the degree of constitutional scrutiny to apply in this case? Compare Section II.D.3 of the majority opinion with the second paragraph of Section I.A of Justice O'Connor's opinion.

(c) Did Justice O'Conner's opinion take into account the fact that non-broadcast programmers could place their programming on commercial "leased access" channels? Does this place them in a better or worse position than broadcasters which negotiate for "retransmission consent"?

5. (a) If the Court were to adopt Justice O'Connor's constitutional reasoning, would it be able to avoid overturning not only must-carry, but also many other provisions of the 1992 Cable Act? Would her analysis jeopardize the viability of the comparative hearing process for broadcast licensing, the political broadcasting rules, and various rules and policies intended to promote program diversity (including multiple-and cross-owner-ship restrictions)?

(b) Will the decision in *Turner Broadcasting* remain valid if telephone companies are permitted to compete with cable television companies by constructing their own networks to distribute video programming?

6. (a) Even if the must-carry rules are properly evaluated as content-neutral regulations, should the Court have remanded the case to the district court, or should it have, nonetheless, struck down the rules for failure to be narrowly tailored? Does Section II of Justice O'Connor's opinion properly analyze this issue, or has Justice O'Connor assumed the answers to questions, that, according to the majority opinion, cannot yet be answered properly because of the lack of an adequate factual record? Do you agree or disagree with Justice Stevens' contention that the majority opinion, in its directions to the district court on remand, asks that court to predict the future and to answer questions that cannot reasonably be answered?

(b) Consider the Court's explanation of the requirement of narrow tailoring. In Section III.A of the majority opinion, the Court quotes from its decision in the *O'Brien* case to state that "a content-neutral regulation will be sustained if ' ... the incidental restriction on alleged First Amendment freedoms is no greater than is essential to the furtherance of that [substantial governmental] interest.' " Do you agree, as the Court then states, that this standard does not require that the regulation in question "be the least speech-restrictive means of advancing the Government's interests"? If a content-neutral regulation must be no broader than is "essential" to further the government's interest, do you agree (as the Court concludes) that a regulation that does not burden "substantially more speech than is necessary" meets this test? Ultimately, how do you think the district court will apply the narrow tailoring element of the constitutional test used by the Court in this case?

(c) How difficult would it be for the FCC to show the need for the must-carry rules? Is it enough for the agency to note the many recent bankruptcies of UHF stations? The decline in network stations' audiences? The general loss of revenues to broadcast stations?

Note: Shopping Channels

1. (a) Section 4(g) of the 1992 Cable Act added a new Section 614(g) to the Communications Act, 47 U.S.C. Sec. 533(g), which required the FCC to determine whether local broadcast stations that carry home shopping programming for all or substantially all of their broadcast days are serving the public interest, convenience, and necessity. If the Commission concluded that these stations were serving the public interest, it was required to declare the stations eligible for must-carry treatment. (Before the Commission's decision on this issue, home shopping broadcast stations were not eligible for mandatory free carriage on their local cable systems.) If the Commission found that one or more such stations were not serving the public interest, then the Commission was required to provide them with a reasonable time to change their programming (or risk losing their station licenses).

In July 1993, the FCC determined that home shopping broadcast stations served the public interest. In the Matter of Implementation of Section 4(g) of the Cable Television Consumer Protection and Competition Act of 1992, Home Shopping Station Issues, 8 F.C.C. Rcd. 5321; 73 Rad. Reg. 2d (P & F) 355 (1993)(Report and Order). In light of that determination, the Commission went on to analyze the must-carry issue:

37. Given our conclusion that home shopping stations are operating in the public interest, Section 4(g)(2) of the 1992 Cable Act seems to suggest that such stations are automatically eligible for mandatory cable carriage. However, the Notice [in this proceeding] stated that another option might be to find that home shopping stations, although operating in the public interest in such a manner as to warrant continued authorization and renewal, do not warrant mandatory cable carriage. * * *

38. Several commenters assert that the Act does not allow the Commission to authorize the continued operation of home shopping stations without making them eligible for mandatory carriage. * * *

39. We are not persuaded that the 1992 Cable Act would allow the continued authorization of home shopping stations without granting

them eligibility for mandatory carriage. The plain language of Section 4(g)(2) provides that the Commission "shall" qualify such stations for mandatory carriage upon a finding that they are serving the public interest. We have made such a finding. Commenters opposing this interpretation have failed to provide a reasonable means to read the statute otherwise. Moreover, we agree that the failure to qualify certain licensed stations based upon their programming decisions would place the content-neutrality of the must-carry rules into serious doubt, thereby jeopardizing their constitutionality. We conclude that as long as a home shopping broadcast station remains authorized to hold a Commission license, it should be qualified for mandatory carriage.

(b) This decision was made before the Court decided the *Turner Broadcasting* case. Leaving aside the Commission's conclusion that Section 4(g) required that home shopping stations be deemed eligible for must-carry status once they were found to be serving the public interest, do you agree, in light of the decision in *Turner Broadcasting*, that a decision denying such stations the benefits of must-carry would undermine the constitutionality of the entire must-carry scheme?

(c) Even if you believe that the Commission's decision properly avoids a content-based classification, do you think it reflects sound public policy? In the home shopping proceeding, consistent with congressional direction in the 1992 Cable Act, the Commission assessed whether home shopping stations were serving the public interest by evaluating primarily three factors: (1) the viewing of home shopping stations by the public; (2) the level of competing demands for the spectrum allocated to such stations; and (3) the role of such stations in providing competition to nonbroadcast services offering similar programming. The Commission found that home shopping stations were widely viewed by the public, were not unfairly depriving other competing users of access to highly-valued spectrum space, and were providing competition with non-broadcast home shopping services. What does the focus on these three factors say about the meaning of the public interest standard generally? Keeping in mind that such determination is a condition for must-carry eligibility, does the Commission's decision support or undermine the premises of the *Turner Broadcasting* decision?

(d) Consider the following analysis (included in the FCC's decision on home shopping stations) of the whether programming activities of home shopping stations satisfy their overall public interest obligations:

29. *Public Interest Obligations.* Commenters were also invited to demonstrate how home shopping stations have satisfied their obligation to address the needs and interests of their communities of license. In response, we have received detailed listings of the public interest programming of many licensees of home shopping stations. According to these submissions, licensees of home shopping stations have addressed such issues as drug and alcohol abuse, AIDS, race relations, homelessness, basic legal knowledge for non-English-speaking viewers, and local political debates and election returns. These commenters assert that home shopping stations utilize a variety of formats for this type of

programming, including public service announcements (PSAs) and program length features.

* * *

31. Based upon the record before us, it appears that the chosen format of home shopping stations generally does not preclude them from adequately addressing the needs and interests of their communities of license. We observe that we have never denied the license renewal application of any home shopping station, thus indicating that these stations have been able to meet the Commission's standards on public affairs programming responsive to issues confronting the local community, as well as standards on indecency and political or emergency broadcasting. Indeed, with regard to serving the needs and interests of children, as with all public interest considerations, home shopping stations must comply with the same rules that apply to other television broadcast stations. * * *

Is the Commission's approach to the issue a convincing one? Should the analysis of this issue have any impact on the decision of whether a station is eligible for must-carry status? Can this issue be relevant to the must-carry question after the decision in *Turner Broadcasting*?

(e) Does the fact that Congress singled out home shopping stations for special consideration undermine the Court's argument that must-carry is a content-neutral regulation? Is it "content-neutral" to require a broadcast station to serve the public interest as a condition of eligibility for must-carry status? Keep in mind that a licensee that does not serve the public interest can have its license revoked altogether.

Note: Later History of Turner

As indicated, the *Turner* Court based its opinion on certain factual assumptions as to the relationship between broadcasting and cable; it thus remanded the case for further findings of fact on these issues. Most observers thought that would be merely a formalistic exercise. As indicated by the following excerpt from Turner Broadcasting System, Inc v. FCC, U.S. (1997) it turned out to be a somewhat closer call than some had expected.

One question to keep in mind as to *Turner II* is whether it is really is a constitutional decision in the first place. To what extent does the majority or dissent really rely on constitutional—as opposed to general administrative law—principles? When the plurality talks about Congress not acting "unreasonably," does that conjure up constitutional decisions or judicial review of administrative action? Is the Court applying the First Amendment or the "arbitrary and capricious" test?

TURNER BROADCASTING SYSTEM v. FCC

Supreme Court of the United States, 1997.
—— U.S. ——, 117 S.Ct. 1174, 137 L.Ed.2d 369.

KENNEDY, J., announced the judgment of the Court and delivered the opinion of the Court, except as to a portion of Part II–A–1. REHNQUIST, C. J., and STEVENS and SOUTER, JJ., joined that opinion in full, and BREYER, J., joined except insofar as Part II–A–1 relied on an anticompetitive rationale. STEVENS, J., filed a concurring opinion. BREYER, J., filed an opinion concurring in part. O'CONNOR, J., filed a dissenting opinion, in which SCALIA, THOMAS, and GINSBURG, JJ., joined.

JUSTICE KENNEDY delivered the opinion of the Court, except as to a portion of Part II–A–1.

* * *

On appeal from the District Court's grant of summary judgment for appellees, the case now presents the two questions left open during the first appeal: First, whether the record as it now stands supports Congress' predictive judgment that the must-carry provisions further important governmental interests; and second, whether the provisions do not burden substantially more speech than necessary to further those interests. We answer both questions in the affirmative, and conclude the must-carry provisions are consistent with the First Amendment.

* * *

I

* * *

[After the Court's remand the] District Court oversaw another 18 months of factual development on remand "yielding a record of tens of thousands of pages" of evidence, comprised of materials acquired during Congress' three years of pre-enactment hearings, sworn declarations and testimony, and industry documents obtained on remand. Upon consideration of the expanded record, a divided panel of the District Court again granted summary judgment to appellees. 910 F. Supp. at 751. The majority determined "Congress drew reasonable inferences" from substantial evidence before it to conclude that "in the absence of must-carry rules, 'significant' numbers of broadcast stations would be refused carriage." The court found Congress drew on studies and anecdotal evidence indicating "cable operators had already dropped, refused to carry, or adversely repositioned significant numbers of local broadcasters," and suggesting that in the vast majority of cases the broadcasters were not restored to carriage in their prior position. Noting evidence in the record before Congress and the testimony of experts on remand, the court decided the noncarriage problem would grow worse without must-carry because cable operators had refrained from dropping broadcast stations during Congress' investigation and the pendency of this litigation, and possessed increasing incentives to use their growing economic power to capture broadcasters' advertising revenues and promote affiliated cable programmers. * * *

The court held must-carry to be narrowly tailored to promote the Government's legitimate interests. It found the effects of must-carry on cable operators to be minimal, noting evidence that: most cable systems had not been required to add any broadcast stations since the rules were adopted; only 1.2 percent of all cable channels had been devoted to broadcast stations added because of must-carry; and the burden was likely to diminish as channel capacity expanded in the future. The court proceeded to consider a number of alternatives to must-carry that appellants had proposed * * * concluding that "even assuming that [the alternatives] would be less burdensome" on cable operators' First Amendment interests, they "are not in any respect as effective in achieving the government's [interests]."

* * *

This direct appeal followed. See 47 U.S.C. § 555(c)(1); 28 U.S.C. § 1253.

* * *

II

We begin where the plurality ended in *Turner*, applying the standards for intermediate scrutiny enunciated in O'Brien. * * * As noted in *Turner*, must-carry was designed to serve "three interrelated interests: (1) preserving the benefits of free, over-the-air local broadcast television, (2) promoting the widespread dissemination of information from a multiplicity of sources, and (3) promoting fair competition in the market for television programming." We decided then, and now reaffirm, that each of those is an important governmental interest. * * *

* * *

A

[As to the factual issues] * * * we turn first to the harm or risk which prompted Congress to act. * * *

In reviewing the constitutionality of a statute, "courts must accord substantial deference to the predictive judgments of Congress." * * * This is not the sum of the matter, however. We owe Congress' findings an additional measure of deference out of respect for its authority to exercise the legislative power. Even in the realm of First Amendment questions where Congress must base its conclusions upon substantial evidence, deference must be accorded to its findings as to the harm to be avoided and to the remedial measures adopted for that end, lest we infringe on traditional legislative authority to make predictive judgments when enacting nationwide regulatory policy.

We have no difficulty in finding a substantial basis to support Congress' conclusion that a real threat justified enactment of the must-carry provisions. We examine first the evidence before Congress and then the further evidence presented to the District Court on remand to supplement the congressional determination.

* * *

The reasonableness of Congress' conclusion was borne out by the evidence on remand, which also reflected cable industry favoritism for integrated programmers.

In addition, evidence before Congress, supplemented on remand, indicated that cable systems would have incentives to drop local broadcasters in favor of other programmers less likely to compete with them for audience and advertisers. Independent local broadcasters tend to be the closest substitutes for cable programs, because their programming tends to be similar, and because both primarily target the same type of advertiser: those interested in cheaper (and more frequent) ad spots than are typically available on network affiliates. The ability of broadcast stations to compete for advertising is greatly increased by cable carriage, which increases viewership substantially. With expanded viewership, broadcast presents a more competitive medium for television advertising. Empirical studies indicate that cable-carried broadcasters so enhance competition for advertising that even modest increases in the numbers of broadcast stations carried on cable are correlated with significant decreases in advertising revenue to cable systems. Empirical evidence also indicates that demand for premium cable services (such as pay-per-view) is reduced when a cable system carries more independent broadcasters. Thus, operators stand to benefit by dropping broadcast stations.

Cable systems also have more systemic reasons for seeking to disadvantage broadcast stations: Simply stated, cable has little interest in assisting, through carriage, a competing medium of communication. * * *

The dissent contends Congress could not reasonably conclude cable systems would engage in such predation because cable operators, whose primary source of revenue is subscriptions, would not risk dropping a widely viewed broadcast station in order to capture advertising revenues. However, if viewers are faced with the choice of sacrificing a handful of broadcast stations to gain access to dozens of cable channels (plus network affiliates), it is likely they would still subscribe to cable even if they would prefer the dropped television stations to the cable programming that replaced them. Substantial evidence introduced on remand bears this out. * * *

It was more than a theoretical possibility in 1992 that cable operators would take actions adverse to local broadcasters; indeed, significant numbers of broadcasters had already been dropped. The record before Congress contained extensive anecdotal evidence about scores of adverse carriage decisions against broadcast stations. Congress considered an FCC-sponsored study detailing cable system carriage practices in the wake of decisions by the United States Court of Appeals for the District of Columbia Circuit striking down prior must-carry regulations. It indicated that in 1988, 280 out of 912 responding broadcast stations had been dropped or denied carriage in 1,533 instances. Even assuming that every station dropped or denied coverage responded to the survey, it would indicate that nearly a quarter (21 percent) of the approximately 1,356 broadcast stations then in existence, had been denied carriage. The same study reported 869 of 4,303 reporting cable systems had denied carriage to 704 broadcast stations in 1,820 instances, and 279 of those stations had qualified for carriage under the prior must-carry rules. A contemporaneous study of public television stations indicated that in the vast majority of cases, dropped stations were not restored to the cable service.

Substantial evidence demonstrated that absent must-carry the already "serious" problem of noncarriage would grow worse because "additional local broadcast signals will be deleted, repositioned, or not carried," The record included anecdotal evidence showing the cable industry was acting with restraint in dropping broadcast stations in an effort to discourage reregulation. There was also substantial evidence that advertising revenue would be of increasing importance to cable operators as subscribership growth began to flatten, providing a steady, increasing incentive to deny carriage to local broadcasters in an effort to capture their advertising revenue.

Additional evidence developed on remand supports the reasonableness of Congress' predictive judgment. Approximately 11 percent of local broadcasters were not carried on the typical cable system in 1989. The figure had grown to even more significant proportions by 1992. According to one of appellants' own experts, between 19 and 31 percent of all local broadcast stations, including network affiliates, were not carried by the typical cable system.

* * *

The dissent cites evidence indicating that many dropped broadcasters were stations few viewers watch, and it suggests that must-carry thwarts noncable viewers' preferences. Undoubtedly, viewers without cable—the immediate, though not sole, beneficiaries of efforts to preserve broadcast television—would have a strong preference for carriage of any broadcast program over any cable program, for the simple reason that it helps to preserve a medium to which they have access. The methodological flaws in the cited evidence are of concern. Even aside from that, the evidence overlooks that the broadcasters added by must-carry had ratings greater than or equal to the cable programs they replaced. * * * On average, even the lowest-rated station added pursuant to must-carry had ratings better than or equal to at least nine basic cable program services carried on the system. * * *

* * *

* * *The issue before us is whether, given conflicting views of the probable development of the television industry, Congress had substantial evidence for making the judgment that it did. We need not put our imprimatur on Congress' economic theory in order to validate the reasonableness of its judgment.

[The Court reviewed conflicting showings as to whether lack of must-carry had caused any diminution in the number of broadcast stations—particularly the fact that more new television stations had gone on the air than had gone bankrupt.]

* * * The question is not whether Congress, as an objective matter, was correct to determine must-carry is necessary to prevent a substantial number of broadcast stations from losing cable carriage and suffering significant financial hardship. Rather, the question is whether the legislative conclusion was reasonable and supported by substantial evidence in the record before Congress. In making that determination, we are not to "re-weigh the evidence de novo, or to replace Congress' factual predictions with our own." Rather, we are simply to determine if the standard is satisfied. * * *

Although evidence of continuing growth in broadcast could have supported the opposite conclusion, a reasonable interpretation is that expansion in the cable industry was causing harm to broadcasting. Growth continued, but the rate of growth fell to a considerable extent during the period without must-carry (from 4.5 percent in 1986 to 1.7 percent by 1992), and appeared to be tapering off further. * * * Broadcast advertising revenues declined in real terms by 11 percent between 1986 and 1991, during a period in which cable's real advertising revenues nearly doubled. While these phenomena could be thought to stem from factors quite separate from the increasing market power of cable (for example, a recession in 1990–1992), it was for Congress to determine the better explanation. * * *

* * *

We think it apparent must-carry serves the Government's interests "in a direct and effective way." Must-carry ensures that a number of local broadcasters retain cable carriage, with the concomitant audience access and advertising revenues needed to support a multiplicity of stations. Appellants contend that even were this so, must-carry is broader than necessary to accomplish its goals. We turn to this question.

The second portion of the *O'Brien* inquiry concerns the fit between the asserted interests and the means chosen to advance them. Content-neutral regulations do not pose the same "inherent dangers to free expression."

* * *

In any event, after careful examination of each of the alternatives suggested by appellants, we cannot conclude that any of them is an adequate alternative to must-carry for promoting the Government's legitimate interests. First, among appellants' suggested alternatives is a proposal to revive a more limited set of must-carry rules, known as the "Century rules" after the 1987 court decision striking them down, see *Century Communications Corp. v. FCC*, 266 U.S. App. D.C. 228, 835 F.2d 292. [The Court held that these rules would be unworkable.]

* * *

[The second alternative proposed was the use of "A/B" switches in combination with antennas, to permit viewers to switch between cable and broadcast input; the Court rejected this on the grounds that Congress had examined the use of A/B switches as an alternative to must-carry and concluded it was "not an enduring or feasible method of distribution and . . . not in the public interest." § 2(a)(18)—and that studies had shown that few subscribers requested switches and even fewer used them. Similarly, the Court dismissed the notion of using "leased access" to provide carriage for broadcast stations, on the ground that it was too complex and potentially expensive to work effectively. The Court also stated that the notion of a guaranteed subsidy for failing stations was too general to be of any substance. Finally it declined to rely on enforcement of the general antitrust laws as an appropriate remedy.]

III

Judgments about how competing economic interests are to be reconciled in the complex and fast-changing field of television are for Congress to make. Those judgments "cannot be ignored or undervalued simply because [appellants] cast [their] claims under the umbrella of the First Amendment." Appellants' challenges to must-carry reflect little more than disagreement over the level of protection broadcast stations are to be afforded and how protection is to be attained. We cannot displace Congress' judgment respecting content-neutral regulations with our own, so long as its policy is grounded on reasonable factual findings supported by evidence that is substantial for a legislative determination. Those requirements were met in this case, and in these circumstances the First Amendment requires nothing more. The judgment of the District Court is affirmed.

It is so ordered.

JUSTICE STEVENS, concurring.

As Justice Kennedy clearly explains, the policy judgments made by Congress in the enactment of legislation that is intended to forestall the abuse of monopoly power are entitled to substantial deference. That is true even when the attempt to protect an economic market imposes burdens on communication. Though I write to emphasize this important point, I fully concur in the Court's thorough opinion.

JUSTICE BREYER, concurring in part.

I join the opinion of the Court except insofar as Part II–A–1 relies on an anticompetitive rationale.* * * My conclusion rests, however, not upon the principal opinion's analysis of the statute's efforts to "promote fair competition," but rather upon its discussion of the statute's other objectives. * * * Whether or not the statute does or does not sensibly compensate for some significant market defect, it undoubtedly seeks to provide over-the-air viewers who lack cable with a rich mix of over-the-air programming by guaranteeing the over-the-air stations that provide such programming with the extra dollars that an additional cable audience will generate. I believe that this purpose—to assure the over-the-air public "access to a multiplicity of information sources," provides sufficient basis for rejecting appellants' First Amendment claim.

I do not deny that the compulsory carriage that creates the "guarantee" extracts a serious First Amendment price. * * *

But there are important First Amendment interests on the other side as well. The statute's basic noneconomic purpose is to prevent too precipitous a decline in the quality and quantity of programming choice for an ever-shrinking non-cable-subscribing segment of the public. This purpose reflects what "has long been a basic tenet of national communications policy," namely that "the widest possible dissemination of information from diverse and antagonistic sources is essential to the welfare of the public." * * *

With important First Amendment interests on both sides of the equation, the key question becomes one of proper fit. That question, in my view, requires a reviewing court to determine both whether there are significantly less restrictive ways to achieve Congress' over-the-air programming objectives, and also to decide whether the statute, in its effort to achieve those objectives, strikes a reasonable balance between potentially speech-restricting and speech-enhancing consequences. The majority's opinion analyzes and evaluates those consequences, and I agree with its conclusions in respect to both of these matters.

* * *

JUSTICE O'CONNOR, with whom JUSTICE SCALIA, JUSTICE THOMAS, and JUSTICE GINSBURG join, dissenting.

In sustaining the must-carry provisions of the Cable Television Protection and Competition Act of 1992 against a First Amendment challenge by cable system operators and cable programmers, the Court errs in two crucial respects. First, the Court disregards one of the principal defenses of the statute urged by appellees on remand: that it serves a substantial interest in preserving "diverse," "quality" programming that is "responsive" to the needs of the local community. The course of this litigation on remand and the proffered defense strongly reinforce my view that the Court adopted the wrong analytic framework in the prior phase of this case. Second, the Court misapplies the "intermediate scrutiny" framework it adopts. Although we owe deference to Congress' predictive judgments and its evaluation of complex economic questions, we have an independent duty to identify with care the Government interests supporting the scheme, to inquire into the reasonableness of congressional findings regarding its necessity, and to examine the fit between its goals and its consequences. The Court fails to discharge its duty here.

I

I did not join those portions of the principal opinion in *Turner* holding that the must-carry provisions of the Cable Act are content neutral and therefore subject to intermediate First Amendment scrutiny. The Court there referred to the "unusually detailed statutory findings" accompanying the Act, in which Congress recognized the importance of preserving sources of local news, public affairs, and educational programming. * * *

Neither the principal opinion nor the partial concurrence offers any guidance on what might constitute a "significant reduction" in the availability of broadcast programming. The proper analysis, in my view, necessarily turns on the present distribution of broadcast stations among the local broadcast markets that make up the national broadcast "system." Whether cable poses a "significant" threat to a local broadcast market depends first on how many broadcast stations in that market will, in the absence of must-carry, remain available to viewers in noncable households. It also depends on whether viewers actually watch the stations that are dropped or denied carriage. The Court provides some raw data on adverse carriage decisions, but it never connects that data to markets and viewership. Instead, the Court proceeds from the assumptions that adverse carriage decisions nationwide will affect broadcast markets in proportion to their size; and that all broadcast programming is watched by viewers. Neither assumption is logical or has any factual basis in the record.

* * *

II

The principal opinion goes to great lengths to avoid acknowledging that preferences for "quality," "diverse," and "responsive" local programming underlie the must-carry scheme, although the partial concurrence's reliance on such preferences is explicit. I take the principal opinion at its word and evaluate the claim that the threat of anticompetitive behavior by cable operators supplies a content-neutral basis for sustaining the statute. It does not.

* * *

What was not resolved in *Turner* was whether "reasonable inferences based on substantial evidence," supported Congress' judgment that the must-carry provisions were necessary "to prevent cable operators from exploiting their economic power to the detriment of broadcasters," Because I remain convinced that the statute is not a measured response to congressional concerns about monopoly power, in my view the principal opinion's discussion on this point is irrelevant. But even if it were relevant, it is incorrect.

1

* * *

In my view, the statute is not narrowly tailored to serve a substantial interest in preventing anticompetitive conduct. I do not understand JUSTICE BREYER to disagree with this conclusion. Congress has commandeered up to one third of each cable system's channel capacity for the benefit of local broadcasters, without any regard for whether doing so advances the statute's alleged goals. To the extent that Congress was concerned that anticompetitive impulses would lead vertically integrated operators to prefer those programmers in which the operators have an ownership stake, the Cable Act is overbroad, since it does not impose its requirements solely on such operators. An integrated cable operator cannot satisfy its must-carry obligations by allocating a channel to an unaffiliated cable programmer. And must-carry blocks an operator's access to up to one third of the channels on the system, even if its affiliated programmer provides programming for only a single channel.

* * *

Finally, I note my disagreement with the Court's suggestion that the availability of less-speech-restrictive alternatives is never relevant to *O'Brien's* narrow tailoring inquiry. The *Turner* Court remanded this case in part because a plurality concluded that "judicial findings concerning the availability and efficacy of constitutionally acceptable less restrictive means of achieving the Government's asserted interests" were lacking in the original record. The Court's present position on this issue is puzzling.

* * *

I therefore respectfully dissent, and would reverse the judgment below.

———

As indicated above, the *Turner* cases are marginally helpful in terms of developing First Amendment doctrine in the field of cable television. The first case seems a bit self-contradictory, while the second resembles a typical administrative law review as to whether government action is "arbitrary or capricious."

Note: Cable Copyright Payments

The broadcast industry receives some direct compensation from cable operators, in terms of the "compulsory copyright fees" of 17 U.S.C. § 111—part of the general Copyright Revision Act of 1976. The amounts range in the hundreds of million of dollars—not exactly huge for an industry with revenues of more than $20,000,000 per year. As the old political remark goes, however, "when you get to a quarter of a billion, pretty soon you're talking real money."

Section 111 is somewhat complex, and becomes more so every year—Despite the difficulty with the details, it may be worthwhile to take a quick look at Section 111's general structure.

Generally, in order for works to be copyrighted under the 1976 Act, they must be "fixed in any tangible medium of expression * * * from which they can be perceived, reproduced, or otherwise communicated, either directly or with the aid of a machine or device." 17 U.S.C. § 102. If sufficiently fixed, video programs may be classified as "motion pictures and other audiovisual works," the latter of which are defined as:

> works that consist of a series of related images which are intrinsically intended to be shown by the use of machines or devices such as projectors, viewers, or electronic equipment, together with accompanying sounds, if any, regardless of the material objects, such as films or tapes, in which the works are embodied.

17 U.S.C. § 101.

As with regulation, the copyright history of cable television began in the courts. The Supreme Court consistently held that retransmission of distant broadcast signals did not infringe the copyright thereon. Fortnightly Corporation v. United Artists Television, Inc., 392 U.S. 390, 88 S.Ct. 2084, 20 L.Ed.2d 1176 (1968); Teleprompter Corporation v. CBS, Inc., 415 U.S. 394, 94 S.Ct. 1129, 39 L.Ed.2d 415 (1974). The Court viewed cable systems as passive intermediaries that "simply carry, without editing whatever programs they receive." Cable systems thus could carry broadcast programming without paying for a license or incurring any copyright liability.

Legislative adjustment of this situation came as part of the general Copyright Act of 1976. Section 111 of the new law created a compulsory copyright scheme, under which cable systems may retransmit broadcast programs in return for statutorily set royalty fees. The Act also created a new administrative agency, the Copyright Royalty Tribunal (CRT), to administer the compulsory copyright. 17 U.S.C. § 801(a). The CRT not only found Section 111 fiendishly difficult, but also was chronically underfunded for its mission; in the early days, CRT commissioners often had to do their own office work. Its members eventually asked Congress to abolish the agency, and Congress transferred its functions to the long-standing Copyright Office.

Section 111 calls for copyright fees to be collected from cable operators and distributes them to producers and other copyright owners under formulae which seem to satisfy no one. For a comparative perspective, see generally *Copyright Royalty Tribunals: Experience in Various Countries*, 34 J. Copyright 1986.

The basic thrust of Section 111 is to give cable systems compulsory licenses for all FCC-authorized signals and to require systems, except in specifically exempted situations, to pay for the use of distant signals. The availability of a compulsory license depends upon whether carriage of a particular signal is "permissible under the rules, regulations, or authorizations of the Federal Communications Commission." 17 U.S.C. § 111(c)(1). Section 111 thus uses the FCC's rules to define the scope of a compulsory copyright.

Tracking the Commission's "must carry" and "may carry" rules, § 111 sets up two primary categories of payments. First, a cable system must pay a flat percentage of its gross revenues for carrying local television signals. Second, cable operators must pay additional royalties for every "distant signal equivalent" (DSE) carried. The Act defines a DSE as "any nonnetwork television programing carried by a cable system in whole or in part beyond the service area of the primary transmitter of such programming", i.e., a distant independent station. 17 U.S.C. § 111(f).

Initially, the fee per DSE was set on a sliding scale, and was relatively low—0.675 percent of gross revenues for the first DSE, 0.425 for the second, third, and fourth DSEs, and 0.2 for each additional DSE. Because Congress foresaw that the Commission might modify its signal carriage rules, however, Section 801(b)(2)(B) gave the Copyright Royalty Tribunal the right to increase compulsory copyright fees to reflect such changes. After the Commission deleted its distant signal and syndicated exclusivity restrictions, the CRT increased royalty fees significantly.

Section 111 limits these payments in three major ways. First, a system pays a percentage only of "the gross receipts from subscribers * * * for the basic service of providing" broadcast signals. This excludes from the royalty calculation revenues earned from pay television programming, which may constitute half of a cable system's gross receipts. Second, § 111 provides a bargain basement rate for small cable systems. For example, a cable system with about 1,000 subscribers would pay very little for carriage of local signals alone. Many systems thus pay only nominal royalties.

Finally, cable systems pay on the basis not of individual distant signals, but rather of "distant signal equivalents". In recognition of the simple fact that educational stations often do not attract large audiences, § 111 treats them as only one-fourth of a "distant signal equivalent." Moreover, partly-carried stations and "station[s] carried pursuant to the late-night or specialty programming rules of the FCC" count only fractionally toward a DSE. A cable system could carry two distant independent signals and four educational signals for the price of three DSEs.

Calculating a system's royalties is complex. The Commission's repeal of the may carry rules means that carriage of any signal is "permissible," and hence within the compulsory copyright. But the royalty is much higher for distant than for local signals. Here, once again, the dead hand of the FCC's signal carriage rules is felt.

Under the Copyright Act, the definition of a local signal depends upon the old must carry rules; a signal is local if a cable system would be required to carry it. Section 111(f) defines "local service area of a primary transmitter" as "the area in which such station is entitled to insist upon its signal being retransmitted by a cable system pursuant to the rules * * * of the Federal Communications Commission in effect on April 15, 1976." A signal's classification as distant or local—and a potential fee difference of several thousand percent—thus depend upon application of the old must carry rules.

Suffice it to say, these are somewhat arcane in nature. Under the old FCC rules, must carry status depended not only upon the size of the market in which a cable system was located, but also upon the type of station seeking carriage. For example, in the top fifty television markets, a cable system had to carry:

(1) Television broadcast stations within whose specified zone [a thirty-five mile radius from a designated reference point in the station's city of license] is located, in whole or in part * * *;

(2) Noncommercial educational television broadcast stations within whose Grade B contours the community of the system is located, in whole or in part;

(3) Television translator stations, with 100 watts or higher power, licensed to the community of the system;

(4) Television broadcast stations licensed to other designated communities of the same major television market (Example: Cincinnati, Ohio–Newport, Kentucky television market);

(5) Commercial television broadcast stations that are significantly viewed in the community of the system. 47 C.F.R. § 76.61(a) (removed 1986).

To say that implementation of § 111 is idiosyncratic would obviously be an understatement. Nevertheless, none of the industries involved seems interested in abandoning the basic notion of a compulsory copyright; the transaction costs of an open marketplace might be staggering.

1. *Access Channels*

As noted before (p. 357 et seq.), the First Amendment status of access channels is unclear. In the following case, however, the Court established that PEG channels had at least some basic constitutional protections.

DENVER AREA EDUCATIONAL TELECOMMUNICATIONS CONSORTIUM, INC., v. FEDERAL COMMUNICATIONS COMMISSION

Supreme Court of the United States, 1996.
___ U.S. ___, 116 S.Ct. 2374, 135 L.Ed.2d 888.

*   Together with No. 95–227, Alliance for Community Media et al. v. Federal Communications Commission et al., also on certiorari to the same court.

JUSTICE BREYER announced the judgment of the Court and delivered the opinion of the Court with respect to Part III, an opinion with respect to Parts I, II, and V, in which JUSTICE STEVENS, JUSTICE O'CONNOR, and JUSTICE SOUTER join, and an opinion with respect to Parts IV and VI, in which JUSTICE STEVENS and JUSTICE SOUTER join.

These cases present First Amendment challenges to three statutory provisions that seek to regulate the broadcasting of "patently offensive" sex-related material on cable television. Cable Television Consumer Protection and Competition Act of 1992 (1992 Act or Act), §§ 10(a), 10(b), and 10(c), 47 U.S.C. §§ 532(h), 532(j). The provisions apply to programs broadcast over cable on what are known as "leased access channels" and "public, educational, or governmental channels." Two of the provisions essentially permit a cable system operator to prohibit the broadcasting of "programming" that the "operator reasonably believes describes or depicts sexual or excretory activities or organs in a patently offensive manner." 1992 Act, § 10(a). The remaining provision requires cable system operators to segregate certain "patently offensive" programming, to place it on a single channel, and to block that channel from viewer access unless the viewer requests access in advance and in writing. 1992 Act, § 10(b).

We conclude that the first provision—that permits the operator to decide whether or not to broadcast such programs on leased access channels—is consistent with the First Amendment. The second provision, that requires leased channel operators to segregate and to block that programming, and the third provision, applicable to public, educational, and governmental channels, violate the First Amendment, for they are not appropriately tailored to achieve the basic, legitimate objective of protecting children from exposure to "patently offensive" material.

I

* * *

In 1992, in an effort to control sexually explicit programming conveyed over access channels, Congress enacted the three provisions before us.

* * *

The upshot is, as we said at the beginning, that the federal law before us (the statute as implemented through regulations) now permits cable operators either to allow or to forbid the transmission of "patently offensive" sex-related materials over both leased and public access channels, and requires those operators, at a minimum, to segregate and to block transmission of that same material on leased channels.

[Petitioners had challenged the constitutionality of the three provisions in the D.C. Circuit; a panel invalidated the statute, but the Circuit *in banc* held it to be constitutional.]

* * *

II

We turn initially to the provision that permits cable system operators to prohibit "patently offensive" (or "indecent") programming transmitted over leased access channels. 1992 Act, § 10(a). * * *

* * *

Like the petitioners, Justices Kennedy and Thomas would have us decide this case simply by transferring and applying literally categorical standards this Court has developed in other contexts. For Justice Kennedy, leased access channels are like a common carrier, cablecast is a protected medium, strict scrutiny applies. § 10(a) fails this test, and, therefore, § 10(a) is invalid. For Justice Thomas, the case is simple because the cable operator who owns the system over which access channels are broadcast, like a bookstore owner with respect to what it displays on the shelves, has a predominant First Amendment interest. Both categorical approaches suffer from the same flaws: they import law developed in very different contexts into a new and changing environment, and they lack the flexibility necessary to allow government to respond to very serious practical problems without sacrificing the free exchange of ideas the First Amendment is designed to protect.

The history of this Court's First Amendment jurisprudence, however, is one of continual development ... * * *

* * *

This tradition teaches that the First Amendment embodies an overarching commitment to protect speech from Government regulation through close judicial scrutiny, thereby enforcing the Constitution's constraints, but without imposing judicial formulae so rigid that they become a straightjacket that disables Government from responding to serious problems. This Court, in different contexts, has consistently held that the Government may directly regulate speech to address extraordinary problems, where its regulations are appropriately tailored to resolve those problems without imposing an unnecessarily great restriction on speech. Justices Kennedy and Thomas would have us further declare which, among the many applications of the general approach that this Court has developed over the years, we are applying here. But no definitive choice among competing analogies (broadcast, common carrier, bookstore) allows us to declare a rigid single standard, good for now and for all future media and purposes. That is not to say that we reject all the more specific formulations of the standard—they appropriately cover the vast majority of cases involving Government regulation of speech. Rather, aware as we are of the changes taking place in the law, the technology, and the industrial structure, related to telecommunications, we believe it unwise and unnecessary definitively to pick one analogy or one specific set of words now.

* * *

Rather than decide these issues, we can decide this case more narrowly, by closely scrutinizing § 10(a) to assure that it properly addresses an extremely important problem, without imposing, in light of the relevant interests, an unnecessarily great restriction on speech. The importance of the interest at stake here—protecting children from exposure to patently offensive depictions of sex; the accommodation of the interests of programmers in maintaining access channels and of cable operators in editing the contents of their channels; the similarity of the problem and its solution to those at issue in *Pacifica*, *supra*; and the flexibility inherent in an approach that permits private cable operators to make editorial decisions, lead us to conclude that § 10(a) is a sufficiently tailored response to an extraordinarily important problem.

First, the provision before us comes accompanied with an extremely important justification, one that this Court has often found compelling—the need to protect children from exposure to patently offensive sex-related material.

Second, the provision arises in a very particular context—congressional permission for cable operators to regulate programming that, but for a previous Act of Congress, would have had no path of access to cable channels free of an operator's control. The First Amendment interests involved are therefore complex, and involve a balance between those interests served by the access requirements themselves (increasing the availability of avenues of expression to programmers who otherwise would not have them), and the disadvantage to the First Amendment interests of cable operators and other programmers (those to whom the cable operator would have assigned the channels devoted to access).

Third, the problem Congress addressed here is remarkably similar to the problem addressed by the FCC in *Pacifica*, and the balance Congress struck is commensurate with the balance we approved there.* * *

All these factors are present here. Cable television broadcasting, including access channel broadcasting, is as "accessible to children" as over-the-air broadcasting, if not more so.

Fourth, the permissive nature of § 10(a) means that it likely restricts speech less than, not more than, the ban at issue in *Pacifica*. The provision removes a restriction as to some speakers—namely, cable operators. Moreover, although the provision does create a risk that a program will not appear, that risk is not the same as the certainty that accompanies a governmental ban. In fact, a glance at the programming that cable operators allow on their own (nonaccess) channels suggests that this distinction is not theoretical, but real. Finally, the provision's permissive nature brings with it a flexibility that allows cable operators, for example, not to ban broadcasts, but, say, to rearrange broadcast times, better to fit the desires of adult audiences while lessening the risks of harm to children. In all these respects, the permissive nature of the approach taken by Congress renders this measure appropriate as a means of achieving the underlying purpose of protecting children.

* * *

The existence of this complex balance of interests persuades us that the permissive nature of the provision, coupled with its viewpoint-neutral application, is a constitutionally permissible way to protect children from the type of sexual material that concerned Congress, while accommodating both the First Amendment interests served by the access requirements and those served in restoring to cable operators a degree of the editorial control that Congress removed in 1984.

* * *

For three reasons * * * it is unnecessary, indeed, unwise, for us definitively to decide whether or how to apply the public forum doctrine to leased access channels. First, while it may be that content-based exclusions from the right to use common carriers could violate the First Amendment, it is not at all clear that the public forum doctrine should be imported wholesale into the area of common carriage regulation. * * * Second, it is plain from this Court's cases that a public forum "may be created for a limited purpose." * * * Finally, and most important, the effects of Congress'. decision on the interests of programmers, viewers, cable operators, and children are the same, whether we characterize Congress' decision as one that limits access to a public forum, discriminates in common carriage, or constrains speech because of its content. If we consider this particular limitation of indecent television programming acceptable as a constraint on speech, we must no less accept the limitation it places on access to the claimed public forum or on use of a common carrier.

* * *

[The opinion also concluded that the definition of materials subject to a cable operator's deletion was not void for vagueness.]

III

The statute's second provision significantly differs from the first, for it does not simply permit, but rather requires, cable system operators to restrict speech—by segregating and blocking "patently offensive" sex-related material appearing on leased channels (but not on other channels). 1992 Act, § 10(b). In particular, this provision and its implementing regulations require cable system operators to place "patently offensive" leased channel programming on a separate channel; to block that channel; to unblock the channel within 30 days of a subscriber's written request for access; and to reblock the channel within 30 days of a subscriber's request for reblocking. Also, leased channel programmers must notify cable operators of an intended "patently offensive" broadcast up to 30 days before its scheduled broadcast date. §§ 76.701(d), (g).

These requirements have obvious restrictive effects. The several up-to-30-day delays, along with single channel segregation, mean that a subscriber cannot decide to watch a single program without considerable advance planning and without letting the "patently offensive" channel in its entirety invade his household for days, perhaps weeks, at a time. These restrictions will prevent programmers from broadcasting to viewers who select programs day by day (or, through "surfing," minute by minute); to viewers who would like occasionally to watch a few, but not many, of the programs on the "patently offensive" channel; and to viewers who simply tend to judge a program's value through channel reputation, i.e., by the company it keeps. Moreover, the "written notice" requirement will further restrict viewing by subscribers who fear for their reputations should the operator, advertently or inadvertently, disclose the list of those who wish to watch the "patently offensive" channel. Further, the added costs and burdens that these requirements impose upon a cable system operator may encourage that operator to ban programming that the operator would otherwise permit to run, even if only late at night.

* * *

* * *[O]nce one examines this governmental restriction, it becomes apparent that, not only is it not a "least restrictive alternative," and is not "narrowly tailored" to meet its legitimate objective, it also seems considerably "more extensive than necessary." That is to say, it fails to satisfy this Court's formulations of the First Amendment's "strictest," as well as its somewhat less "strict," requirements.* * *

Several circumstances lead us to this conclusion. For one thing, the law, as recently amended, uses other means to protect children from similar "patently offensive" material broadcast on unleased cable channels, i.e., broadcast over any of a system's numerous ordinary, or public access, channels. The law, as recently amended, requires cable operators to "scramble or . . . block" such programming on any (unleased) channel "primarily dedicated to sexually-oriented programming." In addition, cable operators must honor a subscriber's request to block any, or all, programs on any channel to which he or she does not wish to subscribe. And manufacturers, in the future, will have to make television sets with a so-called "V-chip"—a device that will be able automatically to identify and block sexually explicit or violent programs.

* * *

No provision, we concede, short of an absolute ban, can offer certain protection against assault by a determined child. * * * [T]he Solicitor General's list of practical difficulties would seem to call, not for "segregate and block" requirements, but, rather, for informational requirements, for a simple coding system, for readily available blocking equipment (perhaps accessible by telephone), for imposing cost burdens upon system operators (who may spread them through subscription fees); or perhaps even for a system that requires lockbox defaults to be set to block certain channels (say, sex-dedicated-channels). * * *

Consequently, we cannot find that the "segregate and block" restrictions on speech are a narrowly, or reasonably, tailored effort to protect children. Rather, they are overly restrictive, "sacrificing" important First Amendment interests for too "speculative a gain." For that reason they are not consistent with the First Amendment.

IV

The statute's third provision, as implemented by FCC regulation, is similar to its first provision, in that it too permits a cable operator to prevent transmission of "patently offensive" programming, in this case on public access channels. 1992 Act, § 10(c). But there are four important differences.

The first is the historical background. [C]able operators have traditionally agreed to reserve channel capacity for public, governmental, and educational channels as part of the consideration they give municipalities that award them cable franchises.* * * Unlike § 10(a) therefore, § 10(c) does not restore to cable operators editorial rights that they once had, and the countervailing First Amendment interest is nonexistent, or at least much diminished.

The second difference is the institutional background that has developed as a result of the historical difference. When a "leased channel" is made available by the operator to a private lessee, the lessee has total control of programming during the leased time slot. Public access channels, on the other hand, are normally subject to complex supervisory systems of various sorts, often with both public and private elements. Municipalities generally provide in their cable franchising agreements for an access channel manager, who is most commonly a nonprofit organization, but may also be the municipality, or, in some instances, the cable system owner.

* * *

Third, the existence of a system aimed at encouraging and securing programming that the community considers valuable strongly suggests that a "cable operator's veto" is less likely necessary to achieve the statute's basic objective, protecting children, than a similar veto in the context of leased channels. Of course, the system of access managers and supervising boards can make mistakes, which the operator might in some cases correct with its veto power. Balanced against this potential benefit, however, is the risk that the veto itself may be mistaken; and its use, or threatened use, could prevent the presentation of programming, that, though borderline, is not "patently offensive" to its targeted audience.

* * *

Finally, our examination of the legislative history and the record before us is consistent with what common sense suggests, namely that the public/nonprofit programming control systems now in place would normally avoid, minimize, or eliminate any child-related problems concerning "patently offensive" programming. We have found anecdotal references to what seem isolated instances of potentially indecent programming, some of which may well have occurred on leased, not public access channels.

* * * Having carefully reviewed the legislative history of the Act, the proceedings before the FCC, the record below, and the submissions of the parties and amici here, we conclude that the Government cannot sustain its burden of showing that § 10(c) is necessary to protect children or that it is appropriately tailored to secure that end. Consequently, we find that this third provision violates the First Amendment.

* * *

[The Court found that the three provisions were severable, since Congress had not intended that operation of all three together was essential to its legislative plan.]

For these reasons, the judgment of the Court of Appeals is affirmed insofar as it upheld § 10(a); the judgment of the Court of Appeals is reversed insofar as it upheld § 10(b) and § 10(c).

It is so ordered.

JUSTICE STEVENS, concurring.

The difference between § 10(a) and § 10(c) is the difference between a permit and a prohibition. The former restores the freedom of cable operators to reject indecent programs; the latter requires local franchising authorities to reject such programs. While I join the Court's opinion, I add these comments to emphasize the difference between the two provisions and to endorse the analysis in Part III–B of JUSTICE KENNEDY's opinion even though I do not think it necessary to characterize the public access channels as public fora. Like JUSTICE SOUTER, I am convinced that it would be unwise to take a categorical approach to the resolution of novel First Amendment questions arising in an industry as dynamic as this.

* * *

I do not agree, however, that § 10(a) established a public forum. Unlike sidewalks and parks, the Federal Government created leased access channels in the course of its legitimate regulation of the communications industry. In so doing, it did not establish an entirely open forum, but rather restricted access to certain speakers, namely unaffiliated programmers able to lease the air time. By facilitating certain speech that cable operators would not otherwise carry, the leased access channels operate like the must-carry rules.

* * *

JUSTICE SOUTER, concurring.

* * *

Nor does the fact that we deal in this case with cable transmission necessarily suggest that a simple category subject to a standard level of scrutiny ought to be recognized at this point; while we have found cable television different from broadcast with respect to the factors justifying intrusive access requirements under the rule in * * * today's plurality opinion rightly observes that the characteristics of broadcast radio that rendered indecency particularly threatening in *Pacifica*, that is, its intrusion into the house and accessibility to children, are also present in the case of cable television. It would seem, then, that the appropriate category for cable indecency should be as contextually detailed as the *Pacifica* example, and settling upon a definitive level-of-scrutiny rule of review for so complex a category would require a subtle judgment; but there is even more to be considered, enough more to demand a subtlety tantamount to prescience.

All of the relevant characteristics of cable are presently in a state of technological and regulatory flux. Recent and far-reaching legislation not only affects the technical feasibility of parental control over children's access to undesirable material. As cable and telephone companies begin their competition for control over the single wire that will carry both their services, we can hardly settle rules for review of regulation on the assumption that cable will remain a separable and useful category of First Amendment scrutiny. And as broadcast, cable, and the cyber-technology of the Internet and the World Wide Web approach the day of using a common receiver, we can hardly assume that standards for judging the regulation of one of them will not have immense, but now unknown and unknowable, effects on the others.

Accordingly, in charting a course that will permit reasonable regulation in light of the values in competition, we have to accept the likelihood that the media of communication will become less categorical and more protean. Because we cannot be confident that for purposes of judging speech restrictions it will continue to make sense to distinguish cable from other technologies, and because we know that changes in these regulated technologies will enormously alter the structure of regulation itself, we should be shy about saying the final word today about what will be accepted as reasonable tomorrow.

* * *

JUSTICE O'CONNOR, concurring in part and dissenting in part.

* * *

The distinctions upon which the Court relies in deciding that § 10(c) must fall while § 10(a) survives are not, in my view, constitutionally significant. Much emphasis is placed on the differences in the origins of leased access and public access channels. To be sure, the leased access channels covered by § 10(a) were a product of the Federal Government, while the public access channels at issue in § 10(c) arose as part of the cable franchises awarded by municipalities, see ante at 30–31, but I am not persuaded that the difference in the origin of the access channels is sufficient to justify upholding § 10(a) and striking down § 10(c). The interest in protecting children remains the same, whether on a leased access channel or a public access channel, and allowing the cable operator the option of prohibiting the transmission of indecent speech seems a constitutionally permissible means of addressing that interest. Nor is the fact that public access programming may be subject to supervisory systems in addition to the cable operator, see ante, at 31–33, sufficient in my mind to render § 10(c) so ill-tailored to its goal as to be unconstitutional. Given the compelling interest served by § 10(c), its permissive nature, and fit within our precedent, I would hold § 10(c), like § 10(a), constitutional.

* * *

JUSTICE KENNEDY, with whom JUSTICE GINSBURG joins, concurring in part, concurring in the judgment in part, and dissenting in part.

* * *

Before engaging the complexities of cable access channels and explaining my reasons for thinking all of § 10 unconstitutional, I start with the most disturbing aspect of the plurality opinion: its evasion of any clear legal standard in deciding this case.

* * *

The plurality seems distracted by the many changes in technology and competition in the cable industry. The laws challenged here, however, do not retool the structure of the cable industry or (with the exception of § 10(b)) involve intricate technologies. The straightforward issue here is whether the Government can deprive certain speakers, on the basis of the content of their speech, of protections afforded all others.

These restatements have unfortunate consequences. The first is to make principles intended to protect speech easy to manipulate. The words end up being a legalistic cover for an ad hoc balancing of interests; in this respect the plurality succeeds after all in avoiding the use of a standard. Second, the plurality's exercise in pushing around synonyms for the words of our usual standards will sow confusion in the courts bound by our precedents. Those courts, and lawyers in the communications field, now will have to discern what difference there is between the formulation the plurality applies today and our usual strict scrutiny. I can offer little guidance, except to note the unprotective outcome the plurality reaches here. This is why comparisons and analogies to other areas of our First Amendment case law become a responsibility, rather than the luxury the plurality considers them to be. The comparisons provide discipline to the Court and guidance for others, and give clear content to our standards—all the things I find missing in the plurality's opinion. The novelty and complexity of the case is a reason to look for help from other areas of our First Amendment jurisprudence, not a license to wander into uncharted areas of the law with no compass other than our own opinions about good policy.

* * *

In all events, the plurality's unwillingness to consider our public-forum precedents does not relieve it of the burden of explaining why strict scrutiny should not apply. Except in instances involving well-settled categories of proscribable speech, strict scrutiny is the baseline rule for reviewing any content-based discrimination against speech. The purpose of forum analysis is to determine whether, because of the property or medium where speech takes place, there should be any dispensation from this rule. * * *

* * *

In agreement with the plurality's analysis of § 10(b) of the Act, insofar as it applies strict scrutiny, I join Part III of its opinion. Its position there, however, cannot be reconciled with upholding § 10(a). In the plurality's view, § 10(b), which standing alone would guarantee an indecent programmer some access to a cable audience, violates the First Amendment, but § 10(a), which authorizes exclusion of indecent programming from access channels altogether, does not. There is little to commend this logic or result. I dissent from the judgment of the Court insofar as it upholds the constitutionality of § 10(a).

JUSTICE THOMAS, joined by the CHIEF JUSTICE and JUSTICE SCALIA, concurring in the judgment in part and dissenting in part.

I agree with the plurality's conclusion that § 10(a) is constitutionally permissible, but I disagree with its conclusion that §§ 10(b) and (c) violate the First Amendment. For many years, we have failed to articulate how and to what extent the First Amendment protects cable operators, programmers, and viewers from state and federal regulation. I think it is time we did so, and I cannot go along with the plurality's assiduous attempts to avoid addressing that issue openly.

* * *

It is one thing to compel an operator to carry leased and public access speech, in apparent violation of Tornillo, but it is another thing altogether to say that the First Amendment forbids Congress to give back part of the operators' editorial discretion, which all recognize as fundamentally protected, in favor of a broader access right. It is no answer to say that leased and public access are content neutral and that §§ 10(a) and (c) are not, for that does not change the fundamental fact, which petitioners never address, that it is the operators' journalistic freedom that is infringed, whether the challenged restrictions be content neutral or content based.

* * *

Notes and Questions

1. What if the "holding" of the case? What parts of the 1992 Act did the Court invalidate? On what constitutional grounds?

2. Which constitutional test does the plurality opinion use? *O'Brien*? A "strict scrutiny" approach? Some version of the traditional "public forum" doctrine? What is the debate between Breyer and Kennedy about?

One commentator has criticized the *Denver Area* decision for its lack of coherence.

> The Court has now made a bad situation even worse in *Denver Area Educational Telecommunications Consortium, Inc. v. FCC* by its treatment of "indecency" on certain cable access channels. In a case with six

contentious opinions, none of which enjoyed a full majority, the plurality assiduously managed not only to avoid defining the First Amendment status of cable within fairly well-established boundaries, but seemed to grope at a new, ad hoc constitutional approach somewhere between intermediate and strict scrutiny. The primary public interest in full First Amendment freedom of the press cannot avoid suffering from the Court's emerging and confusing hierarchy of differing constitutional statuses for various segments of the media, precisely as they all—voice, print, video, and data—are converging technologically into one.

Lawrence H. Winer, *The Red Lion of Cable, and Beyond?—Turner Broadcasting v. FCC*, 15 Cardozo Arts & Ent. L.J.I. (1997).

3.   All of the opinions talk about adopting new constitutional tests for new media, such as cable. Indeed, there is a lively dialogue between various Justices' opinions on this point. Some seem to favor analogies to existing regulatory schemes; others the creation of new constitutional doctrines. And some seem to be willing to live with either one. Which is the better approach? What would a new constitutional doctrine look like?

4.   The Court seems to be in agreement that it is better to develop new doctrines than to analogize to existing law, e.g., the old "reasonably ancillary" test for cable. (p. 78 et seq.) But if this is the case, it raises some questions as to the content of new doctrines.

(a) How would a court develop a new test, without looking at prior rulings, e.g., the *Red Lion* vs. *Tornillo* approaches?

(b) What factors would be relevant to developing new doctrines for new media? And how would they be developed?

In both recent opinions and scholarly literature, there has been a call to give up the old practice of looking for the best possible analogy for regulation of a new medium, e.g., DBS as broadcasting (p. 59), and instead to create new modes of regulation for new media. As indicated above, however, the difficult part with this approach is creating a totally new regulatory scheme. Moreover, this task is complicated by the fact that it usually is difficult if not impossible to foresee with any accuracy the development of a new industry. For example, entrepreneurs first tried to launch DBS in the early 1980s; then again in the early 1990s; and then finally—apparently with some success—in the mid–1990s. Which scenario would it make sense to base regulation on?

5.   The plurality talks about the need for new tests because of developments of "new media." What precisely are these developments? What does Justice Breyer seem to mean by this? Why does Justice O'Conner seem to disagree with this?

6.   Why should PEG channels be treated any differently than leased access channels, since both provide "access"—albeit to different groups? Justice Breyer relies heavily upon the "history" to PEG channels—which first were required by local franchising authorities, then mandated by the FCC, and then allowed by the 1984 and 1992 cable legislation. What is the real difference between leased access and PEG channels? What difference

does the "history" of PEG make? Is PEG more or less intrusive on cable operators than leased access? How many companies would you think have demanded—let alone gotten-leased access?

7. The plurality notes the existence of various means of excluding indecency from the home other than censorship—such as the "V-chip" (p. 562 et seq.) which would allow parents to prevent children from watching certain types of programming. As the plurality notes, however, it is not yet clear whether these system will work, or be held constitutional. What happens to the underpinnings of the plurality opinion if the V-chip ultimately is either scuttled or held to be unconstitutional?

D.   THE ACCESS ALTERNATIVE

1.   ORIGINS IN THE BROADCAST MEDIA

The fairness doctrine provided, and equal opportunities provide, airtime only after a third party performs an initial act of some kind—a "triggering statement." This type of arrangement makes sense where the basic goal is to provide a reply on an important matter. The requirement of a triggering statement does not further the interests, however, of an individual or group concerned with initiating a discussion on what it perceives to be a significant topic.

Providing an electronic forum for these purposes requires a different conceptual and administrative scheme, often described as a "mandatory right of access." (This was the right at issue in the *CBS v. DNC* case. (p. ___)) Instead of making airtime hinge on a perhaps mechanical but clearly ascertainable event—the triggering statement—an access scheme of this type would depend upon some other (and administratively more difficult) means of allocating airtime among potential speakers.

Advocates of access have suggested schemes ranging from lotteries to "first in time, first in right" approaches. None has attracted any widespread support or acceptance; all are fraught with administrative complications and constitutional dilemmas. Nevertheless, the notion of an access scheme continues to have a certain attraction because of its potential to provide an "electronic soapbox" to a broader range of speakers.

Although the access concept does not seem to have any clearly identifiable parent, it has been the subject of debate at least since Professor Chafee sketched it out in 1941. Dean Barron provided more detail in his 1967 article; indeed, the access concept began to attract considerable attention at just about that time. Its support undoubtedly was fueled not only by legal theory, but also by the media-hungry civil rights and anti-war movements and by the newly emerging cable industry, which could provide access channels without displacing other programming.

Z. CHAFEE, FREE SPEECH IN THE UNITED STATES

559–560 (1941).

Speech should be fruitful as well as free. Our experience introduces this qualification into the classical argument of Milton and John Stuart Mill, that only through open discussion is truth discovered and spread. In their simpler times, they thought it enough to remove legal obstacles like the censorship and sedition prosecutions. * * * To us this policy is too exclusively negative. For example, what is the use of telling an unpopular speaker that he will incur no criminal penalties by his proposed address, so long as every hall owner in the city declines to rent him space for his meeting and there are no vacant lots available? There should be municipal auditoriums, schoolhouses out of school hours, church forums, parks in summer, all open to thresh out every question of public importance, with just as few restrictions as possible. * * *

We must do more than remove the discouragements to open discussion. We must exert ourselves to supply active encouragements.

Physical space and lack of interference alone will not make discussion fruitful. We must take affirmative steps to improve the methods by which discussion is carried on. Of late years the argument of Milton and Mill has been questioned, because truth does not seem to emerge from a controversy in the automatic way their logic would lead us to expect. * * * Perhaps Truth will win in the long run; but in the long run, as Walter Lippmann says, we shall all be dead—and perhaps not peacefully in our beds either. * * *

Nevertheless, the main argument of Milton and Mill still holds good. All that this disappointment means is that friction is a much bigger drag on the progress of Truth than they supposed. Efforts to lessen that friction are essential to the success of freedom of speech. * * *

BARRON, ACCESS TO THE PRESS—A NEW FIRST AMENDMENT RIGHT

80 Harvard L.Rev. 1641 (1967).*

There is an anomaly in our constitutional law. While we protect expression once it has come to the fore, our law is indifferent to creating opportunities for expression. Our constitutional theory is in the grip of a romantic conception of free expression, a belief that the "marketplace of ideas" is freely accessible. But if ever there were a self-operating marketplace of ideas, it has long ceased to exist. The mass media's development of an antipathy to ideas requires legal intervention if novel and unpopular ideas are to be assured a forum—unorthodox points of view which have no claim on broadcast time and newspaper space as a matter of right are in a poor position to compete with those aired as a matter of grace.

The free expression questions which now come before the courts involve individuals who have managed to speak or write in a manner that captures public attention and provokes legal reprisal. The conventional constitutional issue is whether expression already uttered should be given First Amendment shelter or whether it may be subjected to sanction as speech beyond the constitutionally protected pale. To those who can obtain access to the media of mass communications First Amendment case law furnishes considerable help. But what of those whose ideas are too unacceptable to secure access to the media? To them the mass communications industry replies: The First Amendment guarantees our freedom to do as we choose with our media. Thus the constitutional imperative of free expression becomes a rationale for repressing competing ideas. First Amendment theory must be reexamined, for only responding to the present reality of the mass media's repression of ideas can the constitutional guarantee of free speech best serve its original purposes. * * *

The aversion of the media for the novel and heretical has escaped attention for an odd reason. The controllers of the media have no ideology. Since in the main they espouse no particular ideas, their antipathy to all ideas has passed unnoticed. What has happened is not that the controllers of opinion, Machiavellian fashion, are subtly feeding us information to the end that we shall acquiesce in their political view of the universe. On the contrary, the communications industry is operated on the whole with an intellectual neutrality consistent with V.O. Key's theory that the commercial nature of mass communications makes it "bad business" to espouse the heterodox or the controversial.

But retreat from ideology is not bereft of ideological and practical consequences. In a commentary about television, but which applies equally well to all mass media, Gilbert Seldes has complained that, in a time demanding more active intelligence than has ever before been necessary if we are to survive, the most powerful of all our media are inducing inertia. The contemporary structure of the mass media directs the media away from rather than toward opinion-making. In other words, it is not that the mass communication industry is pushing certain ideas and rejecting others but rather that it is using the free speech and free press guarantees to avoid opinions instead of acting as a sounding board for their expression. What happens, of course, is that the opinion vacuum is filled with the least controversial and bland ideas. Whatever is stale and accepted in the status quo is readily discussed and thereby reinforced and revitalized. * * *

There is inequality in the power to communicate ideas just as there is inequality in economic bargaining power; to recognize the latter and deny the former is quixotic. The "marketplace of ideas" view has rested on the assumption that protecting the right of expression is equivalent to providing for it. But changes in the communications industry have destroyed the equilibrium in that marketplace. While it may have been still possible in 1925 to believe with Justice Holmes that every idea is "acted on unless some other belief outweighs it or some failure of energy stifles the movement at its birth," it is impossible to believe that now. Yet the Holmesian theory is not abandoned, even though the advent of radio and television has made even more evident that philosophy's unreality. A realistic view of the First Amendment requires recognition that a right of expression is somewhat thin if it can be exercised only at the sufferance of the managers of mass communications. * * *

A corollary of the romantic view of the First Amendment is the Court's unquestioned assumption that the amendment affords "equal" protection to the various media. According to this view, new media of communication are assimilated into First Amendment analysis without regard to the enormous differences in impact these media have in comparison with the traditional printed word. Radio and television are to be as free as newspapers and magazines, sound trucks as free as radio and television.

This extension of a simplistic egalitarianism to media whose comparative impacts are gravely disproportionate is wholly unrealistic. It results from confusing freedom of media content with freedom of the media to restrict access. The assumption in romantic First Amendment analysis that the same postulates apply to different classes of people, situations, and means of communication obscures the fact, noted explicitly by Justice Jackson in *Kovacs v. Cooper*,[24] that problems of access and impact vary significantly from medium to medium: "The moving picture screen, the radio, the newspaper, the handbill, the sound truck and the street corner orator have differing natures, values, abuses and dangers. Each, in my view, is a law unto itself, and all we are dealing with now is the sound truck." * * *

An analysis of the First Amendment must be tailored to the context in which ideas are or seek to be aired. This contextual approach requires an examination of the purposes served by and the impact of each particular medium. If a group seeking to present a particular side of a public issue is unable to get space in the only newspaper in town, is this inability compensated by the availability of the public park or the sound truck? Competitive media only constitute alternative means of access in a crude manner. If ideas are criticized in one forum the most adequate response is in the same forum since it is most likely to reach the same audience. Further, the various media serve different functions and create different reactions and expectations—criticism of an individual or a governmental policy over television may reach more people but criticism in print is more durable. * * *

The late Professor Meiklejohn, who has articulated a view of the First Amendment which assumes its justification to be political self-government, has wisely pointed out that "what is essential is not that everyone shall speak, but that everything worth saying shall be said"—that the point of ultimate interest is not the words of the speakers but

24. 336 U.S. 77, 97 (1949) (concurring opinion).

the minds of the hearers.[29] Can everything worth saying be effectively said? Constitutional opinions that are particularly solicitous of the interests of mass media—radio, television, and mass circulation newspaper—devote little thought to the difficulties of securing access to those media. If those media are unavailable, can the minds of "hearers" be reached effectively? Creating opportunities for expression is as important as ensuring the right to express ideas without fear of governmental reprisal. * * *

The avowed emphasis of free speech is still on a freeman's right to "lay what sentiments he pleases before the public." But Blackstone wrote in another age. Today ideas reach the millions largely to the extent they are permitted entry into the great metropolitan dailies, news magazines, and broadcasting networks. The soap box is no longer an adequate forum for public discussion. Only the new media of communication can lay sentiments before the public and government who can most effectively abridge expression by nullifying the opportunity for an idea to win acceptance. As a constitutional theory for the communication of ideas, laissez-faire is manifestly irrelevant. * * *

The mass communications industry should be viewed in constitutional litigation with the same candor with which it has been analyzed by industry members and scholars in communication. If dissemination of books can be prohibited and punished when the dissemination is not for any "saving intellectual content" but for "commercial exploitation," it would seem that the mass communications industry, no less animated by motives of "commercial exploitation," could be legally obliged to host competing opinions and points of view. If the mass media are essentially business enterprises and their commercial nature makes it difficult to give a full and effective hearing to a wide spectrum of opinion, a theory of the First Amendment is unrealistic if it prevents courts or legislatures from requiring the media to do that which, for commercial reasons, they would be otherwise unlikely to do. Such proposals only require that the opportunity for publication be broadened and do not involve restraint on publication or punishment after publication, as did *Ginzburg* where the distributor of books was jailed under an obscenity statute even though the books themselves were not constitutionally obscene. * * *

The foregoing analysis has suggested the necessity of rethinking First Amendment theory so that it will not only be effective in preventing governmental abridgment but will also produce meaningful expression despite the present or potential repressive effects of the mass media. If the First Amendment can be so invoked, it is necessary to examine what machinery is available to enforce a right of access and what bounds limit that right. * * *

One alternative is a judicial remedy affording individuals and groups desiring to voice views on public issues a right of nondiscriminatory

29. A. Meiklejohn, *Political Freedom: The Constitutional Powers of the People*, pp. 25–38 (1960).

access to the community newspaper. This right could be rooted most naturally in the letter-to-the-editor column and the advertising section. That pressure to establish such a right exists in our law is suggested by a number of cases in which plaintiffs have contended, albeit unsuccessfully, that in certain circumstances newspaper publishers have a common law duty to publish advertisements. In these cases the advertiser sought nondiscriminatory access, subject to even-handed limitations imposed by rates and space. * * *

The courts could provide for a right of access other than by reinterpreting the First Amendment to provide for the emergence as well as the protection of expression. A right of access to the pages of a monopoly newspaper might be predicated on Justice Douglas's open-ended "public function" theory which carried a majority of the Court in *Evans v. Newton*.[74] Such a theory would demand a rather radical conception of "state action," but if parks in private hands cannot escape the stigma of abiding "public character," it would seem that a newspaper, which is the common journal of printed communication in a community, could not escape the constitutional restrictions which quasi-public status invites. If monopoly newspapers are indeed quasi-public, their refusal of space to particular viewpoints is state action abridging expression in violation of even the romantic view of the First Amendment. * * *

Another, and perhaps more appropriate, approach would be to secure the right of access by legislation. A statute might impose the modest requirement, for example, that denial of access not be arbitrary but rather be based on rational grounds. * * *

Constitutional power exists for both federal and state legislation in this area. Turning first to the constitutional basis for federal legislation, it has long been held that freedom of expression is protected by the due process clause of the Fourteenth Amendment. * * *

If public order and an informed citizenry are, as the Supreme Court has repeatedly said, the goals of the First Amendment, these goals would appear to comport well with state attempts to implement a right of access under the rubric of its traditional police power. If a right of access is not constitutionally proscribed, it would seem well within the powers reserved to the states by the tenth amendment of the Constitution to enact such legislation. Of course, if there were conflict between federal and state legislation, the federal legislation would control. Yet, the whole concept of a right of access is so embryonic that it can scarcely be argued that congressional silence preempts the field.

The right of access might be an appropriate area for experimental, innovative legislation. The right to access problems of a small state dominated by a single city with a monopoly press will vary, for example, from those of a populous state with many cities nourished by many competing media. These differences may be more accurately reflected by

74. 382 U.S. 296 (1966).

state autonomy in this area, resulting in a cultural federalism such as that envisaged by Justice Harlan in the obscenity cases. * * *

If a right of access is to be recognized, considerations of administrative feasibility require that limitations of the right be carefully defined. The * * * case of *Office of Communication of the United Church of Christ v. FCC*[99] suggests, by analogy, the means by which such a right of nondiscriminatory access can be rendered judicially manageable. In *Church of Christ* the court, while expanding the concept of standing, did not hold that every listener's taste provides standing to challenge the applicant in broadcast license renewal proceedings. * * *

A right of access, whether created by court or legislature, necessarily would have to develop a similar approach. One relevant factor, using *Church of Christ* as an analogue, would be the degree to which the petitioner seeking access represents a significant sector of the community. But this is perhaps not a desirable test—"divergent" views, by definition, may not command the support of a "significant sector" of the community, and these may be the very views which, by hypothesis, it is desirable to encourage. Perhaps the more relevant consideration is whether the material for which access is sought is indeed suppressed and underrepresented by the newspaper. Thus, if there are a number of petitioners seeking access for a particular matter or issue, it may be necessary to give access to only one. The unimpressed response of Judge Burger in *Church of Christ* to the FCC's lamentations about that enduring tidal phenomenon of the law, the "floodgates," strikes an appropriate note of calm: "The fears of regulatory agencies that their processes will be inundated by expansion of standing criteria are rarely borne out."

Utilization of a contextual approach highlights the importance of the degree to which an idea is suppressed in determining whether the right to access should be enforced in a particular case. If all media in a community are held by the same ownership, the access claim has greater attractiveness. This is true although the various media, even when they do reach the same audience, serve different functions and create different reactions and expectations. The existence of competition within the same medium, on the other hand, probably weakens the access claim, though competition within a medium is no assurance that significant opinions will have no difficulty in securing access to newspaper space or broadcast time. It is significant that the right of access cases that have been litigated almost invariably involve a monopoly newspaper in a community. * * *

With the development of private restraints on free expression, the idea of a free marketplace where ideas can compete on their merits has become just as unrealistic in the twentieth century as the economic theory of perfect competition. The world in which an essentially rationalist philosophy of the First Amendment was born has vanished and what was rationalism is now romance.

99. 359 F.2d 994 (D.C.Cir.1966) see p. 143, above.

Notes and Questions

1. Dean Barron's argument has substantial logical and emotional appeal. Do you think that its force depends upon a judgment that the electronic mass media have aspired to sterility—or at least wholly non-controversial programming? If current programming did (does it?) include a generous amount of debate on public issues, would it still make sense to pursue an access scheme? If an access approach has significant constitutional or public policy value, consider the concerns of the lawmaker who must devise the method for regulating access and of the regulator who must perform, or monitor, the "gatekeeping" function. On what basis could—or should—access be rationed, assuming that there always will be too little room to accommodate all interested speakers? Is it essential that an access principle be fair, or only that it be applied consistently?

2. Evans v. Newton, 382 U.S. 296, 86 S.Ct. 486, 15 L.Ed.2d 373 (1966) cited by Dean Barron, involved a park in Georgia that was open to whites only in accordance with the will of the former U.S. Senator who bequeathed the parkland to the City of Macon. The City sought to be removed as trustee on the ground that it could not operate a racially segregated facility without violating the equal protection clause of the Fourteenth Amendment. A Georgia court approved the transfer of title from the city to a group of private individuals and the appointment of those individuals as the new trustees. The record in the case reflected that the park had been maintained as a "public" facility, benefitting from various municipal services. There was no suggestion that upon transfer of "title," this situation would change. In his opinion for the Supreme Court, Justice Douglas stated that the act of removing the City and installing private "owners" did not immunize the park from the command of the Fourteenth Amendment:

> Golf clubs, social centers, luncheon clubs, schools such as Tuskegee were at least in origin, and other like organizations in the private sector are often racially oriented. A park, on the other hand, is more like a fire department or police department that traditionally serves the community. * * *

> Under the circumstances of this case, we cannot but conclude that the public character of this park requires that it be treated as a public institution subject to the command of the Fourteenth Amendment, regardless of who now has title under state law.

382 U.S. at 301–302, 86 S.Ct. at 490. See also Marsh v. Alabama, 326 U.S. 501, 66 S.Ct. 276, 90 L.Ed. 265 (1946) ("company town" subject to the First Amendment).

Does this line of cases apply to the broadcast media? To the print media? If so, under what circumstances? Are these cases more relevant to cable television? Is it the nature of the activity, or the degree of government control of (or involvement in) the activity, that is relevant to the issue addressed in the *Newton* case? For a slightly different approach to this issue, see Note, *Access to Cable, Natural Monopoly, and the First Amendment*, 86 Colum.L.Rev. 1663 (1986) (access requirements may be justifiable only where natural monopoly results in a "distortion" of program diversity).

3. Public rights of access can come in different forms, each with its own implications for diversity of speech and its own economic consequences. The following analysis compares several approaches to access:

Public access is used to describe what is, quite simply, a first-come, first-served right to free use of valuable channel time. Since time on spectrum imposes costs on a broadcaster or cable operator, however, public access implies subsidized time. If nothing else, access time imposes an opportunity cost, because a cable operator would otherwise put something else on that spectrum.

Who benefits from this subsidy is not evident. Presumably it is either the programmer, the viewer, or both. Why would anyone want to subsidize programmers? One might want to aid them in developing their creative talents by providing an otherwise unaffordable outlet (similar to the rationale for subsidizing experimental theatre), or to enable them to disseminate their messages (as by setting up a "speakers' corner" in a public park).

Why would one want to help viewers receive access programming without paying for it (either directly or through advertising)? The viewers might be narrow groups not served by conventional broadcasting, which generally seeks a mass audience. Thus, they might be unable to purchase the same kind of programming from any available outlets. This type of audience could conceivably have nothing in common except the fact that it prefers a particular program, such as an opera. Access programs, however, will tend to be directed toward organized groups (such as those focused on political or ethnic concerns), which can assert their interest, and not toward an audience (such as opera buffs) that has not otherwise coalesced.

Mandatory leased access is another type of time on spectrum, but unlike public access, it is priced. It is mandatory in one sense, because a broadcaster or cable operator must devote channel time to this use, just as in public access. But it is also typically mandatory in the sense of having to serve all comers, whether they want to use the spectrum to present programs or, in the case of cable, to transmit electronic mail.

A pricing system for mandatory leased access might be either discriminatory or nondiscriminatory. That is to say, there might be either a uniform price for any given amount and type of time, or a different price might be negotiated between the provider and each user. A zero price for public access is necessarily a nondiscriminatory zero price for all comers.

Nondiscriminatory leased access prices might be fixed by regulation or set by a broadcaster or cable operator pursuant to a regulatory injunction against price discrimination. However it is set, a nondiscriminatory pricing scheme can impose welfare losses on society if the uniform price is high enough to bar a user who would derive more value from the time than the marginal cost of providing it.

Discriminatory pricing may help avoid social welfare losses by facilitating sales of spectrum "slots" to those who value access at more than it costs but at less than the single, uniform price. Indeed, price discrimination may be needed to insure the commercial viability of leased access. Depending on the cost structure of a commodity or service, it may be impossible without price discrimination to make enough sales to cover total operating costs, with the result that the service is not provided at all (or is provided at a loss, in the case of mandatory leased access). In these cases, price discrimination is the only means of providing a service on a self-supporting basis.

An alternative approach, economically less efficient than the price system, might be to use a "public interest" standard to allocate public access time. If public access time were allocated under a non-price-based public interest allocation scheme, the results probably would be much the same as in the sorry history of the F.C.C.'s broadcast licensing process. Competing claims would have to be arbitrated, in the cable context presumably in the contracts for and administration of local franchises. These claims could be decided only after lengthy proceedings—albeit not necessarily formal hearings—that primarily would benefit lawyers and impose substantial costs on the intended beneficiaries' ability to get a supposedly free good. This type of system probably would result in allocating time for particular, well-represented purposes, such as children's programming, use by a local school system, or political communication. And the results would be just about as arbitrary as the F.C.C.'s licensing decisions.

An earlier form of this discussion appeared in Douglas H. Ginsburg, *Rights of Excess: Cable and the First Amendment, Communications and the Law*, Oct. 1984, at 71–75.*

Which approaches to access (if any) seem likely to produce greater diversity among broadcast "speakers" than the current commercial system? Do any? How fair to station operators are the various approaches? How likely are underrepresented political, cultural, ethnic, or other groups to be able to broadcast their views under each regime?

4. For many years, various groups have urged the FCC to adopt one or another access scheme for the broadcast media. In some cases, access has been proposed as a substitute for the fairness doctrine; in others, it has been offered as a supplement to that doctrine. The Commission has consistently rejected the proposals. See, e.g., Reconsideration of the 1974 Fairness Report, 58 FCC 2d 691, 699 (1976), remanded in part, NCCB v. FCC, 567 F.2d 1095 (D.C.Cir.1977) (court, noting potential public policy and constitutional infirmities of an access obligation, nonetheless concludes that Commission had not adequately considered access proposal offered as alternative to fairness doctrine); Report and Order in BC Dkt No. 78–60, 74 FCC 2d 164 (1979) (Commission, on remand, concludes that access system would be inferior to fairness doctrine). The access proposals that have been suggested to the Commission include the following:

• As an alternative to case-by-case adherence to the fairness doctrine, a broadcaster could provide one hour each week for "access" programming. Of that hour, 35 minutes would be reserved for spot messages, and the remaining 25 minutes would be saved for "program-length" messages. Half of the time would be offered on a first-come, first-served

* ©1984, Meckler Publishing. Adapted and reprinted with permission.

basis; the other half would be allocated by the broadcaster according to "predetermined, content-neutral" principles. Compliance with this approach would result in a presumption that the broadcaster has satisfied its fairness obligations.

● Also as an alternative to traditional fairness doctrine approaches, a broadcaster operating an 18–hour broadcast day could devote 259 minutes per week to access uses (3.4% of the programming time, roughly equivalent to then-current time devoted to public affairs programming). Each weeknight, 20 minutes would be reserved for "partisan users," defined to be representatives of established political parties. Each week, 40 minutes would be reserved for 10–minute programs from "nonpartisan users" (defined to be representatives of established community and issue-based groups). The balance would be open for spot use, at least 25% of which must be reserved for individuals. Broadcasters also would have to establish "access centers" to assist with production, distribution, and regional coordination of access programming.

● As a supplement to fairness doctrine obligations, commercial broadcasters would be required to grant access for one hour each day during television prime time or radio drive time to a non-profit corporation chartered by Congress. The corporation, called Audience Network, would be a national membership organization funded by membership dues and run by a board elected by the members. Audience Network would air programming that it produced or obtained and would serve as a clearinghouse for other public-interest groups seeking media access.

● In an effort to address perceived deficiencies in the economic forces that affect broadcasters, broadcasters would be required to devote a certain portion of each broadcast day to the carriage of programs from which they receive no financial benefit. This obligation would be in addition to traditional fairness obligations.

In 1987, when considering alternatives to the fairness doctrine, the Commission reviewed these and other access proposals and concluded—once again—that mandatory access was not a desirable approach to regulation:

> 74. There are aspects of access systems that, at first blush, would seem to promote the First Amendment values underlying the Fairness Doctrine. Because access focuses on the right to speak, it would appear to advance the First Amendment principle of encouraging "the widest possible dissemination of information from diverse and antagonistic sources."[74] In addition, those access proposals embracing a first-come, first-served approach appear promising in the sense that they are intended to remove the ubiquitous presence of government, occasioned by our present Fairness Doctrine policies, from the task of overseeing program content on broadcast stations and are designed to ensure that "the government remains neutral in the marketplace of ideas."[76] And,

74. Associated Press v. United States, 326 U.S. 1, 20 (1945).

76. * * * [Certain of the access] proposals would require licensees to make decisions as to what persons constitute "representative spokespersons," "representatives of established political parties," or "representatives of established community and issue-based organizations." Accordingly, these proposals would still require some degree of government supervision to ensure licensee implementation of these require-

unlike the specific defects we found with the Fairness Doctrine in the 1985 Fairness Report, access would not seem, at first glance, to create the "paradoxical effect of actually inhibiting the expression of a wide spectrum of opinion on controversial issues of public importance" nor, similarly, would access have the consequence of "stifling viewpoints which may be unorthodox, unpopular or unestablished," a possibility we found existed with the Fairness Doctrine. Finally, access would appear to contribute to diversity from the standpoint of increasing the number of ideas and viewpoints presented by advocates themselves, rather than by broadcast licensees who speak on their behalf. * * *

75. Although access, as an alternative to the Fairness Doctrine, could theoretically lead to a blending of many of the First Amendment aims and goals actually noted above, the likelihood of any of the access plans achieving these benefits is so speculative and remote as not to outweigh the risks access poses because of the continued presence that would be required of government to supervise the access plans. More fundamentally, these plans would result in the dilution even further of the rights broadcasters enjoy under the First Amendment. None of the access proposals, in our opinion, would achieve both the diversity objective and the objective of not intruding on editorial discretion.

76. Although some of these proposals * * * could lead to new opportunities for presentation of unorthodox, unpopular, or unrepresentative viewpoints and to increased presentations by genuine partisans, they would not necessarily guarantee that discussion of controversial issues of public importance would be greater than what we now have under the Doctrine or, more importantly, greater than what we believe the public could receive without the Doctrine and its accompanying chilling effects. * * *

77. More importantly, we believe it is extremely unlikely that any of these access proposals would yield the public benefits we perceive could be gained under the approach we recommended in the 1985 Fairness Report of according broadcasters the same journalistic freedom as that enjoyed under the First Amendment by the print and other media. Indeed, as noted above, we are skeptical whether the public would gain the benefits under access it receives under the Fairness Doctrine as it has historically been administered. * * * Even if we assumed arguendo that, these access plans were capable of achieving many of the objectives espoused under the First Amendment, we are convinced that the one substantial flaw each of these access proposals shares is that the government would continue to play a significant, if not extensive, role in supervising a regime that would diminish *even further* the journalistic freedoms of broadcasters under the First Amendment. * * *

80. We share many of the concerns that the Court expressed in *CBS v. DNC* about ensuring the wide journalistic freedom of broadcasters * * *.

ments. More specifically, they could require government to [oversee] licensees' judgments with respect to [whether] the views presented by these access users were from appropriate "representatives."

81. * * * [W]hile an access approach which is non-discretionary as to speakers is intended to eliminate * * * [the fairness doctrine] type of government oversight for much of a licensee's programming, it would result in a more fundamental and drastic type of government intervention—complete usurpation of *any* degree of journalistic discretion over access programming. While access as herein proposed would deny licensees the use of their facilities to broadcast for, presumably, only a small portion of the broadcast day, it would result in complete and absolute dispossession during this period. These licensees would be denied all rights of material selection, editorial judgment and discretion enjoyed by other private communications media and would be required to permit the use of their facilities for the transmission of any program regardless of its content, quality, interest, context, relevance, or taste. Thus, contrary to the present system of broadcasting we have today, under which broadcasters are accorded "wide journalistic freedom," such an access plan would deprive the licensee of direct editorial control over the issues to be presented over its facilities.

82. Even if we assumed that access would increase viewpoint diversity more substantially than either the Fairness Doctrine as currently enforced or complete reliance on the marketplace, we would still have serious reservations as to whether any type of procedural alternative that is premised on a virtually total abridgement of a broadcaster's First Amendment rights would be justified. In our judgment, the means used to accomplish this end would not be justified. And, as stated below, we even harbor reservations about the assumption that access would lead to increased viewpoint diversity. * * *

83. We have previously concluded that an access approach would not necessarily guarantee that discussion of controversial issues of public importance would take place during access time. Indeed, our earlier expressed views that access plans appear to exhibit "common difficulty in soliciting public participation" would appear to strengthen our suspicion that access would not necessarily result in coverage of a greater number of issues than now exists under the Doctrine or, more importantly, than might exist without the Doctrine. For similar reasons, we are not confident that access would lead to "the widest dissemination of information from diverse and antagonistic sources." As we have indicated previously, if there is no general demand for access time, individuals or groups "sharing a viewpoint on a single important or unimportant issue could virtually dominate the so-called 'first-come, first-served' access."

84. Apart from the concerns expressed above, we question whether compelling broadcasters to surrender journalistic discretion over issues and ideas to be presented on their facilities during access periods would contribute materially toward a more informed public from the standpoint of increased programming that is informative and comprehensible. * * * The exercise of journalistic discretion and editorial judgments by newspapers and broadcasters alike, in our opinion, contributes toward a better-informed public citizenry and the public appears to value and to benefit significantly from these services performed by the mass media. All of these reasons suggest to us that, as a matter of sound public

policy, it would be unwise to supplant or replace the journalistic freedom of broadcasters for a system of broad access rights.

85. Of perhaps equal importance, regardless of whether the access scheme is structured on a first-come, first-served basis, whether it involves the allotment of time for "representative spokespersons," or whether it entails different categories for different types of access users, e.g., partisan and non-partisan access users, the government would inevitably be drawn into the process of overseeing the broadcaster's day-to-day implementation of the system. In the NCCB case, the D.C. Circuit suggested that the Commission's requirement that a system of access cannot draw government into the role of deciding who and when someone should be allowed on the air would appear to be "furthered even more than it is under present [fairness] doctrine enforcement."[88] As we subsequently pointed out, however, the Commission's attention would necessarily "focus on the licensee selection of representative spokespersons, assignments regarding 'first-come, first-served' access patrons, and even a licensee's compliance with public interest requirements" under any access scheme. As a consequence, access could engender new opportunities for government intervention and scrutiny over a broadcaster's operations with little or no assurance that it would produce significantly greater benefits than under a system which accords broadcasters wide journalistic freedom. * * *

87. Congress has approved limited rights of access to broadcast stations by enacting Section 315 of the Act to afford equal opportunities to candidates for public office and Section 312(a)(7) of the Act to afford "reasonable access" for candidates for federal elective office, but was careful to tailor them narrowly to avoid excessive intrusion upon broadcasters' discretion. In stark contrast, the much broader access rights contemplated under the plans submitted and reviewed here would not preserve the values of private journalism Congress intended when, in 1934, it enacted the Communications Act. * * *

2 FCC Rcd 5272, 5281–83, 63 R.R.2d at 511–17 (1987).

Notes and Questions

Are you convinced by the Commission's arguments that access schemes are "more intrusive" than an approach such as the fairness doctrine? Could it be argued that access, as an alternative to the fairness doctrine, is *less intrusive?* In other words, might government be assuming a narrower role if it were to require a set-aside of a small amount of program time each day or week for access use than it does when it has the potential authority to review the reasonableness of every judgment a broadcaster makes in connection with "controversial issue" programming? Could it be argued that access is simply antithetical to basic First Amendment notions of a speaker's freedom? Does the answer to this question depend upon whether one views a broadcast licensee as either a "speaker" entitled to traditional First Amendment protections or some type of "public trustee" that enjoys a licensed, and limited, right to use the public airwaves?

88. NCCB v. FCC, 567 F.2d 1095 (D.C.Cir.1977).

Does the Commission have statutory authority to impose access obligations on broadcasters? Recall that Section 153(h) of the Communications Act prohibits the imposition of "common carrier" obligations on a broadcaster. See *FCC v. Midwest Video Corp.* (p. 66)

The cases thus leave unclear the question as to whether access channels are constitutional in the first. As indicated, the courts have debated this issue almost from the beginning of access channels. More recently, the Court seems to have shown a willingness not only to accept access channels, but also to protect them against onerous regulation, as in the *Denver Area* case.

2. Legislatively Created New Media: Open Video Systems

The 1996 Telecommunications Act created a new form of multichannel media: "open video systems" ("OVS"). As discussed below, an OVS system is a hybrid of traditional common carrier and cable principles. Most important, it may program its own channels as long as there is room for other programmers on a quasi-common carrier basis. If channel supply outruns demand, an OVS system may not control more than one-third of its total channel capacity.

In terms of technology and economics, and drafters seemed to have had in mind the evolving concept of digital fiberoptic systems, using both fiberoptics and coaxial cable. This type of technology would deliver about 500 digital video channels to the home, using a system known as "hybrid-fiber-coax"—that is, a combination of optical and coaxial cable to carry up to several gigahertz of video signals. This system also would use heavy amounts of digital compression in order to offer this amount of bandwidth; as noted in Chapter I, digital compression allows a channel to carry between six and ten high-quality signals.

This notion of a mixed broadcast/carrier type of approach is hardly new. Indeed, the European Commission proposed a highly similar approach in the early 1990's. Although this approach to "convergence" may make a lot of sense in the long run, when enacted it was a solution without a problem. Although the Regional Bell Operating Companies had complained for a decade that they should be allowed to enter the home video market, none of them immediately responded to the OVS approach—probably for a variety of reasons.

The results indicate some of the problems of legislatively creating new media. The OVS approach very well have been attractive in the 1980's, when the telephone companies were lobbying for it under its previous moniker of "Video Dial Tone." But for reasons discussed below, the same incentives may have ceased to exist by passage of the 1996 Act.

In short, politicians, congressional staffers, and agency officials may not always be the best ones to make strategic decisions about technological deployment. But once they have done so, how can an industry and/or an agency change their statutory standards, without returning to Congress—an obviously difficult procedure.

Whether OVS makes commercial sense to potential entrants is less than clear, as discussed below in Kimberly Auerback, *OVS: A Platform Worth Investing In?*, 1996 Media Law & Policy 1.

INTRODUCTION

On February 8, 1996 President Clinton signed the Telecommunications Act of 1996 ("1996 Act") into law. * * * Section 653 created Open Video Systems ("OVS"), a platform developed primarily for telephone companies ("telcos") to enter the video programming market. This article examines whether the regulatory structure established for OVS by the Federal Communications Commission ("Commission") meets the goals set out in the 1996 Act, including flexible market entry, enhancing competition, streamlining regulation, increasing diversity of programming choices, encouraging investment in infrastructure and technology, and increasing consumer choice.

* * *

I.   What Will an OVS Look Like?

Congress' intent in creating an OVS was to promote competition in the video programming market. The 1996 Act specifically invites local exchange carriers ("LECs") to become OVS operators." The Commission also may allow other interested parties to become OVS operators if so doing provides for the "public interest, convenience and necessity." To encourage entry, the 1996 Act places fewer regulatory burdens on OVS operators than on cable operators. For example, OVS operators will not have to provide leased access channels, pay franchise fees, or be subject to rate regulation.

Despite these reduced burdens, OVS operators will still be subject to some regulation. Most important, if demand exists, OVS operators must relinquish programming control of up to two-thirds of their system to unaffiliated operators. Additionally, although OVS operators do not have to pay local franchise authority fees, they will have to pay local government fees for the use of rights-of-way. Further, an OVS must transmit public, educational and governmental ("PEG") programming and "must-carry" broadcast channels.

Applicants must be certified by the Commission, which has 10 days to approve or deny a request to become an OVS operator, and the Commission has the authority to resolve disputes and award damages, which it must do within 180 days of receiving the complaint.

* * *

Questions

1.   Is OVS a cable operation? To what extent does an OVS system have the discretion to refuse carrying a third party's programming? If the programming is offensive to the operator—on grounds other than indecency? If the operator believes the programming has no interest to its audience? If the operator is concerned that the programming will compete with its own

material—especially since OVS might end up carrying many of the same satellite channels as a cable operator?

2. Conversely, to what extent is OVS a common carrier? What legal standard should govern when it may refuse, as above, to carry a a third party's programming? Must it accept all financially qualified users, as discussed in Chapter III? Can it adopt a "first in time, first in right approach?"

3. May a local cable operator demand carriage of all its signals on an OVS system, even though many of the signals would duplicate those already on the OVS? Would it make a difference if OVS operators could exclude duplicative programming? Or, should a local OVS and cable operator share the revenues from the same programming, e.g., CNN, ESPN?

4. OVS presumably would require some type of "hybrid-fiber-coax" infrastructure. As of the middle of the 1990's, this cost about $1,500 as opposed to roughly $600 per subscriber for cable—or $300 per subscriber for MMDS. If cable or MMDS operators can aggregate 50 percent or more of the viewing audience, they can expect a cash flow of about 30 percent. (DBS is not developed enough yet to make any real judgments as to long-term cash flows.) What does this suggest about the viability of Congress' vision of OVS?

5. How would OVS fare in competition with another digital medium, namely DBS? OVS can offer about 500 channels, DBS about 200. Also, DBS has no "return capability"—for ordering programs, products, and the like—whereas OVS can offer this either over its own network or through telephone lines.

6. Would OVS have a significant competitive edge over DBS, because it carries local over-the-air television channels? To what extent can DBS compete in this respect?

7. In terms of overall profitability for an LEC, is OVS or long distance telephony more attractive?

8. Which enterprise requires more capital to enter? As noted, OVS costs about $1,500 per subscriber, versus $600 for cable and $300 for MMDS. But which one is likely to be more profitable in the long run?

Putting aside OVS and DBS for the moment, how attractive is long distance. Is it relevant that the RBOCs had been part of AT & T—including Long Lines—before the 1984 divestiture? What does this tell you about the expertise (or lack thereof) of RBOC personnel in long distance?

Along these lines, is it relevant that RBOCs already have created local telephone networks—"local calling areas." For example, the former NYNEX (now Bell Atlantic) has fiber connections with Bell Atlantic for each of their "regional" areas. What does this suggest in terms of (a) the amount of competition between the two for long distance traffic; and (b) the ability of the two companies to interconnect quickly to offer long-distance service?

9. In short, after the changes wrought by the courts, the Commission, and the Congress, is it very clear in what directions the RBOCs will go?

10. Most important, is it at all clear that there will be significant entry into OVS by the RBOCs? If not, then by whom? And if no one joins the

party, what is the effect on the marketplace envisioned by the drafters of the 1996 Telecommunications Act?

E.   EMERGING PROBLEMS OF COMPUTER COMMUNICATIONS: THE INTERNET ET. AL.

We generally approach media law issues in the context of audio and/or visual content—most commonly, of course, radio and television. But as has been evident since the first electronic medium—that is, telegraphy—these media can distribute many other types of material.

The most common and most important type of content today is data—the binary codes already seen in Chapter I. (p. 2) Data transmission is important for several reasons. First, since increasing amounts of financial information are in the form of data, large and small businesses transact increasingly large amounts of transaction through data transmission, e.g., credit card purchases, stock trades, sales of goods etc. In addition, in today's much-touted "information age," professionals and others depend upon the availability of accurate and high-speed information in making economic decisions, e.g., amount of goods sold, price of securities, and current inventories. Finally, the boundary line between commercial and casual applications of data is becoming increasingly tenuous; the same CD ROM drive that loads a word-processing program can present a videogame, motion picture, or the like.

Probably the most dramatic development for the general public is the Internet, and the attendant World Wide Web. This gives access to thousands—and, as people develop individual data bases, eventually perhaps millions of "websites"—in the form of data bases hooked into the Internet network. But there actually is nothing at all new about the Internet; it has existed for almost 30 years as a means for researchers, primarily in the hard sciences, to exchange information, scholarly papers, and the like. The development of the Web, faster modems, and extensive graphics programs has made it of interest to a broader audience.

Given its humble beginnings, it is important to understand that the Internet is not an entity of any kind. Instead, it is the result of solely voluntary activities by hundreds of universities, research departments, and businesses around the world. There is no systematic funding of the Internet, beyond the few million dollars per year that the U.S. government contributes to its operation. As a result, transmission companies can withdraw from the cooperative effort; and there would be no fund available to buy or build replacements for them. Moreover, creating this type of fund would be somewhat difficult, since Internet operations produce little real revenue; by the middle of the 1990's, "electronic commerce" was producing only a few hundred million dollars per year.

The Internet thus is not really a network in the traditional sense, in terms of having central management and financial control. It is important to understand the decentralized and informal way in which it operates. An excellent description of the Internet is contained in the federal district court opinion challenging the constitutionality of the Communications Decency Act (part of the 1996 Telecommunications Act). Judge Slovitzer's opinion is a good and unfortunately rare example of a court's coming to grips with a new medium. *American Civil Liberties Union v. Reno*, 929 F.Supp. 824 (E.D.Pa.1996). This understanding of the process may have had a significant impact on the Court's ultimate opinion, as will be seen.

* * *

The Nature of Cyberspace

The Creation of the Internet and the Development of Cyberspace

1. The Internet is not a physical or tangible entity, but rather a giant network which interconnects innumerable smaller groups of linked computer networks. It is thus a network of networks. This is best understood if one considers what a linked group of computers— referred to here as a "network"—is, and what it does. Small networks are now ubiquitous (and are often called "local area networks"). For example, in many United States Courthouses, computers are linked to each other for the purpose of exchanging files and messages (and to share equipment such as printers). These are networks.

* * *

3. The nature of the Internet is such that it is very difficult, if not impossible, to determine its size at a given moment. It is indisputable, however, that the Internet has experienced extraordinary growth in recent years. In 1981, fewer than 300 computers were linked to the Internet, and by 1989, the number stood at fewer than 90,000 computers. By 1993, over 1,000,000 computers were linked. Today, over 9,400,000 host computers worldwide, of which approximately 60 percent located within the United States, are estimated to be linked to the Internet. This count does not include the personal computers people use to access the Internet using modems. In all, reasonable estimates are that as many as 40 million people around the world can and do access the enormously flexible communication Internet medium. That figure is expected to grow to 200 million Internet users by the year 1999.

4. Some of the computers and computer networks that make up the Internet are owned by governmental and public institutions, some are owned by non-profit organizations, and some are privately owned. The resulting whole is a decentralized, global medium of communications—or "cyberspace"—that links people, institutions, corporations, and governments around the world. The Internet is an international system. This communications medium allows any of the literally tens of millions of people with access to the Internet to exchange information. These communications can occur almost in-

stantaneously, and can be directed either to specific individuals, to a broader group of people interested in a particular subject, or to the world as a whole.

5. The Internet had its origins in 1969 as an experimental project of the Advanced Research Project Agency ("ARPA"), and was called "ARPANET." This network linked computers and computer networks owned by the military, defense contractors, and university laboratories conducting defense-related research. The network later allowed researchers across the country to access directly and to use extremely powerful supercomputers located at a few key universities and laboratories. As it evolved far beyond its research origins in the United States to encompass universities, corporations, and people around the world, the ARPANET came to be called the "DARPA Internet," and finally just the "Internet."

6. From its inception, the network was designed to be a decentralized, self-maintaining series of redundant links between computers and computer networks, capable of rapidly transmitting communications without direct human involvement or control, and with the automatic ability to re-route communications if one or more individual links were damaged or otherwise unavailable. Among other goals, this redundant system of linked computers was designed to allow vital research and communications to continue even if portions of the network were damaged, say, in a war.

7. To achieve this resilient nationwide (and ultimately global) communications medium, the ARPANET encouraged the creation of multiple links to and from each computer (or computer network) on the network. Thus, a computer located in Washington, D.C., might be linked (usually using dedicated telephone lines) to other computers in neighboring states or on the Eastern seaboard. Each of those computers could in turn be linked to other computers, which themselves would be linked to other computers.

* * *

9. Messages between computers on the Internet do not necessarily travel entirely along the same path. The Internet uses "packet switching" communication protocols that allow individual messages to be subdivided into smaller "packets" that are then sent independently to the destination, and are then automatically reassembled by the receiving computer. While all packets of a given message often travel along the same path to the destination, if computers along the route become overloaded, then packets can be re-routed to less loaded computers.

10. At the same time that ARPANET was maturing (it subsequently ceased to exist), similar networks developed to link universities, research facilities, businesses, and individuals around the world. These other formal or loose networks included BITNET, CSNET, FIDONET, and USENET. Eventually, each of these net-

works (many of which overlapped) were themselves linked together, allowing users of any computers linked to any one of the networks to transmit communications to users of computers on other networks. It is this series of linked networks (themselves linking computers and computer networks) that is today commonly known as the Internet.

11. No single entity—academic, corporate, governmental, or non-profit—administers the Internet. It exists and functions as a result of the fact that hundreds of thousands of separate operators of computers and computer networks independently decided to use common data transfer protocols to exchange communications and information with other computers (which in turn exchange communications and information with still other computers). There is no centralized storage location, control point, or communications channel for the Internet, and it would not be technically feasible for a single entity to control all of the information conveyed on the Internet.

How Individuals Access the Internet

12. Individuals have a wide variety of avenues to access cyberspace in general, and the Internet in particular. In terms of physical access, there are two common methods to establish an actual link to the Internet. First, one can use a computer or computer terminal that is directly (and usually permanently) connected to a computer network that is itself directly or indirectly connected to the Internet. Second, one can use a "personal computer" with a "modem" to connect over a telephone line to a larger computer or computer network that is itself directly or indirectly connected to the Internet. As detailed below, both direct and modem connections are made available to people by a wide variety of academic, governmental, or commercial entities.

* * *

14. Similarly, Internet resources and access are sufficiently important to many corporations and other employers that those employers link their office computer networks to the Internet and provide employees with direct or modem access to the office network (and thus to the Internet). Such access might be used by, for example, a corporation involved in scientific or medical research or manufacturing to enable corporate employees to exchange information and ideas with academic researchers in their fields.

15. Those who lack access to the Internet through their schools or employers still have a variety of ways they can access the Internet. Many communities across the country have established "free-nets" or community networks to provide their citizens with a local link to the Internet (and to provide local-oriented content and discussion groups). * * *

* * *

18.   Individuals can also access the Internet through commercial and non-commercial "Internet service providers" that typically offer modem telephone access to a computer or computer network linked to the Internet. Many such providers * * * are commercial entities offering Internet access for a monthly or hourly fee. Some Internet service providers, however, are non-profit organizations that offer free or very low cost access to the Internet. For example, the International Internet Association offers free modem access to the Internet upon request. Also, a number of trade or other non-profit associations offer Internet access as a service to members.

19.   Another common way for individuals to access the Internet is through one of the major national commercial "online services" such as America Online, CompuServe, the Microsoft Network, or Prodigy. These online services offer nationwide computer networks (so that subscribers can dial-in to a local telephone number), and the services provide extensive and well organized content within their own proprietary computer networks. In addition to allowing access to the extensive content available within each online service, the services also allow subscribers to link to the much larger resources of the Internet. * * *

20.   In addition to using the national commercial online services, individuals can also access the Internet using some (but not all) of the thousands of local dial-in computer services, often called "bulletin board systems" or "BBSs." With an investment of as little as $2,000.00 and the cost of a telephone line, individuals, non-profit organizations, advocacy groups, and businesses can offer their own dial-in computer "bulletin board" service where friends, members, subscribers, or customers can exchange ideas and information. BBSs range from single computers with only one telephone line into the computer (allowing only one user at a time), to single computers with many telephone lines into the computer (allowing multiple simultaneous users), to multiple linked computers each servicing multiple dial-in telephone lines (allowing multiple simultaneous users). Some (but not all) of these BBS systems offer direct or indirect links to the Internet. * * *

* * *

Methods to Communicate Over the Internet

22.   Once one has access to the Internet, there are a wide variety of different methods of communication and information exchange over the network. These many methods of communication and information retrieval are constantly evolving and are therefore difficult to categorize concisely. The most common methods of communications on the Internet (as well as within the major online services) can be roughly grouped into six categories:

(1) one-to-one messaging (such as "e-mail"),

(2) one-to-many messaging (such as "listserv"),

(3) distributed message databases (such as "USENET news-groups"),

(4) real time communication (such as "Internet Relay Chat"),

(5) real time remote computer utilization (such as "telnet"), and

(6) remote information retrieval (such as "ftp," "gopher," and the "World Wide Web").

Most of these methods of communication can be used to transmit text, data, computer programs, sound, visual images (i.e., pictures), and moving video images.

* * *

34. Purpose. The World Wide Web (W3C) was created to serve as the platform for a global, online store of knowledge, containing information from a diversity of sources and accessible to Internet users around the world. Though information on the Web is contained in individual computers, the fact that each of these computers is connected to the Internet through W3C protocols allows all of the information to become part of a single body of knowledge. It is currently the most advanced information system developed on the Internet, and embraces within its data model most information in previous networked information systems such as ftp, gopher, wais, and Usenet.

* * *

36. Basic Operation. The World Wide Web is a series of documents stored in different computers all over the Internet. Documents contain information stored in a variety of formats, including text, still images, sounds, and video. An essential element of the Web is that any document has an address (rather like a telephone number). Most Web documents contain "links." These are short sections of text or image which refer to another document. Typically the linked text is blue or underlined when displayed, and when selected by the user, the referenced document is automatically displayed, wherever in the world it actually is stored. Links for example are used to lead from overview documents to more detailed documents, from tables of contents to particular pages, but also as cross-references, footnotes, and new forms of information structure.

37. Many organizations now have "home pages" on the Web. These are documents which provide a set of links designed to represent the organization, and through links from the home page, guide the user directly or indirectly to information about or relevant to that organization.

* * *

42. Information to be published on the Web must also be formatted according to the rules of the Web standards. These

standardized formats assure that all Web users who want to read the material will be able to view it. Web standards are sophisticated and flexible enough that they have grown to meet the publishing needs of many large corporations, banks, brokerage houses, newspapers and magazines which now publish "online" editions of their material, as well as government agencies, and even courts, which use the Web to disseminate information to the public. At the same time, Web publishing is simple enough that thousands of individual users and small community organizations are using the Web to publish their own personal "home pages," the equivalent of individualized newsletters about that person or organization, which are available to everyone on the Web.

43.   Web publishers have a choice to make their Web sites open to the general pool of all Internet users, or close them, thus making the information accessible only to those with advance authorization. Many publishers choose to keep their sites open to all in order to give their information the widest potential audience. In the event that the publishers choose to maintain restrictions on access, this may be accomplished by assigning specific user names and passwords as a prerequisite to access to the site. Or, in the case of Web sites maintained for internal use of one organization, access will only be allowed from other computers within that organization's local network.

* * *

46.   A distributed system with no centralized control. Running on tens of thousands of individual computers on the Internet, the Web is what is known as a distributed system. The Web was designed so that organizations with computers containing information can become part of the Web simply by attaching their computers to the Internet and running appropriate World Wide Web software. No single organization controls any membership in the Web, nor is there any single centralized point from which individual Web sites or services can be blocked from the Web. From a user's perspective, it may appear to be a single, integrated system, but in reality it has no centralized control point.

47.   Contrast to closed databases. The Web's open, distributed, decentralized nature stands in sharp contrast to most information systems that have come before it. Private information services such as Westlaw, Lexis/Nexis, and Dialog, have contained large storehouses of knowledge, and can be accessed from the Internet with the appropriate passwords and access software. However, these databases are not linked together into a single whole, as is the World Wide Web.

48.   Success of the Web in research, education, and political activities. The World Wide Web has become so popular because of its open, distributed, and easy-to-use nature. Rather than requiring those who seek information to purchase new software or hardware,

and to learn a new kind of system for each new database of information they seek to access, the Web environment makes it easy for users to jump from one set of information to another. By the same token, the open nature of the Web makes it easy for publishers to reach their intended audiences without having to know in advance what kind of computer each potential reader has, and what kind of software they will be using.

* * *

Content on the Internet

74. The types of content now on the Internet defy easy classification. The entire card catalogue of the Carnegie Library is on-line, together with journals, journal abstracts, popular magazines, and titles of compact discs. The director of the Carnegie Library, Robert Croneberger, testified that on-line services are the emerging trend in libraries generally. Plaintiff Hotwired Ventures LLC organizes its Web site into information regarding travel, news and commentary, arts and entertainment, politics, and types of drinks. Plaintiff America Online, Inc., not only creates chat rooms for a broad variety of topics, but also allows members to create their own chat rooms to suit their own tastes. The ACLU uses an America Online chat room as an unmoderated forum for people to debate civil liberties issues. Plaintiffs' expert, Scott Bradner, estimated that 15,000 newsgroups exist today, and he described his own interest in a newsgroup devoted solely to Formula 1 racing cars. America Online makes 15,000 bulletin boards available to its subscribers, who post between 200,000 and 250,000 messages each day. * * *

77. The ease of communication through the Internet is facilitated by the use of hypertext markup language (HTML), which allows for the creation of "hyperlinks" or "links". HTML enables a user to jump from one source to other related sources by clicking on the link. A link might take the user from Web site to Web site, or to other files within a particular Web site. Similarly, by typing a request into a search engine, a user can retrieve many different sources of content related to the search that the creators of the engine have collected.

92. The Government offered no evidence that there is a reliable way to ensure that recipients and participants in such fora can be screened for age. The Government presented no evidence demonstrating the feasibility of its suggestion that chat rooms, newsgroups and other fora that contain material deemed indecent could be effectively segregated to "adult" or "moderated" areas of cyberspace.

93. Even if it were technologically feasible to block minors' access to newsgroups and similar fora, there is no method by which the creators of newsgroups which contain discussions of art, politics or any other subject that could potentially elicit "indecent" contri-

butions could limit the blocking of access by minors to such "indecent" material and still allow them access to the remaining content, even if the overwhelming majority of that content was not indecent.

94. Likewise, participants in MUDs (Multi–User Dungeons) and MUSEs (Multi–User Simulation Environments) do not know whether the other participants are adults or minors. Although MUDs and MUSEs require a password for permanent participants, they need not give their real name nor verify their age, and there is no current technology to enable the administrator of these fantasy worlds to know if the participant is an adult or a minor.

95. Unlike other forms of communication on the Internet, there is technology by which an operator of a World Wide Web server may interrogate a user of a Web site. An HTML document can include a fill-in-the-blank "form" to request information from a visitor to a Web site, and this information can be transmitted back to the Web server and be processed by a computer program, usually a Common Gateway Interface (cgi) script. The Web server could then grant or deny access to the information sought. The cgi script is the means by which a Web site can process a fill-in form and thereby screen visitors by requesting a credit card number or adult password.

96. Content providers who publish on the World Wide Web via one of the large commercial online services, such as America Online or CompuServe, could not use an online age verification system that requires cgi script because the server software of these online services available to subscribers cannot process cgi scripts. There is no method currently available for Web page publishers who lack access to cgi scripts to screen recipients online for age.

Notes and Questions

1. How did a communications device for government and non-profit researchers turn into a popular entertainment and advertisement medium—within the space of a few years? What forces drove this development? Universal deployment of computers and modems? But as of 1997, only about 15 percent of U.S. households had both. Lack of interest in existing media? But at the same time, cable systems had begun offering 80–90 channels, and DBS 50–150. Given the fact that both audio and video quality on the Internet are low, why was there such a rush to use it?

2. As noted before, the Internet has generated comparatively little revenue. If this is likely to be the case in the future, does it need to be regulated in any way? Does it explain why it has not been regulated in the past? Is it somewhat like "citizens band" radio ("CB"), which largely has gone unregulated?

3. Where does the Internet fall in terms of the tri-partite scheme-broadcasting, carriage, hybrid regulation—discussed in Chapter III? Does it have aspects of all three? What if a user contracts with an information service provider to send identical messages to a number of affiliated companies? To a limited number of potential customers?

4. For the past and at present, the Internet has been maintained by voluntary donations of computer and communications time. As noted above, what would happen if key computer/communications centers simply pulled out of the whole scheme? Would the U.S. government increase its funding of the Internet in order to keep it going? What has been its track record in terms of public broadcasting?

5. Whether or not the Internet has sufficient funding for its current operations, does it have enough bandwidth to handle future demands? After all, when the Internet was created, few modems transmitted at more than 1,200 baud; by the middle of the 1990s, most ran at 10–15 times that rate. If bandwidth begins to be scarce, who will provide more? Non-profit institutions? Commercial operators? The federal government?

These and other questions obviously cannot be answered now. Nevertheless, some of the Internet's legal issues have begun to be resolved. The following case deals fairly straightforwardly with the First Amendment issues—perhaps because informed by the district court opinion excerpted above. It also suggests that the Internet's legal status may change as its nature does.

RENO v. AMERICAN CIVIL LIBERTIES UNION

Supreme Court of the United States, 1997.
___ U.S. ___, 117 S.Ct. 2329, 138 L.Ed.2d 874.

STEVENS, J., delivered the opinion of the court, in which SCALIA, KENNEDY, SOUTER, THOMAS, GINSBURG, and BREYER, JJ., joined. O'CONNOR, J., filed an opinion concurring in the judgment in part and dissenting in part, in which REHNQUIST, C. J., joined.

JUSTICE STEVENS delivered the opinion of the court.

At issue is the constitutionality of two statutory provisions enacted to protect minors from "indecent" and "patently offensive" communications on the Internet. Notwithstanding the legitimacy and importance of the congressional goal of protecting children from harmful materials, we agree with the three-judge District Court that the statute abridges "the freedom of speech" protected by the First Amendment.

I

The District Court made extensive findings of fact, most of which were based on a detailed stipulation prepared by the parties. See 929 F. Supp. 824, 830–849 (E.D.Pa.1996). * * *

THE INTERNET

* * *

The Internet has experienced "extraordinary growth." The number of "host" computers—those that store information and relay communication-increased from about 300 in 1981 to approximately 9,400,000 by the time of the trial in 1996. Roughly 60% of these hosts are located in the United States. About 40 million people used the Internet at the time of trial, a number that is expected to mushroom to 200 million by 1999.

Individuals can obtain access to the Internet from many different sources, generally hosts themselves or entities with a host affiliation. * * *

SEXUALLY EXPLICIT MATERIAL

Sexually explicit material on the Internet includes text, pictures, and chat and "extends from the modestly titillating to the hardest-core." These files are created, named, and posted in the same manner as material that is not sexually explicit, and may be accessed either deliberately or unintentionally during the course of an imprecise search. "Once a provider posts its content on the Internet, it cannot prevent that content from entering any community." Thus, for example, "when the UCR/California Museum of Photography posts to its Web site nudes by Edward Weston and Robert Mapplethorpe to announce that its new exhibit will travel to Baltimore and New York City, those images are available not only in Los Angeles, Baltimore, and New York City, but also in Cincinnati, Mobile, or Beijing—wherever Internet users live. Similarly, the safer sex instructions that Critical Path posts to its Web site, written in street language so that the teenage receiver can understand them, are available not just in Philadelphia, but also in Provo and Prague."

Some of the communications over the Internet that originate in foreign countries are also sexually explicit.

Though such material is widely available, users seldom encounter such content accidentally. "A document's title or a description of the document will usually appear before the document itself . . . and in many cases the user will receive detailed information about a site's content before he or she need take the step to access the document. Almost all sexually explicit images are preceded by warnings as to the content." For that reason, the "odds are slim" that a user would enter a sexually explicit site by accident. Unlike communications received by radio or television, "the receipt of information on the Internet requires a series of affirmative steps more deliberate and directed than merely turning a dial. A child requires some sophistication and some ability to read to retrieve material and thereby to use the Internet unattended."

Systems have been developed to help parents control the material that may be available on a home computer with Internet access. A system may either limit a computer's access to an approved list of sources that have been identified as containing no adult material, it may block designated inappropriate sites, or it may attempt to block messages containing identifiable objectionable features. "Although parental control software currently can screen for certain suggestive words or for known sexually explicit sites, it cannot now screen for sexually explicit images." Nevertheless, the evidence indicates that "a reasonably effective method by which parents can prevent their children from accessing sexually explicit and other material which parents may believe is inappropriate for their children will soon be available."

AGE VERIFICATION

The problem of age verification differs for different uses of the Internet. The District Court categorically determined that there "is no effective way to determine the identity or the age of a user who is accessing material through e-mail, mail exploders, newsgroups or chat rooms." The Government offered no evidence that there was a reliable way to screen recipients and participants in such fora for age. Moreover, even if it were technologically feasible to block minors' access to newsgroups and chat rooms containing discussions of art, politics or other subjects that potentially elicit "indecent" or "patently offensive" contributions, it would not be possible to block their access to that material and "still allow them access to the remaining content, even if the overwhelming majority of that content was not indecent."

Technology exists by which an operator of a Web site may condition access on the verification of requested information such as a credit card number or an adult password. Credit card verification is only feasible, however, either in connection with a commercial transaction in which the card is used, or by payment to a verification agency. Using credit card possession as a surrogate for proof of age would impose costs on non-commercial Web sites that would require many of them to shut down. For that reason, at the time of the trial, credit card verification was "effectively unavailable to a substantial number of Internet content providers." Moreover, the imposition of such a requirement "would completely bar adults who do not have a credit card and lack the resources to obtain one from accessing any blocked material."

Commercial pornographic sites that charge their users for access have assigned them passwords as a method of age verification. The record does not contain any evidence concerning the reliability of these technologies. Even if passwords are effective for commercial purveyors of indecent material, the District Court found that an adult password requirement would impose significant burdens on noncommercial sites, both because they would discourage users from accessing their sites and because the cost of creating and maintaining such screening systems would be "beyond their reach."

* * *

II

The Telecommunications Act of 1996, Pub. L. 104–104, 110 Stat. 56, was an unusually important legislative enactment. * * * The major components of the statute have nothing to do with the Internet; they were designed to promote competition in the local telephone service market, the multichannel video market, and the market for over-the-air broadcasting. The Act includes seven Titles, six of which are the product of extensive committee hearings and the subject of discussion in Reports prepared by Committees of the Senate and the House of Representatives. By contrast, Title V— known as the "Communications Decency Act of 1996" (CDA)— contains provisions that were either added in executive committee after the hearings were concluded or as amendments offered during floor debate on the legislation. An amendment offered in the Senate was the source of the two statutory provisions challenged in this case. They are informally described as the "indecent transmission" provision and the "patently offensive display" provision.

The Telecommunications Act of 1996, Pub. L. 104–104, 110 Stat. 56, was an unusually important legislative enactment.* * * An amendment offered in the Senate was the source of the two statutory provisions challenged in this case. They are informally described as the "indecent transmission" provision and the "patently offensive display" provision.

The first, 47 U.S.C. A. § 223(a) (Supp. 1997), prohibits the knowing transmission of obscene or indecent messages to any recipient under 18 years of age. It provides in pertinent part:

"(a) Whoever—

"(1) in interstate or foreign communications—

     * * *

"(B) by means of a telecommunications device knowingly—

"(i) makes, creates, or solicits, and

"(ii) initiates the transmission of,

     "any comment, request, suggestion, proposal, image, or other communication which is obscene or indecent, knowing that the recipient of the communication is under 18 years of age, regardless of whether the maker of such communication placed the call or initiated the communication;

     * * *

     "(2) knowingly permits any telecommunications facility under his control to be used for any activity prohibited by paragraph (1) with the intent that it be used for such activity,

     "shall be fined under Title 18, or imprisoned not more than two years, or both."

The second provision, § 223(d), prohibits the knowing sending or displaying of patently offensive messages in a manner that is available to a person under 18 years of age. It provides:

"(d) Whoever—

"(1) in interstate or foreign communications knowingly—

"(A) uses an interactive computer service to send to a specific person or persons under 18 years of age, or

"(B) uses any interactive computer service to display in a manner available to a person under 18 years of age,

"any comment, request, suggestion, proposal, image, or other communication that, in context, depicts or describes, in terms patently offensive as measured by contemporary community standards, sexual or excretory activities or organs, regardless of whether the user of such service placed the call or initiated the communication; or

"(2) knowingly permits any telecommunications facility under such person's control to be used for an activity prohibited by paragraph (1) with the intent that it be used for such activity,

"shall be fined under Title 18, or imprisoned not more than two years, or both."

The breadth of these prohibitions is qualified by two affirmative defenses. See § 223(e)(5). One covers those who take "good faith, reasonable, effective, and appropriate actions" to restrict access by minors to the prohibited communications. § 223(e)(5)(A). The other covers those who restrict access to covered material by requiring certain designated forms of age proof, such as a verified credit card or an adult identification number or code. § 223(e)(5)(B).

"(5) It is a defense to a prosecution under subsection (a)(1)(B) or (d) of this section, or under subsection (a)(2) of this section with respect to the use of a facility for an activity under subsection (a)(1)(B) of this section that a person—

"(A) has taken, in good faith, reasonable, effective, and appropriate actions under the circumstances to restrict or prevent access by minors to a communication specified in such subsections, which may involve any appropriate measures to restrict minors from such communications, including any method which is feasible under available technology; or

"(B) has restricted access to such communication by requiring use of a verified credit card, debit account, adult access code, or adult personal identification number."

III

On February 8, 1996, immediately after the President signed the statute, 20 plaintiffs filed suit against the Attorney General of the United States and the Department of Justice challenging the constitutionality of §§ 223(a)(1) and 223(d). A week later, based on his conclusion that the term "indecent" was too vague to provide the basis for a criminal prosecution, District Judge Buckwalter entered a temporary restraining order against enforcement of § 223(a)(1)(B)(ii) insofar as it applies to indecent communications. A second suit was then filed by 27 additional plaintiffs, the two cases were consolidated, and a three-judge District Court was convened pursuant to § 561 of the Act. After an evidentiary hearing, that Court entered a preliminary injunction against enforcement of both of the challenged provisions. Each of the three judges wrote a separate opinion, but their judgment was unanimous.

* * *

IV

In arguing for reversal, the Government contends that the CDA is plainly constitutional under three of our prior decisions: (1) *Ginsberg v. New York*; (2) *FCC v. Pacifica Foundation;* and (3) *Renton v. Play time Theatres, Inc.* A close look at these cases, however, raises—rather than relieves—doubts concerning the constitutionality of the CDA.

In *Ginsberg*, we upheld the constitutionality of a New York statute that prohibited selling to minors under 17 years of age material that was considered obscene as to them even if not obscene as to adults. * * * In four important respects, the statute upheld in *Ginsberg* was narrower than the CDA. First, we noted in Ginsberg that "the prohibition against sales to minors does not bar parents who so desire from purchasing the magazines for their children." Under the CDA, by contrast, neither the parents' consent—nor even their participation—in the communication would avoid the application of the statute. Second, the New York statute applied only to commercial transactions, whereas the CDA contains no such limitation. Third, the New York statute cabined its definition of material that is harmful to minors with the requirement that it be "utterly without redeeming social importance for minors." *Id.*, at 646. The CDA fails to provide us with any definition of the term "indecent" as used in § 223(a)(1) and, importantly, omits any requirement that the "patently offensive" material covered by § 223(d) lack serious literary, artistic, political, or scientific value. Fourth, the New York statute defined a minor as a person under the age of 17, whereas the CDA, in applying to all those under 18 years, includes an additional year of those nearest majority.

In *Pacifica*, we upheld a declaratory order of the Federal Communications Commission, holding that the broadcast of a recording of a 12–minute monologue entitled "Filthy Words" that had previously been delivered to a live audience "could have been the subject of administrative sanctions." The Commission had found that the repetitive use of certain words referring to excretory or sexual activities or organs "in an afternoon broadcast when children are in the audience was patently offensive" and concluded that the monologue was indecent "as broadcast." * * * After rejecting respondent's statutory arguments, we confronted its two constitutional arguments: (1) that the Commission's construction of its authority to ban indecent speech was so broad that its order had to be set aside even if the broadcast at issue was unprotected; and (2) that since the recording was not obscene, the First Amendment forbade any abridgement of the right to broadcast it on the radio.

[The] * * * plurality stated that the First Amendment does not prohibit all governmental regulation that depends on the content of speech. Accordingly, the availability of constitutional protection for a vulgar and offensive monologue that was not obscene depended on the context of the broadcast. * * *

As with the New York statute at issue in *Ginsberg*, there are significant differences between the order upheld in *Pacifica* and the CDA. First, the order in *Pacifica*, issued by an agency that had been regulating radio stations for decades, targeted a specific broadcast that represented a rather dramatic departure from traditional program content in order to designate when—rather than whether—it would be permissible to air such a program in that particular medium. The CDA's broad categorical prohibitions are not limited to particular times and are not dependent on any evaluation by an agency familiar with the unique characteristics of the Internet. Second, unlike the CDA, the Commission's declaratory order was not punitive; we expressly refused to decide whether the indecent broadcast "would justify a criminal prosecution." Finally, the Commission's order applied to a medium which as a matter of history had "received the most limited First Amendment protection," in large part because warnings could not adequately protect the listener from unexpected program content. The Internet, however, has no comparable history.

Moreover, the District Court found that the risk of encountering indecent material by accident is remote because a series of affirmative steps is required to access specific material.

In *Renton*, we upheld a zoning ordinance that kept adult movie theatres out of residential neighborhoods. The ordinance was aimed, not at the content of the films shown in the theaters, but rather at the "secondary effects"—such as crime and deteriorating property values—that these theaters fostered, * * * According to the Government, the CDA is constitutional because it constitutes a sort of "cyberzoning" on the Internet. But the CDA applies broadly to the entire universe of cyberspace. And the purpose of the CDA is to protect children from the primary effects of "indecent" and "patently offensive" speech, rather than any "secondary" effect of such speech. Thus, the CDA is a content-based blanket restriction on speech, and, as such, cannot be "properly analyzed as a form oftime, place, and manner regulation."

These precedents, then, surely do not require us to uphold the CDA and are fully consistent with the application of the most stringent review of its provisions.

V

In *Southeastern Promotions, Ltd. v. Conrad*, 420 U.S. 546, 557, 43 L. Ed. 2d 448, 95 S. Ct. 1239 (1975), we observed that "each medium of expression ... may present its own problems." Thus, some of our cases have recognized special justifications for regulation of the broadcast media that are not applicable to other speakers, see *Red Lion Broadcasting Co. v. FCC*; *FCC v. Pacifica Foundation,* U.S. In these cases, the Court relied on the history of extensive government regulation of the broadcast medium; the scarcity of available frequencies at its inception and its "invasive" nature, see *Sable Communications of Cal., Inc. v. FCC*, 492 U.S. 115, 128, 106 L. Ed. 2d 93, 109 S. Ct. 2829 (1989).

Those factors are not present in cyberspace. Neither before nor after the enactment of the CDA have the vast democratic fora of the Internet been subject to the type of government supervision and regulation that has attended the broadcast industry. Moreover, the Internet is not as "invasive" as radio or television. The District Court specifically found that "communications over the Internet do not 'invade' an individual's home or appear on one's computer screen unbidden. Users seldom encounter content 'by accident.'" It also found that "almost all sexually explicit images are preceded by warnings as to the content," and cited testimony that" 'odds are slim' that a user would come across a sexually explicit sight by accident."

We distinguished *Pacifica* in Sable on just this basis. In Sable, a company engaged in the business of offering sexually oriented prerecorded telephone messages (popularly known as "dial-a-porn") challenged the constitutionality of an amendment to the Communications Act that imposed a blanket prohibition on indecent as well as obscene interstate commercial telephone messages. We held that the statute was constitutional insofar as it applied to obscene messages but invalid as applied to indecent messages. In attempting to justify the complete ban and criminalization of indecent commercial telephone messages, the Government relied on Pacifica, arguing that the ban was necessary to prevent children from gaining access to such messages.

We agreed that "there is a compelling interest in protecting the physical and psychological well-being of minors" which extended to shielding them from indecent messages that are not obscene by adult standards, but distinguished our "emphatically narrow holding" in *Pacifica* because it did not involve a complete ban and because it involved a different medium of communication. We explained that "the dial-it medium requires the listener to take affirmative steps to receive the communication." * * *

Finally, unlike the conditions that prevailed when Congress first authorized regulation of the broadcast spectrum, the Internet can hardly be considered a "scarce" expressive commodity. It provides relatively unlimited, low-cost capacity for communication of all kinds. * * * This dynamic, multifaceted category of communication includes not only traditional print and news services, but also audio, video, and still images, as well as interactive, real-time dialogue.

Through the use of chat rooms, any person with a phone line can become a town crier with a voice that resonates farther than it could from any soapbox. Through the use of Web pages, mail exploders, and newsgroups, the same individual can become a pamphleteer. As the District Court found, "the content on the Internet is as diverse as human thought." We agree with its conclusion that our cases provide no basis for qualifying the level of First Amendment scrutiny that should be applied to this medium.

VI

* * *

[The Court declined to pass upon plaintiffs' challenge that the statute was void for vagueness; it noted, however, that the generality of the provisions aggravated the possibilities of misapplication.]

In contrast to Miller and our other previous cases, the CDA thus presents a greater threat of censoring speech that, in fact, falls outside the statute's scope. Given the vague contours of the coverage of the statute, it unquestionably silences some speakers whose messages would be entitled to constitutional protection. That danger provides further reason for insisting that the statute not be overly broad. The CDA's burden on protected speech cannot be justified if it could be avoided by a more carefully drafted statute.

VII

We are persuaded that the CDA lacks the precision that the First Amendment requires when a statute regulates the content of speech. In order to deny minors access to potentially harmful speech, the CDA effectively suppresses a large amount of speech that adults have a constitutional right to receive and to address to one another. That burden on adult speech is unacceptable if less restrictive alternatives would be at least as effective in achieving the legitimate purpose that the statute was enacted to serve.

* * *

The District Court was correct to conclude that the CDA effectively resembles the ban on "dial-a-porn" invalidated in Sable. In Sable, this Court rejected the argument that we should defer to the congressional judgment that nothing less than a total ban would be effective in preventing enterprising youngsters from gaining access to indecent communications. Sable thus made clear that the mere fact that a statutory regulation of speech was enacted for the important purpose of protecting children from exposure to sexually explicit material does not foreclose inquiry into its validity. As we pointed out last Term, that inquiry embodies an "over-arching commitment" to make sure that Congress has designed its statute to accomplish its purpose "without imposing an unnecessarily great restriction on speech." *Denver Area*.

* * *

The District Court found that at the time of trial existing technology did not include any effective method for a sender to prevent minors from obtaining access to its communications on the Internet without also denying access to adults. The Court found no effective way to determine the age of a user who is accessing material through e-mail, mail exploders, newsgroups, or chat rooms. * * *

* * *

For the purposes of our decision, we need neither accept nor reject the Government's submission that the First Amendment does not forbid a blanket prohibition on all "indecent" and "patently offensive" messages communicated to a 17–year old—no matter how much value the message may contain and regardless of parental approval. It is at least clear that the strength of the Government's interest in protecting minors is not equally strong throughout the coverage of this broad statute. Under the CDA, a parent allowing her 17–year-old to use the family computer to obtain information on the Internet that she, in her parental judgment, deems appropriate could face a lengthy prison term. Similarly, a parent who sent his 17–year-old college freshman information on birth control via e-mail could be incarcerated even though neither he, his child, nor anyone in their home community, found the material "indecent" or "patently offensive," if the college town's community thought otherwise.

The breadth of this content-based restriction of speech imposes an especially heavy burden on the Government to explain why a less restrictive provision would not be as effective as the CDA. It has not done so. * * *

VIII

In an attempt to curtail the CDA's facial overbreadth, the Government advances three additional arguments for sustaining the Act's affirmative prohibitions: (1) that the CDA is constitutional because it leaves open ample "alternative channels" of communication; (2) that the plain meaning of the Act's "knowledge" and "specific person" requirement significantly restricts its permissible applications; and (3) that the Act's prohibitions are "almost always" limited to material lacking redeeming social value.

[The Court rejected all of these arguments, on the ground that the CDA did not make explicit for the limitations or defenses at issue.]

* * *

For the foregoing reasons, the judgment of the district court is affirmed.

It is so ordered.

JUSTICE O'CONNOR, with whom the CHIEF JUSTICE joins, concurring in the judgment in part and dissenting in part.

I write separately to explain why I view the Communications Decency Act of 1996 (CDA) as little more than an attempt by Congress to create "adult zones" on the Internet. Our precedent indicates that the creation of such zones can be constitutionally sound. Despite the soundness of its purpose, however, portions of the CDA are unconstitutional because they stray from the blueprint our prior cases have developed for constructing a "zoning law" that passes constitutional muster.

* * *

The creation of "adult zones" is by no means a novel concept. States have long denied minors access to certain establishments frequented by adults. States have also denied minors access to speech deemed to be "harmful to minors." The Court has previously sustained such zoning laws, but only if they respect the First Amendment rights of adults and minors. That is to say, a zoning law is valid if (i) it does not unduly restrict adult access to the material; and (ii) minors have no First Amendment right to read or view the banned material. As applied to the Internet as it exists in 1997, the "display" provision and some applications of the "indecency transmission" and "specific person" provisions fail to adhere to the first of these limiting principles by restricting adults' access to protected materials in certain circumstances. Unlike the Court, however, I would invalidate the provisions only in those circumstances.

* * *

Cyberspace differs from the physical world in another basic way: Cyberspace is malleable. Thus, it is possible to construct barriers in cyberspace and use them to screen for identity, making cyberspace more like the physical world and, consequently, more amenable to zoning laws. This transformation of cyberspace is already underway. Internet speakers (users who post material on the Internet) have begun to zone cyberspace itself through the use of "gateway" technology. Such technology requires Internet users to enter information about themselves—perhaps an adult identification number or a credit card number—before they can access certain areas of cyberspace, much like a bouncer checks a person's driver's license before admitting him to a nightclub. * * *

Although the prospects for the eventual zoning of the Internet appear promising, I agree with the Court that we must evaluate the constitutionality of the CDA as it applies to the Internet as it exists today. Given the present state of cyberspace, I agree with the Court

that the "display" provision cannot pass muster. Until gateway technology is available throughout cyberspace, and it is not in 1997, a speaker cannot be reasonably assured that the speech he displays will reach only adults because it is impossible to confine speech to an "adult zone." Thus, the only way for a speaker to avoid liability under the CDA is to refrain completely from using indecent speech.
* * *

* * *

Thus, the constitutionality of the CDA as a zoning law hinges on the extent to which it substantially interferes with the First Amendment rights of adults. Because the rights of adults are infringed only by the "display" provision and by the "indecency transmission" and "specific person" provisions as applied to communications involving more than one adult, I would invalidate the CDA only to that extent. Insofar as the "indecency transmission" and "specific person" provisions prohibit the use of indecent speech in communications between an adult and one or more minors, however, they can and should be sustained. The Court reaches a contrary conclusion, and from that holding that I respectfully dissent.

Notes and Questions

1. Is this really a constitutional decision? Or, like some of the cases seen above, is the Court looking at the reasonableness of the statute, again along the line of judicial review of administrative action? Is this appropriate, though, when dealing with dealing with a coordinate branch of government, such as Congress?

Is this development over the last few years a healthy one? Does it involve courts too much in legislative decisions? In factfinding in somewhat difficult technological areas, where judges have no expertise? Does it violate the notion of separation of powers?

2. If this is a constitutional decision, what is its basis? What First Amendment test does the majority seem to be using? Strict scrutiny? Intermediate review? Is it very clear? How does the CDA fit within each one?

3. Why didn't the Court take the easy way out of just finding the provisions to be overly broad and void for vagueness? Wouldn't this have taken a lot less doctrinal development than trying to figure out the impact of a "dynamic" medium, whose future none of the parties claim to be able to predict very well? Which approach is likely to be more confining in terms of future decisionmaking?

4. How well did the Court understand the technology and industry at issue? If it did, would that have made it more likely to reach into the merits? To that extent, did Judge Sloviter's excellent description of the Internet above end up having an impact on the substantive outcome of this case? Should judges attempt to influence other judges by making it easy to understand an otherwise complex issue? Compare the Court's willingness to

deal with the Internet with its decisions in the Chapter III jurisdictional cases.

5. Is the availability of blocking software outcome-determinative, since it allows adults to control what their children—much like the infamous "V–Chip" discussed later. (p. 562) For somewhat puzzling reasons, the Court—and apparently the parties—ignored the fact that several programs already existed at the time of this case for preventing access to websites. To be sure, they required a parent to block either particular sites or domain names—rather than the simplistic rating system used with the V–Chip—but they were at least as effective as the type of control over telephones involved in *Sable*. Even by 1997 technological standards, did Internet users have more or less control over access than telephone customers (*Sable*) or cable subscribers (*Cruz v. Ferre*)? (p. 553) Indeed, if worse comes to worst, couldn't a parent simply use an external modem, and disconnect it when using the computer? Is this any more onerous that lock boxes for cable television?

Note: Tort Liability of On–Line Services

During the early 1990s, a number of on-line service providers developed. As indicated in the *Prodigy* case below, these operations commonly use large main-frame computers and telecommunications facilities to offer not only their own data-quality content, but also material "uploaded" by their subscribers. (It should be noted that the relatively limited bandwidth of present telecommunications networks prevents on-line or other programmers from offering voice or video programming—of the type associated with recurring problems of "indecency" and the like.)

The status of on-line carriers is relatively unclear in terms of regulation, defamation, and intellectual property. First, they "cast" material to a large number of people, but on an individual basis. Second, and of more concern in recent litigation, some services exercise considerably more content control than do traditional common carriers. The control factor played a large part in a lower court decision, Stratton Oakmont, Inc. v. Prodigy Services Co., 23 Media L. Rep. 1794, (Sup.Ct. Nassau Cnty.1995). The plaintiff investment banking services firm claimed that defendant Prodigy had allowed defamatory comments to be made about it by users of its "Money Talk" computer "bulletin board," as follows:

(a) STRATTON OAKMONT, INC. ("STRATTON"), a securities investment banking firm, and DANIEL PORUSH, STRATTON's president, committed criminal and fraudulent acts in connection with the initial public offering of stock of Solomon–Page Ltd.;

(b) the Solomon–Page offering was a "major criminal fraud" and "100% criminal fraud";

(c) PORUSH was "soon to be proven criminal"; and,

(d) STRATTON was a "cult of brokers who either lie for a living or get fired."

In denying plaintiff's motion for partial summary judgment, the court viewed the key issue as to whether Prodigy was deemed to be a "publisher" of the allegedly defamatory statements—or, conversely, whether it had a common carrier's immunity. The court went on to note that:

PRODIGY contracts with bulletin Board Leaders, who, among other things, participate in board discussions and undertake promotional efforts to encourage usage and increase users. * * *

Plaintiffs base their claim that PRODIGY is a publisher in large measure on PRODIGY's stated policy, starting in 1990, that it was a family oriented computer network. In various national newspaper articles * * * PRODIGY held itself out as an online service that exercised editorial control over the content of messages posted on its computer bulletin boards, thereby expressly differentiating itself from its competition and expressly likening itself to a newspaper. * * *

In opposition, PRODIGY insists that its policies have changed and evolved since 1990 and that the latest article on the subject, dated February, 1993, did not reflect PRODIGY's policies in October, 1994, when the allegedly libelous statements were posted. * * *

The court noted that Prodigy also had "content guidelines" prohibiting offensive material, automatic screening of certain types of offensive language, the presence of "Board Leaders" to control each bulletin board, and an "emergency delete function" to remove potentially offensive material. The court defined a "publisher's" status as follows.

A finding that PRODIGY is a publisher is the first hurdle for Plaintiffs to overcome in pursuit of their defamation claims, because one who repeats or otherwise republishes a libel is subject to liability as if he had originally published it. In contrast, distributors such as book stores and libraries may be liable for defamatory statements of others only if they knew or had reason to know of the defamatory statement at issue. * * * In short, the critical issue to be determined by this Court is whether the foregoing evidence establishes a prima facie case that PRODIGY exercised sufficient editorial control over its computer bulletin boards to render it a publisher with the same responsibilities as a newspaper.

* * *

As for legal authority, PRODIGY relies on Cubby Inc. v. CompuServe Inc., 776 F.Supp. 135, 139. There the defendant CompuServe was a computer network providing subscribers with computer related services or forums including an online general information service or "electronic library". One of the publications available on the Journalism Forum carried defamatory statements about the Plaintiff, an electronic newsletter. * * * The [*Cubby*] Court noted that CompuServe had no opportunity to review the contents of the publication at issue before it was uploaded into CompuServe's computer banks. Consequently, the Court found that CompuServe's product was, "in essence, an electronic for-profit library" that carried a vast number of publications, and that CompuServe had "little or no editorial control" over the contents of those publications.

* * *

The key distinction between CompuServe and PRODIGY is two fold. First, PRODIGY held itself out to the public and its members as controlling the content of its computer bulletin boards. Second, PRODI-GY implemented this control through its automatic software screening program, and the Guidelines which Board Leaders are required to enforce. By actively utilizing technology and manpower to delete notes from its computer bulletin boards on the basis of offensiveness and "bad taste", for example, PRODIGY is clearly making decisions as to content and such decisions constitute editorial control. That such control is not complete and is enforced both as early as the notes arrive and as late as a complaint is made, does not minimize or eviscerate the simple fact that PRODIGY has uniquely arrogated to itself the role of determining what is proper for its members to post and read on its bulletin boards. Based on the foregoing, this Court is compelled to conclude that for the purposes of plaintiffs' claims in this action, PRODIGY is a publisher rather than a distributor.

[The court went on to hold that the Board Leader should be considered Prodigy's agent, because it not only gave him very explicitly orders as to supervising the bulletin board, but also reviewed his activities on a regular basis.]

Chapter VII

BEHAVIORAL REGULATION

The constitutional issues examined in Chapter VI have arisen because regulators and legislators have tried various approaches to influencing—and sometimes prescribing—the content of the electronic mass media. Although such activity would incite outrage (and judicial rejection) if applied to print media, it has drawn mixed reactions when applied to the electronic media. Quite simply, public policy toward broadcast and cable communications has reflected uncertainty and consternation, perhaps more than anything else.*

In a purely legal sense, the root of the problem may be that policy makers have never decided who truly "owns"—or should own—an electronic medium. Is it the licensee or the franchisee, at least for the period of the license or franchise? Is it the government, which serves as the landlord and grants leases in the forms of licenses and franchises? Is it the public, which "owns" the necessary airwaves and the public rights-of-way? Without a clear sense of "owners" and "users," it is understandably difficult to define the rights and responsibilities of the different parties involved in electronic communications.

The fact that they were building on a very unstable legal foundation, however, has not deterred the Congress, the FCC, or the courts from trying to construct a scheme of behavioral regulation for the electronic media. The need to define the rights and responsibilities of "owners" and "users" is unquestionable. Thus, the law has charged—or, perhaps, stumbled—forward in search of a sensible regulatory scheme. As should be apparent from Chapter VI, this effort has come up against the First Amendment at almost every turn. Largely because of the uncertainty about "ownership" of the electronic media, the various First Amendment doctrines have been applied in many different and often inconsistent ways, making the task of lawmakers and regulators immeasurably more difficult.

Ultimately, this unfortunate legal problem has been consumed by a much broader public policy debate about the proper role of government.

* Recall Chief Justice Taft's remarks, as reported by Professor Coase, (p. 31).

This debate will be evident as we consider in this Chapter the various approaches to behavioral regulation. These regulatory efforts have sparked vigorous debates about social responsibility, morality, citizenship, fairness, and other similarly fundamental social concerns.

At bottom, the unanswered question is whether to permit the "marketplace of ideas" to govern the electronic media (as it does the print media) or to impose at least the "guiding hand" of the government on that market. As is almost always the case in these situations, there is debate about whether an unfettered marketplace is sufficient. Can it adequately and accurately reflect certain social values, such as morality and fairness? For many years, government answered this question in the negative—and behavioral regulation thrived. More recently, policy makers have grown skeptical about the ability and the wisdom of government imposition of social values, and thus have withdrawn substantially from the business of overseeing behavior.

We begin our examination of behavioral regulation with a relatively indirect attempt by the government to influence content.

A. REGULATION BY RAISED EYEBROW

YALE BROADCASTING CO. v. FCC

United States Court of Appeals, District of Columbia Circuit, 1973.
478 F.2d 594, certiorari denied 414 U.S. 914, 94 S.Ct. 211, 38 L.Ed.2d 152.

WILKEY, CIRCUIT JUDGE:

* * *

I. SUBSTANCE OF THE FIRST AND SECOND NOTICES

In the late 1960s and early 1970s the FCC began receiving complaints from the public regarding alleged "drug oriented" songs played by certain radio broadcasters.* In response to these complaints the Commission issued a Notice, the stated purpose of which was to remind broadcasters of their duty to broadcast in the public interest.[2] To fulfill this obligation licensees were told that they must make "reasonable efforts" to determine before broadcast the meaning of music containing drug oriented lyrics. The Notice specified that this knowledge must be in the possession of a management level executive of the station, who must then make a judgment regarding the wisdom of playing music containing references to drugs or the drug culture.

This initial Notice led to substantial confusion within the broadcast industry and among the public. Confusion centered around the meaning

---

* What the court does not mention is the fact that the most serious complaint came from a seemingly unlikely source—the Department of Defense (DOD). The armed services were concerned that "drug lyrics" would increase the existing problem of drug use in Vietnam. DOD officials thus orga-nized a meeting with then-FCC Chairperson Dean Burch, and asked him to reduce the amount of drug-related music. They also apparently provided the list of 22 songs referred to by the Court of Appeals.

2. Public Notice, 28 F.C.C.2d 409 (1971).

of phrases such as "knowing the content of the lyrics," "a certain before broadcast," and "reasonable efforts."

In order to clarify these ambiguities, the FCC issued a second Memorandum and Order clarifying and modifying certain parts of the original Notice.[3] The thrust of this Order was that (1) the Commission was not prohibiting the playing of "drug oriented" records, (2) no reprisals would be taken against stations that played "drug oriented" music, but (3) it was still necessary for a station to "know" the content of records played and make a "judgment" regarding the wisdom of playing such records.

II.   INTERPRETATION OF THE DEFINITIVE ORDER

Many of appellant's fears and arguments stem from the apparent inconsistencies between the Notice and the subsequent Order. * * * [W]e treat the Notice, as we believe the Commission intends, as superseded by the Order. Reference to the Commission's requirements is to those established by the Order.

Once the Order is taken as definitive, it becomes fairly simple to understand what the FCC asks of its licensees. The Order recognizes the gravity of the drug abuse problem in our society. From this basis, the Order proceeds to remind broadcasters that they may not remain indifferent to this severe problem and must consider the impact that drug oriented music may have on the audience. The Commission then makes the common sense observation that in order to make this considered judgment a broadcaster must "know" what it is broadcasting.[5]

The Commission went to great lengths to illustrate what it meant by saying that a broadcaster must "know" what is being broadcast. The Order emphasizes that it is not requiring the unreasonable and that the Commission was "not calling for an extensive investigation of each * * * record" that dealt with drugs. It also made clear that there was no general requirement to pre-screen records.

The Commission in its Order was obviously not asking broadcasters to decipher ever syllable, settle every ambiguity, or satisfy every conceivable objection prior to airing a composition. A broadcaster must know what he can reasonably be expected to know in light of the nature of the music being broadcast. It may, for example, be quite simple for a broadcaster to determine that an instrumental piece has little relevance to drugs. Conversely, it may be extremely difficult to determine what thought, if any, some popular lyrics are attempting to convey. In either

---

3. Memorandum Opinion and Order, 31 F.C.C.2d 377 (1971).

5. "The Commission did make clear in the Notice that the broadcaster could jeopardize his license by failing to exercise license responsibility in this area." Except as to broadcasts by political candidates, the licensee is responsible for the material broadcast over his facilities. * * * The thrust of the Notice is simply that this concept of licensee responsibility extends to the question of records which may promote or glorify the use of illegal drugs. The licensee should know whether his facilities are being used to present again and again a record which urges youth to take heroin or cocaine—that it is a wonderful, joyous experience." *Id.* at 379.

case, only what can reasonably be understood is demanded of the broadcaster.

Despite all its attempts to assuage broadcasters' fears, the Commission realized that if an Order can be misunderstood, it will be misunderstood—at least by some licensees. To remove any excuse for misunderstanding, the Commission specified examples of how a broadcaster could obtain the requisite knowledge. A licensee could fulfill its obligations through (1) pre-screening by a responsible station employee, (2) monitoring selections while they were being played, or (3) considering and responding to complaints made by members of the public. The Order made clear that these procedures were merely suggestions, and were not to be regarded as either absolute requirements or the exclusive means for fulfilling a station's public interest obligation.

* * *

III. AN UNCONSTITUTIONAL BURDEN ON FREEDOM OF SPEECH

Appellant's first argument is that the Commission's action imposes an unconstitutional burden on a broadcaster's freedom of speech. This contention rests primarily on the Supreme Court's opinion in Smith v. California, [361 U.S. 147, 80 S.Ct. 215, 4 L.Ed.2d 205 (1959)], in which a bookseller was convicted of possessing and selling obscene literature. The Supreme Court reversed the conviction. Although the State had a legitimate purpose in seeking to ban the distribution of obscene materials, it could not accomplish this goal by placing on the bookseller the procedural burden of examining every book in his store. To make a bookseller criminally liable for all the books sold would necessarily "tend to restrict the books he sells to those he has inspected; and thus the State will have imposed a restriction upon the distribution of constitutionally protected as well as obscene literature * * *."

Appellant compares its own situation to that of the bookseller in *Smith* and argues that the Order imposes an unconstitutional burden on a broadcaster's freedom of speech. The two situations are easily distinguishable.

Most obviously, a radio station can only broadcast for a finite period of twenty-four hours each day; at any one time a bookstore may contain thousands of hours' worth of readable material. Even if the Commission had ordered that stations pre-screen all materials broadcast, the burden would not be nearly so great as the burden imposed on the bookseller in *Smith*. As it is, broadcasters are not even required to pre-screen their maximum of twenty-four hours of daily programming. Broadcasters have specifically been told that they may gain "knowledge" of what they broadcast in other ways.

A more subtle but no less compelling answer to appellant's argument rests upon *why* knowledge of drug oriented music is required by the Commission. In *Smith,* knowledge was imputed to the purveyor in order that a criminal sanction might be imposed and the dissemination halted. Here the goal is to assure the broadcaster has adequate knowledge. Knowledge is required in order that the broadcaster can make a judgment about the wisdom of its programming. It is beyond dispute that the Commission requires stations to broadcast in the public interest. In order for a broadcaster to determine whether it is acting in the public interest, knowledge of its own programming is required. The Order issued by the Commission has merely reminded the industry of this fundamental metaphysical observation—in order to make a judgment about the value of programming one must have knowledge of that programming.

We say that the licensee must have *knowledge* of what it is broadcasting; the precise *understanding* which may be required of the licensee is only that which is reasonable. No radio licensee faces any realistic possibility of a penalty for misinterpreting the lyrics it has chosen or permitted to be broadcast. If the lyrics are completely obscure, the station is not put on notice that it is in fact broadcasting material which would encourage drug abuse. If the lyrics are meaningless, incoherent, the same conclusion follows. The argument of the appellant licensee, that so many of these lyrics are obscure and ambiguous, really is a circumstance available to some degree in his defense for permitting their broadcast, at least until their meaning is clarified. Some lyrics or sounds are virtually unintelligible. To the extent they are completely meaningless gibberish and approach the equivalent of machinery operating or the din of traffic, they, of course, do not communicate with respect to drugs or anything else, and are not within the ambit of the Commission's order. Speech is an expression of sound or visual symbols which is intelligible to some other human beings. At some point along the scale of human intelligibility the sounds produced may slide over from characteristics of free speech, which should be protected, to those of noise pollution, which the Commission has ample authority to abate.

We not only think appellant's argument invalid, we express our astonishment that the licensee would argue that before the broadcast it has no knowledge, and cannot be required to have any knowledge, of material it puts out over the airwaves. * * * No producer of pork and beans is allowed to put out on a grocery shelf a can without knowing what is in it and standing back of both its contents and quality. The Commission is not required to allow radio licensees, being freely granted the use of limited air channels, to spew out to the listening public canned music, whose content and quality before broadcast is totally unknown.

* * * Far from constituting any threat to freedom of speech of the licensee, we conclude that for the Commission to have been less insistent on licensees discharging their obligations would have verged on an evasion of the Commission's own responsibilities.

* * *

V. ASSERTED VAGUENESS

[The court here rejects arguments "(1) that the Order is unconstitutionally vague, or (2) that the Order is so vague that the Commission abused its discretion in refusing to clarify it."]

VI. CONCLUSION

In spite of the horrendous foreboding which brought appellant into court the fact is that appellant has recently had its license renewed. Likewise, there has been no showing or suggestion that the standard enunciated in the Order has been employed to deny any license to a broadcaster. If such a denial does occur and can be shown to be unfair or due to a misapplication of the Commission's own guidelines (as described in Part II of our opinion), then redress may be sought in the courts. Until that time, appellant might commit its energies to the simple task of understanding what the Commission has already clearly said, rather than instituting more colorful but far less fruitful actions before already heavily burdened federal courts.

For the reasons given above, the action of the Federal Communications Commission is

Affirmed.

On Motion for Rehearing En Banc

Separate Statement by CHIEF JUDGE BAZELON as to why he would grant rehearing *en banc, sua sponte.*

BAZELON, CHIEF JUDGE:

* * *

The panel opinion found that the language of the Commission's directives does not purport to censor popular songs. But that language can only be understood in the light of the Commission's course of conduct.

The Commission's initial statement in the area of "drug-oriented" songs was a "Public Notice" issued on March 5, 1971. The Notice, entitled "Licensee Responsibility to Review Records Before Their Broadcast", did not specifically prohibit the playing of particular songs. But broadcasters might well have read it as a prohibition. For one thing, two members of the Commission, including the member reported to be the originator of the Notice, appended to it a formal statement explaining that their goal was to "discourage, if not eliminate, the playing of records which tend to promote and/or glorify the use of illegal drugs." Five weeks after the Notice was issued, the Commission's Bureau of Complaints and Compliance provided broadcasters the names of 22 songs which had come to its attention as "so-called drug-oriented song lyrics."[6]

* * * It appears that radio stations moved quickly to ban certain songs. In some cases stations stopped playing, regardless of subject or lyric, all the works of particular artists whose views might lift the

---

6. In its subsequent Order, infra, the Commission reported that the 22 songs had been identified by the Department of the Army. Apparently the Commission conferred with military officials before issuing the initial Public Notice. 31 FCC 2d 79 (1971). The Commission did not consult with the Bureau of Narcotics and Dangerous Drugs. N.Y. Times, March 28, 1971, p. 41, c. 1.

Commission's eyebrow. Broadcasters circulated the list of 22 songs throughout the industry as a "do not play" list.

The Commission's subsequent "Memorandum Opinion and Order", issued on April 16, 1971, and designated by the Commission as its "definitive statement" on the subject, appeared to backtrack somewhat. The Order repudiated the list of 22 songs. It stated that the evaluation of which records to play "is one solely for the licensee", and that "[t]he Commission cannot make or review such individual licensee judgment."

But the Commission's order went further. Instead of rescinding the Public Notice, the Order restated its basic threat: "the broadcaster could jeopardize his license by failing to exercise licensee responsibility in this area." As we have recognized, "licensee responsibility" is a nebulous concept. It could be taken to mean—as the panel opinion takes it—only that "a broadcaster must 'know' what it is broadcasting." On the other hand, in light of the earlier Notice, and in light of the renewed warnings in the Order about the dangers of "drug-oriented" popular songs, broadcasters might have concluded that "responsibility" meant "prohibition".

* * * The confusion was crystallized later in 1971 in Congressional testimony by FCC Chairman Burch. At one point, the Chairman offered this assurance:

> Chairman Burch: * * * [C]ontrary to Commissioner Johnson's statement that we banned drug lyrics, we did not ban drug lyrics. * * *

Moments later, however, the following ensued:

> Senator Nelson: All I am asking is: If somebody calls to the FCC's attention that a particular station is playing songs that, in fact, do promote the use of drugs in the unanimous judgment of the Commission, if you came to that conclusion, what would you do?

> Chairman Burch: I know what I would do, I probably would vote to take the license away.

* * *

In NAACP v. Button, [371 U.S. 415, 438, 83 S.Ct. 328, 340, 9 L.Ed.2d 405 (1963)], Mr. Justice Brennan observed that "precision of regulation must be a touchstone" in the area of freedom of expression. There is no precision here. The Commission's chameleon-like directives reflect the spectrum from confusion to deliberate obfuscation. The Court must look to the impact of these directives, not merely their language. Such review is all the more necessary where the Commission's directives are couched in code words for licensee renewal such as "public interest" or "license responsibility". Seven years ago, a member of the Commission explained:

> Talk of "responsibility" of a broadcaster in this connection is simply a euphemism for self-censorship. It is an attempt to shift the onus of action against speech from the Commission to the broadcaster, but

it seeks the same result—suppression of certain views and arguments. Since the imposition of the duty of such "responsibility" involves Commission compulsion to perform the function of selection and exclusion and Commission supervision of the manner in which that function is performed, the Commission still retains the ultimate power to determine what is and what is not permitted on the air.

Judge (later Chief Justice) Burger found this reasoning to be "unanswerable." Anti–Defamation League of B'Nai B'Rith v. FCC, 131 U.S.App. D.C. 146, 148, 403 F.2d 169, 171 (1968). In the differing circumstances of this case, that reasoning might be answerable. But the court cannot abdicate its responsibility to face the question.

The panel opinion indicates that the present challenges to the Commission's directives are premature; that the Commission's final sanction is denial of a license, and until that sanction is imposed, the petitioners cannot demonstrate any harm from the Commission's actions. Opposed to this viewpoint is the often recognized principle that the threat of legal sanction can have as much effect on the conduct of threatened parties as the sanction itself.[22] If that principle applies here, as petitioners argue, then there is a judicially cognizable injury as soon as broadcasters begin to alter their programming to avoid governmental reprisal.

This case presents several other questions of considerable significance: Is the popular song a constitutionally protected form of speech? Do the particular songs at which these directives were aimed have a demonstrable connection with illegal activities?[24] If so, is the proper remedy to "discourage or eliminate" the playing of such songs? Can the FCC assert regulatory authority over material that could not constitutionally be regulated in the printed media?

Clearly, the impact of the Commission's order is ripe for judicial review. And on review, it would be well to heed Lord Devlin's recent warning:

> If freedom of the press * * * [or freedom of speech] perishes, it will not be by sudden death. * * * It will be a long time dying from a debilitating disease caused by a series of erosive measures, each of which, if examined singly, would have a good deal to be said for it.

Questions

1. Is *Smith v. California* convincingly distinguished by the court?

---

22. * * * [C]f. the candid statement of Clay T. Whitehead, Director of Telecommunications Policy in the White House, as to why the threat of license removal is an effective means of program control: "The main value of the sword of Damocles is that it hangs, not that it drops. Once you take a guy's license away, you no longer have any leverage against him." The Washington Post, March 9, 1973, at p. A 17, col. 3.

24. The only evidence in the record on this point is the statement of the Director of the Bureau of Narcotics and Dangerous Drugs expressing strong doubt that there is any connection between "drug-oriented song lyrics" and the use of drugs. The New York Times, March 28, 1971, p. 41, c. 1 * * *

(a) Concerning the "burden" distinction, assume that a radio station with a contemporary music format receives 250 new records per week, many of which are quite difficult to interpret. Is it reasonable to compare the time it would take to pre-screen "twenty-four hours of daily programming" with the "thousands of hours' worth of readable material" in a bookstore? See *Comment*, 5 Loyola L.A.L.Rev. 329, 355 (1972).

(b) Concerning the "more subtle" distinction between the state's purpose in *Smith* and the FCC's purpose here—to assure broadcaster knowledge—is the court implying that a broadcaster might discharge its public interest obligation by knowingly playing drug-oriented music? If so, is that a realistic proposition, in light of the FCC's implied distaste for such programming? If not, does the court's distinction still obtain?

2. Even a broadcaster with knowledge of what it is broadcasting is held only to a reasonable understanding of the material, i.e., as to whether it is "drug-oriented." How would you advise a broadcaster to make that determination? Consider both substance and procedure. As to substance, would you say that "Lucy in the Sky with Diamonds," by the Beatles, is "drug-oriented"? Why? As to procedure, bear in mind that many "drug-oriented songs do not explicitly promote or glorify the use of drugs, and such meanings must be drawn out of innuendo, *double entendre,* and special lingo." Note, *Drug Songs and the FCC,* 5 U.Mich.J.L.Reform 334, 337 (1972). What procedures are therefore indicated to the broadcaster anxious to take reasonable steps to know the contents of what it broadcasts?

3. How would you argue against the court's analogy between "canned-music" and canned food, the producers of which are required to know the contents and to "stand back of" both contents and quality? Are broadcasters being required to warrant the quality of their product? Are broadcasters more like the producers or the retailers of canned goods?

4. Compare the court's rather unruffled attitude toward the potential impact of the FCC Order (e.g., "no * * * suggestion that the * * * Order has been employed to deny any license") with Judge Bazelon's concern for its potential chilling effect on expression. As Judge Bazelon recognizes, the relevance of that concern turns ultimately upon whether "the popular song [is] a constitutionally protected form of speech." How should that question be answered? Does the answer depend upon whether a particular song is "drug oriented," or, in the FCC's phrase the song "promote[s] or glorif[ies] the use of illegal drugs"?

5. If the FCC can deny a broadcaster's license renewal on public interest grounds for having played songs promoting illegal drug use, does it follow that a state could ban the sale of the same songs in another form, such as sheet music or a tape or disc? Could it ban their sale to children only?

6. How seriously do broadcasters take FCC pronouncements such as this one? Despite Judge Bazelon's observations, would it surprise you to learn that the vast majority of licensees viewed the Commission's statements as purely a public relations move that had no impact upon their day-to-day operations? In the late 1980s, however, the FCC announcement that it would punish licensees for transmitting "indecent" programs received far more serious attention from licensees.

7. What happens when a broadcast trade group adopts a program content guideline to be observed by members? In 1975 the National Association of Broadcasters ("NAB") amended its Television Code, observance of which was a condition of NAB membership, by adding the following "family viewing policy":

> Entertainment programming inappropriate for viewing by a general family audience should not be broadcast during the first hour of network entertainment programming in prime time and in the immediately preceding hour [i.e., not before 9:00 p.m. (8:00 p.m. Central Time)]. In the occasional case when an entertainment program is deemed to be inappropriate for such an audience, advisories should be used to alert viewers.

The policy was the product of meetings between then Chairperson Richard Wiley and network executives. In October, 1974, Wiley summoned the vice-presidents from the then-three commercial networks to a meeting in Washington.

> The meeting was scheduled for four-thirty on a Friday afternoon. For most of the participants it was the last meeting of the week, and all of the network officials had flown down to Washington specially for the meeting. * * *

> None of the network executives was enthusiastic about attending the meeting. * * * They concluded that it would be improper for them to take any action or even to express any opinion as to actions proposed by the FCC.

* * *

> As the executives assembled in the chairman's office, it seemed that the room outside was jammed with journalists, all clamouring for interviews. * * * At Wiley's request, his staff had arranged the office chairs in two semicircles. The chairman was seated behind his desk, with two staff members on either side. Chairs for the six network people were arranged in a semicircle facing him in front of his desk.

* * *

> Wiley used the opportunity to suggest that since CBS and, he hoped, the other networks agreed that there was a problem, perhaps they would be willing to issue a statement, jointly or individually, describing their networks' policies. When the networks agreed that it might be possible for them to release their policies separately, Wiley continued, "Let's see whether or not there might be anything else you want to include in such a statement." He then suggested that the networks consider implementing the various scheduling and warning ideas that he and his staff had discussed earlier that afternoon.

* * *

Geoffrey Cowan, *See No Evil* 93 et. seq. (1978).

A television writers union and others sued the FCC, the seven FCC commissioners, the NAB and the three commercial television networks, challenging the so-called "family viewing policy" as censorship. The district court agreed, finding that the policy had been adopted as a result of government action and thus was subject to the same constitutional and procedural requirements as if it had been adopted by the FCC directly:

> * * * Based on the totality of the evidence accumulated in this case the court finds that [FCC] Chairman Wiley, acting on behalf of the Commission (and with the approval of the Commissioners) in response to congressional committee pressure launched a campaign primarily designed to alter the content of entertainment programming in the early evening hours. * * * The court finds that Chairman Wiley in the course of his campaign threatened the industry with regulatory action if it did not adopt the essence of his scheduling proposals. On some occasions, when the persuasive demands of the situation so dictated, he would withdraw his threats or assume a low profile. But the Commission's pressure in this case was persistent, pronounced and unmistakable. Chairman Wiley's actions were the direct cause of the implementation of the family viewing policy: were it not for the pressure he exerted, it would not have been adopted by any of the networks nor by the NAB. The threat of regulatory action was not only a substantial factor leading to its adoption but a crucial, necessary, and indispensable cause.

* * *

> The existence of the threats, and the attempted securing of commitments coupled with the promise to publicize non-compliance in this case constituted *per se* violations of the First Amendment. * * * Here the Commission compromised licensee independence in two ways: first, it pressured the networks to adopt the family viewing policy; second, it participated in a conspiracy to usurp licensee independence through the vehicle of the NAB. Those activities violated the First Amendment.

Writers Guild of America, West, Inc. v. FCC, 423 F.Supp. 1064 (C.D.Cal. 1976), vacated and remanded 609 F.2d 355 (9th Cir.1979), cert. denied 449 U.S. 824, 101 S.Ct. 85, 66 L.Ed.2d 27 (1980). The court of appeals did not reach the merits; it held that claims against the government defendants should have been pursued first before the FCC, and instructed the district court to hold in abeyance the claims against the private defendants pending the FCC's resolution.

(a) How is a court to distinguish between a Commissioner's speeches that have no special legal significance and "speeches [used] as one form of regulatory tool"? Suppose that the Chairman concludes unilaterally to respond in a speech to broadcast practices that are of concern to the Commission. Does the speech become a "regulatory tool"? What if a senior staff person gives the speech? A Commissioner makes extemporaneous remarks about a pending matter? Does the distinction depend upon the Commission's intent, as determined perhaps from testimony concerning its internal proceedings? Must the Commission then publicly disavow any speech in which a single Commissioner is speaking only for himself, lest it be considered agency action? The court also struggled with the characterization of a speech in Illinois Citizens Committee for Broadcasting v. FCC, 515 F.2d 397 (D.C.Cir.1974).

(b) What should the networks have done, in the face of Chairman Wiley's threats and pressure on them, if they were to avoid liability under the First Amendment?

(c) Suppose that the FCC had resisted the congressional pressure to "do something" about violence on television, and one of the committees that had been pressing the issue announced that it was considering legislation to regulate early evening program content. At hearings to which it invited the networks, the committee obtained undertakings from each network to program only family fare before 9:00 p.m., so as to make formal legislation unnecessary. Is the resulting network programming conduct "government action" for the purposes of the First Amendment? Has the committee run afoul of the court's distinction between "government encouragement" and "government pressure"? If so, what remedy would be appropriate?

(d) In the actual case, the court predicated its conclusion that there had been "government pressure" on the threat, delivered implicitly by Chairman Wiley, of imposing on the networks "the burden of a full-fledged administrative proceeding together with necessary appeals therefrom." Is this sort of threat—of presumptively lawful regulatory proceedings—normally a cognizable harm? Cf. Dombrowski v. Pfister, 380 U.S. 479, 85 S.Ct. 1116, 14 L.Ed.2d 22 (1965) (federal injunctive relief against state prosecution undertaken in bad faith to harass defendant).

(e) At one point, the court attributes the FCC's ability to apply pressure successfully to "the uncertainty of the relicensing process and the vagueness of the standards which govern it." This perception leads it to require that any agency content regulation be precisely articulated in formal regulations, yet the court stops short of prohibiting the agency from offering "*suggestions* when it believes it has information or ideas which broadcasters may wish to consider in making their independent [programming] determinations."*

Does this bring the court into essential congruence with the opinion in *Yale Broadcasting*? Could the Commission's approach to "drug lyrics" be adapted to accomplish a similar broadcaster sensitivity to demands for "family viewing," e.g., by requiring broadcasters to know whether their early evening programming is harmful or disturbing to children, so that they can then make a programming decision in the public interest with full knowledge of its consequences?

(f) Could the NAB now lawfully re-adopt a new family viewing policy, free of the taint of governmental pressure? In fact, the NAB discontinued the Television Code in 1982 after certain of its provisions relating to advertising practices were challenged by the Department of Justice on antitrust grounds.

---

* But cf. Kalven, as quoted in CBS v. DNC, at p. 329 above (Douglas, J., concurring):

The government cannot reciprocally criticize the performance of the press, its officers, and its policies without its criticism carrying implications of power and coercion. The government simply cannot be another discussant of the press's performance. Whether it will it or not, it is a critic who carries the threat of the censor and more often than not it wills it. Nor is it at all clear that its voice will be needed; surely there will be others to champion its view of the performance of the press.

6 *The Center Magazine*, No. 3, pp. 36–37 (May/June 1973).

8. In recent years, there has been a series of efforts launched to require—or induce—record companies to label as such albums that contain "explicit" lyrics. The object of these efforts has been music alleged to advocate or glorify sex, drugs, alcohol, and violence. See Comment, *Regulating Rock Lyrics: A New Wave of Censorship?*, 23 Harv.J.Legis. 595 (1986). Some advocates of labeling portray it as being no more intrusive than the "voluntary" system of movie ratings used by the Motion Picture Association of America. If ratings were adopted, could radio broadcasters constitutionally be required to read the applicable label before playing a labeled album or a single? Could television broadcasters or cable systems constitutionally be required to display an applicable label before showing a music video? What about applying the requirement to programming networks? Would voluntary labeling of records or videos by record companies, radio stations, or television stations, infringe the First Amendment rights of musicians?

B. THE FAIRNESS DOCTRINE: A GRAND EXPERIMENT IN THIRD PARTY ACCESS?

1. THE FAIRNESS DOCTRINE, 1929–87

As seen in Chapter VI, one of the common themes of regulation is giving media "have-nots" the ability to use broadcasting to communicate matters of interest to them—ranging from news to special interest entertainment programming. This concern is evident in a wide variety of regulatory policies, such as local programming, diversification of ownership, and minority participation. To a certain extent, it is a means of preventing civil unrest; as Dr. Martin Luther King said, "violence is the language of the unheard."

The Commission has at its disposal means of both encouraging and discouraging particular types of programming. On the affirmative side, it has tried to allocate frequencies in order to produce local programming. On the negative side, it has attempted to forbid certain types of "offensive" programming, as discussed later in this Chapter.

Between these two polarities, the FCC for many years enforced the "fairness doctrine." This essentially gave third parties a right to use a broadcast station's facilities to reply to statements made on the station— particularly "personal attacks" or "editorial endorsements." It does not, however, require a station either to produce or to suppress a particular type of programming. In First Amendment terms, it thus is easier to justify than other, more intrusive requirements.

This type of reply right is not unusual. Although *Tornillo* (pp. ___) indicated that it would be unconstitutional as applied to the print media, many other countries have imposed it upon both print and broadcast media as a matter of course. The French "droit de reponse" goes back more than a century; and the Federal of Australian Commercial Television Stations ("FACTS") long ago adopted the language of the Fairness Doctrine as part of its voluntary Code.

The Fairness Doctrine was an accepted part of FCC doctrine until its repeal in 1987. Although the Federal Radio Commission initially banned all editorializing by broadcasting, the Federal Communications Commission later not only authorized editorials, but required reply time to certain types of broadcast stations.

As we will see, the FCC eventually decided that the Fairness Doctrine not only was unnecessary, but was inconsistent with both the Communications Act and the First Amendment.

This section briefly summarizes a number of relatively recent fairness cases, highlighting the application of the fairness doctrine to investigative reporting and advertising. In reading this material, you should consider the Commission's eventual position, expressed below, that the fairness doctrine produced a chilling effect on broadcasters and did little to promote diversity or a vigorous debate of controversial issues.

a. *Background of the Fairness Doctrine*

MARK CONRAD THE DEMISE OF THE FAIRNESS DOCTRINE: A BLOW FOR CITIZEN ACCESS

41 Fed. Com. L. J. 161 (1989).

The roots of the Fairness Doctrine go back to the very beginnings of broadcast regulation. The Federal Radio Act of 1927, which created the Federal Radio Commission to ensure that broadcasters operated in the "public interest," also contained a provision requiring radio broadcasters to provide equal time to political candidates. Efforts to broaden this section to require licensees "to permit equal opportunity for presentation of both sides of public questions" were debated at the time of the creation of the Radio Act and again in 1932. In 1927, Congress decided not to include this provision in the final version of the Act. In 1932, President Hoover vetoed a measure which would have added this language.

Similarly, the Communications Act of 1934, which replaced the Radio Act, did not make specific mention of a fairness requirement. Neither section 315, the equal opportunities provision that required equal access to broadcast outlets by candidates for public office, nor section 312(a)(7), which created a right of reasonable access to facilities for federal candidates, incorporated language mandating citizen access to the media.

Lacking statutory codification, it was up to the Federal Radio Commission and later the FCC to conceive the Fairness Doctrine. The germination of this doctrine came in 1929 in *Great Lakes Broadcasting*,[20] a case involving New York and Chicago radio stations owned by labor organizations. The two stations applied for increases in power but were

---

20. 3 FRC ANN Rep 32 (1929), rev'd on other grounds, 37 F.2d 993 (D.C.Cir.), cer-   tiorari denied 281 U.S. 706 (1930).

turned down by the FRC on the ground that the stations had been used almost exclusively as propaganda outlets for labor interests. The FRC, in criticizing the stations' broadcasts, stated that "the public interest requires ample play for the free and fair competition of opposing views . . . [T]his principal applies . . . to all discussion of importance to the public."

In 1941, the FCC took *Great Lakes Broadcasting* one step further when it ruled that a license renewal could only be granted to a licensee that agrees not to editorialize. In *Mayflower Broadcasting*, [21]the Commission ordered a comparative license renewal between an established Boston radio station and Mayflower Broadcasting, which sought the frequency. Although Mayflower's claim was rejected, the Commission criticized the present licensee, the Yankee Network, for its acceptance of inflammatory commentaries and editorials. The FCC stated that "radio can serve as an instrument of democracy only when devoted to the communication of information and exchange of ideas fairly and objectively presented." Licensees were thus put on notice that advocacy broadcasting would not be tolerated.

The Mayflower doctrine lasted for only eight years. With the end of World War II, relative tranquility returned to the nation, and commercial television began to challenge the dominance of radio. These developments caused the Commission to reexamine Mayflower in 1949. The subsequent FCC report[25] reversed the Commission's previous position and permitted licensees to editorialize, with the stipulation that the editorials must be "fair" and that programming in general must be "balanced." More importantly, this order also required broadcasters to "devote a reasonable amount of broadcasting time to the discussion of public issues of interest in the community served by their stations. * * * [S]uch programs [must] be designed so that the public has a reasonable opportunity to hear opposing positions on the public issues" raised. Thus, the Fairness Doctrine was born.

b. *Application of the Fairness Doctrine*

i. *In General*

Not surprisingly, the Fairness Doctrine was quite fact-oriented. Most cases depended upon the nature of both the initial, "triggering" statement and the proposed response. For example, identifying someone as a "Communist" was deemed to be a personal attack; but criticizing a person's Marxist analysis of a particular problem was not.

As with many basically common law doctrines, it was difficult to identify with any precision where the Doctrine did or did not apply. The Doctrine thus always created a certain amount of uncertainty. A brief overview of its application to different types of programming thus may be useful in understanding its reach, as indicated by the examples below.

---

21. 8 FCC 333 (1941).

25. Editorializing by Broadcast Licensees, 13 FCC 1246 (1949).

i.   Denny Mulloy's infant son died while sleeping in a woven wooden cradle. The cause of death apparently was inhalation of toxic fumes, and the coroner's report raised questions about whether the cradle was unsafe. A local television station in Columbus, Ohio covered an ensuing dispute about whether the infant's death was in fact caused by the cradle. Mr. Mulloy filed a fairness complaint with the Commission, alleging that the television station had distorted its coverage of the story because the cradle manufacturer advertised on the station. Mr. Mulloy claimed that although he and the county coroner were interviewed, their views were used only as "responses" to statements by the manufacturer. Mr. Mulloy submitted a series of newspaper articles showing that the coroner's findings prompted the U.S. Consumer Product Safety Commission to undertake a investigation of the safety of the cradle and that its safety was a legitimate question. The station responded that the issue was not a controversial one of public importance and that, therefore, no fairness obligations attached to its coverage. What result? Denny Mulloy, FCC Mimeo No. 4828 (released May 30, 1985), recon. denied, FCC Mimeo No. 1750 (released Jan. 3, 1986), review denied, FCC No. 86–360 (released Aug. 13, 1986) (no violation for want of a controversial issue of public importance).

ii. A television station in Georgia aired a program entitled "Should the Constitution be Amended ... or Repealed?", examining a ballot proposition for significant amendments to the State constitution. Charles Littlejohn filed a fairness complaint with the Commission alleging that (a) during the first thirty minutes of the program, all of the live guests and interviewees advocated adoption of the proposition, and (b) during the subsequent sixty minutes of the program, all of the panelists responding to viewer calls "showed avid advocacy for ratification." He further alleged that, as a regular viewer of the station, he has seen no other contrasting viewpoints presented. The station was owned by the state, and the ballot proposition was being put forth by the state government.

The station responded to a Commission letter of inquiry stating that it had attempted, although unsuccessfully, to locate spokespersons opposed to ratification. It also argued that the ballot proposition was not controversial; the only controversy had arisen—and been resolved—in the process of drafting the amendments. What result? Charles E. Littlejohn, FCC Mimeo No. 2936 (released March 16, 1984), review denied, FCC No. 84–448 (released Oct. 5, 1984):

> Even [though no opposing spokesperson was presented during the program], the Commission will not attempt to second-guess its licensees or require them to follow a rigid formula for fulfilling fairness obligations. This is not to say we condone the practice of not having a spokesperson for the opposing point of view. However, where the licensee has made reasonable, good faith efforts to inform the public on an issue, the Commission will not step in and impose its own formulation of how it may have handled a particular fairness matter.

iii. Lawrence Krak filed a fairness complaint with the Commission, alleging that a Wisconsin television station "did not make an honest attempt to fairly present the reasons for opposition to the restoration of wolves in Wisconsin" in its program "The Return of the Wolf." The licensee responded that (a) Mr. Krak had not properly identified the issue on which the program focused; (b) the issue being covered was simply the methods used to track the reemergence of wolves within the state; (c) the program had nevertheless stated several times that there was opposition to the protection of wolves within the state; and (d) Mr. Krak had been interviewed on the program. What result? *Letter to Lawrence Krak from the Mass Media Bureau* (October 14, 1984), review denied, FCC No. 85–268 (released May 21, 1985) (finding no violation because no evidence of unbalanced coverage had been presented).

iv. When defending the fairness doctrine, the Commission often noted that it had erected substantial procedural hurdles for complainants in order to protect broadcasters from undue intrusion into their editorial processes. In this regard, the Commission had stated that a prima facie fairness complaint (which, in theory, would prompt the Commission to seek a response from a licensee) was required to include the following: (a) a basis for concluding that the issue covered was controversial; (b) the specific issue in question, including a summary of views presented; (c) the date and time of the broadcast of the issue; (d) the basis for believing the issue was one of public import; (e) reasonable grounds for believing that only one side of the issue had been presented (such as regular viewership of the station); (f) copies of correspondence between the complainant and the broadcaster (showing that the complainant had sought corrective action from the broadcaster before coming to the Commission); and (g) information as to whether the broadcaster has afforded, or intended to afford, reasonable opportunity for the presentation of contrasting views.

ii. *Investigative Reporting*

i. A classic fairness doctrine case that highlighted the difficulty of government involvement in decisions about programming arose from NBC's airing of a documentary entitled "Pensions: The Broken Promise." In May 1973, on the day that it won a Peabody Award for the documentary, the Commission notified NBC that its broadcast had violated the fairness doctrine. In general, the program was highly critical of private pension plans. Accuracy in Media ("AIM"), a public interest group, complained to the FCC that the program had distorted events to present an ideological view of the issues and had failed to provide a reasonable opportunity for presentation of views supportive of private pension programs. NBC argued that (a) the issue was not a controversial one, (b) it had not distorted the news, and (c) in NBC's judgment, the program had presented views that the private pension system was functioning well overall. The Commission rejected the news distortion claim, but concluded that NBC had violated its fairness doctrine obligations and ordered it promptly to present contrasting views. The court of appeals reversed. National Broadcasting Co. v. FCC, 516 F.2d 1101 (D.C.Cir.1974), vacated as moot 516 F.2d at 1180 (D.C.Cir.), cert. denied 424 U.S. 910, 96 S.Ct. 1105, 47 L.Ed.2d 313 (1976) (the Commission had improperly substituted its editorial judgment for that of the licensee, whereas its "function" in administering the fairness doctrine was limited to "correcting the licensee for *abuse* of discretion"). The court's decision emphasized the special need to protect a broadcaster's discretion in matters of investigative reporting and news coverage:

> The point is fundamental. In a case where NBC has made a reasonable judgment that a program relates to, and the public has an interest in knowing about, the "broken promise" abuses that its reporters have identified in various private pension plans, and there is no controversy concerning the existence in fact of such abuses, then the balancing of the fairness doctrine cannot permit the intrusion of a government agency to make its own determination of the subject and thrust of the program as a report that such abuses feature private pensions generally, and with such enlargement to a controversial status to burden the reporting with the obligation of providing an opposing view of the escalated controversy.

Does this decision envision a two-level review process, in which a station (or network) reviews its program and then the FCC, in response to a complaint, reviews the station's editorial decisions? Was the court seeking to prevent the FCC from reviewing the actual content of the program at issue? If a station has made a good faith editorial judgment, can the FCC ever reverse or penalize that judgment?

ii. The Central Intelligence Agency ("CIA") filed a complaint with the Commission alleging that ABC World News Tonight violated the fairness doctrine and engaged in news distortion in a series of news segments aired in late 1984. The segments concerned allegations of the CIA's involvement in various illegal activities, including attempts to assassinate American citizens. Much of the CIA's complaint alleged that ABC News had knowingly presented false information. The Commission initially rejected the news distortion complaint, on the ground that there was no extrinsic evidence of an intent to present false information. Cf. Hunger in America, 20 FCC 2d 143 (1969). With respect to the fairness doctrine issue, the Commission concluded that the CIA had not identified a "controversial" issue and had not presented evidence of its regular viewing to support a prima facie showing of a fairness doctrine violation. Central Intelligence Agency, 57 R.R.2d 1543 (1985).

The CIA amended its complaint. On the news distortion claim, the Commission found that extrinsic evidence was still lacking; accordingly, the Commission would not "second-guess" ABC's news judgment. On the fairness doctrine issue, the CIA, then joined by the American Legal Foundation, claimed that the issue was whether the CIA condoned or participated in murder, that such issue was a controversial one of great public import, and that regular monitoring of ABC News programming indicated that no reasonable opportunities for contrasting views were provided.

After reviewing the programs, the Commission stated that the identified issue was not the subject of the news segments; they concerned only an allegation that the CIA had planned an assassination in connection with its involvement with an investment firm that went bankrupt. The Commission went on to hold that no evidence had been presented to demonstrate that, even if the CIA had correctly identified the issue being examined by ABC News, the issue was one on which there was vigorous public debate. The amended complaint was dismissed. 58 R.R.2d 1544 (1985). In addressing the complaint, the Commission denied a request for a declaratory ruling that a government agency should not be permitted to file a fairness doctrine complaint because of the severe chilling effect such complaints may have. The Commission stated that the chilling effect "is the result of the Fairness Doctrine generally and not particularly due to the fact that the complaint is generated by a governmental source."

iii. Advertising

i.   John F. Banzhaf, III requested that WCBS–TV, New York, make free air time available to anti-smokers to respond to the claims made in cigarette advertisements regularly carried by the station. The broadcaster responded that its news programs, as well as public service announcements by the American Cancer Society that it aired without charge, satisfied any fairness doctrine obligation it might have. WCBS added that, in any event, the fairness doctrine should not be applied to purely commercial advertisements. Banzhaf then turned to the Commission. What result? See Banzhaf v. FCC, 405 F.2d 1082 (D.C.Cir.1968), cert. denied 396 U.S. 842, 90 S.Ct. 50, 24 L.Ed.2d 93 (1969) (affirming the Commission's ruling that, in the case of cigarettes, product commercials, which tout smoking as a good or desirable practice, give rise to a fairness doctrine obligation, but the obligation can be satisfied in a variety of ways, including the ways in which WCBS had presented contrasting views). The court stated that "as a public health measure addressed to a unique danger * * *, the cigarette ruling is not invalid on account of its unusual particularity. It is in fact the product singled out for special treatment which justifies the action taken."

Would a station that carried anti-smoking messages and no cigarette commercials have to give time to the pro-smoking viewpoint? See Larus & Bro. Co. v. FCC, 447 F.2d 876 (4th Cir.1971). In 1969, Congress passed a statute that prohibited cigarette advertising "on any medium of electronic communication subject to the jurisdiction of the [FCC]." 15 U.S.C. § 1335. The broadcast industry appealed the constitutionality of the statute, which deprived it of a substantial source of advertising revenue. The ban was upheld, in part on the ground that commercial speech was not entitled to full First Amendment protection. Capital Broadcasting Co. v. Mitchell, 333 F.Supp. 582 (D.D.C.1971), affirmed 405 U.S. 1000, 92 S.Ct. 1289, 31 L.Ed.2d 472 (1972). In 1986, a similar ban on advertising of smokeless tobacco, passed the House but failed in the Senate. Since then, similar efforts to ban alcohol advertisements have also failed.

ii.   Should fairness doctrine obligations extend to stations that carry commercials for automobiles with large engines and for "high-test" gasoline, both of which contribute significantly to air pollution? Friends of the Earth v. FCC, 449 F.2d 1164 (D.C.Cir.1971) (remanding to the Commission the issue of whether carriage of the advertisements created a fairness doctrine obligation in light of the *Banzhaf* case, discussed above). See Jaffe, *The Editorial Responsibility of the Broadcaster: Reflections on Fairness and Access,* 85 Harv.L.Rev. 768, 771–80 (1972).

iii.   In the mid–1980s, CBS became the target of a takeover battle when Ted Turner, the owner of Superstation WTBS in Atlanta and head of Cable News Network and associated cable programming services, proposed to acquire the company. At the same time, a group called Fairness in Media ("FIM") suggested that it might wage a proxy fight for control of CBS. FIM had been formed to work with Sen. Jesse Helms and Rep. Phil Crane to urge individuals concerned with CBS's alleged "liberal bias" to acquire stock of the company. While the corporate battles ensued, FIM filed a complaint with the FCC, alleging that a CBS affiliate in North Carolina had violated the fairness doctrine by running advertisements touting the "accuracy, integrity, objectivity, and fairness" of the CBS Evening News, and had refused to present FIM's contrasting view that CBS News was biased. According to FIM, the issue was controversial and of public importance. What result? *Fairness in Media,* FCC Mimeo No. 1751 (released Jan. 3, 1986) (finding no violation; FIM was complaining about the station's refusal to accept its contrasting ads, and the fairness doctrine did not entitle any particular individual or group access to a broadcast station).

C.   REPEAL OF THE FAIRNESS DOCTRINE

In 1985, the Commission instituted an inquiry to consider whether the fairness doctrine continued to promote the public interest. The result was a lengthy report in which the Commission concluded, tentatively, that the fairness doctrine no longer served either the public interest or the goals of the First Amendment. *Inquiry into Section 73.1910 of the Commission's Rules and Regulations Concerning the General Fairness Doctrine Obligations of Broadcast Licensees* (1985 Fairness Report), 102 FCC 2d 143 (1985). Despite those conclusions, the FCC did not go on to repeal the fairness doctrine at that time. As discussed at length in the *1985 Fairness Report,* there was a substantial issue as to whether Congress had codified the fairness doctrine when it amended the Communications Act in 1959. If so, then the FCC would not have the authority to repeal the fairness doctrine. In addition, at the time of the *1985 Fairness Report,* Congress was considering various legislative proposals concerning the fairness doctrine and had cautioned the FCC about repealing it before Congress had been given a full opportunity to consider the proposals. The FCC already was having its share of problems with the Congress; many members of the committees responsible for overseeing the FCC's activities believed that, in its rush to deregulate the broadcast media, the FCC was implementing an ideology and not its statutory mandate.

As a result, the Commission laid out its basic conclusions as to the status of the fairness doctrine, but did not actually invalidate it. Its reasoning is noteworthy, because it represented perhaps the high point of deregulatory concerns during the 1970s and 1970s. But after all, the then Chairperson of the Commission once had quipped that for regulatory purposes a television set was to different than a toaster. In Fairness Doctrine Obligations of Broadcast Licensees, 102 FCC 2d 145, 55 R.R. 2d 1137 (1985), the Commission laid out the reasoning which was to govern the ultimate repeal of the doctrine.

> 5. On the basis of the voluminous factual record compiled in this proceeding, our experience in administering the doctrine and our general expertise in broadcast regulation, we no longer believe that the fairness doctrine, as a matter of policy, serves the public interest. In making this determination, we do not question the interest of the listening and viewing public in obtaining access to diverse and antagonistic sources of information. Rather, we conclude that the fairness doctrine is no longer a necessary or appropriate means by which to effectuate this interest. We believe that the interest of the public in viewpoint diversity is fully served by the multiplicity of voices in the marketplace today and that the intrusion by government into the content of programming occasioned by the enforcement of the doctrine unnecessarily restricts the journalistic freedom of broadcasters. Furthermore, we find that the fairness doctrine, in operation, actually inhibits the presentation of controversial issues of public importance to the detriment of the public and in degradation of the editorial prerogatives of broadcast journalists.

* * *

II. The Constitutionality of the Fairness Doctrine is Suspect

> 17. In light of the significant changes that have occurred in the communications marketplace, a number of commenters have taken the position that the application of a disparate First Amendment standard to cases involving broadcast journalists is no longer appropriate. * * * We do not believe, however, that it is necessary or appropriate for us to make that determination in this proceeding.

> 18. Administrative agencies are not tasked with the duty to adjudicate the constitutionality of a federal statute.* * * [W]e are mindful that it is the province of the federal judiciary—and not this Commission—to interpret the Constitution. We do not purport, therefore, to definitely resolve whether or not the fairness doctrine is constitutional. However, for several reasons we believe that it is

appropriate for us to state our opinion on this issue. First, as noted above, constitutional considerations are an integral component of the public interest standard and we believe that an evaluation of the constitutionality of the doctrine is necessary in order to make a meaningful evaluation as to whether or not retention of the doctrine is in the public interest. Second, as the expert administrative agency charged by the Congress with the day-to-day implementation of broadcast regulation, we believe that our opinions on these matters provide a unique perspective which may prove useful. Third, as noted above, in upholding the constitutionality of the fairness doctrine in the *Red Lion* decision, the Supreme Court relied upon our representation that the fairness doctrine did not operate to inhibit the coverage of controversial issues of public importance; the evidence in this proceeding, however, compels the conclusion that this assumption is no longer valid.

19. We believe that there are serious questions raised with respect to the constitutionality of the fairness doctrine whether or not the Supreme Court chooses to continue to apply the less exacting standard which it has traditionally employed in assessing the constitutionality of broadcast regulation. * * * [T]he compelling evidence in this proceeding demonstrates that the fairness doctrine, in operation, inhibits the presentation of controversial issues of public importance. As a consequence, even under a standard of review short of the strict scrutiny standard applied to test the constitutionality of restraints on the press, we believe that the fairness doctrine can no longer be justified on the grounds that it is necessary to promote the First Amendment rights of the viewing and listening public. Indeed, the chilling effect on the presentation of controversial issues of public importance resulting from our regulatory policies affirmatively disserves the interest of the public in obtaining access to diverse viewpoints. In addition, we believe that the fairness doctrine, as a regulation which directly affects the content of speech aired over broadcast frequencies, significantly impairs the journalistic freedom of broadcasters. * * * Were the balance ours alone to strike, the fairness doctrine would thus fall short of promoting those interests necessary to uphold its constitutionality. * * *

20. A number of commenters have argued that the limited availability of the electromagnetic spectrum is sufficient to justify the fairness doctrine. * * * While it is true that the limited availability of the electromagnetic spectrum may constitute a *per se* justification for certain types of government regulation, such as licensing, it does not follow that all other types of governmental regulation, particularly rules which affect the constitutionally sensitive area of content regulation, are similarly justified. * * *

21. * * * We will now specifically address the factors which, in our view, mandate a reassessment of our historical position that the fairness doctrine is consistent with the public interest.

III.   A NUMBER OF FACTORS JUSTIFY A REASSESSMENT
OF THE FAIRNESS DOCTRINE

B.   *The Fairness Doctrine in Operation Lessens the Amount of Diverse Views Available to the Public*

1.   *Broadcasters Perceive That the Fairness Doctrine Involves Significant Burdens.*

* * *

29.   * * * [T]he fairness doctrine in its operation encourages broadcasters to air only the minimal amount of controversial issue programming sufficient to comply with the first prong [which requires a broadcaster to provide coverage of controversial issues of public importance to the community]. * * *

30.   There are a variety of reasons why a broadcaster might be inhibited from providing comprehensive coverage of controversial issues of public importance by operation of the fairness doctrine. One reason is the fear of government sanction. * * *[73]

33.   The potential of a "chilling effect," however, is not restricted to the fear by a broadcaster that the Commission will find a violation of the fairness doctrine and impose sanctions on the licensee. A licensee may also be inhibited from presenting controversial issue programming by the fear of incurring the various expenses and other burdens which may arise in the context of fairness doctrine litigation regardless of whether or not it is ultimately found to be in violation of the doctrine.

35.   Broadcasters can also be deterred by the financial costs involved in defending a fairness doctrine complaint. The record reflects that such costs can be substantial. For example, a fairness doctrine complaint was brought against KREM–TV, a television station in Spokane, Washington charging the station with unbalanced coverage of a bond issue for an international exposition entitled "Expo–74."[81] While the Commission ultimately made the determination that the licensee did not violate the fairness doctrine, the administrative process extended for more than 20 months. The licensee incurred legal costs of at least $20,000 and other expenses, such as travel expenses, significantly added to that total. As the total profits reported by all three Spokane television stations in 1972 were approximately $494,000, the financial burden borne by the station in defending this single fairness doctrine complaint was considerable. Moreover, in addition to the legal costs and other out-of-pocket expenses incurred by the station, the licensee was further burdened by the dislocation of normal operational functions that

---

73. The evidence of record from a fairness doctrine supporter demonstrates that organizations have effectively used the threat of license revocation in fairness doctrine negotiations in order to pressure broadcasters to give them air time for their specific programming. * * * [Footnote relocated]

81. Sherwyn M. Heckt, 40 F.C.C.2d 1150 (1973).

necessarily resulted from the significant amount of time expended by high-level management and station employees with respect to this matter.

38. We also reject the contention that we should be unconcerned with the administrative and financial burdens that result from the fairness doctrine because they merely represent the cost of doing business. Indeed, the United States Supreme Court has recognized that financial considerations "may be markedly more inhibiting than the fear of prosecution under a criminal statute." * * *

2. The Record Demonstrates that the Fairness Doctrine Causes Broadcasters to Restrict Their Coverage of Controversial Issues.

42. The record reflects that, in operation, the fairness doctrine—in stark contravention of its purpose—operates as a pervasive and significant impediment to the broadcasting of controversial issues of public importance. * * *

46. Equally or perhaps even more disturbing than the self-censorship of individual broadcasts is the fact that the avoidance of fairness doctrine burdens has precipitated specific "policies" on the part of broadcast stations which have the direct effect of diminishing, on a routine basis, the amount of controversial material presented to the public on broadcast stations. For example, the owner of a broadcast station and two newspapers regularly prints editorials in his newspapers but, inhibited by regulatory restrictions, is reluctant to repeat the same editorials on his radio station. * * *

* * *

61. A number of commenters argue that there is no inhibiting effect because the Commission has been careful to administer the fairness doctrine in a manner which attenuates the regulatory burdens on broadcasters. It is true that we have enforced the doctrine with a view toward minimizing editorial intrusion on broadcast journalists. But the record in this proceeding has convinced us that the fairness doctrine generally operates to inhibit the presentation of controversial issues of public importance on the airwaves. * * *

C. The Administration of the Fairness Doctrine Operates to Inhibit the Expression of Unorthodox Opinions

* * *

70. First, the requirement to present balanced programming under the second prong of the fairness doctrine is in itself a government regulation that inexorably favors orthodox viewpoints. * * * [O]nly "major" or "significant" opinions * * * are within the scope of the regulatory obligation to provide contrasting viewpoints. As a consequence, the fairness doctrine makes a regulatory distinction between two different categories of opinions: those which are "significant enough to warrant broadcast coverage [under the fair-

ness doctrine]" and opinions which do not rise to the level of a major viewpoint of sufficient public importance that triggers responsive programming obligations. While the broadcaster in the first instance is responsible for evaluating the "viewpoints and shades of opinion which are to be presented," we are obligated to review the reasonableness of the broadcaster's evaluation. As a consequence, the fairness doctrine in operation inextricably involves the Commission in the dangerous task of evaluating the merits of particular viewpoints. This evaluation has serious First Amendment ramifications. * * *

* * *

D. In Operation the Fairness Doctrine Places the Government Into the Intrusive and Constitutionally Disfavored Role of Scrutinizing Program Content

72. * * * In evaluating whether or not a broadcaster met his or her balanced programming obligations under the fairness doctrine, we are obligated to determine whether or not the broadcaster made a reasonable determination as to whether or not the programming presented controversial issues of public importance, and if so, we must assess whether or not the broadcaster provided reasonable opportunities for the presentation of contrasting viewpoints. In evaluating the adequacy of the responsive programming, we have had to draw conclusions as to the reasonableness of the selected program formats and spokespersons.

73. Moreover, in making these assessments, we must necessarily take into account the amount of time in which a specific viewpoint was broadcast. Our staff often performs this task by mechanistically weighing the minutes and even the seconds of time devoted to each expression of opinion.[174] In addition, we must assess the frequency of the broadcast and the degree of audience exposure. Further, because the opportunity to present responsive programming may lose its utility if the controversial issue of public importance triggering the obligation subsequently becomes moot, we must

---

174. At the *en banc* hearing [of the Commission], James C. McKinney, Chief of the Mass Media Bureau, described the detailed scrutiny of program content that necessarily results from the enforcement of the fairness doctrine:

[I]t might be interesting for you to know the process that we go through here at the agency at the lower staff level before the Commissioners get [a case] for final decision. We * * * sit down with tape recordings [and] video tapes of * * * what has been broadcast on a specific station. We compare that to newspapers [and] other public statements that are made in the community. We try to make a decision as to whether the issue is controversial and whether it is of public importance in that community, which may be 2000 miles away. * * * [W]hen it comes down to the final analysis, we take out stop watches and we start counting [the] seconds and minutes that are devoted to one issue compared to [the] seconds and minutes devoted to the other side of that issue. * * * [I]n the final analysis we start giving our judgment as what words mean in the context of what was said on the air. What was the twist that was given that specific statement, or that commercial advertisement? Was it really pro-nuclear power or was it pro some other associated issue?

Hearings on the Fairness Doctrine; Panel IV (Statement of James C. McKinney) (February 8, 1985).

also make judgments as to the timeliness of the opportunity for the discussion of contrasting viewpoints. The minute and subjective scrutiny of program content resulting from the enforcement of the fairness doctrine is at odds with First Amendment principles. * * *

 E. The Fairness Doctrine Creates the Opportunity for Intimidation of Broadcasters by Governmental Officials

* * *

75. Political officials have been loathe to criticize the manner in which broadcasters have aired controversial matters of public concern and at times the criticism has been accompanied by overt pressure to influence the manner in which these issues are covered.[180] For example, a White House official during the Nixon Administration suggested to the President's Chief of Staff that the Administration respond to the alleged "unfair coverage" of the broadcast media by showing "favorites within the media," establishing "an official monitoring system through the FCC" and making "official complaints from the FCC." * * *

 G. Need for the Fairness Doctrine in Light of the Increase in the Amount and Type of Information Sources in the Marketplace

81. * * * The Commission's last assessment of the information marketplace, and its necessary relationship to the legal and policy underpinnings of the fairness doctrine, occurred in 1974. At that time the Commission concluded:

> The effective development of an electronic medium with an abundance of channels through the use of cable or otherwise is still very much a thing of the future. *For the present,* we do not believe that it would be appropriate—or even permissible—for a government agency charged with the allocation of the *channels now available* to ignore the legitimate First Amendment interests of the public. (*emphasis added*)

82. More than a decade has passed since this examination. During this time, we have witnessed explosive growth in various communications technologies. We find the information marketplace of today different from that which existed in 1974, as many of the "future" electronic technologies have now become contributors to the marketplace of ideas. * * * [T]he growth of traditional broadcast facilities, as well as the development of new electronic information technologies, provides the public with suitable access to the marketplace of ideas so as to render the fairness doctrine unnecessary. Moreover, we find that the dynamics of the information

---

180. An internal memorandum of one high level official of the Nixon Administration reveals that the President directed his staff on twenty-one occasions during a single thirty-day period to take "specific action relating to what could be considered unfair news coverage." Memorandum to H.R. Haldeman from Jeb S. Magruder, *The Shotgun Versus the Rifle* (Oct. 17, 1969), *reprinted in* D. Bazelon, *FCC Regulation of the Telecommunications Press,* 1975 Duke L.J. 213, 247–51 (1975).

services marketplace overall insures that the public will be sufficiently exposed to controversial issues of public importance. * * *

1. *Nature and Scope of the Information Services Marketplace*

* * *

86. * * * [F]or the purpose of analyzing the fairness doctrine, we believe it is appropriate to consider traditional broadcast services, new electronic media and print as all part of the information services marketplace.

87. Several commenters argued that broadcasting, particularly television, is such a dominant information source that there are no other realistic information alternatives. * * * We do not believe that the purported dominance of one media voice necessarily detracts from the significance of other voices with respect to the availability of antagonistic and diverse sources of information. The success of one particular medium in attracting large audiences does not necessarily provide an appropriate justification for imposing governmentally mandated fairness. Moreover, the data do not suggest that other media voices are somehow unavailable. * * *

88. Similarly, we are not persuaded by those who argue that newspapers and broadcast facilities are in different information markets because newspapers must be read as opposed to television or radio which may be casually watched or monitored. For the purposes of the policies adopted herein, we can find no important regulatory distinction in the fact that an individual watches television, listens to the radio or reads a newspaper. * * *

89. A related argument concerns the fact that broadcasting, unlike almost all other media sources, is subject to substantial and direct government regulation. We do not believe that a system of government licensing affects the substitutability of information among the various media voices. While such a system may influence entry into the information service marketplace, a licensing scheme, in and of itself, does not provide a proper distinction for the purpose of assessing the impact of broadcasting as a diverse information voice. * * *

90. In addition, we do not believe that purported price differences among the various information sources necessarily place them in separate information markets. While programming from traditional advertiser based broadcast facilities has been considered a "zero priced good," there is no evidence in the record suggesting that the alleged price differentials between these facilities and other "pay" media are significant enough to preclude interchangeability among information systems. Indeed, the monthly cost of a daily newspaper may be comparable to or even less than the monthly cost of basic cable service.

91. Several commenters suggested that newer technologies such as pay cable, STV, MDS, DBS are not adequate information

substitutes with respect to the provision of issue related programming. * * * [W]e believe there are sufficient incentives to insure the presentation of programming that addresses controversial issues of public importance. These incentives exist not only for traditional broadcast facilities, but also for the newer electronic technologies.

[The Commission here describes at length the growth of broadcast radio and television and cable television, as well as the emergence of other newer media, including DBS, MDS, STV, SMATV, LPTV, FM subcarriers, and videotex.]

3. Availability in the Information Market

125. Several parties have argued that * * * overall increases in information service outlets are not necessarily sufficient to provide each market with diverse and antagonistic sources of information. The argument is predicated on two assumptions. First it assumes that the growth of information sources nationwide has had no impact on local markets. Second it assumes that these sources will not provide coverage to controversial issues of public importance. * * *

126. On the record before us, we find that the nationwide development of these diverse information sources has had a direct impact on the availability of the information in each media market. For example, even in small markets such as El Paso, Texas (ADI market No. 104), there are a significant number of media voices. According to data submitted by NAB, this market has seven television stations, twenty-seven radio stations, two MDS channels, thirty thousand VCR's and cable penetration at 47 percent. * * *

129. Several commenters have argued that absent the fairness doctrine there will be no incentive for broadcasters to provide coverage to controversial issues of public importance. These parties also assert that the new electronic technologies are unable to address these types of issues, particularly at the local level. We are not persuaded by these arguments.

* * *

131. Apart from the incentives of traditional broadcast facilities, we believe that other media systems will provide sufficient amounts of programming covering controversial issues of public importance. Cable television, for example, is already providing various informational programming such as CNN and the Financial News Network [now CNBC]. Moreover, many cable systems are originating their own programming and have local community access channels. Increased availability of VCR's will also provide an important outlet for discussion of issues in each market. Most importantly, local newspapers will remain as an important source of

locally oriented information. All of these sources will make significant contributions to the marketplace of ideas.

* * *

VI. CONCLUSION

* * *

176. Notwithstanding [our] conclusions, we have decided not to eliminate the fairness doctrine at this time. The doctrine has been a longstanding administrative policy and a central tenet of broadcast regulation in which Congress has shown a strong although often ambivalent interest. * * * In addition, we recognize that the United States Supreme Court in *FCC v. League of Women Voters of California* has similarly demonstrated an interest in our examination of the constitutional and policy implications underlying the fairness doctrine. Because of the intense Congressional interest in the fairness doctrine and the pendency of legislative proposals, we have determined that it would be inappropriate at this time to eliminate the fairness doctrine. Given our decision to defer to Congress on this matter, we also believe that it would be inappropriate for us to act on the various proposals to modify or restrict the scope of the fairness doctrine. It is also important to emphasize that we will continue to administer and enforce the fairness doctrine obligations of broadcasters and to underscore our expectation that broadcast licensees will continue to satisfy these requirements.

* * *

Notes and Questions

1. (a) The final paragraph of the FCC's Report stresses the political aspect of its decision not to modify or eliminate the fairness doctrine. Not insignificant, as well, is the fact that the political broadcasting rules (p. 499), which are closely related to the fairness doctrine, provide federal office-seekers with substantial media access benefits. Repeal of the fairness doctrine could have provided substantial support for efforts to eliminate the political broadcasting rules—either on public policy or on constitutional grounds—despite the fact that there are significant distinctions (constitutional and otherwise) between fairness obligations and the equal opportunities and reasonable time requirements contained in the political broadcasting rules. The fairness doctrine also had the support of vocal constituents, who feared that without it they would be denied the opportunity to "correct" perceived biases among broadcasters.

In this politically charged environment, the FCC decided to tread very carefully. It ended the *1985 Fairness Report* with an extended discussion of its authority to modify or repeal the fairness doctrine. Its authority turned on the question of whether the fairness doctrine was a statutory requirement (which could be altered only by the Congress) or simply an agency rule or policy (which the FCC could change). Although the Commission maintained that Congress had not codified the fairness doctrine, it stopped short of a definitive answer to the question and deferred instead to the Congress and the courts—at least temporarily.

(b) Slightly more than a year after the FCC issued the *1985 Fairness Report,* the court of appeals concluded that the fairness doctrine had *not* been codified by Congress. Telecommunications Research and Action Center v. FCC, 801 F.2d 501 (D.C.Cir.1986), rehearing denied 806 F.2d 1115 (D.C.Cir.), cert. denied 482 U.S. 919, 107 S.Ct. 3196, 96 L.Ed.2d 684 (1987) (*"TRAC"*).

The court reasoned that although Congress had not nullified the fairness doctrine in several different general amendments to the Communications Act, it also had not taken any clear action to adopt it. The court thus concluded that the Congress had not implicitly codified the fairness doctrine—and thus that the Commission was free to repeal it on any rational basis. This left the FCC legally free to modify or repeal the doctrine—although it continued to face substantial political pressure not to act.

The proceeding that resulted in release of the *1985 Fairness Report* was begun at the same time that the Commission was deciding a case in which it concluded that a television licensee had failed to comply with its fairness doctrine obligations. The case involved the construction of the Nine Mile Point II nuclear power plant in upstate New York. In 1982, WTVH–TV (Syracuse), owned by Meredith Broadcasting Corp., had aired a series of editorial advertisements for the Energy Association of New York, which advocated the nuclear plant as a "sound investment" for New York. In 1983, the Syracuse Peace Council ("SPC") filed a fairness doctrine complaint with the FCC, alleging that WTVH had failed to provide coverage of contrasting views on the construction of the nuclear plant. SPC alleged that the question of whether the plant was a "sound investment" was a controversial issue of public importance and that its members, who regularly watched WTVH, had not observed the presentation of any contrasting views on the issue.

In response to the complaint, the FCC asked WTVH to comment. WTVH first argued that SPC had mischaracterized the issue; according to WTVH, the issue actually was the danger of dependence on foreign oil. Even assuming that SPC had identified the proper issue, WTVH argued that such issue was neither controversial nor of public importance. According to WTVH, SPC was really focusing on the issue of potential rate increases for electricity; at the time of the advertisements, WTVH noted, no rate increases were pending. Accordingly, WTVH concluded that SPC's issue was not the topic of debate or the focus of public comment. Finally, WTVH advised the FCC, even if the issue was a controversial one of public importance, the station had satisfied any fairness doctrine obligations by providing regular and extensive coverage of the "anti-nuclear viewpoint" throughout 1981 and 1982.

The FCC rejected WTVH's positions in all respects. *Syracuse Peace Council v. Television Station WTVH,* 99 FCC 2d 1389 (1984). First, the FCC determined that WTVH's definition of the "issue" raised by the editorial advertisements was unreasonable. Based on a review of the text of the ads, the FCC noted that "U.S. dependence on foreign oil was mentioned only in the first two," whereas "all three advertisements ended with the tag line

'Nine Mile Point . . . a *sound investment* for New York's future.' "The FCC also noted that the ads "are framed in terms of problems facing New York * * *." Although stressing its inclination to defer to the licensee whenever possible, the Commission concluded, on the basis of its review, that "we cannot find that reasonable people could differ on the conclusion that the issue discussed and the point to be made by each of these ads is that the Nine Mile II plant is an economically sound investment * * *."

Second, the FCC found that WTVH could not reasonably conclude that the issue was not a controversial one of public importance at the time:

> The question of whether an issue is controversial is determined by measuring the degree of attention paid to an issue by government officials, community leaders, and the media. The key issue here is whether the issue is the subject of vigorous debate with substantial elements of the community in opposition to one another. [The FCC noted the many newspaper articles cited by SPC that discussed the wisdom of constructing the Nine Mile II plant and documented the concerns of government officials about the project.]

> As to the public importance of the issue addressed in the announcement[s], the complainant asserts [the potential impact of Nine Mile II on utility rates was of great import]. WTVH provides no information to negate these allegations.

Finally, the Commission determined that WTVH had not presented programming to satisfy its fairness doctrine obligations. The Commission focused on the fact that WTVH had presented programming that generally opposed nuclear power, "which is not the specific issue discussed in the advertisements." Thus, the Commission assessed WTVH's actions only in light of the programming it had presented specifically addressing the soundness of building the Nine Mile II plant. After noting that fairness doctrine obligations are not judged on the basis of any rigid mathematical formulae, the Commission determined:

> The record shows that the total time devoted to the [pro-Nine Mile II] viewpoint * * * was more than 187 minutes, which includes approximately five minutes of news stories and 182 minutes of paid advertising. When compared to the total time allotted to the contrasting viewpoint, approximately 22 minutes, the result is a ratio of more than 9:1 * * *.

The FCC also noted that the pro-Nine Mile II viewpoint was aired 261 times, the contrasting viewpoint just 20 times.

Meredith moved for reconsideration. The Commission responded to the motion by concluding that Meredith had not raised any new arguments that warranted a reversal of the original finding that WTVH had failed to satisfy its fairness doctrine obligations. The FCC found, however, that WTVH had acted in good faith following the Commission's decision by giving air time to SPC; thus, it decided not to take any action against WTVH. In a footnote, the Commission noted Meredith's constitutional arguments against the fairness doctrine, but it declined to address those arguments in light of its conclusion in the *1985 Fairness Report* to leave the constitutional questions to Congress and the courts.

Meredith appealed the FCC's decision to the court of appeals, and the case was argued together with a petition to review the *1985 Fairness Report.* In the appeal of the *1985 Fairness Report,* it was alleged that the Commission, in light of findings, was obligated—as a matter of administrative procedure—to institute a rulemaking proceeding to consider the need to eliminate or modify the fairness doctrine. The two cases were decided on the same day.

In the *Meredith* appeal, the court first affirmed the FCC's decision that WTVH had not satisfied its fairness doctrine obligations. Noting that "the Commission's task in administering the fairness doctrine is one of great delicacy and difficulty, and that the Commission's experience in this matter accordingly is entitled to 'great weight[,]' "the court stated that "[a]pplying that deferential standard here, we have no doubt that the Commission's application of its fairness precedent must be sustained." *Meredith Corporation v. FCC,* 809 F.2d 863 (D.C.Cir.1987). The court took issue, however, with the Commission's decision on reconsideration not to address Meredith's constitutional challenges to the fairness doctrine:

> * * * Although the Commission's 1985 Fairness Report would appear to foreshadow its conclusion as to the constitutionality of this enforcement proceeding against Meredith, nonetheless, we may well benefit—in the event of further review—from the Commission's analysis. The Commission might choose to decide the issue narrowly, resting on the particular circumstances of Meredith's case, or if the Commission reasons more broadly, it might explicitly discuss the interrelationship between supposed constitutional infirmities of the fairness doctrine and the basic statutory licensing scheme.[10]

> * * * Of course, the fair inference to be drawn from the Commission's report was that the Commission believed the doctrine was not specifically mandated; otherwise, it would have been irresponsible for the Commission gratuitously to cast constitutional doubt on a congressional command. Nonetheless, because the Commission felt intense political, if not legal, pressure from Congress, it chose not to reach a final conclusion regarding the origins of the doctrine. We think, however, the Commission was obliged to resolve that issue, at least in the context of an enforcement proceeding in which a party raises a constitutional defense.

> * * * The Commission, however, confuses its quasi-judicial role with its quasi-legislative one. Whether or not it may refuse to initiate a rulemaking in light of its Fairness Report—the question presented in our companion case—it may not simply ignore a constitutional challenge in an enforcement proceeding. The Commission's finding that Meredith violated the fairness doctrine is, under the Commission's rules, a first step that can lead to a license revocation proceeding, see 47 C.F.R. § 1.80 (1985), a formal adjudication under the APA. See 47 U.S.C. § 312 (1982). And in a formal adjudication, an administrative agency is obliged to consider and respond to substantial arguments a respondent presents

---

10. It is, of course, conceivable that the Commission, faced with the necessity of responding to Meredith's challenge to the fairness doctrine on the merits would determine to hold, in an adjudicatory context, that the doctrine cannot be enforced because it is contrary to the public interest and thereby avoid the constitutional issue.

in its defense, 5 U.S.C. § 557(c) (1982) * * *. To be sure, the Commission has not as yet initiated a license revocation proceeding, but its finding, as we have already noted, has its own coercive impact.

* * *

* * * The Commission's failure to [consider Meredith's constitutional claims] * * * seems to us the very paradigm of arbitrary and capricious administrative action.

Accordingly, we remand the case to the FCC with instructions to consider Petitioner's constitutional arguments. Of course, the Commission need not confront that issue if it concludes that in light of its Fairness Report it may not or should not enforce the doctrine because it is contrary to the public interest.

In the companion case, the court further set the stage for a constitutional examination of the fairness doctrine. The case involved two procedural issues. First, the court decided that it could not review the FCC's conclusions with respect to the constitutionality of the fairness doctrine. The Commission's report on the constitutional issues, the court stated, was not an "agency action subject to review" in the court of appeals. Thus, any constitutional challenge to the fairness doctrine would have to be brought in district court. The court went on to hold, however, that it could address the claim that, in light of the *1985 Fairness Report,* the Commission acted arbitrarily and capriciously in failing to institute a rulemaking to eliminate or modify the fairness doctrine. Radio–Television News Directors Ass'n v. FCC, 809 F.2d 860 (D.C.Cir.1987), vacated as moot 831 F.2d 1148 (D.C.Cir.1987) (court of appeals' willingness to review the procedural claim against the FCC was rendered moot by the FCC's decision to address the substantive issues in the reconsideration order, which appears below). The result of these two court decisions was the FCC's further reconsideration of the WTVH fairness doctrine decision, which follows. Syracuse Peace Council, 2 FCC Rcd. 5043, reconsideration denied 3 FCC Rcd. 2035, affirmed 867 F.2d 654 (D.C.Cir.1989), cert. denied 493 U.S. 1019, 110 S.Ct. 717, 107 L.Ed.2d 737 (1990).

III.   Discussion

A.   Scope of This Proceeding—Procedural Issues

1.   Discussion of Policy and Constitutional Issues

* * *

19.   * * * [I]n this Memorandum Opinion and Order, we consider whether the fairness doctrine is consistent with the guarantees of the First Amendment and whether it comports with the public interest. As noted above, the court ordered the Commission to consider Meredith's constitutional arguments unless it decided, on policy grounds, not to enforce the fairness doctrine. As we began to examine the policy issues, however, it became evident to us that the policy and constitutional considerations in this matter are inextricably intertwined and that it would be difficult, if not impossible, to isolate the policy considerations from the constitutional as-

pects underlying the doctrine. We believe, as a result, that it is appropriate and necessary to address the policy and constitutional issues together for a number of reasons.

20. First, in an analysis of any Commission regulation, it is well-established that First Amendment considerations are an integral component of the public interest standard. * * * A meaningful assessment of the propriety of the Doctrine, therefore, necessarily includes an evaluation of its constitutionality. If the doctrine impedes the realization of First Amendment objectives—and, as explained more fully below, we believe that it does—a fortiori it disserves the public interest.

21. A second, but related, reason that the policy and constitutional issues are inextricably intertwined is that the promotion of First Amendment values was the Commission's core policy objective in establishing and maintaining the doctrine. The parameters defining the need and desirability of government intervention under the fairness doctrine are coextensive with those of the First Amendment. Therefore, if the doctrine fails to further First Amendment principles, or if it strays from those parameters established by the Constitution, it necessarily follows that the doctrine does not achieve the specific purpose for which it was intended and can no longer be sustained.

22. Third, this Commission was established by Congress as the expert agency in broadcast matters and possesses more than fifty years of experience with the day-to-day implementation of communications regulation. As a consequence, the courts, when considering the constitutionality of broadcast regulation, have found our perspective informative. * * *

2. Consideration of the Doctrine on its Face

* * * We believe that the relevant issue in this proceeding is whether the doctrine itself complies with the strictures of the First Amendment and thereby comports with sound public policy. Therefore, in order to resolve the issues that the court directed us to consider, we conclude that we have no choice but to consider Meredith's challenge to the facial validity of the fairness doctrine itself.

* * *

32. In short, broadcasters are faced daily with editorial decisions concerning what types of commercial or noncommercial material on controversial public issues to present to their listeners and viewers. The fundamental issue embodied in this fairness doctrine litigation is the same as that presented in all other fairness doctrine cases: whether it is constitutional and thereby sound public policy for a government agency to oversee editorial decisions of broadcast journalists concerning the broadcast of controversial issues of public importance. * * *

33. Nor do we believe that it would be appropriate, in passing on the constitutional and policy issues raised by our enforcement of the fairness doctrine to limit our consideration of such issues to the one part of the fairness doctrine that we determined had been violated in this case. The fairness doctrine, although consisting of two parts,* is a unified

* Part one is the obligation to cover controversial issues of public importance. Part two is the obligation to provide a reasonable opportunity for the presentation of con-

doctrine; without both parts, the doctrine loses its identity. The litigants and courts in this and, indeed, the Red Lion case have all considered the validity of the doctrine as a whole, and not as two separate policies. They have considered the doctrine as such because neither part of the doctrine, standing separately, constitutes the fairness doctrine, for both parts of the doctrine are interdependent and integral to the overall regulatory scheme. Consequently, if the constitutional infirmity of the doctrine arises from the enforcement of one of its parts, we do not believe it appropriate to sever that part of the doctrine and to continue enforcing only the other part.

* * *

B. Constitutional Considerations Under Red Lion

36. * * * [T]he extraordinary technological advances that have been made in the electronic media since the 1969 *Red Lion* decision, together with a consideration of fundamental First Amendment principles, provide an ample basis for the Supreme Court to reconsider the premise or approach of its decision in *Red Lion*. Nevertheless, while we believe that the Court, after reexamining the issue, may well be persuaded that the transformation in the communications marketplace justifies alteration of the *Red Lion* approach to broadcast regulation, we recognize that to date the Court has determined that governmental regulation of broadcast speech is subject to a standard of review under the First Amendment that is more lenient than the standard generally applicable to the print media. Until the Supreme Court reevaluates that determination, therefore, we shall evaluate the constitutionality of the fairness doctrine under the standard enunciated in *Red Lion* and its progeny.[104]

2. *Application of the Red Lion Standard*

39. Under the standard enunciated by the Supreme Court for assessing the constitutionality of broadcast regulation, * * * the government * * * [may] regulate the speech of broadcasters in order to promote the interest of the public in obtaining access to diverse viewpoints.

(a) *Chilling Effect of the Doctrine*

42. In the 1985 Fairness Report, the Commission evaluated the efficacy of the fairness doctrine in achieving its regulatory objective. Based upon the compelling evidence of record, the Commission determined that the fairness doctrine, in operation, thwarts the purpose that it is designed to promote. Instead of enhancing the discussion of controversial issues of public importance, the Commission found that the fairness doctrine, in operation, "chills" speech. [The Commission here summarized the findings of the 1985 Fairness Report.]

trasting viewpoints–that is, a right of reply—on the controversial issues covered.—Ed.

104. * * * [F]or the reasons set forth below, we believe the rationale employed by the Court in *Red Lion* compels the conclusion that the fairness doctrine contravenes the First Amendment today, when evaluated consistent with the principles of *Red Lion*. Furthermore, the relationship between the application of constitutional principles in this area and the advances in technology are such, as the Supreme Court has indicated, that it is necessary to review past decisions to ensure their consistency with current technology.

(b) The Extent and Necessity of Government Intervention into Editorial Discretion

52.   * * * Historically, the Commission has taken the position that the agency had an affirmative obligation, derived from the First Amendment, to oversee the content of programming through enforcement of the fairness doctrine in order to ensure the availability of diverse viewpoints to the public. After careful reflection, however, the Commission, with respect to the fairness doctrine, repudiated the notion that it was proper for a governmental agency to intervene actively in the marketplace of ideas. * * *

(c) Conclusion

* * *

59.   * * * Because the net effect of the fairness doctrine is to reduce rather than enhance the public's access to viewpoint diversity, it affirmatively disserves the First Amendment interests of the public. This fact alone demonstrates that the fairness doctrine is unconstitutional under the standard of review established in *Red Lion*.

60.   Furthermore, almost two decades of Commission experience in enforcing the fairness doctrine since *Red Lion* convince us that the doctrine is also constitutionally infirm because it is not narrowly tailored to achieve a substantial government interest. Because the fairness doctrine imposes substantial burdens upon the editorial discretion of broadcast journalists and, because technological developments have rendered the doctrine unnecessary to ensure the public's access to viewpoint diversity, it is no longer narrowly tailored to meet a substantial government interest and therefore violates the standard set forth in *League of Women Voters*. The doctrine requires the government to second-guess broadcasters' judgment on such sensitive and subjective matters as the "controversality" and "public importance" of a particular issue, whether a particular viewpoint is "major," and the "balance" of a particular presentation. The resultant overbreadth of the government's inquiry into these matters is demonstrated by the chill in speech that we have identified. The doctrine exacts a penalty, both from broadcasters and, ultimately, from the public, for the expression of opinion in the electronic press. As a result, broadcasters are denied the editorial discretion accorded to other journalists, and the public is deprived of a more vigorous marketplace of ideas, unencumbered by governmental regulation.

C.   Preferred Constitutional Approach

[The Commission then went on to reiterate many of its conclusions from its *1985 Report and Order* (discussed above) It concluded once again that the fairness doctrine had a chilling effect on broadcasters, that the "scarcity doctrine" no longer had any validity, with the development of new media, that the broadcast media thus should be subject to the same constitutional protections as the print media, and that broadcasters' "journalistic discretion" should be protected.]

IV. Conclusion

98. The court in *Meredith Corp. v. FCC* "remand[ed] the case to the FCC with instructions to consider [Meredith's] constitutional arguments." In response to the court's directive, we find that the fairness doctrine chills speech and is not narrowly tailored to achieve a substantial government interest.

* * *

Notes and Questions

1. Does the Commission's reasoning reflect "changed circumstances" in the media marketplace, or does it reflect a radically different view of the public interest? Of the First Amendment? See Conrad, *The Demise of the Fairness Doctrine: A Blow for Citizen Access*, 41 Comm.L.J. 161, 163 (1989):

> Unless this opinion is overruled, or the Fairness Doctrine is codified by Congress, citizen access to the media will remain severely limited for the foreseeable future. The broadcast media, which should serve as a lightning rod for differing viewpoints, will remain in the firm control of those interests with large accumulations of wealth.

Sound familiar? Is it sound? See also Labunski, *May It Rest in Peace: Public Interest and Public Access in the Post–Fairness Doctrine Era*, I1 Hastings Comm/Ent L.J. 219 (1989).

2. The Commission denied all petitions for reconsideration. 3 FCC Rcd. 2035 (1988). One petition, filed by the Freedom of Expression Foundation, requested that the Commission expand the scope of its order and strike down the political broadcasting rules imposed by the Commission in accordance with Sections 312(a)(7) and 315 of the Communications Act. The Commission denied the request on the ground that it was outside of the scope of the *WTVH* proceeding. Would the Commission have any basis for ceasing to enforce those rules, which are imposed in accordance with statutory command? Does the Commission have discretion to cease enforcing the rules because of its statutory duty to promote the public interest? Is there a constitutional distinction between the fairness doctrine and the political broadcasting rules?

3. Was it appropriate or necessary for the Commission to "overrule" *Red Lion* and its progeny? The Court of Appeals, when it considered the *WTVH* case for the second time, clearly was uncomfortable with the Commission's constitutional "ruminations." In affirming the Commission's decision to cease enforcement of the fairness doctrine, Judge Williams sought to unhinge the Commission's public interest and constitutional analyses:

> * * * [T]he Commission's reasoning behind its "intertwining" assertion belies any inference that its policy judgment *depends* upon its constitutional view. * * * Surely both decisions encompass goals of stimulating fair, balanced, and diverse treatment of controversial issues * * *; of minimizing any chilling effect that may flow from governmental requirements * * *; and of minimizing the risks of abuse and other adverse effects that may flow from having governmental officials sit in judgment on editorial decisions. But it plainly does not follow from this

congruity of values that the Commission can make a policy finding against the fairness doctrine only by relying on constitutional grounds.

Quite the reverse. Indeed the Commission's third argument for "intertwining," namely that in resolving broadcast-related constitutional issues courts "have found our perspective informative," * * * pinpoints a clear distinction. In making a public interest judgment under the Communications Act, the Commission is exercising both its congressionally-delegated power and its experience; it clearly enjoys broad deference on issues of both fact and policy. * * * Its role in constitutional judgments, while uncertain, is more limited. * * * [A]n ultimate constitutional decision on the doctrine necessarily melds raw facts with First Amendment value judgments, * * * and that melding process is for the courts.

* * *

Of course, if the Commission had written its opinion in purely constitutional terms, we would have no choice but to address the constitutional issue or—more likely—to remand to the Commission for it to re-arrange horse and cart. * * *

Happily, the Commission's opinion is not written in exclusively constitutional terms. * * *

Syracuse Peace Council v. FCC, 867 F.2d 654, 658–59 (D.C.Cir.1989), cert. denied 493 U.S. 1019, 110 S.Ct. 717, 107 L.Ed.2d 737 (1990). This result was a happy one for the court, because it allowed a decision that did not become enmeshed in a very sensitive—and politically explosive—constitutional issue. The court simply determined that the Commission's policy decision was neither arbitrary nor capricious.

Judge Starr, who concurred in the result, was less comfortable with the court's approach:

* * * After elaborate briefing on the constitutional issue resolved by the Commission in conformity with the *Meredith* remand, my colleagues have arrived at the view—urged by no one in the case—that our analysis can properly proceed by, in effect, blue penciling the Commission's language purporting to base the agency's action on constitutional grounds. The majority's methodology of restraint flows, quite understandably, from the salutary principle that courts must avoid deciding constitutional issues where nonconstitutional grounds of decision are available. * * * But the applicability of that venerable principle here is very much in doubt. * * * [T]he issue comes to us in an administrative law setting with the agency expressly relying upon constitutional considerations and rendering a constitutional judgment. * * * The agency's analysis must, perforce, shape the contours of the court's consideration. * * *

* * * [I]f the Commission were deciding a public-interest issue alone, without more, all it would have needed to do was dust off and press into service the 1985 Report. Indeed, there is not the slightest hint that the FCC in 1987 viewed its *magnum opus* of only two years earlier as sufficient to the purpose at hand. Rather, the Commission decided, in light of the *Meredith* remand, to tangle with *Red Lion* itself. * * * It has

switched gears from three years ago and gone beyond the less heroic, public-interest reach of the 1985 Report. * * *

* * * Under governing standards,[6] the Commission's decision to view the public interest as driven by First Amendment values (when other considerations, e.g., broad notions of broadcasters as public trustees, were available) is eminently reasonable. The FCC has never wavered from justifying the fairness doctrine, instrumentally, by reference to the fostering of First Amendment values. * * * In view of the fairness doctrine's unique, constitutionally-charged history, it is hardly unreasonable for the FCC to view the public interest through First Amendment lenses.

* * *

The foregoing satisfies me that a remand to delink that which the agency has viewed as inextricably intertwined would be painfully inappropriate. It would also be a bit cheeky, in light of *Meredith*'s generous terms of remand. In short, the Commission's determination that the public interest is inextricably related to First Amendment values is, I believe, fully consistent with the statute and explained with sufficient clarity and cogency to constitute a valid exercise of discretion. * * *

Vindication of the constitutional reasoning in the Order thus would *not* constitute a judicial determination that the fairness doctrine (as currently administered) is "unconstitutional." To reiterate: I would hold only that the FCC's decision to eliminate the fairness doctrine correctly interprets *Red Lion* and is based, as the court's opinion effectively demonstrates, on an adequate factual record. Such a decision would therefore not automatically foreclose a future FCC (or Congress) from reestablishing the fairness doctrine in its present (or some modified) form. The fate of any future attempt to resurrect (or refashion) the fairness doctrine would depend, obviously, on the Supreme Court's articulation of applicable constitutional doctrine (e.g., *Red Lion*); but it would also be affected by the scope of review applied to the facts upon which the "new" fairness doctrine was sought to be justified. * * *

As to the constitutional principles applicable to this case, the parties are congenially in accord (1) that *Red Lion* principles govern; and (2) that, under the *Red Lion* framework, government restrictions on broadcasters' speech are valid only if "narrowly tailored to further a substantial government interest, such as ensuring adequate and balanced coverage of public issues." * * *

[A]s petitioners see it, the fairness doctrine is constitutionally permissible so long as *allocational scarcity* exists, namely, that demand for broadcast frequencies exceeds supply. * * * The FCC, in contrast, asserts that the constitutionality of the doctrine depends on *numerical*

6. As the fairness doctrine itself is not required by statute, Telecommunications Research and Action Center v. FCC, 801 F.2d 501 (D.C.Cir.1986), the Commission's decision to view the public interest in First Amendment terms is subject only to limited review. Specifically, the FCC's position as to the public interest must not be "so implausible that it could not be ascribed to a difference in view or the product of agency expertise," and must evince "a rational connection between the facts found and the choice made."

scarcity in the sense that, without government intervention, the public is not provided with access to diverse viewpoints.

* * * As I see it, the FCC's position is much better founded; indeed, in my view, petitioners have fallen badly into error by misreading *Red Lion.* * * *

* * * [T]he FCC has correctly discerned that, under *Red Lion,* the constitutionality of the fairness doctrine is closely related to the incapacity of the communications marketplace to give expression to diverse voices. * * *

The governing constitutional doctrine therefore recognizes that the communications marketplace may be sufficiently responsive to the public's need for controversial issue programming so that government regulation is unnecessary. * * * As a corollary of that principle, the FCC also recognized that, where the communications marketplace itself provides a plethora of voices, the fairness doctrine is not only superfluous, it is positively harmful. This is of singular importance in the analysis. * * *

As to the FCC's finding that the fairness doctrine so chilled speech as to result in a net reduction in the coverage of controversial issues, * * * [p]etitioners' main argument in this particular is that the Commission gave undue weight to testimony of chilling effect and insufficient weight to evidence that the doctrine stimulated speech.

* * *

* * * [M]y reading of the Order suggests that the Commission, based on its regulatory experience and testimony before the agency concerning chilling effects, reasonably determined that the fairness doctrine's predominant effect on speech was inhibitory. * * * Specifically, the Commission found that the fairness doctrine chilled individual program decisions *and* induced broadcasters to adopt categorical policies against carrying editorials, political advertisements or nationally-produced public affairs programs. * * * The Commission further noted that, by virtue of the fairness doctrine, many broadcasters were encouraged not to air controversial issue programming above that minimal amount required by the first part of the doctrine. * * * The Commission was also entitled to take into account the fact that the doctrine, by requiring coverage only of "major" contrasting viewpoints, fell with particular severity on broadcasters who express unorthodox views, thus tending to deprive the public of "uninhibited, robust and wide-open" debate. * * * Finally, the Commission pointed to the fact that "no broadcaster indicated to us that its station's coverage of controversial issues has increased as a result of the fairness doctrine." * * *

These findings, taken together, reasonably support the Commission's ultimate conclusion that elimination of the fairness doctrine would unleash a substantial amount of controversial issue programming. In light of our limited scope of review, this factually supported conclusion withstands judicial scrutiny in the absence of powerfully contradictory evidence. * * *

If the FCC determines that the communications marketplace now has the capacity, without regulatory intervention, "to give expression to diverse voices," will the difference between the constitutional standard in *Red Lion* and the standard in *Tornillo* have any practical impact? That is, can there plausibly be any government interest in behavioral regulation when the unregulated marketplace is functioning "properly"? Has Judge Starr created an intriguing, but perhaps elusive, distinction between the condition that justifies the constitutional standard (scarcity) and the application of the constitutional standard to the facts? In other words, if, although there will never be enough broadcast spectrum to license all interested speakers, this "scarcity" produces no negative impact on vigorous expression in the media marketplace, is there any basis for creating a separate constitutional standard for broadcasting?

What does the court's decision ultimately say about the public interest standard? Is there anything surprising about the Commission's view that the public interest necessarily implicates First Amendment values? Do you think Judge Williams strained unreasonably to distinguish between constitutional and public policy considerations in an effort to avoid difficult constitutional issues?

When the Supreme Court denied certiorari, the prospect for a resolution of the constitutionality of the fairness doctrine (and perhaps the confusing progression from *Red Lion* to *Tornillo*) dimmed substantially; unless Congress enacts the fairness doctrine into law (again?), the issue may never be finally resolved. But some of the cases in Chapter VI, e.g., *Denver Area*, indicate that the Court might be receptive to a right of reply.

4. In response to a congressional request that it consider "alternative means of administration and enforcement of the Fairness Doctrine and * * * report to Congress * * * ", the FCC issued a report (on the same day that it decided to stop enforcing the fairness doctrine) concluding that "the best alternative to the Doctrine, the one that best achieves the underlying First Amendment principles and thereby serves our public interest objectives, continues to be an unregulated 'free marketplace of ideas.' " *Inquiry into Section 73.1910 of the Commission's Rules and Regulations Concerning Alternatives to the General Fairness Doctrine Obligations of Broadcast Licensees,* 63 R.R.2d 488, 499 (1987). Among the alternatives that the Commission evaluated (but found inferior to reliance on market forces), are the following:

(a) *Renewal Time Review:* Two proposals suggested that the Commission might consider fairness doctrine compliance only at the time of license renewal. Under one proposal, the Commission would consider only whether a licensee had acted with malice—deliberately violating the doctrine. Under the second proposal, the Commission would consider more broadly a licensee's overall record in carrying out its fairness obligations. The Commission rejected both alternatives. Although it recognized that the proposals sought to remove the FCC from day-to-day editorial judgments, the Commission concluded that, despite the lenient standards for enforcement, the chilling effect of enforcement would remain and the policy would not be likely to stimulate additional coverage of controversial issues.

The Commission also suggested that a "delayed" fairness ruling could have an even greater chilling effect on speech. Because the merits of fairness complaints would not be heard until license renewal time, a licensee would be deprived of the opportunity to correct a violation by airing contrasting programming. Thus, alleged fairness violations would hang over the licensee during the license period and magnify the possibility that the licensee would lose the license at the end of its term.

(b) *Marketwide Approach to Enforcement:* The Commission, without the support of any commenting parties, suggested that considering the programming of all media outlets in a market in order to evaluate the balance of coverage of controversial issues might be preferable to the fairness doctrine as it existed before the *WTVH* decision:

> The foremost advantage of a marketwide approach is that it would take into account a more realistic view of today's diverse and ever-expanding communications marketplace. * * * [B]y taking into account the programming offered by a variety of sources, marketwide enforcement comes closer to protecting the interest of the public in obtaining access to diverse and antagonistic sources of information * * *.

> 63 R.R.2d at 534. See also Robinson, *The FCC and the First Amendment,* 52 Minn.L.Rev. 67 (1987) (arguing that constitutional considerations compel the Commission to consider all the various media presenting views to the public).

(c) *Other Proposals:* The Commission also rejected—as being too limited a response to the changed market conditions documented in the *1985 Fairness Report*—limiting enforcement of the fairness doctrine to smaller media markets, limiting enforcement to television (to reflect the enormous growth in the number of radio outlets), enforcing only the "first prong" of the fairness doctrine (an alternative rejected by the Commission in the *1985 Fairness Report* and in the *WTVH* decision) and implementing an experimental moratorium on enforcement of the fairness doctrine. The Commission also considered, but did not embrace, various concepts of access. (Access as an alternative to behavioral regulation is considered in Part B of this chapter.)

5. *Personal Attacks.* The Commission's personal attack rule, although a corollary of the fairness doctrine, was not repealed along with the general fairness doctrine. See 47 C.F.R. § 73.1920. Under that rule, if an attack is made on the "honesty, character, integrity or like personal qualities of an individual or group" during a broadcast concerning a controversial issue of public importance, then the broadcaster must give the attacked individual or group notice and a reasonable opportunity to respond on the broadcaster's station. Personal attacks made during certain types of news programs are exempt. Also exempt are attacks on a legally qualified candidate for political office, his or her authorized spokesperson, or another person associated with the candidate's campaign, made by another legally qualified candidate, that candidate's authorized spokesperson, or someone associated with that candidate's campaign. What do you think the reasoning is for singling out a personal attack made in the course of a discussion of a controversial issue?

In 1983, partly in response to the Supreme Court's analysis of the constitutionality of requiring access to the broadcast media in the *CBS v. DNC* case, the Commission put out a rulemaking proposal for the *Repeal or Modification of the Personal Attack and Political Editorializing Rules,* 48

Fed.Reg. 28295 (June 21, 1983), which was still outstanding when the general fairness doctrine obligations were repealed. Does the Commission's reasoning in the *WTVH* decision leave any public policy or constitutional basis for continued enforcement of the rule?

For examples of the application, and a discussion of the purposes, of the personal attack rule, see Galloway v. FCC, 778 F.2d 16 (D.C.Cir.1985) (affirming the Commission's decision that the personal attack rule did not apply because the statements at issue were not made during discussion of a controversial issue of public importance); and Raymond J. Donovan, FCC Mimeo No. 3143 (released March 17, 1986) (complainant failed to state a prima facie case).

6. After the Commission repealed the fairness doctrine, a significant number of congressmen advocated legislation to codify the doctrine. In 1987, Congress adopted such legislation, but President Reagan vetoed the law as being inconsistent with his Administration's policies. Congress failed to override the veto and has not since passed another fairness doctrine bill.

D. POLITICAL BROADCASTS

Although the Commission has stopped enforcing the fairness doctrine, the political broadcasting rules promulgated in accordance with Sections 312(a)(7) and 315 of the Communications Act remain in force. See 47 C.F.R. §§ 73.1940 (broadcasting) & 76.205 (cable television); see also 47 C.F.R. §§ 73.1930 & 76.209(d) (political editorials). Before reading the material that follows, you should review the two statutory provisions and the Commission's rules carefully. The fairness doctrine and the political broadcasting rules are clearly—and closely—related, as suggested by the *Red Lion* decision, but they should not be confused. They also may be constitutionally distinguishable. As you read the material that follows, look for possible bases for drawing a constitutional distinction between them.

Notes and Questions

1. Under Section 315(a) of the Communications Act, when a "legally qualified candidate" for any political office "uses" a broadcast station or a cable system channel that is under the control of the cable system operator, all other legally qualified candidates for that office must be afforded "equal opportunities" to use the same facility. In addition, Section 315 prohibits the broadcast licensee or cable system operator from censoring the candidate's "use." (p. 503) The statute also exempts from the equal opportunities requirements certain types of news broadcasts and imposes limits on the amounts that candidates can be charged for uses of the media.

The application of the "equal opportunities" requirement depends upon the meaning given to several key phrases in the statute: (1) Who is a "legally qualified candidate"? (2) When is there a "use" of a licensed broadcast or cable facility that triggers the requirements of Section 315? (3) What must be done to afford other candidates "equal opportunities"? The interpretation and application of these various terms and requirements are examined at length in the Commission's *Primer on Political Broadcasting and Cablecast-*

ing, 100 FCC 2d 1476 (1984) (*1984 Primer*). The fundamental definitions of
the three phrases noted above are as follows:

> *Legally Qualified Candidate:* " * * * [A] person who has publicly an-
> nounced that he is a candidate *and* who meets the qualifications
> prescribed by the applicable laws to hold the office for which he is a
> candidate *and* who: (1) Has qualified for a place on the ballot *or* (2) Has
> publicly committed himself to seeking election by the write-in method
> *and* is eligible under applicable laws to be voted for by sticker, by
> writing in his name on the ballot, or other method, *and* makes a
> substantial showing that he is a bona fide candidate for nomination for
> office."

> *Qualifying Use:* "In general, any broadcast or cablecast of a candidate's
> voice or picture [other than the four types of broadcasts exempted by
> the statute] is a 'use' * * * if the candidate's participation in the
> program or announcement is such that he will be identified by members
> of the audience."

> *Equal Opportunities:* " * * * '[E]qual opportunities' * * * does not nec-
> essarily mean the same thing as equal time. For example, if Candidate
> Smith receives an hour of free time at 8 p.m. on a television station and
> his opponent Jones merely gets an hour early in the morning or after
> midnight, Jones will be getting 'equal time' but not 'equal opportuni-
> ties,' since he probably won't be seen or heard by nearly as many people
> as Smith. Similarly, if a station gives Smith free time but charges Jones
> for his time, Jones will again get 'equal time' but not 'equal opportuni-
> ties.' The Commission's rules forbid any kind of discrimination between
> competing candidates." Id. at 1503–04. See also Section 315(b), which
> sets forth limits on the amounts that legally qualified candidates can be
> charged for programming time.

The material that follows explores more fully the meaning of these fundamental terms, as well as other significant issues that arise in connection
with the application of Section 315.

2.   As noted above, Section 315 explicitly exempts four types of broadcasts from the application of the equal opportunities obligations.

(a) *Bona Fide Newscast (§ 315(a)(1)):* On its nightly news programs, a
broadcaster interviews some, but not all, of the legally qualified candidates
for a particular office. Can the candidates not interviewed demand equal
opportunities? See KRON–TV, 47 FCC 2d 1204 (1974) (interviews exempt
because part of a bona fide newscast). Suppose that one of the newscasters is
a legally qualified candidate; would opposing candidates be entitled to equal
opportunities? See Branch v. FCC, 824 F.2d 37 (D.C.Cir.1987) (newscaster-
candidates not exempt from Section 315). What if, prior to a broadcast news
conference, the President, a candidate for re-election, makes opening remarks of a political nature? Of any sort? See National Unity Campaign for
John Anderson, 88 FCC 2d 467 (1980); see also Kennedy for President
Committee v. FCC, 636 F.2d 417 (D.C.Cir.1980).

(b) *Bona Fide News Interview (§ 315(a)(2)):* During interview segments
of its morning television show, "The Morning Program," CBS occasionally
schedules appearances by legally qualified candidates. Are equal opportuni-

ties obligations triggered? See In re CBS Inc., FCC No. DA 87–922 (released July 21, 1987) (staff ruling that such interview segments were within the "news interview" exemption). See also In re National Broadcasting Company, Inc., FCC Mimeo No. 5824 (released July 17, 1986) (staff ruling that interviews on the weekly program "1986" are exempt). But see Socialist Workers Party, 65 FCC 2d 234 (1976) (the "Tomorrow" show, which often selected interviewees for reasons other than newsworthiness, was not within the Section 315(a)(2) exemption).

What about interviews on the "Donahue" television program, which often features entertainment subjects and depends heavily upon audience participation? See Multimedia Program Productions, Inc., 84 FCC 2d 738 (1981). Is there—or should there be—a distinction between a news conference held by a candidate that is currently in office and a "call in" program in which the incumbent participates in the selection of questions and the format of the program? See Hon. Michael V. DiSalle, 40 FCC 348 (1962) (press conference exempt, but call-in program is not). Live coverage of press conferences may be exempt under Section 315(a)(4), discussed below.

(c) *Bona Fide News Documentary (§ 315(a)(3)):* In some instances, a "significant" appearance by a candidate in a program that is clearly a documentary may not be exempt from the equal opportunities requirements. See Henry Geller, 54 R.R.2d 1246 (1983).

(d) *On–the–Spot Coverage of Bona Fide News Events (§ 315(a)(4)):* In 1975, the Commission considerably expanded the scope of this exemption by reversing a number of earlier decisions and holding that press conferences and debates are exempt when the event is aired live, in its entirety, and is not sponsored or controlled by the licensee or a candidate. See Aspen Institute, 55 FCC 2d 697 (1975), aff'd sub nom. Chisholm v. FCC, 538 F.2d 349 (D.C.Cir.1976), cert. denied 429 U.S. 890, 97 S.Ct. 247, 50 L.Ed.2d 173. Eight years later, the FCC ruled that delayed broadcasts of such events would also be exempt if the event is aired in its entirety and the delay does not extend beyond the next day. It also decided that broadcaster-sponsored debates would qualify for the Section 315(a)(4) exemption. See Henry Geller, 54 R.R.2d 1246 (1983). Is a televised debate exempt even if it does not include legally qualified minor party candidates for the particular office? See American Independent Party and Eugene McCarthy, 62 FCC 2d 4 (1976), aff'd sub nom. McCarthy v. FCC, No. 76–1915 (D.C.Cir. 1976), cert. denied 430 U.S. 955, 97 S.Ct. 1599, 51 L.Ed.2d 804 (1977); see also Johnson v. FCC, 829 F.2d 157 (D.C.Cir.1987). Should the exemption for debates also apply to "in-studio" taped appearances of two candidates that are run back-to-back in the course of an interview-style program in which questions are selected by the broadcaster? See King Broadcasting Co. v. FCC, 860 F.2d 465 (D.C.Cir.1988). What about a "town meeting" in which a single candidate is involved? See Chicago Educational Television Ass'n, 58 FCC 2d 922 (1976).

3. In accordance with Section 315, a broadcaster or cablecaster may not censor either a candidate's statement or "anything said or shown by anyone else on a program in which a candidate appears to the extent that it becomes a 'use.' "1984 Political Primer, 100 FCC 2d at 1510. In light of this prohibition, the Supreme Court has held that Section 315 preempts state defamation laws and creates an absolute privilege protecting a broadcaster or cablecaster from liability for statements made in programming subject to

Section 315. Farmers Educational & Cooperative Union v. WDAY, Inc., 360 U.S. 525, 79 S.Ct. 1302, 3 L.Ed.2d 1407 (1959).

The prohibition on censorship is applied strictly. For example, the Commission has ruled that a broadcaster may not refuse material that is libelous, see, e.g., Port Huron Broadcasting Co., 12 FCC 1069 (1948); vulgar, see, e.g., Gloria Sage, 62 FCC 2d 135 (1976), review denied 83 FCC 2d 148 (1977); or has the potential to incite racial violence, see, e.g., Atlanta NAACP, 36 FCC 2d 635 (1973). Candidates may not be required to submit scripts or tapes for prior review on criteria such as "taste," "accuracy," or "libelousness." 1984 Political Primer, 100 FCC 2d at 1511–12. This strong prohibition of censorship became a subject of substantial controversy in 1983, when Larry Flynt, publisher of Hustler magazine, suggested that he was going to run for the presidency and use clips of X-rated movies in his "equal opportunity" programming. See Flynt causes X-rated worry, *Broadcasting*, Nov. 21, 1983, at 59. Flynt failed to become a legally qualified candidate, however, and the immediate concern subsided.

4. Section 312(a)(7) imposes on broadcasters the additional obligation to provide candidates with "reasonable access" to their stations. You should review this statutory provision, as well as the CBS v. FCC case (p. 326), and consider the constitutionality of the requirement. The 1984 Primer, 100 FCC 2d at 1523–28, provides the following information about the Section 312(a)(7) obligations:

Reasonable Access for Federal Candidates

73. Like all general terms, "reasonable access" needs some sort of a definition so candidates and broadcasters will know their rights and obligations. It cannot be defined exactly, however, because what is reasonable for station A may not be reasonable for station B. Suppose that station A is a powerful New York City station whose signal covers an area including parts of three States in which there are at least six Senatorial candidates in the current election campaign, plus scores of Congressional candidates in dozens of districts and hundreds of State and local candidates. On the other hand, station B is in a sparsely populated area, and the only Federal candidate within range of its signal are two candidates for one U.S. Senate seat and two candidates in each of two Congressional districts—a total of six Federal candidates. Also, there are few State and local races in the station's area during the period of the current national campaign. A station with as few candidates to accommodate as B would be expected to provide more access to Federal candidates than A. However, the Commission has stated:

> Congress clearly did not intend, to take the extreme case, that during the closing days of the campaign, stations should be required to accommodate requests for political time to the exclusion of all or most other types of programming or advertising. Important as an informed electorate is in our society, there are other elements in the public interest standard, and the public is entitled to other kinds of programming than political. It was not intended that all or most time be preempted for political broadcasts. The foregoing appears to be the only definite statement that may be made about the new section, since no all-embracing standard can be set. The test of

whether a licensee has met the requirement of the new section is one of reasonableness. The Commission will not substitute its judgment for that of the licensee but, rather, it will determine in any case that may arise whether the licensee can be said to have acted reasonably and in good faith in fulfilling his obligations under this section.

We are aware of the fact that a myriad of situations can arise that will present difficult problems. One conceivable method of trying to act reasonably and in good faith might be for licensees, prior to an election campaign for Federal offices, to meet with candidates in an effort to work out the problem of reasonable access for them on their stations. Such conferences might cover, among other things, the subjects of the amount of time that the station proposes to sell or give candidates, the amount of types of its other programming. . . .[190]

Thus, "reasonable access" for Federal candidates will depend on a number of factors, as will be explained in the following paragraphs. First, however, the reader should note that under Section 312(a)(7) of the Act the reasonable access requirement applies only to:

(a) *Uses* of stations by candidates themselves. * * *

(b) Uses of stations by *legally qualified candidates* for Federal elective office. * * *

The reader also should note that the law does not require a station to provide time free. It says the station either must provide reasonable access free or "permit purchase of reasonable amounts of time." Thus, if a station gives away enough time to a candidate to amount to "reasonable access" under the circumstances of the case, it is not required to sell time to the candidate, and if it sells the candidate "reasonable amounts" it need not provide free time.

Principles to Be Followed in Applying Statute

74. On July 12, 1978, the Commission adopted a *Report and Order* clarifying its policy in enforcing Section 312(a)(7).[192] The document reaffirmed the Commission's policy of relying "generally on the reasonable, good faith judgments of licensees as to what constitutes reasonable access under all of the circumstances present in particular cases." It stated, however, that in deciding whether a licensee's judgments on this subject can be considered reasonable, the Commission will follow these general principles:

(a) Reasonable access must be provided to Federal elective candidates through the gift or sale of time for "uses" of the station by legally qualified candidates for public office.

(b) Reasonable access must be provided at least during the 45 days before a primary and the 60 days before a general or special election. The question of whether access should be afforded before

---

190. Public Notice, Use of Broadcast and Cablecast Facilities by Candidates for Public Office, 34 FCC 2d 510, 536 (1972).

192. Report and Order in the Matter of Commission Policy in Enforcing Section 312(a)(7) of the Communications Act, 68 FCC 2d 1079 (1978).

these periods begin and when access should apply before a convention or caucus will be determined by the Commission on a case-by-case basis.

(c) Both commercial and noncommercial educational stations must make available program time during prime-time periods unless unusual circumstances exist.

* * *

(f) In view of the fact that Section 315(a) prohibits censorship of the material that a candidate uses during a personal appearance, noncommercial broadcasters may not reject material submitted by candidates merely on the basis that it was originally prepared for broadcast on a commercial station.

(g) Although both educational and commercial licensees may suggest the format for appearances by candidates who exercise their Section 312(a)(7) rights, candidates need not accept these suggestions and may not be penalized by loss of "equal opportunities" if they decline to appear on programs designed by the broadcasters.
* * *

Time for State and Local Candidates

76.   * * * [T]he law does not require stations to provide access to every State, county, and local candidate. However, the Commission, the courts, and Congress have recognized that political broadcasting is one of the most important services that a station can provide to the public. Therefore, stations are expected to allocate reasonable amounts of time to other political races, based on the licensee's judgment of the importance of the races and the amount of public interest in them.

Examples of Rulings in Non-federal Campaigns

77.   Following are some examples of ways in which the Commission has applied Section 315 to non-Federal political candidates:

(a) *Station need not sell time at all if it gives time.* Even when a station decides a race is important enough to justify presentation of the candidates on the air, it need not sell time to them if it makes time available without charge.[195]

(b) *Station can limit sale of time to certain races.* A station may use its judgment as to which races are most significant and of greatest interest to the public, and refuse to sell or give time for "uses" of the station by candidates for other offices.[196]

(c) *Need not sell time far in advance of election or accept particular format.* A station need not sell time many months in advance of an election or accept a particular length of paid announcement that a candidate wishes to use.[197]

---

195. Rockefeller for Governor Campaign (WAJR), 59 FCC 2d 646 (1976); Charles O. Porter, Esq., 35 FCC 2d 664 (1972).

196. Foster Furcolo (WCVB–TV), 48 FCC 2d 565 (1974); *Lew Breyer,* 31 FCC 2d 548 (1968).

197. Dan Walker (WMAQ), 57 FCC 2d 799 (1975).

(d) *Need not sell a specific period of time.* Neither the Act nor the Commission's rules require a station to sell specific periods of time for political broadcasts.[198]

(e) *Need not sell less than 5 minutes to candidate.* A station which plans to make program time free to candidates in major races and to give "in depth" reports on news programs on these candidates is justified in exercising its judgment that the public interest will be better served by paid political appearances of 5 minutes or more.[199]

* * *

Notes and Questions

1. Why do you think Section 312(a)(7) is limited to candidates for federal elective office? Does this seem fair or equitable? Does it affect your view of the constitutionality of the provision? What is the basis for the Commission's statement that "stations are expected to allocate reasonable amounts of time to other [non-federal] political races * * * "? Could the Commission deny an application for renewal of a broadcast license if it found that a licensee had devoted an "unreasonably small" amount of time to such other races? Would the denial be consistent with the Communications Act? With the First Amendment?

You should keep the political broadcasting rules in mind as you read the material concerning access obligations generally.

2. Is there a public policy basis for distinguishing between the political broadcasting rules and the fairness doctrine? Is there a valid constitutional distinction? Is it possible that the political broadcasting rules have a firmer constitutional footing because (1) Congress has spoken clearly in the area (identifying the governmental interest) and (2) the direct beneficiaries are candidates for federal elective office (raising issues of political organization in which courts might be reluctant to interfere)? Do you think the Commission should recommend to Congress that the political broadcasting rules be repealed? Keep in mind the political controversy sparked by repeal of the fairness doctrine, which does not apply specifically to political uses of broadcast and cable television facilities.

3. The Commission's political editorializing rule, 47 C.F.R. § 73.1930, requires licensees to afford response time to a legally qualified candidate (or a candidate's spokesperson) who is either not endorsed or is expressly opposed in a station editorial. The *1984 Primer* included the following interpretations of the rule:

(a) *What is a station editorial?* Basically, a station editorial is a statement representing the view of the licensee of the station, such as its owner, a principal officer, the manager, or another employee if he is permitted by the licensee to speak for the station. Even if a statement is not labeled an editorial, it may be one. For example, on the day before the primary elections the president and controlling stockholder of a station endorsed several candidates during an interview with him broad-

198. W. Roy Smith, 18 FCC 2d 747 (1969).   **199.** Louis Rosenbush, Jr. (WBAL–TV), 31 FCC 2d 782 (1971).

cast by his station. The station president claimed later that his statements about the candidates represented only his personal feelings and were not an editorial endorsement of candidates by the station itself. The Commission stated that "when the president and controlling stockholder of a licensee ... endorses candidates for public office, such endorsements are indistinguishable from a station editorial within the meaning of [the political editorializing rule]."[208] * * * On the other hand, a statement of an employee or commentator of a station is not a station editorial unless it is represented to be one.[210]

* * *

(c) *"Reasonable opportunity to respond."* There can be no single definition of what is a reasonable offer of an opportunity to respond to a political editorial, because the reasonableness of the opportunity may vary with the circumstances * * *. The Commission [has] stated that "In many instances a comparable opportunity in time and scheduling will be clearly appropriate; in others, such as where the endorsement of a candidate is one of many and involves just a few seconds, a 'reasonable opportunity' may require more than a few seconds if there is to be a meaningful response." Thus, if the station's editorial stated merely that it believed that the following candidates were best qualified for election to the city council and then listed 20 persons, the entire editorial might be less than a minute long, but a "reasonable opportunity" for a response by any of the candidates who were not endorsed certainly would require more than one-twentieth of the time occupied by the editorial. In a specific case, the Commission found that the station had not given a candidate a reasonable opportunity to respond when it devoted 25 lines of script to endorsing his two opponents and opposing him, and offered him the equivalent of six lines for his responses.[213]
* * *

(d) *When does an editorial endorse or oppose a candidate?* If an editorial simply urges the election of one candidate to a certain office or recommends that the public vote against another candidate, there is no question as to whether the editorial falls within the scope of the rule. However, all cases have not been this clear, as illustrated by the following three:

(i) Two of the five members of the Board of Town Commissioners were running for reelection. Without identifying any candidate by name, a station broadcast editorials criticizing the current Board and urging the public to vote for "a change." The Commission ruled that even though the two Board members seeking reelection were not named, the editorial was in effect a statement of the station licensee's opposition to their candidacies and therefore, was a political editorial under the

208. Richard A. Karr (WJOB), 32 FCC 2d 285 (1971); see also, *Port Jervis Broadcasting Co.* (forfeiture order) June 24, 1976; application in mitigation or remission denied, March 14, 1977.

210. Accuracy in Media, Inc., 45 FCC 2d 297 (1973); *Letter to Edward L. Fanning,* December 3, 1975.

213. Dolph Pettey Broadcasting Co. (KUDE), 30 FCC 2d 675 (1971).

rules.[215]

(ii) During the second week before an election, station editorials referred to the fact that a State Senator announced that he would introduce legislation to create a commission to investigate corruption in government. Without referring to the election or the fact that the State Senator was a candidate for reelection, the editorial praised the idea of creating such a commission. The Senator's campaign workers distributed a campaign flier on which the editorial was printed, along with the station's logotype. The station broadcast a disclaimer of the flier three times, stating that use of its logo was unauthorized and that the station had a policy of not endorsing individual candidates. It also wrote to the Senator demanding that he stop using its trademark. The Senator's opponent claimed that the need for strengthened ethics legislation for state officials was a principal issue in his campaign, and that the station's editorial was interpreted by some persons as an endorsement of the Senator. The station denied that the editorial endorsed him or even inferentially advocated his election. The Commission ruled that although the favorable reference to the Senator's proposal "could arguably and with some logic be viewed as an endorsement . . . [t]o apply our political editorializing rules in these situations—where no clear-cut endorsement of a candidacy is involved, would make little practical or legal sense . . . [i]nstead of encouraging 'uninhibited, robust and wide-open debate' . . . the effect of our ruling would be to inhibit it."[216]

(iii) A county prosecuting attorney was a candidate for Democratic nomination for governor. The day before the primary, a station broadcast an editorial six times, strongly criticizing the candidate's record as a prosecutor but making no mention of the primary election for governor or the fact that he was a candidate in it. The licensee of the station denied that the editorial was one opposing the prosecutor's candidacy for governor. The station acknowledged, however, that the prosecutor's record was a controversial issue with "political implications" and that the broadcaster had been aware of the "political significance of the editorial." The Commission ruled that the editorial was a political one opposing the prosecutor's candidacy for governor, because the station took "a partisan position on a politically significant issue which is readily and clearly identified with a legally qualified candidate." The editorial "inferentially . . . challenged the qualifications of this official to obtain nomination as his party's Gubernatorial candidate." Also, "The editorial was broadcast on election eve, even though . . . the issue was one of public concern long before . . . [.]"[217] The Commission found a difference between this and the *Stephen M. Slavin* case above in that the editorial in this case dealt with the candidate's "capacity to function as a public official," whereas in the *Slavin* case "it was the need for legislation to control government corruption that the station sought to endorse, not the candidacy of Senator Berning *per se*." The Commission

215. Bel Air Broadcasting Co., Inc., 47 FCC 2d 985 (1974).

216. Stephen M. Slavin, 45 FCC 2d 639, 641–42 (1973).

217. Taft Broadcasting Co., 53 FCC 2d 126, 132, 133 (1975).

noted, as another distinction, the fact that in the *Slavin* case the station had broadcast denials that an endorsement had been intended.

E. INDECENCY AND OBSCENITY: MANAGING MORALITY IN THE MEDIA

Most developed nations have taboos against the exhibition of nudity or pornographic acts. In some cases, these concerns seem to arise from religious or other ideological bases; in others, from an often unarticulated feeling that "indecency" somehow will hurt the general moral fiber of a community. Over the years, the Commission and the courts have responded in different ways to these concerns, as discussed below.

At the beginning, however, it may be useful to ask the simple question as to what role indecency plays in our society—positive or negative. The follow excerpt suggests that it may be more of the former than many observers would like to admit.

PETER JOHNSON

PORNOGRAPHY DRIVES TECHNOLOGY: WHY NOT TO CENSOR THE INTERNET
49 Fed Com. L. J. 217 (1996).

Throughout the history of new media, from vernacular speech to movable type, to photography, to paperback books, to videotape, to cable and pay-TV, to "900" phone lines, to the French Minitel, to the Internet, to CD–ROMs and laser discs, pornography has shown technology the way. "Great art is always flanked by its dark sisters, blasphemy and pornography."[4] The same is true of the more mundane arts we call media. Where there is the Gutenberg Bible, there is also Rabelais; where the U.S. mails, dirty postcards; where the three-volume hardback novel, paperback pulp fiction; where HBO, Midnight Blue; where CompuServe, the Plain Brown Wrapper library.

Pornography, far from being an evil that the First Amendment must endure, is a positive good that encourages experimentation with new media. The First Amendment thus has not only intellectual, moral, political, and artistic value, but practical and economic value as well. It urges consenting adults, uninhibited by censorship, to look for novel ways to use the new media and novel ways to make money out of the new uses. Therefore, while it may be politically impossible and socially unwise to encourage computer pornography, legislators should at least leave it alone and let the medium follow where pornography leads.

Both English and Italian can trace their emergence as popular tongues partly to pornography. Before the fourteenth century, the gentry of England spoke as much French as English, while the Italian language was a hodgepodge of Latin-derived tongues varying from city-state to

---

4. Camille Paglia, *Sexual Personae* 24–25 (1990).

city-state. Geoffrey Chaucer's *Canterbury Tales* (1387) and Giovanni Boccaccio's *Decameron* (1349–51), larded with the sexy and the scatological, passed in manuscript from hand to hand and read aloud to a largely illiterate populace, helped create national languages in both countries. By writing long and popular works in London English and in Florentine, Chaucer and Boccaccio transformed local vernaculars into national speech. Pornography helped.

The printing press appeared a half-century after Chaucer's death in 1400 and soon spread throughout Europe. Early printing, though voluminous, was largely devoted to the Bible, to other theological, legal, and scientific works, to texts for scholars like the Greek and Latin classics, to popular sheet music, and to local religious and political broadsides. Martin Luther's ninety-five theses, for instance, nailed to the church door in Wittenberg on October 31, 1517, leafleted Germany in two weeks and Europe in two months, thanks to the printing press.

But two less noble works did more to popularize print and bring literacy to the masses than the scholarly works. These were Pietro Aretino's Postures (1524) and Francois Rabelais' Gargantua and Pantagruel (1530–40). Of the two, the Postures was the more pornographic in the strict sense, a series of engravings of sexual positions, each with a ribald sonnet. Rabelais' work, on the other hand, instantly entered the canon, where it has remained ever since. His tales of the two courtly giants, Gargantua and his son Pantagruel, the vinous monk Friar John and the reprobate scholar Panurge, are classics of satire and adventure, spoofing every vestige of the Middle Ages from feudal war to scholasticism to law to religion, with hearty doses of sex and scatology.

Playful governesses introduce Gargantua to sex; Gargantua's horse pisses an army away; a woman scares the devil away by exposing her vagina; Panurge scatters musk on a fine lady who scorned him, exciting the dogs of Paris to rapine and rut. Both Aretino's and Rabelais' works were censured, but since censure at the time made no distinction between political, religious, and social heresies, one cannot be sure they were banned for smut. What is sure is that both were popular, Aretino remaining the underground porn classic for centuries, Rabelais traveling a somewhat higher road.

Rabelais' boast in Gargantua and Pantagruel that "more copies of it have been sold by the printers in two months than there will be of the Bible in nine years" was first, probably true, and second, prescient advice to new media: sex sells.

Three hundred years after Rabelais, photography became a new medium for porn to exploit. Begun as a staid art, requiring long exposures and great stillness, including a headclamp to immobilize the seated subject, photography first lent itself to portraits and landscapes. It was not long, however, before the Civil War taught photography two new uses. The first and more famous was the battlefield photography of Mathew Brady.

The second, the more infamous, was pornography. Soldiers demanded more than letters from home, they demanded erotica. So great was the traffic to the front, not only of dirty books, but soon of erotic daguerreotypes and photographs, that Congress passed the first U.S. law proscribing obscenity via the mails. Congress, as usual, was late. By the time the bill passed, it was 1865, the war was over, and the boys were home with their pictures in their pockets.

* * *

By the mid–1980s a new communications revolution was in full swing, of which the Telecommunications Act of 1996[33] is late acknowledgment. The key term in this revolution is convergence. Telephone, television, computer, and recording technologies are converging upon one another and commingling in so many ways that it will soon be nonsense to speak of media as if they were distinct. * * *

* * * One of the first uses of pay-cable was pornography: people would pay to watch X-and R-rated films at home. When cable systems began competing to wire up entire communities, one of the things communities demanded was leased—or public-access—channels, to keep the cable operator from entirely dominating local programming. What they wanted was worthy alternative programming produced by local civic and educational groups. What they got was porn. * * *

Videotape first emerged as a cheap and efficient alternative to film (later kinescope) for TV production. Its development for home use owes its birth to Sony and Betamax but its maturity to porn. Predicting that the greatest use of home VCRs would be time-shifting, that is, recording TV shows off the air for later viewing, Sony designed Betamax tape with a one hour playing time. When the market for videotape proved not to be time shifting, but prerecorded movies instead, longer-playing tape was demanded, and VHS arose to meet the demand. Though Beta eventually went to a four hour format, it was too late. Within years, two-, four-, and six-hour VHS tape became the industry standard.

* * *

Other participants in the communications revolution that have been helped by pornography include "900" phone numbers, CD–ROMs, and laser discs. In fact, the French Minitel, which many see as the prototype of the computer-mediated telephone system, owes whatever success it has attained largely to its use for exchanging sexual messages.

1. TREATMENT OF BROADCASTING

FCC v. PACIFICA FOUNDATION

Supreme Court of the United States, 1978.
438 U.S. 726, 98 S.Ct. 3026, 57 L.Ed.2d 1073.

MR. JUSTICE STEVENS delivered the opinion of the court * * *.

33. 110 Stat. 1101 (1996).

This case requires that we decide whether the Federal Communications Commission has any power to regulate a radio broadcast that is indecent but not obscene.

A satiric humorist named George Carlin recorded a 12–minute monologue entitled "Filthy Words" before a live audience in a California theater. He began by referring to his thoughts about "the words you couldn't say on the public, ah, airwaves, um, the ones you definitely wouldn't say, ever." He proceeded to list those words and repeat them over and over again in a variety of colloquialisms. The transcript of the recording * * * indicates frequent laughter from the audience.

At about 2 o'clock in the afternoon on Tuesday, October 30, 1973, a New York radio station owned by respondent, Pacifica Foundation, broadcast the "Filthy Words" monologue. A few weeks later a man, who stated that he had heard the broadcast while driving with his young son, wrote a letter complaining to the Commission. He stated that, although he could perhaps understand the "record's being sold for private use, I certainly cannot understand the broadcast of same over the air that, supposedly, you control."

The complaint was forwarded to the station for comment. In its response, Pacifica explained that the monologue had been played during a program about contemporary society's attitude toward language and that immediately before its broadcast listeners had been advised that it included "sensitive language which might be regarded as offensive to some." Pacifica characterized George Carlin as "a significant social satirist" who "like Twain and Sahl before him, examines the language of ordinary people * * *. Carlin is not mouthing obscenities, he is merely using words to satirize as harmless and essentially silly our attitudes towards those words." Pacifica stated that it was not aware of any other complaints about the broadcast.

On February 21, 1975, the Commission issued a Declaratory Order granting the complaint and holding that Pacifica "could have been the subject of administrative sanctions." 56 FCC 2d 94, 99 (1975). The Commission did not impose formal sanctions, but it did state that the order would be "associated with the station's license file, and in the event that subsequent complaints are received, the Commission will then decide whether it should utilize any of the available sanctions it has been granted by Congress."[1]

In its Memorandum Opinion the Commission stated that it intended to "clarify the standards which will be utilized in considering" the growing number of complaints about indecent speech on the airwaves. * * * Advancing several reasons for treating broadcast speech differently

---

1. *Ibid.* The Commission noted: "Congress has specifically empowered the FCC to (1) revoke a station's license (2) issue a cease and desist order, or (3) impose a monetary forfeiture for a violation of Section 1464, 47 U.S.C.A. 312(a), 312(b), 503(b)(1)(E). The FCC can also (4) deny license renewal or (5) grant a short term renewal, 47 U.S.C.A. 307, 308." *Id.*, at 96 n. 3.

from other forms of expression,[2] the Commission found a power to regulate indecent broadcasting in two statutes: 18 U.S.C.A. § 1464, which forbids the use of "any obscene, indecent, or profane language by means of radio communications," and 47 U.S.C.A. § 303(g), which requires the Commission to "encourage the larger and more effective use of radio in the public interest."

The Commission characterized the language used in the Carlin monologue as "patently offensive," though not necessarily obscene, and expressed the opinion that it should be regulated by principles analogous to those found in the law of nuisance where the "law generally speaks to *channeling* behavior more than actually prohibiting it. * * * [T]he concept of 'indecent' is intimately connected with the exposure of children to language that describes, in terms patently offensive as measured by contemporary community standards for the broadcast medium, sexual or excretory activities and organs, at times of the day when there is a reasonable risk that children may be in the audience."[5]

Applying these considerations to the language used in the monologue as broadcast by respondent, the Commission concluded that certain words depicted sexual and excretory activities in a patently offensive manner, noted that they "were broadcast at a time when children were undoubtedly in the audience (i.e. in the early afternoon)," and that the prerecorded language, with these offensive words "repeated over and over," was "deliberately broadcast." In summary, the Commission stated: "We therefore hold that the language as broadcast was indecent and prohibited by 18 U.S.C.A. 1464."

* * *

The United States Court of Appeals for the District of Columbia reversed * * *.

II

The relevant statutory questions are whether the Commission's action is forbidden "censorship" within the meaning of 47 U.S.C.A. § 326 and whether speech that concededly is not obscene may be restricted as "indecent" under the authority of 18 U.S.C.A. § 1464. The questions are not unrelated, for the two statutory provisions have a common origin. Nevertheless, we analyze them separately.

* * *

2. "Broadcasting requires special treatment because of four important considerations: (1) children have access to radios and in many cases are unsupervised by parents; (2) radio receivers are in the home, a place where people's privacy interest is entitled to extra deference, see Rowan v. Post Office Dept., 397 U.S. 728 (1970); (3) unconsenting adults may tune in a station without any warning that offensive language is being or will be broadcast; and (4) there is a scarcity of spectrum space, the use of which the government must therefore license in the public interest. Of special concern to the Commission as well as parents is the first point regarding the use of radio by children." 56 FCC 2d, at 97.

5. Thus, the Commission suggested, if an offensive broadcast had literary, artistic, political or scientific value, and were preceded by warnings, it might not be indecent in the late evening, but would be so during the day, when children are in the audience.

The prohibition against censorship unequivocally denies the Commission any power to edit proposed broadcasts in advance and to excise material considered inappropriate for the airwaves. The prohibition, however, has never been construed to deny the Commission the power to review the content of completed broadcasts in the performance of its regulatory duties.

During the period between the original enactment of the provision in 1927 and its re-enactment in the Communications Act of 1934, the courts and the Federal Radio Commission held that the section deprived the Commission of the power to subject "broadcasting matter to scrutiny prior to its release," but they concluded that the Commission's "undoubted right" to take note of past program content when considering a licensee's renewal application "is not censorship."[10]

* * * And, until this case, the Court of Appeals for the District of Columbia has consistently agreed with this construction. * * *

Entirely apart from the fact that the subsequent review of program content is not the sort of censorship at which the statute was directed, its history makes it perfectly clear that it was not intended to limit the Commission's power to regulate the broadcast of obscene, indecent, or profane language. A single section of the 1927 Act is the source of both the anticensorship provision and the Commission's authority to impose sanctions for the broadcast of indecent or obscene language. Quite plainly, Congress intended to give meaning to both provisions. Respect for that intent requires that the censorship language be read as inapplicable to the prohibition on broadcasting obscene, indecent, or profane language.

* * *

We conclude, therefore, that § 326 does not limit the Commission's authority to impose sanctions on licensees who engage in obscene, indecent, or profane broadcasting.

III

The only other statutory question presented by this case is whether the afternoon broadcast of the "Filthy Words" monologue was indecent within the meaning of § 1464. Even that question is narrowly confined by the arguments of the parties.

The Commission identified several words that referred to excretory or sexual activities or organs, stated that the repetitive, deliberate use of those words in an afternoon broadcast when children are in the audience was patently offensive, and held that the broadcast was indecent. Pacifica takes issue with the Commission's definition of indecency, but does not dispute the Commission's preliminary determination that each of the components of its definition was present. Specifically, Pacifica does not quarrel with the conclusion that this afternoon broadcast was patently

---

10. KFKB Broadcasting Ass'n v. Federal Radio Com'n, 60 App.D.C. 79, 47 F.2d 670 (1931); Trinity Methodist Church, South v. Federal Radio Com'n, 61 App.D.C. 311, 62 F.2d 850 (1932), cert. denied 288 U.S. 599, 53 S.Ct. 317, 77 L.Ed. 975 (1933).

offensive. Pacifica's claim that the broadcast was not indecent within the meaning of the statute rests entirely on the absence of prurient appeal.

The plain language of the statute does not support Pacifica's argument. The words "obscene, indecent, or profane" are written in the disjunctive, implying that each has a separate meaning. Prurient appeal is an element of the obscene, but the normal definition of "indecent" merely refers to nonconformance with accepted standards of morality.

Pacifica argues, however, that this Court has construed the term "indecent" in related statutes to mean "obscene," as that term was defined in *Miller v. California*, 413 U.S. 15. Pacifica relies most heavily on the construction this Court gave to 18 U.S.C.A. § 1461 in *Hamling v. United States*, 418 U.S. 87. *Hamling* rejected a vagueness attack on § 1461, which forbids the mailing of "obscene, lewd, lascivious, indecent, filthy or vile" material. In holding that the statute's coverage is limited to obscenity, the Court followed the lead of Mr. Justice Harlan in Manual Enterprises, Inc. v. Day, 370 U.S. 478. In that case, Mr. Justice Harlan recognized that § 1461 contained a variety of words with many shades of meaning. Nonetheless, he thought that the phrase, "obscene, lewd, lascivious, indecent, filthy or vile," taken as a whole, was clearly limited to the obscene, a reading well-grounded in prior judicial constructions: "the statute since its inception has always been taken as aimed at obnoxiously debasing portrayals of sex." 370 U.S. at 483. In *Hamling* the Court agreed with Mr. Justice Harlan that § 1461 was meant only to regulate obscenity in the mails; by reading into it the limits set by *Miller v. California*, 413 U.S. 15, the Court adopted a construction which assured the statute's constitutionality.

The reasons supporting *Hamling*'s construction of § 1461 do not apply to § 1464. Although the history of the former revealed a primary concern with the prurient, the Commission has long interpreted § 1464 as encompassing more than the obscene. The former statute deals primarily with printed matter enclosed in sealed envelopes mailed from one individual to another; the latter deals with the content of public broadcasts. It is unrealistic to assume that Congress intended to impose precisely the same limitations on the dissemination of patently offensive matter by such different means.

Because neither our prior decisions nor the language or history of § 1464 supports the conclusion that prurient appeal is an essential component of indecent language, we reject Pacifica's construction of the statute. When that construction is put to one side, there is no basis for disagreeing with the Commission's conclusion that indecent language was used in this broadcast.

IV

[Parts IV–A and IV–B of Justice Stevens' opinion, joined only by the Chief Justice and Justice Rehnquist, are omitted.]

C

We have long recognized that each medium of expression presents special First Amendment problems. And of all forms of communication, it is broadcasting that has received the most limited First Amendment protection. Thus, although other speakers cannot be licensed except under laws that carefully define and narrow official discretion, a broadcaster may be deprived of his license and his forum if the Commission decides that such an action would serve "the public interest, convenience, and necessity." Similarly, although the First Amendment protects newspaper publishers from being required to print the replies of those whom they criticize, Miami Herald Publishing Co. v. Tornillo, 418 U.S. 241, it affords no such protection to broadcasters; on the contrary, they must give free time to the victims of their criticism. Red Lion Broadcasting Co., Inc. v. FCC, 395 U.S. 367.

The reasons for these distinctions are complex, but two have relevance to the present case. First, the broadcast media have established a uniquely pervasive presence in the lives of all Americans. Patently offensive, indecent material presented over the airwaves confronts the citizen, not only in public, but also in the privacy of the home, where the individual's right to be let alone plainly outweighs the First Amendment rights of an intruder. Because the broadcast audience is constantly tuning in and out, prior warnings cannot completely protect the listener or viewer from unexpected program content. To say that one may avoid further offense by turning off the radio when he hears indecent language is like saying that the remedy for an assault is to run away after the first blow. * * *

Second, broadcasting is uniquely accessible to children, even those too young to read. Although Cohen's written message might have been incomprehensible to a first grader,* Pacifica's broadcast could have enlarged a child's vocabulary in an instant. Other forms of offensive expression may be withheld from the young without restricting the expression at its source. Bookstores and motion picture theaters, for example, may be prohibited from making indecent material available to children. We held in Ginsberg v. New York, 390 U.S. 629, that the government's interest in the "well being of its youth" and in supporting "parents' claim to authority in their own household" justified the regulation of otherwise protected expression.[28] The ease with which

---

* "Cohen's written message" was "Fuck the Draft," which appeared on the back of a jacket that he wore into a Los Angeles courthouse. On his way out of the courthouse, he was arrested for disturbing the peace and was later convicted and sentenced to a 30–day jail term. The Court overturned the conviction on First Amendment grounds. *Cohen v. California*, 403 U.S. 15, 91 S.Ct. 1780, 29 L.Ed.2d 284 (1971).—Ed.

28. The Commission's action does not by any means reduce adults to hearing only what is fit for children. Cf. Butler v. Michigan, 352 U.S. 380, 383. Adults who feel the need may purchase tapes and records or go to theaters and nightclubs to hear these words. In fact, the Commission has not unequivocally closed even broadcasting to speech of this sort; whether broadcast audiences in the late evening contain so few children that playing this monologue would be permissible is an issue neither the Commission nor this Court has decided.

children may obtain access to broadcast material, coupled with the concerns recognized in *Ginsberg,* amply justify special treatment of indecent broadcasting.

It is appropriate, in conclusion, to emphasize the narrowness of our holding. This case does not involve a two-way radio conversation between a cab driver and a dispatcher, or a telecast of an Elizabethan comedy. We have not decided that an occasional expletive in either setting would justify any sanction or, indeed, that this broadcast would justify a criminal prosecution. The Commission's decision rested entirely on a nuisance rationale under which context is all-important. The concept requires consideration of a host of variables. The time of day was emphasized by the Commission. The content of the program in which the language is used will also affect the composition of the audience, and differences between radio, television, and perhaps closed-circuit transmissions, may also be relevant. As Mr. Justice Sutherland wrote, a "nuisance may be merely a right thing in the wrong place—like a pig in the parlor instead of the barnyard." Euclid v. Ambler Realty Co., 272 U.S. 365, 388. We simply hold that when the Commission finds that a pig has entered the parlor, the exercise of its regulatory power does not depend on proof that the pig is obscene.

The judgment of the Court of Appeals is reversed.

[The concurring opinion of Justice Powell, joined by Justice Blackmun, is omitted. The dissenting opinion of Justice Stewart, joined by Justices Brennan, White, and Marshall, is omitted. Justice White would have construed "indecent" in 18 U.S.C. § 1464 to mean no more than "obscene," thereby avoiding the constitutional issue and reversing the FCC for want of statutory authority to bar non-obscene speech.]

MR. JUSTICE BRENNAN, with whom MR. JUSTICE MARSHALL joins, dissenting. * * *

I

A

Without question, the privacy interests of an individual in his home are substantial and deserving of significant protection. In finding these interests sufficient to justify the content regulation of protected speech, however, the Court commits two errors. First, it misconceives the nature of the privacy interests involved where an individual voluntarily chooses to admit radio communications into his home. Second, it ignores the constitutionally protected interests of both those who wish to transmit and those who desire to receive broadcasts that many—including the FCC and this Court—might find offensive.

"The ability of government, consonant with the Constitution, to shut off discourse solely to protect others from hearing it is ... dependent upon a showing that substantial privacy interests are being invaded in an essentially intolerable manner. Any broader view of this authority would effectively empower a majority to silence dissidents simply as a matter of personal predilections." Cohen v. California, [403 U.S.] at

21.* * * However, I believe that an individual's actions in switching on and listening to communications transmitted over the public airways and directed to the public at-large do not implicate fundamental privacy interests, even when engaged in within the home. Instead, because the radio is undeniably a public medium, these actions are more properly viewed as a decision to take part, if only as a listener, in an ongoing public discourse. * * * [T]he residual privacy interests he retains vis-à-vis the communication he voluntarily admits into his home are surely no greater than those of the people present in the corridor of the Los Angeles courthouse in Cohen who bore witness to the words "Fuck the Draft" emblazoned across Cohen's jacket. Their privacy interests were held insufficient to justify punishing Cohen for his offensive communication.

* * * [T]he very fact that those interests are threatened only by a radio broadcast precludes any intolerable invasion of privacy; for unlike other intrusive modes of communication, such as sound trucks, "[t]he radio can be turned off," and with a minimum of effort. * * * Whatever the minimal discomfort suffered by a listener who inadvertently tunes into a program he finds offensive during the brief interval before he can simply extend his arm and switch stations or flick the "off" button, it is surely worth the candle to preserve the broadcaster's right to send, and the right of those interested to receive, a message entitled to full First Amendment protection. * * *

The Court's balance, of necessity, fails to accord proper weight to the interests of listeners who wish to hear broadcasts the FCC deems offensive. It permits majoritarian tastes completely to preclude a protected message from entering the homes of a receptive, unoffended minority. No decision of this Court supports such a result. Where the individuals comprising the offended majority may freely choose to reject the material being offered, we have never found their privacy interests of such moment to warrant the suppression of speech on privacy grounds. Compare Lehman v. [City of] Shaker Heights, supra. Rowan v. Post Office Dept., 397 U.S. 728 (1970), relied on by the FCC and by the [Court], confirms rather than belies this conclusion. In Rowan, the Court upheld a statute, 39 U.S.C.A. § 4009, permitting householders to require that mail advertisers stop sending them lewd or offensive materials and remove their names from mailing lists. Unlike the situation here, householders who wished to receive the senders' communications were not prevented from doing so. Equally important, the determination of offensiveness vel non under the statute involved in Rowan was completely within the hands of the individual householder; no governmental evaluation of the worth of the mail's content stood between the mailer and the householder. In contrast, the visage of the censor is all too discernable here.

B

Most parents will undoubtedly find understandable as well as commendable the Court's sympathy with the FCC's desire to prevent offensive broadcasts from reaching the ears of unsupervised children. Unfortunately, the facial appeal of this justification for radio censorship masks its constitutional insufficiency. Although the government unquestionably has a special interest in the well-being of children and consequently "can adopt more stringent controls on communicative materials available to youths than on those available to adults," Erznoznik v. City of Jacksonville, supra, at 212; see Paris Adult Theatre I v. Slaton, 413 U.S. 49, 106–107 (1973) (BRENNAN, J., dissenting), the Court has accounted for this societal interest by adopting a "variable obscenity" standard that permits the prurient appeal of material available to children to be assessed in terms of the sexual interests of minors. Ginsberg v. New York, 390 U.S. 629 (1968). * * *

Because the Carlin monologue is obviously not an erotic appeal to the prurient interests of children, the Court, for the first time, allows the government to prevent minors from gaining access to materials that are not obscene, and are therefore protected, as to them. It thus ignores our recent admonition that "[s]peech that is neither obscene as to youths nor subject to some other legitimate proscription cannot be suppressed solely to protect the young from ideas or images that a legislative body thinks unsuitable for them." The Court's refusal to follow its own pronouncements is especially lamentable since it has the anomalous subsidiary effect, at least in the radio context at issue here, of making completely unavailable to adults material which may not constitutionally be kept even from children. * * *

In concluding that the presence of children in the listening audience provides an adequate basis for the FCC to impose sanctions for Pacifica's broadcast of the Carlin monologue, the [Court stresses] the time-honored right of a parent to raise his child as he sees fit—a right this Court has consistently been vigilant to protect. See Wisconsin v. Yoder, 406 U.S. 205 (1972); Pierce v. Society of Sisters, 268 U.S. 510 (1925). Yet this principle supports a result directly contrary to that reached by the Court. Yoder and Pierce hold that parents, *not* the government, have the right to make certain decisions regarding the upbringing of their children. As surprising as it may be to individual Members of this Court, some parents may actually find Mr. Carlin's unabashed attitude towards the seven "dirty words" healthy, and deem it desirable to expose their children to the manner in which Mr. Carlin defuses the taboo surrounding the words. Such parents may constitute a minority of the American public, but the absence of great numbers willing to exercise the right to raise their children in this fashion does not alter the right's nature or its existence. Only the Court's regrettable decision does that.

* * *

III

It is quite evident that I find the Court's attempt to unstitch the warp and woof of First Amendment law in an effort to reshape its fabric to cover the patently wrong result the Court reaches in this case dangerous as well as lamentable. Yet there runs throughout the opinions of my Brothers POWELL and STEVENS another vein I find equally disturbing: a depressing inability to appreciate that in our land of cultural pluralism, there are many who think, act, and talk differently from the Members of this Court, and who do not share their fragile sensibilities. It is only an acute ethnocentric myopia that enables the Court to approve the censorship of communications solely because of the words they contain.

* * * The words that the Court and the Commission find so unpalatable may be the stuff of everyday conversations in some, if not many, of the innumerable subcultures that comprise this Nation. Academic research indicates that this is indeed the case. See B. Jackson, Get Your Ass in the Water and Swim Like Me (1974); J. Dillard, Black English (1972); W. Labov, Language in the Inner City: Studies in the Black English Vernacular (1972). As one researcher concluded, "[w]ords generally considered obscene like 'bullshit' and 'fuck' are considered neither obscene nor derogatory in the [Black] vernacular except in particular contextual situations and when used with certain intonations." C. Bins, "Toward an Ethnography of Contemporary African American Oral Poetry," Language and Linguistics Working Papers No. 5, at 82 (Georgetown University Press 1972).

Today's decision will thus have its greatest impact on broadcasters desiring to reach, and listening audiences comprised of, persons who do not share the Court's view as to which words or expressions are acceptable and who, for a variety of reasons, including a conscious desire to flout majoritarian conventions, express themselves using words that may be regarded as offensive by those from different socioeconomic backgrounds. In this context, the Court's decision may be seen for what, in the broader perspective, it really is: another of the dominant culture's inevitable efforts to force those groups who do not share its mores to conform to its way of thinking, acting, and speaking.

* * *

The following is a verbatim transcript of "Filthy Words" prepared by the Federal Communications Commission.

Aruba-du, ruba-tu, ruba-tu. I was thinking about the curse words and the swear words, the cuss words and the words that you can't say, that you're not supposed to say all the time, ['cause] words or people into words want to hear your words. Some guys like to record your words and sell them back to you if they can, (laughter) listen in on the telephone, write down what words you say. A guy who used to be in Washington knew that his phone was tapped, used to answer, Fuck Hoover, yes, go ahead. (laughter) Okay, I was thinking one night about the words you couldn't say on the public, ah, airwaves, um, the ones you definitely wouldn't say, ever, [']cause I heard a lady say bitch one night on television, and it was cool like she was talking about, you know, ah, well, the bitch is the first one to notice that in the litter Johnie right (murmur) Right. And, uh, bastard you can say, and hell and damn so I have to figure out which ones you couldn't and ever and it came down to seven but the list is open to amendment, and in fact, has been changed, uh, by now, ha, a lot of people pointed things out to me, and I noticed some myself. The original seven words were, shit, piss, fuck, cunt, cocksucker, motherfucker, and tits. Those are the ones that will curve your spine, grow hair on your hands and (laughter) maybe, even bring us, God help us, peace without honor (laughter) um, and a bourbon. (laughter) And now the first thing that we noticed was that word fuck was really repeated in there because the word motherfucker is a compound word and it's another form of the word fuck. (laughter) You want to be a purist it doesn't really—it can't be on the list of basic words. Also, cocksucker is a compound word and neither half of that is really dirty. The word—the half sucker that's merely suggestive (laughter) and the word cock is a half-way dirty word, 50% dirty—dirty half the time, depending on what you mean by it. (laughter) Uh, remember when you first heard it, like in 6th grade, you used to giggle. And the cock crowed three times, heh (laughter) the cock—three times. It's in the Bible, cock in the Bible. (laughter) And the first time you heard about a cock-fight, remember—What? Huh? naw. It ain't that, are you stupid? man. (laughter, clapping) It's chickens, you know, (laughter) Then you have the four letter words from the old Anglo–Saxon fame. Uh, shit and fuck. The word shit, uh, is an interesting kind of word in that the middle class has never really accepted it and approved it. They use it like, crazy but it's not really okay. It's still a rude, dirty, old kind of gushy word. (laughter) They don't like that, but they say it, like, they say it like, a lady now in a middle-class home, you'll hear most of the time she says it as an expletive, you know, it's out of her mouth before she knows. She says, Oh shit oh shit, (laughter) oh shit. If she drops something, Oh, the shit hurt the broccoli. Shit. Thank you. (footsteps fading away) (papers ruffling).

Read it! (from audience).

Shit! (laughter) I won the Grammy, man, for the comedy album. Isn't that groovy? (clapping, whistling) (murmur) That's true. Thank you. Thank you man. Yeah. (murmur) (continuous clapping) Thank you man. Thank you. Thank you very much, man. Thank, no, (end of continuous clapping) for that and for the Grammy, man, [']cause (laughter) that's based on people liking it man, yeh, that's ah, that's okay man. (laughter) Let's let that go, man. I got my Grammy. I can let my hair hang down now, shit. (laughter) Ha! So! Now the word shit is okay for the man. At work you can say it like crazy. Mostly figuratively, Get that shit out of here, will ya? I don't want to see that shit anymore. I can't cut that shit, buddy. I've had that shit up to here. think you're full of shit myself. (laughter) He don't know shit from Shinola. (laughter) you know that? (laughter) Always wondered how the Shinola people feel about that (laughter) Hi, I'm the new man from Shinola. (laughter) Hi, how are ya? Nice to see ya. (laughter) How are ya? (laughter) Boy, I don't know whether to shit or wind my watch. (laughter) Guess, I'll shit on my watch. (laughter) Oh, the shit is going to hit de fan. (laughter) Built like a brick shit-house. (laughter) Up, he's up shit's creek. (laugh-

ter) He's had it. (laughter) He hit me, I'm sorry. (laughter) Hot shit,
holy shit, tough shit, eat shit, (laughter) shit-eating grin. Uh, whoever
thought of that was ill. (murmur laughter) He had a shit-eating grin! He
had a what? (laughter) Shit on a stick. (laughter) Shit in a handbag. I
always like that. He ain't worth shit in a handbag. (laughter) Shitty. He
acted real shitty. (laughter) You know what I mean? (laughter) I got the
money back, but a real shitty attitude. Heh, he had a shit-fit. (laughter)
Wow! Shit-fit. Whew! Glad I wasn't there. (murmur, laughter) All the
animals—Bull shit, horse shit, cow shit, rat shit, bat shit. (laughter)
First time I heard bat shit, I really came apart. A guy in Oklahoma,
Boggs, said it, man. Aw! Bat shit. (laughter) Vera reminded me of that
last night, ah (murmur). Snake shit, slicker than owl shit. (laughter) Get
your shit together. Shit or get off the pot. (laughter) I got a shit-load full
of them. (laughter) I got a shit-pot full, all right. Shit-head, shit-heel,
shit in your heart, shit for brains, (laughter) shit-face, heh (laughter) I
always try to think how that could have originated; the first guy that
said that. Somebody got drunk and fell in some shit, you know. (laughter) Hey, I'm shit-face. (laughter) Shitface, today. (laughter) Anyway,
enough of that shit. (laughter) The big one, the word fuck that's the one
that hangs them up the most. [']Cause in a lot of cases that's the very
act that hangs them up the most. So, it's natural that the word would,
uh, have the same effect. It's a great word, fuck, nice word, easy word,
cute word, kind of. Easy word to say. One syllable, short u. (laughter)
Fuck. (Murmur) You know, it's easy. Starts with a nice soft sound fuh
ends with a kuh. Right? (laughter) A little something for everyone. Fuck
(laughter) Good word. Kind of a proud word, too. Who are you? I am
FUCK. (laughter) FUCK OF THE MOUNTAIN. (laughter) Tune in
again next week to FUCK OF THE MOUNTAIN. (laughter) It's an
interesting word too, [']cause it's got a double kind of a life—personality—dual, you know, whatever the right phrase is. It leads a double life,
the word fuck. First of all, it means, sometimes, most of the time, fuck.
What does it mean? It means to make love. Right? We're going to make
love, yeh, we're going to fuck, yeh, we're going to fuck, yeh, we're going
to make love. (laughter) we're really going to fuck, yeah, we're going to
make love. Right? And it also means the beginning of life, it's the act
that begins life, so there's the word hanging around with words like love,
and life, and yet on the other hand, it's also a word that we really use to
hurt each other with, man. It's a heavy. It's one that you have toward
the end of the argument. (laughter) Right? (laughter) You finally can't
make out. Oh, fuck you man. I said, fuck you. (laughter, murmur) Stupid
fuck. (laughter) Fuck you and everybody that looks like you. (laughter)
man. It would be nice to change the movies that we already have and
substitute the word fuck for the word kill, wherever we could, and some
of those movie cliches would change a little bit. Madfuckers still on the
loose. Stop me before I fuck again. Fuck the ump, fuck the ump, fuck the
ump, fuck the ump, fuck the ump. Easy on the clutch Bill, you'll fuck
that engine again. (laughter) The other shit one was, I don't give a shit.
Like it's worth something, you know? (laughter) I don't give a shit. Hey,
well, I don't take no shit, (laughter) you know what I mean? You know

why I don't take no shit? (laughter)) [']Cause I don't give a shit. (laughter) If I give a shit, I would have to pack shit. (laughter) But I don't pack no shit cause I don't give a shit. (laughter) You wouldn't shit me, would you? (laughter) That's a joke when you're a kid with a worm looking out the bird's ass. You wouldn't shit me, would you? (laughter) It's an eight-year-old joke but a good one. (laughter) The additions to the list. I found three more words that had to be put on the list of words you could never say on television, and they were fart, turd and twat, those three. (laughter) Fart, we talked about, it's harmless It's like tits, it's a cutie word, no problem. Turd, you can't say but [* * *53] who wants to, you know? (laughter) The subject never comes up on the panel so I'm not worried about that one. Now the word twat is an interesting word. Twat! Yeh, right in the twat. (laughter) Twat is an interesting word because it's the only one I know of, the only slang word applying to the, a part of the sexual anatomy that doesn't have another meaning to it. Like, ah, snatch, box and pussy all have other meanings, man. Even in a Walt Disney movie, you can say, We're going to snatch that pussy and put him in a box and bring him on the airplane. (murmur, laughter) Everybody loves it. The twat stands alone, man, as it should. And two-way words. Ah, ass is okay providing you're riding into town on a religious feast day. (laughter) You can't say, up your ass. (laughter) You can say, stuff it! (murmur) There are certain things you can say its weird but you can just come so close. Before I cut, I, uh, want to, ah, thank you for listening to my words, man, fellow, uh space travelers. Thank you man for tonight and thank you also. (clapping whistling).

Notes and Questions

1.   Under Miller v. California, 413 U.S. 15, 93 S.Ct. 2607, 37 L.Ed.2d 419 (1973) and related cases, material may be deemed "obscene" if (a) the average person applying contemporary community standards would find that the work, taken as a whole, appeals to the prurient interest; (b) the work depicts or describes, in a patently offensive way, sexual or excretory conduct specifically defined by the applicable state law; and (c) the work, taken as a whole, lacks serious literary, artistic, political, or scientific value. For purposes of applying these tests, the "community" whose standards are applied is the local community where the material is uttered or displayed.

Under *Pacifica*, "indecent" language as used in 18 U.S.C. § 1464, it seems, "merely refers to nonconformance with accepted standards of morality." Accepted by whom? The Court does not indicate whether the applicable standards are those of the community of broadcast, the national "community," or perhaps just those of the FCC. How should this issue be resolved? Does the Commission have access to information on local standards, such as a jury provides in criminal prosecutions? Should it conduct rulemaking proceedings to determine a set of national standards of decency? Or should it issue regulations or guidelines explicating its own expectations of broadcasters in this area? Keep these questions in mind as you read the materials that follow concerning the FCC's recent attempts to regulate obscene and indecent broadcasts.

Footnote: The Court recites that the Commission acted upon a single letter of complaint about the "Filthy Words" monologue, which was broadcast in New York City. The complaint was received from one John R. Douglas—a Floridian who was a member of the national planning board of Morality in Media. The "young son" whom he said was with him in this car when they heard the monologue was 15 years old at the time. *Broadcasting,* July 10, 1978, at 20.

2. The Court "emphasize[s] the narrowness" of its holding, which is said to be a function of "a host of variables," including the time of day and the content of the program in which indecent language is broadcast—both presumably relevant to audience composition—and whether it is used on radio or television. These and other variables, it suggests, would determine whether the language as broadcast, was a "nuisance," something to be "channeled" rather than prohibited, a "right thing in a wrong place." What does all this mean in practice? May the Carlin monologue ever be aired?

(a) According to a study cited by the court of appeals, 556 F.2d 9, 14 (D.C.Cir.1977), the number of children watching television does not fall below one million until 1:00 a.m. Would this fact justify the Commission, in a later case, determining that indecent language may not lawfully be broadcast before that hour? Is the Commission obliged by the Court's opinion to take account of any countervailing interests, among adults in the audience or among broadcasters, in being able to hear and to say indecent words?

(b) Can the "channeling" concept, or any other scheme of accommodation (such as warnings regarding content) protect the speech interests of those AM licensees authorized to operate during daytime hours only?

(c) The usefulness of channeling became a major point of contention in the late 1980s, when the Commission began to scrutinize allegedly indecent broadcasts for the first time since *Pacifica.* After reading that material, you may want to reconsider your responses to the preceding questions.

(d) Note that 18 U.S.C. § 1464 proscribes "profane" as well as "indecent" and "obscene" language. Could any of these categories be applied to prohibit speech other than "filthy words" on the ground that "the government's interest in the well being of its youth and in supporting parents' claim to authority in their own household justified the regulation of otherwise protected expression"? Suppose that the FCC determined as a fact that the great majority of parents would not want their children to hear atheism presented in a favorable light; could such a presentation be prohibited?

3. Illinois Citizens Committee for Broadcasting v. FCC, 515 F.2d 397 (D.C.Cir.1974), arose from the Commission's response to certain radio call-in programs on sex-related topics, so-called "topless radio." On March 27, 1973, the FCC announced an inquiry into the broadcast of obscene, indecent, or profane material. On the following day, Chairman Burch, in a speech before the National Association of Broadcasters, urged licensees to exercise self-restraint. On April 11 a Notice of Apparent Liability proposing a forfeiture of $2000 against one licensee was issued. The licensee paid the forfeiture but the Citizens Committee and the Illinois division of the American Civil Liberties Union, as representatives of the listening public, filed an Applica-

tion for Remission of the Forfeiture and a Petition for Reconsideration. The Commission denied the petition.

The court of appeals affirmed the Commission on the merits, but specifically upheld the appellants' standing. The government had urged that the public, as distinguished from the licensee, has no interest in a forfeiture proceeding. The court was concerned, however, that the public's interest in the flow of information would not be vindicated if the licensee that is subjected to a forfeiture proceeding found the burden too great, in terms of its own interest, to warrant its undertaking the risk and expense involved in contesting the Commission's action. In a supplemental opinion, Judge Leventhal conceded that "no Supreme Court case * * * goes this far in a situation where the producer or distributor directly affected has acquiesced. However, we found such a requirement implicit in the contours of the statute, a procedural right that furthers the substantive rights of the public under the First Amendment."

What substantive interests should an intervenor such as the Illinois Citizens Committee be heard to assert: those of the broadcaster as well as the listeners? Do listeners have a right to any particular type of programming, including that which plays at the brink of indecency? Should it matter whether the sex-related call-in show under sanction was "unique" in the area?

4. In March 1973, sex-related discussion shows had been ratings leaders in their time slots in several cities, including Chicago. Storer Broadcasting had syndicated one such show to twenty-one stations. Yet in June of that year, one month after Chairman Burch's speech, a National Association of Broadcasters survey showed that sex discussion shows had almost completely disappeared from the air.

5. See generally Note, *Filthy Words, The FCC, and the First Amendment: Regulating Broadcast Obscenity*, 61 Va.L.Rev. 579 (1975), which concludes that the Commission's regulation of offensive speech should be limited to the control of obscenity, and that it should use its rule-making power to bring to this narrow area "more consistency and rationality" than case-by-case adjudication yields. On the general chilling effect created when the FCC retains any wider discretion than there proposed, the author states: "Broadcaster overreaction to protect the valuable license exacerbates this effect."

6. Apparently sensitive to the potential chilling effect of aggressive regulation of "indecent" broadcasts—whatever they might be—the Commission for some years construed *Pacifica* very narrowly. The Commission essentially took the position that only repetitive use of the "seven dirty words" was of concern, and that broadcasts after 10:00 p.m., when unsupervised children were less likely to be watching or listening, were permissible. In effect, the Commission chose not to become involved in making judgments about the decency of broadcast material. See WGBH Educational Foundation, 69 FCC 2d 1250, 1254 (1978) (Commission will "strictly * * * observe the narrowness of the [*Pacifica*] * * * holding."). In fact, between 1975 and 1987, the FCC took no action against any allegedly "indecent" broadcast. See Dyk & Schiffer, *The FCC, the Congress and Indecency on the Air*, 8 Comm. Lawyer 8 (Winter 1990).

The Commission's approach reflected, in part, satisfaction with industry self-regulation. The three television networks, for example, had active "Standards and Practices" departments that imposed strict limits on the degree to which nudity, violence, and "foul" or "suggestive" language could be shown on television. See generally Report on the Broadcast of Violent, Indecent, and Obscene Material, 32 R.R.2d 1367 (1975).

Over time, however, a number of broadcasters—particularly in radio— became more aggressive (or less "discriminating," as one likes) in their choice of programming. Viewers had gained new access to sexually more explicit and more violent programming from pay television services, cable television, and the explosive home video market. (The special case of cable television, which traditionally had not abided by the limits on nudity, language, and violence followed in the broadcast industry, is discussed later in this Chapter.) The result was a growing concern among large segments of the population that the mass media were contributing to a general decline in morality, particularly among younger, highly impressionable viewers. (There was also significant concern that pornography—both hard-core and soft-core—contributed to violence against women and a general degradation of the images that men have of women). See, e.g., Andrea Dworkin, *Pornography: Men Possessing Women* (1979).

As a result of these concerns, in the early-to mid–1980s, Congress and the Reagan Administration began to express a desire for more active FCC enforcement of 18 U.S.C. § 1464. In 1987, to the shock of the broadcast industry, the Commission concluded that three broadcasters had aired programs that constituted actionable indecency. Infinity Broadcasting Corp. of Pa. (WYSP–FM), 2 FCC Rcd 2705 (1987); Pacifica Foundation, Inc. (KPFK–FM), 2 FCC Rcd 2698 (1987); The Regents of the University of California (KCSB–FM), 2 FCC Rcd 2703 (1987). Because of the possibility that the Commission's prior position on indecency may have caused confusion among broadcasters, the Commission issued only warning letters to the three licensees.* The Commission also issued a Public Notice to advise broadcasters generally that henceforth it would be applying the "generic" definition of indecency set forth in the Court's decision in *Pacifica*. Thus, "language or material that depicts or describes in terms patently offensive as measured by contemporary community standards for the broadcast medium, sexual or excretory activities or organs" would be considered indecent. The Commission went on to eliminate any safe harbor arrangement by stating that indecency will be actionable "if broadcast or transmitted at a time of day when there is a reasonable risk that children may be in the audience." Public Notice, FCC No. 87–153 (released April 29, 1987).

The decision marked a dramatic departure from the prior narrow application of *Pacifica*. It also alarmed broadcasters, who claimed that they would be unable to determine whether they were transmitting actionable indecency because the Commission's standard was too vague. In response to requests for reconsideration or clarification of its new indecency policy, the Commission issued the following further order. Infinity Broadcasting Corporation of Pennsylvania, 3 FCC Rcd 930, affirmed in part sub. nom. Action for

---

* The Commission referred the *Pacifica* case to the Justice Department for possible criminal prosecution under the obscenity prong of Section 1464; the Department, however, declined to take any action.

Children's Television v. FCC, 1332 (D.C. Cir. 1988) set forth the FCC's reasoning as below.

7. Petitioner NAB [National Association of Broadcasters] asks the Commission to clarify, and petitioner ACT [Action for Children's Television] asks us to reconsider, not our rulings themselves, but the rulings as characterized in the public notice summarizing the cases. Petitioners do not challenge the Commission's authority to channel indecent broadcasts to late night hours. Instead, they maintain that our construction of Section 1464 is unconstitutionally vague and overbroad. To remedy these asserted constitutional failings, petitioners ask us to adopt several revisions. Collectively, they urge us to: (1) provide more precise guidance as to the elements pertinent to whether material is "patently offensive" and violates "contemporary community standards for the broadcast medium"; (2) consider the literary, artistic, political and scientific value of programming in judging whether it is patently offensive and, thus, indecent; (3) exempt news and informational programming from a finding of indecency; (4) defer to reasonable good faith judgments made by licensees applying the requirements set forth by the Commission; (5) apply rulings prospectively, not sanctioning licensees until they have notice that particular material has been judged to be indecent; and (6) adopt a fixed time of day after which non-obscene, adult oriented programming may be aired, or articulate a similar "bright line" test.

8. In contrast, [Morality in Media ("MIM")] argues in its comments that the Commission has not gone far enough in its regulation of indecency. MIM asserts that indecent material cannot be aired by a broadcaster at any time because the prohibition set out in 18 U.S.C. § 1464 is, on its face, absolute and unqualified. MIM also suggests that the present definition of indecency be expanded to encompass a wide range of material, including that which is "more than indelicate and less than immodest." * * *

III. Discussion

* * *

11. * * * In exercising its authority to enforce the prohibition against indecency expressed in Section 1464, the Commission is advancing the government interest in safeguarding children * * *. The United States Court of Appeals for the Second Circuit has held that this "interest in protecting children from salacious material is no doubt quite compelling."*

12. MIM urges us to apply Section 1464 in a manner that would prohibit at all times of the day the broadcast of certain sexually explicit, yet non-obscene material. When the Supreme Court affirmed the Commission's *Pacifica* ruling in 1978, however, it made plain that our authority under Section 1464 is limited to the imposition of reasonable time, place and manner restrictions on the broadcast of indecent material in order to advance the government's interest in protecting children

---

* Carlin Communications, Inc. v. FCC,   New York, 390 U.S. 629 (1968).
749 F.2d 113, 121 (1984), citing Ginsberg v.

and in enabling parents to determine when and how their children are to be exposed to this material. It is clear that our application of Section 1464 must be consistent with the constitutional principles derived from the *Pacifica* decision. Thus, under Section 1464, we may only do that which is necessary to restrict children's access to indecent broadcasts * * *.

Patent Offensiveness and the Role of Merit

* * *

14. "Patently offensive" is a phrase that must, of necessity, be construed with reference to specific facts. We cannot and will not attempt to provide petitioners with a comprehensive index or thesaurus of indecent words or pictorial depictions that will be considered patently offensive. There is no way to construct a definitive list that would be both comprehensive and not over-inclusive in the abstract, without reference to the specific context. All we hold here, therefore, is that, in the three cases before us, we properly found the material identified as indecent to be patently offensive.

* * *

16. As we stated in our April rulings, and as we reemphasize today, the question of whether material is patently offensive requires careful consideration of context. The Supreme Court has said that the term "context" encompasses a "host of variables." These variables, whose interplay will vary depending on the facts presented, included, as the Court noted, an examination of the actual words or depictions in context to see if they are, for example, "vulgar" or "shocking," a review of the manner in which the language or depictions are portrayed, an analysis of whether allegedly offensive material is isolated or fleeting, a consideration of the ability of the medium of expression to separate adults from children, and a determination of the presence of children in the audience.

17. The merit of a work is also one of the many variables that make up a work's "context," as the Court implicitly recognized in *Pacifica* when it contrasted the Carlin monologue to Elizabethan comedies and works of Chaucer. But merit is simply one of many variables, and it would give this particular variable undue importance if we were to single it out for greater weight or attention than we give other variables. We decline to do so in deciding the three cases before us. We must, therefore, reject an approach that would hold that if a work has merit, it is *per se* not indecent. At the same time, we must reject the notion that a work's "context" can be reviewed in a manner that artificially excludes merit from the host of variables that ordinarily comprise context.

18. The material that the Commission identified in the *KPFK–FM* case as indecent occurred in the context of a 10:00 p.m. radio broadcast of excerpted portions of a theatrical play. The excerpted portions that were broadcast contained the concentrated and repeated use of vulgar and shocking language to portray graphic and lewd depictions of excre-

tion, anal intercourse, ejaculation, masturbation, and oral-genital sex.
* * *

19.   * * * The fact that the material presented was excerpted from a dramatic performance that dealt with homosexual relations and Acquired Immune Deficiency Syndrome (AIDS) does not affect our determination that the *manner* in which these subjects were dealt with in the excerpts was patently offensive. Nor does Pacifica's claim that the play from which the excerpts were taken has been critically acclaimed and long-running in Los Angeles area theaters change the determination.
* * *

* * *

Contemporary Community Standards for the Broadcast Medium

24.   Petitioners also ask for clarification of the phrase "contemporary community standards for the broadcast medium," as that term is used in the indecency definition and was used in each of our three April rulings. * * * [I]n a Commission proceeding for indecency, in which the Commission applies a concept of "contemporary community standards for the broadcast medium," indecency will be judged by the standard of an average broadcast viewer or listener. * * *

The Role of Reasonable Licensee Judgments

25.   Petitioner ACT urges us to defer to reasonable, good faith judgments of licensees in deciding whether a licensee has violated Section 1464. In this way, ACT contends, we will help to avoid inhibiting programming decisions and intruding into the broadcast editorial process. In a related vein, petitioner NAB advocates a policy under which Commission rulings would have prospective effect only. Under this approach, the Commission would refine its standards of what is indecent on a case-by-case basis, but would not penalize a licensee for a broadcast unless the licensee had specific notice that the Commission or a court had previously found that broadcast to be indecent. Absent a ruling squarely on point, a licensee's decision to air programming would be considered reasonable and automatically beyond the reach of Section 1464 under this scenario.

26.   ACT does not contend that deference to reasonable licensee judgments in interpreting Section 1464 is required as a matter of law, and we find no basis on the record before us to allow such judgment to preclude a finding that a licensee has violated its statutory duties. Indeed, given the variety of programming aired by licensees, such a policy would largely read the prohibition against indecent transmissions out of Section 1464. Congress cannot have intended such a result, and we find no basis for reading such a provision into the statute. Although we acknowledge that the statute requires a broadcaster to make judgments as to whether certain material would violate the statute, the fact that the decision may not always be an easy one cannot excuse the broadcaster from having to exercise its judgment, any more than it can excuse the Commission from exercising its enforcement responsibilities. We note, however, that it is standard procedure for the Commission, in

deciding whether to impose a sanction for violation of the law and, if so, what those sanctions should be, to give weight to the reasonable determinations of licensees endeavoring to comply with the law. Because licensees demonstrating reasonable judgment have no cause to fear the imposition of unjustified sanctions, we reject the petitioners' contentions that the editorial decisions of broadcasters will be inappropriately chilled by continuation of this approach.[30] * * *

Notes and Questions

1. (a) Who is the "average broadcast viewer or listener" instanced (at ¶ 24) by the FCC? (b) Consider the Commission's explication of "contemporary community standards for the broadcast medium" in a subsequent decision involving allegations of obscene programming by a Chicago station (known as "Video 44") that had converted from conventional broadcasting to an STV operation in the early 1980s. In 1986 the Commission had refused to consider an obscenity allegation against the operator of Video 44, choosing instead to rely on local officials to make the local determination of whether programming was obscene under "contemporary community standards." In 1988, the Commission used a petition for reconsideration of the *Video 44* decision as the occasion to clarify its position on the handling of obscene broadcasts:

11. Although it may be preferable, in most cases, to deal with questions of obscenity in the context of a previously adjudicated prosecution in a local judicial district, we are persuaded, on reflection, that we should retain the ability to pursue a range of options when allegations of a violation of section 1464 are raised against a licensee. * * * To the extent, therefore, that our previous order in this proceeding suggested that we would never undertake our own administrative determination of an obscenity issue in the first instance, we now reverse that conclusion.

12. In our previous order, we concluded that obscenity determinations require the application of local community standards and that, consequently, the Commission was precluded from making those determinations in the first instance. Video 44, 103 FCC 2d at 1210–11. * * * Two of the three criteria for obscenity [set forth in Miller v. California, 413 U.S. 15 (1973)]—whether a work appeals to the prurient interest and whether it is patently offensive—are to be judged according to contemporary community standards. E.g., Smith v. United States, 431 U.S. 291, 300–01 (1977). The third criterion—whether the work lacks serious value—is to be judged according to a reasonable person test. Pope v. Illinois, 107 S.Ct. 1918 (1987).

14. We recognize that, in the application of the obscenity standard in the context of, for example, the enforcement of 18 U.S.C. § 1461 (prohibiting the mailing of obscene material), lower courts have focused

---

30. Whereas previously we indicated that 10:00 p.m. was a reasonable delineation point, we now indicate that 12:00 midnight is our current thinking as to when it is reasonable to expect that it is late enough to ensure that the risk of children in the audience is minimized and to rely on par-ents to exercise increased supervision over whatever children remain in the viewing and listening audience. Indeed, parents will be on notice that their supervision of any children still awake must be increased after midnight.

on the local nature of the contemporary community standards criterion and the value of local decisionmakers in the application of that criterion. * * * That focus, however, has developed in the context of a judicial system capable of using local decisionmakers in criminal prosecutions of obscenity. Our review suggests that these cases may be inapplicable in the context, as here, of an administrative action by a national agency. We do not believe, therefore, that they necessarily preclude us from undertaking obscenity determinations in the first instance. Indeed, we note that, in the past, the Commission undertook an obscenity determination without focusing on a particular community and was upheld by the Court of Appeals. Sonderling Broadcasting Corp., 27 R.R.2d 285, recon. denied, 41 FCC 2d 777 (1973), aff'd sub nom. Illinois Citizens Committee for Broadcasting v. FCC, 515 F.2d 397 (D.C.Cir.1974). Hence, we believe that we may, as a constitutional matter, apply a broader contemporary community standard for broadcasting generally in obscenity cases. We do not—and need not—decide here whether, as a policy matter, we might choose to attempt to approximate a more local community standard in an appropriate case presenting an obscenity issue.[31]

* * *

Video 44, 3 FCC Rcd 757, 758–59 (1988).

What do you think the Commission means (in ¶ 14) by "a broader contemporary community standard for broadcasting generally"? Should the same standard be applied to STV as to conventional broadcasting? What is meant by "approximat[ing] a more local standard in an appropriate case"? Do you think the Commission is well-equipped to make judgments about local tastes and mores? On what basis should the Commission choose between application of a "broader" and of a local standard? Would it be reasonable, for example, to hold a national network to a national standard and an independent station to a local standard? Under "traditional" obscenity analysis, the network would have to be concerned about an obscenity prosecution in the most restrictive community that any of its affiliates serves; would a national standard be more lenient? Why?

(c) In the *Video 44* case, the Commission went on to hold that it would not decide the obscenity issue raised against the licensee. It concluded that First Amendment considerations required that allegations of the transmission of obscene programs must be made contemporaneously with the transmission of the program; untimely complaints, if actionable, would create an excessive chilling effect. If only timely complaints are considered, the Commission said, violations can be addressed and remedied promptly. If the

---

31. The effect of an obscenity determination is to ban certain speech altogether, rather than merely to channel it to late night hours, as with non-obscene, adult oriented programming. Therefore, applying a standard that attempts to approximate a local standard might appropriately take into account the development of obscenity law by the lower courts, as discussed above. Furthermore, as mentioned below, in a pro-

ceeding in which the Commission issued a forfeiture against a licensee without a full hearing, the licensee could avail itself of a trial de novo in a local district court. This procedure may also afford the opportunity to have the obscenity issue judged by local decisionmakers. These issues, however, are not raised by this case, and we need not definitively resolve them here.

Commission were willing to entertain complaints years after a program had been broadcast (such as at renewal time), however, licensees might fear that they would be found to have aired obscene programs repeatedly and, therefore, have endangered their licenses. According to the Commission, that threat would be so great that it could unduly discourage the airing of controversial programming. The Commission also noted that only a contemporaneous complaint permits the application of the "contemporary community standard" test. The Commission's decision was reversed and remanded on appeal. Monroe Communications Corp. v. FCC, 900 F.2d 351, 357 (D.C.Cir.1990) ("the Commission did not adequately justify its adoption and application of a contemporaneous complaint requirement"). On remand, the FCC revoked the Video 44 license and awarded it to a competing applicant, without resolving the obscenity issue. 5 F.C.C.Rcd. 6383 (1990).

Note also that this was an easy position for the Commission; by the early 1990s, STV effectively had ceased to exist; it could not use one channel to compete with cable's many. Aside from a few LPTVs, STV seems to have disappeared.

2.   In June 1987, Pacifica Foundation filed a request for a declaratory ruling by the Commission regarding its intention to broadcast a reading of a portion of James Joyce's novel, *Ulysses*. (In its request, Pacifica submitted the excerpt to be read but did not identify *Ulysses* as its source.) The broadcast was planned for 11:00 p.m. and would be preceded by a warning that it might be objectionable to some listeners. Pacifica stated its concern that the passage, which contained various sexually explicit phrases, would be considered "indecent" under the Commission's 1987 standard. (In 1933, a federal district court ruled that *Ulysses* was not obscene and, therefore, could be imported into the United States. United States v. One Book Called "Ulysses," 5 F.Supp. 182 (S.D.N.Y.1933)). The Mass Media Bureau declined to rule on the passage's decency, instructing the licensee to make its own judgment on the basis of the Commission's enunciated standard. *Letter to William J. Byrnes, Esq.*, June 5, 1987. The Bureau noted that the Commission was reluctant to issue declaratory rulings on these issues because of their potential to constitute prior restraints and to interfere with licensees' editorial judgments. To assist the licensee in making an informed judgment, however, the letter stated that the Commission has stressed that the context of a broadcast is critical in assessing decency, and that isolated use of an offensive word would not be considered to be indecent. Having learned of the source of the excerpt, the Bureau also evidenced some irritation with Pacifica's apparent effort to "trap" it into declaring a classic literary work to be indecent.

3.   In a concurring opinion in the *Infinity* case, Commissioner Dennis suggested that the Commission should establish a "safe harbor" at the end of the prime time programming period on Sunday–Thursday nights. Dennis noted that teenage (12–17) radio listenership radio peaks at 10:00 p.m., declines significantly from 10:00–11:00 p.m., and drops to 66% of the 10:00 p.m. level during the following hour. Nielsen data showed that just 5–6% of teenagers' television viewing occurred between 11:00 p.m. and 1:00 a.m. For children between 2 and 11, this figure was just 2%. Because "both children and adults may well stay up later on" Friday and Saturday nights, she concurred with the midnight prohibition for those nights. Do you agree with

her approach? How limited must the non-adult audience be in a particular time slot to support a "channeling" requirement? The Commission's decision to impose an effective prohibition on "indecent" broadcasts before midnight was the focus of the court of appeals' criticism in reviewing the Commission's 1987 indecency rulings. Action for Children's Television v. FCC, 852 F.2d 1332 (D.C.Cir.1988).

The court generally upheld the Commission's approach to and definition of "indecency." Noting that the concept was inherently vague, the court held that it nevertheless made sense in the context of a particular goal: namely, "to permit the channeling of indecent material, in order to shelter children from exposure to words and phrases their parents regard as inappropriate for them to hear." But the court had somewhat more difficulty with the Commission's restrictions on appropriate times for broadcast of indecent material—the "safe harbour." It noted:

* * *

We agree that, in view of the curtailment of broadcaster freedom and adult listener choice that channeling entails, the Commission failed to consider fairly and fully what time lines should be drawn. We therefore vacate, in the *Pacifica Foundation* [KPFK] and *Regents of U.C.* [KCSB] cases, the FCC's ruling that the broadcast under review was actionable, and we remand those cases to the agency for thoroughgoing reconsideration of the times at which indecent material may be aired.

We are impelled by the Supreme Court's *Pacifica* decision, however, to affirm the declaratory ruling in *Infinity* ["The Howard Stern Show"]. The FCC in that case held actionable portions of a talk show that airs 6:00–10:00 a.m. Monday through Friday. In *Pacifica,* the Court affirmed a similar declaratory order regarding material broadcast 2:00 p.m. on a Tuesday. No principle has been suggested to us under which we might rationally command different treatment of the *Infinity* early morning program and the *Pacifica* early afternoon broadcast, viewing those broadcasts in the context of the parent-child concerns underpinning the FCC's indecent speech regulation. Having upheld the Commission's standard for "indecent material," we conclude that the FCC's adjudication in *Infinity* must remain in place just as the Supreme Court ordered with respect to the Commission's adjudication in *Pacifica.* The FCC itself, however, would be acting with utmost fidelity to the First Amendment were it to reexamine, and invite comment on, its daytime, as well as evening, channeling prescriptions. * * *

Each of the April 29, 1987 rulings reported an FCC finding that the broadcast occurred at a time of day when there was a reasonable risk that children may have been in the audience. In *Pacifica Foundation,* involving a 10:00–11:00 p.m. broadcast, the Commission relied on ratings data indicating that "approximately 112,200 children aged 12–17 are in the Los Angeles metro survey area radio audience per average quarter hour between 7 p.m. and midnight on Sunday night." 2 FCC Rcd at 2699.

* * *

More troubling, the FCC ventures no explanation why it takes teens aged 12–17 to be the relevant age group for channeling purposes. In the Commission's 1976 legislative proposal, cited to the Supreme Court in the FCC's *Pacifica* brief, the Commission would have required broadcasters to minimize the risk of exposing to indecent material children *under* age 12. The FCC reasoned: "Age 12 was selected since it is the accepted upper limit for children's programming in the industry and at the Commission. The Commission considered using the generally recognized age of majority—18—but concluded that it would be virtually impossible for a broadcaster to minimize the risk of exposure to 18–year-olds." 122 Cong. Rec. at 33,367 n. 119. The FCC further referred to the distinction between obscene and merely indecent material in observing that "a reduced age seemed in order." *Id.* We cannot tell from the record before us whether the Commission is now spreading the focus of its concern to children over 12. * * * If it is thus widening its sights, that apparent change in policy warrants explanation. If, on the other hand, the FCC continues to consider children under 12 as the age group of concern, it should either supply information on the listening habits of children in that age range, or explain how it extrapolates relevant data for that population from the available ratings information.

Furthermore, we note that in the Los Angeles case there is no basis for comparison between the number of teens estimated to be in the radio audience and the total number of teens in the listening area. In Santa Barbara, for which comparative data are available, the figure attracting the FCC's concern amounts to, at most 4.3 percent of the age group population. The Commission published no reason why it determined that the potential exposure of four percent of all children amounts to a "reasonable risk" for channeling purposes.

We do not, however, remand solely for reconsideration of the individual rulings. * * * [On reconsideration,] the FCC [suggested the "after midnight" safe harbor] * * *.

* * * We agree that the FCC's midnight advice, indeed its entire position on channeling, was not adequately thought through.

————

Postscript: In October 1988, shortly after the court's decision, Congress enacted an appropriations rider requiring the Commission to adopt rules to prohibit broadcast indecency 24 hours a day "in accordance with section 1464." Pub.L. No. 100–459, § 608, 102 Stat. 2186, 2228 (1988). In December 1988, the Commission, without notice or comment by interested parties, adopted a rule banning indecent broadcasts entirely. Enforcement of Prohibitions Against Broadcast Obscenity and Indecency, 18 U.S.C. § 1464, 4 FCC Rcd 457 (1988).

The congressional requirement and the FCC rule were promptly challenged, and enforcement of the rule was stayed pending resolution of the case. This led to other challenges to the Commission's indecency rules, culminating the *"ACT III"* case, in which the District of Columbia

Circuit Court of Appeal in banc granted substantial discretion to the Commission in channelling indecent programming.

ACTION FOR CHILDREN'S TELEVISION v. FCC

United States Court of Appeals, District of Columbia Circuit, 1995.
58 F.3d 654

D.H. GINSBURG, CIRCUIT JUDGE

Various broadcasters and public-interest groups representing listeners and viewers appeal a judgment of the district court dismissing their constitutional and statutory challenges to the Federal Communication Commission's scheme for imposing forfeitures for the broadcast of indecent material. The appellants' central argument is that the procedures for enforcement set out in 47 U.S.C. §§ 503(b) and 504(c) lack appropriate safeguards—including prompt judicial review—which forces broadcasters to conform with potentially unconstitutional restrictions upon their speech. We hold that the provisions at issue are capable of constitutional implementation and therefore reject the appellants' facial challenge to the statutes. Though we agree that the FCC's implementation of its enforcement scheme is potentially troubling in some respects, we also conclude that the appellants have not alleged facts sufficient to show that the FCC is currently applying the statutes in an unconstitutional manner. We therefore affirm the judgment of the district court.

I. BACKGROUND

Section 1464 of 18 U.S.C. provides: "Whoever utters any obscene, indecent, or profane language by means of radio communication shall be fined not more than $10,000 or imprisoned not more than two years, or both." In addition, the FCC may impose a civil forfeiture for each violation of the same statute. * * *

* * * While other cases have examined the substantive limits of the Government's ability to regulate broadcast indecency, * * *, the questions we address today concern only the procedures by which it does so.

A. The Enforcement Scheme

Section 503(b) of the Communications Act of 1934 authorizes the Commission to impose a forfeiture for the violation of a Commission order or regulation. * * *

* * * [I]n practice the exclusive means of imposing a forfeiture for the broadcast of indecent material is for the Commission to issue a "notice of apparent liability" to the broadcaster, setting forth the relevant facts and granting the potentially liable party "an opportunity to show, in writing, ... why no such forfeiture penalty should be imposed." 47 U.S.C. § 503(b)(4). The Commission initiates the forfeiture process only after receiving a complaint from a listener or viewer. The agency staff reviews each complaint to determine whether it suggests that there has been a violation of the ban on indecent broadcasting. In the course of this review, the staff may send the broadcaster a Letter of

Inquiry seeking more information or inviting the broadcaster to respond to the complaint. After further consideration, the Commission decides whether to issue a Notice of Apparent Liability (NAL). The stipulated facts in this case concerning the indecency cases pending when the complaint was filed in district court show that the Commission issues a NAL anywhere from six months to three years after the broadcast to which it relates. During that time, the broadcaster may or may not be aware that the agency is considering whether the broadcast at issue contained indecent material.

The NAL is both sent to the broadcaster and published in the FCC Record. The NAL advises the broadcaster of its "apparent liability for a forfeiture" in a stated amount for an "apparent violation of 18 U.S.C. § 1464," and gives the broadcaster 30 days to pay or otherwise to respond. * * * Once the broadcaster has responded or the 30 days have run, the Commission decides whether to order the forfeiture. As far as we can discern from the current record, the FCC has never failed to impose a forfeiture after issuing a NAL.

* * * In the seven instances in which the Commission imposed a forfeiture between January 1987 and March 1993, it took from two to 23 months—and an average of approximately nine months—for the FCC to make its decision.

* * * As with any Commission order, the broadcaster may petition for reconsideration, * * * but it may not obtain judicial review at that stage. * * * If the order becomes final and the broadcaster does not pay the forfeiture, the Commission issues progressively stiffer dunning letters, and threatens to refer and after 165 days does indeed refer the matter to the Department of Justice "for commencement of [a] civil action ... to recover the forfeiture," * * *. In defending that suit the broadcaster is entitled to a trial de novo on the question whether its broadcast was indecent. * * *

* * *[A]s far as we can discern, no broadcaster has yet gone to trial on the merits of an FCC indecency determination, as envisioned by the statute; every one has either paid the forfeiture imposed or is awaiting action by the Commission or the Department of Justice.

Although the issue has never been litigated, we assume that the general five-year period of limitations on forfeiture proceedings, * * * would effectively prevent the Government from filing a civil action more than five years after the indecent material was aired. Once an action is timely filed, however, there is no law limiting the amount of time that may pass before the case is actually tried. In an extreme case, therefore, a broadcaster could wait as long as six or seven years from the time a program was aired until its first opportunity for judicial review of the Commission's decision that the material was indecent.

By all indications, a long wait promises to be the rule rather than the exception. * * *

This delay is unfortunate enough, but a number of other factors serve to exacerbate the effects of uncertainty about the outcome. First, a broadcaster claiming that a forfeiture is unconstitutional runs the risk of incurring an increased forfeiture for any subsequent indecency violation, * * *, and the possibility that the Commission will invoke the ultimate sanction, revocation of the broadcaster's license. * * * Second, individual Commissioners have taken an active public role in criticizing broadcasters for airing indecent material and have let it be known that sanctions for such activity are likely to increase. Furthermore, the Commission will not, as a matter of policy, issue a declaratory ruling on whether a proposed broadcast is indecent. Thus, the only official guidance about the Commission's standards of decency available to a broadcaster is what can be gleaned from published NALs and forfeiture orders.

Against this background, the parties to this case have stipulated that:

At a hearing, plaintiff broadcasters would testify that because of the delays of securing administrative and judicial determinations in indecency forfeiture proceedings, and uncertainties as to the permissible scope of FCC indecency regulation, they attempt to conform their conduct to the indecency standards articulated by the FCC and its Commissioners, whether or not they believe those standards are constitutional, especially because of the various sanctions to which broadcasters are potentially subject.

The FCC does not concede that this testimony would be credible, but in light of the district court's grant of summary judgment to the Commission we must accept the appellants' version of the facts.

B. The Appellants' Claims

The appellants * * * claim that the delay allows the FCC to take action against them without affording them the procedural safeguards necessary to avoid any abridgment of their First Amendment rights.

The appellants * * * claim that by forcing broadcasters to comply with the Commission's unreviewed determinations of indecency the scheme operates as a system of "informal censorship" similar to the one held unconstitutional in *Bantam Books, Inc. v. Sullivan*, 372 U.S. 58, 9 L. Ed. 2d 584, 83 S. Ct. 631 (1963). * * *

II. JURISDICTION

[The jurisdictional discussion is omitted.]

III. THE MERITS

* * *

A. The Facial Challenge

* * * Certainly nothing in the statutes or regulations prevents the Commission from issuing a NAL, imposing a forfeiture, and if need be

referring a case to the Department of Justice all within a period of time short enough virtually to eliminate any concern with delay. The whole course could probably be run in most cases within, say, 90 days. No case of this type is very complex; each turns simply upon whether a certain broadcast was indecent. Indeed, under the Commission's own internal guidelines, after a broadcaster has had 30 days to respond to the NAL, the target for imposing a forfeiture is only 60 more days. If the FCC met this goal and then allowed the broadcaster to stipulate that it will not pay unless ordered by a district court to do so, then judicial review could begin almost immediately. * * * In practice, no case has moved through the pipeline that quickly, but we are aware of no reason why the Commission could not, in principle, act with such dispatch. Reducing delay would also cabin the Commission's opportunity to rely upon its own unreviewed forfeiture decisions in setting standards of decency, thereby reducing the tendency for one unconstitutional decision to beget others.

[Accordingly, the court concluded, the statute is not unconstitutional on its face.] * * *

B.   The Challenge to the Statutes as Applied

The more difficult question is whether the statutes as applied pass muster under the teaching *of Bantam Books* * * *. We agree with the appellants that some of the Commission's procedures are troubling but, on the basis of the record before us, we cannot agree that those procedures violate the First Amendment. The centerpiece of the appellants' grievance is that:

Because of the delays of securing administrative and judicial determinations in indecency forfeiture proceedings, and uncertainties as to the permissible scope of FCC indecency regulation they attempt to conform their conduct to the indecency standards articulated by the FCC and its Commissioners, whether or not they believe those standards are constitutional.

That simply does not establish a violation of the Constitution.

In *Bantam Books*, Rhode Island had established a Commission to Encourage Morality in Youth and authorized it to determine whether publications were "objectionable for sale, distribution or display to youths." * * * Upon an affirmative finding, the Morality Commission would send a letter urging the distributor of the offending material not to carry the publication, and would refer the matter to the local police for investigation and possible prosecution under the state obscenity law. * * * The Supreme Court struck down this scheme because it "amounts to . . . governmental censorship devoid of the constitutionally required safeguards for state regulation of obscenity, and thus abridges First Amendment liberties." * * *

The lesson of *Bantam Books* is that the state may not move to suppress speech by means of a scheme that, as a practical matter, forecloses the speaker from obtaining a judicial determination of whether the targeted speech is unprotected, lest the state be able effectively to suppress protected speech. In that case it was established, as a matter of fact, that a notice from the Commission would cause the distributor to cease selling the listed publications without a judicial determination of whether the material was legally subject to proscription. * * *

The appellants argue that the FCC has similarly implemented a system of "prior administrative restraint" that, for want of appropriate procedural safeguards, forces protected and unprotected material alike off the air. * * * [H]owever, the Commission is not administering anything akin to a literal prior restraint. Broadcasters are free to air what they want; if and only if what they air turns out to transgress established guidelines do they face a penalty—but that is very much after the fact, not prior thereto. * * *

As the Court recognized in *Bantam Books*, however, a scheme may also be a prior restraint in effect even though specific materials are not evaluated prior to publication (or here broadcast) if that scheme in practice causes a speaker of reasonable fortitude to censor itself in order to conform with an unconstitutional standard. This case therefore turns upon the question whether the regime that leads broadcasters to "attempt to conform their conduct to [FCC] indecency standards" is analogous to the scheme that forced booksellers in Rhode Island to drop publications officially declared "objectionable" for fear of a possible prosecution for selling obscene materials.

We cannot help but conclude that the appellants have failed to establish any essential similarity between this case and *Bantam Books*. Unlike the Rhode Island Commission, which sought to regulate materials that could not be proscribed as obscene, * * * so far as this record shows the FCC is not enforcing the statutory ban on indecency against material that is not indecent. Again unlike the Rhode Island Commission, which could and did avoid judicial oversight because the mere threat of prosecution coerced booksellers into complying with its recommendations, * * *, we have no indication that the FCC has done anything actively to discourage judicial review of any indecency forfeiture it imposed. That no case has yet progressed to judicial review may be the effect of any of several inoffensive causes: the Commission has only recently stepped up its enforcement efforts; the violators penalized thus far may very well have broadcast the indecency as charged and thus seen no point in contesting the forfeiture in court; and broadcasters may be self-censoring only indecent material, eliminating the need for many prosecutions. Indeed, some degree of self-censorship is inevitable and not necessarily undesirable so long as proper standards are available. * * *

Finally, there is no indication that the FCC—unlike Rhode Island's free-roving Commission to Encourage Morality in Youth, * * *—has failed or will fail to follow judicial guidelines for determining what is indecent and what is not, as they have developed and will develop in judicial decisions. The suggestion that every determination of indecency must be a judicial one simply proves too much; the Commission could then play no role in developing or enforcing the Congress's declared policy of banning indecency from the airwaves during certain hours of the day. We have no indication that the Commission is developing a body of precedent in any way at odds with the First Amendment, or that the agency would continue to do so in the face of a corrective court decision. While the prospect of a forfeiture trial may understandably cause some broadcasters to forego judicial review of a Commission determination that a program was indecent, we find no indication in this record that the FCC is taking the opportunity afforded thereby to impose unconstitutional restrictions upon broadcast speech.

Under the statute as administered, a broadcaster need do nothing at all until it is served with a complaint, at which point it is entitled to a trial de novo in district court. Nothing but the timing would be different if the Congress were to change the current scheme so as to allow the Commission to bring a forfeiture action in district court immediately after the airing of an allegedly indecent broadcast, which would be unquestionably constitutional. The distinction, i.e., the delay inherent in the current scheme, is of constitutional significance only if it burdens broadcast speech that is not indecent. The parties have stipulated that some speech is being burdened in that broadcasters "conform their conduct to the indecency standards articulated by the FCC ... whether or not they believe those standards are unconstitutional." The broadcasters would go one step farther and argue that the delay thereby chills protected as well as indecent speech; however, they have failed to make any such showing.

Alternatively, the broadcasters' claim might be more compelling if in a particular case the Commission increased the fine for a subsequent violation or decided not to renew a license when the broadcaster had neither acquiesced in the former determination of indecency nor yet had its day in court. Such a situation creates a greater risk that material that is not indecent is being kept off the air. Even that, however, would still be the stuff upon which an individual, not a generic, challenge to enforcement would be built. * * *

IV. CONCLUSION

Although the appellants have failed to show that the Commission's administration of the statute is unconstitutional, we cannot fail to acknowledge that the agency's practices could give rise to some of the evils that the appellants claim are already at hand. Two avenues of relief are available, however, to any broadcaster that in fact comes to the grief alleged in this case. First, the broadcaster could stipulate the facts giving rise to the Notice of Apparent Liability and state that it will not pay the forfeiture unless ordered to do so in district court; the Commission could then forward the matter to the Department of Justice immediately, so that the broadcaster could get a trial on the merits of the forfeiture relatively quickly.

Alternatively, if the Commission will not cooperate in order to expedite judicial review as outlined above, then * * * a broadcaster "suffering from demonstrably adverse consequences from government delay in initiating the collection proceeding . . . could bring a declaratory judgment action against the United States in the district court." * * *

For the reasons stated in Parts II and III above, the judgment of the district court is Affirmed.

[The Concurring Opinion of CHIEF JUDGE EDWARDS and the Dissenting Opinion of JUDGE TATEL are omitted.]

Notes and Questions

1.   (a) What do you understand the potential constitutional infirmity of the forfeiture process to be? The substance of the FCC's decisions? The length of time required before an FCC decision is reviewed by a court? Both?

For general history see, *Case Comment, Constitutional Law—Freedom of Speech—D.C. Circuit Upholds Daytime Ban on Broadcast Indecency—Action for Children's Television v FCC*, 109 Harv.L.Rev. 864 (1996).

Although the *in banc* reconsideration and reversal of the panel decision was a companion case to *Denver Area* (p. 404), the Supreme Court declined to review it. What does this tell you about the Court's interest in "new" media vs. traditional pornography problems?

In *Action for Children's Television v. FCC*, the Court of Appeals for the D.C. Circuit revisited the issue of broadcast indecency. The court held that a statutory ban on daytime broadcasting of indecent material did not violate the First Amendment. In so holding, the court failed to require Congress to tailor its regulations narrowly enough to account for the constitutional rights of adults. By misapplying the relevant constitutional mandates, the court undervalued free expression and underestimated the impact of new technologies.

Congress had responded to previous court rulings on broadcast indecency by passing the Public Telecommunications Act of 1992. Section 16(a) of the Act required the FCC to prohibit indecent broadcasting during most hours of the day. A range of broadcasters and other interested parties petitioned for judicial review of the FCC regulations promulgated to implement this ban. The petitioners argued that the provisions were insufficiently limited to accommodate First Amendment concerns, that they unconstitutionally discriminated between commercial and public broadcasters, and that the FCC's definition of indecency was overly vague.

In a divided *in banc* decision, the D.C. Circuit rejected the First Amendment challenge. Although the court noted that Pacifica's strict scrutiny analysis for broadcast media was of more deferential character than review for other forms of media, it acknowledged that indecent speech restrictions are acceptable only if they meet the standard strict scrutiny analysis, which requires that the ends of the statute be compelling and its means carefully tailored to accomplish those ends. The court characterized at least two of the government's interests as compelling: assisting parents' supervision of their children's exposure to broadcasting and protecting children's psychological health. It reasoned that both goals were compelling because parents in modern society cannot adequately screen all broadcast programming that their children might see or hear, and because it is not obvious that indecent programming is harmless to children.

Turning to the means used to accomplish these governmental ends, the court established that, under Supreme Court precedent, constitutionally protected speech may only be regulated by the 'least restrictive means' necessary to accomplish a compelling interest. The court reasoned that because far fewer children watch television and listen to the radio between the hours of midnight and 6 a.m. than during the day, and because many adults do so late at night, the statutory 'safe harbor' during those hours was well-tailored to accommodate the interest of both those wishing to view indecent materials and parents hoping to protect their children. Because the court found that the restriction did not disturb the rights of adults unnecessarily, it held that a daytime ban on broadcast indecency was constitutional.

(b) Can you quibble with the point that authorizing the FCC to impose monetary forfeitures and other penalties on broadcasters that transmit indecent programming is constitutionally permissible? Should a court, rather than an agency, be the only entity permitted to impose a penalty for speech? Even where the involved agency is delegated with broad authority to regulate the conduct of the speakers?

(c) Does the forfeiture process amount to censorship? Consider the "prior restraint" argument that is noted by Judge Ginsburg in light of the decisions in *Near* and *Trinity Methodist Church*. Does the regulatory scheme become like a prior restraint, or does a prior restraint—for purposes of First Amendment jurisprudence—exist only where the government directly bans particular speech in advance? In other words, if a regulatory scheme is difficult to understand and abide by, and if the penalties for violating the scheme are potentially great (e.g., license revocation), is that regulatory scheme different from a prior restraint in a way that has—or should have—constitutional significance?

2.   (a) What do you make of Judge Ginsburg's observation that the FCC had not used a prior ruling on indecent programming, which has not been subjected to judicial review, to support a severe penalty such as license revocation? Is it relevant to the analysis in this case that many broadcasters (particularly Infinity Broadcasting, which has been fined more than any other for broadcasting indecent programming) did not pay their forfeitures, and do not intend to do so absent a court enforcement order upholding the FCC's ruling and directing payment?

(b) What if the FCC used a broadcaster's past violations of the indecent programming rules as a basis for delaying approval of that broadcaster's subsequent application for permission to acquire an additional broadcast station—on the theory that a broadcaster that transmits indecent programming should not have additional outlets to disseminate such programming? Does it matter if the application ultimately is approved? Even if the delay costs the broadcaster millions of dollars? Suppose the basis for such delay is not stated by the Commission, but is only alluded to in private remarks of certain commissioners?

How easy is it for the FCC to persuade the Department of Justice or a local U.S. attorney to bring actions for collecting forfeitures? Do these offices have more pressing agendas—ranging from drug prosecutions to antitrust cases?

3. How would you analyze the situation if Congress required that if any party appealed an FCC decision finding a program to be indecent, the court was required to decide the case within 120 days? Would this change the analysis of the dissenting opinion? Would broadcasters prefer such a scheme, understanding that it could result in fines having to be paid quickly? Do you think broadcasters may be more interested in preserving the status quo, where the FCC's indecency rulings have not really been enforced, to date. Would such an approach be constitutional under notions about separation of powers?

F. DIFFERENTIAL TREATMENT OF SUBSCRIBER–CONTROLLED MEDIA

1. TELEPHONY

As seen above, the major complaint about indecent material is that children cannot avoid it, and parents cannot prevent their children from viewing it. Presumably, therefore, if a parent had complete control over the programming which a child could view, there would be little or no concern for indecent or other content. As indicated below, some cases give support for this proposition; but even the best technological fixes, e.g., the "V–Chip"—(p. 562) have not fully satisfied many persons' desire to ban programming outright.

The effect of parental content control traditionally has come up in two main contexts—carriage of material by common carriers and by cable television systems. The cases below seem to give some answers to the question of control; as seen before in the *Denver* litigation, however, they apparently do not satisfy a general urge to censor.

SABLE COMMUNICATIONS OF CALIFORNIA v. FCC

Supreme Court of the United States, 1989.
492 U.S. 115, 109 S.Ct. 2829, 106 L.Ed.2d 93.

JUSTICE WHITE delivered the opinion of the Court.

The issue before us is the constitutionality of § 223(b) of the Communications Act of 1934. 47 U.S.C. § 223(b). The statute, as amended in 1988, imposes an outright ban on indecent as well as obscene interstate commercial telephone messages. * * *

I

In 1983, Sable Communications, Inc., a Los Angeles-based affiliate of Carlin Communications, Inc., began offering sexually-oriented pre-recorded telephone messages[32] (popularly known as "dial-a-porn") through the Pacific Bell telephone network. * * *

32. A typical prerecorded message lasts anywhere from 30 seconds to two minutes and may be called by up to 50,000 people hourly through a single telephone number.

In 1988, Sable brought suit in District Court seeking declaratory and injunctive relief against enforcement of the recently amended § 223(b). * * * Sable also sought a declaratory judgment, challenging the indecency and the obscenity provisions of the amended § 223(b) as unconstitutional, chiefly under the First and Fourteenth Amendments to the Constitution.

* * * The District Court * * * struck down the "indecent speech" provision of § 223(b), holding that in this respect the statute was overbroad and unconstitutional and that this result was consistent with *FCC v. Pacifica Foundation,* 438 U.S. 726 (1978). * * *

II

While dial-a-porn services are a creature of this decade, the medium, in its brief history, has been the subject of much litigation and the object of a series of attempts at regulation.[33] The first litigation involving dial-a-porn was brought under 82 Stat. 112, 47 U.S.C. § 223 which proscribed knowingly "permitting a telephone under [one's] control" to be used to make "any comment, request, suggestion or proposal which is obscene, lewd, lascivious, filthy, or indecent." However, the FCC concluded in an administrative action that the existing law did not cover dial-a-porn. In re Application for Review of Complaint Filed by Peter F. Cohalan, FCC File No. E–83–14 (memorandum opinions and orders adopted May 13, 1983).

In reaction to that FCC determination, Congress made its first effort explicitly to address "dial-a-porn" when it added a subsection 223(b) to the 1934 Communications Act. The provision, which was the predecessor to the amendment at issue in this case, pertained directly to sexually-oriented commercial telephone messages, and sought to restrict the access of minors to dial-a-porn. The relevant provision of the Act, Federal Communications Commission Authorization Act of 1983, Pub.L. 98–214, § 8(b), 97 Stat. 1470, made it a crime to use telephone facilities to make "obscene or indecent" interstate telephone communications "for commercial purposes to any person under eighteen years of age or to any other person without that person's consent." 47 U.S.C. § 223(b)(1)(A) (1982 ed., Supp. II). The statute criminalized commercial transmission of sexually oriented communications to minors and required the FCC to promulgate regulations laying out the means by which dial-a-porn sponsors could screen out underaged callers. § 223(b)(2). The enactment provided that it would be a defense to prosecution that the defendant restricted access to adults only, in accordance with procedures established by the FCC. The statute did not criminalize sexually-oriented messages to adults, whether the messages were obscene or indecent.

Comment, *Telephones, Sex, and the First Amendment,* 33 UCLA L.Rev. 1221, 1223 (1986).

33. Dial-a-porn is big business. The dial-a-porn service in New York City alone re-ceived six to seven million calls a month for the six-month period ending in April of 1985. *Carlin Communications, Inc. v. FCC,* 787 F.2d 846, 848 (C.A.2, 1986).

The FCC initially promulgated regulations that would have established a defense to message providers operating only between the hours of 9:00 p.m. and 8:00 a.m. Eastern Time ("time channeling") and to providers requiring payment by credit card ("screening") before transmission of the dial-a-porn message. Restrictions on Obscene or Indecent Telephone Message Services, 47 CFR § 64.201 (1988). In *Carlin Communications, Inc. v. FCC,* 749 F.2d 113 (C.A.2, 1984) (*Carlin I*), the Court of Appeals for the Second Circuit set aside the time channeling regulations and remanded to the FCC to examine other alternatives, concluding that the operating hours requirement was "both overinclusive and underinclusive" because it denied "access to adults between certain hours, but not to youths who can easily pick up a private or public telephone and call dial-a-porn during the remaining hours." *Id.,* at 121. The Court of Appeals did not reach the constitutionality of the underlying legislation.

In 1985, the FCC promulgated new regulations which continued to permit credit card payment as a defense to prosecution. Instead of time restrictions, however, the Commission added a defense based on use of access codes (user identification codes). Thus, it would be a defense to prosecution under § 223(b) if the defendant, before transmission of the message, restricted customer access by requiring either payment by credit card or authorization by access or identification code. 50 Fed.Reg. 42699, 42705 (1985). The regulations required each dial-a-porn vendor to develop an identification code database and implementation scheme. Callers would be required to provide an access number for identification (or a credit card) before receiving the message. The access code would be received through the mail after the message provider reviewed the application and concluded through a written age ascertainment procedure that the applicant was at least eighteen years of age. The FCC rejected a proposal for "exchange blocking" which would block or screen telephone numbers at the customer's premises or at the telephone company offices. In *Carlin Communications, Inc. v. FCC,* 787 F.2d 846 (C.A.2 1986) (*Carlin II*), the Court of Appeals set aside the new regulations because of the FCC's failure adequately to consider customer premises blocking. Again, the constitutionality of the underlying legislation was not addressed.

The FCC then promulgated a third set of regulations, which again rejected customer-premises blocking but added to the prior defenses of credit card payment and access code use a third defense: message scrambling. 52 Fed.Reg. 17760 (1987). Under this system, providers would scramble the message, which would then be unintelligible without the use of a descrambler, the sale of which would be limited to adults. On January 15, 1988, in *Carlin Communications, Inc. v. FCC,* 837 F.2d 546 (*Carlin III*), cert. denied, 488 U.S. 924 (1988), the Court of Appeals for the Second Circuit held that the new regulations, which made access codes, along with credit card payments and scrambled messages, defenses to prosecution under § 223(b) for dial-a-porn providers, were supported by the evidence, had been properly arrived at, and were a "feasible and effective way to serve" the "compelling state interest" in protecting minors, 837 F.2d, at 555; but the Court directed the FCC to reopen proceedings if a less restrictive technology became available. The Court of Appeals, however, this time reaching the constitutionality of the statute, invalidated § 223(b) insofar as it sought to apply to nonobscene speech. * * *

Thereafter, in April 1988, Congress amended § 223(b) of the Communications Act to prohibit indecent as well as obscene interstate commercial telephone communications directed to any person regardless of age. The amended statute, which took effect on July 1, 1988, also eliminated the requirement that the FCC promulgate regulations for restricting access to minors since a total ban was imposed on dial-a-porn, making it illegal for adults, as well as children, to have access to the sexually explicit messages, Pub.L. 100–297, 102 Stat. 424. It was this version of the statute that was in effect when Sable commenced this action.[33]

III

* * * [T]he District Court upheld § 223(b)'s prohibition of obscene telephone messages as constitutional. We agree with that judgment. * * *

In its facial challenge to the statute, Sable argues that the legislation creates an impermissible national standard of obscenity, and that it places message senders in a "double bind" by compelling them to tailor all their messages to the least tolerant community. * * *

IV

* * * [T]he District Court concluded that while the government has a legitimate interest in protecting children from exposure to indecent dial-a-porn messages, § 223(b) was not sufficiently narrowly drawn to serve that purpose and thus violated the First Amendment. We agree.

Sexual expression which is indecent but not obscene is protected by the First Amendment; and the government does not submit that the sale of such materials to adults could be criminalized solely because they are

---

33. After Sable and the FCC filed their jurisdictional statements with this Court, but before we noted probable jurisdiction, § 223(b) was again revised by Congress in § 7524 of the Child Protection and Obscenity Enforcement Act of 1988 * * *.

Section 223(b) states in pertinent part:

"(b)(1) Whoever knowingly—

(A) in the District of Columbia or in interstate or foreign communication, by means of telephone, makes (directly or by recording device) any obscene communication for commercial purposes to any person, regardless of whether the maker of such communication placed the call; or

(B) permits any telephone facility under such person's control to be used for an activity prohibited by clause (i), shall

be fined in accordance with title 18 of the United States Code, or imprisoned not more than two years, or both.

(2) Whoever knowingly—

(A) in the District of Columbia or in interstate or foreign communication, by means of telephone, makes (directly or by recording device) any indecent communication for commercial purposes to any person, regardless of whether the maker of such communication placed the call; or

(B) permits any telephone facility under such person's control to be used for an activity prohibited by clause (i), shall be fined not more than $50,000 or imprisoned not more than six months, or both." * * *

indecent. The government may, however, regulate the content of constitutionally protected speech in order to promote a compelling interest if it chooses the least restrictive means to further the articulated interest. We have recognized that there is a compelling interest in protecting the physical and psychological well-being of minors. This interest extends to shielding minors from the influence of literature that is not obscene by adult standards. * * * The government may serve this legitimate interest, but to withstand constitutional scrutiny, "it must do so by narrowly drawn regulations designed to serve those interests without unnecessarily interfering with First Amendment freedoms." *Schaumburg v. Citizens for a Better Environment,* 444 U.S. 620, 637 (1980). It is not enough to show that the government's ends are compelling; the means must be carefully tailored to achieve those ends.

* * *

In attempting to justify the complete ban and criminalization of the indecent commercial telephone communications with adults as well as minors, the government relies on *FCC v. Pacifica Foundation,* 438 U.S. 726 (1978) * * *. In an emphatically narrow holding, the *Pacifica* Court concluded that special treatment of indecent broadcasting was justified.

Pacifica is readily distinguishable from this case, most obviously because it did not involve a total ban on broadcasting indecent material. * * *

The *Pacifica* opinion also relied on the "unique" attributes of broadcasting * * *. The private commercial telephone communications at issue here are substantially different from the public radio broadcast at issue in *Pacifica.* In contrast to public displays, unsolicited mailings and other means of expression which the recipient has no meaningful opportunity to avoid, the dial-it medium requires the listener to take affirmative steps to receive the communication. There is no "captive audience" problem here; callers will generally not be unwilling listeners. * * *

The Government nevertheless argues that the total ban on indecent commercial telephone communications is justified because nothing less could prevent children from gaining access to such messages. We find the argument quite unpersuasive. The FCC, after lengthy proceedings, determined that its credit card, access code, and scrambling rules were a satisfactory solution to the problem of keeping indecent dial-a-porn messages out of the reach of minors. The Court of Appeals, after careful consideration, agreed that these rules represented a "feasible and effective" way to serve the Government's compelling interest in protecting children. * * *

The Government now insists that the rules would not be effective enough—that enterprising youngsters could and would evade the rules and gain access to communications from which they should be shielded. There is no evidence in the record before us to that effect, nor could there be since the FCC's implementation of § 223(b) prior to its 1988 amendment has never been tested over time. In this respect, the Government asserts that in amending § 223(b) in 1988, Congress expressed its view that there was not a sufficiently effective way to protect minors short of the total ban that it enacted. The Government claims that we must give deference to that judgment.

* * *

* * * It may well be that there is no fail-safe method of guaranteeing that never will a minor be able to access the dial-a-porn system. * * * No Congressman or Senator purported to present a considered judgment with respect to how often or to what extent minors could or would circumvent the rules and have access to dial-a-porn messages. On the other hand, [in hearings] the committee heard testimony from the FCC and other witnesses that the FCC rules would be effective and should be tried out in practice. Furthermore, at the conclusion of the hearing, the chairman of the subcommittee suggested consultation looking toward "drafting a piece of legislation that will pass constitutional muster, while at the same time providing for the practical relief which families and groups are looking for." * * * The bill never emerged from Committee.

For all we know from this record, the FCC's technological approach to restricting dial-a-porn messages to adults who seek them would be extremely effective, and only a few of the most enterprising and disobedient young people will manage to secure access to such messages. If this is the case, it seems to us that § 223(b) is not a narrowly tailored effort to serve the compelling interest of preventing minors from being exposed to indecent telephone messages. * * *

Accordingly, we affirm the judgments of the District Court * * *.

JUSTICE SCALIA, concurring.

* * *

In joining Part IV, I do so with the understanding that its examination of the legislative history * * * is merely meant to establish that no more there than anywhere else can data be found demonstrating the infeasibility of alternate means to provide (given the nature of this material) adequate protection of minors. * * *

[JUSTICE BRENNAN, joined by JUSTICE MARSHALL, dissenting in part, would have struck down the statute in its entirety. In his view, even the prohibition on obscene telephonic messages was unconstitutional. He found no evidence that less restrictive alternatives, such as those proposed by the FCC's rules, would not have served the government's interest in protecting children from harm.]

Notes and Questions

1.   The Court rejects the notion that Congress deserves deference in making judgments about the constitutionality of particular types of speech. Do you agree with Justice Scalia's reading of the Court's opinion, in which

he suggests that the absence of justifying data may well be the fatal flaw in Congress' decision to ban indecent phone services? Do you think the Court would defer to Congress if it were to compile extensive data showing that minors were readily able to circumvent blocking and screening mechanisms? Where, as Justice Scalia asks, should the line be drawn? That is, how many "clever" minors must be able to get access to dial-a-porn services before a total ban would be justifiable? What constitutional basis is there for making such a judgment?

2.   Do you agree with the Court's apparent conclusion that the technological differences between telephonic and broadcast communications are of constitutional significance? Does the Court's reasoning support greater constitutional tolerance for content regulation of broadcasting because of the medium's uniquely intrusive nature? Do you think that the government should be permitted to play a "parental" role in determining the listening and viewing options of children? Is it more appropriate for the government to take steps simply to "assist" parents in supervising children, such as through the adoption of screening requirements for dial-a-porn or channeling requirements for broadcasting?

3.   In 1989, the FCC acted on 95 broadcast indecency complaints that had accumulated over a two-year period. It issued four notices of apparent liability, to four different radio stations, with penalties ranging from $2,000 to $10,000. It also sent letters to four other stations requesting additional information about complaints. In letters to 51 complainants, the Commission stated that as a result of the *Action for Children's Television* decision, it could not take action against broadcasts aired after 8 p.m. One proceeding against a broadcaster that had aired allegedly indecent material at 8 p.m. was terminated. See Order Vacating Proceeding in the Matter of KZKC(TV), 4 FCC Rcd 6706 (1989). Other complaints were dismissed as lacking sufficient information, as involving material that was not indecent, or as moot. Public Notice, FCC Mimeo No. 348 (released Oct. 26, 1989).

4.   The FCC responded to the decision in *Sable* by asking the court of appeals to stay all proceedings in the case challenging the 24–hour ban on indecent broadcasts until the Commission could compile evidence to support a conclusion that a 24–hour ban was the least restrictive means of protecting children from indecent broadcast material. The court granted the stay. Action for Children's Television v. FCC, 932 F.2d 1504 (D.C.Cir. 1991).

In August 1990, the Commission released a report in which it compiled information provided in more than 90,000 formal and informal filings. According to the Commission, 95% of the comments filed with it supported the 24–hour ban. *Enforcement of Prohibitions Against Broadcast Indecency in 18 U.S.C. § 1464*, 5 FCC Rcd 5297 (1990) (the "*1990 Indecency Report*").

(a) In light of the decisions in *Action for Children's Television* and *Sable* (particularly Justice Scalia's concurring opinion), which, if any, of the following findings set forth in the *1990 Indecency Report* would support the constitutionality of a 24–hour ban on indecent broadcasts?

i.   Nearly 750,000 children (ages 12–17) listen to radio between midnight and 6 a.m.

ii.   Radio listening for children 12–17 after midnight peaks at 12:15 a.m., when almost 1.5 million children are in the audience. It hits a low of 300,000 between 3:45 a.m. and 4:00 a.m., and grows to almost 1.5 million again between 5:45 a.m. and 6:00 a.m.

iii.   On any given day, an average of 3.5 million children listen to radio for at least five minutes between midnight and 6:00 a.m.

iv.   According to a survey by Infinity Broadcasting Corporation, in 99.6% of surveyed households, no children between 6 and 11 years old listen to "The Howard Stern Show." Data from other sources, however, indicate that the New York station that carries the show is the fifth-highest rated station in the market for children ages 12–17 between 7 a.m. and 8 a.m. and more than 10,000 children in that age group are estimated to listen to at least five minutes of the show between 7 a.m. and 8 a.m.

v.   During school hours and between midnight and 6 a.m., approximately 1–4% of the total radio listening audience consists of children between 12 and 17 years old. During these periods, virtually no children listen to public radio stations. The Commission relied on other data that suggest that between midnight and 6 a.m., children between 12 and 17 years of age made up approximately 10% of the average total listening audience.

vi.   There are no reported data for television viewing by age group between 2 a.m. and 6 a.m. Available data indicate, however, that from 6:00 p.m. through 1:45 a.m., the viewing audience consists of approximately equal percentages of children between 12 and 17 and adults. Between 3% (ages 2 to 5) and 8% (ages 12–17) of children's weekly viewing occurs between 11:00 p.m. and 1:00 a.m.

vii.   It is estimated that 4.8% of children ages 12–17 (slightly less than 1 million children) are watching television between 1:45 a.m. and 2:00 a.m.

viii.   Almost 70% of U.S. television households have videocassette recorders, which permit children to record late-night programs for subsequent playback.

ix.   According to a survey of 1,000 homes conducted by broadcasters, 98% of children under 17 are under adult supervision between 8:00 p.m. and 6:00 a.m. Between midnight and 6 a.m., 98% of such children are under parental supervision, and 99% are under adult supervision. Proponents of the 24–hour ban and the FCC noted that the survey measured the presence of an adult, and did not necessarily demonstrate that the adult was supervising television viewing. The FCC also noted that the survey revealed that from 1:00 a.m. through 6:00 a.m., 1.2% of children under 17 are neither with an adult nor asleep.

x.   Parental supervision of broadcast programming is difficult because technology does not currently assist such supervision. Television receivers do not typically permit blocking of specified channels, and channel-blocking devices are not available for radio. Many commenters also advised the FCC that it is not feasible for parents to monitor their children's viewing and listening choices, particularly because of the availability of broadcast programming outside of the home and the access to portable televisions and radios that can be carried around by children.

Based on this evidence, the Commission concluded that a 24–hour ban was constitutional:

> * * * [G]iven the pervasiveness and accessibility of radio and television, unsupervised children in pursuit of entertainment need be neither "enterprising" nor "disobedient" to turn on a television or radio, or to record a program on a VCR, at any time of day or night. Accordingly, we conclude that there exists a reasonable risk that a sufficient number of children are in the broadcast audience at all times to warrant narrowly-tailored government regulation of indecent broadcasting aimed both at facilitating parental supervision and promoting the well-being of youth. Such regulation is particularly necessary since, * * *, a wide range of sexually explicit and patently offensive material may be encompassed within the definition of "indecency."

1990 Indecency Report, 5 FCC Rcd at 5306.

Has the Commission sufficiently addressed the court of appeals' complaint that, in its earlier proceeding, the Commission relied upon population figures that "appear to estimate the number of teens in the *total* radio audience," rather than the number of teens listening to the program or station in question? Does the following statement by the Commission assist its constitutional case?

> 89.   * * * [I]n the future we will consider, on a case-by-case basis, evidence from a station charged with indecent broadcasting that the data concern[ing] children's viewing or listening are not applicable in its specific market. * * * In this regard, stations will not be required to show that children were not in the market audience on the specific date and at the specific time that the allegedly indecent program was aired * * *. Rather, stations will be permitted to demonstrate through ratings data or other probative evidence that children typically are not in the audience on the day and at the time in question. This policy will ensure that enforcement of the broadcast indecency statute will be narrowly tailored * * *. * * *

> 90.   We note that in several prior instances, parties have * * * argue[d] * * * that few or no children were likely to have been listening to their particular station when the alleged indecent language was aired. Listeners and viewers, however, often switch indiscriminately from station to station and, particularly in the case of radio, "tune into a station generally without the benefit of a schedule of programs or warning as to potentially offensive content." * * * Accordingly, to ensure that children are not exposed to indecent programming, we will require a station defending against a broadcast indecency complaint to demonstrate that children in fact are not in the broadcast audience for the entire market, not just the particular station, at the time it aired allegedly indecent material.

Id. at 5309.

(b) The court of appeals also questioned why the Commission selected children between the ages of 12 and 17 as "the relevant age group for channeling purposes." In the *1990 Indecency Report*, the Commission again concluded that children ages 17 and under were the appropriate group to be protected from indecent broadcasts. That conclusion was based on four factors. First, the legislative history of Section 1464 suggests that Congress sought to protect children between 12 and 17, as well as those under 12. Second, other federal statutes, such as the one at issue in the *Sable* case, sought to protect "persons under the age of 18." Third, most of the 48 state laws brought to the attention of the Commission imposed penalties for the distribution of "sexually explicit" (but not necessarily obscene) materials to persons under 17. Finally, the Supreme Court has twice found that the government has a compelling interest in protecting persons between 12 and 17 from indecent materials, see Bethel School District No. 403 v. Fraser, 478 U.S. 675, 106 S.Ct. 3159, 92 L.Ed.2d 549 (1986); *Ginsberg v. New York*, 390 U.S. 629, 88 S.Ct. 1274, 20 L.Ed.2d 195 (1968). *1990 Indecency Report*, 5 FCC Rcd at 5301. Is the Commission's rationale convincing?

(c) What does this statement in the court of appeals opinion mean: "[W]e have upheld the FCC's generic definition of indecency in light of the sole purpose of that definition: to permit the channeling of indecent material, in order to shelter children from exposure to words and phrases their parents regard as inappropriate for them to hear"? Will the FCC's definition of indecency be subjected to greater scrutiny if it is used to define programs that are prohibited rather than channeled? On what grounds? The FCC has stated that "the D.C. Circuit * * * explicitly affirmed this definition [of 'indecency']" in the *Action for Children's Television* decision. 1990 Indecency Report, 5 FCC Rcd at 5301. Do you agree with this Commission's reading of the court's opinion?

(d) In the *1990 Indecency Report*, the FCC wrote that it would "continue to give weight to reasonable licensee judgments when deciding to impose sanctions in specific cases." Id. Clearly, however, the Commission means that it, not the licensee, will decide finally what is indecent. Reread the definition of "indecent" set out in the *Pacifica* decision. Could a licensee, based on this definition, reasonably be expected to anticipate with some precision what the FCC will consider indecent? On what basis will the Commission determine "contemporary community standards"? Are such standards readily identifiable? Should a government agency determine the standards of decency?

(e) The FCC's decision is intended not only to protect children, but also to assist parents in supervising their children. When does government action intended to assist parental supervision impermissibly intrude upon children's rights as viewers and listeners of the broadcast media? What rights do children have in this regard? Consider a policy of a public library in Montgomery County, Maryland. The library cautions parents about obtaining a library card in the name of a young child because it is the library's policy to refuse to disclose to anyone but the cardholder the books that have been checked out by the cardholder. Does the library's nondisclosure policy, coupled with the caution it gives to parents, impair parents' ability to supervise their children's reading choices? Is your answer different in the case of a 7–year old than in the case of a 17–year old? Should the library further parental supervision by permitting disclosure to a cardholder's parent or guardian if the cardholder is younger than a certain age?

5.   With the elimination of the congressional ban on indecent telephone messages, the FCC was again faced with a statute contemplating that the Commission would issue regulations designed to guard against access by minors to dial-a-porn services. The Commission again proposed to require dial-a-porn services to use access codes, credit card verification, or scrambling. Regulations Concerning Indecent Communications by Telephones, 5 FCC Rcd 1011 (1990).

6.   Can a telephone company refuse to permit a dial-a-porn service to use its network? One court of appeals has held that a telephone company may refuse such access without violating the dial-a-porn provider's First Amendment rights—under certain circumstances. The decision depends upon an assessment of whether the telephone company's refusal represents "state action," which is subject to First Amendment constraints by virtue of the Fourteenth Amendment. In that case, Mountain Bell was threatened with state criminal prosecution if it did not promptly terminate service to a dial-a-porn provider. The court held that, by threatening prosecution, the state had converted Mountain Bell's action into state action. The court went on to conclude, however, that Mountain Bell's subsequent decision to ban all adult telephone services was not state action and, therefore, was not subject to constitutional limits. Carlin Communications, Inc. v. Mountain States Tel. & Tel. Co., 827 F.2d 1291 (9th Cir.1987). For a critical analysis of the court's reasoning, see Tovey, *Dial-a-Porn and the First Amendment: The State Action Loophole*, 40 Fed. Comm. L.J. 267 (1988). See also Use of Common Carriers for the Transmission of Obscene Materials, 2 FCC Rcd 2819 (1987) (licensed MDS common carriers may prohibit use of their facilities to transmit obscene programming).

7.   The *Sable* decision makes clear that different media are to be treated differently when it comes to government regulation of indecent material. In its *1990 Indecency Report*, the FCC noted that the federal requirement that cable systems offer lock boxes to subscribers, in order to permit them to "lock out" specific channels, makes it much easier for parents to limit their children's access to indecent cable programming. 1990 Indecency Report, 5 FCC Rcd 5305. What other characteristics of cable television make indecency in that medium less intrusive than indecency in broadcasting? In recognition of the distinctions between cable and broadcast television, courts have tended to be far more skeptical of government regulations aimed at indecent cable television programs. The next section examines the treatment of cable indecency.

8.   To what extent does *Denver* read off of *Sable*? Does the Supreme Court in *Denver* mean to suggest that programming on various types of access channels should receive more protection than those on traditional broadcast stations, because the public has become used to the "open" nature of access channels?

2. CABLE TELEVISION

CRUZ v. FERRE

United States District Court, Southern District of Florida, 1983.
571 F.Supp. 125, affirmed 755 F.2d 1415 (11th Cir.1985).

HOEVELER, DISTRICT JUDGE:

The issue presented in this case is whether the Defendant City of Miami may constitutionally regulate the dissemination of material through cable television defined by the City as "indecent."

* * *

While the Court is sympathetic with the defendant's attempt to protect the perceived deterioration of the "moral fiber" of the City, the ruling in this case must and shall be based upon the Constitution and the Supreme Court interpretations of it. Despite good intentions, however, the means used by the City exceed the limits of proper constitutional action.

* * *

BACKGROUND

On October 19, 1981, the City of Miami adopted Ordinance No. 9223, effective November 19, 1981. Ordinance No. 9223 ("the cable television ordinance") set forth a comprehensive system for regulating cable television in Miami. On November 19, 1981, pursuant to Ordinance No. 9223, the City enacted Ordinance No. 9332 ("the licensing ordinance"). This ordinance granted Miami Cablevision, Inc. ("Cablevision") a nonexclusive, revocable license to operate a cable television system in Miami. Section 203(a) of the licensing ordinance reiterated a similar provision in the cable television ordinance. It states: "In accepting this license, the licensee acknowledges that its privileges hereunder are subject to the police power of the City ... and the licensee ... agrees to comply with all applicable general laws, resolutions and ordinances presently in force or subsequently enacted by the City pursuant to such power."

On January 13, 1983, the City enacted its third cable ordinance, Ordinance No. 9583, which is the subject of this lawsuit. Ordinance No. 9583 ("the indecency ordinance") provides for the regulation of "indecent" and "obscene" material on cable television. The ordinance states, in pertinent part:

Section 1. No person shall by means of a cable television system knowingly distribute by wire or cable any obscene or indecent material.

Section 2. The following words have the following meanings:

* * *

(f) The test of whether or not material is "obscene" is: (i) whether the average person, applying contemporary community standards, would find that the work, taken as a whole, appeals to the prurient interest; (ii) whether the work depicts or describes, in a patently offensive way, sexual conduct specifically defined by the applicable state law; and (iii) whether the work, taken as a whole, lacks serious literary, artistic, political or scientific value.

(g) "Indecent material" means material which is a representation or description of a human sexual or excretory organ or function which the average person, applying contemporary community standards, would find to be patently offensive.

The indecency ordinance further provides that all complaints under Section 1 shall be brought before the City Manager, Ord. No. 9538 sec. 3(a), including those initiated by the City Manager. The City Manager reviews each complaint to determine whether there is probable cause to believe that a violation of section 1 has occurred. If he finds probable cause, a hearing is held. The hearing is to be "informal," but the licensee may be represented by counsel, the parties may present evidence, and the proceedings must be transcribed by a court reporter. The licensee is opposed at the hearing by the City, which has the burden of proving that the licensee is in violation of sec. 1. The purpose of the hearing is to provide the licensee with an opportunity to refute the alleged violations of the ordinance. The City Manager presides over the hearing, determines the admissibility of evidence, and, within ten days of the hearing's conclusion, must make his finding and decision. If the City Manager determines that the cable licensee has violated section 1, he may impose sanctions, including suspension or termination of the cable television license.

* * *

The Cable Television Medium

* * *

Cablevision is presently the sole Miami cable television licensee. It provides basic cable services, which include improved reception of local broadcast television and the reception of more remote broadcast signals. It also has offered and continues to offer subscribers up to six private television services for a separate fee. Subscribers may opt for these services on a monthly basis and must make supplemental payments each month for the services to be maintained.

One private service currently offered by Cablevision is Home Box Office, Inc. ("HBO"). Approximately seventy-five percent of the 2,000 or so Miami households receiving cable television subscribe to HBO. * * * By agreement, Cablevision retransmits HBO's entire viewing daily.

HBO shows films rated "G," "PG," or "R" by the Motion Picture Association of America, as well as unrated films which would have received such ratings if rated. It is HBO's policy not to exhibit films receiving an "X" rating or its equivalent.

Monthly HBO program guides list the times and dates of all program offerings, and they describe and give the ratings, if any, of the programs. Subscriber-households may control family access to the cable system by using "lockboxes" and "parental keys." These are available from Cablevision free of charge.

* * *

THE FIRST AMENDMENT

* * *

Indecent speech * * * does not fall within the confines of the definition of obscenity and is accorded some First Amendment protection. FCC v. Pacifica Foundation, 438 U.S. 726, 98 S.Ct. 3026, 57 L.Ed.2d 1073 (1978). Therefore, in regulating the distribution of "indecent" materials, the ordinance sweeps within its bounds "speech" subject to constitutional protection. By transgressing the carefully crafted limits of the *Miller* "obscenity" test, the ordinance is overly broad and facially defective. See Community Television of Utah v. Roy City, 555 F.Supp. 1164 (D.Utah 1982).

The defendants oppose this analysis and argue that the leading case on the regulation of "indecent" speech, *Pacifica*, supports the ordinance's proscription of "indecent" speech. I quite agree that *Pacifica* is, from defendants' standpoint, the most attractive case upon which to shape their argument. However, a careful consideration of *Pacifica* serves defendants' position poorly and, indeed, highlights the distinctions which render the case inapplicable to the facts herein.

The ordinance subject to review by this court prohibits far too broadly the transmission of indecent materials through cable television. The ordinance's prohibition is wholesale, without regard to the time of day or other variables indispensable to the decision in *Pacifica*. The rationale of *Pacifica* applies only to broadcasting. The medium of cable television presents different First Amendment concerns; therefore, *Pacifica* is inapposite.

A COMPARISON OF CABLE AND BROADCAST

The comparison of the broadcast and cable television media reveals the extent to which *Pacifica* is inapplicable here. In *Community Television of Utah, Inc. v. Roy City,* supra, which involved circumstances identical to the case at bar, the District Court explored some of the many differences between broadcast and cable television.

In *Roy City,* the Court found that a City ordinance regulating the transmission through cable television of material defined as indecent was constitutionally defective because it inhibited protected communication. The Court, in so finding, meticulously charted the dissimilarities of cable and broadcast:

Cable	Broadcast
1. User needs to subscribe.	User need not subscribe.
2. User holds power to cancel subscriptions.	User holds no power to cancel.
	May complain to FCC, station, network, or sponsor.
3. Limited advertising.	Extensive advertising.
4. Transmittal through wires.	Transmittal through public airways.
5. User receives signal on private cable.	User appropriates signal from public airwaves.
6. User pays a fee.	User does not pay a fee.
7. User receives preview of coming attractions.	User receives daily and weekly listing in public press or commercial guides.
8. Distributor or distributee may add services and expand spectrum of signals or choices.	Neither distributor nor distributee may add services or signals or channels and choices.
9. Wires are privately owned.	Airways are publicly controlled.

* * *

Significantly, in addition to offering greater quantitative choice, cable also provides greater overall viewing control to the subscriber. Cable is "offered to users of television sets on terms the users are free to accept or reject." It is totally up to the user to decide to bring Cablevision into his home. * * * Viewers of cable television may also avoid the surprise that sometimes occurs in broadcast programming. Cable subscribers need only consult the monthly viewing guides for information. And to protect children or other immature viewers from unsuitable programming, subscribers need only use a free "lockbox" or "parental key" available from Cablevision. This opportunity to completely avoid the potential harm to minor or immature viewers sounds the death-knell of *Pacifica*'s applicability in the cable television context.

* * *

DUE PROCESS OF LAW

Plaintiffs also contend that the methods and procedures which provide for the enforcement of the ordinance violate the fundamental notion of fairness implicit in due process. The Court concurs.

* * *

Due process requires, however, not only that certain procedures such as hearings be provided, but also that the procedures which are provided be fair. * * *

* * *

The indecency ordinance permits the City Manager to initiate complaints against the licensee, assess the validity of the complaint, preside over the hearing on the complaint, admit evidence at the hearing, make a determination, and issue sanctions, all in an area of moral judgment that might well try the neutrality and impartiality of Solomon. The risk of arbitrary or capricious governmental action under these circumstances is intolerably high. The Court consequently finds that these procedures, by concentrating the functions of complainant, jury, judge and "executioner" in one person, do not comport with the fundamental notion of fairness implicit in due process.

* * *

CONCLUSION

A somewhat more detailed discussion of the City's undertaking seems appropriate. In so doing, I succumb to the urge to comment on one of the directions of our time, and to make some observations, born, no doubt, of the reality which increasingly surrounds us. From antiquity, the smut peddlers have been with us. Hadrian (AD 76–138) one of the "five good emperors of Rome" wrote in his memoirs "the story-tellers and spinners of erotic tales are hardly more than butchers who hang up for sale morsels of meat attractive to flies." (Memoirs of Hadrian, Yourcenar, Marguerite; Farrar, Straus and Giroux, N.Y.1981, p. 22). The butchers of our times press forward, their appetites for profit obscured by the banners of the First Amendment which they thrust forward with each new attempt to enlarge the ambit and prurience of their offerings. The potential for corporate moral enervation does not, of course, present an impediment to entrepreneurs; but general concerns, no doubt, present the background for the City's well meant effort to regulate or eliminate "indecency." While our collective zeal to stem the tide of smut must always be tempered by ongoing and careful reference to the Constitution, we must, nonetheless, be sympathetic to the thought that in our avid pursuit of the most generous view of "free" speech in this area, we exercise caution. By constitutional indulgence in an area which should be more carefully scrutinized, reactions are born which could ultimately infect the much most important of the First Amendment speech freedoms.

The suggestion that much of what we see today on our newsstands, in some book stores and many screens, has some socially redeeming value, seems born of the vertical exercise of viewing each new incursion into boldness in the light of the one most recently justified. It is difficult to predict where our tolerance of licentiousness will end. The "end," however, cannot be induced by the use of a blunderbuss. The understandable anxieties of the City fathers cannot provide the basis for approving legislation which in its reach exceeds the dangers they contemplate and which they have the power to control. That I am sympathetic with the general objective of the City is unimportant. My course has been charted by the Supreme Court. In *Stanley v. Georgia*, 394 U.S. at 565, 89 S.Ct. at 1248, the Court stated:

If the First Amendment means anything, it means that a State has no business telling a man, sitting alone in his own house what books he may read or what films he may watch.

I do not suggest by reference to *Stanley* that government may have no say about indecent material projected into citizens' living rooms. In some circumstances involving conventional broadcast programming, the *Pacifica* opinion may well be held to apply. It does not apply here.

Passing the question of whether the state has preempted regulation of obscenity, no one questions the right of the City to properly legislate in this area. Again, the fatal defects are the broadness of the ordinance and its due process deficiencies.

Finally, a fitting conclusion to this case is a reference to the Supreme Court conclusion in [*Erznoznik v. City of Jacksonville*, 422 U.S. 205, 95 S.Ct. 2268, 45 L.Ed.2d 125 (1975) (invalidating an ordinance that prohibited drive-in movies from showing films containing nudity if the screen was visible from a public street)]:

> In concluding that this ordinance is invalid, we do not deprecate the legitimate interests asserted by the City of Jacksonville. We hold only that the present ordinance does not satisfy the vigorous constitutional standard that apply when government attempts to regulate expression. Where First Amendment freedoms are at stake we have repeatedly emphasized that precision of drafting and clarity of purpose are essential. These prerequisites are absent here.

The defect of overbroadness will not be solved by redrafting. The procedural problems—the precursor to sanctions—can be. In its present form, the ordinance cannot be saved.

* * *

Notes and Questions

1. Do you agree that technological differences between cable and broadcast television make the analysis of *Pacifica* inapplicable to cable? In 1982, Judge Posner wrote that "the universal access to the home that television enjoys and a resulting felt need to protect children * * * is independent of whether the television signal comes into the home over the air or through coaxial cable." Omega Satellite Products Co. v. City of Indianapolis, 694 F.2d 119, 128 (7th Cir.1982). Do you agree or disagree with his reasoning? Does the availability of VCRs make a difference to your analysis? Recall that the FCC considered the prevalence of VCRs in determining that time channeling is not sufficient to protect minors from exposure to indecent broadcasts.

2. Is cable television more like telephone service than broadcasting? Access to indecent cable programming requires taking affirmative action, such as signing up for cable service and, in some cases, subscribing separately to a premium channel or service tier. Is this comparable to becoming a telephone subscriber? Or to calling a dial-a-porn service? Is the sensory difference (audio only vs. audio-visual)—and the potentially different impact on minors—between telephone and cable service relevant?

3. The *Roy City* case cited in the *Cruz* decision is one of three federal court decisions striking down efforts in Utah to restrict the transmission of "offensive" cable programming. The battle began in 1981, when Utah made it a crime to transmit "pornographic or indecent" programs over a cable system. The term "pornographic" was defined in other state statutes; the term "indecent" was not defined. In a suit brought by Home Box Office, several cable companies, and a satellite company, the federal district court in Utah struck down the statute as incurably overbroad. In its analysis, the court noted that the statute made it a crime to cablecast (1) a number of Academy Award-winning movies, such as "Annie Hall" and "Coal Miner's Daughter," and (2) many programs that were readily available on videocassettes and videodiscs. Home Box Office, Inc. v. Wilkinson, 531 F.Supp. 987 (D.Utah 1982).

Soon after that decision, the same judge decided the *Roy City* case, in which he struck down a local ordinance that prohibited distribution of "indecent" material, defined to include "the representation or verbal description of (a) an erotic human sexual activity; (b) erotic nudity; (c) erotic ultimate sexual acts, normal or perverted, actual or simulated, or (d) erotic masturbation; which under contemporary community standards is patently offensive." The term "erotic" was defined as "tending to arouse sexual feelings or desires."

The State legislature tried once more in 1983, adopting two laws over the Governor's veto. The first made it a misdemeanor to transmit material harmful to minors over a cable system. The second imposed fines for the cable transmission of indecent programming, which was defined in a specific way similar to the ordinance overturned in *Roy City*. The court struck down both statutes, noting that the Cable Communications Policy Act of 1984 clearly had made cable television "not an intruder but an invitee whose invitation can be carefully circumscribed." Community Television of Utah, Inc. v. Wilkinson, 611 F.Supp. 1099, 1113 (D.Utah 1985), affirmed sub nom. Jones v. Wilkinson, 800 F.2d 989 (10th Cir.1986), affirmed 480 U.S. 926, 107 S.Ct. 1559, 94 L.Ed.2d 753 (1987).

On appeal, Judge Baldock, concurring in the court's affirmance, agreed that the statute was overbroad, but also argued that cable television was no less intrusive than broadcasting:

> * * * Even though cable television is transmitted by cable and regular television is transmitted by broadcasting, there is an undeniable similarity between the two. Both rely on television receivers and provide a similar, and often interchangeable, product. * * * To permit the regulation of indecency in radio and television broadcasting, but not on cablecasting, based merely on the differences in transmission, is to deemphasize that the programming transmitted on both emanates from outside the home and is received identically.

> Just as radio and television are pervasive, so too is cable television * * *. * * * The pervasiveness of television simply is not related to how the signal reaches the set. Pervasiveness is related to the location of the television set in the home, the scanning activity of viewers, and other qualities of the television medium.

Much has been made of the fact that a television household must elect to have cable installed and then pay a monthly fee for its use.* * * * Merely because cable television is a subscriber medium does not mean that it is so unlike traditional broadcasting that indecency cannot be regulated. * * * When further analyzed, it is apparent that merely subscribing to cable does not alter its basic nature. A subscription to cable presumably is purchased to enhance the viewers' choice of programs. It is easy to get a general idea of the contents of a book or magazine, but with television it may be more difficult because of the tremendous diversity of programming, the large number of programs and the scanning which occurs. This is particularly true when indecent programming is interspersed with programming generally thought suitable for minors.

Practically, cable television reception does not require activity of a purchasing nature for each program. The cable viewer is not purchasing a particular program at the time of viewing, rather he is purchasing a wider range of programs than available on broadcast television. He is purchasing program choice. Cable programs are then disseminated generally to the public, and like programs on conventional television or radio, are frequently viewed or heard in the home where the right to be free of "patently offensive indecent material" outweighs an unlimited right to present such material. *F.C.C. v. Pacifica*, 438 U.S. at 748, 98 S.Ct. at 3039.

Not only does cable television come directly into the home, it frequently is viewed without any effective advance warning of patently offensive, indecent material. This is true for several reasons. Out of the hundreds of programs offered on cable television, it is unreasonable to shift an affirmative duty onto every parent to study all cable television program listings each week, even assuming that such listings provide adequate warning. No such duty was even considered by the Court in *Pacifica*. While it is true that lockboxes may be used to prevent reception of entire channels, the unwanted complexity that these devices introduce into television viewing is attested to by their lack of use. Most importantly, there is no reason to believe that frequent scanning, often a factor in the regulation of broadcasting, does not occur with cablecasting. This means that viewing often will be unplanned and incomplete. Viewers will tune into scenes of programs in progress, reducing the effectiveness of warnings preceding such programs.

Over and over the argument has been made that a subscriber voluntarily chooses cable television service and should not be heard to complain if some of the programming is indecent because the service may be canceled. Stated another way, the subscriber consents to the indecency for himself and his household. This argument is too simplistic and is akin to the notion that one who hears an indecent broadcast has an adequate remedy by turning it off. This notion was expressly rejected in *F.C.C. v. Pacifica*, 438 U.S. at 748–49, 98 S.Ct. at 3039–40. The record indicates that the basic cable service and the optional services provide

---

* Although broadcast television is not a subscriber medium, a decision to obtain a television set is a prerequisite to viewing. Moreover, broadcast television is supported, at least indirectly, by viewers who purchase the products advertised.

plenty of programming without patently offensive indecent material. As a developing medium, cable television provides a remarkable opportunity for viewing programming in other distant cities, recent movies, sports and other features for a nominal fee. That opportunity should be available to all who are willing to subscribe, even those who object to patently offensive indecent material being presented during family viewing hours. Quite simply, in enacting the Cable Decency Act, the Utah legislature seems to have wanted to take the good (increased choice) without the bad (indecent material). 800 F.2d at 1004–1006.

4.   Do you find Judge Baldock's reasoning convincing? Is it valid in the era of the "V-chip," discussed below?

5.   How does the reasoning in *Sable* and *Cruz* fit with that in *Denver*? The governing concern in the two cases above seems to be that a communications user has the power to exclude undesireable types of programming from his or her household. Although this was implicit in the access channels involved in *Denver*, Justice Breyer did not seem to make a major issue out of it—although he did note the long custom and usage of non-censorship of access channels.

On the other hand, the parental (or other) control element did not seem to factor into the somewhat ill-defined combination of strict scrutiny/intermediate scrutiny which Justice Breyer seemed to use. There was little or no attempt to show that user control gave either the user or the programmer any greater rights. Would it be fair to argue that subscriber control in fact should "empower" both users and operators? That users need less protection from either government or cable operators? That cable operators need afford less protection to subscribers?

As with so many aspects of relatively new media, once again, factual contexts often seem to be controlling. For example, how might Justice Breyer have reacted to a local government's refusal to grant more than one franchise for any geographic area?

G.   EFFECT OF THE POWER TO EXCLUDE PROGRAMMING: HEREIN OF THE V–CHIP

As suggested above, not everyone necessarily would be satisfied with even a near-complete ability to control—exclude—programming available in his or her home. Again, this may result from religious, ideological, or other reasons. Whatever the cause, however, it certainly is not consistent with the notion that government should be concerned only about programming with allegedly bad results. A "macro" view of the V-chip is offered by Prof. Balkin.

Despite its name, the V-chip is not a single chip at all, but a combination of different technologies. All television programs currently have the capacity to carry extra information—like closed captioning—as well as sound and pictures. An electronic circuit in a television or cable box can be designed to block programs by reading a numerical code broadcast along the same band used for closed captioning. Viewers then use a remote control device to select from a menu of choices as to how much violence, bad language, sex, and nudity they wish to tolerate. A rating system now being tested in Canada features a five-number scale, with higher numbers signifying more sex and violence. When the V-chip circuitry reads a rating equal to or higher than the consumer's preselected number, the picture is replaced by a large black box.

Critics charge that the V-chip raises serious First Amendment problems. This essay explores a few of them. But my more important goal is to use the debate over the V-chip to rethink the foundations of broadcast regulation. The federal courts, including the Supreme Court, have justified content-based restrictions on broadcast indecency partly on the grounds of the special nature of the mass media. Yet their justifications for special treatment have been, on the whole, unconvincing. I will argue that the real issues have little to do with traditional justifications of scarcity, public interest, and pervasiveness. They have to do with how different media permit the filtering of information. Different communication technologies are better adapted to different kinds of informational filters. For example, broadcast media permit different and more limited filters than print media. The V-chip promises to change all that by creating a new system for filtering broadcast information. But this new technology raises many new and unexpected problems. In particular, it raises the possibility that in the Information Age, control of filters may be one of the most important forms of power over human thought and human expression. In the Information Age, the informational filter, not information itself, is king.

J.M Balkin, Media Filters, *The V–Chip, and the Foundations of Broadcast Regulation*, 45 Duke L.J. 1131 (1996). See also, Laurence H. Winer, *The Red Lion of Cable, and Beyond?—Turner Broadcasting v. FCC*, Cardozo Arts & Ent. L.J. 41 (1997)

Is it clear that violent programming causes violent behavior? Consider the following discussion.

PETER JOHNSON
THE IRRELEVANT V–CHIP:
AN ALTERNATE THEORY OF TV AND VIOLENCE
4 U.C.L.A. Enter. L. Rev. 185 (1997).

I. Introduction

The Telecommunications Act of 1996, signed by President Clinton on February 8, 1996, contains a two-prong attack on TV violence. The first prong is a technological one, requiring that a "V-chip" (V for violence) be installed on all new TV sets greater than 13″. When TV programs are rating-encoded, parents will be able to decide whether to activate the V-chip on their home sets and block whatever rated programs they choose. The second prong is a substantive one, providing that, if "distributors of video programming" do not establish a voluntary rating system for "sexual, violent, or other indecent material" within one year, the government will do it for them.

The "distributors of video programming" fell quickly into line. At a White House meeting on February 29, 1996, network and cable executives promised a rating system by year's end. By year's end, they delivered.

The content of the proposed rating system, and the controversy it has spawned, is not at issue in this paper. What is at issue is that the President, Congress, and now the TV industry have endorsed the "violence hypothesis," i.e. that viewing violent television programming causes violent or aggressive behavior, usually by children. This hypothesis has been in the air almost as long as TV has been on the air, since at least 1954. Of late, proponents and opponents have become so polarized that not even the data are safe: Each side uses the same study to reach an opposite conclusion. Now, however, the proponents have won Congress' and the country's hearts if not quite their minds. Although Congress, in the Telecommunications Act, was unwilling to adopt the violence hypothesis in so many words, it still managed hedgingly to "find" that [s]tudies have shown that children exposed to violent video programming at a young age have a higher tendency for violent and aggressive behavior later in life than children not so exposed, and that children exposed to violent video programming are prone to assume that acts of violence are acceptable behavior.

On its own, Congress less boldly found only that children watch a lot of TV, that TV contains a lot of violence, and that there is a compelling government interest in empowering parents to limit same.

The problem with the sweeping endorsement of the violence hypothesis is that it is just that—a hypothesis. Despite what Congress finds about what studies have shown, there is great disagreement not only about what the studies show, but even about how many studies there are. What is needed to break the logjam is a tertium quid, a third way of looking at television and violence that, without doing violence to the data, explains the discrepancies in interpreting it. This paper offers that third view.

The tertium quid is the following hypothesis. (1) Violence is antisocial behavior. (2) Television-watching is antisocial behavior. (3) Therefore, the more a child watches television, to the exclusion of other, more socializing activities, the more likely it is that the child will grow up antisocial and, perhaps, violent, regardless of the content of what he watches. In other words, there is something in the nature of TV-watching, rather than in the content of TV programs, that is more likely to cause antisocial behavior, including violence, than the content itself. Excessive, solitary TV-watching robs a child of socializing activities, such as sports and games, even computer games, that would accustom her to dealing regularly and nonviolently with other people.

This thesis explains, without reaching the content of TV programs, several findings that have puzzled researchers. Among them are, first, the failure of the data to connect more than a few individual acts of violence to specific violent TV programs; second, the findings of several studies that, as TV becomes more pervasive in a community or a country, so does violence; and third, why children are as likely to come to blows over the remote while watching "Gumby" as while watching "Mighty Morphin Power Rangers."

This thesis is not novel. * * * [T]he effect of art upon the individual and society has interested philosophers for centuries. To Plato, the representations of drama have a direct and immediate effect on people's behavior. To Aristotle, the effect of art has more to do with its structure than its content. To our contemporary Marshall McLuhan, both the content and the structure of particular works of art pale before the impact of the medium itself.

* * *

[T]he tertium quid hypothesis potentially invites more, rather than less, government restriction of TV. If it is, in fact, true that too much TV-watching by children, to the exclusion of other socializing play, leads to a violent adult populace, it follows that the government has a compelling interest in restricting not the content of TV, but the amount of TV that children may watch. This invites the paradoxical conclusion from accepting the tertium quid hypothesis that merely restricting violent content is far more narrowly tailored than limiting the total amount of what children can watch.

VI. CONCLUSION

Though the violence hypothesis has won wide acceptance, the alternate hypothesis that excess TV-watching of any sort is at fault seems to account equally well for the connection between TV-watching and social violence. Unfortunately, if this tertium quid hypothesis is true, it carries the unappetizing baggage that might let Congress restrict, not the content, but the amount of television children may watch.

Neither restriction is necessary. The point of the tertium quid hypothesis is not that it is true, but that Congress is on shaky constitutional grounds legislating as if the violence hypothesis were true while an alternate hypothesis explains the same data. Given this philosophical stalemate, Congress's only recourse is to leave television alone and face up to the real sources of societal violence—poverty and ignorance—that the Constitution empowers it to do something about.empowers it to do something about.

Notes and Questions

1.   Is there "state action" present if the video industries adopt program ratings on a "voluntary" basis? What is the real force behind their action? Remember the "Family Viewing Hour" litigation discussed in Chapter VI. (p. 267) What is the remedy if a station strips the V-chip codes from its

programs, thus rendering the device inoperable? Can the FCC take any action? On what theory? Does the 1996 Act give it any power to act?

2. Is the V-chip technology too much of a shotgun rather than rifle shot approach? Note that technology proposed for the V-chip is not capable of eliminating particular channels, series, or program. The technology to allow a narrow degree of parental control—e.g., show by show—currently exists, and is not particularly expensive.

3. Does the V-chip make sense for adults? What happens if parents set their V-chip to reject any program involving bloody murderers; when the parents settle in to watch *Macbeth* and cannot access it, is their reaction likely to be very positive? Especially when they have to input a PIN number in order to watch the show, and then put it and a code in again in order to restore the blocking effect? Given the millions of VCRs in the U.S. perpetually blinking "12:00," are most people likely to use the V-chip on a regular basis?

4. Note that the V-chip provision does not require installation in sets under 13 inches. What size set are privileged children likely to have in their rooms?

H. OTHER BEHAVIORAL POLICIES

1. CHILDREN'S TELEVISION

As indicated in *Pacifica*, children have a special—albeit largely undefined and unarticulated—status in media regulation. It seems axiomatic that the child audience is less sophisticated than the adult; as the Commission once noted, children are "far more trusting of and vulnerable to commercial 'pitches' than are adults * * *" and "very young children cannot distinguish conceptually between programming and advertising." Children's Television Report and Policy Statement, 50 FCC 2d 1, 11 (1974) ("1974 Report"), affirmed sub nom. Action for Children's Television v. FCC, 564 F.2d 458 (D.C.Cir.1977); see also Memorandum Opinion and Order, 53 FCC 2d 161 (1975), reconsideration denied 63 FCC 2d 145 (1977).

The Commission has almost continuously debated whether to impose restrictions against overcommercialization on children's programs. A 1963 Commission proposal was abandoned as a result of congressional pressure. In 1974, FCC Chairman Wiley held "extensive discussions" with the NAB and the Association of Independent Television Stations, after which they agreed to limit industry practice to a maximum of 9.5 minutes of commercials per hour on Saturday and Sunday mornings, and 12 minutes per hour at other times. (According to B. Cole and M. Dettinger, Reluctant Regulators, 276–77, the Chairman "employed the tactics of a Kojak.") In addition, the Commission required separation of commercials from programs and prohibited "host-selling." *1974 Report*, 50 FCC 2d at 15–16, 31. The FCC also explored—but never adopted— other types of regulations. Second Notice of Inquiry, 68 FCC 2d 1344 (1978); Notice of Proposed Rulemaking, 75 FCC 2d 138 (1979). And in

1997, the Commission adapted "procedural" rules to flag for special attention any renewal applications proposing less than three hours of children's *educational* programming per week.

This paternalistic attitude toward the child came into conflict with the Commission's general policy favoring deregulation, which included removal of limits on commercials generally. In 1984, the Commission repealed advertising limitations on television for all types of material, including children's programming. Revision of Programming and Commercialization Policies, 98 FCC 2d 1076 (1984), reconsideration denied 104 FCC 2d 358 (1986). The FCC's only basis for refusing to continue special treatment for children's programming was that:

> Elimination of the policy is consistent with [the] Commission's general de-emphasis regarding quantitative guidelines * * *. Moreover, the Commission has consistently noted the importance of advertising as a support mechanism for the presentation of children's programming.

On review, the Court of Appeals required a better explanation to support the Commission's change of heart. See Action for Children's Television v. FCC, 821 F.2d 741 (D.C.Cir.1987):

> It is axiomatic that an agency choosing to alter its regulatory course "must supply a reasoned analysis indicating that its prior policies and standards are being deliberately changed, not casually ignored." * * * If an agency does not supply a reasoned basis for its action, the courts are not to supply one. * * *

> Despite ACT's specific comments on the subject during the 1984 rulemaking, the FCC appears at first to have overlooked entirely the existence of the children's guidelines. Only when NAB specifically requested clarification as to the *1984 Report's* scope did the Commission come forward and indicate that the general deregulation of television commercialization extended to children's television as well. Even in response to that call for clarification, the Commission deigned to fashion only two sentences (and two moderately pertinent footnotes) * * *.

> Far be it from us to demand long-winded, tiresome explanations. But the Commission's barebones incantation of two abbreviated rationales cannot do service as the requisite "reasoned basis" for altering its long-established policy. * * *

> To make bad matters worse, this latter-day inspiration is barely articulated, much less explained; the Commission's rather economical language tells us only that eliminating the children's quantitative guidelines is "consistent with" elimination of guidelines generally. True, but insufficient. * * * In view of the importance of the Commission's volte face, we have not the slightest hesitation in concluding that this explanation crosses the line from "the tolerably terse to the intolerably mute." *Greater Boston*, 444 F.2d at 851–52.

Similarly, the Commission's assertion of the obvious—that commercials help support children's television programming—scarcely justifies elimination of all children's television commercialization guidelines. The FCC's quantitative commercialization guidelines never eliminated commercials from children's television. As the Commission itself pointed out in 1974, "[a]lthough advertising should be adequate to insure that the station will have sufficient revenues with which to produce programming which will serve the children of its community meaningfully, the public interest does not protect advertising which is substantially in excess of that amount." *1974 Report,* 50 F.C.C.2d at 12. The FCC has not found, say, that present levels of children's programming are inadequate; that additional commercialization is necessary to provide greater diversity in children's programming; or that increased levels of children's television commercialization pose no threat to the public interest. Bereft of bolstering findings of this sort, the Commission's invocation of the obvious fact that commercials pay the tab for children's programming hardly explains the leap to a "hands off" commercialization policy.

* * *

First, the FCC argues that the existence of children's television commercialization guidelines depended on the existence of the overall television commercialization guidelines. If so, the Commission points out, then general elimination of the industrywide guidelines made it entirely appropriate (and perhaps even necessary) to eliminate the children's guidelines. * * *

Upon analysis, however, this argument falls flat, in view of the long history of the Commission's separate treatment of the children's television policy. * * * As the agency has seen it, kids are different; the Commission cannot now cavalierly revoke its special policy for youngsters without reexamining its earlier conclusions.

[The court here rejected the Commission's argument that repeal of the children's television rules flowed inevitably from the National Association of Broadcasters' elimination of its Code guidelines in 1982, as part of the settlement of an antitrust challenge to the Code. United States v. National Ass'n of Broadcasters, 553 F.Supp. 621 (D.D.C.1982).] [T]he Commission offers nothing to suggest a perceived indissoluble link between the NAB standards and the children's television guidelines.

In sum, we find the Commission has failed to explain adequately the elimination of its long-standing children's television commercialization guidelines, and we therefore remand to the Commission for elaboration on that issue.

Following the court's decision, the Commission reopened the proceeding in which it addressed the commercialization practices for children's television. Revision of Programming and Commercialization Policies, 2 FCC Rcd 6822 (1987). In addition to the court's remand, the Commission had before it two petitions filed by ACT. The first requested that the Commission conclude that the public interest is not served by programs that are intended to be viewed together with an interactive toy. (Such programs contain signals that interact with the toy.) The second requested that the Commission find that so-called program-length commercials (programs built around a commercial product) do not serve the public interest. Among the issues on which the Commission sought public comment were the following:

(1) Do children tend not to be sensitive to the distinction between commercials and programs?

(2) Does parental or sibling monitoring create a market environment in which over-commercialized programs will be turned off?

(3) Has increased variety in the video marketplace given children and their parents greater choice, which limits a broadcaster's ability to "force" viewing of overly commercial programs?

(4) Can the Commission reimpose commercialization guidelines in view of the greater constitutional protection given to commercial speech today, as compared to 1974?

(5) How should the Commission distinguish among "programs" that involve toys, "commercials," and "program-length commercials"?

(6) On what basis might the Commission distinguish between a program intended primarily to interact with a toy and a program that adds interactivity as an extra feature of the program?

For a psychological discussion of the impact of television on young children, see Singer & Singer, *Psychologists Look at Television: Cognitive, Developmental, Personality, and Social Implications*, American Psychologist, July 1983, at 826.

Notes and Questions

1. Should parents be expected to teach their pre-school age children to distinguish between programs and commercials? Consider the arguments concerning the difficulty of relying upon parents to supervise their children's television viewing. If not, what is the government interest in doing so? Is that a compelling, or even a strong, interest? How does it compare to the government's interest in compulsory schooling? See Wisconsin v. Yoder, 406 U.S. 205, 221–229, 92 S.Ct. 1526, 1536–1540, 32 L.Ed.2d 15 (1972).

2. What justification is there for government affirmatively promoting or requiring children's television programming of a desirable sort? What is "children's" television? Who should decide whether a particular program qualified? See B. Cole & M. Oetinger, Reluctant Regulators 283–84 (1978) (noting that despite the policy adopted in the *1974 Report* requiring broadcast applicants to demonstrate a commitment to children's programming, the FCC Staff was unwilling to "get into the problem of deciding what is and what isn't a children's program and how much is enough").

(a) In the *1974 Report,* the Commission had pointed to the reasoning in *Red Lion* to support its view that it could use its licensing process to encourage broadcasters to provide programming that served the needs of children. 50 FCC 2d at 4–5. Should *Red Lion* be applied in this fashion?

(b) How would you analyze the constitutionality of a requirement that broadcasters carry a certain amount of children's programming or demonstrate a certain commitment to such programming? Note that in its 1997 action, the FCC in theory dealt only in "procedural" terms.

3. In October 1990, the Communications Act was amended to add provisions directed at concerns about adequate provision of children's programming and excessive advertising on children's programs.

(a) The Children's Television Act of 1990 required the Commission, within six months, to complete a rulemaking to define "standards applicable to commercial television licensees [defined to include a cable television operator] with respect to the time devoted to commercial matter in conjunction with children's television programming." Any rules must provide that "advertising" on children's programs may not exceed 10.5 minutes per hour on weekends and 12 minutes per hour on weekdays.

Is the congressional finding that "special safeguards are appropriate to protect children from overcommercialization on television" sufficient to withstand a constitutional attack on the advertising limits? Is the governmental interest in this issue similar to, and as strong as, the interest in protecting children from obscenity? Can truthful advertising of lawful products and activities be regulated more strictly than other video programming? Is "overcommercialization" of television in general a public harm that Congress should address?

(b) The legislation also states that in future decisions regarding applications for renewals of broadcast television licenses, the Commission should consider (1) a licensee's compliance with the advertising standards, and (2) "the extent to which the [television broadcast] licensee * * * has served the educational and informational needs of children through the licensee's overall programming, including programming specifically designed to serve such needs."

At least the second obligation would seem to apply to noncommercial as well as commercial licensees; cable television operators are not covered by either obligation. Was there no jurisdictional "hook" on which Congress could hang these obligations with respect to cable systems? Should Congress have amended Section 546 of the Communications Act to permit franchising authorities to consider children's programming in evaluating an application for renewal of a cable franchise? Can the "public interest" obligations of a broadcaster practically be applied to a cable operator?

In support of the legislation, Rep. Markey stated, "Children's television should and can be the video equivalent of textbooks and the classics, rather than the video equivalent of the Toys–R–Us catalog." 136 Cong. Rec. H8538 (Oct. 1, 1990). Is this useful guidance for broadcasters seeking to comply with the law? For the FCC in evaluating a broadcaster's performance at renewal time? Where do superhero cartoons fit on the broad spectrum between textbooks and toy catalogs? What about Walt Disney cartoons? Is

"Fantasia" to be valued more than "The Little Mermaid" because only the former contains the music of the world's most renowned classical composers?

(c) Finally, Congress established a National Endowment for Children's Educational Television, under the direction of the Secretary of Commerce. The endowment was to be used to support the planning and production of children's programs "specifically directed toward the development of fundamental intellectual skills," either through contracts with the Corporation for Public Broadcasting or through direct grants to any other person. Grants were to be made in person. In 1991 and 1992, any programs produced with the assistance of grants can be provided only to public and noncommercial television licensees. Grants are to be made in consultation with a new Advisory Council on Children's Educational Television, to be appointed by the Secretary of Commerce.

More recently, concerns about children's television have focused on the lack of any substantial amount of educational programming—particularly during the "Saturday morning wasteland," when there is limited parental supervision. The major political and conceptual problem has been how to define broadcasters' obligations in terms not only of deleting offensive material, but also of offering positive programming.

On the negative or prohibitory side, the concern has been with protecting children from viewing programs—primarily with sex of violence—which arguably interfere with their development into healthy adults. As seen, however, the relationship between pornographic or violent television and anti-social behavior is less than clear. Moreover, even "failsafe" restrictions on children's viewing habits seem less than effective.

The other, positive side of the issue is providing children with sources of high-quality educational programming. This concern is perhaps even more difficult to treat than pornography and the like, for several reasons. First, defining "educational" or similar developmental programming is even more difficult than identifying pornographic and other "bad" material. Traditional instructional programming is relatively easy to define; but it also has relatively little interest for children's traditional Saturday morning viewing habits. On the other hand, more attractive programs—particularly cartoons—may be somewhat lacking in any real educational content. (Witness the attempt of many stations to characterize programs such as "The Flintstones" as children's programming.)

Moreover, First Amendment questions presumably are more sensitive in terms of affirmatively requiring specific types of programming than in creating safe harbours for others. To the extent that the Commission or any other government agency requires particular types of educational programs, it obviously moves from intermediate to the strict scrutiny under the First Amendment.

As the indecency discussion shows, the prohibitory side of children's television regulation has been around for quite a while, and shows no real tendency to change. The notion of affirmative programming obligations is relatively new, however, and raises issues which have not been carefully reviewed by the Commission, the courts, of commentators—as indicated by the material below.

The discussion above focusses mainly on preventing broadcasters and advertisers from airing manipulative or untruthful advertisements for children. (By the way, note that the Federal Trade Commission (FTC) has overlapping jurisdiction here by way of its power over "deceptive" advertising, and occasionally has proceeded again children's advertising when the FCC has not. In theory, the two agencies are supposed to coordinate their enforcement activities; in fact, they generally do not.)

Only during the beginning of the 1990's has there been any real pressure from Congress or the FCC to require broadcasters to broadcast a minimum amount of educational or similar programming. This was mainly the product of Reed Hundt, Chair of the Commission during most of the Clinton Administration. His basic agenda was to require television stations to air at least three hours per week of educational television. Since this obviously would have created serious First Amendment problems, the Commission ultimately in 1996 adopted the requirement as a "processing guideline." If a license renewal application did not show the minimum three hours, it would be put to the side for more intensive—and undefined— examination. Although the Commission's use of similar "guidelines" in the past, e.g., for news and public affairs, never had cost a license, the very threat of delay and negotiations—including attorneys' fees—was enough to make most broadcasters avoid the process and comply with the non-substantive guidelines.

TELEVISION BUSINESS INTERNATIONAL

COMPETING FOR KIDS: NEW
SHOWS, NEW NETWORKS
September, 1996.

Competition for children's viewing in the U.S. is getting hotter than ever before, with new timeslots multiplying the number of hours on offer. And as distributors beat a path of global expansion, the competitive temperature is spreading to other markets around the world. Opening TBI's annual focus on the kids' business, Louise McElvogue profiles the new Fall season

When Saban, the company behind the Power Rangers, started to sell its new show The Why Why Family on its educational content, it became clear that something different was happening in U.S. children's television.

What's new is the Federal Communications Commission regulations, which from September 1997 will demand the major television stations show three hours a week of educational children's television.

While these changes were decided only this summer, children's television producers have been refocusing their business for some time to make way for the FCC changes and the coming of the V-chip.

Still, three hours a week will not make such a huge difference in the evolution of U.S. children's television, and there is still plenty of the karate-kicking action-adventure in the Fall schedules. But producers and broadcasters are learning that the name of the game is to have more than one programming string to their bow.

While Saban pushes The Why Family for syndication, its big new series on Fox Children's Network is Big Bad Beetleborgs, a half-hour live action show which follows three kids who can turn into comic book heroes—apparently dressed by the Power Rangers tailor—to fight evil.

Another change in FCC rules—namely the phasing out of fin-syn—has made U.S. broadcasters much more rights-acquisitive now they can own the shows they air. Indeed, some producers complain privately that it is nigh on impossible to make a network sale without giving the network a cut of broadcasting rights. Similarly, the broadcasters are strengthening their position in merchandising and licensing rights—potentially, a huge revenue-generator. * * *

* * *

The biggest forces in U.S. children's television broadcasting continue to be the Fox Children's Network and Nickelodeon.

Nickelodeon has been the success story of cable and has significantly eaten into the networks' share of kids audiences and the $700 million kids tv ad market. While the networks—excluding Fox—focus on Saturday morning as kids' time, Nickelodeon has been hammering away with a weekly schedule and this Fall will move into early prime and primetime, where children have traditionally been under-served.

* * *

The other big changes within the networks' children's schedules are inspired by the change of network ownership. At ABC, the first effects of new parent company Disney on the children's service will be seen this season. Disney brings a huge library and a trusted brand name in children's television together with experienced executives. Geraldine Laybourne, former president of Nickelodeon, and Anne Sweeney, another Nick alumnus who was president of the fX cable channel, will both have input into ABC's children's schedule.

2. RADIO FORMATS

The demand for programming to serve children is somewhat similar to the demand that has been made in connection with a number of radio licensing proceedings for programming that fits a particular format, such as classical music or jazz, and thus serves a particular audience. As you read the material in this section, consider how to account for the fact that while the Commission was, at least initially, sympathetic to demands for children's programming, it has been steadfastly hostile to demands for regulation of radio formats.

As laid out in the *Sanders Brothers* case (p. 162), broadcasting traditionally has been considered an medium of "free competition"—as opposed to common carriage—with no direct control of programming by either the audience or the FCC. This proposition seemed to be in question at least for a while, however, in terms of a station's ability to change its "format"—that is, the general type of programming aired, ranging from country-and-western to classical.

As noted below, during the 1970s a series of court of appeals cases held that if there were a significant "public outcry" when a station changed its format, a hearing was necessary. And as seen above, the expense and aggravation of a full adjudicatory hearing usually is enough to deter a station from almost any change.

Moreover, by definition format change challenges invariably came in the context of station sales, for two reasons. First, the only other time at which a station was vulnerable to a protest was during its license renewal—which was 3 then 5 and now 8 years; in theory, a group could file a petition for revocation at any time during a station's license, but these invariably were dismissed out of hand. Second, and more realistically, after the sale of a station, the new owner was quite likely to change its format; after all, presumably a buyer would have some reason to believe that it could increase an operation's revenues—and a format change usually was a major consideration. By way of illustration, after the Commission approved the sale of a New York City classical music station, the new buyer made its programming plans quite clear by beginning its first broadcast day at midnight with a rendition of the rock classic, "Roll Over, Beethoven."

In principle, protests to format changes should have been treated no differently than the complaints authorized in *United Church of Christ* (p. 234) As with children's television, however, there were several major definitional problems. What was a format—e.g., the Boston Pops versus the New York Philharmonic? What was a "public outcry"—a large percentage of the general public, or of those interested in a particular format, such as jazz or classical music? What were suitable alternatives, e.g., a "middle of the road" as opposed to a "serious" classical station.

In principle, format change protests may have had as much validity as other petitions to deny—once again, as in the *United Church of Christ* case. Because of the difficulty in difficulty in defining the nature of the harm, however, the Supreme Court basically put an end to format litigation in FCC v. WNCN Listeners Guild, 450 U.S. 582, 101 S.Ct. 1266, 67 L.Ed.2d 521 (1981).

* * *

This issue arose when, pursuant to its informal rulemaking authority, the Commission issued a "Policy Statement" concluding that the public interest is best served by promoting diversity in entertainment formats through market forces and competition among broadcasters and that a change in entertainment programming is therefore not a material factor that should be considered by the Commission in ruling on an application for license renewal or transfer. Respondents, a number of citizen groups interested in fostering and preserving particular entertainment formats, petitioned for review in the Court of Appeals for the

District of Columbia Circuit. That court held that the Commission's Policy Statement violated the Act. We reverse the decision of the Court of Appeals.

I

Beginning in 1970, in a series of cases involving license transfers,* the Court of Appeals for the District of Columbia Circuit gradually developed a set of criteria for determining when the "public-interest" standard requires the Commission to hold a hearing to review proposed changes in entertainment formats.**

* * *

In January 1976 the Commission responded to these decisions by undertaking an inquiry into its role in reviewing format changes.*** In particular, the Commission sought public comment on whether the public interest would be better served by Commission scrutiny of entertainment programming or by reliance on the competitive marketplace.****

Following public notice and comment, the Commission issued a Policy Statement*** pursuant to its rulemaking authority under the Act. The Commission concluded in the Policy Statement that review of format changes was not compelled by the language or history of the Act, would not advance the welfare of the radio-listening public, would pose substantial administrative problems, and would deter innovation in radio programming. In support of its position, the Commission quoted from *FCC v. Sanders Brothers Radio Station,* 309 U.S. 470, 475, 60 S.Ct. 693, 697, 84 L.Ed. 869 (1940): "Congress intended to leave competition in the business of broadcasting where it found it, to permit a licensee ... to survive or succumb according to his ability to make his programs attractive to the public.**** The Commission also emphasized that a broadcaster is not a common carrier and therefore should not be subjected to a burden similar to the common carrier's obligation to continue to

---

* Citizens Committee to Save WEFM v. FCC, 165 U.S.App.D.C. 185, 506 F.2d 246 (1973) (en banc); *Citizens Committee to Keep Progressive Rock v. FCC,* 156 U.S.App. D.C. 16, 478 F.2d 926 (1973); *Lakewood Broadcasting Service, Inc. v. FCC,* 156 U.S.App.D.C. 9, 478 F.2d 919 (1973); *Hartford Communications Committee v. FCC,* 151 U.S.App.D.C. 354, 467 F.2d 408 (1972); *Citizens Committee to Preserve the Voice of the Arts in Atlanta v. FCC,* 141 U.S.App. D.C. 109, 436 F.2d 263 (1970).

** We shall refer to the Court of Appeals' views on when the Commission must review changes in entertainment format as the "format doctrine," and we shall often refer to a change in entertainment programming by a radio broadcaster as a change in format.

*** *Notice of Inquiry, Development of Policy re: Changes in the Entertainment For-* *mats of Broadcast Stations,* 57 F.C.C.2d 580 (1976).

**** The Commission also invited interested parties to consider the impact of the format doctrine on First Amendment values.

*** *Memorandum Opinion and Order,* 60 F.C.C.2d 858 (1976) ("Policy Statement"), reconsideration denied, 66 F.C.C.2d 78 (1977).

**** The Commission observed that radio broadcasters naturally compete in the area of program formats since there is virtually no other form of competition available. A staff study of program diversity in major markets supported the Commission's view that competition is effective in promoting diversity in entertainment formats. *Policy Statement,* [60 F.C.C.2d], at 861. * * *

provide service if abandonment of that service would conflict with public convenience or necessity."[†]

The Commission also concluded that practical considerations as well as statutory interpretation supported its reluctance to regulate changes in formats. Such regulation would require the Commission to categorize the formats of a station's prior and subsequent programming to determine whether a change in format had occurred; to determine whether the prior format was "unique";[††] and to weigh the public detriment resulting from the abandonment of a unique format against the public benefit resulting from that change. The Commission emphasized the difficulty of objectively evaluating the strength of listener preferences, of comparing the desire for diversity within a particular type of programming to the desire for a broader range of program formats and of assessing the financial feasibility of a unique format.

Finally, the Commission explained why it believed that market forces were the best available means of producing diversity in entertainment formats. First, in large markets, competition among broadcasters had already produced "an almost bewildering array of diversity" in entertainment formats. Second, format allocation by market forces accommodates listeners' desires for diversity within a given format and also produces a variety of formats. Third, the market is far more flexible than governmental regulation and responds more quickly to changing public tastes. Therefore, the Commission concluded that "the market is the allocation mechanism of preference for entertainment formats, and * * * Commission supervision in this area will not be conducive either to producing program diversity [or] satisfied radio listeners."

The Court of Appeals, sitting en banc, held that the Commission's policy was contrary to the Act as construed and applied in the court's prior format decisions.

* * *

The Commission has provided a rational explanation for its conclusion that reliance on the market is the best method of promoting diversity in entertainment formats. The Court of Appeals and the Commission agree that in the vast majority of cases market forces provide sufficient diversity. The Court of Appeals favors government intervention when there is evidence that market forces have deprived

---

[†] * * * The Commission also addressed the "constitutional dimension" of the format doctrine. It concluded that the doctrine would be likely to deter many licensees from experimenting with new forms of entertainment programming, since the licensee could be burdened with the expense of participating in a hearing before the Commission if for some reason it wished to abandon the experimental format. Thus, "[t]he existence of the obligation to continue service . . . inevitably deprives the public of the best efforts of the broadcast industry and results in an inhibition of constitution-ally protected forms of communication with no offsetting justifications, either in terms of specific First Amendment or diversity-related values or in broader public interest terms." *Policy Statement, supra,* at 865.

[††] * * * [T]he Commission discussed the difficult task of categorizing formats, noting that the Court of Appeals had suggested in the WEFM case that 19th–century classical music should be distinguished from 20th–century classical music. *Notice of Inquiry, supra,* at 583, and n. 2.

the public of a "unique" format, while the Commission is content to rely on the market * * *. The Court of Appeals places great value on preserving diversity among formats, while the Commission emphasizes the value of intra-format as well as inter-format diversity. Finally, the Court of Appeals is convinced that review of format changes would result in a broader range of formats, while the Commission believes that government intervention is likely to deter innovative programming.

In making these judgments, the Commission has not forsaken its obligation to pursue the public interest. * * * [The Commission] did not assert that reliance on the marketplace would achieve a perfect correlation between listener preferences and available entertainment programming. Rather, it recognized that a perfect correlation would never be achieved, and it concluded that the marketplace alone could best accommodate the varied and changing tastes of the listening public. These predictions are within the institutional competence of the Commission.

* * * [D]iversity is not the only policy the Commission must consider in fulfilling its responsibilities under the Act. The Commission's implementation of the public-interest standard, when based on a rational weighing of competing policies, is not to be set aside by the Court of Appeals, for "the weighing of policies under the 'public interest' standard is a task that Congress has delegated to the Commission in the first instance." FCC v. National Citizens Committee for Broadcasting, 436 U.S. at 810, 98 S.Ct. at 2119.

* * *

III

* * *

Under its present policy, the Commission determines whether a renewal or transfer will serve the public interest without reviewing past or proposed changes in entertainment format. This policy is based on the Commission's judgment that market forces, although they operate imperfectly, will not only more reliably respond to listener preference than would format oversight by the Commission but will also serve the end of increasing diversity in entertainment programming. * * *

A major underpinning of its Policy Statement is the Commission's conviction, rooted in its experience, that renewal and transfer cases should not turn on the Commission presuming to grasp, measure and weigh the elusive and difficult factors involved in determining the acceptability of changes in entertainment format. To assess whether the elimination of a particular "unique" entertainment format would serve the public interest, the Commission would have to consider the benefit as well as the detriment that would result from the change. Necessarily, the Commission would take into consideration not only the number of listeners who favor the old and the new programming but also the intensity of their preferences. It would also consider the effect of the format change on diversity within formats as well as on diversity among formats. The Commission is convinced that its judgments in these respects would be subjective in large measure and would only approximately serve the public interest. It is also convinced that the market, although imperfect, would serve the public interest as well or better by responding quickly to changing preferences and by inviting experimentation with new types of programming. Those who would overturn the Commission's Policy Statement do not take adequate account of these considerations.

* * *

We decline to overturn the Commission's Policy Statement, which prefers reliance on market forces to its own attempt to oversee format changes at the behest of disaffected listeners. Of course, the Commission should be alert to the consequences of its policies and should stand ready to alter its rule if necessary to serve the public interest more fully. * * *

* * *

[The Court went on to hold that the Commission's refusal to consider format changes did not violate the listening public's First Amendment right to receive diverse points of view.]

JUSTICE MARSHALL, with whom JUSTICE BRENNAN joins, dissenting.

* * * In my judgment, the Court of Appeals correctly held that in certain limited circumstances, the Commission may be obliged to hold a hearing to consider whether a proposed change in a licensee's entertainment program format is in the "public interest." Accordingly, I would affirm the judgment of the Court of Appeals insofar as it vacated the Commission's "Policy Statement."

II

* * *

I agree with the majority that predictions of this sort [diversity resulting through reliance on market forces] are within the Commission's institutional competence. I am also willing to assume that a general policy of disregarding format changes in making the "public interest" determination required by the Act is not inconsistent with the Commission's statutory obligation to give individualized consideration to each application. The Commission has broad rulemaking powers under the Act, and we have approved efforts by the Commission to implement the Act's "public interest" requirement through rules and policies of general application. * * *

The problem with the particular Policy Statement challenged here, however, is that it lacks the flexibility we have required of such general regulations and policies. * * * The Act imposes an affirmative duty on the Commission to make a particularized "public interest" determination for each application that comes before it. * * *

* * *

IV

* * *

Although it has abandoned the "administrative nightmare" argument before this Court, the Commission nonetheless finds other "intractable" administrative problems in format regulation. For example, it insists that meaningful classification of radio broadcasts into format types is impractical, and that it is impossible to determine whether a proposed format change is in the public interest because the intensity of listener preferences cannot be measured.* Moreover, the Commission argues that format regulation will discourage licensee innovation and experimentation with formats, and that its effect on format diversity will therefore be counterproductive.

None of these claims has merit. Broadcasters have operated under the format doctrine during the past 10 years, yet the Commission is unable to show that there has been no innovation and experimentation with formats during this period. Indeed, a Commission staff study on the effectiveness of market allocation of formats indicates that licensees have been aggressive in developing diverse entertainment formats under the format doctrine regime. This "evidence"—a welcome contrast to the Commission's speculation—undermines the Commission's claim that format regulation will disserve the "public interest" because it will inhibit format diversity.

The Commission's claim that it is impossible to classify formats, is largely overcome by the Court of Appeals' suggestion that the Commission could develop "a format taxonomy which, even if imprecise at the margins, would be sustainable so long as not irrational."** 197 U.S.App. D.C., at 334, 610 F.2d, at 853. Even more telling is the staff study relied on by the Commission to show that there is broad format diversity in major radio markets, for the study used a format classification based on industry practice. As the Court of Appeals noted, it is somewhat ironic that the Commission had no trouble "endorsing the validity of a study largely premised on classifications it claims are impossible to make." Ibid. To be sure, courts do not sit to second-guess the assessments of specialized agencies like the Commission. But where, as here, the agen-

* The Commission also insists that any findings about the financial viability of a particular format would be entirely speculative.

** There have been a number of comments and suggestions about how the Commission might best accomplish this task. See *e.g.,* * * * D. Ginsburg, [Regulation of Broadcasting, 1st ed.], at 316; Note, *Judicial Review of FCC Program Diversity Regulation,* 75 Colum.L.Rev. 401, 436–437 (1975).

The Court of Appeals suggested that the Commission could consider an alternative approach of "dispensing altogether with the need for classifying formats by simply taking the existence of significant and bona fide listener protest as sufficient evidence that the station's endangered programming has certain unique features for which there are no ready substitutes." The court indicated that "this approach would focus attention on the essentials of the format doctrine," namely, that when a significant sector of the populace is aggrieved by a planned programming change, this fact raises a legitimate question as to whether the proposed change is in the public interest. 197 U.S.App.D.C., at 334–335, n. 47, 610 F.2d at 853–854, n. 47.

cy's position rests on speculations that are refuted by the agency's own administrative record, I am not persuaded that deference is due.***

* * *

I respectfully dissent.

Notes and Questions

1. At the time of the *WNCN* decision, the Commission was substantially deregulating radio program service (as opposed to technical operations, equal employment opportunities, etc.). A central feature of that deregulation was the elimination of various content guidelines, in favor of deference to licensee discretion in how best to serve the public. Justice Marshall's dissent proceeds from a fundamentally different view of the Commission's obligations under the "public interest" standard of the Communications Act. He is particularly unmoved by arguments about administrative inconvenience or the difficulty of making certain regulatory judgments.

2. An argument against the desirability of "diversity" in broadcast programming is difficult to imagine. But what does "diversity" mean? How would one measure a change in diversity in order to make the public interest determination called for by the dissent in a "unique format" case? Would diversity mean something different in the context of television programming?

3. The court of appeals opinion in *WEFM,* with which the Supreme Court disagreed in *WNCN,* reasoned that the process by which advertising forces determine programming is "inherently inconsistent" with the Communications Act's purpose "to secure the maximum benefits of radio to all the people."

There is, in the familiar sense, no free market in radio entertainment because over-the-air broadcasters do not deal directly with their listeners. They derive their revenue from the sale of advertising time. More time may be sold, and at higher rates, by a station that has a larger *or* a demographically more desirable audience for advertisers. Broadcasters therefore find it to their interest to appeal, through their entertainment format, to the particular audience that will enable them to maximize advertising revenues. If advertisers on the whole prefer to reach an audience of a certain type, i.e., young adults with their larger discretionary incomes, then broadcasters, left entirely to themselves by the FCC, would shape their programming to the tastes of that segment of the public.

This is inherently inconsistent with "secur[ing] the maximum benefits of radio to all the people of the United States," and not a situation that we can square with the statute as construed by the Supreme Court. We think it axiomatic that preservation of a format [that] would otherwise disappear, although economically and technologically viable

*** All this suggests that the "practical difficulties" the Commission has identified are not intractable, and that these problems could be solved if the Commission channelled as much energy into devising workable standards as it has devoted to mischaracterizing the Court of Appeals' format doctrine.

and preferred by a significant number of listeners, is generally in the public interest. 506 F.2d at 268.

Accord, Barrow, *The Attainment of Balanced Program Service in Television*, 52 Va. L. Rev. 633 (1966). Do you agree?

4. Would the format change doctrine apply to television as well as radio stations? What would be a substantial change for a television station? Moving to foreign language programming? Becoming all-news? Changing its network affiliation? How easily can you resolve these issues?

5. And what would be the effect on multichannel media, such as cable or MDS? When does a 70–channel medium change its "format"? If it drops one of two news channels? If it reduces its voluntary commitment to PEG access? If it changes its tiers to move popular services from a "basic" to an "enhanced" (that is, more expensive) tier?

6. Do you see why the Supreme Court did not want to get involved with the whole format change issue? How would Chief Justice Taft have felt?

I. REASSESSING STRUCTURAL REGULATION: ALTERNATIVES FOR TELEVISION?

Having considered the various behavioral approaches to content regulation presented in this chapter, it may be useful to revisit the role of structural regulation in promoting diversity, which was a central theme of Chapter V. The following article suggests, based upon economic theory, that viewer satisfaction might be improved if the broadcast industry were structured so that a "licensee" received the right to program all available channels during a single time period (so-called "temporal monopoly"). Competition would occur from one time period to the next ("intertemporal competition"). As you read this article, consider whether the growth of media other than broadcasting (particularly cable television) has undermined the utility of the proposal. Does the proposal assume that only a relatively small number of channels are available to the temporal monopolist? Might the proposal still represent a useful alternative for restructuring at least the allocation of rights to use the broadcast spectrum? Consider carefully what values would be served by the proposed restructuring of the market. Are these values the most important ones? Who should make such a decision?

BEEBE AND OWEN

ALTERNATIVE STRUCTURES FOR TELEVISION

Office of Telecommunications Policy.
Staff Research Paper OTP–SP–10 (1972).

There has been a long and heated debate concerning the quality of commercial television and whether it can be improved by altering the structure of the industry. Some of this debate has centered on the motivation of the executives of stations and networks, and proceeds on the premise that television would be "better" if only the media owners would make it better. Implicit in these criticisms is the idea that there is a subterranean conspiracy to deprive the public of high quality television either because of laziness or because of greed on the part of the media owners.

The other side of the debate has been more academic, and takes the economic motivation of media owners as given, if not proper. This approach does not attempt to rationalize firm behavior on philosophical or sociological grounds. Nor does it reflect traditional methods of regulation, which for the most part attempt to regulate firm behavior directly. Instead, it is directed at developing positive policies for regulation through altering market structures. The problem is to propose alternative industry structures in which the natural economic incentives of media owners work to the greater satisfaction of consumers, by "the invisible hand."

Public policy has over the years undertaken a number of changes in the structure of television in order to improve it. [The authors also note that cable television, which was starting to develop rapidly at the time, offered the most significant potential for structural change up to that time.]

This paper examines in some detail the idea of monopoly control of a few channels as a structural alternative to the present system—competition (or at least rivalry) among a few channels, principally the three national networks. We shall not consider here the possibility of many channels (cable) and of pay-television. The question is whether the current system of broadcasting can be changed structurally, preserving the existing stations and networks, and not increasing the number of channels available, so as to "improve" broadcast programming.

An immediate difficulty lies in the problem of defining "better" programming. To the economist, the "best" allocation of resources among programs is that which consumers would be willing to pay the most for, net of production costs. But we have no information on this point, and are unlikely to get any in the absence of pay-TV. An alternative welfare criterion is to count noses on a one-man, one-vote basis. * * * This turns out to be a reasonably practical welfare criterion, and it is the one we use for the election of public officials. But note that it is not the decision rule which an economist would prefer for the allocation of resources. It is used here with that caveat.

Suppose there are three viewers and two programs. Two of the viewers prefer Program A to B, while the third prefers Program B to A. We propose to these viewers two alternative states: (1) in which Program A is aired, (2) in which Program B is aired. By vote, state (1) wins, 2 to 1. We shall then say that state (1) is "better than" state (2), keeping in mind that the out-voted viewer, if he had been able to vote with dollars, might have been able to win. The phrase "better than" in this context has a highly populist connotation.

The academic literature on television makes a distinction between "diversity" and "duplication." * * * If there are two [different "types" of] programs, A and B, and if there are two stations, then the production of both A and B is a state "more diverse" than the production of two programs of Type A. The latter is said to constitute "duplication" and is wasteful of resources employed in program production.

[The authors here "compare the behavior of a few competitors with that of a monopolist in the context of an advertiser-supported television system of limited channel capacity."] * * *

* * *

Up to this point, we have shown that under limited channel capacity, one cannot say for certain whether monopoly or competition is likely to yield higher viewer satisfaction. Duplication under competition displaces potential "minority" programming; the monopolist's search for "lowest common denominator" programming does not ensure the production of preferred programming. In the context of a pre-cable world with limited channels, can we conceive of a structure under which profit maximizing producers might avoid both of these tendencies—one in which producers avoid duplication at any point of time and produce preferred programs even though viewers will watch lesser choices?

Consider now the possibility of intertemporal competition. In order to explore this possibility, we will add a new assumption: Each viewer is assumed to have a finite upper limit on the time he will spend watching television. * * * We make two further assumptions, which are sufficient for our result, but perhaps not necessary: [the amount of time that each viewer group will view is independent of the actual programs offered, and viewers are indifferent as to the periods in which they allocate their viewing time within S, the span of time considered, e.g., an evening.]

* * *

Take the monopoly case first. The joint profit maximum is described by the following table for three time periods and three channels:

Period	Channel 1	Channel 2

Program patterns of the monopolist clearly do not result in a high level of viewer satisfaction. Only group 3 receives its preferred choice, the reason being simply that it refuses to watch anything else. (This is the typical result under monopoly.)

Compare the above result with that which obtains when stations compete in parallel through time, as they do at present:

2 stations

Period	3–hour day	4–hour day
	AA	AA
	AA	AA
	AA	AA
	—	AB

Groups 1 and 2 both prefer this structure to monopoly, but group 3 is now clearly worse off. The "minority" program never appears. (This is the typical result of competitive duplication under constrained channel capacity.)

Now consider program patterns offered viewers under the structure of "competitive temporal monopolists":

Without resorting to interpersonal comparisons, we can rank temporal monopoly as preferable to monopoly since a vote between the two would favor temporal monopoly. Similarly, we can rank it preferable to competition for the same reason. Everyone is at least as well off with temporal monopoly as with any other structure. * * * So long as considerable duplication occurs under competition (due to the skewed distribution of viewer preferences), the vote will come out in favor of "competitive temporal monopoly" [over] competition. The reasons are twofold: (1) the temporal monopolist will always avoid duplication within his own time period s_i; (2) at the same time, if viewers are restrictive as to their total viewing, the temporal monopolists must compete for viewers (across time periods) by offering preferred choices.

Notes and Questions

1. With the foregoing analysis of intertemporal monopoly, compare the conclusion drawn in McGowan, *Competition, Regulation, and Performance in Television Broadcasting*, 1967 Wash.U.L.Q. 499, 511–12. Professor McGowan begins by assuming that broadcasters, such as the three (or four) networks, do not collude to determine their programming policies or schedules nor do they make side payments to each other; thus, each competes to maximize its own profits rather than industry profits.

> Our question then becomes, will program diversity be the same as it would under the assumption that the broadcasters behaved to maximize industry profits [i.e., as monopolists would]? The answer is "yes", provided: (1) that * * *broadcasters find it profitable to broadcast for the whole programming period [as they do], and (2) each broadcaster makes his program decisions in full knowledge of the other's decisions. * * *If the second condition is not satisfied, then industry program policy will only eventually correspond to the joint maximum policy as the broadcasters revise their program policies from period to period. Since this second condition will in general not be satisfied then there is no collusion, whether facit or explicit, between broadcasters, industry performance under competition may at times be characterized by less diversity than would occur under conditions where all broadcasters were under unified management. However, so long as broadcaster markets are highly oligopolistic, some degree of cooperative behavior among broadcasters is likely to arise.

> The foregoing considerations lead us to conclude that, on the average, competition among broadcasters is an efficient means of promoting diversity in programming. By this we mean that industry performance given the number of broadcast stations will, on the average, be

the same when the several broadcast facilities are independently operated as it would be if they were operated under unified management.

(a) In what ways does McGowan's analysis differ from that of Beebe and Owen?

(b) Does the industry practice of "counter-programming" tend to confirm or to refute the relevance of McGowan's analysis to the real world?

(c) Notice that both the Beebe and Owen and the McGowan analyses, being structural, focus on the process by which programming decisions are made under different industry configurations—monopoly and competition, respectively. As they illustrate, structural analyses do not have to address the question of whether a resulting output—an array of programs offered at any given hour—is in fact more "diverse" than would be some other mixture. They do not need to resolve, that is, the programming-categorizing questions that were at issue in the radio format cases, because they predict analytically rather than empirically that the most diverse array of programs possible will result.

2.   Another proposal for restructuring the television industry appears in Crandall, *The Economic Case for a Fourth Commercial Television Network*, 22 Pub. Pol'y 513, 532–34 (1974). The author calculates that a viable fourth network reaching almost 60 million homes (44 million of them on VHF) could be created by transferring to UHF all VHF educational stations in markets with fewer than four commercial VHFs; "dropping in" additional VHFs where feasible under the present allocation scheme; interconnecting these two groups of stations with existing independents and enabling the resulting network also to build UHFs in markets with fewer than four commercial stations. He estimates that "[t]he shifting of noncommercial stations to the UHF band might reduce their audiences by as much as 25 to 30 percent, or less than 100,000 viewers [in prime time]. But a fourth network would be worth nearly $1 billion to viewers" a gain which he estimates to be substantially more than the value of the loss imposed upon the audience for noncommercial television.

Crandall predicts that under his proposal, the three existing networks' audiences would erode and the rents earned by performers would decline as a result; affiliation payments to stations would decline only somewhat, while total industry network advertising revenues would be "very nearly the same as for a three-network market."

How do you evaluate the proposal? Is Crandall's single welfare criterion—value to viewers as measured by their willingness to pay—the only one you would use? Have the Fox Network and the many new "cable networks" begun to move the market closer to the structure envisioned by Crandall? Is there a danger of excess fractionalization of the broadcast video market? If so, what is the harm?

Chapter VIII

CODA

This book has focused almost exclusively on the U.S. regulatory system and an evaluation of it in terms of both procedure and substance. This is perfectly natural, of course, since most students live in and will work in this policy environment.

Nevertheless, it may be useful to compare the U.S. norms with another country's—particularly when on their face they seem relatively similar. The following comparison of the U.S. and Japanese broadcast licensing schemes thus may test some of your conclusions about broadcast licensing in this country.

JONATHAN WEINBERG

BROADCASTING AND THE ADMINISTRATIVE PROCESS IN JAPAN AND THE UNITED STATES

39 Buffalo L. Rev. 615 (1991).

* * *

My focus in this Article * * * is on how contrasting regulatory approaches and philosophies in two countries—the United States and Japan—have shaped the doctrines and practices those countries' broadcast regulators have selected. The basic documents for the governance of the electronic media in Japan are based on American models; they were drafted by or under the supervision of Americans, during the Occupation period following World War II. The two countries, however, are characterized by fundamentally different regulatory styles. * * *

* * *

The Japanese regulatory model * * * has provided no magic cure for the problems of choosing broadcast allocation policies, selecting broadcast licensees, and planning for new electronic mass media technology. Japanese regulators have limited their license awards to entities that represent coalitions among the powerful and well-connected, with the regulator subsequently protecting the market position of the regulated. The Japanese experience has tended to protect the position of old technology, and to suppress or marginalize the development of new technology. Japanese policymakers have instituted a decisionmaking process less incoherent and wasteful than our own, but with drawbacks that we would find unacceptable.

* * *

I. REGULATORY MODELS AND LEGAL IDEOLOGY

A. *Two approaches to regulation*

I hope to explain U.S. and Japanese broadcast regulation in this Article, and to illuminate the enterprise of regulation more generally, through the use of two stylized models to describe day-to-day agency interaction with regulated parties. I refer to these as a "formal rationality" model on the one hand, and a "bargaining" model on the other. They are ideal-types, and oversimplified; most regulation incorporates elements of both.

Under the formal rationality model, regulatory enforcement emphasizes detecting and prosecuting violations of the law, and punishing violators through the imposition of legal sanctions. The enforcement style is adversarial, and stresses formal legal process as a routine device. In the United States, OSHA enforcement has provided the paradigmatic example of such an approach to regulation.

Policymaking under this model emphasizes formal procedures, focusing on the promulgation of rational rules in a clear, objective, and unbiased manner. The formal rationality approach to enforcement demands that regulated parties be in a position easily to ascertain the law and to follow it. Since the regulator does not seek to work informally with regulated parties in the enforcement process—and, indeed, rejects such contacts as inconsistent with fairness and objectivity—informal bargaining of rules only serves to undermine the values on which the system depends.

Regulators under the bargaining model, by contrast, hinge their enforcement efforts on low-visibility negotiation, involving "accommodations, threats, and tradeoffs between enforcement official and violator that result in compromises and modifications of the [effective] law." The process de-emphasizes the actual imposition of formal sanctions as stigmatizing and counterproductive; such sanctions are commonly threatened but rarely imposed. The agency hopes to induce compliance by combining flexibility on its own part with threats, education and exhortation.

Such regulation is characterized by continuing personal contact between regulator and regulated. Close relationships, social and otherwise, are seen as important to facilitate negotiation and to keep regulators informed of problems and violations. In seeking to achieve effective industry-wide compliance at minimum cost, regulators deal with regulated parties on a political basis; that is, they reach results based on relative bargaining power and appeals to shared values.

The bargaining model in policymaking yields a pluralist process, with policymaking accomplished largely through negotiation among regulators and affected interests. The close contacts intrinsic to informal rule enforcement foster informal action in the policymaking arena as well. An administrator oriented towards a bargaining approach to enforcement will pursue the input and agreement of regulated parties for policymaking, so as to come up with rules that industry members will be willing to obey.

Bargaining-minded enforcement tends to merge rulemaking and enforcement. Where the agency sees itself as enforcing flexible, "real-world" law, rather than mechanically imposing the formal text of official rules, ongoing policymaking becomes a part of the enforcement process.

B. *Regulation in the United States*

It has become a commonplace that regulation in the U.S. follows a formal rationality model. Formal rationality characterizes much of our thinking about administrative law, and most of our judicial rulings. Our bureaucrats sometimes are said to stress formality unduly; to insist on the letter of the regulatory law at the cost of common sense. That characterization, though, slights the role in our society of bargaining-oriented, accommodationist approaches. One can observe both modes of regulation by United States agencies; indeed, informal policymaking and rule enforcement seem to be the norm, "the 'bread and butter' of the process of administration."

* * *

Federal Communications Commission policymaking illustrates the ubiquity of informal ex parte contacts. In FCC rulemaking, "political deals and interest group bargaining ... are present in considerable degree." The Commission has negotiated proposed rules with industry groups, and has in the rulemaking process adopted the results of bargaining among industry groups. Indeed, until 1977, AT & T rates were set not by formal procedures but by negotiated settlements between AT & T and FCC common carrier staff.

Pure negotiation, further, is not the only informal tool at the agency's disposal. In appropriate cases, an agency can use informal techniques in order to deflect the judicial and political weapons that an industry party might otherwise bring to bear against an agency decision. For example, the FCC successfully applied informal pressures to bring about the adoption of a "family viewing policy" by the networks and the National Association of Broadcasters, under which programming deemed inappropriate for viewing by a general family audience was not shown during certain evening hours. * * *

Powerful elements of United States legal ideology, however, significantly check those aspects of regulatory practice, and oblige agencies to conform more closely to the formal rationality model. That ideology is embodied in part in a line of cases, beginning around 1970, establishing what came to be known as "hard look" review. * * * Courts * * * tighten[ed] their review of agency decisionmaking, insisting that agency procedures be transparent, that agency reasoning be clear, and that agency goals be tightly rooted in what the courts deemed to be acceptable readings of the underlying statutes. * * *

The role of the administrative agency, when subjected to such review, is far from that suggested by the bargaining model: The agency, in making the decisions that are at the heart of its job, is expected to apply neutral criteria, in a rational and unbiased manner, to the parties before it. It is expected to follow a process under which it determines its goals with reference to its statutory mandate; considers which of various courses of action will most nearly achieve those goals; and adopts the course that this analytical process generates. Moreover, the agency must structure its processes so as to make its actions amenable to judicial review, which in turn will test those actions against a rationality standard. * * *

Such a requirement of "reasoned decisionmaking," however, is incompatible with a negotiated, political decisionmaking process. A bargaining-oriented process leads the agency to compromise neutrality, by giving greater weight to the views of those parties with greater bargaining power. It leads the agency to compromise rationality, by choosing the policy most acceptable to the contending parties rather than the policy most directly advancing statutory goals. The substantive rule most acceptable to the negotiating parties, indeed, may advance goals completely at odds with those Congress members thought important, and may call upon the agency to assert authority Congress members did not intend to give it. Bargaining-oriented proceedings, thus, notwithstanding their practical merits, are problematic when set up against the formal rationality model's requirements of neutrality, reasoned decisionmaking and transparency.

* * *

C. Regulation in Japan

Japanese administrative practice is consistent with a pure version of the bargaining model. Regulatory practice and legal ideology do not cut against each other, as they do in the United States; rather, they reinforce each other.

The typical form of regulation in Japan is *gyosei shido*, or administrative guidance; over 80% of Japanese regulatory activity, it is said, takes that form. Under the administrative guidance approach, rule enforcement or other agency action is accomplished informally, through meetings between the regulator and regulated, and in the absence of formal process. Administration is oriented around the notion that "the formal use of regulatory power is not considered desirable.... The approach preferred in Japan is to create a situation that is acceptable to both the administrative organs and the other parties through informal negotiation." That regulatory mode is justified by Japanese scholars in tones familiar to American students of the bargaining model: "[R]esort to authoritative modes of regulation based on 'orders and coercion' [may] lead to friction in the relationship between the administration and the public, or it may even lead to negative resistance and law-evading behavior."

* * *

The Japanese pattern, under which regulators consult with affected groups and seek to achieve consensus among them before making and enforcing policy decisions, * * * seems largely congruent with the approach urged by American advocates of regulatory negotiation. In some respects the Japanese pattern of consultation could have been scripted as a regulatory negotiation model for Americans. I argued earlier, however, that regulatory negotiation places severe strain on American legal ideology; the approach does not cause similar problems in Japan.

That pattern can succeed in Japan and fail in the United States in substantial degree because Japan lacks what this country has: judicial rationality review. Judicial review of administrative action in Japan is largely unavailable. Administrative law doctrine excludes most agency decisions from the scope of reviewable agency action. Agency behavior is not subject to judicial review unless it constitutes an "administrative disposition [*shobun*] or other exercise of public power," that is, unless it immediately and directly changes private legal rights or obligations. This test excludes from review most administrative acts with general effect. It also excludes any agency actions that can be construed as mere internal government behavior, not formally altering the specific legal rights or duties of private citizens. It, of course, excludes from review the informal agency action characteristic of administrative guidance.

* * *

III.   Broadcast licensing

B.   Broadcast Licensing in Japan

When the Occupation forces in Japan turned to reconstituting the Japanese broadcast system after World War II, they concluded that the existing monopoly broadcasting system should be dismantled, and replaced with a competitive system overseen by an independent government agency. MacArthur's staff drafted a new set of broadcasting regulation laws on the American model, establishing a formal system similar to the U.S. communications regime. The agency in charge of regulating Japanese broadcasting pursuant to these laws after 1952 was the Ministry of Posts and Telecommunications (MPT).

MPT, notwithstanding that the formal law it was applying was drafted according to an American model, constructed a system of broadcast regulation sharply different from that of the United States. Enforcing American drafted statutes through pure bargaining-oriented regulation, MPT developed broadcast allocation policies more restrictive than those of the U.S., and mechanisms for choosing individual licensees that bypass formal adjudicatory proceedings altogether. MPT chooses individual license recipients through a process emphasizing compromise between *all* politically influential applicants in the formation of a single joint-venture licensee. That license selection process has had significant consequences, one of which has been to confine media power almost completely within the structure of the socially acceptable and politically influential mainstream.

1.   Initial choices. In Japan, as in the United States, regulators had to resolve basic questions of license allocation: Would the regulator award licenses to the limits of spectrum availability? If not, what procedures would it use to exercise control over whether a frequency would be made available, and what substantive criteria would it apply? Japanese regulators were able to answer those questions on a clean slate; there were no private broadcasters when Japan's 1950 broadcast regulatory scheme went into effect.

Japanese regulators initially contemplated that broadcast diffusion would be quite slow. MPT's first broadcast allocation policy * * * contemplated licensing only two commercial television stations in Tokyo and one each in the cities of Osaka and Nagoya, far fewer than the spectrum technically could support. MPT revised its table of assignments in 1956, but still contemplated slow diffusion of television stations, broadcasting on four stations made available for civilian use. * * * MPT bureaucrats opposed any more rapid expansion, notwithstanding frequency availability, emphasizing that television was best brought along in an unhurried and steady manner.

A year later, however, the Ministry completely reversed course, awarding forty-three new television licenses on eleven channels; it thus increased the number of licensees over one thousand percent. Why was MPT so initially cautious, and why did it undertake this sudden shift? To understand Japan's allocation policy choices, one must first understand its unique method of dealing with competing applications. The question of how to resolve competing applications, in the Japanese context, drove the broadcast allocation and licensing process from its earliest moments.

2.   *Ipponka chosei.* In December 1950, the Radio Regulatory Commission (RRC) announced that it would grant two preliminary commercial AM radio licenses in Tokyo, and one in each of thirteen other cities. Large numbers of applicants sought each of these scarce authorizations. How was the regulator to select licensees? Language in its regulations apparently provided for competitive selection: "When there is a shortage of availability in frequencies assignable to the applying broadcast stations ... priority shall be given to the applicant whose plan can be considered to contribute most to the public welfare." Instead, however, the RRC rejected the American approach of formal, competitive hearings, and substituted an approach of its own: *ipponka chosei.* The phrase is

commonly translated as "coordination" * * *. It means that when many different entities file applications for a single license, the regulator, instead of engaging in a competitive selection process, facilitates the creation of a joint venture representing, to the extent possible, all influential applicants.

The RRC, as a result, notwithstanding that it was established on an American model, did not follow the American approach to licensee selection. It instead sought

> to bring about voluntary mergers of plural applicants in each city by clarifying the prospects for commercial stations in areas where there were large numbers of applicants. It was particularly intended for Tokyo and Osaka as there were many applicants in each city. In the process of mergers of applicants in Tokyo and Osaka, serious troubles developed between those of opposing interests and there were cases in which political and financial leaders had to intervene to adjust matters.

In the end, the RRC approved two stations in Osaka rather than one, because "no agreement could be reached among the applicants."

Ipponka, rather than competitive selection, to this day remains the dominant mode of selecting Japanese broadcast licensees. The key national players in the ipponka process today are Japan's five major media groups, centered around Japan's five nationwide daily newspapers. Each nationwide newspaper is associated with a "key station" television station in Tokyo, which in turn serves as the hub of a nationwide television network. When a new license is made available, these networks approach an assortment of former employees or shareholders, or former employees or shareholders of related firms, to file applications on their behalf with the relevant regional Telecommunication Administration Bureau. Applications typically number in the hundreds; in Nagano prefecture recently, over 1300 applications were filed for a single license. Not all of these applications, however, are legitimate. Almost all are filed by camouflage entities acting as proxies for a few real parties in interest, including the national media groups and leading local businesses.

MPT selects a person with a high degree of influence in the prefecture to "guide" the coordination process. This person must be familiar with the prefecture, credible with the applicants, and (in theory) neutral among them. As a practical matter, according to broadcasters, if the prefectural governor is a member of the ruling * * * party, then MPT will typically approach him first; governors who are members of the main opposition Socialist Party are not approached. If the governor belongs to an inconvenient political party, the Ministry will typically approach the head of the local economic association or the head of an influential local company. Alternatively, MPT may bypass the governor if a Diet member with particular clout in communications matters represents part of the area in question.

* * *

3. Allocation Policy. [MPT's 1957 table of assignments, including forty-three new television licenses on eleven channels,] produced an explosion in TV licensing, making licenses available in each prefecture and filling up the VHF band. * * *

Increasing the number of licenses available necessitated selection or creation, through *ipponka chosei*, of new licensees. In most prefectures, the process was relatively simple. A company had been formed a few years earlier to receive the radio licenses allocated to the prefecture * * *. It typically counted the most important companies and banks of the local area as its major stockholders, and took one in five of its directors from the prefectural newspaper. That company was awarded the new VHF license as well.

In the large cities, however, competition was more keen. The major newspapers, already heavily involved in radio broadcasting, realized that the award of television licenses presented a one-in-a-lifetime opportunity. Six new licenses were awarded in the cities of Tokyo, Osaka, and Nagoya in 1958–59, and extensive coordination was required in the *ipponka* process. The coordination did not always treat all applicants equally; some ended up with greater stakes. Through that process, [Kakuei Tanaka, then Minister of Posts and Telecommunications, later Prime Minister] is said to have gained substantial influence over the regulated companies and their newspaper sponsors. He is also said to have raised extensive sums of money from would-be-licensees.

[In 1968–70, MPT approved over thirty licenses for UHF television stations.] * * *

In the establishment of each new station, it was (again) necessary to sort out the participation of local capital as well as that of national news interests. According to one industry analyst, the process was (again) valuable as a fund-raising device for the governing Sato faction. The process, moreover, afforded opportunities for the exercise of local power. The dominant figure in the UHF *ipponka* process in Yamanashi prefecture, for example, was Shin Kanemaru: a Diet member, a close associate of then-LDP President Tanaka, and a figure of growing influence in telecommunications matters. Kanemaru is now a managing director and the largest shareholder of the television station (TV Yamanashi) established in that process.

* * *

Japanese regulators, early on, adopted a table-of-assignments approach to control frequency allocation, rather than the ad hoc approach characteristic of United States AM radio. This did not mean, however, that they were adopting an objective system of license allocation, characterized by formal rationality; MPT assignment plans were informal, internal agency documents, largely unconstrained by procedural requirements, and could be revised conveniently without formal processes or explanation. These revisions served as the vehicle for almost all of Japan's major broadcast policymaking. MPT's discretion was increased by its reluctance to award licenses to the limits of spectrum availability; notwithstanding marked shifts in MPT allocation approaches, MPT adhered to a policy of not granting licenses unless it felt that economic conditions ensured new broadcasters' financial success.

4. *Ipponka* Explained. The narrative I have set out so far raises a number of questions. Most importantly, why have Japanese regulators chosen to select licensees via *ipponka?* MPT officials explained to me that *ipponka* is necessary in part because it is difficult to select the one applicant out of many who is most suitable and deserving of the license. More importantly, selection of only a single applicant will make all the rest unhappy. *Ipponka,* they told me, is the natural and inevitable result of the need for consensus in matters such as the distribution of valuable resources. It represents an attempt to conduct governmental allocation of scarce resources on the principle that, as one Japanese communications scholar explained to me, "to fight each other is not good behavior."

This Article's earlier discussion of administrative guidance, however, suggests another way of looking at the problem. *Ipponka* seems a natural extension of the principles of administrative guidance to the licensing context. In the process of administrative guidance, the regulator consults with selected interested parties in the hope of finding common ground regarding the agency's ultimate action. In order to achieve anything resembling consensus, the regulator must limit the sphere from which it draws those contacts, staying within the realm of government and industry representatives who share more or less common interests. The government selects people with whom it can do business, and attempts to achieve consensus within that group.

Ipponka reflects a similar approach. Here, too, the agency selects the "serious" applicants–those it can or must do business with–and seeks to achieve a consensus among them. That effort at consultation and voluntary or imposed consensus serves the goals of the pure bargaining model, in that it discourages broadcast applicants from seeking to challenge the agency's decisions through judicial or political channels. The agency, by making concessions to include various industry members in the joint-venture entity, can exert significant influence in that entity's final makeup. The process further serves the goals of the bargaining model in that the ultimate licensee, a creature of the local corporate and national media power structures and of the Ministry as well, may be more amenable to agency guidance than a less broad-based, more self-made licensee.

* * *

MPT's role as the Ministry of Posts and Telecommunications * * * suggests a second way of looking at this question. Japan has some 23,000 post offices, of which almost 18,000 are family-owned rural branch offices, usually with no more than two or three employees. MPT's predecessor began setting up these post offices through the award of franchises to prominent local families over a century ago; since 1875 they have not only delivered the mail but also served as branch banks for the postal savings system. MPT gave its rural postmasters land tax exemptions, commissions on postage-stamp sales, and bounties on their savings accounts above a certain amount. The postmasters got a reasonably lucrative business; MPT got partial control of large sums of depositor savings and the allegiance of a local institution uniquely situated to mobilize voters in the rural stronghold of the [ruling] party.

When Tanaka became MPT Minister in 1957, he emphasized and exploited the existing post office symbiosis by tripling the number of commissioned postmasters, adding about 2000 to the existing 1150 * * * . He thus continued the process of distributing scarce and valuable resources–here, the right to participate in a monopoly delivery business and an administratively favored banking business–to prominent members of the local and economic power structure. In return, the regulatees helped turn out the vote for [ruling-party] politicians who provided political support for MPT.

MPT's radio and television licensing followed the same model. * * * Through the distribution process, the regulator singled out its licensees for governmental largesse and, due to the debt thus created, gained political influence over them. The licensees, members of the local business structure and thus predisposed to support the business-oriented ruling party, were in a position to support politicians who could, in turn, provide the regulator support in its battles with other elements of the bureaucracy. Through *ipponka,* MPT was able to mobilize the entire political structure in this process, with a minimum of playing favorites or creating unhappiness, and thus could maximize the political benefits that would accrue.

* * *

[Japanese allocation policy can be seen as an uneasy blend of bureaucratic and political components. From the bureaucratic standpoint, *ipponka*, requires some limitation on the number of licensees. From the perspective of administrative guidance, MPT must limit the number of licensees in order to preserve for itself the threat of licensing competitors, the regulator's greatest weapon in exerting administrative-guidance pressure on industry members. From the perspective of the post office model, MPT must limit the number of licensees in order to protect licenses' profit-making potential and ensure their value.

* * *

[On the other hand], Japanese politicians have had a simultaneous interest in *increasing* the number of broadcast stations, at least in their home districts. New broadcast stations are welcomed by the electorate and are easier and cheaper to provide than new railway lines. Voters in rural areas served by only one or two commercial television stations strongly favor new stations, providing additional television programming at zero cost to them. The creation of new licenses may give prominent local figures, shut out of earlier stations, opportunities to participate in the new one. Getting a broadcast license for one's constituency affords a

Diet member the opportunity to build political capital, demonstrate his political power, increase his connections, and accumulate political credit. * * *

5. Some Consequences of the Japanese Approach. The Japanese approach to broadcast allocation has yielded some problematic results. Most obviously, if one assumes that some broadcasters MPT chose not to license would have flourished, then, for an extended period of time, Japanese listeners have received less broadcasting than they would have otherwise. This is most obvious with regard to radio, for which MPT to this day has made few station assignments.

In an ideal world, one could compare the number of stations MPT chose to license in each market with the number that the market might have supported absent such policies, and thus determine the extent of MPT's limitation on market entry. The question of how many broadcasters an area's economy can "support," however, is an enigmatic one. Cross-national comparisons are unsatisfying; it is hard to know just what to do with the fact, for example, that different countries spend vastly different sums, per capita and as a percentage of GNP, on advertising. Do low advertising expenditures mean that an area can support little over-the-air broadcasting, or would an increase in the number of broadcast stations stimulate greater advertising spending? While one cannot determine precisely the extent to which MPT artificially limited the number of broadcast stations, it seems clear that the Ministry deliberately chose to move slowly on allocation. That limitation on the number of licensees may have been necessary to the smooth functioning of the *ipponka*-based system.

A second consequence of the ipponka process is its tendency to centralize media power. In most prefectures, the RRC or MPT awarded the prefecture's single radio license to an ipponka-created consortium led by the prefectural newspaper, and MPT later awarded the single VHF television license to the radio licensee. These awards were quite natural, given *ipponka's* internal logic. The obvious consortium to receive the radio license was a coalition of the prefectural newspaper and prominent local businesses; that coalition, once created, incorporated the most important members of the local power structure and thus was a natural candidate that receive the television license as well. Policies of limiting the number of broadcast licensees checked the licensing of new radio or television stations to compete with the existing ones. Mass communications, thus, was an effective monopoly until the licensing of UHF in the late 1960s.

* * *

A further possible consequence of *ipponka* allocation is blandness and mainstream orientation in programming. * * * *Ipponka* helps ensure that broadcast licensees (1) are drawn from the conventional power structure, and thus are unlikely to have unusual views; and (2) are joint ventures comprising a large number of individuals and organizations, so that even if one shareholder should have unusual views, those views are unlikely to be reflected in station programming. * * *

                              * * *

* * * Japanese broadcasters have hardly been uniformly pro-government. While the factors discussed above, I believe, make Japanese broadcast stations more supportive of the status quo than they would otherwise be, broadcasters have in times of crisis have staked out positions strongly in the political opposition. [H]owever, government officials have found weapons to retaliate against the broadcast press when it has strayed from appropriate behavior; this provides yet another factor reinforcing the natural tendencies of the *ipponka*-based system to mainstream reporting and views.

A final consequence of *ipponka* allocation worth considering is its contribution to the interplay of political considerations in the licensing process. The 1957–59 VHF licensing under Tanaka and the 1967–70 UHF licensing each demonstrate that interplay. Japan, of course, is not alone in having a broadcast licensing system marked by political considerations in the licensing and policymaking process. The same can easily be said of the United States, notwithstanding the demands of formal rationality. * * *

The two systems, however, are different in important ways. Japanese regulation, centered around administrative guidance and the bargaining model, provides few checks against the exercise of political influence in the regulatory process to the extent of the political actors' bargaining power. Indeed, the crux of the system is that *all* parties with a voice in the process be given an opportunity to exercise their bargaining power. Political considerations can be suppressed only to the extent that politicians lack bargaining power, or bureaucrats consider direct negotiation with politicians illegitimate.

Because procedures for making allocation policy and licensing decisions are informal and bargaining-oriented, there is extensive opportunity for negotiation with political actors in the regulatory process. No external institution such as judicial review limits that negotiation. [I]nter-bureaucratic competition extensively shapes regulatory policy in Japan today, and plays a role comparable in some ways to the role played in the United States by judicial review. That competition, though, only increases the role of political actors in the regulatory process.

The United States system also offers extensive opportunities for the exercise of political bargaining power in the regulatory process. With Congressional committees controlling the FCC's budget and statutory authority, things could hardly be otherwise. Nor is political influence on agency policymaking even controversial; the D.C. Circuit has declared it "entirely proper for Congressional representatives vigorously to represent the interests of their constituents before administrative agencies engaged in informal, general policy rulemaking." The ideology of procedural fairness and rationality, however, has to some degree helped to delegitimize political influence at least in resolving specific licensing questions. * * *

7. Conclusion. In Japan, the informal, bargaining-oriented system, together with the force of the post office model, allowed—perhaps even mandated—an ipponka-based license award process. That process supports the positions of both the Ministry and the LDP within the political status quo. It limits the number of licensees, both because *ipponka* is inherently self-limiting—as the important local players are all drawn into broad-based license coalitions, one quickly runs out of suitable coalition members—and because licensee protection forms an important part of the administrative guidance interplay. At the same time, however, the informal nature of the license award process makes it highly vulnerable to political pressure, including pressures to award additional licenses on a politically motivated basis. Judicial review is unavailable to check any of these on a fairness-oriented or doctrinal basis.

The effect of *ipponka* in Japan has been to place media power squarely within the establishment consensus of the socially and politically acceptable, and to diffuse it through shared authority within that class, perpetuating communications power through negotiation among power-structure groups. Granting licenses only to "consensus," and thus mainstream, licensees has to some degree obviated the need for content control of their later broadcasts. Compared to the United States allocation system, *ipponka* is less wasteful. It is also even more cozy, safe, and supportive of the status quo.

Notes and Questions

1. Which system is better of terms of procedural efficiency? In terms of procedural fairness?

Would the Japanese *ipponka* approach be acceptable under U.S. administrative procedure? Or, was the recent demise of the 1965 Policy Statement the right result for the wrong reasons?

To what extent does it go on in the United States in a *sub rosa* manner? Remember the *WHDH* case. (p. 133). To what extent is it allowed in certain types of U.S. procedures, particularly hybrid situations involving elements of both rulemaking and adjudication? E.g., Sierra Club v. Costle, 657 F.2d 298 (D.C.Cir.1981). There, Senator Byrd played a major role in pushing the electric power industry and the EPA into adopting a compromise set of emission standards. Cf. Home Box Office, Inc. v. FCC, 567 F.2d 9 (D.C.Cir.), cert denied, 434 U.S. 829, 98 S.Ct. 111, 54 L.Ed.2d 89 (1977). There the court invalidated a rule governing programming of pay movies, because of extensive contacts between various industry representatives and FCC staff and well as commissioners.

Is the Japanese system somewhat similar to the relatively new U.S. procedure of "negotiated rulemaking"? Under this approach, an administrative agency can institute a proceeding in which a "convenor" brings together representatives of various interest groups and works with them to find an acceptable solution to a common problem. Administrative Conference of the United States, *Negotiated Rulemaking Sourcebook* (1990). At this stage it is somewhat difficult to evaluate the usefulness of the procedure; very few cases have invoked the system, because of natural fears about a totally new approach.

2. As to the Japanese favoritism for mergers, compare the FCC's historically ambivalent approach.

The FCC, historically, was wary of settlements and mergers in the comparative-hearing process. (Why?) As early as 1946, it adopted rules requiring applicants designated for comparative hearing to disclose any payments they had received in return for dismissing their applications, and to obtain Commission approval of the dismissal; section 311(c) of the Communications Act codified that policy. See also 47 C.F.R. § 73.3525. While comparative-hearing applicants were free to enter into mergers, the Commission did not allow the merged applicants to assert, against the remaining applicants, any comparative advantages they achieved by virtue of the merger. See Proposals to Reform the Commission's Hearing Process, 6 F.C.C.Rcd. 157 (1990); , 101 F.C.C.2d 1010 (1986).

On the other hand, Congress and the Commission have been much more friendly towards license-applicant mergers in situations where the agency would make no public-interest determination. 47 U.S.C. 309(j), granting the FCC authority to distribute licenses via auction, states that the Commission has an "obligation in the public inheres* * *to use* * *negotiation* * * to avoid mutual exclusivity in application and licensing proceedings." And section 3002 of the 1997 Balanced Budget Act, directing the Commission to settle existing initial-licensing conflicts via auction, directs the agency to waive any provision of its regulations that would interfere with pre-auction settlements among the parties.

In other licensing contexts, the FCC has sought ways to split the pot among the applicants rather than hold a comparative hearing. See, e.g., Continental Satellite Corp., 4 F.C.C.Rcd. 6292 (1989) (satellite orbital slots). How different are the U.S. and Japanese systems today?

3. Would the Japanese system be workable if judicial review were available to the extent that it is under U.S. procedures? Would a limited form of judicial review—i.e., solely as to abuse of discretion—be feasible?

4. Which system is better in terms of reaching equitable results? How can you tell? What assumptions go into your answer?

5. With your accumulated wisdom from this course, which system is better overall?

6. For more on the Japanese process, F. Upham, *After Minimata: Current Prospects and Prospects and Problems in Japanese Environmental Litigation*, 8 Ecology L. Q. 213 (1979); see also Dzuibala, *The Impotent Sword of Japanese: The Doctrine and Shobunsei as a Matter to Administrative Litigation*, 18 Cornell Int'l L.J. 37 (1985).

Index

References are to Pages

References are to Pages

0–314–21122–5

90000

9 780314 211224